Introduction to Modern Macroeconomics

Introduction to Modern Macroeconomics

second edition

Thomas M. Havrilesky
DUKE UNIVERSITY

HARLAN DAVIDSON, INC.
ARLINGTON HEIGHTS, ILLINOIS 60004

Library of Congress Cataloging-in-Publication Data

Havrilesky, Thomas M.
Introduction to modern macroeconomics.

Bibliography: p.
Includes indexes.
1. Macroeconomics. I. Title.
HB172.5.H38 1988 339 87-24456
ISBN 0-88295-414-8

Manufactured in the United States of America

92 91 90 89 88
7 6 5 4 3 2 1

MG

Contents

Preface to the Second Edition

The teaching of macroeconomics continues to change rapidly. Since the 1950s the $C + I + G$, 45° line paradigm had been considered the basic starting point in standard courses in intermediate macroeconomic theory. This model made it easy to explain Keynes' famous multiplier principle and rationalized an entire era of government fiscal and monetary policy activism. It also had other, somewhat more salient, advantages: it was easy to teach, and it seemed to be popular with students. However, the $C + I + G$, 45° line apparatus had one major disadvantage: it virtually ignored the existence of all other sectors of the economy. During a one-semester course in intermediate macroeconomic theory, this shortcoming was typically corrected through the introduction of asset-holding behavior and the interest rate, usually incorporated in the form of the legendary *LM-IS* curves.

Generations of students labored arduously at the mechanics of *LM-IS* curve derivation and manipulation. As with the $C + I + G$, 45° line approach, the main advantages of *LM-IS* analysis seemed to be that it was the easiest way to teach Keynesian multipliers and that it was relevant to a macroeconomic policy environment in which monetary and fiscal fine-tuning of the economy was held up as a somewhat remote but not unachievable ideal. For a long time the only major disadvantage of the *LM-IS* approach appeared to be that it ignored an important sector of the economy—the labor market. This deficiency was usually corrected through the introduction of the aggregate supply curve. The only trouble with this tack was that it required the parallel derivation of the aggregate demand curve. Unfortunately, the student effort required for these exercises was formidable, especially coming on the heels of the tedium of *LM-IS* curve manipulation. Moreover, because of the time typically consumed in deriving all these hybrid functions, the semester was usually over before the labor market was ever mentioned.

Throughout this process, the conscientious instructor continually assured students that all of these exercises in the derivation and manipulation of highly aggregative curves were terribly relevant for macroeconomic stabilization policy. Unfortunately, two elemental flaws were visible, even to those who embraced the relevance argument. First, little of the apparatus appeared to be related to *micro*economics. Supply and demand analysis, the theories of the firm, and consumer behavior seemed, at the elementary level, only remotely related to the hybrid aggregate equilibrium curves of macroeconomics. For example, how many of those schooled only in the $C + I + G$, 45° line approach can translate it into supply and demand behavior?

Second, as the number of sectors introduced into the conventional analysis grows, the mounting level of aggregation obscures more and more of the interesting variables. For example, when using the aggregate demand-aggregate supply apparatus to explain a supply shock, how many students can tell what is happening to the interest rate or the real wage level?

Nevertheless, convention weighs heavily in teaching and even more heavily in publishing. Instructors frequently invest their human capital in particular methods, and retooling is costly. Publishers not only understand this but, more and more, they are burdened with overhead that militates against risky new forays away from convention. As a result, year after year and generation after generation, macroeconomics textbooks, no matter how exciting their peripheral innovations, still paid homage to the standard pedagogy just outlined.

Perhaps this is the ordinary state of academic practice, but I think that the teaching of macroeconomics will not remain mired in this convention. While economists and publishers may have been unable to wrest themselves away from the irksome pedagogy of the standard macroeconomics textbook, the dramatic events of the past decade are beginning to force an evacuation. Fundamental changes have occurred in the nature of the problems facing modern economies and in the standard macroeconomic theory which attempts to explain those problems. Both these changes in problems and in theory require thoroughgoing improvement in macroeconomics textbooks.

Even though ideologues might disagree, the issues that are involved here are not ideological. Many of the conventions of today's textbooks are simply too rigid to handle the contemporary advances in macroeconomic analysis that purport to explain modern problems. Labeling these conventions "Keynesian" or "Monetarist" and their revision as "anti-" is counterproductive.

The 1970s and early 1980s provided us all with a crash course in macroeconomic problems. In the cauldron of an inflationary environment, analysis of the behavior of market participants requires explicit recognition of expectational alternatives. Inflationary expectations seem to have a marked impact on labor market behavior. As a result, the old notion of a stable Phillips curve came under attack. Inflationary expectations also seem to have an effect on behavior in asset and credit markets. As a result, the paradigm of the liquidity effect of the money supply on interest rates was dethroned.

Macroeconomics texts have tried several inappropriate responses to the new problems. One is to ignore the obsolescence of existing pedagogic methods and blithely continue to try to apply them to modern problems. Such is the textbook that draws the aggregate demand and aggregate supply curves and then applies these tools to the new problems. The result may appear to be relevant, but it is not good or even adequate macroeconomic theory. Moreover, as the newer expectational problems are bolted on to the old engines of *LM-IS* and aggregate supply-aggregate demand analysis, the result is a Ptolemaic nightmare consisting of different, special-case models for different problems.

Another inappropriate response to the new problems facing modern economics is to make textbooks more mathematical. Several textbooks use mathematical tools beyond college algebra to present modern macroeconomic theory. Their contribution to scholarship is commendable. Unfortunately, few students of elementary and intermediate macroeconomic theory are properly trained to handle the resulting analysis.

Yet another inappropriate answer is to invent new aggregate hybrids. Occasionally, a textbook will use new forms of excess demand analysis or dynamic modeling to explain modern macroeconomics. These contributions are interesting; however, they require that the student learn the derivation and manipulation of an entire new mode of analysis. This generates the same misplaced emphasis on the derivation and manipulation of hybrid curves that plagues the *LM-IS* and aggregate demand-aggregate supply approaches.

I believe that the appropriate solution is not to make teaching methods more complex but rather to simplify them. As a result, as did the first edition, *Introduction to Modern Macroeconomics, Second Edition,* uses only the tools of supply and demand analysis. Part II of the text begins by analyzing the labor market in a partial equilibrium framework. Next, it considers the credit (goods and services) market in a partial equilibrium framework. Then, it examines the money (asset) market in a partial equilibrium framework.

In each market only supply and demand are used. In each market the application of these tools to contemporary problems is immediate, providing quick reward for the student. In the labor market the different varieties of Phillips curves are derived, and cyclical and secular changes in unemployment, the business cycle, and macroeconomic forecasting are examined. In the credit market the problems of crowding out and the effects of inflationary expectations on interest rates are explored, and the Keynesian $C + I + G$, 45° line model is shown to be a socially powerful but diametrically opposite way of explaining the equilibration of credit flows. In the money market, the problems of alternative linkages from money to the rest of the economy and instability in the income velocity of various measures of money are introduced. Throughout these partial equilibrium analyses, expectational alternatives—rational expectations and adaptive expectations—are given (where relevant) full and explicit consideration.

The advantages of this approach are obvious. The student is required only to work with the simplest of models as a foundation for exposure to many of the most interesting and vexing problems of modern macroeconomics. Onerous derivation and manipulation of hybrid aggregate relations is not a prerequisite to macroeconomic understanding. Therefore, the only prerequisite for the student is a one-semester course in microeconomic principles. In addition, *Introduction to Modern Macroeconomics, Second Edition,* does not dwell on one sector of the economy such as the flow sector while ignoring other sectors. There is a balanced treatment of demand-side (flow and stock) markets as well as supply-side markets. Moreover, the method is simple—consistently applying supply and demand analysis to contemporary problems.

Part III of the text is cast in a general equilibrium rather than a partial equilibrium framework. Here, the individual markets are viewed simultaneously and solution processes are seen to rest on alternative expectational assumptions. Therein, the Neoclassical and Keynesian models are treated as easily reconciled variations of the same general theory. The general equilibrium model in three markets (labor, credit, and money markets) is then shocked in a series of experiments. These experiments consist of observing the effects on the model of an increase in the supply of money, an increase in the government deficit, and a supply shock in the form of an increase in the price of an imported raw material. The supply shock case is expanded in a discussion of the real business cycle. In all experiments assumptions regarding the formulation of expectations in each of the three markets are made explicit, and the resulting alternative views of the linkage mechanism are illustrated.

The alternative linkage mechanisms are labeled Keynesian, Neoclassical, and New Classical. These labels are not applied because there are hard and fast boundaries between different schools. Rather, *Introduction to Modern Macroeconomics, Second Edition,* emphasizes the common foundations of all alternative models. However, because it clearly identifies distinct alternative views of the economy, this text is able to examine efficiently alternative views on the concepts of supply shock and cost push inflation, the effectiveness of price controls, and the effectiveness of macroeconomic stabilization policy.

Another innovation of this text is that disturbances to the economy—monetary, fiscal, and supply shocks—are viewed as being interrelated. The general equilibrium, supply and demand model is applied to examine the operation of monetary policy as it is used in the real world to correct, cover, or compensate for fiscal and supply shock perturbations, especially when these disturbances imply crowding out and/or a reduction in employment and output. Thus, this textbook is able to apply a simple, supply and demand, general equilibrium model to an examination of the political economy of and effectiveness of monetary and fiscal policy. Moreover, because of the explicit treatment of alternative expectational assumptions and resulting alternative views of the linkage mechanism, this textbook is able to generate easy-to-follow pictures of the alternative time paths that the interest rate, inflation, output, and financial asset prices will follow under different expectational regimes in different markets. This dramatic visual presentation permits a close, critical inspection of the likelihood that specialists can profitably forecast movements in interest rates, stock and bond prices, and the efficient markets hypothesis. Moreover, it suggests a healthy skepticism toward the bold claims of prognosticators of the future paths of employment and output, and it permits further critical inspection of the proper role for macroeconomic stabilization policy.

Perhaps the greatest advantage of this textbook is that, throughout these exercises, the use of a supply and demand, general equilibrium model allows full visibility of movements in all of the variables of the model. Nothing of importance is obscured by the sort of needless aggregation that prevails in many other textbooks. In addition, the close ties to microeconomics are clear and apparent to the student, and time is not wasted in the derivation and manipulation of hybrid aggregative relations.

Introduction to Modern Macroeconomics, Second Edition, also contains a treatment not found in most textbooks. An entire chapter is devoted to an inspection of supply-side economic policy and a related discussion of economic growth. The presentation involves another application of the supply and demand, general equilibrium model. Here again, the student does not have to learn a new model in order to understand the causes and consequences of economic growth. Moreover, because the familiar general equilibrium model is used, the connection between the crowding out that occurs at the initial stages of a supply-side tax cut and subsequent political pressure for tax increases, tax reform, and/or monetary ease can be easily pointed out.

The text closes by developing a general equilibrium model of an open economy. Once again, three markets are presented, and all of the interesting variables—including the exchange rate, the terms of trade, the price of domestic goods, and the overall price level—are visible. The expectational assumptions and their implications for alternative views of the linkage mechanism are clearly presented. Two disturbances are considered, each under regimes of either fixed or flexible exchange rates: a money supply increase and an increase in the government deficit. Using this analysis, implications are presented for crowding out and monetary and fiscal policy in open economies. A discussion of various international payments systems, including the managed float, is included.

Innovative Contents

This book contains many topics of interest to modern macroeconomists and macroeconomic policymakers that are not usually found in other texts. A synoptic list of these topics includes:

—the New Classical, rational expectations hypothesis featured as an integral part of many chapters.

—explicit and balanced treatment of expectational alternatives and their effect on the linkage mechanism (Chapters Eleven, Twelve, Thirteen, and Fifteen).

—careful examination of nominal wage contracting in labor markets (Chapter Four).

—balanced treatment of demand-side (flow and stock) markets as well as supply-side markets.

—coverage of the effects of an increase in the deficit in closed and open economy models of the credit market (Chapters Five and Fifteen).

—thorough discussion of the Ricardian Equivalence Principal (Chapters Five and Eleven).

—unbounded growth in the government debt (Chapters Five and Thirteen).

—crowding out in partial and in general equilibrium models in open and closed economies (Chapters Five, Eleven, Thirteen, and Fifteen).

—crowding out in a partial equilibrium model under the actual and the high employment budgets (Chapter Five).

—the cyclical effects of price inflation on interest rates in partial and general equilibrium models (Chapters Six and Thirteen).

—comparison, contrast, and reconciliation of Keynesian and Neoclassical models in a partial equilibrium model (Chapter Seven), in general equilibrium context (Chapters Twelve and Thirteen), and in an open economy framework (Chapter Fifteen).

—derivation of long- and short-run Phillips curves from a model of the labor market (Chapters Three and Four).

—the explicit derivation of expansion coefficients (money multipliers) for narrowly and broadly defined measures of the money stock (Chapter Eight).

—discussion of the operation of modern depository institutions, including innovations such as liability management and gap management (Chapter Eight).

—examination of recent secular and cyclical movements in the income velocity of narrow and broad measures of money (Chapter Nine).

—the supply shock and cost push concepts in a general equilibrium framework (Chapters Eleven, Twelve, and Thirteen).

—the operation of monetary policy to compensate for fiscal policy and supply shock disturbances (Chapter Thirteen).

—an analysis of alternative views of the supply shock concept (Chapter Eleven).

—extension of the supply shock discussion into coverage of the real business cycle (Chapter Eleven).

—supply-side economic policy and an analysis of the modifications in the tax cut program and tax reform proposals (Chapter Fourteen).

—the process of economic growth in a general equilibrium context (Chapter Fourteen).

—illustrations of alternative time paths of inflation, interest rates, stock and bond prices, and output, given an increase in the money supply under assumptions of different expectational formations by market participants (Chapter Thirteen).

—the efficacy of stock market and business cycle forecasts (Chapters Four and Thirteen).

—the efficient markets hypothesis (Chapter Thirteen).

—the proper role for macroeconomic stabilization policy in closed and open economies (Chapters Twelve, Thirteen, and Fifteen).

Alternative Uses

This book is primarily intended for use in courses in intermediate macroeconomic theory. The chapters can most profitably be used in the order in which they are presented, but the instructor can emphasize or delete chapters and segments of chapters as time and interests permit. There are several ways to reduce the work load. Some instructors may not have the time to justify assigning the supply-side and economic growth material in Chapter Fourteen. Others might choose to omit the open economy model of Chapter Fifteen. Some might also pare down the work load by eliminating the money supply material in Chapter Eight or by deleting crowding out and inflationary expectations discussions in the partial equilibrium model of the credit market in Chapter Six. Chapter Seven can be omitted by those not interested in a comparison and contrast of the $C + I + G$, 45° line model and all the attendant multipliers with the Neoclassical model of the credit market. Finally, the work load can be reduced by omitting the discussion of causes and consequences of changes in money supply growth in Chapter Thirteen.

Any combination of the deletions and omissions will not detract from an efficient, effective course in intermediate macroeconomic theory. The essential core of this book is in Chapters One through Five and Chapters Nine through Twelve.

Field trials by different instructors at Duke University indicate that this text can also be used in courses in macroeconomic principles. For this usage, a one-semester course in microeconomic principles is a recommended prerequisite. Because progress will usually be slower at the principles level, the core chapters (One through Five and Nine through Twelve) are recommended. Other chapters can be added to this core as time and interest permit.

This text is also intended for use in MBA programs where up to a full semester of macroeconomics is taught, or as a theory-review text for courses in money and banking. Here again, at least a one-semester course in microeconomic analysis or its equivalent is a recommended prerequisite. The book is eminently suited to the abilities and interests of MBA candidates. There is a pronounced emphasis on supply and demand analysis in individual markets. The student can proceed to rewarding real-world applications of supply and demand analysis in a partial equilibrium context. The hybrid aggregative equilibrium (*LM-IS*, aggregate supply-aggregate demand) curves are totally absent.

This book contains a strong emphasis on the concepts and terminology with which modern business people must deal. The topics and concepts include various measures of the money stock (Chapter Eight), the management of depository institutions (also Chapter Eight), the operation of credit markets and the magnitude of credit flows (Chapter Five), crowding out, and the effect of inflationary expectations on interest rates (Chapter Six), the income velocity of various measures of the money stock (Chapter Nine), and business cycle forecasting (Chapter Four).

As time and resources permit, general equilibrium analysis can be explored. After working through the short Chapter Ten on the solution process for the Neoclassical general equilibrium model, the student can proceed directly to a number of rewarding real-world applications. These might include: the effects of money supply on government deficit and supply shock disturbances, a critical examination of the supply shock and cost push concepts, and the efficiency of price and wage controls (all in Chapter Eleven), predicting dynamic movements in interest rate and stock and bond prices, the efficiency of economic forecasting, the efficient markets hypothesis, and the proper rate for macroeconomic stabilization policy (all in Chapter Thirteen). Chapter Fourteen presents material on tax incentives, supply-side economic policy, tax reform, and the real world of fiscal policy. Finally, for business school students with an international orientation, Chapter Fifteen, on the open economy, is invaluable.

Special Features

This textbook has a number of features that should prove useful. All key phrases and terminology are italicized in the text, then defined in the glossary which follows Chapter Fifteen.

Each chapter also has a sizable set of carefully selected and tested questions. These questions usually require a recall of major points in the chapter. Sometimes they challenge the student's ability to reflect, compare, and contrast. A *Student's Assistance Manual,* designed to accompany both the first and second editions of the text, is available. It synopsizes each chapter, presents tried and tested exercises, and gives the answers to the questions at the end of each chapter in the text.

Each chapter also contains a carefully selected bibliography. Usually the items in the bibliography are source references and survey articles. Because of size limitations, these bibliographies do not necessarily reflect the latest research in the field but are rather selected for balanced coverage of each chapter's topics.

Many people have been helpful in the preparation of this book. Readers to whom I am deeply indebted have included Art Benavie and Harold Black of the University of North Carolina, Robert Schweitzer of the University of Delaware, Art Selender of the University of Chicago, John Campanella of the Pittsburgh National Bank, and my colleagues at Duke University: Martin Bronfenbrenner, Dave Nickerson, Kent Kimbrough, Ed Tower, Dale Stahl, Phil Brock, Neil DeMarchi, Mike Luger, David Feldman, Robert Boylan, John Gildea, Janet Seiz, Khuan Gon, Hasashi Yamada, Cliff Goalstone, John Geweke, Robert Marshall, and William Yohe. I would also like to thank Dudley Wallace, who, as department chairman, encouraged this project. Invaluable editorial assistance was rendered by Steve Bauer, Jennifer Horner, Alice Fins, Maureen Hewitt, Nancy Maybloom, Martha Kreger, George Cook, and Andy Bray. Special thanks goes to the people who assisted in typing the manuscript: Pat Williams, Stacy Miller, Peggy East, and Pat Johnson.

Finally, there is no way to express adequately my gratitude to my students at Duke University who are ever vigilant in exposing the untenable stories of conventional textbook analysis, who suffered through earlier drafts of this manuscript and were unrelenting in their helpful comments. At the risk of doing a disservice to the many who were helpful, let me thank a number of them who more clearly stand out in my mind. They include Lewis Sarasohn, Manny Perlman, Chris Phelan, Amy Cozwith, David Wombwell, Darryl

Creighton, Cam Hewell, Jon Langford, John Featherston, Nick Beare, Alan Voorhees, Craig Leese, Al Bagget, Brian Simpson, Phil Fresen, Bobby Hinson, Tim Bryan, Don Burton, Nat Henshaw, David Rice, Joe Larisa, Ed Mitchell, Yvette Chocolaad, Adam Schwarz, David Cohen, Jon Libman, Thomas Mincher, Jr., Charles Roos, Jon Blank, Michael Greenberg, Gary Goldsholle, Vernon Johnson, and Reid Lewis. Special thanks go for the outstanding efforts of Stephen Siegel and Christopher Olson.

Introduction

TO THE STUDENT

This book is divided into three parts. Part I, "Basic Concepts, Meanings, and Measurements," includes the first two chapters. Part II, "Partial Equilibrium Models," incorporates Chapters Three through Nine. Part III, "General Equilibrium Models," includes Chapters Ten through Fifteen.

Chapters One and Two identify the basic problems of macroeconomics and present an economist's view of the economy as a whole. The conceptual tools, terminology, methods, and measurements of macroeconomics are discussed in these chapters. These chapters provide an overview of the economy as it consists of different types of markets. This big picture discloses the role played by the decision-making entities—households, business firms, and government—in these markets. These chapters develop the meanings of terms such as income, expenditures, saving, investment, government deficit, transfer payments, wealth, and the price level and show how each is measured.

Part II of this book presents partial equilibrium models of individual markets of the economy. In partial equilibrium analysis variables influenced by behavior in other markets are assumed constant. One of the markets incorporated in the big picture discussed in Chapters One and Two is the labor market.

As discussed in Chapter Three, in the labor market, households make the decision to allocate their time to labor or leisure, and business firms decide to hire labor. Both decisions depend upon the level of wages and prices. When labor suppliers (workers) and labor demanders (employers) come together in the labor market, the level of wage and employment are determined. These are the matters covered in Chapter Three.

Does an increase in inflation cause higher employment? If the price level rises and workers and employers can anticipate it, and if wages are flexible, wages will rise to reflect fully the higher price level. The level of employment will not change. If the labor market participants do not anticipate rises in the price level, or if wages are not immediately adjustable, employment will change. The rate of change of the price level over time is called inflation. Discussion of how employment is affected by inflation is the focus of Chapter Four.

What determines the interest rate? One of the markets incorporated into the big picture of the economy featured in Chapter Two is the credit market. Chapter Five examines the decision of a household to save (to lend in the credit market). Saving is viewed as being dependent on the interest rate and the level of the household's income after taxes. Chapter Five further demonstrates that the decision of a business firm to borrow in the credit market to finance investment expenditures also depends on the interest rate. Therefore, the interest rate affects both the supply of and demand for credit. It is the "price" of credit that brings supply and demand into balance in the credit market.

In recent years the deficit of government has grown. Since government must borrow in the credit market to obtain the funds to spend in excess of its tax receipts, this pushes up the interest rate. If credit flows in from abroad the deficit forces up the value of the dollar in terms of foreign currencies. A higher interest rate causes a crowding out of private investment and private consumption expenditures. Another source of a high interest rate is inflation. When inflation is expected to occur, lenders insist on being compensated for erosion in the purchasing power of the funds they lend. They obtain this compensation in the form of a higher interest rate. The effects of changes in the government deficit and changes in inflation on interest rates are the subject matter of Chapter Six.

Chapter Seven looks at the credit market in an alternative way. John Maynard Keynes contended that the interest rate should be viewed as being inflexible in the short run. Since saving also depends upon income, he argued that it is changes in income rather than changes in the interest rate that brings the credit market into balance. Therefore, a change in the government deficit could be used to influence the level of income in the economy.

Another market included in the big picture of Chapter Two is the money market. Chapter Eight investigates the determination of the supply of money. It examines various measures of the money stock and how the behavior of depository institutions, individuals, and the Federal Reserve influence these measures.

The supply of money can be controlled by the Federal Reserve. What are the variables that determine the demand for money? Is the demand for money stable over time? If the Federal Reserve knew the answers to these questions, examined in Chapter Nine, its job of influencing the economy would be much easier.

Chapters Ten through Fifteen, Part III of this textbook, bring the individual markets of Chapters Three through Nine together in a general equilibrium model of the economy as a whole. Chapter Ten illustrates the process of finding solution values for the variables of a general equilibrium model.

In Chapter Eleven, a Neoclassical, general equilibrium model is used in three experiments. The first experiment involves observing the effects of an increase in the money supply; the second experiment considers the effects of increasing the government deficit; the third experiment examines the effect of a supply shock in the form of an increase in the price of an imported raw material. Because many analysts view supply shocks and related phenomena as independent causes of inflation, this chapter carefully examines some alternative views of the supply shock concept. Under what conditions can an increase in the price of an imported raw material significantly shock the economy? How do significant supply shocks set off a real business cycle? Are the perpetrators of these shocks merely used as scapegoats for a mismanaged monetary and fiscal policy? Can government price and wage controls suppress the inflationary effects of these and other shocks?

Chapter Twelve presents a Keynesian general equilibrium model of the economy as a whole. The solution process and two experiments using the Neoclassical model in Chapters Ten and Eleven, respectively, are performed with the Keynesian model in Chapter Twelve. This chapter shows how Keynesian and Neoclassical views of the economy can be reconciled, despite their contrasting implications for macroeconomic stabilization policy.

Throughout Chapters Eleven and Twelve, alternative assumptions regarding the way labor, credit, and money market participants form their expectations are shown to affect the way the money supply and the deficit affect the rest of the economy. These alternative linkage mechanisms are clearly illustrated.

Money supply changes, variations in the deficit, and supply shocks are treated in Chapters Eleven and Twelve as independent disturbances. In reality, they are interrelated because the Federal Reserve frequently increases the money supply in response to the crowding out effects of an increased deficit and the effect on real income and interest rates caused by a supply shock. Chapter Thirteen describes how these interactions take place. Using the alternative linkage mechanisms derived from the general equilibrium models of Chapters Eleven and Twelve, this chapter portrays the alternative paths that inflation, interest rates, stock and bond prices, and output would follow over time, given a change in the money supply growth rate. The alternative time paths depend on the alternative assumptions regarding how market participants form their expectations.

Can well-informed prognosticators systematically predict movements in interest rates and the prices of stocks and bonds, and, thereby, speculate profitability? Can economic forecasters foresee movements in employment and output? What is the proper role for macroeconomic stabilization policy in a world where such predictions are available to market participants? Chapter Thirteen outlines the answers to these questions.

In 1981 a massive series of income tax cuts was enacted by Congress, but in 1982 and 1983 Congress raised taxes but cut them again in 1986. Why the turnabouts? The tax cuts were predicated on the idea of supply-side economic policy that reductions in the income tax rate are incentives for productive effort. Supply-side advocates contend that more saving, investment, and labor will spur greater economic growth. Chapter Fourteen describes the relationships between tax cuts, the level of productive input into production processes, and the rate of economic growth. Then, using the general equilibrium model of previous chapters, it illustrates the step-by-step effect of a cut in the income tax on the size of the deficit, productive effort, and the level of real income. The model shows how the increases in the deficit and the related crowding out of private expenditures resulted in the tax increases of 1982 and 1983 that threatened the promised incentive effects of the initial tax cuts and led to the 1986 cuts.

The final chapter of this text presents a model of an open economy. Like the closed economy model of previous chapters, it focuses on the labor, credit, and money markets in a general equilibrium perspective. This open economy model generates solution values for new variables such as exports, imports, the exchange rate, and the terms of trade. The model has both Neoclassical and Keynesian forms under alternative regimes of fixed or flexible exchange rates. Two experiments are performed on these four variants of the model. The experiments involve an increase in the money supply and an increase in the government deficit. As in previous chapters, alternative assumptions regarding the formation of expectations by market participants have a substantial effect on the linkage mechanisms. A number of interesting implications are shown for fiscal and monetary policy including the impact of crowding out and the proper role for macroeconomic stabilization policy. The chapter closes with a description of the evolution of the international payments mechanism from a fixed to a flexible exchange rate system and to the present arrangement of a managed float.

Basic Concepts, Meanings, and Measurements

Part I

Basic Concepts

Chapter 1

THE THREE BIG QUESTIONS OF MACROECONOMICS

Why the Questions Are Important

This is a book about macroeconomic theory. A theory is a hypothetical answer to a question. All answers began with questions. The three big questions in macroeconomics are: what determines the level of employment (and output)? what determines the level of interest rates? and, what determines the price level and its rate of change?

These are very important problems. The level of aggregate employment affects well-being, especially if you are one of the unfortunate workers who is unable to find employment at the prevailing wage rate. The word *aggregate* means "sum of." Aggregate output, the sum total of newly produced goods and services over a period of time, is of great interest to many people because it is an important reflection of our standard of living. For example, one measure of our standard of living, *per capita output,* is defined as aggregate output divided by the population. Therefore, when aggregate output declines with the population unchanged, our standard of living is often said to fall.

The *interest rate* actually refers to an average of many rates. Interest rates capture the attention of borrowers and lenders because they influence the interest income of lenders as well as the cost of credit to borrowers. At very high rates of interest the ordinary citizen may find prospective mortgage payments unbearably high and business people may be reluctant to borrow to finance the acquisition of new *capital goods*. Capital goods are the produced means of producing more goods and services. The expansion of the stock of capital goods usually has a fruitful impact on the growth of production and output per worker. It improves the overall efficiency of firms and industries in our economy and enhances the ability of our business firms and industries to compete in international markets. It also affects the prosperity and well-being of regions of the country where the output of domestic industries must compete with foreign imports.

The *price level* is an average of many prices. The rate of change of the price level over time (the rate of inflation) has an immense effect on most citizens. Few individuals have not experienced the dramatic loss of purchasing power associated with an acceleration of inflation when the growth rate of his or her disposable income did not accelerate. Inflation erodes the purchasing power of noninterest-earning assets such as currency. By causing the nominal or money value of incomes to rise, inflation pushes private tax payers into higher income tax brackets. It also raises the taxable value of property. Finally, inflation hurts the market system because it requires the individual to spend more time in comparison shopping to keep abreast of price changes.

To appreciate the three big questions regarding the level of employment, interest rates, and the price level, the reader should understand how economists view the economy as a whole. This book presents a picture of the economy as a whole as economists tend to view it.

In Chapter Two the concepts of aggregate output, aggregate wealth, the price level, and equilibrium are introduced. The chapter contains a discussion of how the flow of aggregate output is measured, and how it relates to the flow of credit, and the stock of aggregate wealth. This basic concepts chapter describes how economists conceive of our economic system as a market economy. Economists agree—virtually unanimously—that employment, interest rates, and the price level are determined within markets. However, despite the importance of these problems, economists have not agreed on *how* the level of employment, interest rates, and the price level are determined within our market economy and *why* these variables fluctuate over time, establishing an up-and-down pattern commonly called *the business cycle*.

The Disagreement Between Keynesian and Neoclassical Theories

The two opposing theories regarding the determination of employment, output, interest rates, and the price level have traditionally been termed Keynesian theory and the Neoclassical theory.[1]

The term *Keynesian* is used in this text to refer to macroeconomic analysis that indicates that changes in government expenditures, taxation, and the money supply can and should be applied to affect systematically interest rates, employment, and aggregate

[1]Compartmentalization can be very misleading because new subcategories are continually invented and because a lot of serious research effort is not, and should not be, compartmentalized. Nevertheless, this book deals with a number of policy issues and the labels Keynesian and Neoclassical frequently emerge in these policy debates.

output. The term *Neoclassical* is used in this text to refer to macroeconomic analysis that predicts that changes in government expenditures, taxation, and the money supply may affect employment and aggregate output, but that such effects either are too short-lived or too unsystematic to serve as a basis for government macroeconomic stabilization policy. The label *Monetarist* has so many interpretations that it is seldom used in this text. It is commonly applied to the part of the Neoclassical macroeconomic analysis that emphasizes the role of the money supply in macroeconomic stabilization policy and concludes that stable money supply growth is an optimal foundation for such policy. The term *New Classical* is used in this text to refer to macroeconomic analysis associated with the rational expectations hypothesis that predicts that changes in government expenditures, taxation, and the money supply can affect employment and aggregate output only when unsystematic and, hence, only when unanticipated by market participants and concludes that such a basis is not a justifiable premise for macroeconomic stabilization policy. New Classical analysis is frequently considered a branch of Neoclassical theory.[2]

Most economists are influenced by both Keynesian and Neoclassical theories of the determination of employment, output, interest rates, and the price level: some economists favoring one theory over the other, other economists being skeptical of both theories, others, including many noneconomists, being just plain confused. Table 1.1 presents a highly simplified sketch of some of the contrasting implications of the two theories.

Such apparent disagreement over the determination of employment, output, interest rates, and prices keeps economists up late at night trying to reconcile these theories (yawn!). This disagreement also leaves policymakers and decision makers in government and industry with little certainty regarding the "best" course of action for government economic policy. For example, suppose there were broad consensus on the need to reduce interest rates. According to Table 1.1, a Keynesian economic adviser in government might recommend increasing the money supply. A Neoclassical economic adviser would insist that the Keynesian course of action would only cause the price level to rise and would suggest instead that if interest rates are to be brought down, some part of aggregate spending should be reduced. As another example, if too high a level of unemployment and too low a level of production were the perceived social problem, a Keynesian adviser in government might insist on policies to stimulate aggregate spending. A Neoclassical purist might protest that such policies could only drive up interest rates. If policymakers subsequently heeded the Keynesian's advice and if interest rates rose, they might then try to reduce interest rates by increasing the money supply. The Neoclassical economist would predict that any action to increase the money supply in this instance would result in a rise in the level of prices.

Such ongoing disagreement among Keynesian and Neoclassical economists about the proper course of economic policy leaves government officials and business people highly uncertain. While this uncertainty provides economists with lucrative employment, it also

[2]There are yet other types of macroeconomic analyses. For instance, the term *Post Keynesian* macroeconomic analysis refers to the small band of economists who insist that other analysts have misinterpreted the original theories of John Maynard Keynes. In this text, Post Keynesian analysis is ignored on the basis that if you've met one Post Keynesian, you've met them both. However, for an excellent description of the Post Keynesian program, see the book by A. G. Hines that is cited in the Bibliography to Chapter 12.

Table 1.1 A Simplified View of the Contrasting Implications of Neoclassical and Keynesian Theories

	Primarily Affected By	
Variables	Neoclassical Theory	Keynesian Theory
Employment and output	The labor market	Aggregate spending and the money market
Interest rate	Aggregate spending	Aggregate spending and the money market
Price level	The money market	Aggregate spending and the money market

gives them a well-deserved reputation for being disorganized. Unfortunately, it also keeps students of macroeconomics in a state of high anxiety.

There Is But One Economics

The preceding portrait of the opposition of Neoclassical and Keynesian economists is extremely simplified. Unfortunately, this overly simplistic dichotomy tends to prevail in the media, and especially in political circles. Simpleminded theories make good copy for the media and, if their implications are politically convenient, they tend to be embraced by politicians. Later chapters demonstrate that the two theories are readily reconcilable, and that both Keynesian economics and Neoclassical economics are part of a unified body of knowledge. The two theories draw from the same foundations. Small changes in the underlying assumptions about human behavior account for the differences between the conclusions and policy implications of each theory given in Table 1.1. These differences in underlying assumptions will be clearly delineated.

This book will show that Keynesian economics may sometimes be viewed as a special, short-run case of a more general Neoclassical theory, or that Neoclassical economics may sometimes be viewed as a special, long-run case of a more general Keynesian theory. Short run and long run refer to different intervals of time. The choice between theories is often simply a matter of perspective and value judgment. A person who might be more concerned about problems which typically persist over long intervals of time, such as inflation, would weigh the long run more heavily. This individual would probably place more credence in Neoclassical economics. Another person who might be worried about problems which typically occur over short intervals of time, such as upswings in unemployment, would place more emphasis on the short run. This individual would have more faith in the Keynesian perspective. Many of the promising developments in modern macroeconomics cannot be so readily reconciled by use of the long- and short-run taxonomy. Another classification used in this book differentiates Keynesian and Neoclassical economics in terms of whether periodic shocks to the economy are anticipated or unanticipated by market participants. In a world where shocks to the economy are anticipated by market participants, the results are Neoclassical; in a world where shocks are not anticipated, the results are Keynesian (see footnote 1). The purpose of this book is not to make judgments on individual values but rather to show *why* economists occasionally disagree. With this perspective in mind, this book can broaden the scope of common agreement and understanding of macroeconomic theories.

The Market System as Part of the Social System

People seem to take the market system for granted. Yet, it is an important organizer. The market system enables people and groups in the social system to reach their goals. It does so efficiently—in a way that does not unnecessarily waste resources.

The market system reflects the general principle of reciprocity. Reciprocity means "give and take." Market exchange is a special kind of give and take. Specifically, because it involves equal exchange between individuals, market exchange may be characterized by the statement: "You do something good for me, and I'll do something equally good for you." Other types of reciprocity may not involve ostensibly equal exchanges.

A market mode of organizing society obviously has certain advantages when compared to some of the alternatives. One alternative to market exchange as a social organizer is coercion. Coercion may be characterized by the statement, "You do something good for me or I'll do something bad for you." Historically, coercion has been a dominant social organizer in most societies. Institutions that are basically coercive are the police, the military, and indeed the state itself. Even seemingly noncoercive institutions such as the family and the church have elements of coercion in them. For coercion to be credible it must be backed up with threats and/or the use of force. Thus, coercion is wasteful of resources. For example, the state can only sustain its coercive power if it maintains visible means of enforcing its threats—the entire apparatus of criminal law, police forces, and standing armies.

Coercion as a social organizer can be contrasted to market exchange as a social organizer. Unlike coercion the implicit payoff from exchange is not negative. There is no punishment or threat of punishment. Rather, the payoff is positive—gain for both parties to the exchange. For example, when you purchase a candy bar, you do not threaten the storekeeper; you are not coerced into consuming candy, and he is not coerced into selling it. Rather, you do something good for him—pay him 35 cents—and he does something good for you—gives you a candy bar. No costly and cumbersome apparatus of enforcement and punishment is necessary to bring the candy into your possession or to direct the producer to make it available. When consumers decide that they prefer candy to cigarettes, the price of candy rises, the price of cigarettes falls, and profit-seeking manufacturers produce more candy and less cigarettes. Through the price system more resources are automatically allocated to candy production because wages and profits rise in the candy industry. Fewer resources are allocated to cigarette production. In contrast, coercive organization of cigarette and candy production, such as exists in many socialist nations, requires the costly and cumbersome arrangement of planning ministries, production quotas, penalties, and chronic surpluses and/or shortages in industry. Horror stories of failures in planned economies are legend. Consider the persistent shortages of agricultural goods in socialist economies. For example, the Soviet press reported last year that the Soviet Union had its sixty-eighth annual drought.

Microeconomics and Macroeconomics

Macroeconomics is concerned with aggregate economic variables like national income and employment, total consumption spending, and the stock of money. Microeconomics is the study of behavior of individual consumers and producers in market-exchange relationships. Microeconomic theory is an attempt to analyze the way relative prices and outputs (of candy and cigarettes, for example) are determined and distributed. Microeconomics and macroeconomics are not inconsistent with one another. The processes of individual microeconomic behavior actually determine the movement of these broad macroeconomic aggregates. The development of a macro relation from a micro hypothesis involves problems of aggregation or adding up across individual behavioral entities. Problems of aggregation occasionally make micro- and macroeconomics seem virtually incompatible. In the first nine chapters of this book the macroeconomic relations that are to be used in the latter part of the text are derived from specific microeconomic hypotheses.

Economic Models

An *economic model* is a set of relationships among economic variables used to formulate, express, and analyze economic theories. Economic theories, in turn, are hypothetical answers to economic questions such as the three big questions of macroeconomics discussed at the outset of this chapter.

Models abstract from the complexities of the real world by the use of simplifying assumptions. These are necessary in order to make models manageable and should be as realistic as possible. Economic theories are often scored for the lack of realism of their assumptions. Sometimes assumptions that are not very realistic are acceptable if making them more realistic would only complicate the model without substantively changing its conclusions.

TYPES OF ECONOMIC VARIABLES

Stocks and Flows

An elemental distinction among economic variables is between *stocks* and *flows*. Many economic analysts confuse the classification of variables. A *stock* variable can be measured at a point in time. A *flow* variable can be measured only over an interval of time. In nature, a stock variable is the size of a lake in terms of volume; a flow variable is the volume of water passing into that lake. The stock variable can be measured at a point in time (gallons of water); the flow variable must be expressed in terms of the amount *per unit of time* (millions of gallons per minute, per hour, or per day). Stock measures can be converted into flow measures only if the *change* in the stock is considered over some time interval.

Noneconomists often apply stock terms to flow concepts and vice versa. They say they make "money" when economists would say they earn "income." Money is a *stock,* a way of holding one's wealth. Income is a *flow* of earnings over a period of time. The confusion arises because most people are paid in money; the stock of money changes hands because it is used as a medium of exchange. Even when money changes hands, it remains a stock and not a flow.

Even trained economists make grievous errors with stocks and flows. In the financial press the word "savings" (plural), which is a stock and a way of holding wealth (as in a savings account or savings bonds), is often confused with the flow of saving (singular) out of income. Similar stock-flow confusion arises commonly with the terms investment and capital. For example, when one sees the term "investment" one cannot always be sure it means the holding of a stock of wealth such as one's investment in the securities of a corporation or "investment expenditures" on a newly produced capital good such as a piece of machinery, a flow. Chapter Two clarifies these and other distinctions.

In economics, ratio variables permit relating flows to flows, stocks to stocks, flows to stocks, and stocks to flows. All prices and interest rates are ratio variables because they express one magnitude in terms of another. For example, the nominal wage is the ratio of a flow of labor services per hour to the stock of money paid in exchange for that flow.

Endogenous and Exogenous Variables

Economic models have two types of variables, exogenous and endogenous. An *exogenous variable* is one whose value is assumed to be determined outside a model. An *endogenous variable* is one whose value is determined within a model. Endogeneity and exogeneity of variables depend on the breadth of the model. Narrow models that purport to explain only a few variables have many exogenous variables. Broader models that purport to explain more things have fewer exogenous variables.

For example, to describe the determination of the price of a candy bar (an *endogenous* variable) in the Redneck, New Jersey, market, one would only need to know the quantity supplied and quantity demanded of candy in Redneck, New Jersey, for a specific period of time. Other variables such as the wage of workers in the Amazon in Brazil would be *exogenous,* even though the Amazon Valley is a leading producer of cocoa beans. In contrast, to describe the determination of world candy prices, one needs more endogenous variables, such as the quantity supplied and demanded in Redneck as well as all of the other major cities of the world, and the wage rate in the Amazon. (Let no one ever ask what the Amazon has to do with the price of candy in New Jersey.)

This suggests that the size of economic models is related to the number of endogenous variables they contain. For very large macroeconomic models (which try to explain a lot) the number of endogenous variables increases. This is because each model must contain as many equations as it does endogenous variables. Thus, categorizing some variables as exogenous helps model builders to keep their models of manageable size.

Exogenous variables require no explanation in an economic model, because they are assumed to be determined outside the model. Sometimes, variables are classed as exogenous because the model builder has little idea what determines them. For example, rainfall can be predicted by meteorologists, but in models of agricultural output and agricultural prices, economists are even more confused about the causes of rainfall than they are about the causes of purely economic phenomena such as inflation, interest rates, and unemployment. Therefore they usually consider rainfall to be exogenous and do not try to predict it. At other times variables are classified as exogenous because they are not affected by market behavior. For example, government policy determines the money supply, tax rates, and the deficit. These are usually called policy variables and are often considered exogenous.

Types of Relationships

In economic models there are four general kinds of relations: (1) identities, (2) technical relations, (3) equilibrium conditions, and (4) behavioral relations.

An *identity* is a definition; it is always true. A key macroeconomic identity is the aggregate budget identity which says

$$Y \equiv C + S + T \tag{1.1}$$

where aggregate income (Y) is defined as either being spent on consumption goods and services (C), saved (S), or taxed away by government (T). The aggregate budget identity, like all identities, is *always* true for *any* values of the variables involved. It does not depend on behavior, equilibrium, or anything else. Identities are very important because they help model builders to ascertain certain conservation or "adding up" conditions for their models. For example, if in the above identity income (Y) is unchanged, the effect of any variable on consumption spending (C) must be equal in magnitude but opposite in algebraic sign from its combined effect on saving (S) and taxation (T), since the effect on saving (S) and taxation (T) must just offset the effect on consumption spending (C) for the aggregate budget identity to hold.

A *technical relation* specifies that the variables are related through their physical properties. A key technical relation in macroeconomics is the aggregate production function

$$Q = F(L, K) \tag{1.2}$$

where the quantity of production (Q) depends on the quantity of labor input (L) and the quantity of capital input (K) used in production.[3]

An *equilibrium condition* describes a system that has no tendency to change. In terms of market equilibrium this means that the quantity that suppliers plan to supply equals the quantity that demanders plan to demand. A common equilibrium condition in macroeconomics is the money market equilibrium condition

$$M_s = M_d \tag{1.3}$$

[3]The notation $F(\ )$ simply means that a relationship exists between the arguments within the parentheses on the right-hand side and the dependent variable on the left-hand side of the equation. It is general in that it does not specify the form of the relationship. This is elaborated later. To denote that various functions are different, separate letters will be used for each technical and behavioral relation, e.g., $F(\ ), f(\ ), g(\ )$.

where the quantity of money supplied (M_s) is equal to the quantity of money demanded (M_d). If this equation holds, there is no need for the variables which determine the quantity demanded and the quantity supplied to change.

A *behavioral relation* describes a stimulus and a response. It reflects the behavior of individuals. In macroeconomics one such behavioral relation is the aggregate saving function

$$S = j(i, Y) \tag{1.4}$$

where the level of saving (S) depends on income (Y) and the rate of interest (i). The letter j simply denotes that some systematic but unspecified relationship exists between Y and i as the stimuli and S as the response. The letter does not tell us the nature of the relationship. It only says that one exists. The Equation 1.4 may be rewritten to be a bit more specific:

$$S = j(\underset{+}{i}\,, \underset{+}{Y}) \tag{1.5}$$

Now Equation (1.5) has plus (+) signs beneath each right-hand side variable. This signifies that there is a positive linkage between i and Y as stimuli and S as a response. It indicates that when income rises, aggregate saving goes up, and that when the interest rate increases, aggregate saving goes up. Equation (1.5) is much more informative about behavior than Equation (1.4). However, Equation (1.5) is still fairly general. It does not say specifically what the mathematical form of the positive linkage between Y and i and S is. For instance, Equation (1.5) would be perfectly consistent with certain types of linear equations or certain types of logarithmic equations. This text describes all behavioral relations in the simple, general notation of Equation (1.5). Therefore, only a minimal level of mathematics is required to understand this book.

Real versus Nominal Magnitudes

The term *real* is synonymous with the terms "dollars of constant purchasing power" or "constant dollars." The term *nominal* in economics is synonymous with the term "current dollars."

The concepts of real expenditures, real income, or real money balances abstract from price changes and measure what the dollar amounts would be if prices remained constant. Economists use the word *real* in a specific way. Real measures may be expressed by dividing ("deflating") nominal measures by a price index. Nominal magnitudes are expressed in dollars of current purchasing power, current dollars. A price index is a weighted average of a number of actual prices expressed in dollars per unit. Therefore, a real measure of something is equal to its nominal measure divided by a price index.

For example, assume that in 1988 aggregate nominal investment expenditures (total spending on newly produced capital goods) in the United States economy were $500 billion and in 1989 aggregate nominal investment expenditures were $600 billion. Assume further that in 1988 an index or weighted average of the price of newly produced capital goods was 1.0 and in 1989 the index was 1.5. Because the average cost of capital goods rose from 1.0 to 1.5, real expenditures on newly produced capital goods in the economy in 1989, measured in dollars of constant 1988 purchasing power, were $600 billion divided by 1.5 = $400 billion. In other words, if the price of newly produced capital goods had not risen by 50 percent from 1.0 to 1.5, only $400 billion would have been spent on new capital goods in 1989. Said in another way, in dollars of constant 1988 purchasing power $400 billion of investment expenditures were made in 1989. Nominal investment expenditures were $600 billion in 1989; real investment expenditures in dollars of 1988 purchasing power were $600 billion divided by 1.5 = $400 billion.

Since changes in real measures reflect what would have happened if prices had not changed, they are measures of volume. In contrast, changes in nominal measures include the effect of price changes and are measures of current dollar value (price times volume). For example, economists regularly talk about nominal aggregate income and real aggregate income. One measure of nominal aggregate income is the nominal *gross national product* or GNP. Nominal aggregate income (Y) is the product of a measure of the volume of newly produced goods and services (Q) times an index of the average prices at which these newly produced goods and services are exchanged (P). Since $Y \equiv P \cdot Q$, then real aggregate income equals the volume of newly produced goods and services, $Y/P \equiv Q$.

Static and Dynamic Analysis

In static analysis the equilibrium values of endogenous variables are determined. Exogenous variables have known values that are placed into the relations of the model—and a solution is sought. If one of the exogenous variables changes, new equilibrium values are found for the endogenous variables. In static analysis neither the path involved in moving from the first set of equilibrium values to the second nor the length of the period of adjustment is examined.

Dynamic analysis is concerned primarily with paths of adjustment, disequilibrium, and change. Paths of adjustment are the equilibrium paths followed by the endogenous variables of the model.

Almost all of the analysis in this book is static. The focus is on equilibrium and changes in exogenous variables that generate a new equilibrium. Neither tracing the values taken on by the endogenous variables between equilibria nor estimating how long it takes to reach a new equilibrium will be addressed. This should not suggest that dynamic analysis is not used or is unimportant in macroeconomics. In fact, dynamic analysis is extraordinarily useful—for example, in tracing out the paths of endogenous variables in models of economic growth. Dynamic analysis is not discussed because the complex mathematical formulations it requires are beyond the scope of this text.

Long-Run and Short-Run Equilibrium

Equilibrium is defined as a set of values for the endogenous variables of a model from which there is no tendency to change. In reality, a set of values for the endogenous variables may allow them to remain in equilibrium only for a limited time. Such an equilibrium is called a *short-run equilibrium*. Processes may be occurring that will upset the system from its temporary position of rest and propel it to a new equilibrium position. When equilibrium values for the endogenous variables are found that will persist no matter how much time passes (unless a change occurs in some exogenous variable), the situation is referred to as *long-run equilibrium*. One of the best examples of short-run and long-run equilibrium in macroeconomic theory occurs in the labor market when there is a change in an exogenous variable such as the price level. If employers are aware that they can sell their output at higher prices, they will demand more labor at the prevailing wage. This will cause wages to rise slightly. If workers are unaware of the price level change, they will supply more labor at the slightly higher wages. As a result, the equilibrium level of employment of labor will increase. However, this is only a short-run equilibrium. As time passes, workers will learn about the increase in the price level and ask for much higher wages to compensate for the higher cost of living. When this learning is completed, the level of employment will return to its position of long-run equilibrium.

Partial and General Equilibrium Models: Plan of Development

This book began with three basic economic questions that will be answered hypothetically by formulating economic models. The first question is: what determines the level of employment for the economy as a whole? This question is addressed in Chapters Three and Four where a static *partial equilibrium* model is presented. It involves the labor market only; all other markets are ignored, and the variables affected by other markets are assumed exogenous.

The second question, what determines the level of the interest rate? is considered in Chapters Five, Six, and Seven. In these chapters a static partial equilibrium model of the credit market alone is developed. The term *credit* refers to the volume of borrowing and lending. Again, all other markets are ignored, and the variables affected by other markets are assumed exogenous.

The third question, what determines the price level? is considered in Chapters Eight and Nine. There a static partial equilibrium model of the money market is developed. Money is one form in which people hold their wealth.[4]

Chapters Ten, Eleven, and Twelve combine all three markets in a static *general equilibrium* model of the economy as a whole. In these chapters, many variables that were considered exogenous in the partial equilibrium treatments of earlier chapters are made endogenous and the system is solved for all of the variables of the model. By altering a key assumption or two within the general equilibrium model of the economy as a whole—a model involving labor, credit, and money markets—hypothetical answers to the three big questions of macroeconomics may be changed from Neoclassical answers to Keynesian ones.

Chapters Ten and Eleven present a general equilibrium model of the Neoclassical theory. Chapter Twelve presents a general equilibrium model of the Keynesian theory. In

[4]In each of the models of the first nine chapters macroeconomic relations are derived from *micro*-economic hypotheses.

these chapters both the Neoclassical and the Keynesian models are subject to three experiments. For each model the effects of changes in each of three exogenous variables are examined. These are the effect of a change in the money supply, in the government deficit, and in the relative price of a key input into production processes such as imported petroleum. This latter change is sometimes called a *supply shock*. Both short-run and long-run equilibrium responses to these three exogenous changes are analyzed.

Though many of the problems of macroeconomics benefit from dynamic analysis, the presentation of this book is static. Chapters Thirteen and Fourteen address several inherently dynamic problems using the static general equilibrium models of Chapters Ten, Eleven, and Twelve. Chapter Thirteen probes the dynamics of macroeconomic policy. Why is money so difficult for the policymaker to control? What implications does this have for the (dynamic) time path of key macroeconomic variables such as employment, inflation, and the interest rate?

Chapter Fourteen examines the problems of economic growth. In the 1970s economic growth slowed precipitously. In the 1980s the Reagan administration enacted massive tax cuts to stimulate growth. The static general equilibrium models of Chapters Ten, Eleven, and Twelve are used to analyze the sources of and promised cure for this economic malaise.

Chapter Fifteen develops a model of an *open economy*—an economy that is influenced by imports, exports, international capital flows, and exchange rates. The static general equilibrium models of Chapters Ten, Eleven, and Twelve are used as a starting point.

What the Models Do—An Overview

As indicated previously, the first nine chapters of this book show how economists perceive the economic behavior of individuals in a partial equilibrium context. Table 1.2 presents the behavior that is involved in each market. Chapters Three and Four examine labor market behavior. Chapters Five, Six, and Seven consider credit market behavior—lending and borrowing. The credit market is often called the loanable funds market.

Table 1.2 Behavior in the Three Markets

Chapters	Markets	Behavior
Three and Four	Labor market	Demand for labor Supply of labor Labor market equilibrium Production function
Five, Six, and Seven	Credit market (Loanable funds market)	Supply of credit—saving Demand for credit—investment expenditures plus government deficit Credit market equilibrium
Eight and Nine	Money market	Demand for money Supply of money Money market equilibrium

Table 1.3 How Disturbances Typically Affect the Economy: Neoclassical and Keynesian General Equilibrium Perspectives

Market Type	Neoclassical Model	Keynesian Model[4]
Increase in Money Supply		
Labor:	No change in employment	Increased employment
	Higher nominal wages[1]	Higher nominal wages[1]
	Unchanged real wages[2]	Lower real wages[2]
Credit:	No change in saving and investment	Increased saving and investment
	No change in interest rate	Lower interest rate
Money:	No change in real money stock	Increased real money stock
	Higher price level	Slightly higher price level
Increase in Government Deficit		
Labor:	No change in employment	Increased employment
	Higher nominal wages	Higher nominal wages
	Unchanged real wages	Lower real wages
Credit:	Decreased investment, increased saving	Increased saving, slightly decreased investment
	Higher interest rate	Slightly higher interest rate
Money:	Lower real money stock	Slightly lower real money stock
	Higher price level	Slightly higher price level
Increase in Price of Imported Raw Material[3] (a "Supply Shock")		
Labor:	Decrease in employment	Decrease in employment
	Higher nominal wages	Higher nominal wages
	Lower real wages	Lower real wages
Credit:	Reduction in saving and investment	Reduction in saving and investment
	Increase in interest rate	Increase in interest rate
Money:	Fall in real money stock	Fall in real money stock
	Increase in price level	Increase in price level

Notes:
[1]Nominal wages are wages expressed in dollars.
[2]Real wages are wages expressed in dollars of constant purchasing power: the nominal wage divided by the price level.
[3]This assumes an effect on the economy's productive capacity. If there were no significant reduction in productive capacity, employment, real wages, saving and investment, the interest rate, and the price level would not be affected.
[4]The model described here does not assume that nominal wages are fixed in the short run, only that there is an imperfect response by labor suppliers to price information.

Chapters Eight and Nine examine money market behavior—holding and disposing of financial assets.

In Chapters Ten through Twelve, the economist's perspective on individual human behavior is applied to basic disturbances that regularly occur in the economy. These disturbances are an increase in the money supply, an increase in the government deficit, and an increase in the price of an imported raw material, a "supply shock." In the past three decades the economy has been periodically perturbed by huge increases in the money supply, tremendous jumps in the federal deficit, and enormous swings in the prices of imported raw materials such as oil.

Table 1.3 simplistically categorizes the typical effects of these types of economic disturbances as perceived from Keynesian and Neoclassical general equilibrium perspectives. These effects are not explained here but are developed in detail in later chapters. The table shows that in the Neoclassical model an increase in the money supply has no effect on the interest rate or level of real income; it only affects the price level. In the Keynesian model, an increase in the money supply has a small effect on the price level but also lowers the interest rate and raises real income.

Table 1.3 shows that from the Neoclassical perspective an increase in the government deficit has no impact on real income but does boost both the interest rate and the price level. In contrast, from the Keynesian viewpoint, a greater deficit raises the interest rate and the price level only slightly and has a stimulating effect on real income.

When the price of an imported raw material increases, as long as it does not significantly curtail our capacity to produce, the Neoclassical and Keynesian theories both predict similar effects on employment, interest, and the price level.

Concluding Comment

This chapter provides an overview of key economic concepts and outlines the goals and methods of this textbook. To achieve these goals, it is necessary to understand exactly how economists view the economy as a whole and to learn their language. Chapter Two describes how economists view the economy and how they define and measure its important variables.

EXERCISES

1. Indicate whether the following are stocks, flows, or neither:
   a. the money supply of the United States
   b. total government expenditures
   c. the number of houses in the United States
   d. the interest rate
   e. the rate of inflation
   f. the level of a household's income
2. In a supply and demand model of the market for cantaloupes, label the following variables as exogenous or endogenous:

a. the quantity of cantaloupe demanded
b. the price of cantaloupes
c. rainfall in the cantaloupe fields
d. the wages of cantaloupe pickers
e. the quantity of cantaloupe supplied
f. household income

3. Discuss the alternative(s) that exist to organizing an economy along market-exchange lines.

4. If your wage is $10 per hour and rises to $12 per hour, but the cost of living doubles, what happens to your *real wage*?

5. What is meant when economists say that a variable is measured in dollars of constant purchasing power?

6. Several economists have proposed and use a "Misery Index," which adds the level of unemployment to the rate of inflation. What other variables that commonly measure economic distress would you add to this Index?

Meanings and Measurements

Chapter 2

Theories are necessary to make sense of the complexities of the world. Simplification through the use of theory is a requisite for usable economic predictions. Economists have developed a highly simplified conception of the economy. This chapter examines that conception in detail. As a result of this examination, the reader should come to understand many of the essential concepts and variables used by macroeconomists. In later chapters, these concepts are applied.

OVERVIEW

To economists the economy consists of three sectors: household, business, and government. These sectors participate in three types of markets:

1. *product markets*—in which households, business firms, and governments (local, state, and federal) buy goods and services from business firms at market prices,
2. *factor markets*—in which households sell the services of the factors of production to business firms at market prices, and
3. *credit (loanable funds) markets*—in which households, business firms, and governments lend and borrow.

In product markets, the quantity of goods exchanged multiplied by their market-determined prices generate a dollar-denominated magnitude called *expenditures*. In factor markets, the services of the factors of production exchanged multiplied by their market-determined prices is called *income*. Income is also measured in terms of dollars. In credit markets, sometimes called loanable funds markets, the household sector's income that is earned in the factor markets and not spent in the product markets is loaned out. This dollar-denominated magnitude is called *saving*. When a sector's expenditures in the product markets exceed its income from the factor markets, borrowing occurs. Typically, business firms borrow to finance their *investment expenditures* and governmental entities borrow to finance their *deficits*.

Economists assume that households own all factors of production (labor, capital, land, and entrepreneurial talent), and that households receive all of the income in the economy (wages, interest, rent, and profit) by selling the services of these factors. The assumption of household ownership of all capital is simplistic but not unrealistic because households do own all business firms either through ownership of single proprietorships and partnerships, or through their holdings of equity claims (common and preferred stock) issued by corporations. Thus, households make the decision to sell the services of their factors of production and, using the derived income, make the decision to consume either in the present or in the future. Business firms are also decision makers. They make the decisions both to produce and to sell goods and services, and concomitantly, make the decision to hire the factors of production. Governmental entities make the decisions to tax and to spend.

Throughout this chapter and throughout this book except for part of Chapter Six and all of Chapter Fifteen, it is assumed that there are no imports or exports—that is, that the economy is a *closed economy*. In Chapters Five and Fifteen the concepts of imports, exports, exchange rates, and international capital flows are introduced. Economies that are viewed in an international context are called *open economies*.

Stocks and Flows

In Chapter One, a distinction was made between *stocks* and *flows*. Aggregate income and aggregate expenditures are examples of flows—they can only be measured between two points in time. The supply of money and the supply of physical capital goods are examples of *stocks*—they are specifically measurable only at a given point in time. As an example, consider a keg of beer. The amount of beer pouring from an open tap can only be measured in, say, ounces per minute, a value between two points in time—one point and another point sixty seconds later. Yet, the amount of beer in the keg at any one instant can be specifically measured in, say, gallons. Here, measurement requires no time dimension other than a point in time.

Figure 2.1 is a simplified diagram of the circular flow of income and expenditures. Each level of the diagram signifies different markets. Level I shows the factor markets in which the services of the factors of production are exchanged for factor earnings (i.e., labor for wages, capital for interest, land for rent, and entrepreneurial talent for profit).

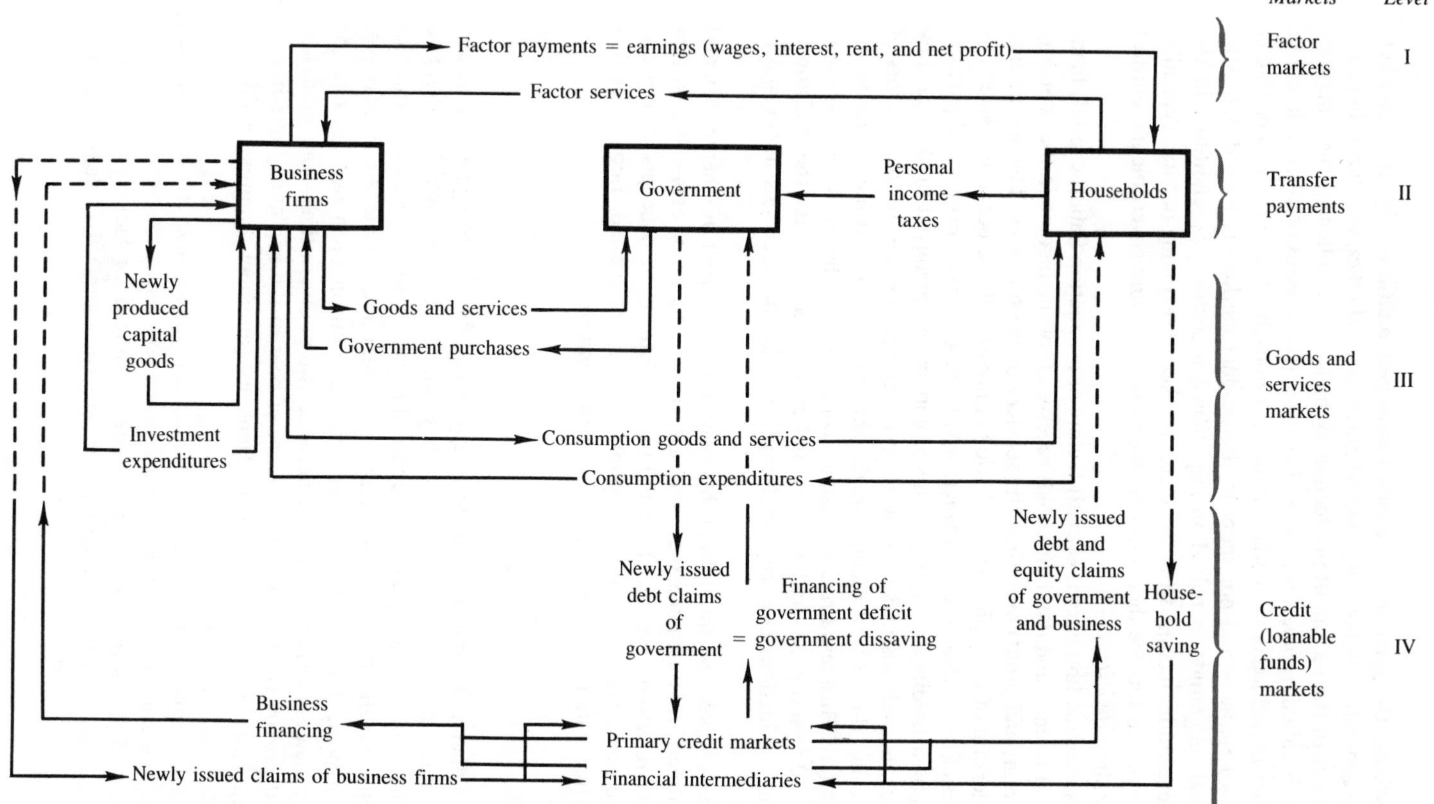

Figure 2.1 Circular Flow of Income and Expenditures

Households, which own all factors of production, supply the services of these factors to business firms in exchange for a flow of income.

Notice that in this simplified flow diagram, governments receive no earnings, and business firms retain no earnings. All income is earned and received by households. Later in the chapter these two assumptions are relaxed.

Transfer payments at Level II are one-way, nonmarket flows. Economists envision transfer payments as unreciprocated flows. To keep matters simple, the only transfer payment included in Figure 2.1 is the personal income tax. Households do not expect a remunerative flow of services for their tax payments and do not make a direct exchange of taxes for government services. Later in this chapter other transfer payments, such as corporate income taxes, dividends, and social security contributions, are introduced.

Level III is the goods and services markets. Here, households buy newly produced goods and services from business firms in exchange for *consumption expenditures*. Governments buy newly produced goods and services from business firms in exchange for *government purchases,* and business firms buy newly produced capital goods from other business firms in exchange for *investment expenditures*. For each flow of goods and services there is a related flow of expenditures in the opposite direction.

Budget Identities

As seen in Level I, all aggregate income is received by households. This income can either be transferred to the government sector (Level II), expended on consumption goods and services (Level III), or saved (Level IV). Thus the budget identity of the household sector is

$$Y \equiv C + S + T \tag{2.1}$$

where Y is aggregate income, C is aggregate consumption expenditures, S is aggregate personal saving, and T is aggregate transfer payments to the government sector. As seen in Level I, the government sector earns no income. However, at Level II it receives receipts from households in the form of tax receipts (e.g., personal income taxes). These receipts can either be spent on goods and services (Level III), or saved (Level IV). The budget identity of the government sector is

$$T \equiv G + S_g \tag{2.2}$$

where T is tax receipts, G is government purchases, and S_g is the deficit (or surplus) of government. *Government expenditures* are the sum of government purchases (G) and transfer payments from governments to households. The latter are not shown in Figure 2.1 but will be introduced later. In recent decades the expenditures of the government sector have chronically exceeded its receipts, so the government sector has engaged in *dissaving,* that is, it has a deficit and S_g is negative.

In this simplified scheme the business sector pays out to households all of its earnings and neither receives nor makes transfer payments. In short, the business sector has zero receipts.

Budget identities allow economists to impose consistency conditions on their models. For example, suppose there is a change in household income. That change must be distributed across the three uses of income: consumption, transfer payments, and saving.

$$\Delta Y \equiv \Delta C + \Delta S + \Delta T \tag{2.3}$$

where Δ always stands for "change in."

In another example, consider what happens if income is unchanged. Suppose a variable such as the interest rate or aggregate wealth changes, causing one of the three elements—consumption, saving, or transfer payments—to change. Since income on the left-hand side of Equation (2.1) is unchanged, the effect of a change in the interest rate or wealth on the sum of consumption, saving, and transfer payments must also be zero. This means that whatever the effect of a change in the interest rate or wealth on consumption, the combined effect of this change on saving and transfer payments must be opposite in algebraic sign but equal in absolute magnitude.

Decision Loci and Financing Constraints

Each sector has specific decisions to make regarding its resource allocation. Assuming that transfer payments are nonvoluntary, households make the decision to consume (Level III) and concomitantly, by the household budget identity, the decision to save (Level IV).

Household saving goes into credit markets (Level IV) where it earns a market-determined rate of interest. Business firms and government borrow at this market "price" (rate of interest). Business firms use the funds to purchase newly produced capital goods from the businesses which produce such goods. Thereby, business firms make the decision to carry out investment expenditures.

At Level I it is assumed that business firms retain no earnings. At Level II, it is assumed that business firms make or receive no transfer payments (e.g., corporate income taxes, dividend payments). Therefore, only by borrowing from the flow of household saving can business firms obtain funds with which to carry out investment expenditures. In exchange for their saving households receive debt and equity claims that are newly issued by business firms. These debt and equity claims represent claims against the future earnings of the business firms, earnings which firms hope will be enhanced by new investment expenditures. In short, the business sector is constrained to finance investment expenditures by issuing claims of ownership or debt, stocks or bonds, to households.

The government sector faces a similar constraint. If government purchases are greater than government receipts (if government has a deficit), it must obtain household saving in exchange for newly issued debt claims (bonds). (Governmental entities do not issue equity claims.) Generally, financing constraints say that if a sector spends more than its receipts, it must borrow in credit markets at the market rate of interest.

Financial Intermediaries

Financial intermediaries are business firms which acquire the debt claims of other businesses and governmental entities as their earning assets and issue *specialized debt claims* against themselves. They profitably "intermediate" in the credit markets (at Level IV), more efficiently mobilizing the flow of saving. For example, financial intermediaries such as commercial banks may profit if they buy debt claims (such as loan paper) from business firms at one interest rate and then issue specialized debt claims (such as savings accounts) to households at a lower interest rate. The role of financial intermediaries in the credit (loanable funds) markets will be covered in greater detail in Chapter Five.

Some of the specialized debt claims of financial intermediaries are interest bearing and some are noninterest bearing. The specialized debt claims of certain financial intermediaries can be transferred by check, wire, or preauthorized arrangement. These "checkable deposits" together with privately held noninterest bearing claims against government (currency in circulation) are usually counted as part of the nation's money supply. (The operations of financial intermediaries and the determination of the money supply will be discussed in Chapter Eight.) The outstanding stock of debt and equity claims are traded in financial markets. As the interest rates that are established in financial markets have an effect on the economy, the supply and demand for existing claims will have a significant influence on the economy. Therefore, theories concerning the supply of and demand for the outstanding stock of debt and equity claims (that is, bonds, equities, and money) are of considerable importance in economics.

Wealth

When an individual household acquires newly issued debt or equity claims out of its own saving, it is increasing its holdings of assets without increasing its liabilities. Therefore, it is increasing its wealth. Economists call such claims *financial assets*. Debt and equity claims (both are types of financial assets) are additions to an individual household's wealth because such assets represent claims on future income. The household saving that is used to purchase these claims at Level IV of Figure 2.1 is employed by business firms to invest in newly produced *capital goods*. Capital goods are productive; if used efficiently, they increase the level of future production in the economy. As such, capital goods are "the produced means of production." Since the stock of financial assets held by a household are claims against future income of business firms, such assets are considered part of the household's wealth. When fluctuations occur in the expected future profits of the firms that have issued equity claims, fluctuations also occur in the value of these equity claims. Thus the wealth of the household will vary with the expected level of business profits.

Debt claims issued by the government sector are also often considered part of an individual household's wealth. This is rationalized because of government's power to finance interest payments through taxation of future earnings. In a sense, these financial assets, like debt and equity issues of the business sector, are claims against future earnings, and thus are part of an individual household's wealth.

Economists conceive of the total wealth of an individual household as consisting of:

1. the value of its holdings of debt claims and equity claims issued by firms,
2. the value of its holdings of debt claims issued by government,

3. the value of its stock of consumer durables, and

4. the present value of its future labor services.

Until now just the wealth of an individual household was considered; all households taken as a whole were not considered. If for the sake of simplicity the stock of consumer durables is ignored, the wealth of the entire household sector consists of:

1. the value of equity claims issued by business firms, and

2. human wealth, the present value of all future labor services.

Private debt claims issued by business firms are not included because when economists aggregate across all households, those claims cancel out. For example, if X-Rated Video Games, Inc., issued a debt claim to a certain household, the debt claim is an asset to that household yet a liability to the households which have equity claims in X-Rated. Thus, in the aggregate, all privately issued debt cancels out.[1]

Many economists believe that government debt should not be counted as part of aggregate private wealth. While the debt of government is an asset of the households which hold it, it represents a liability to households which will pay the future taxes to meet the future interest payments on that debt. These economists insist that even if it is assumed that government goes into debt to develop social overhead or public capital goods which enhance the future productivity of business firms and households, government debt is still not part of aggregate private wealth. For example, if the government borrows to build new roads into Mount Escondido, California, the "Kumquat Capital of the World," no returns will accrue to the government. However, since the roads are social overhead capital goods, kumquat farmer Joe Sixpack will acquire higher profits because it will be less costly to bring his kumquats to market on the new, paved roads than on the old mule trails. The owners of the Sixpack farm are made wealthier. The households that use the roads and sell labor services to Joe are wealthier, too, because their time is more productive. In this sense, debt-financed government expenditures could be viewed as increasing the value of private human and nonhuman capital only if one assumes that resources absorbed (borrowed) by government to finance its deficit had less productive private uses. This assumption is rather debatable. However, the government debt itself should *not* be counted as aggregate wealth because the net benefits of these debt-financed expenditures are already captured by private capital owners. Despite these formidable arguments, many economists continue to count the government debt as part of aggregate private wealth.[2]

[1]Even though all privately issued debt cancels out in the measurement of aggregate private wealth, debt-financed acquisition of capital goods still adds to aggregate private wealth. This holds because those capital goods enhance the future profits of firms and thereby are reflected in an increased market value of the existing equity claims of firms which are part of aggregate private wealth.

[2]Occasionally a distinction is made between aggregate *private net worth*, which includes the debt of government, and aggregate *private wealth*, which does not. If we were discussing an open economy aggregate, wealth would include net claims held against foreigners.

Table 2.1 X-Rated Video Games, Inc., Statement of Operations, Year Ending 12/31/88

*Purchases of materials		$ 300	Sales	$1050
Beginning inventory	$200			
Less ending inventory	100			
Change in inventory		100		
Indirect business taxes (sales, property, and excise taxes)		25		
Wages and salaries		175		
Rent		50		
Interest		60		
*Advertising		15		
*Heat, light, and power		150		
Depreciation		25		
Profit		150		
		$1,050		$1,050

Note: An asterisk * represents purchases of goods or services from other business firms.

THE MEASUREMENT OF AGGREGATE INCOME

Value Added

To measure the flow of income, begin with the accounting statements of business firms, since they are assumed to make all production decisions and factor payments. The basic building block is the firm's statement of operations (profit and loss statement), a simplified version of which is shown in Table 2.1.

To measure precisely the contribution which a firm makes to the flow of aggregate income during a given year, economists consider the *value added* by the firm. To derive a firm's value added, deduct from each side of a firm's statement of operations those contributions to aggregate income that are reflected in other firms' statements of operation. For example, included in the statement of operations for X-Rated Video Games, Inc., are the expense categories: purchases of materials, advertising, and heat, light, and power. These expenses are payments to other firms and represent income generated for the factors of production by other firms. These expenses, marked by asterisks, must be subtracted from each side of the statement of operations of X-Rated to obtain the value it added to the flow of the aggregate income. When this is done, the categories marked by asterisks are removed from the left side of the statement, and the figure on the right side of the statement represents the firm's "final sales."[3]

If this subtracting of "intermediate transactions" were not done, intermediate sales from one business firm to another would be counted in aggregate income. This would result in double counting since goods are often processed and sold many times among producers and distributors before they are sold to the final purchaser.

[3]Rent and interest are assumed to be paid to households. If paid to firms, they too would be deducted as payments to other firms.

Table 2.2 X-Rated Video Games, Inc., Statement of Value Added, Year Ending 12/31/88

Sales, property, and excise taxes	$ 25	Sales	$1,050
Wages and salaries	175	Less payments to other firms	465
Rent	50	Final sales	585
Interest	60	Plus increase (less decrease)	
Depreciation	25	in inventory	$ (100)
Profit	150	Value added	$ 485
Value added	$485		

The only remaining step to determine the value added to aggregate income is to adjust for goods sold this year but produced in previous years or produced this year but sold in future years. The objective is to capture value added in the year something is produced, not in the year it is sold. In the example given in Table 2.1, X-Rated experienced a decrease in its inventory. Beginning inventory minus ending inventory represents an expense to X-Rated since its assets were reduced by that amount. So, goods sold out of inventory this year do not represent value added in the current year, even though their value is reflected in the sales figure. Goods produced earlier and not sold (kept as an increase in inventory) represent value added in the year they were produced, regardless of when they are sold. Thus, a decrease in inventory should be subtracted from both sides of the statement of operations, whereas an increase in inventory should be added to both sides.

The two steps of subtracting intermediate transactions and adjusting for changes in inventory levels will yield the statement of value added shown as Table 2.2.

Even though X-Rated had $1050 in sales, its value added is only $485, since $465 worth of goods and services were purchased from other firms and its inventory decreased by $100.

Aggregate Income

To derive the aggregate income for the entire economy, first combine all the values added by all firms. Table 2.3 represents an aggregation across all of the statements of value added for all of the business firms in the economy. For each firm we subtract payments made to other firms and add the increase or subtract the decrease in inventory. Thus, in Table 2.3, no payments to other firms or changes in inventories appear on the left-hand side.

All that remains on the left-hand side of Table 2.3 are the sum of all factor payments (wages, net interest, rental income of persons, and profits), depreciation, and indirect business taxes. Because they go directly to the government, indirect business taxes (e.g., sales taxes, excise taxes, and property taxes) are an expense to firms, the cost of which is passed directly to the unlucky consumer by way of higher prices. Profits include proprietors' income because many firms are not incorporated. Net interest is the interest paid by business firms less the interest they receive. (Government interest payments are considered a transfer payment.)

Table 2.3 Statement of Aggregate Income, Year Ending 12/31/88

Compensation of employees plus Rental income of persons plus Net interest plus Depreciation plus Profits plus Indirect business taxes equals Aggregate income (gross national product)	Sales minus Payment to other firms equals Final sales, which consists of: Consumption expenditures (C) (final sales to households on current account) plus Investment expenditures (I) (final sales to business firms on capital account) plus Government purchases (G) (final sales to government on current and capital account) equals Final sales ($C + I + G$) plus (or minus) Increase (or decrease) in inventories (I) equals Aggregate income (gross national product)

Depreciation is also an expense to the firm, not paid out, however, but retained in order to someday replace the capital stock as it wears out. It is a cost of production. Depreciation will be discussed at greater length later in this chapter.

On the right-hand side of the statement of aggregate income in Table 2.3 is the sum of all final sales, defined as sales minus payments to other firms plus or minus the required adjustments for changes in inventory. These final sales are made up of final sales of noncapital goods to either households (C) or government (G), and final sales of newly produced capital goods to business firms (I) or government (G). All noncapital goods sold to business firms are canceled out by the subtraction of "payments to other firms" in deriving value added, because these, by definition, are "intermediate" (nonfinal) transactions. Increases or decreases in inventories are not part of final sales, but, as explained previously, must nevertheless be included. Net increases in inventories are measured as part of investment expenditures on the right-hand side of the statement because an inventory is part of a firm's stock of capital goods.

Imputations

The initial assumption that all production (value added) comes from business firms is not wholly realistic. Adjustments must be made for the following sources of value added that are not included in business firms' value added:

1. consumption by farmers of their own production,
2. the rental value of owner-occupied dwellings, and
3. government processing of the goods and services it purchases.

Value added must be imputed to aggregate income for these activities. The imputation of farmers' consumption of their own output is made since this consumption circumvents the marketplace; thus, it is not reflected in any firm's value added.

When a household purchases a new home it is part of the value added by the firm that built the home and is measured as investment expenditures. However, throughout the useful life of the owner-occupied house, rent, and depreciation expenditures are imputed on the left side, and an equivalent amount of consumption is imputed on the right side of the statement of aggregate income.

Value added by government is measured only by the wages and salaries paid by government. This amount is added to wages and salaries on the left-hand side and to government purchases on the right-hand side of the statement of aggregate income. No imputation is made for the value added to the flow of production from the capital goods and natural resources owned by government. This treatment flies in the face of reality; it results from the practical difficulty of measuring government's capital stock, and from the conceptual reluctance of economists to treat government as a locus of the decision to produce.

No imputation is made for do-it-yourself production. This may seriously understate GNP. As individuals are pushed into higher income tax brackets, the incentive for do-it-yourself activity rises. Rather than earn the income, pay income taxes on part of it, and with what is left over hire someone to perform a service, individuals may be better off doing it themselves. If you take your car to a mechanic the services performed on it end up in GNP, but if you repair it yourself, they do not.

No imputation is made for illegal activities nor for legal activities that are not reported on income tax returns. People such as racketeers, smugglers, pushers, and prostitutes who earn income from illegal activities, as well as noncriminals such as waitresses, musicians, accountants, executives, and plumbers who do not report part of their income, are part of the *underground economy*. This underground economy generates production that does not add to GNP because the income from these activities is not reported. It has been estimated that if the income generated by the underground economy were reported, GNP would increase by 15 to 20 percent.

Finally, no imputation is made for household production. Housepersons are responsible for a vast amount of production that is excluded from aggregate income largely because of difficulties in measurement. Yet, the value of the cooking, cleaning, repair work, yardwork, and other kinds of care and attention generated by housepersons is enormous. If these services had to be purchased in the market, aggregate income would explode.

The main difficulty with not making imputations for houseperson production, do-it-yourself activity, the underground economy, and natural resources owned by government is that it casts doubt on the validity of comparisons of GNP over time. For example, over the past two decades as a share of measured aggregate income—measured GNP—the underground economy has grown, houseperson production has fallen, do-it-yourself activity has risen, and the scope of government has increased. With all of these trends in unmeasured production, it becomes very difficult to interpret the meaning of changes in per capita GNP over such a long interval of time.

After all imputations are made, each side of the statement of aggregate income equals the *gross national product*. However, even though the left-hand side equals the right-hand side, one cannot infer that the economy is in equilibrium. As discussed in Chapter One equilibrium refers to equality between planned magnitudes, not measured or actual magnitudes.

Earnings, Receipts, and Expenditures

Table 2.4 breaks down the statement of aggregate income (GNP) by sector. Row 1 depicts the earnings of each sector, the sum of which is GNP. For this table, like Figure 2.2, assume that all corporations initially retain all profits and depreciation as *earnings* rather than pay them automatically to households. The earnings of unincorporated enterprises are listed as proprietors' income received by households. Next, assume that the earnings of government consist of indirect business taxes minus subsidies. Although these are not factor payments, they are reflected in the price of goods and services so they are included as earnings.

Row 2 depicts transfer payments. As previously stated, these are unilateral, nonmarket flows which contribute nothing to output. The transfer payments in Table 2.4 are self-explanatory except for the catchall phrase *government transfers*. These include government interest payments to persons, unemployment compensation, veterans' benefits, and social security benefits. In the business sector, after-tax dividends and corporate income taxes are treated as transfer payments since they are established by law or custom and do not directly affect market prices. Aggregating across all three sectors, transfer payments sum to zero.

Row 3 depicts final receipts by sector, that is, earnings plus or minus transfer payments. These also sum to GNP. Row 4 shows current (that is, noncapital) expenditures. After these are deducted from final receipts, saving or dissaving by sector remains in row 5.

Row 6 represents capital expenditures by the business sector. Conventionally, all government expenditures are considered current expenditures. The sum of current expenditures and capital expenditures, rows 4 and 6, is equal to GNP. This means of measuring GNP is found on the right-hand side of the statement of aggregate income in Table 2.3.

Row 7 gives the budget identities of each sector with earnings items (row 1) on the left-hand side and transfer payments (row 2), saving (row 5), and current expenditures (row 4) on the right-hand side of each identity.

The household sector's budget identity is similar to the one discussed earlier, except that *gross corporate profits* (net corporate profits plus depreciation) are not part of household earnings on the left-hand side, and that several classes of transfer payments are included on the right-hand side. As shown in row 3, the difference between household earnings and these transfer payments is called *personal disposable income*.

The business sector's budget identity contains earnings consisting of net corporate profits plus depreciation. Dividends and corporate income taxes are the relevant transfer

Table 2.4 Income and Expenditures by Sector

Row	Item	Household	Business	Government	Total
1	earnings	wages and salaries (w) rental income of persons (r) net interest (i) proprietors' income (u)	net corporate profits (π) and depreciation (d)	indirect business taxes minus subsidies (T_i)	GNP
		$(w+i+r+u) = Y_h$	$(\pi+d) = Y_b$	$T_i = Y_g$	Y
	minus				
2	transfer payments	+ government transfers + dividends − personal income taxes − social security contributions	− dividends − corporate income taxes	− government transfers + personal and corporate income taxes + social security contributions	
		$-T_h$	$-T_b$	$+(T_h + T_b) = T_g$	0
	equals				
3	final receipts	personal disposable income Y_d	gross business saving S_b	net government receipts T_n	GNP Y
	equals				
4	current expenditures	consumption expenditures		government purchases	
		C_h	0	G	$C + G$
	plus or minus				
5	saving	personal saving	gross business saving	government saving (+ surplus or − deficit)	
		S_h	S_b	S_g $-S_g$	S
6	capital expenditures		gross investment expenditures		
		0	I_g	0	I_g
7	budget identities	$w+i+r+u \equiv C_h+S_h+T_h$	$\pi + d \equiv T_b + S_b$	$T_i \equiv -T_g + G - S_g$	$Y \equiv C_h + S_h + S_b + T_n$
8	financing constraints	$S_n + S_h = \Delta K + \Delta V_g + \Delta M_g$	$\Delta K = I_n = S_n$ + external financing	$S_g = T_n - G = \Delta M_g + \Delta V_g$	
9	private balance sheet identity	$W_n \equiv K + V_g + M_g$			

payments. The final receipts of the business sector, earnings minus transfer payments, called gross business saving, are in row 3.

As discussed, the government sector has one source of "earnings": indirect business taxes. These plus or minus the various transfer payments generate net government receipts, shown in row 3. When government purchases (G) are subtracted from this figure, as in row 4, the remainder is called *government saving* (government surplus or deficit) as shown in row 5. Another way of looking at the deficit is to view it as government expenditures (which are defined as the sum of government purchases plus transfer payments from government) minus transfer payments to government (tax receipts).

The terms on the left-hand sides of the budget identities displayed in row 7 are the same as those on the left-hand side of the statement of aggregate income and sum to GNP in row 1, Table 2.4 and Level I, Figure 2.2. The terms on the right-hand sides of the budget identities also sum to GNP, and, in turn, are equal to the sum of rows 4 and 6 in Table 2.4 which corresponds to the right-hand side of the statement of aggregate income and Level III in Figure 2.2.

Row 9 presents the private balance sheet identity which defines aggregate private nonhuman wealth (W_n) as the value of the private capital stock (K), plus the value of the interest-earning and the noninterest-earning debt claims of government, (V_g) and (M_g) respectively.[4]

$$W_n = K + V_g + M_g$$

Increases in the outstanding debt of government ($\Delta V_g + \Delta M_g$) occur when the government runs a deficit ($G > T_n$). (The term Δ stands for *change in.*) Increases in the private capital stock (ΔK) occur because of net investment expenditures (I_n).

Net investment expenditures (I_n) are financed in two ways: (1) internally, out of net business saving (S_n), and (2) externally, out of household saving (S_h). Net business saving, retained earnings, is defined as gross business saving (S_b) minus depreciation, capital consumption allowances (d). Net investment expenditures are defined as gross investment expenditures (I_g) minus depreciation, capital consumption allowances (d). Both types of saving add to wealth because the value of equities held by the household sector will increase as a result of this saving flowing into net investment expenditures. The rest of private saving finances the government deficit. This is portrayed in Level IV of Figure 2.2.

Figure 2.2 differs from Figure 2.1 by depicting the more complicated view of the economy seen in Table 2.4. Net corporate profits and depreciation are separated from the earnings flow to households and are instead channeled to the business sector to contribute

[4]Despite the cogent reasons for not doing so (given earlier), many economists still view the debt of government in terms of this balance sheet identity as part of aggregate private wealth. From this balance sheet perspective, inclusion of government debt in the definition of wealth may appear to be reasonable because all saving flows are reflected as increases in the value of outstanding debt claims of government and equity claims of business firms. However, to the extent that the benefits of debt-financed government expenditures already are captured as increases in the value of private human and nonhuman capital, this balance sheet approach involves double counting. As indicated in footnote 2 above, a better label for this concept might be aggregate private *net worth*.

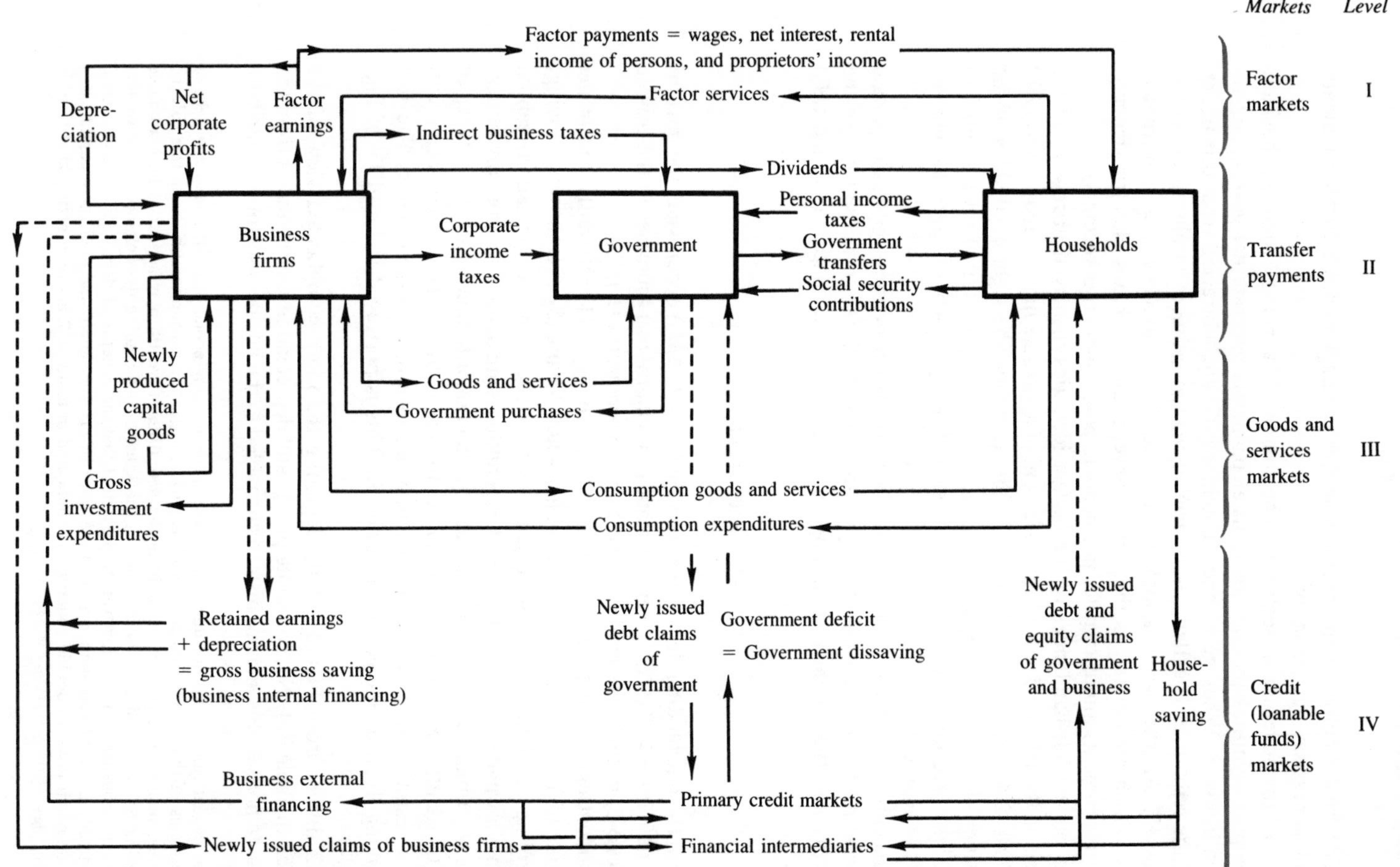

Figure 2.2 Circular Flow of Income and Expenditures

Table 2.5 Statement of U.S. Gross National Product, 1985 (in billions)

Compensation of employees	$2,372.7	Personal consumption expenditures	$2,581.9
Rental income of persons	14.0	Gross private investment expenditures	670.4
Corporate profit	299.0	Government purchases	814.6
Proprietors' income	242.4	Net exports	−74.4
Net interest	287.7		
Capital consumption allowances	438.2		
Indirect business taxes	338.5		
Total	$3,992.5		$3,992.5

Source: U.S. Department of Commerce

to internal financing of gross investment expenditures after dividends and corporate income taxes are paid.

Indirect business taxes are also introduced and treated as earnings of government, and thus included in the factor markets. Another difference between the two figures is that Figure 2.2 includes a much more extensive network of transfer payments in Level II.

Imputations for government wages and salaries, the value added by owner-occupied dwellings and farmers' consumption of their own production could also be added, but this would excessively complicate the diagram.

Table 2.5 reports the statement of GNP for 1985. On the right-hand side, the level of consumption expenditures is $2,581.9 billion, the level of investment expenditures is $670.4 billion, the level of government purchases is $814.6 billion, and net exports are $−74.4 billion. On the left-hand side, compensation of employees is $2,372.7 billion, rental income of persons is $14 billion, corporate profit is $299 billion, proprietors' income is $242.4 billion, net interest is $287.7 billion, capital consumption allowances are $438.2 billion, and indirect business taxes are $338.5 billion.

NET AGGREGATE INCOME

Net National Product

Economists traditionally have defined net aggregate income as the total amount of production that could be consumed without depleting the physical capital stock of the economy. Depreciation is used as a measure of how much of the physical capital stock wears out each year. If the capital stock is to remain intact, replacement investment expenditures must match depreciation. Depreciation for the firm is the "writing off" each year as an expense a portion of the historical cost of that firm's stock of capital goods, as they wear out. (The use of historical cost rather than replacement cost is an accounting convention.) Since depreciation is an expense, it is included in the price of the product that the firm sells. Unlike other expenses, depreciation expense is not paid out by the firm; rather it is retained as part of the firm's inward cash flow.

Net national product (NNP) is equal to *gross national product* (GNP) minus *capital consumption allowances*. Capital consumption allowances are the sum total of estimated depreciation in the economy. When capital consumption allowances are subtracted from both sides of the statement of aggregate income, they cancel out on the left-hand side and are deducted from gross investment expenditures on the right-hand side, yielding *net investment expenditures*. Using the data in Table 2.5, net national product for 1985 is \$3,992.5 billion minus \$438.2 billion, which equals \$3,554.3 billion; and net investment expenditures are \$670.4 billion minus \$438.2 billion, which equals \$232.2 billion.

Net investment expenditures and net national product are often considered superior to gross investment expenditures and gross national product because they avoid the double counting of investment expenditures. For example, assume that X-Rated Video Games, Inc. wants to purchase a new capital good. When that capital good is produced, it is counted as investment expenditures on the right-hand side of the statement of aggregate income and as factor payments on the left-hand side of the statement, because earnings were generated for the factors of production employed by the firm that produced the capital good. If the gross national product and gross investment expenditures concepts are used, part of the value of that capital good is counted in each subsequent year as the replacement portion of gross-investment expenditures on the right-hand side and as depreciation on the left-hand side. If the gross national product (GNP) concept is used, then the capital good is being counted twice, first when it is purchased, and later as it wears out. By deducting capital consumption allowances from both sides of the statement of aggregate income, the concepts of net national product (NNP) and net investment expenditures avoid double counting. Thus, many economists prefer NNP to GNP when measuring aggregate income.

National Income

An even more "net" measure is called *national income*. National income is found by subtracting indirect business taxes from both sides of the statement of aggregate income (NNP). National income measures aggregate income at factor cost by excluding those types of taxes which are not factor payments but are merely added to product prices. In Table 2.5, national income is \$3,554.3 billion minus \$338.5 billion, which equals \$3,215.8 billion.

What Is Income?

Other net measures of aggregate income are possible. Consider again the traditional definition of net income: "Net aggregate income is everything the economy can consume while keeping its capital stock intact." If capital is defined to include human capital, a good deal of what is measured as net income consists of consumption expenditures that are necessary to keep the human capital stock intact. If these social subsistence consumption expenditures (human capital consumption allowances) were deducted from either side of the statement of aggregate income, aggregate income would shrink considerably. From this perspective a high per capita GNP would not necessarily indicate a high standard of living if a high level of consumption expenditures were necessary to keep the human capital stock of the economy intact.

Deducting human capital consumption allowances, as well as physical capital consumption allowances from aggregate income, suggests that people influence the economy in the same way as physical capital goods. The measurement of social subsistence consumption expenditures, what is spent to keep the economy's human capital stock intact, could prove very controversial. How much of the $2,581.9 billion in aggregate consumption expenditures in 1985 was necessary to keep the human capital stock intact? Should this figure include just the part of total consumption expenditures used for basic food, clothing, and shelter? What part of total food expenditures is essential for social subsistence? What part of medical expenditures and expenditures for transportation are essential for social subsistence? However social subsistence is measured, one thing is certain: net income, by this definition, is a good deal less than GNP.[5]

Income Is Not Welfare (Or the Best Things in Life Are Free)

A common assumption is that aggregate real income per capita is a good indicator of how well off a nation is. Per capita real income shows the quantity of newly produced goods and services at market prices that is available per person. Therefore, for purposes of intertemporal (between points in time) and international comparisons, per capita income is often used as a measure of a nation's standard of living. Unfortunately, real income per capita is not always a good measure of the true well-being or welfare of a nation. In addition to adjusting aggregate income downward for wear and tear on the nation's physical capital stock, one should also consider the competitive structure of the nation's markets and the overall *quality* of life, defined to include leisure time, the quality of the environment, and the lack of wear and tear on the nation's human capital stock.

For example, consider the mythical island kingdom of Banalia, where there is but one newly produced good—a mysterious liquid that pours from a spring in the center of the island. Centuries of experience show that this natural tonic is good for everything: it is a perfect drink, an excellent food, a terrific libation for entertainment, and an all-purpose cleaner. Moreover, it is all organic, pH balanced, tamper-proof, unpasteurized, and free of preservatives and coloring. Since the climate on Banalia is marvelous year round, and disease and tourism are unknown, there is no need for clothing, shelter, or any other type of production. The natives of Banalia ingenuously call their native drink "The Elixir of Life."

Now these assumptions may seem a bit unrealistic even for an economics textbook. However, they are made in the interest of analytical simplicity. In addition, one more simplifying assumption is made: the Elixir of Life is costlessly produced. Thus, there is a zero marginal cost of production. The denizens of Banalia simply, costlessly visit the spring and enjoy an absolutely delicious, cost-free drink, meal, or bath of Elixir.

[5]To better capture a nation's "net" well-being, it has been suggested that we switch to income measures that decline when leisure time decreases, when the environment is spoiled, or when human capital is consumed. These measures would also reclassify as net investment those consumption expenditures which increase the value of human capital as well as those consumption expenditures which increase the stock of consumer durables. For further reading see the book by Ruggles and Ruggles which is cited in the Bibliography.

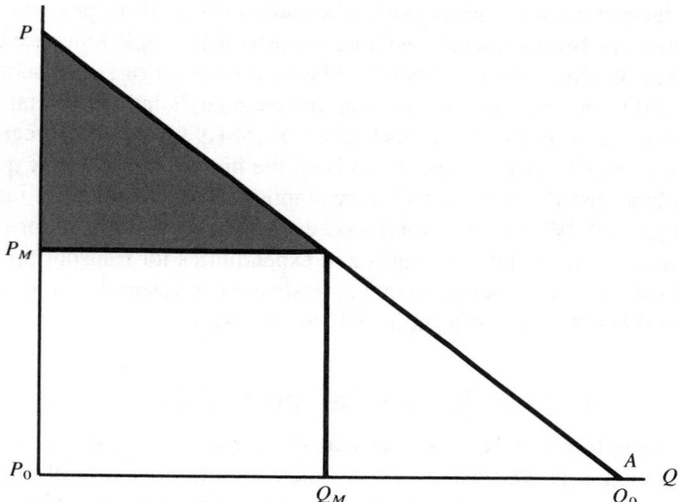

Figure 2.3 The Demand Curve for Elixir

Figure 2.3 shows exactly how much Elixir the Banalians will produce. Since the cost of production is zero, Elixir will be produced to the point where marginal benefit—measured by what the natives would be willing to pay for an extra dose of it—is just equal to marginal cost. Since the marginal cost is zero, the natives will consume Elixir to the point where they would be willing to pay zero for it. This occurs at point *A* in Figure 2.3 with quantity produced Q_0 at price P_0.

Under these circumstances the aggregate nominal income of Banalia may be calculated. Since the quantity produced is positive, Q_0, and the price is zero, P_0, the aggregate nominal income of the Banalian economy is $Q_0 \times P_0 = Q_0 \times 0 = 0$. Alas, poor Banalia will rank rock-bottom in the economic honor roll of nations. Its GNP per capita is zero. Its ambassadors, at august international meetings, will be humiliated as representatives of the least developed country. International loans will be planned by world bankers, and charitable organizations will arrange for missions to be sent to the ailing land. International revolutionaries of every stripe will plot insurrections to be exported there. Pictures of prospective Banalian refugees will flood the media.

Nevertheless, students of economics must inquire whether this attention is justified. Exactly how badly off are the Banalians? What is their true "standard of living"? Or as economists put it, "what is their social welfare?" Since the benefits per unit of Elixir are measured by the price people would pay for that unit, the true welfare—economists call it "consumer surplus"—of Banalia is the entire area under the demand curve in Figure 2.3. In other words, if you would be willing to pay $10,000 for a pitcher of Elixir and it is free, you are $10,000 better off. Since the price of Elixir is zero, the welfare of anybody who would pay a positive price for it is measured by that price times the quantity they would consume.

Therefore, the per capita income of Banalia is not an accurate measure of its overall, or social, welfare. Since the people of this paradise get all of their Elixir free and Elixir is the only thing they have to produce, their social welfare is positive and equal to the area under the demand curve in Figure 2.3. In contrast, of course, their aggregate income is zero.

With bankers, altruists, revolutionaries, anthropology majors, and tourists descending on Banalia, this blissful paradise is doomed. Among the visitors is Colonel Liberator and a squad of heavily armed military advisers. Liberator annexes Banalia because it obviously is a threat to international security. One of the colonel's first acts under martial law is to erect a barbed wire fence and plant anti-personnel mines around the Elixir spring. Next to a 50 caliber machine gun emplacement, his pacification teams erect a sign reading "Elixir, $5 a glass."

Figure 2.3 shows the effect on the Banalian economy. At the price of $P_M = \$5$, only Q_M of Elixir will be demanded and the welfare of Banalia falls to the shaded area above P_M. However, all is not lost, for now Banalia has a nonzero GNP. The aggregate nominal income of Banalia soars to $P_M \times Q_M$. Banalia's ambassador at the United Nations can hold his head high. Banalia now has a growth rate and has become, in one fell swoop, a developing country. Even though welfare has fallen, nominal income per capita has skyrocketed.

THE MEASUREMENT OF THE PRICE LEVEL

This chapter has discussed how economists conceptualize and measure aggregate income and expenditures. As previously stated, income and expenditures are dollar-denominated as the product of the quantities exchanged and their market prices. The story of Banalia shows, among other things, that a rise in dollar-denominated income may be caused by an increase in prices rather than an increase in output. Thus, it is necessary to devise a way to measure income and expenditures in *real* or *purchasing power* terms. This may be accomplished by dividing (deflating) a dollar-denominated magnitude by the price level.

It is difficult to measure the price level, because there is no such thing. There are only price indices. Each index is an average of the prices of individual commodities weighted by the quantities purchased of those commodities.

For example, consider an economy which consists of only two commodities, briefs and body oils. Assume that the quantities and prices consumed of these commodities for two consecutive years is as reported in Table 2.6.

Table 2.6 Measurement of Price Level

	Commodity One		Commodity Two	
	Briefs		Body Oils	
Year	Price	Quantity	Price	Quantity
0	$10	100	$20	50
1	15	200	25	150

GNP is \$2,000 (\$10 × 100 + \$20 × 50) in the base year and \$6,750 (\$15 × 200 + \$25 × 150) in the present year. To accurately assess the increase in real GNP (that is, the value of goods and services produced at unchanged prices) between the two years, it is necessary to determine how much the price index rose.

One way to calculate a price index is to use a weighted average of the prices, using the quantities of each commodity produced in the base year as a weight:

$$P = \frac{\sum_{i=1}^{n} p_i^1 q_i^0}{\sum_{i=1}^{n} p_i^0 q_i^0} \times 100$$

Using the data in Table 2.6, the price index is 137.5, indicating that it would cost 37.5 percent more to purchase the same market basket in year one than in the base year, year zero.

Base year quantity weights are used in calculating the *consumer price index* (CPI). The weights are based on the typical market basket of an urban household, compiled periodically by the Bureau of Labor Statistics (BLS). The last market basket was compiled in 1972–1973. The BLS compiles about 125,000 prices every month for this index.

An alternate technique is called the *implicit GNP price deflator*. It uses the quantities produced in the present year as weights. These weights are the actual quantities produced in the GNP.

$$P = \frac{\sum_{i=1}^{n} p_i^1 q_i^1}{\sum_{i=1}^{n} p_i^0 q_i^1} \times 100$$

Using the data in Table 2.6, the price index is 135.0. This indicates that it would cost 35 percent more to purchase present quantities in the present year than it would have cost to purchase that same market basket in the base year.

Neither technique is without deficiencies. In inflationary times, the CPI overestimates the rise in prices because it does not allow for substitution of cheaper products for more expensive ones in the present year. Thus the numerator has an upward bias. The implicit GNP price deflator tends to underestimate inflation for the same reason. It disallows substitution of cheaper products for more expensive ones in the base year. Thus, the denominator has an upward bias, giving the index a downward bias. Additionally, both indices have an upward bias because the quality of products, and hence prices, are likely to have increased. Both may also have some downward bias as improved technology permits higher quality often at lower prices.

The implicit price deflator differs from the CPI in other ways. First, it is based on prices of a much wider group of goods and services than the CPI. Second, the basket-of-goods weights in the implicit price deflator changes every year, depending on what is produced in the economy, while the CPI basket is unchanged over time. Third, the deflator includes only domestically produced goods, while the CPI includes the prices of imports. Fourth, the CPI includes interest costs while the implicit price deflator does not. The latter two differences account for the upward bias of the CPI during years of rising imported oil prices and rising interest rates as well as the downward bias during years of falling oil import prices and falling interest rates.[6]

Throughout this text, nominal income (Y) will be the product of real income (Y/P) and the price index (P). The index used will be the implicit price deflator because it is based on all goods and services counted in GNP.

MEASURING EMPLOYMENT AND UNEMPLOYMENT

Labor force statistics indicate the current population of the economy of age sixteen and over that is employable. People who do not seek work, students at school, disabled people, and retired people are not counted in the labor force. Labor force figures can vary with structural changes in the composition of the working population. In recent years the labor force has had a smaller percentage of older workers because of increased preference for early retirement and the incentive of more generous pension funds. In the mid-1980s the labor force had over 120 million members.

Employment statistics measure the number in the civilian, noninstitutionalized population who are currently working at paid jobs. The *employment rate* is the number of employed workers divided by the noninstitutionalized adult civilian population. It is possible that the employment rate can fall at the same time that the number of those employed rises. The discrepancy arises because changes in the denominator, the noninstitutionalized adult civilian population, can affect the employment rate statistic so that it may move inversely to the employment level. During a recession the employment rate may rise as the labor force shrinks.

Unemployment statistics are collected by the Labor Department in a telephone survey of about 50,000 households. Surveyors ask, "Are you currently working?" and, if not, "Are you actively seeking work?" If a respondent answers "no" to the first question but "yes" to the second, he or she is counted as unemployed. People are also classified as unemployed if they are waiting to report to a new job within thirty days or to be recalled to a job from which they were laid off. People who are neither employed nor unemployed by this definition are not counted in the labor force. A statistic on average duration of unemployment is also collected.

Probably, the most frequently used unemployment statistic is the figure on the *unemployment rate* as a percentage of the labor force. Again, this rate is the result of two sets of data, and it is possible that the unemployment rate may rise at the same time that the

[6]There is yet another index, called the producer price index (PPI), which is generated by the BLS from prices of a larger number of commodities that are not purchased directly by consumers. These include raw materials such as coal and crude oil and intermediate goods such as steel and capital goods such as machinery.

employment level rises. Again, changes in the denominator of the unemployment rate, that is, the labor force statistic, can be responsible for such an apparent contradiction. Because discouraged workers leave the labor force during recessions and encouraged workers enter the labor force during economic booms, the unemployment rate underestimates true joblessness during recession and overestimates true joblessness during boom periods. The unemployment rate also fails to reflect workers who are forced to go from full-time to part-time employment during recessions. Some argue that it is not the unemployment *rate* but the average *duration* of unemployment that is important, since we should only be concerned with individuals who are unemployed for a long period of time.

The welfare meaning of the unemployment rate—like the total number unemployed—is quite ambiguous. Considerations discussed previously suggest that the unemployment rate is often an overestimate. The unemployment rate is much more important—or at least selectively useful—in the political sphere than for macroeconomic analysis. For macroeconomists, the unemployment rate is a useful index with a somewhat arbitrary normal level. Generally, the relative size of (statistically significant) deviations of the unemployment rate from this normal level is all that is meaningful for economic analysis.

Concluding Comment

This chapter describes how economists view the economy as a whole. It presents the big picture, outlining the decisions made by the three behavioral entities (households, business firms, and governments) in the three basic markets (factor, goods and services, and credit—loanable funds—markets). The key variables of income, consumption expenditures, saving, transfer payments, investment expenditures, government expenditures, government deficits, wages, interest, the general price level, unemployment, and wealth are defined. In the rest of this text the concepts discussed in this chapter are applied to the development of theories which answer the three big questions of macroeconomics. The three questions are, what determines the level of employment and output? what determines the interest rate? and what determines the price level?

EXERCISES

1. If the debt of a business firm is the wealth of an individual household, why is the total outstanding debt of the business sector not part of the wealth of the household sector?
2. If government debt is issued in order to finance the acquisition of public capital goods (sometimes called social overhead capital) such as highways and fire protection equipment, why might it be reasonable not to count government debt as wealth?
3. What is the value to society of continually functioning stock and bond markets?
4. If monopoly power increases in an economy, its real GNP will fall.
   a. true
   b. false

5. "The further back in time the base year is, the less relevant the price index is."
   a. true
   b. false

6. If a business firm issues some debt to acquire newly produced capital goods, how is the wealth represented by those capital goods reflected in the household sector?

7. Indicate whether the following are measured as consumption expenditures (C), investment expenditures (I), government expenditures (G), value added but not specifically identifiable on the right-hand side of the statement of GNP (Y), or not measured in GNP (N).
   a. the value of land sold at auction
   b. a share of stock sold on the New York Stock Exchange from one household to another
   c. an automobile purchased by the Xerox Corporation
   d. an automobile purchased by the U.S. Treasury Department
   e. an automobile purchased by a household
   f. legal fees paid by Xerox Corporation
   g. salaries paid by Xerox Corporation

8. In 1988 The Mineral Spring Water Corporation pays its workers wages of $10,000 to bottle 100 cases of mineral spring water. There are no other costs of production. In 1989 these cases are sold to households for $11,000. Show the effect of these transactions on the income and expenditures sides of the GNP account for 1988 and 1989.

9. I. M. Flush purchases a diamond ring for his housekeeper. It is sold out of the inventory of Stoned, Incorporated, where it is valued in inventory at $5,000. The markup is 20 percent. The salesperson's commission is 10 percent, and the sales tax is 5 percent. Record the effect on the GNP by sector, in terms of income and expenditures, by using Table 2.4.

10. What happens to GNP when Mr. Flush marries his housekeeper and she continues to perform the same housework but is no longer paid?

11. What is personal disposable income? Develop a list of reasons why it might not be a satisfactory measure of how well off an economy is.

12. Why does the unemployment rate underestimate true joblessness in a recession?

13. What does the legend of Banalia, told in this chapter, teach with regard to the relationship between the following concepts?
    a. nominal income and real income
    b. welfare and the competitive structure of the economy
    c. real income and real income minus wear and tear on the human capital stock, environmental deterioration, and the loss of leisure time.

BIBLIOGRAPHY

Barro, Robert J. "Are Government Bonds Net Wealth?" *Journal of Political Economy* (December 1974), pp. 1095–1117.

Fisher, Irving. *The Nature of Income and Capital*. New York: Macmillan, 1930.

Hicks, John. *Value and Capital*, 2nd ed. Oxford: Clarendon Press, 1946.

Kendrick, John W. *Economic Accounts and Their Uses*. New York: McGraw-Hill, 1972.

Powelson, John P. *National Income and Flow of Funds Analysis*. New York: McGraw-Hill, 1960.

Ruggles, Richard, and Nancy O. Ruggles. *The Design of Economic Accounts*. New York: National Bureau of Economic Research, 1970.

Von Furstenburg, George M., and Burton Malkiel. "The Government and Capital Formation: A Survey of Recent Issues." *Journal of Economic Literature* (September 1977), pp. 835–878.

Partial Equilibrium Models

Part II

The Labor Market: First Principles

Chapter 3

Introduction

The previous chapter showed that economists view the United States economy as a market economy. In a market economy the equilibrium quantities and prices of goods, services, and productive inputs are determined in their respective markets by supply and demand.

Labor is a productive input. The labor market consists of a demand for labor, a supply of labor, and an equilibrium condition which specifies that, in equilibrium, quantity supplied equals quantity demanded. The study of the labor market in this chapter begins with the theory of the demand for labor, followed by the theory of the supply of labor. Finally, supply and demand are discussed. A major finding is that the aggregate labor market automatically attains full employment equilibrium. This equilibrium is not affected by changes in the price level or rate of inflation as long as labor suppliers and labor demanders have perfect information and wages are free to adjust. The automatic attainment of full employment equilibrium is the essence of the Neoclassical theory of the labor market.

LABOR DEMAND

Fundamental Assumptions

The theory of the demand for labor is derived from five basic assumptions. These assumptions are:

1. the law of diminishing returns,
2. output markets are purely competitively structured,
3. labor markets are purely competitively structured,
4. business firms are profit-maximizers,
5. firms have perfect information regarding prices and wages.

If and when these assumptions are modified, the related conclusions about the theory of the demand for labor will be modified also.

As pointed out in Chapter One, typically economists rely heavily on their assumptions. A classic example is found in the story of an economist, a zoologist, and a clergyman who were trapped in a pit of vipers. True to their callings the zoologist tried to determine which of the snakes were poisonous, while the clergyman began praying. Not to be outdone, the economist began, "Assume a ladder. . . ."

Since assumptions play such a vital role in economic analysis, the reasoning that lies behind them should be examined. The first assumption is the *law of diminishing returns*. As seen in Chapter Two, the aggregate demand for labor is linked to the decision by individual business firms to produce goods and services. Labor is one of the productive services needed to produce output of goods and services. Economists envision a simple relation between an individual firm's productive inputs, such as labor hours, and its output. This relation is called the firm's production function. On the horizontal axis in Figure 3.1 one of the productive inputs—person hours of labor (L)—is plotted; and on the vertical axis the quantity of output (Q) is plotted. All other inputs, such as units of capital, are held constant. The firm's short-run production function is assumed to be concave to (bowed outward from) the origin, exhibiting the property of *diminishing marginal productivity* of labor.

Columns 1 and 2 of Table 3.1 show, in stepwise form, an example of a firm's production function. As inputs of labor hours increase, output increases but at a decreasing rate. In other words, the increment to the firm's output (ΔQ) relative to the increment to labor hours of input (ΔL) is positive but decreases as labor input increases.[1] The quotient, $\Delta Q/\Delta L$, is called the *marginal physical product of labor*. The marginal physical product is shown in column 3 of Table 3.1. For every level of employment of labor hours on the horizontal axis in Figures 3.1 and 3.2, there is a unique level of output in Figure 3.1, and a unique marginal physical product of labor in Figure 3.2. This ever-decreasing marginal physical product of labor reflects the *law of diminishing returns*.

[1]Throughout this book the notation Δ, the "delta" of the Greek alphabet, always stands for "change in."

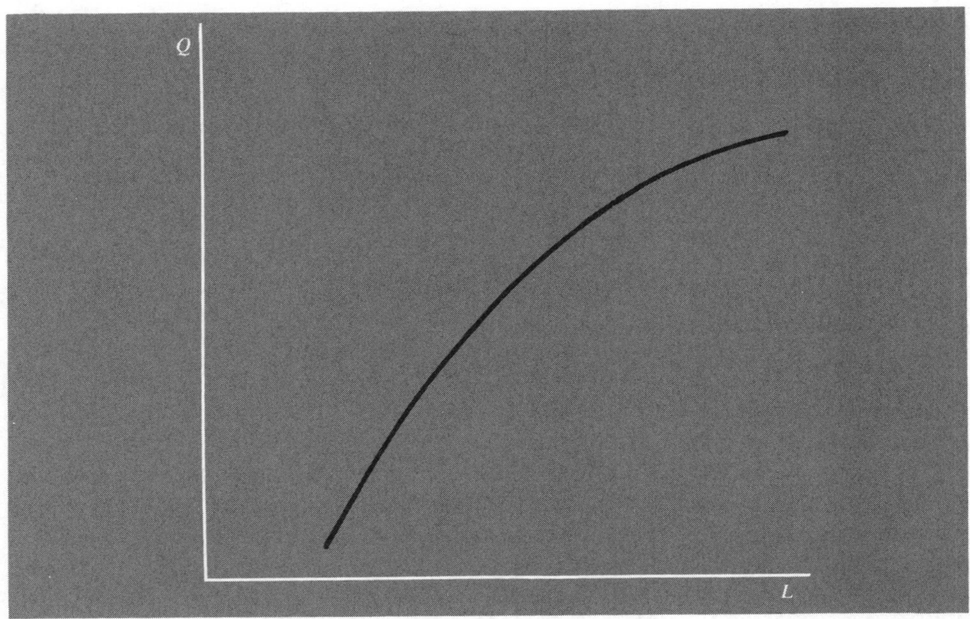

Figure 3.1 The Firm's Production Function

Table 3.1 The Firm's Demand Schedule for Labor

1 Labor Hours L	2 Output Q	3 Marginal Physical Product of Labor $(\Delta Q/\Delta L)$	4 Price of Output P	5 Marginal Revenue Product of Labor $(\Delta Q/\Delta L)\cdot P$	6 Nominal Wage w	7 Total Revenue $P\cdot Q$	8 Total Cost $w\cdot L$	9 Profit $(P\cdot Q)-(w\cdot L)$
1	10	10	$1	$10	$4	$10	$ 4	$ 6
2	19	9	1	9	4	19	8	11
3	27	8	1	8	4	27	12	15
4	34	7	1	7	4	34	16	18
5	40	6	1	6	4	40	20	20
6	45	5	1	5	4	45	24	21
7	49	4	1	4	4	49	28	21
8	52	3	1	3	4	52	32	20
9	54	2	1	2	4	54	36	18
10	55	1	1	1	4	55	40	15
11	55	0	1	0	4	55	44	11

Note: nominal wage = $4/hour
price of output = $1/unit

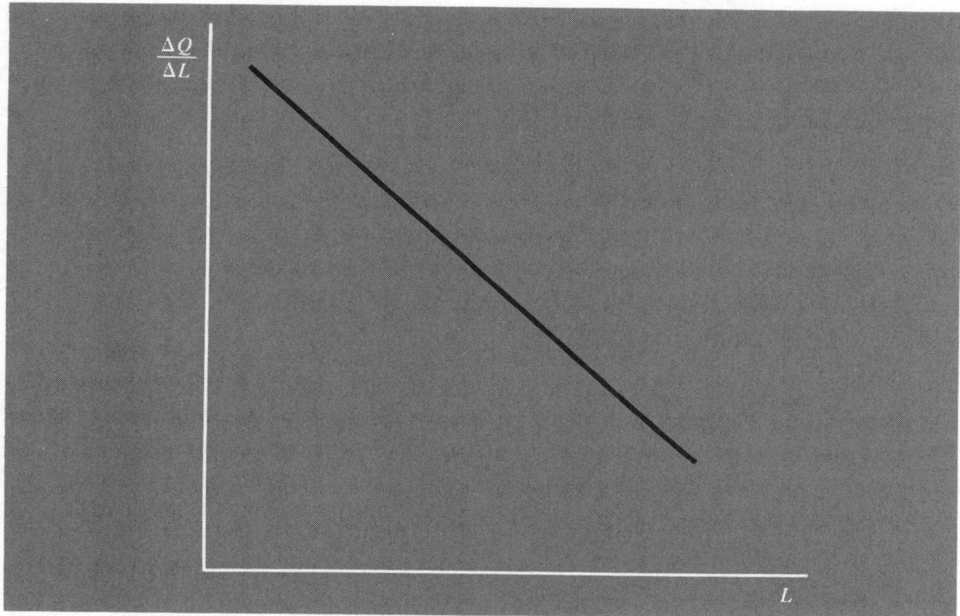

Figure 3.2 The Marginal Physical Product of Labor

The law of diminishing returns is a time-honored principle in economics. It indicates that as successive equal-sized doses of a productive input, such as an hour of labor, are applied to a productive activity (such as growing tomatoes), the quantity of output (bushels of tomatoes) ascribable to the last dose of input that is applied will fall. A traditional old saw in economics is that if the law of diminishing returns were not true, one could feed the world with tomatoes from one's garden simply by applying more and more of a productive input.

The second basic assumption in the theory of the demand for labor is of purely competitively structured output markets. This means that an individual firm can sell all of its output at a market-determined price. In short, if the market for the firm's output is purely competitively structured it may sell all the output that it wants to sell at the price (P). The market-determined price (P) is shown in column 4 of Table 3.1.

If the price at which output sells is multiplied by the marginal physical product of labor, the *marginal revenue product of labor* is obtained. This translates the increment to output with respect to the increment of labor hours (a quantity of output) into an increment to dollars of revenue with respect to the increment of labor hours (a dollar amount). It is the increment to the firm's revenue relative to the increment of labor hours of input. The marginal revenue product of labor is given in column 5 of Table 3.1. Notice that marginal revenue product $[(\Delta Q/\Delta L) \cdot P]$ in column 5 declines as labor input is increased because the marginal physical product of labor ($\Delta Q/\Delta L$) in column 3 declines as labor hours of input increase. Thus, the ever-decreasing *marginal revenue product of labor* is a direct consequence of the ever-decreasing marginal physical product of labor.

The third basic assumption in the theory is the idea of purely competitively structured labor markets. This means that a firm may hire all the hours of labor it needs at the market-determined nominal wage. In the example, assume a market-determined wage of $4 per hour. That wage ($w$) is listed in column six.

The two assumptions of purely *competitively structured markets* for output and labor imply that the individual firm, being one of a very large number of output market sellers and labor market buyers, can have no effect either on the price of output when it sells its production or on the price of labor (the nominal wage) when it hires its workers. As such, these assumptions simplify the analysis because they allow treatment of the price of output and the nominal wage as given. These assumptions are made for analytical convenience. Unlike the assumption of *diminishing returns,* these two assumptions may not always hold true in all labor and output markets. For example, the only employer in a geographic region often may bid up the local wage rate when it hires more workers, or the sole producer of a product in an economy may cause the price of that product to rise when it cuts back production. In short, these two simplifying assumptions, like the assumption of the economist trapped in the snake pit, may not always be completely realistic. However, assumptions need not be judged on the basis of their lack of realism if, when they are made more realistic, they do not alter the fundamental conclusions derived from them. For example, if these assumptions were modified to allow for markets that were not perfectly competitively structured, the analysis would be complicated but the general theory of the demand for labor would hardly be modified. In contrast, if the "ladder assumption" of the trapped economist were made more realistic, his analysis would not only be complicated, but his conclusions about how to behave would be greatly altered.

The fourth assumption of the theory is the idea of profit-maximizing business firms. This means simply that a firm chooses to produce output and hire labor up to the point where its profit is maximized. In Table 3.1 profit reaches a maximum of $21 where seven hours of labor are hired. At this point marginal revenue product of $4 is equal to nominal wage of $4. The (first-order) condition for a profit maximum is to hire labor input to the point where the increment to profit with respect to the increment to labor input is zero. Since profit is defined as the difference between total revenue and total cost, this condition is satisfied where the increment to revenue with respect to the increment to labor input, the marginal revenue product of labor, is equal to the increment cost with respect to the increment to labor input, the nominal wage.[2]

The fifth assumption of the theory of the demand for labor is the idea that firms have perfect knowledge of prices and wages. In Table 3.1 the firm has perfect information regarding the $4 per hour nominal wage paid to labor, as well as the $1 per unit price at

[2]Profit is defined as the difference between total revenue and total cost. Total revenue is the product of price and quantity of output. Total cost is assumed to consist only of labor cost which is defined as the product of the wage and the number of person hours of labor.

In this and all subsequent examples the profit-maximizing quantity of labor appears to be two numbers (in this case six or seven person hours). This occurs because of the discrete, stepwise, nature of the example. In all such cases, the greater number will be chosen.

which it may sell the output it produces. If it did not have such knowledge, it could not readily attain a profit-maximizing position.

Deriving the Firm's Demand Curve for Labor

The firm's demand curve for labor indicates the relationship between the quantity of labor hours demanded by the firm (as a dependent variable) and the nominal wage paid for a labor hour and the price at which output sells (as explanatory variables). What would happen in the example in Table 3.1 if the nominal wage changed? Suppose that the market-determined nominal wage fell from $4 per person hour, in Table 3.1, to $3 per person hour as in Table 3.2. Following the assumption that the firm would maximize its profit, the quantity of labor hours demanded would increase to eight person hours. At eight person hours, profit is at a maximum of $28, where the marginal revenue product of $3 is equal to the new nominal wage of $3. As in Table 3.1, where the marginal revenue product equals the nominal wage, profit is maximized.

Now, to understand the effect of a change in the nominal wage on the quantity of labor hours demanded, compare Table 3.1 to Table 3.2. It becomes clear that for the profit-maximizing firm, as the nominal wage declines, the quantity of labor hours demanded increases because the firm hires labor until the wage is equal to the marginal revenue product of labor. The individual firm's demand curve for labor is its marginal revenue product curve. The graphical relationship between nominal wage and labor hours demanded, the marginal revenue product curve, is shown in Figure 3.3. Figure 3.3 and Tables 3.1 and 3.2 show that as the nominal wage declines, the quantity of labor demanded increases. In order to satisfy the profit-maximizing condition, $(\Delta Q/\Delta L) \cdot P = w$,

Table 3.2 The Firm's Demand Schedule for Labor

1 Labor Hours L	2 Output Q	3 Marginal Physical Product of Labor $(\Delta Q/\Delta L)$	4 Price of Output P	5 Marginal Revenue Product of Labor $(\Delta Q/\Delta L) \cdot P$	6 Nominal Wage w	7 Total Revenue $P \cdot Q$	8 Total Cost $w \cdot L$	9 Profit $(P \cdot Q) - (w \cdot L)$
1	10	10	$1	$10	$3	$10	$ 3	$ 7
2	19	9	1	9	3	19	6	13
3	27	8	1	8	3	27	9	18
4	34	7	1	7	3	34	12	22
5	40	6	1	6	3	40	15	25
6	45	5	1	5	3	45	18	27
7	49	4	1	4	3	49	21	28
8	52	3	1	3	3	52	24	28
9	54	2	1	2	3	54	27	27
10	55	1	1	1	3	55	30	25
11	55	0	1	0	3	55	33	22

Note: nominal wage = $3/hour
price of output = $1/unit

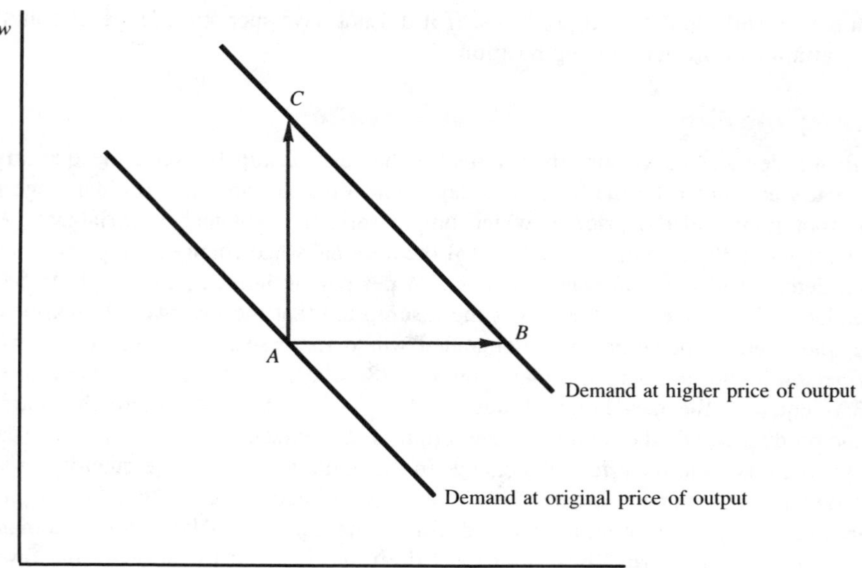

Figure 3.3 Shift in Firm's Demand for Labor Caused by an Increase in the Price of Output

as w, the nominal wage, falls, the marginal physical product of labor, $\Delta Q/\Delta L$, must fall; $\Delta Q/\Delta L$ will fall only if the level of employment, L, rises. Therefore, an inverse relationship exists between the price of labor (the nominal wage, w) and the quantity of labor hours demanded by the firm (L). This inverse relationship is reflected in the firm's marginal revenue product curve.

What is the relationship between the price at which output sells and the quantity of labor hours demanded? Suppose the price (P) at which output sells rose from $1 per unit in Table 3.1 (column 4) to $2 per unit in Table 3.3 (column 4). When this occurs, the marginal revenue product of labor doubles at all possible levels of labor input because the marginal revenue product is simply marginal physical product times price, which has doubled from $1 to $2 per unit. For the first unit of labor, the marginal revenue product in Table 3.3 (column 5) is $20; for the second person hour of labor, it is $18; for the third $16; and so on. How many hours of labor would be hired at a nominal wage of $4 per hour? The answer is nine hours because at nine person hours of labor, the marginal physical product is two units, which at the price of $2 per unit, yields a marginal revenue product of $4, which is equal to the nominal wage of $4. At this level of employment profit is at a maximum of $72.

To understand the relationship between the price at which output sells and the demand for labor, compare Table 3.1 to Table 3.3. Clearly, as the price at which output sells increases, the marginal revenue product of labor *increases in the same proportion*. Because the profit-maximizing firm hires labor up to the point where the nominal wage equals the marginal revenue product of labor, as the price of output rises, the demand for

Table 3.3 The Firm's Demand Schedule for Labor

1 Labor Hours L	2 Output Q	3 Marginal Physical Product of Labor $(\Delta Q/\Delta L)$	4 Price of Output P	5 Marginal Revenue Product of Labor $(\Delta Q/\Delta L)\cdot P$	6 Nominal Wage w	7 Total Revenue $P\cdot Q$	8 Total Cost $w\cdot L$	9 Profit $(P\cdot Q)-(w\cdot L)$
1	10	10	$2	$20	$4	$20	$ 4	$16
2	19	9	2	18	4	38	8	30
3	27	8	2	16	4	54	12	42
4	34	7	2	14	4	68	16	52
5	40	6	2	12	4	80	20	60
6	45	5	2	10	4	90	24	66
7	49	4	2	8	4	98	28	70
8	52	3	2	6	4	104	32	72
9	54	2	2	4	4	108	36	72
10	55	1	2	2	4	110	40	70
11	55	0	2	0	4	110	44	66

Note: nominal wage = $4/hour
price of output = $2/unit

labor increases. Therefore, as shown in Figure 3.3 the firm's demand curve for labor shifts upward and rightward as the price at which it sells its output increases.

Thus, as the price at which output sells increases, the firm would either be willing to hire more labor hours at any given nominal wage, as shown by the segment *AB* in Figure 3.3. In order to satisfy the profit-maximizing condition, $(\Delta Q/\Delta L)\cdot P = w$, with the nominal wage, w, held conceptually constant, if the price at which output sells, P, rises, the marginal physical product of labor, $\Delta Q/\Delta L$, must fall; $\Delta Q/\Delta L$ will fall only if employment, L, rises. Alternatively, the firm would be willing to pay a higher nominal wage at any given level of employment, as shown by segment *AC* in Figure 3.3. In the latter case, the increase in the nominal wage that the firm would be willing to pay at any given level of employment would be proportional to the increase in the price at which output sells. This holds because, as an arithmetical product, the marginal revenue product of labor rises in proportion to the increase in price, and the profit-maximizing firm will hire labor until the marginal revenue product equals the nominal wage.

Earlier, it was indicated that for every level of employment there is a unique, marginal physical product of labor (see Figure 3.2). Therefore, if employment is held constant, the marginal physical product of labor is also unchanged. The profit-maximizing condition for the firm is

$$(\Delta Q/\Delta L)\cdot P = w \qquad (3.1)$$

Where $(\Delta Q/\Delta L)$, the marginal physical product of labor, is unchanged because employment is held constant, the nominal wage (w) must increase in the same proportion as the price of output (P). Put another way, dividing through by P, the profit-maximizing condition becomes

$$(\Delta Q/\Delta L) = w/P \tag{3.2}$$

With $\Delta Q/\Delta L$ unchanged, if P rises, w must rise in the same proportion.

Implicit in the foregoing analysis is the fifth assumption: that firms have perfect knowledge of prices and wages. For example, if the firm did not have perfect knowledge of the price it could receive for its output, the demand for labor would not shift vertically in proportion to the increase in price. The firm would not be able to maximize its profit.

The preceding analysis allows specification, in general notation, of the firm's demand-for-labor function:

$$L_D = \underset{-\;\;\,+}{f(w,\ P)} \tag{3.3}$$

The general notation $f(\ )$ simply indicates that labor hours demanded is a function, $f(\ )$, of the terms within the parentheses. The minus sign under the nominal wage term indicates that while holding the price of output constant, the quantity of labor demanded (L_D) varies inversely with the nominal wage (w). The demand curve is downward sloping in the two-dimensional w, L space, as in Figure 3.3. The plus sign under the price-of-output term indicates that while holding the nominal wage constant, the quantity of labor demanded (L_D) varies directly with the price of output (P). The demand curve shifts rightward as the price of output increases, as in Figure 3.3.

In summary, the five assumptions from which this theory of labor demand is derived are:

1. the law of diminishing returns,
2. purely competitively structured output markets,
3. purely competitively structured labor markets,
4. profit-maximizing business firms (labor demanders), and
5. perfect information regarding prices and wages by business firms (labor demanders).

The foregoing discussion specified that when drawing a demand relation between the nominal wage and the quantity of labor hours demanded, all other "things" (in Latin *cetera*) are "being held constant" or "equal" (in Latin *paribus*). The phrase *ceteris paribus* finds continual usage in economics. It means *holding other things equal or constant*.

If labor is viewed as a homogeneous input, then the aggregate demand for labor by all business firms is simply the sum of the demand curves for labor of individual firms. The aggregate demand curve for labor is the sum of the quantity of labor demanded by each firm in the economy at each possible nominal wage level with the price level held constant and the sum of the quantity of labor demanded by each firm in the economy at each possible price level with the nominal wage level held constant.[3]

[3]The use of the term *price level* in this context implies that there is only one kind of output that is produced by all firms. If there are several kinds of output the aggregation procedure is more complicated. See footnote 8 for additional assumptions involved in the aggregation procedure.

LABOR SUPPLY

Introduction

While the theory of the demand for labor is viewed from the perspective of the business firm—specifically the business firm's demand for productive inputs—the theory of the supply of labor is viewed from the perspective of the household. The demand for the services of the factors of production comes from the business sector. As seen in Chapter Two, business firms are assumed to make the decision to hire the services of the factors of production, which include labor. As also seen in Chapter Two, the household sector of the economy is assumed to make the decision to sell the services of the factors of production that it owns; these factors of production include labor hours.

The theory of the supply of labor is, therefore, properly viewed from the perspective of the household's decision to allocate its time between either labor hours or leisure hours. Since the amount of time that a household has is fixed at twenty-four hours per day, the decision of a household to *supply* labor hours is the obverse of its decision to *demand* leisure hours. Thus, the theory of the supply of labor is identically related to the demand for leisure hours. Since leisure hours are a good, like automobiles or stereos, the theory of the demand for leisure is a subset of the general theory of household demand for goods and services.

Fundamental Assumptions

The four assumptions from which the theory of labor supply is derived are:

1. households maximize their utility,
2. the substitution effect dominates the income effect,
3. households have perfect information regarding wages and prices, and
4. there is perfect nominal wage flexibility.

If and when these assumptions are modified, the related conclusions about the theory of the supply of labor will be modified also.

In conformity with the general theory of demand (taught in principles of economics courses), the first assumption in deriving the theory of the supply of labor is that the household maximizes the amount of its utility or satisfaction subject to a budget constraint and an array of prices. The budget constraint of the household is the condition that it has a budget of twenty-four hours per day that can be allocated to either labor or leisure. Being completely consistent with the general theory of demand, the household makes the decision to allocate its budget of twenty-four hours per day between labor hours and leisure hours so as to maximize its utility or satisfaction.

Generally speaking, leisure is a "good" as opposed to a "bad." It increases one's satisfaction. However, like many goods, leisure is not free. It has a price. A key variable in the allocation decision of any household is the price of the good in question. The key variable in the time-allocation decision of the household is the price of an hour of leisure.

The price of an hour of leisure is the amount of purchasing power that the household could have obtained if that hour had been devoted to labor instead. The price of leisure is really an *opportunity cost;* it is the purchasing-power value of the nominal wage that the household could have received for that hour. The value in terms of purchasing power of the nominal or dollar wage is sometimes called the *real wage*. *Real* should always be interpreted as "purchasing power value of." The real wage is denoted as w/P, where w is the nominal wage in dollars per hour and P is the average price level of newly produced goods and services, a cost-of-living index.[4]

For example, if the nominal wage (w) is \$5 per hour, and the price index is 1, then the real wage is \$5/1 or \$5 per hour. If the nominal wage stays at \$5 per hour, but the cost of living doubles, the purchasing-power value of the nominal wage, the real wage, declines by half to \$5/2 = \$2.50 per hour. The nominal wage purchases only half as much, in real terms, as it did before the price level doubled. Thus, the real wage varies directly with the nominal wage but inversely with the price level.

This discussion of the theory of labor supply began with the idea that since there is a budget of twenty-four hours in a day, hours not devoted to labor are, by definition, hours of leisure. Thus, the *supply* of labor hours is related to the *demand* for leisure hours. As mentioned earlier, the demand for leisure can be viewed as part of the general theory of household demand—the household maximizing its utility subject to a budget constraint and an array of prices. In the demand for leisure hours, the budget constraint is twenty-four hours per day and the array of prices is the nominal wage (w) and the price index (P), conveniently combined as the real wage (w/P).

Since the real wage is the price or opportunity cost of leisure hours, how does the demand for leisure hours vary with their price? To answer this question, the *substitution* and *income effects* of a change in the real wage on the demand for leisure hours have to be examined.

The *substitution effect* derives from the fact that when the price of a good declines, a utility-maximizing household can increase its total utility by substituting the good whose price has fallen for other goods whose prices have not fallen. For example, when the price of French wine declines, the household can increase its utility by substituting French wines for domestic wines whose prices have not fallen. Thus, when the price of leisure declines—when the real wage falls—the substitution effects implies that the household will substitute leisure hours for labor hours, thereby increasing its total utility or satisfaction. The substitution effect, therefore, implies that the demand for leisure hours varies inversely with the real wage. Under the budget constraint, labor hours per day plus leisure hours per day equal twenty-four hours per day. Therefore, the substitution effect implies that the quantity of labor hours supplied varies directly with the real wage.

Figure 3.4 shows that the substitution effect causes the quantity of leisure hours demanded to vary inversely with the real wage. Because of the constraint that twenty-four hours per day minus leisure hours demanded per day equals labor hours supplied per day, the quantity of labor hours supplied varies directly with the real wage. Thus, viewing

[4]More properly, the opportunity cost of leisure is the real wage less income tax payments plus unemployment compensation and "welfare" benefits, if any.

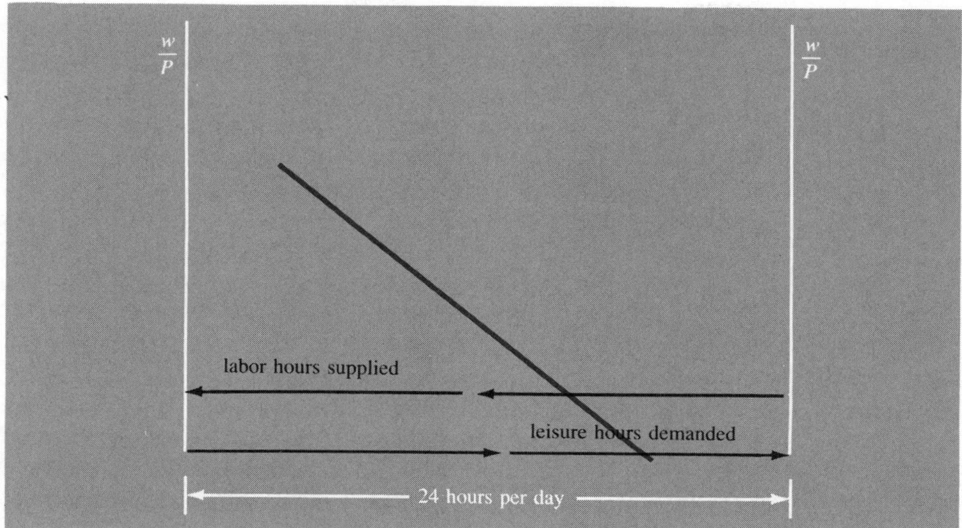

Figure 3.4 Substitution Effect of a Change in the Real Wage on Leisure Hours Demanded and on Labor Hours Supplied

Figure 3.4 from left to right, the substitution effect will always cause a downward-sloping demand curve for leisure hours. Viewing Figure 3.4 from right to left, the substitution effect will always cause an upward-sloping supply curve for labor hours.

The *income effect* of a decline in the real wage on the demand for leisure hours (and supply of labor hours) works as follows: When the real wage falls, the income of the household falls, *ceteris paribus,* because wages are a source of income. Therefore, the household has less purchasing power and will buy less of all goods including leisure hours. Therefore, as the real wage declines, the income effect causes the quantity of leisure hours demanded to fall and, by definition, the quantity of labor hours supplied will rise.

Figure 3.5 shows that the income effect causes the quantity of leisure hours demanded to vary directly with the real wage. Because of the budget constraint that twenty-four hours per day equals leisure hours demanded per day plus labor hours supplied per day, the quantity of labor hours supplied varies inversely with the real wage. Thus, viewing the curve in Figure 3.5 from left to right, the income effect will always cause an upward-sloping demand curve for leisure hours. Viewing the curve in Figure 3.5 from right to left, the income effect will always cause a downward-sloping supply curve of labor hours.

Which effect is dominant—the substitution effect or the income effect? In this case, one should not choose the substitution effect over the income effect (or vice versa) as a matter of convenience. Rather, one should appeal to the facts by asking: Which effect seems to dominate the actual behavior of labor suppliers, the substitution effect or the income effect?

Usually, economists cannot perform laboratory experiments. They cannot readily isolate a worker in a controlled environment (consisting, for example, of a twenty-four hour

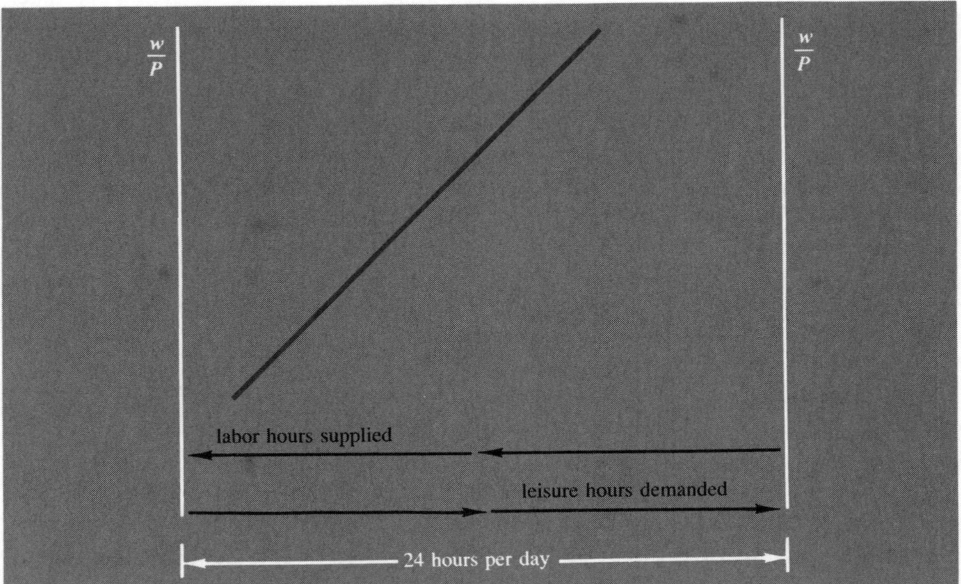

Figure 3.5 Income Effect of a Change in the Real Wage on Leisure Hours Demanded and on Labor Hours Supplied

period in a bare room containing only a fully equipped workbench and a television set that plays only M.A.S.H. reruns), raise the nominal hourly wage, hold the cost of living constant, and observe whether the worker applies more hours to labor or to watching television. However, economists can gather data on nominal wages and hours spent at work and, statistically holding the effect of all other variables constant, estimate the relationship between the two by various techniques. When this is done, a graphical result similar to the one in Figure 3.6 is often obtained.

Clearly, between points *A* and *B* (in Figure 3.6) as the real wage rises, labor hours supplied fall. Over this range, the income effect dominates the substitution effect. This suggests that when real wages are relatively low, a reduction in real wages will, on balance, induce workers to work more to preserve their income in order to survive. In contrast, between points *B* and *C* the substitution effect dominates the income effect. When real wages are relatively high, a reduction in real wages will, on balance, induce workers to work less.[5]

There have been historical periods in which the income effect has dominated the substitution effect. For example, during the forty-year period from 1890 to the Great Depression of 1929, there were vast increases in labor productivity, real wages, and real labor income in the United States. These were closely followed by sizable reductions in

[5]Empirical estimates in the *BC* range indicate that for a 10 percent increase in the real, after-tax wage, labor supplied by married males increases between 2 and 3 percent and labor supplied by married females increases by 8 percent. For further evidence see the articles by Jerry Hausman and Don Fullerton cited in the bibliography to this chapter.

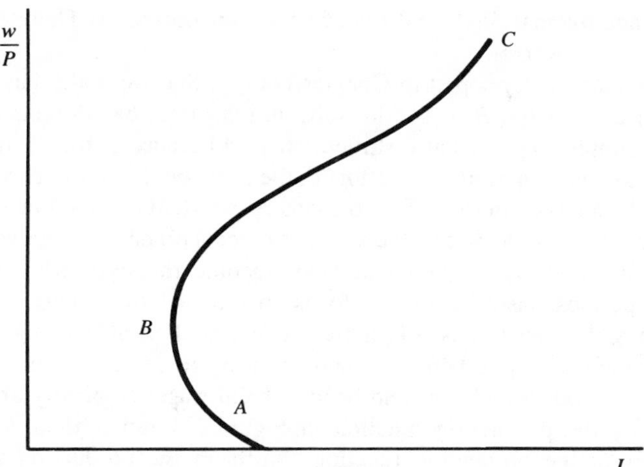

Figure 3.6 An Empirical Labor Supply Relation

the average work week from about 60 hours to about 44 hours. One explanation for this is that technological changes and the increase in capital stock shifted the production function upward (in Figure 3.1) and made it steeper. This increased the marginal productivity of labor, the real wage, and the level of real labor income at every possible level of employment. As real labor income rose above the level required for workers to acquire the basic necessities of life, leisure hours became more important relative to consumption goods. The labor supply curve was negatively sloped (as in the *AB* range in Figure 3.6) because the income effect dominated the substitution effect. As the demand for labor by firms increased due to the increased marginal physical productivity of labor, labor market equilibrium moved along the *AB* locus. Thus, between 1890 and 1929, as real wages and real labor income initially rose from very low levels, the average work week declined.

This explanation is fortified by another hypothesis: the *leisure time valuation hypothesis*. In order to extract a flow of services from a stock of luxury (nonnecessity) consumption goods, considerably more leisure time is required as a complementary input. For example, one cannot derive benefits from a new sound system unless one allocates the leisure time to listen to it. Therefore, as the real wage and real income rise, purchases of stocks of consumption goods increase. Since leisure time is a complementary input, together with these stocks of goods, in producing a flow of consumption services, it becomes more valuable. This leisure time valuation effect can be viewed as working in the same direction as the income effect and moderating the substitution effect.

In contrast to the period from 1890 to 1929, in the forty-year period since World War II labor productivity, real wages, and real labor income have continued to rise but the average work week has remained virtually unchanged. One explanation for this is that we have been moving along the nearly vertical range of the supply curve shown in Figure 3.6 and the income and substitution effects have been canceling each other out. As real labor income rises and more time is allocated to leisure, the marginal utility of leisure time decreases and the marginal disutility of labor time decreases. Therefore, the income effect becomes less powerful.

Another explanation, developed in Chapter Four, is that we really have moved rightward along the curve from B to C (the substitution effect has dominated the income effect), but the supply curve has also shifted leftward because of the disincentive of ever higher income tax rates on productive effort in the post–World War II period.

Throughout the analysis in the next two chapters, we shall assume that the substitution effect dominates the income effect. We will not be concerned with the vast increases in labor productivity, real wages, and real labor income that typically occur over long historical time periods. Instead, we will focus on the analytical short run. In the short run, changes in real wages are usually not associated with sizable swings in the productivity and real income of workers. Put another way, in the short run changes in the marginal physical product of labor, and hence in real wages, typically arise from small movements *along* the production function in Figure 3.1 rather than from upward or downward *shifts in* the production function. Shifts in the production function imply sizable changes in real labor income at each level of employment. (*Real labor income* is defined as the real wage times the level of employment.) Thus, in the short run, the income effect can reasonably be assumed to be dominated by the substitution effect. (The income effect will be discussed in later chapters, when we consider changes in the economy's productive capacity.)

Since the range from B to C is the more prevalent case, in all of the short-run analysis that follows, the (second) basic assumption is that the substitution effect dominates the income effect. The demand curve for leisure hours of the household is downward sloping and its supply curve for labor hours is upward sloping, as shown in Figure 3.7.[6]

Figure 3.7 is an example of the dominance of the substitution effect over the income effect. At an hourly real wage of $9, nine hours of leisure are demanded and fifteen hours of labor are supplied. At $7 per hour, twelve hours of leisure are demanded and twelve hours of labor supplied. At a $5 per hour real wage, fifteen hours of leisure are demanded and nine hours of labor are supplied.

If the assumption is that the supply curve of labor hours is upward sloping for each household in the economy (the substitution effect dominates the income effect), then in the labor market for the aggregate of households the aggregate supply curve of labor is upward sloping, as depicted in Figure 3.8. If labor is homogeneous, then the aggregate supply of labor of all households is simply the sum of the quantity supplied by each household in the economy at each possible real wage level. The aggregate supply schedule indicates that as the nominal wage (w) rises, or as the price level (P) falls, the quantity of labor hours will rise because the real wage (w/P) will rise. This allows the specification of the aggregate labor supply relation in general notation

$$L_s = \underset{+}{g}(w/P) \tag{3.4}$$

[6]It is also possible to derive the upward-sloping supply curve of labor from the assumption of *homothetic preferences* on the part of households. This concept usually is reserved for advanced economic theory courses. The intellectually curious may consult the bibliography following this chapter.

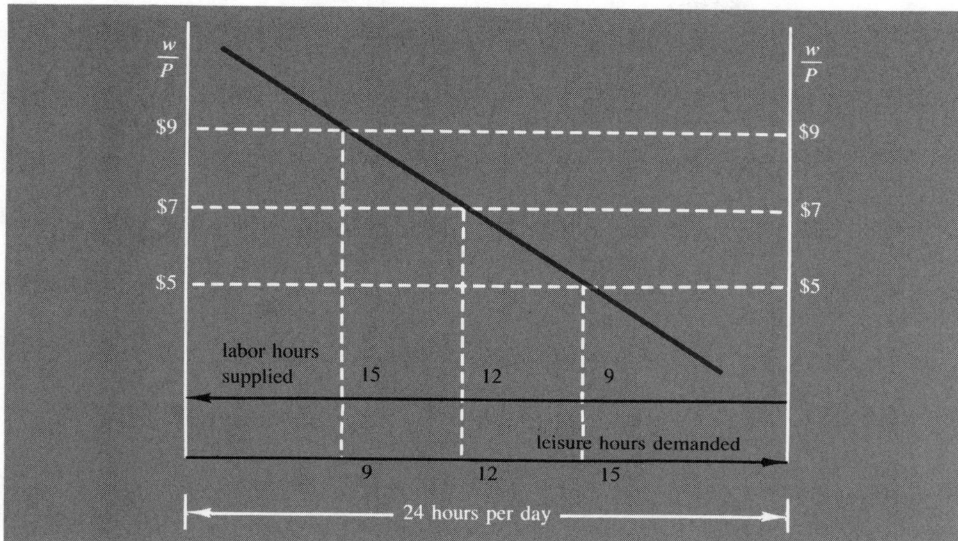

Figure 3.7 The Household Demand for Leisure and Supply of Labor

The notation $g(\ )$ simply means that the quantity of labor hours supplied (L_s) is a function, $g(\ )$, of the variables within the parentheses. The plus sign under the real wage term indicates that the quantity of labor supplied (L_s) varies directly with the nominal wage and inversely with the price level in the two-dimensional (w/P), L space. It also indicates that a change in the nominal wage level that matches, in percentage terms, a change in the price level will have no effect on the quantity of labor supplied.[7]

The third basic assumption in the theory of the supply of labor is that households have perfect information regarding wage and price levels. The fourth and final assumption is that the nominal wage level is perfectly flexible. These two assumptions imply that labor suppliers respond to the real or purchasing-power value of the nominal wage. If the price level were imperfectly known, workers could not readily respond to changes in the real wage that are caused by changes in the price level. If the nominal wage were inflexible, say because of contracts with employers that fix the nominal wage for a period of time, responses of labor suppliers to changes in the nominal wage would not be feasible. In either case, the household could not immediately maximize its utility.

[7]It can also reasonably be argued that the interest rate affects labor supply. In Chapter Five, the interest rate is seen as the opportunity cost of current consumption. It may also be seen as another opportunity cost—the opportunity cost of leisure (in addition to the real wage). The higher the interest rate, the more future consumption we sacrifice by allocating time to current leisure. Therefore, the higher the interest rate, the less time we allocate to current leisure. It follows that an increase in the interest rate encourages a greater allocation of current time to labor. Because of this effect, the quantity of labor supplied varies positively with the interest rate. Increased current labor boosts current income, causing greater current saving, which results in greater future consumption. Thus, a rise in the interest rate is an incentive to work more today in order to enjoy greater consumption in the future.

At the end of Chapter Four, we argue that the income tax rate on labor income and other factors can also affect labor supply.

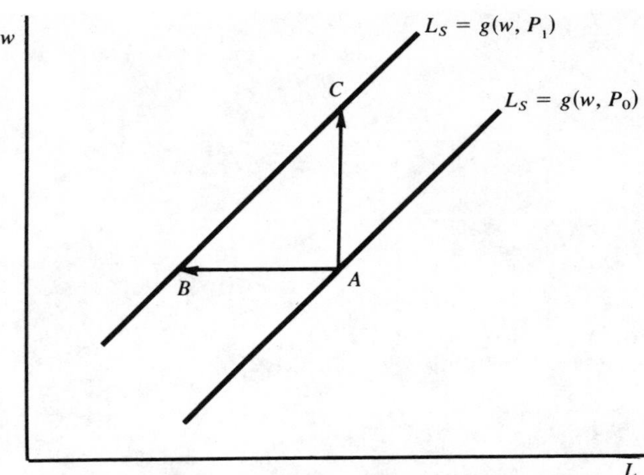

Figure 3.8 Aggregate Supply Curve of Labor in *w, L* Space

The preceding analysis allows specification of the aggregate labor supply relation with two right-hand side variables, *w* and *P*, as in Equation (3.5):

$$L_s = g(\underset{+}{w}, \underset{-}{P}) \tag{3.5}$$

The plus sign under the nominal wage term indicates that the quantity of labor supplied varies directly with the nominal wage. The minus sign under the price level term indicates that the quantity of labor supplied varies inversely with the price level. These algebraic signs should be viewed as the logical implications of the four basic assumptions expressed above. In Figure 3.8 the aggregate labor supply curve is drawn in *w, L* space consistent with Equation (3.5). With the labor supply curve expressed in this way, the analysis can progress more smoothly.

A unique aggregate labor supply curve exists for every possible price level. As the price level rises, say from P_0 to P_1, the labor supply curve shifts leftward and upward. This is entirely consistent with Figure 3.8 and Equation (3.5) which show that the quantity of labor hours supplied varies inversely with the price level. Thus, at any given nominal wage, as the price level rises labor suppliers are willing to work fewer hours as shown by segment *AB* in Figure 3.8, because the real wage declines. Looking at this another way, labor suppliers would be willing to work the same number of hours at a higher nominal wage, as shown by segment *AC* in Figure 3.8. In the latter case, if the quantity of labor hours supplied does not change, then, when the price level increases by a certain percentage, the nominal wage that workers would require has to increase by the same percentage. This follows directly from Equation (3.4) and Figure 3.8. Thus, given an increase in the price level, in order for labor hours to remain unchanged, the nominal wage must rise in the same proportion as the price level. In other words, the opportunity cost of leisure is the real wage. When the real wage is unchanged, no alteration will occur in the allocation of time between labor hours and leisure hours.

Equilibrium in the Labor Market

When the aggregate supply curve of labor and the aggregate demand curve for labor are combined with a *labor market equilibrium condition*—when labor hours supplied equal labor hours demanded—an equilibrium real wage and an equilibrium quantity of labor are found. As shown in Figure 3.3, there is a unique labor demand curve for every price level at which the firm's output will sell. As shown in Figure 3.8, there is also a unique labor supply curve for every price level. As a matter of convenience, assume that the price at which output sells (which influences the demand for labor) is identical to the price "level" (which influences the supply of labor). This implies that P is the price of a homogeneous output. (Price indexes were discussed in Chapter Two.)

Given a price level such as P_0 in Figure 3.9, unique labor supply and labor demand curves may be identified. Where these supply and demand curves intersect, the equilibrium nominal wage (w_0) and the equilibrium quantity of labor (L_0) are determined. Where the price level is known (P_0), the solution yields the equilibrium nominal wage (w_0).

The graphical treatment in Figure 3.9 shows a system of three equations:

$$L_D = f(w, P) \quad \text{labor demand} \tag{3.3}$$

$$L_S = g(w, P) \quad \text{labor supply} \tag{3.5}$$

$$L_D = L_S \quad \text{equilibrium condition} \tag{3.6}$$

in *four* unknowns, L_D, L_S, w, and P.

Generally a value for one of the four unknowns must be given before the system can be solved for its equilibrium values. In Figure 3.9 a given price level P_0 is assumed, and the system is solved for w_0, L_D and L_S. This means that the price level is not determined

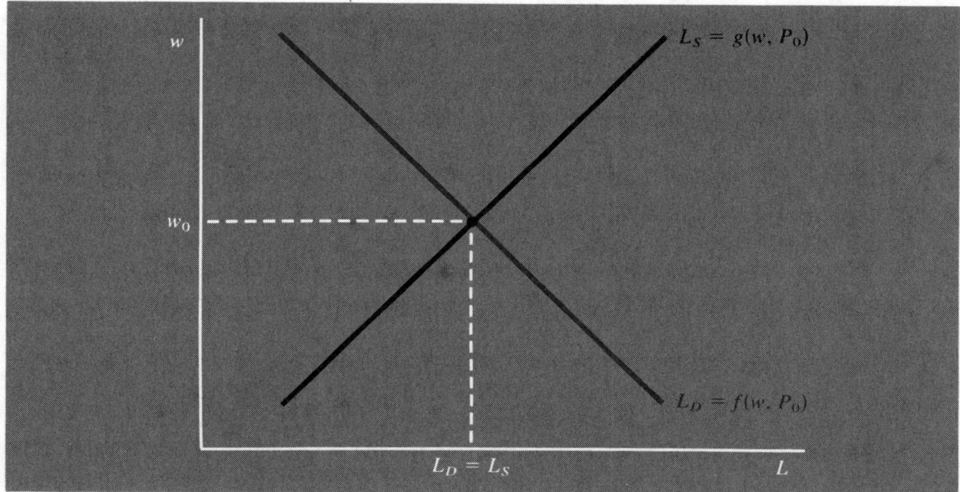

Figure 3.9 Equilibrium in the Aggregate Labor Market

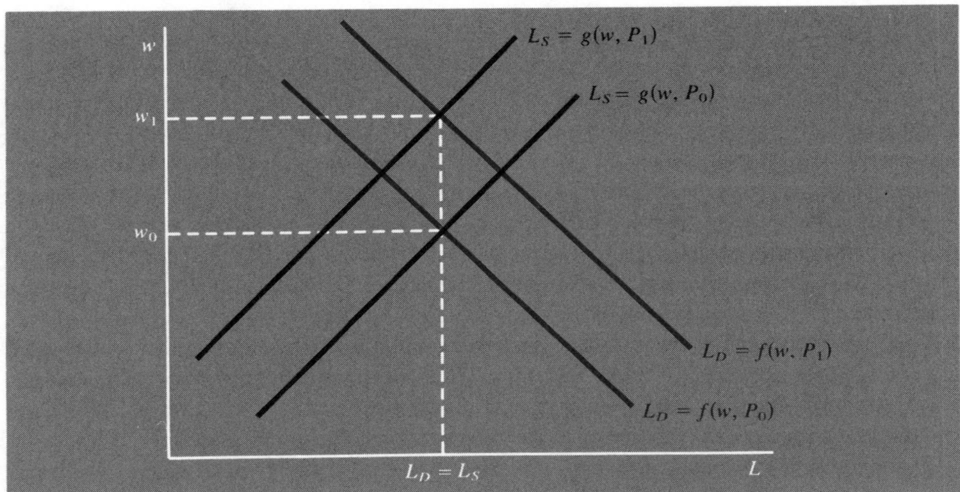

Figure 3.10 Effect of a Change in the Price Level on the Demand for Labor and on the Supply of Labor with Perfect Information and Nominal Wage Flexibility

by the working of the labor market but is assumed to be exogenous to it. With an exogenously determined price level, we may solve for the endogenous variables, w_0, L_D and L_S.

Now, assume another value for the exogenous variable, the price level (P_1), where P_1 is greater than P_0 (Figure 3.10). Earlier it was shown that when the price at which output sells increases, the marginal revenue product of labor increases in the same proportion. Since profit-maximizing firms are assumed to have perfect knowledge of wages and prices, they will be willing to pay a nominal wage equal to the marginal revenue product of labor, and the demand curve for labor shifts upward in Figure 3.10 in the same proportion as the increase in P.

Thus, at every possible level of employment of labor hours (L) firms are willing to pay a nominal wage that increases in the same proportion as the increase in the price level, $\Delta w/w_0 = \Delta P/P_0$. Therefore, at every possible level of employment (L) the real wage (w/P), and hence the marginal physical product of labor, are unchanged, $w_0/P_0 = w_1/P_1$. It follows that as long as employment is unchanged, firms are on the same point of the production function, and the marginal physical product of labor will also be unchanged. Since the profit-maximizing firm hires labor up to the point where the marginal physical product of labor equals the real wage, if employment is unchanged, the real wage is also unchanged.

On the supply side of the labor market, if there is no change in the quantity of labor supplied, an increase in the exogenously determined price level will result in a proportionately higher nominal wage request by labor suppliers. This is shown in Figure 3.10. The result reflects the four basic assumptions of the theory of labor supply. Under these assumptions when the price level increases by a certain percentage ($\Delta P/P_0$), labor suppliers require an increase in the nominal wage of the same percentage, $\Delta w/w_0 = \Delta P/P_0$, to work the same number of hours. Thus, if the allocation of time between labor hours and leisure hours is unchanged, the real wage (w/P) is unchanged, $w_0/P_0 = w_1/P_1$. The opportunity cost of leisure is the real wage. At each real wage level there is a unique number of hours that workers would be willing to work. When the price level changes, if there is no alteration in the number of hours of labor supplied, the nominal wage must vary in the same proportion, such that the real wage, the opportunity cost of leisure, is unchanged. With an invariant real wage, there is no alteration in the allocation of time between labor and leisure.

Earlier in this chapter the concept of the short-run production function for the firm was discussed. Consider the *aggregate* short-run production function.[8] *Aggregate* implies a summation across all of the production functions of each individual firm in the economy. This concept is usually easier to understand if a homogeneous type of output and a homogeneous type of labor are assumed. Figure 3.1 shows the one-to-one relationship between labor input (aggregate employment) and production (aggregate output) for the economy as a whole.

In Chapter Two the level of aggregate output of the economy was related, by definition, to the level of real income of the economy. By producing output, business firms generate real income for the factors of production that they employ. Therefore, aggregate output and aggregate real income are often used synonymously. Nominal aggregate income (Y) is simply a product of the price level (P) times the level of aggregate output (Q), that is,

$$Y \equiv P \times Q$$

The term Y/P stands for aggregate real income, and aggregate real income is identical to aggregate output, $Y/P \equiv Q$.

If there is perfect information regarding the new price level and if the nominal wage is flexible, both the aggregate labor supply and aggregate labor demand curves shift upward in the same proportion as the change in the price level. Therefore, in Figure 3.11A, given an increase in the price level from P_0 to P_1, the nominal wage will change proportionally from w_0 to w_1 and aggregate employment will not vary. If aggregate employment does not change, then neither aggregate output nor aggregate real income will be altered. Except for workers switching jobs, everyone seeking a job at the prevailing nominal wage and price level will have one. In this situation, the full employment level of employment, and the full employment level of output are achieved. Full employment is defined as the perfect information-flexible wage equilibrium in the labor market.

Figure 3.11 shows the labor market with an initial price level of P_0, an initial equilibrium nominal wage of w_0, and an equilibrium real wage of w_0/P_0. Equilibrium employment is L_0 and, using the aggregate production function, at the bottom of Figure 3.11, the equilibrium level of aggregate output is Q_0. In Figure 3.11A, when the price level increases to P_1, labor suppliers request a proportionately higher nominal wage, w_1. This

[8]To derive an aggregate production function and an aggregate demand for labor from the production functions of different firms in static models, it is necessary to assume that the production functions of all firms are concave and homogeneous of degree one. The latter concept is discussed in the references cited in the bibliography at the end of this chapter.

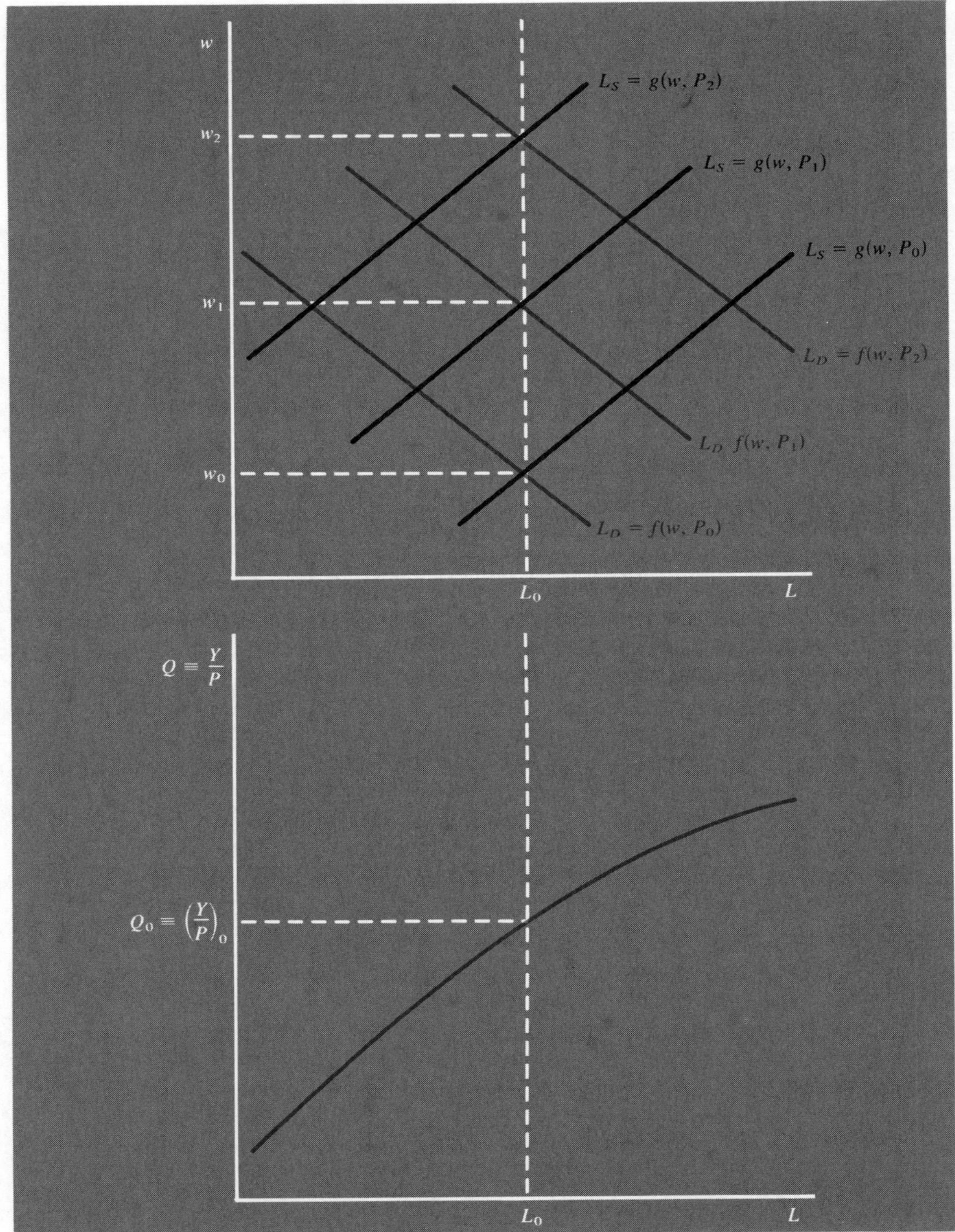

Figure 3.11 The Effect of a Change in the Price Level on the Labor Market and Production Function with Perfect Nominal Wage Flexibility and Perfect Information

occurs because of the basic assumptions of the theory of labor supply. Especially important are the assumptions of perfect information and perfectly flexible nominal wages.

Labor demanders are willing to pay this higher wage (w_1), and still hire the same number of workers for the same number of hours. Because they are assumed to have perfect knowledge of the increase in the price level, they realize that the marginal revenue product of labor increases in the same proportion as the increase in the price level. In short, both supply and demand curves shift upward in the same proportion. When this occurs, in Figure 3.11A the nominal wage increases to w_1. With employment unchanged at L_0, in Figure 3.11B output is unaltered at Q_0. The real wage in Figure 3.11A is also unchanged, $w_0/P_0 = w_1/P_1$.

Since firms are still at the same point on the aggregate production function in Figure 3.11B, the marginal physical product of labor is the same. With the marginal physical product of labor unchanged, firms will not pay a different real wage because, in equilibrium, the real wage is equal to the marginal physical product of labor.

With the real wage unchanged, labor suppliers have no incentive to alter the allocation of their time between leisure and labor because the real wage is the opportunity cost of leisure. If the price level increases to P_2 in Figure 3.11A, the supply and demand curves shift in the same proportion once again and intersect vertically above L_0. The nominal wage rises to w_2, but the real wage is unchanged, $w_0/P_0 = w_1/P_1 = w_2/P_2$. Thus, under conditions of perfect information regarding nominal wage and price levels on both sides of the labor market and nominal wage flexibility, a change in the price level can have no effect on full employment production and employment.

The levels of full employment production and employment are determined exclusively by the preferences of households, which determine the supply curve of labor, and the technical conditions of production (the aggregate production function) and the stock of capital goods, which determine the demand curve for labor. The equilibrium level of real income is invariant with respect to the general price level. No matter what price level is assumed, it will have no effect on employment or real income.[9]

The Long-Run Phillips Curve

A slight modification allows the preceding analysis to be expressed in terms of a Phillips curve. A *Phillips curve* depicts the relationship between the rate of inflation and the rate of unemployment. The rate of inflation is the change in the price level expressed as a percentage over some period of time. For example, if the price index, discussed in Chapter Two, goes from a value of 200 on January 1, 1988, to 220 on January 1, 1989, the rate of inflation for 1988 is (220 − 200)/200 = 20/200 = 10 percent. The *rate of unemployment* is defined as the civilian labor force, measured in terms of persons avail-

[9]It is interesting to note here that *supply-side economic policy* contends that a reduction in the tax rate on labor income will stimulate an increase in the supply of labor because it will increase the *after-tax* real wage. The increase (rightward shift) in the supply of labor will increase the equilibrium level of employment and raise the level of output in the economy. The success of supply-side policy with regard to the supply of labor depends on the dominance of the substitution effect over the income effect of a change in the after-tax real wage. This policy will be discussed again in Chapter Four and examined in detail in Chapter Fourteen.

able for work, minus the level of employment, the difference divided by the civilian labor force. For example, if the labor force consists of 120 million people, and 114 million people are employed, the level of unemployment is 6.0 million. The unemployment rate (6 million/120 million) is 5 percent.

In the preceding analysis, all nominal wages and prices were expressed as levels. Now they will be expressed as *rates of change*—rates of nominal wage inflation and rates of price inflation. A dot over a variable signifies that it is expressed as a percentage rate of change over an interval of time:

$$\dot{P} = \frac{\Delta P/\Delta t}{P} \text{ and } \dot{w} = \frac{\Delta w/\Delta t}{w}$$

where Δt is a year, $\Delta P/\Delta t$ is the change in the price level over the year, and $\Delta w/\Delta t$ is the change in the nominal wage level over the year.

In Figure 3.12, at the initial level of full employment, A, labor suppliers and labor demanders both have perfect information regarding the prevailing rate of price inflation, $\dot{P}_0$. This is reflected in an equilibrium rate of nominal wage increase, $\dot{w}_0$, that equals the rate of increase of the price level, $\dot{P}_0$. Assume that labor suppliers and labor demanders have perfect information regarding any new rate of inflation and that the rate of nominal

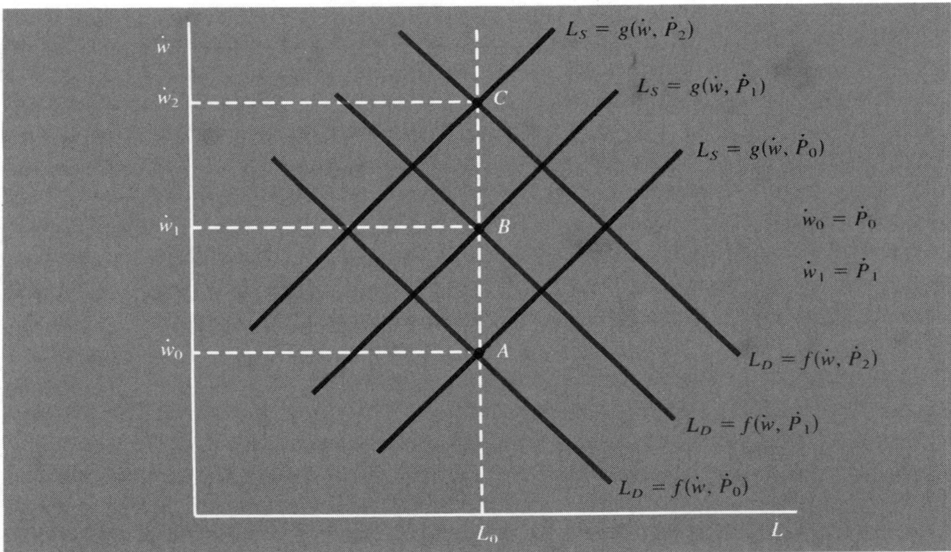

Figure 3.12 The Labor Market with Price and Nominal Wage Variables Expressed in Terms of Rates of Change and with Perfect Information and Nominal Wage Flexibility

wage increase is perfectly flexible. If the exogeneously determined rate of price inflation rises from $\dot{P}_0$ to $\dot{P}_1$, then labor demand and labor supply curves will shift upward in the same proportion as the increase which matches the rate of inflation, $\dot{P}_1$.

Employers anticipate that the marginal revenue product will rise because they expect to sell output at higher prices. Therefore, employers are willing to offer a higher rate of nominal wage increase at each possible level of employment. Workers realize that unless nominal wages increase at a rate commensurate with the new rate of inflation, $\dot{P}_1$, the level of real wages will fall. Because of this loss of purchasing power, workers have an incentive to work less. Therefore, in order to work the same number of hours, laborers are willing and able to require a rate of nominal wage increase which matches the new rate of inflation, $\dot{P}_1$. Since both curves shift upward in the same proportion, the new equilibrium is at point B, with employment unchanged at level L_0, the full employment level of employment. The equilibrium rate of nominal wage increase is now at $\dot{w}_1$. Since the equilibrium rate of nominal wage inflation matches the rate of price inflation, the real wage w/P is not going to change. This is consistent with the unchanged level of employment and, therefore, the unchanged marginal product of labor and the unchanged real wage.

Similarly, if the rate of price inflation goes to $\dot{P}_2$, equilibrium will occur at C with no deviation from the full employment equilibrium level of employment. This occurs as long as labor demanders and labor suppliers have perfect information regarding inflation and the rate of nominal wage increase is perfectly flexible. The equilibrium rate of nominal wage increase will now be $\dot{w}_2$, matching the rate of price inflation $\dot{P}_2$. Again, the level of the real wage is unchanging.

Since unemployment is defined as the labor force minus employment, a unique level of unemployment is associated with the full employment level of employment (L_0) in Figure 3.12. (The labor force minus employment, L_0, expressed as a percentage of the labor force equals the unemployment rate, U_0.) As the equilibrium level of employment is invariant with the rate of inflation ($\dot{P}$), the rate of unemployment also will be invariant with the inflation rate. This result hinges on the assumptions of perfect information on both sides of the labor market and the assumption of perfect nominal wage flexibility. Since these conditions are often thought likely to exist in the long run, the invariant relationship between price inflation and unemployment is often considered a long-run relationship.

Early in this century, an American economist named Irving Fisher first probed the relationship between price and wage inflation and the unemployment rate. Decades later, a British economist named A. W. Phillips plotted a statistical relationship between inflation and the unemployment rate. Today, economists call any mapping between inflation and the unemployment rate a Phillips curve. The Phillips curve is further discussed in the next chapter.

Figure 3.12 suggests a long-run Phillips curve of the sort depicted in Figure 3.13. Figure 3.12 shows that as the rate of inflation increases, there is no effect on the full employment equilibrium level of employment (L_0). If the labor force is unchanged, it follows that there will be no change in the full employment rate of unemployment in

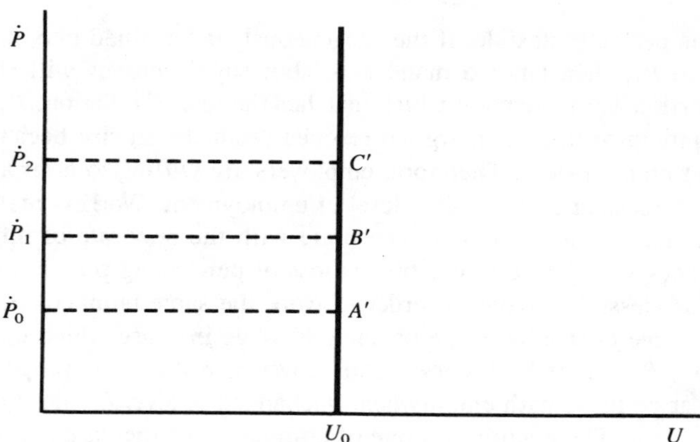

Figure 3.13 A Long-Run Phillips Curve

Figure 3.13. Points A′, B′, and C′ in Figure 3.13 correspond to points A, B, and C in Figure 3.12. The full employment equilibrium rate of unemployment (U_0) is positive instead of zero because there will always be a certain percentage of the labor force changing jobs. This is called *frictional unemployment*. At full employment equilibrium, all unemployment is frictional.[10] In Chapter Four, trends in frictional unemployment are discussed in detail.

Concluding Comment

The level of employment and the rate of unemployment are key macroeconomic variables that are determined by the working of the labor market. This chapter derived the theory of the demand for labor and the theory of the supply of labor from nine basic assumptions. In general, it was shown that modifying one of these assumptions may significantly change the conclusions of the theory. One key assumption is the assumption of nominal wage flexibility. The other key assumptions are the assumptions of perfect information on both sides (supply and demand) of the labor market. Under these assumptions, the employment level is invariant with respect to a change in the price level, and the unemployment rate is invariant with respect to a change in the inflation rate. The long-run Phillips curve depicts an invariant relationship between the rate of inflation and the rate of unemployment. In the next chapter the assumptions of perfect information and perfect nominal wage flexibility are relaxed, and its effect on the theory of employment and production is observed. This modification of the working of the labor market has a substantial impact on the conclusions that are drawn about the overall economy in later chapters.

[10]If the average worker quit his or her job once every two years and remained unemployed for one month, the frictional rate of unemployment associated with a full employment equilibrium would be 1/24 = 4.2 percent.

EXERCISES

1. Why does the profit-maximizing assumption imply that the firm will hire labor until the incremental cost of hiring labor equals the incremental revenue from hiring labor?
2. Assume that the income effect of a wage change exceeds the substitution effect. Draw the labor supply curve for this case in w, L space. Explain the result in words.
3. Why will a business firm demand more labor when the price at which it sells its product rises? Draw the effect on the demand curve for labor in w, L space.
4. List the assumptions that are used to derive a labor demand curve where the quantity demanded varies inversely with the wage and directly with the price at which output sells.
5. Consider the supply of labor with wage and price variables expressed in the rate-of-change form; what exactly are workers asking for in their employment contracts?
6. Why would the nominal wage requested by workers vary proportionately with the price level as long as employment is unchanged?
7. Derive a long-run Phillips curve from a model of the labor market.
8. What effect would a cut in the income tax rate applied to labor income have on the labor supply curve? Will such a tax cut increase aggregate employment and output?
9. A recent college campus survey revealed that students with lower grade point averages spend more time watching daytime soap operas and sports events than their counterparts with higher grades. Analyze this in terms of income and substitution effects.

BIBLIOGRAPHY

Fullerton, Don. "Can Tax Revenues Go Up When Tax Rates Go Down?" Washington, D.C.: Department of the Treasury, Office of Tax Analysis, Paper 41, September 1982.

Hausman, Jerry A. "Labor Supply." In *How Taxes Affect Economic Behavior,* ed. Henry J. Aaron and Joseph A. Pechman. Washington, D.C.: Brookings Institution, 1981.

Hicks, John R. *Theory of Wages*. London: Macmillan, 1932.

Malinvaud, Edmund. *Lectures in Microeconomic Theory*. Amsterdam: North Holland, 1972.

Rees, Albert. *The Economics of Work and Pay*. 2d ed. New York: Harper and Row, 1979.

The Labor Market: Nominal Wage Inflexibility, Imperfect Information, and Unanticipated Information

Chapter 4

Introduction

The previous chapter described how the aggregate labor market automatically attains a full employment equilibrium that is invariant with respect to changes in the price level or the rate of inflation, as long as it is assumed that labor demanders and labor suppliers have perfect information and nominal wages are perfectly flexible. In the present chapter these assumptions are relaxed, and quite a different result is obtained. For example, if participants in the labor market do not have perfect information regarding the price level or rate of inflation, or if nominal wages are not perfectly flexible, then the economy need not be at a full employment equilibrium, and the level of employment and production need not be invariant with respect to changes in the price level or the rate of inflation.

The Labor Market Revisited

Assume a labor demand relation, Equation (4.1), that is identical to the one used in Chapter Three:

$$L_D = f(\underset{-}{w}, \underset{+}{P}) \tag{4.1}$$

This indicates that the demand for labor varies inversely with the nominal wage and positively with the price level. This is shown by the minus sign under the nominal wage variable and the plus sign under the price level variable.

The modification of the model occurs entirely on the supply side of the labor market:

$$L_S = \underset{\infty}{g(w,} \underset{0}{P)} \tag{4.2) I}$$

In Equation (4.2) I, the zero under the price level variable indicates either that workers have no information about the price level or have information but cannot respond to it because of labor contracts. The infinity sign beneath the nominal wage variable means that the quantity of labor is infinitely sensitive to variations in the nominal wage. (An infinitely small decrease in the nominal wage results in the quantity of labor supplied falling to zero.) This implies essentially that the nominal wage is fixed.

This type of labor supply function will be shown to result in the level of employment and output being responsive to shifts in the demand for labor caused by changes in the price level. The responsiveness of employment and output to changes in the price level is an extremely important property and will be referred to throughout this book.

This link between output and price level changes may arise from supply decisions in many markets, not just the labor market. From a more general perspective, there are two alternative conditions under which a rise in the price level will stimulate higher levels of productive inputs to be supplied and outputs to be produced in markets including the labor market.

The first is *imperfect information*. Under this condition, the increase in the general price level is incorrectly perceived as causing an increase in the input supplier's own price relative to the general price level or reflecting an increase in the output producer's own price relative to the general price level. As a result of this condition, more input is supplied and more output is produced because suppliers and producers incorrectly believe that their relative prices have increased. In this chapter, when there is imperfect information in the labor market, workers (input suppliers) confuse a rise in their nominal wage, brought about by the increases in the demand for labor caused by a higher price level, with a rise in their real wage (the nominal wage relative to the general price level) and, as a result, supply more labor hours.

The second condition is that input suppliers or output producers engage in *fixed price or nominal wage contracting* under which their own prices cannot be instantaneously adjusted in the face of a rise in the price level. Thus, when the demand for their input or output increases because of an increase in the general price level, they are contractually obligated to respond without raising their own prices. In this chapter, when there is nominal wage contracting in the labor market, workers are bound by contracts to supply more labor hours whenever the demand for labor increases.[1]

[1]The imperfect information approach is associated with the seminal research of Friedman and Phelps. This approach was justified in the works of Lucas and Sargent and Wallace. The alternative to the imperfect information approach is that nominal wages are set for the finite period of a labor contract and therein cannot respond to price level changes that were unanticipated when the contract was made. This approach is exemplified in the research of Taylor. All of the researchers above are cited in the bibliography for this chapter.

Fixed nominal wages can result from nominal wage contracting. Imperfect nominal wage responses to changes in the price level can also result from nominal wage contracting. In addition, imperfect responses to changes in the price level may reflect *imperfect information*. A special type of imperfect information is *money illusion*. Money illusion occurs when workers do not respond to real, purchasing-power values of the wage but instead react only to nominal or money values. The failure of labor suppliers, who are not prevented by contracts from doing so, to respond to a change in the price level is, therefore, tantamount to money illusion. Workers may have money illusion either because they have imperfect information regarding the price level or because they have good price level information and are simply not concerned about their real wage. Keynes suggested that workers in one industry will have money illusion because they will be far more concerned about their nominal wages relative to the nominal wages of their cohorts in other industries rather than their nominal wages relative to the price level.

Because of the high cost of workers' finding a satisfactory job and employers' finding satisfactory employees, labor markets are not typically organized as a continuous auction. Instead, labor markets are characterized by contracts. The fact that contracts are made in nominal terms does not necessarily imply that workers have money illusion or imperfect information either before or after a contract is signed. Labor contracts that are made in nominal terms may be either explicit or implicit. Nominal wage contracts might result if rational workers are reluctant to bear the cost of periodically pressuring their employers for raises when the demand for their services unexpectedly increases and to bear the cost of resisting nominal wage cuts when the demand for their services unexpectedly decreases. Nominal wage contracts might also result if employers are reluctant to bear the costs of recruiting new workers when nominal wages are cut. When nominal wage contracts exist, labor suppliers may have good, or even perfect, current information regarding the price level but will be unable to respond to it because of the contract.

Nominal wage contracts might also result if rational workers are averse to bearing the risk of changes in the price level that were unanticipated when the contract was negotiated. Workers, who depend entirely on their jobs for their livelihood, may be risk-averse and not want to see their real incomes fall even if it means that they periodically must give up gains in real income. Firms, on the other hand, are owned by stockholders who diversify their holdings, do not depend on one firm's profits for their livelihood, and are therefore risk-neutral. They may forego some profit in one period in exchange for even greater profit in another.

Under these circumstances, if the price level falls, contracts may permit eventual nominal wage reductions but will allow workers to keep their jobs. Productivity and real wages will decline because of overemployment during recessions. This overemployment will cause greater decreases in profit than would be the case if employment were severely cut at the contracted nominal wage. Later, if the price level rises, contracts may permit eventual nominal wage increases but will require workers to abide by the contracts and continue to work at the contracted nominal wage. With workers more efficiently utilized, productivity and real wages will rise. Firms' profits will also rise to a level that will more than compensate for recessionary losses. The procyclical pattern in real wages that emerges from risk-averse contracting behavior on the part of labor suppliers runs counter to the pattern predicted by the theory developed in this chapter. See footnote four for further discussion.

Finally, nominal wage contracts will result if rational and fully informed workers and employers have a higher cost of organizing, monitoring, and enforcing more complicated kinds of contracts, such as those with detailed contingency clauses.

A prominent feature of modern nominal wage contracting is a *cost of living adjustment* (*COLA*) clause. This feature indexes the nominal wage to published price level changes that have occurred in the recent past. Only about 60 percent of all workers are covered by COLAs, and most of these adjustments are less than 100 percent of the price level increase. Moreover, indexing takes effect after a considerable time lag and adds complexity to the contract. Therefore, the presence of COLAs will result in labor suppliers not fully and immediately responding to a change in the price level that was unanticipated when the contract was negotiated even though they may have good or even perfect current price level information.

Whatever the reason for nominal wage contracting and hence a rigid nominal wage and an imperfect response to price level information, characterized by Equation (4.2) I, such contracts clearly play an important part in today's labor market despite theoretical arguments aligned against them.[2] Nonindexed two- and three-year contracts are commonplace in the unionized sector of the economy. Nonunion workers typically have wage adjustments about once a year. Union and nonunion wage contracts do not all lapse at once; rather, wage negotiations are occurring continually. The result of staggered indexed and unindexed contracts is that nominal wages are rigid in the short run and respond with a lag to price level changes. The lag in the response of nominal wages to price level changes makes it appear that labor suppliers have imperfect information regarding the price level when what is really involved is imperfect response to what may be good, if not perfect, current information. The key here is that the new information was not anticipated when the contract was made and that, even if it is required in the contract, indexation is never immediate and is seldom complete. Therefore, when referring to the labor supply relation, the presence of imperfect price level information or imperfect response to price level information is synonymous with an unanticipated change in the price level.

The labor supply relation, Equation (4.2) I, reflects an extreme case: one of nominal wage inflexibility and either imperfect price level information or imperfect response to price level information. It indicates that workers are assumed to stand ready to supply labor at the fixed nominal wage.

Equation (4.3) reflects the labor market equilibrium condition,

$$L_D = L_S \tag{4.3}$$

[2]There is considerable debate over why nominal wage contracts of fairly inflexible length, featuring (backward-looking) lagged responses to price level information, would persist in a world of rational, well-informed, utility-maximizing workers and profit-maximizing employers. See, for example, Robert J. Barro, "Long Term Contracting, Sticky Prices and Monetary Policy," *Journal of Monetary Economics* 3 (July, 1977), pp. 305–316; Robert E. Hall and David Lilien, "Efficient Wage Bargains under Uncertain Supply and Demand," *American Economic Review* 69 (December, 1979), pp. 868–879; and Milton Harris and Bengt Holmstrom, "Microeconomic Developments and Macroeconomics," *American Economic Review* 73 (May, 1983), pp. 223–227.

It indicates that the labor market will clear when quantity supplied equals quantity demanded.

The final relation, Equation (4.4), is the aggregate production function:

$$Q = \underset{+\ +}{\phi(L, K)} \tag{4.4}$$

This function shows that the level of aggregate output varies positively with the input of labor and capital. (The notation ϕ means "function of.") In the short run, the capital stock (K) is assumed constant so the relevant variable is labor output (L). (See footnote 8, Chapter Three, for the assumptions involved in the aggregation procedure.)

This system of four equations in five unknowns (L_S, L_D, Q, w, and P) is identical to the system developed in the previous chapter except for the specification of the labor supply relation. Figure 4.1 shows that the labor supply relation will not shift when the price level changes and is perfectly elastic (a horizontal line), indicating that the nominal wage is fixed at w_0.

The system begins in full employment equilibrium at points X and X' in Figure 4.1. The exogenously determined price level is P_0, the nominal wage is w_0, and full employment and aggregate output are L_0 and Q_0, respectively. If the price level increases from P_0 to P_2, at higher prices the marginal revenue product of labor will increase. Employers are assumed to be close to the market, to have perfect price information, and to respond to that information. As a result, the demand for labor increases. It shifts upward from $f(w, P_0)$ to $f(w, P_2)$. In contrast, labor suppliers neither ask for higher nominal wages as the price level rises to P_2 nor ask for higher wages as employment increases from L_0 to L_2, a greater-than-full-employment-equilibrium or "super-full-employment"-equilibrium level of employment.

Equilibrium now occurs at point K, at the top of Figure 4.1. At the bottom of Figure 4.1, the higher level of employment, L_2, prompts an increase in aggregate output to Q_2 at K' on the aggregate production function.

With the rise in employment we move out along the production function at the bottom of Figure 4.1. At K' the marginal physical product of labor is lower than at X'. The profit-maximizing firm hires labor until its marginal physical product equals the real wage. Therefore, at the top of Figure 4.1, the real wage at $X(w_0/P_0)$ exceeds the real wage at $K(w_0/P_2)$.

Going further, at the top of Figure 4.1, as the price level rises again from P_2 to P_4, employment rises from L_2 to L_4 and at the bottom of Figure 4.1 aggregate output increases from Q_2 to Q_4. The points of equilibrium are Z and Z'.

In this system, unlike the one of the previous chapter (the Neoclassical model), aggregate employment and aggregate output are not invariant with respect to the price level. An increase in the price level stimulates an increase in employment and output. As the price level rises, because of the inflexibility of the nominal wage and imperfect information or imperfect response to price level information on the supply side of the labor market, output increases sharply. The increase in output occurs because as the demand for labor increases, laborers are perfectly willing to offer more labor hours at the prevail-

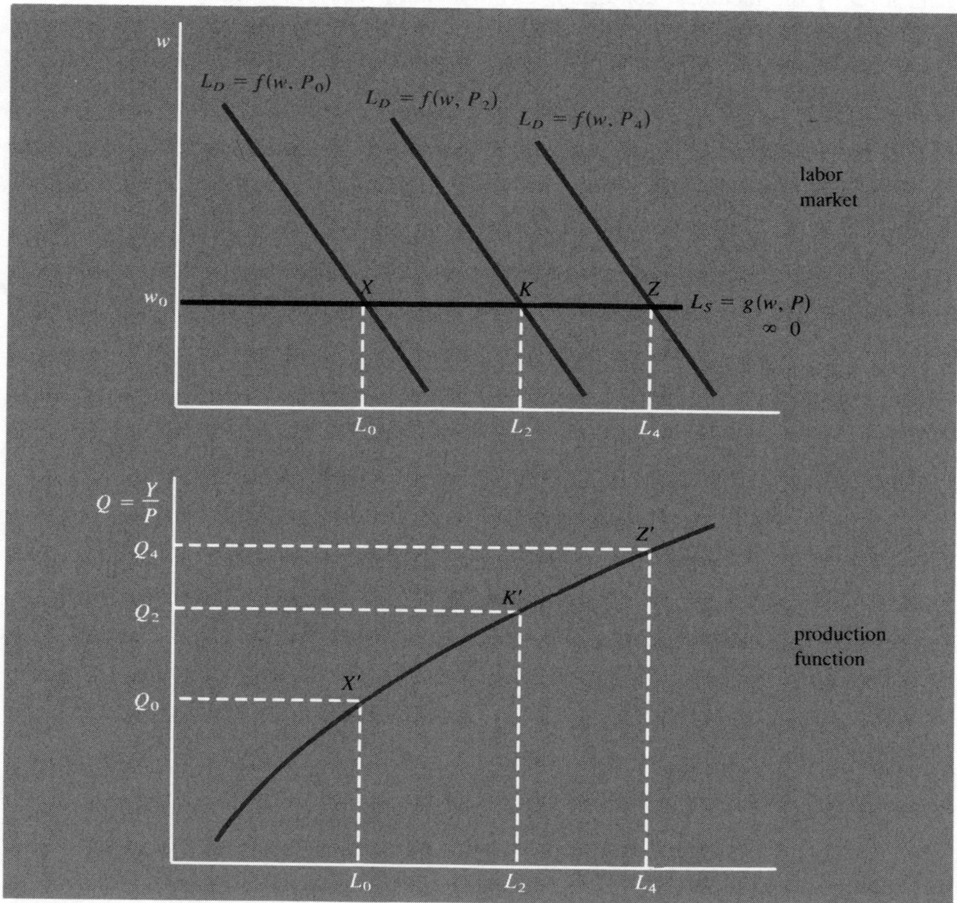

Figure 4.1 The Labor Market and Aggregate Production Function with Imperfect Price Level Information or Imperfect Response to Price Level Information and Nominal Wage Rigidity on the Supply Side of the Labor Market

ing nominal wage. They lack the contractual power to ask for a higher nominal wage, at least in the short run. In Figure 4.1, the model of the labor market under the condition of a perfectly rigid nominal wage may be called *Keynesian*.[3] In contrast, under conditions of perfect information and perfect nominal wage flexibility, developed in Chapter Three, aggregate employment and aggregate output are invariant with respect to changes in the price level. In that Neoclassical case employment and output were fixed at a full employ-

[3]This follows from the basic distinction between Neoclassical and Keynesian economics outlined in Chapter One. A Keynesian perspective lends itself to the view that macroeconomic policy, in affecting the price level, can effectively influence employment and output and interest rates.

ment level by the technical conditions of production, reflected in the demand for labor, and by the preferences of laborers, reflected in the supply of labor.

The Keynesian model reveals that because of imperfect information or imperfect response to information and a rigid nominal wage, employment and output will actually exceed the full employment level as the price level increases. Would this fixed nominal wage (w_0) be expected to persist over time? The answer to this question can be determined by considering what normally occurs as employment increases above the full employment level. Labor shortages begin to develop and more and more labor contracts expire; ever increasing numbers of workers are able to obtain a higher nominal wage. One would, therefore, expect that within a short period of time, labor suppliers would negotiate higher nominal wages at employment levels greater than L_0. Thus, this case should be considered a very short-run phenomenon.

Now, examine the labor market and assume that the nominal wage is flexible. Laborers realize that they can obtain a higher nominal wage at greater levels of employment. However, retain the assumption that the quantity of labor supplied does not respond to the price level. These assumptions are reflected in the algebraic signs beneath the nominal wage and the price level variables in Equation (4.2) II.

$$L_D = f(\underset{-}{w}, \underset{+}{P}) \tag{4.1}$$

$$L_S = g(\underset{+}{w}, \underset{0}{P}) \tag{4.2) II}$$

$$L_S = L_D \tag{4.3}$$

$$Q = \phi(\underset{+}{L}, \underset{+}{K}) \tag{4.4}$$

This model reflects neither the very short-run world of the case where the nominal wage is perfectly inflexible nor the long-run world of the Neoclassical model. Here, while the nominal wage is flexible, workers either have imperfect information regarding the price level or have perfect information but cannot respond to it because of labor contracts that do not feature complete and immediate adjustments of the nominal wage to changes in the price level. Like the previous model, this is a Keynesian model; however, it may be useful to think of it as a short-run model instead of a *very* short-run model.

In this system, the labor demand, equilibrium, and production function equations (4.1, 4.3, and 4.4) are identical to the Neoclassical case of Chapter Three and the Keynesian case just discussed. Only the labor supply relation, Equation (4.2) II, differs.

In Figure 4.2 the labor supply curve is no longer perfectly horizontal as it is in the previous Keynesian case. Now, as the price level rises and the demand for labor increases, laborers request higher nominal wages. As a result the nominal wage rises and employers

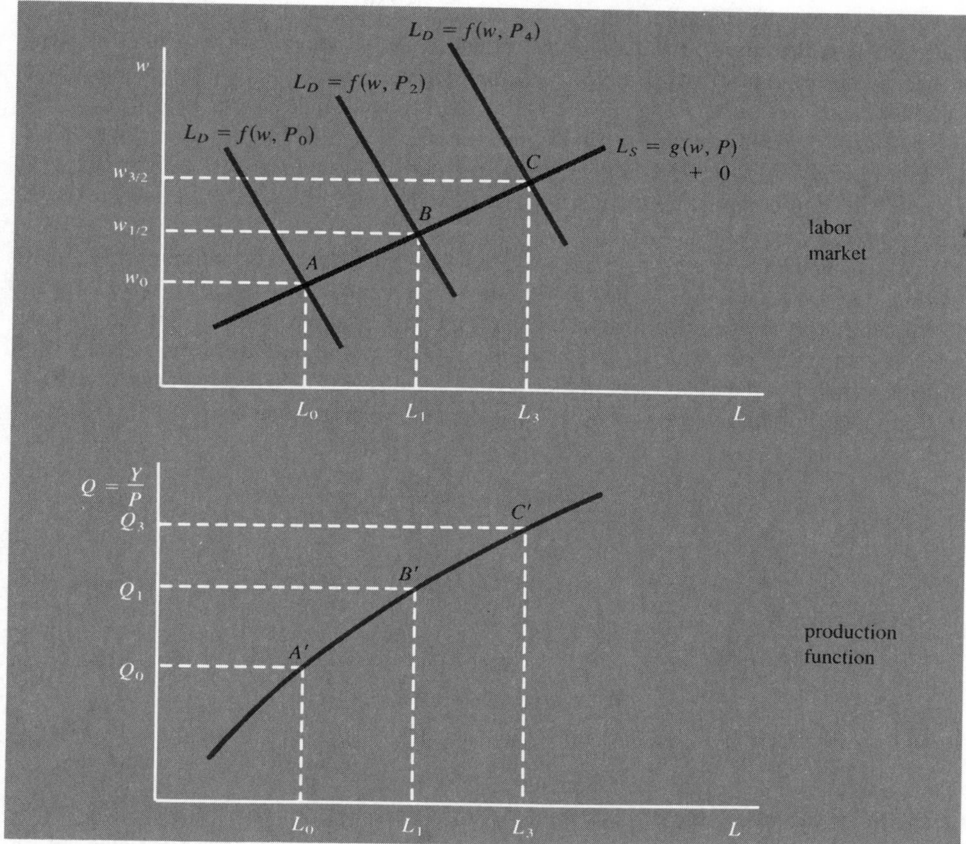

Figure 4.2 The Labor Market and Aggregate Production Function with Flexible Nominal Wages but with Imperfect Price Level Information or Imperfect Response to Price Level Information on the Supply Side of the Labor Market

do not find it profitable to increase employment as much as in the case of the fixed nominal wage.

The system begins again in full employment equilibrium at points A and A' in Figure 4.2. The exogenously determined price level is P_0, the nominal wage is w_0, full employment is L_0, and aggregate output is Q_0. If the price level increases to P_2, employers, facing a higher marginal revenue product of labor, increase the demand for labor. Instead of responding by working more hours at an unchanged nominal wage, workers are able to negotiate for higher nominal wages. As a result of the higher nominal wage, profit-maximizing employers can only increase employment to L_1 (instead of L_2 depicted in Figure 4.1). Equilibrium occurs at points B and B' in Figure 4.2, greater-than-full-employment-equilibrium levels of employment and output, respectively.

Firms will employ labor at the point where the marginal revenue product of labor equals the nominal wage. As the nominal wage now rises with increased employment, there is a smaller increase in employment than in the previous case of a fixed nominal wage. If the price level increases to P_2, employment rises to L_1, and aggregate output increases to Q_1 at point B' along the aggregate production function. If the price level increases to P_4, employment rises to L_3, and output rises to Q_3 at point C' in Figure 4.2. In this Keynesian system, while employment and production are not invariant with respect to the price level, they are not as sensitive to changes in the price level as in the rigid nominal wage world.

Is it reasonable to expect imperfect (response to) price level information on the part of workers to persist over time? The answer can be determined by examining what happens to the real wage as the price level rises in Figure 4.2. Despite the fact that the nominal wage is rising, the real wage actually declines. In the initial equilibrium position with a price level of P_0 and employment of L_0, the real wage is w_0/P_0. When the price level rises to P_2 and the nominal wage goes up to $w_{1/2}$, the real wage declines to

$$\frac{w_{1/2}}{P_2} < \frac{w_0}{P_0} \quad \text{where} \quad \frac{w_{1/2} - w_0}{w_0} < \frac{P_2 - P_0}{P_0}$$

When the price level rises to P_4 and the nominal wage ascends to $w_{3/2}$, the real wage declines further to

$$\frac{w_{3/2}}{P_4} < \frac{w_{1/2}}{P_2} \quad \text{where} \quad \frac{w_{3/2} - w_{1/2}}{w_{1/2}} < \frac{P_4 - P_2}{P_2}$$

Thus, even though hours worked increase, laborers receive a lower real wage. In fact, the decrease in the real wage is consistent with the increase in employment. This occurs because the marginal physical product of labor declines as employment rises and, for the profit-maximizing firm, the real wage equals the marginal physical product of labor. The initial equilibrium position represented an optimal allocation of workers' time between labor hours and leisure hours. Allocating more time to labor and less to leisure as the real wage falls is clearly suboptimal. Therefore, one would expect that, over time, labor suppliers would request higher nominal wages at employment levels greater than L_0. Thus, the Keynesian cases should be considered short-run conditions. Eventually, labor suppliers either learn about the higher price level or are able to respond to it by negotiating for or by automatically receiving (through a lagged cost-of-living adjustment clause) a correspondingly higher nominal wage and the long-run Neoclassical world of Chapter Three—a world of perfectly flexible nominal wages and perfect information—is entered.

A simplistic view of the labor market's response to an increase in the price level is as follows: In the very short run, nominal wages are rigid, and the responses of aggregate employment and output are sizable, as illustrated in Figure 4.1. As time passes and we move from the very short run to the short run, workers learn that they can negotiate a higher nominal wage and nominal wages become flexible. Nevertheless, workers either are still not aware of the higher price level or cannot respond to it—perhaps because their implicit or explicit nominal wage contracts do not feature complete and immediate adjustments to price level changes. Because it is not profitable for firms to hire as many workers at a higher nominal wage, employment and output cannot be sustained at the "super-full" levels of the previous model. Yet, because of the persistence of imperfect (response to) price level information, the increase in the price level still causes employment and output to exceed the full employment levels, shown in Figure 4.2. As more time passes, either workers learn that, despite the higher nominal wage, their real wage has declined and are able to contract for an even higher nominal wage or else, the indexation provisions of existing contracts become fully effective. The decline in the real wage that occurred because nominal wage increases did not match increases in the price level is now corrected. As the nominal wage is raised to match the hike in the price level, firms do not find it profitable to increase employment and output beyond the full employment level.

Therefore, in this sense, the difference between the Keynesian and Neoclassical models of the labor market is time. In the very short run, the nominal wage is rigid and price level information or the response to that information is imperfect. As time passes, price level information or the response to price level information is still imperfect, but as contracts expire workers are able to negotiate higher nominal wages in response to the greater demand for labor. As even more time passes, price level information or the (contractual) response to that information becomes perfect, and the Neoclassical perspective prevails. In the very short run and in the short run, which are fraught with imperfect informational responses, the Keynesian view may accurately describe reality. In the long run, when informational responses are perfect, the Neoclassical model may better describe how the world really works.

How long is the short run? How short is the long run? To Keynesians, who (as discussed in Chapters Seven and Twelve) see the economy as being bombarded by a steady barrage of shocks, the long run is a series of short runs. As a result of these shocks, in these short runs price level information and/or related responses are always imperfect, and employment is always changing. Some Neoclassical economists, as discussed in Chapter Thirteen, see the policies of government as the major source of shocks. They believe that government policies should be made less erratic.

Later in this chapter, we shall see that the Keynesian/Neoclassical distinction may be viewed in another way. Instead of using the short-run versus long-run perspective, it may be useful to determine whether or not price level shocks are anticipated by labor market participants. In a world where price level changes are anticipated by labor market participants, such changes are swiftly reflected in a corresponding nominal wage adjustment with employment and output unaffected, even in the short run. In this case, the labor market model may be described as Neoclassical. Where price level changes are not anticipated, they may have effects on employment and output. Here the labor market model may be described as Keynesian. As discussed above, Keynesian economists see the economy as being barraged by shocks that are difficult for market participants to anticipate. Neoclassical economists tend to view the policies of government as the primary source of unanticipated shocks. They believe that government policies should be made more predictable.

The Short-Run Phillips Curve: An Acceleration of Inflation

As in Chapter Three, a slight modification allows the preceding analysis to be expressed in terms of rates of change. Instead of writing nominal wages and prices as levels, they will now be expressed as rates of change, as follows:

$$\dot{P} = \frac{\Delta P / \Delta t}{P} \text{ and } \dot{w} = \frac{\Delta w / \Delta t}{w}$$

As described previously, the notation Δ means change in; Δt stands for an interval of time. Therefore, a dot over a variable depicts it in a rate-of-change form, such as percentage change per year.

In Figure 4.3 at the initial level of full employment, A, labor suppliers and labor demanders both have perfect information about the prevailing rate of price inflation, $\dot{P}_0$. The rate of nominal wage increase $\dot{w}_0$ matches the rate of inflation $\dot{P}_0$, and the level of the real wage is unchanging.

Suppose that the rate of price inflation, which is assumed to be exogenously determined, rises from $\dot{P}_0$ to $\dot{P}_1$. Assuming that the rate of nominal wage increase is perfectly rigid, ($\dot{w}_0$), equilibrium employment will increase to L_2. Employers demand more labor because they anticipate a higher marginal revenue product of labor as they expect to sell output at higher prices. Workers are willing to supply more labor hours at an unchanged rate of nominal wage increase ($\dot{w}_0$).

A temporary greater-than-full employment equilibrium level of employment occurs at point C at the top of Figure 4.3. A concomitant temporary, greater-than-full employment equilibrium level of aggregate output occurs at point C' of Figure 4.3. These positions show how a transitory boom in output and employment can occur as a result of a rise in inflation that is imperfectly anticipated or responded to by labor suppliers but fully anticipated by labor demanders. This boom cannot be sustained as it is based on a perfectly rigid rate of nominal wage increase. With the rate of inflation $\dot{P}_1$ exceeding the rate of nominal wage increase $\dot{w}_0$, the level of the real wage falls, as it logically must since employment has increased.[4] When employment increases, the marginal productivity of labor falls; the level of the real wage is lower at C' than it is at A'. The Keynesian, very short-run points of equilibrium C and C' in Figure 4.3 are dynamic analogs of points K and K' in Figure 4.1.

[4]There is considerable evidence that average real wages do not vary inversely with employment in the short run as this model of the labor market would predict. As discussed earlier in this chapter, this could occur because of risk-averse contracting behavior on the part of labor suppliers. In this set-up, firms overemploy workers in periods of less-than-full employment, sustaining a lower marginal productivity than would otherwise occur. Employers are, therefore, off (to the right of) their demand curve for labor during periods of less-than-full employment. When production picks up, firms do not add more labor in the short run, and marginal productivity rises rather than falls.

The procyclical behavior of real wages might also occur because of the rise in overtime employment during booms. Since employers typically pay a premium for overtime, the average real wage may rise during booms while the underlying straight-time real wage falls, as suggested by our theory. As the economy enters a recession, overtime is reduced and the average real wage may fall even though the underlying straight-time real wage rises.

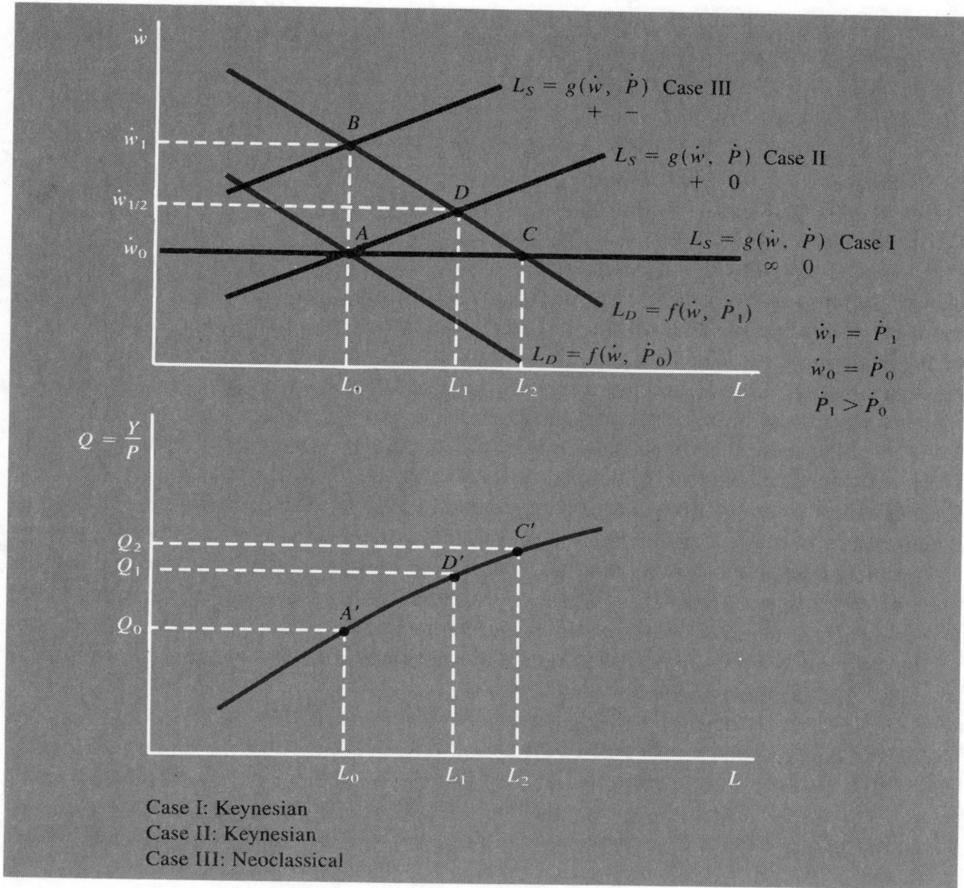

Figure 4.3 The Labor Market with Price and Nominal Wages Variables Expressed in Terms of Rates of Change: An Acceleration of Inflation

As time passes, we leave the very short run. Workers obtain better information regarding the increased demand for labor and/or can negotiate a greater rate of nominal wage increase. However, it will be assumed that either workers are not aware of the new rate of inflation $\dot{P}_1$ or are unable to respond to it because their new labor contracts do not feature complete and immediate adjustment for inflation. As employers grant higher rates of nominal wage increase, employment level L_2 can no longer be sustained. The next,

---

Finally, the procyclical behavior of real wages could also result because of "supply shocks." As discussed in Chapter Eleven, supply shocks affect the productivity of and demand for labor; increases in productivity increase the demand for labor, decreases in productivity reduce it. If these supply shocks were also the cause of cyclical swings in employment, they could explain the observed positive correlations between real wages and employment. This explanation is often called the *real business cycle*, since it explains cyclical movement in output and employment as arising from "real" (supply and productivity) shocks rather than nominal (price level) shocks. The real business cycle is discussed in detail in Chapter Eleven.

temporary, greater-than-full employment equilibrium level of employment *(L_1)* occurs at point D in Figure 4.3. Output is at point Q_1. While these levels of output and employment are lower than they were initially at points C and C', they are still higher than the full employment levels. Therefore, even these levels cannot be sustained. They are based on imperfect information or imperfect response to good information regarding inflation on the supply side of the labor market. The economy is still in a period of a temporary, although fading, boom. The short-run equilibrium points D and D', in Figure 4.3, are the dynamic analogs of points B and B' in Figure 4.2

As more time passes, we leave the Keynesian short run. Workers learn of the higher rate of inflation and/or are able to receive a proportionately higher rate of nominal wage increase. They realize that at the old rate of nominal wage increase $\dot{w}_{1/2}$, the level of the real wage fell. The labor supply curve shifts leftward. Long-run full employment equilibrium occurs at B in Figure 4.3. Here, the rate of nominal wage increase, $\dot{w}_1$, matches the rate of inflation $\dot{P}_1$, and the level of the real wage is unchanging.

All of this can be translated into Phillips curve analysis. Assuming a fixed labor force, the rate of unemployment U is defined as the difference between the labor force and the level of employment expressed as a percentage of that labor force. In Figure 4.3 at point A there is an initial full employment level of employment of L_0. The number of workers temporarily between jobs *(frictional unemployment)* is equal to the labor force minus this level of employment *(L_0)*. The difference expressed as a percentage of the labor force, U_0, is sometimes said to represent the *natural rate of unemployment*. The natural rate of unemployment is sometimes said to reflect the notion that normally some percentage of the labor force is changing jobs.

In Figure 4.3, as the rate of inflation goes up, employment initially and temporarily rises to L_2 (and output rises to Q_2). Correspondingly, in Figure 4.4, the rate of unemployment initially and temporarily falls to U_2 (the labor force minus L_2, divided by the labor force). There is movement upward along the very short-run Phillips curve I, as depicted by the arrows in Figure 4.4. This very short-run Phillips curve I, in Figure 4.4, is the dynamic analog of Case I in Figure 4.3. Point C in Figure 4.3 corresponds to point C in Figure 4.4. The decline in the unemployment rate to U_2 (in Figure 4.4) reflects a period of sharp boom in the economy. As it is based on rigid rates of nominal wage increase, this boom is only temporary.

As time passes, labor suppliers become aware of a greater demand for their services and are able to extract a higher rate of nominal wage increase. The movement from C to D in Figure 4.4 traces a clockwise rotation from the very short-run Phillips curve I to the short-run Phillips curve II. This corresponds to the movement from C to D in Figure 4.3, as employment and output fall temporarily to L_1 and Q_1, respectively. This new higher rate of unemployment at U_1 is still lower than the full employment rate of unemployment at U_0. The economy is still in a period of boom. However, because unemployment is rising, it is obvious that the boom is fading. Moreover, even this weakened boom is temporary because, while rates of nominal wage increase are now rising, they are not rising rapidly enough, and the level of real wage is falling. The supply side of the labor market either still has poor information about the higher rate of inflation or has good information but cannot respond to it because of the nature of the labor contract. In Figure

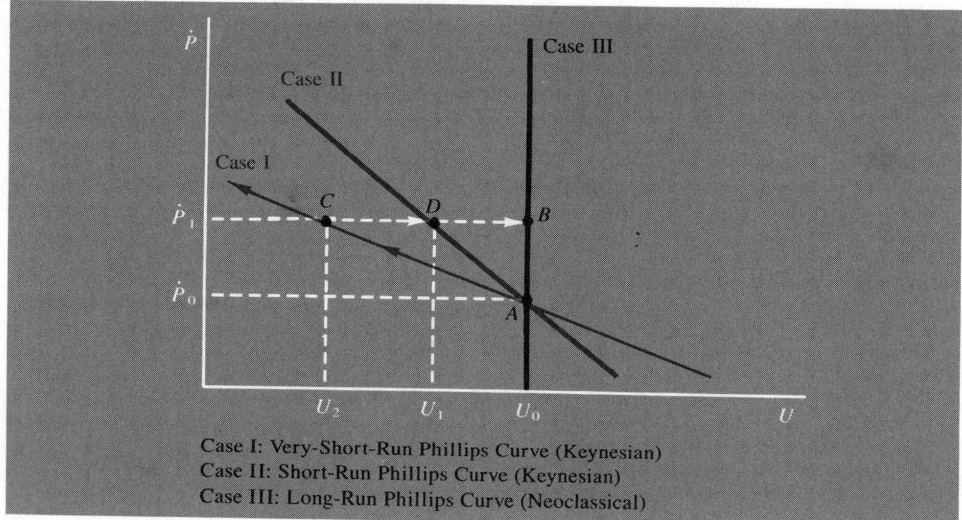

Figure 4.4 Short- and Long-Run Phillips Curves: An Acceleration of Inflation

4.3, workers will soon realize that at the rate of nominal wage increase $\dot{w}_{1/2}$ with a rate of price inflation $\dot{P}_1$, the level of the real wage is declining because $\dot{w}_{1/2} < \dot{P}_1$. In Figure 4.4, as the rate of the nominal wage increases comes to reflect the new anticipated rate of inflation, $\dot{P}_1$, the Phillips curve again rotates clockwise from the Keynesian Phillips curve II to the Neoclassical Phillips curve III, moving from *D* to *B* in Figure 4.4. This corresponds to the movement from *D* to *B* in Figure 4.3

The vertical line above U_0 in Figure 4.4 represents the long-run Phillips curve. The economy will be at a full employment equilibrium at the new fully anticipated rate of price inflation. Only imperfect (response to) information, unexpected acceleration and deceleration of the rate of inflation, and rigidity in the rate of change of the nominal wage can induce (temporary) changes in employment and production.

The Short-Run Phillips Curve: A Deceleration of Inflation

The preceding analysis showed the effect of an increase in inflation, which is imperfectly anticipated or imperfectly responded to by labor suppliers, in stimulating a short-lived boom period in the economy. With the initial acceleration of inflation, unemployment declined greatly. Then, as workers began to demand higher rates of nominal wage increase, the unemployment rate rose. When the wage demands of workers finally caught up with the rate of inflation, the period of economic boom came to an end as the labor market returned to full employment equilibrium.

A similar perspective can be applied to periods of recession in the economy. The labor market is in long-run, full employment equilibrium at point *B* in Figure 4.5 with the rate of inflation at $\dot{P}_1$ and the unemployment rate at U_0. Initially, assume a decrease in the rate of inflation from $\dot{P}_1$ to $\dot{P}_0$ that is fully anticipated and responded to by labor de-

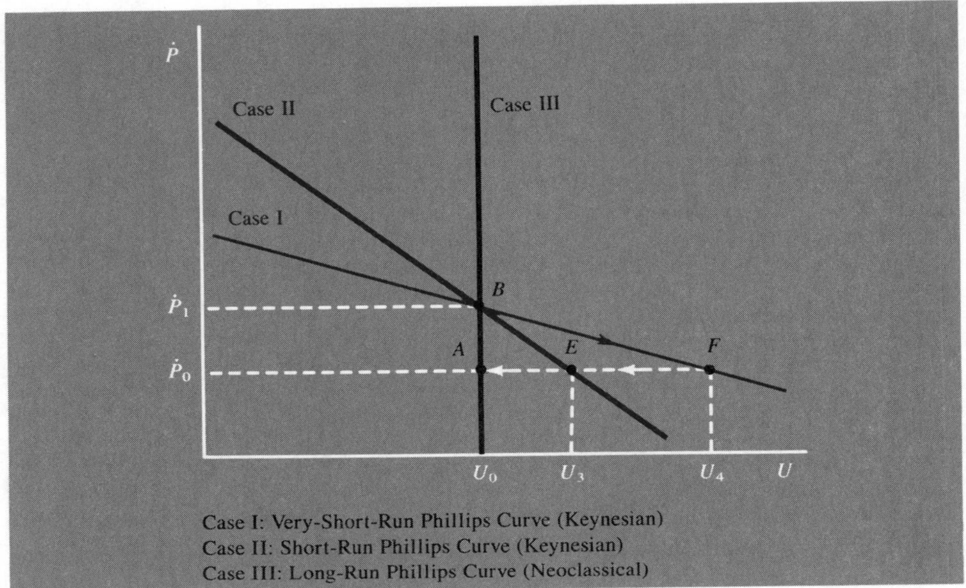

Figure 4.5 Short- and Long-Run Phillips Curves: A Deceleration of Inflation

manders but not by labor suppliers. With an initial rigid rate of nominal wage increase, there will be a temporary rise in unemployment to U_4, a less-than-full employment equilibrium or underemployment equilibrium rate of unemployment. There is movement downward along the short-run Phillips curve, Case I, to point F, as depicted by the arrows in Figure 4.5. There occurs a period of sharp recession in the economy, but this phase of the recession is temporary, since it is based on a rigid rate of nominal wage increase in the very short run.

As time passes, labor suppliers become aware of abnormally higher levels of unemployment and become more inclined to settle for a lower rate of nominal wage increase. When this occurs, there is clockwise rotation in the Phillips curve from Case I to Case II and movement from F to E in Figure 4.5 as unemployment falls to U_3. The new, lower rate of unemployment is still higher than a full employment rate of unemployment U_0. The economy is still in a recession. However, because unemployment has fallen the recession is less severe. Moreover, even this weakened recession is temporary because while rates of nominal wage increases are now falling, they are still not falling rapidly enough. There is still imperfect information regarding the lower rate of inflation or imperfect response to that information on the supply side of the labor market.

Workers will soon realize that at the old rate of nominal wage increase with a lower rate of inflation $\dot{P}_0$, the level of real wage is rising. They will be (contractually) willing and able to accept lower rates of nominal wage increase which fully reflect the new anticipated rate of inflation $\dot{P}_0$. The Phillips curve rotates clockwise from Case II to Case III, and there is movement from E to A in Figure 4.5.

The vertical line above U_0 represents the long-run Phillips curve. The economy returns to a full-employment equilibrium rate of unemployment and level of output at the new fully anticipated rate of inflation.

Rational Expectations versus Adaptive Expectations

Mechanisms for the formulation of inflationary expectations are implicit in the preceding specifications of the labor market and Phillips curves. There are two alternative theories of the way expectations are formulated and learning occurs. First, we focus on an *adaptive expectations* mechanism; then we examine the *rational expectations* hypothesis.

To be logically correct the labor supply relation and the labor demand relation should be written in terms of the expected rate of inflation $(\dot{P}_e)$ as follows:

$$L_S = g(\underset{+}{\dot{w}}, \underset{-}{\dot{P}_e}) \tag{4.5}$$

$$L_D = f(\underset{-}{\dot{w}}, \underset{+}{\dot{P}_e}) \tag{4.6}$$

In Equations (4.5) and (4.6), labor suppliers and labor demanders always respond to their expected rate of inflation $(\dot{P}_e)$. In the preceding analysis it was assumed that labor demanders were able to anticipate correctly and respond to the rate of inflation in the current period. This allows Equation (4.6) to be written as:

$$L_D = f(\underset{-}{\dot{w}}, \underset{+}{\dot{P}}) \tag{4.7}$$

It was further assumed that labor suppliers were unable in the short run either to anticipate or to respond to the actual rate of inflation in the current period. Thus, Equation (4.5) may be written as it appears in Figure 4.5, the Keynesian Case II:

$$L_S = (\underset{+}{\dot{w}}, \underset{0}{\dot{P}}) \tag{4.8}$$

When the expected rate of inflation equals the actual rate of inflation in the current period and workers are completely responsive to this rate of inflation, Equation (4.5) may be written as it appears in Figure 4.3, the Neoclassical Case III:

$$L_S = g(\underset{+}{\dot{w}}, \underset{-}{\dot{P}}) \tag{4.9}$$

Therefore, when $\dot{P}_e = \dot{P}$, the rate of inflation expected by labor suppliers equals the actual rate of inflation. The model is Neoclassical, yielding the long-run Phillips curve. If $\dot{P}_e \neq \dot{P}$, the rate of inflation expected by labor suppliers is different from the actual rate of inflation. The model is Keynesian, yielding a short-run Phillips curve.

Under an *adaptive expectations* mechanism, the expected rate of inflation may be specified as a weighted average of past rates of inflation with the weights summing to unity:

$$\dot{P}_e = a_1\dot{P}_{t-1} + a_2\dot{P}_{t-2} + \ldots + a_n\dot{P}_{t-n} \qquad (4.10)$$

where t–1 is the previous period, t–2 is the period prior to that, and so on; with regard to the weights, $a_1 > a_2 > \ldots > a_n$, and $a_1 + a_2 + \ldots + a_n = 1$. Equation (4.10) indicates that labor suppliers formulate their expectation of inflation by looking at the past. The weights, a_j, decline as time recedes. How fast they fall depends on the strength of memories. Rapidly declining weights mean that workers have short memories so that price inflation expectations depend on the recent past. The learning process embodied in Equation (4.10) explains how, as time passes, the rate of inflation that is expected by labor suppliers gets closer and closer to the actual rate of inflation. Thus, the learning process accounts for the shifting of the short-run Phillips curve over time. The process begins with the nominal shock of an acceleration or deceleration of the rate of inflation that is fully anticipated and responded to by labor demanders but not labor suppliers. The result is a fairly flat short-run Phillips curve such as the curve for Case II in Figures 4.4 and 4.5. Assuming no intervening additional acceleration or deceleration of inflation, the process ends with the long-run Phillips curve for Case III in Figures 4.4 and 4.5.

Critics have argued that an adaptive expectations generating scheme such as Equation (4.10) is naïve. It postulates that labor suppliers learn about current inflation entirely from past inflation and ignore all other data that could be used to reduce expectational error. It seems implausible that individuals would fail to exploit information that would improve expectational accuracy. Critics contend that it would be irrational for individuals to continue to form expectations of inflation from *any* scheme that is inconsistent with the actual way inflation is generated. Being different from the true inflation-generating mechanism, such schemes will produce expectations that are systematically wrong over time. If learning schemes are systematically wrong, rational individuals will abandon them because not doing so will result in these individuals systematically harming themselves over time. In short, it is claimed that the adaptive expectations mechanism is incompatible with rational behavior.

The reason that labor suppliers would hurt themselves systematically over time if they formed their expectations adaptively can be seen in Figures 4.3 and 4.5. In Figure 4.3, when inflation virtually rises to $\dot{P}_1$, the real wage falls because the rate of nominal wage increase does not rise as much (it rises only to $\dot{w}_{1/2}$). Thus, workers are being harmed. In Figure 4.5, when inflation decreases to $\dot{P}_0$, the rate of unemployment rises. Again workers are being harmed. The assumption of adaptively formed expectations implies that whenever inflation changes, labor suppliers will lose in one way or another. Individuals who behave in a way that harms them systematically over time are clearly irrational.

According to the *rational expectations* hypothesis of the "New Classical" branch of Neoclassical economics,[5] individuals will exploit all information about the inflation process when making inflation forecasts. All *systematic* elements for predicting the rate of inflation will become known, and the consensual inflationary expectations of individual market participants will be the most accurate forecast consistent with that knowledge. This implies that except for unavoidable surprises arising from random shocks, the market consensus expectation of inflation will not be systematically different over time from the actual rate of inflation. In a world in which expectations are formed rationally, only an inflationary surprise that is random and unsystematic can generate movement along a short-run Phillips curve.[6]

The rational-versus-adaptive inflationary expectations perspective is similar, but not analogous, to the perfect-versus-imperfect inflation information scheme discussed earlier. Both schemes generate unemployment that temporarily varies inversely with changes in inflation because of asymmetrical responses between labor suppliers and labor demanders. If labor demanders have perfect inflation information or form inflationary expectations rationally and labor suppliers have imperfect (responses to) information or form inflationary expectations adaptively, the unemployment rate will vary inversely with changes in inflation. More generally, this result obtains as long as the inflation learning–response lag of labor suppliers is greater than that of labor demanders.

However, there is a significant difference between the two views. The rational expectations hypothesis does not assume that information is perfect. Nor does it assume that everyone is rational. The rational expectations hypothesis assumes only that errors in the consensual expectations of market participants are not correlated over time with inflation. In other words, expectations of inflation are not systematically different over time from actual inflation. The rational expectations hypothesis, nevertheless, does make the fairly strong assumption that systematic, stable methods for predicting inflation can be learned at a cost that is lower than the benefits of not making systematic errors.

In order to explain the short-run Phillips curve, rather than assume asymmetry in the adaptive formulation of expectations it is more plausible to assume that there are asymmetrical responses between labor suppliers and labor demanders such that demand curves shift in response to price changes before supply curves. As discussed earlier in this chapter, there are a number of reasons why labor suppliers might reasonably accept contracts featuring an indexation adjustment of nominal wages to price level (cost-of-living) changes that are unanticipated when the contract is made.[7] Such cost-of-living adjustments would necessarily be lagged because dependable cost-of-living data are always released with a lag. In addition, wage adjustments to reliable data are often made

[5]The terms Neoclassical, Monetarist, New Classical, Keynesian, Neo- and Post-Keynesian were identified in Chapter One. These expressions find considerable application in business and government but are used here only to categorize models, not because hard and fast boundaries between schools of thought isolate economic researchers from one another.

[6]For students with knowledge of statistics, a rational expectation coincides with a conditional mathematical expectation, given the available information.

[7]For example, labor market participants might bear a much higher cost of organizing, maintaining, and enforcing alternative, more complicated types of labor contracts, such as contracts with detailed contingency clauses. In addition, labor suppliers might be more averse than labor demanders to accepting the risks of unanticipated changes in the price level.

with a lag, and some aspects of nominal compensation such as fringe benefits are difficult to index to the cost of living. Under this type of contractual arrangement, as long as labor demanders formulate expectations rationally, there will be asymmetrical responses of labor supply and labor demand to changes in the inflation rate that cause unemployment temporarily to vary inversely with a change in the rate of inflation. In this case, it can be said that labor suppliers and demanders form their price expectations rationally, but that suppliers cannot immediately respond to their current expectations because of the nature of the labor contract.

Another possibility is that both suppliers and labor demanders formulate their inflationary expectations rationally but because of unanticipated changes in the rate of inflation, revert to adaptive formulation of expectations or, in an attempt to predict the policy-making behavior that is causing the unanticipated inflation, behave *as if* they were forming their expectations adaptively. In these circumstances, asymmetrical responses to unanticipated inflation could also cause unemployment to vary inversely with a change in inflation.

The (Limited) Ability of Macroeconomic Policy to Affect Employment and Output

While the preceding is only a partial equilibrium model of the labor market, with the price level or rate of inflation determined exogenously, it is still possible to formulate some policy implications. Assume that government policymakers under the direction of the President and Congress can control the rate of inflation. While this is a strong assumption, it is not unrealistic. As is discussed in the general equilibrium models of Chapters Ten through Fifteen, Keynesian and Neoclassical theories both agree that government policymakers can greatly influence the rate of inflation.

Both the adaptive expectations and rational expectations hypotheses indicate that it is possible for the authorities to bring unemployment below the natural (full employment) level only at the cost of accelerating inflation. Further, if inflation is stabilized, unemployment returns to its natural rate. Both the adaptive expectations and rational expectations hypotheses also show that the more severe the inflationary shock, the greater the impact on (the likelihood of) unemployment. Beyond this the adaptive and rational hypotheses disagree. The adaptive expectations mechanism allows a role for *systematic* policy shocks. Increases or decreases in inflation can bring about lower or higher unemployment and movement along the short-run Phillips curve only because expectations do not adjust instantaneously. In contrast if both labor suppliers and labor demanders form their expectations of inflation rationally, the rational expectations hypothesis does not allow systematic policy to affect employment. If policy is systematic, it is also predictable and is built into wage contracts when they are negotiated. Actual inflation will not be systematically different from expected inflation, thereby, allowing a change in inflation to have no systematic effect on employment over time. Only completely unpredictable or surprise policy tactics can affect employment and generate movement along a short-run Phillips curve.[8]

[8]One of the major shortcomings of modern labor market models is that contracts are not invariant with respect to economic policy. For further reading, see the recent articles cited in the bibliography to this chapter.

The Business Cycle: Predicting the Length and Severity of Boom and Recession

The property that only surprise inflationary shocks can affect employment, together with the idea that policymakers can control inflation, leads us to the concept of the *political business cycle*. Assume that policymakers desire to increase the reelection chances of incumbent politicians. It would seem to be in their interest to cause a surprise increase in inflation prior to elections. However, as long as labor market participants formed their expectations rationally, they would not be systematically fooled by increases in inflation because they would come to expect these increases prior to elections. The political business cycle would not work unless policymakers were able to deceive market participants by publicly pledging themselves to anti-inflationary militance but then engaging in pre-election inflationary surprises. Whether real-world policymakers are really adept at such deception is a debatable question.

The preceding discussion of short- and long-run Phillips curves and rational and adaptive expectations suggest that given an increase (or decrease) of inflation, the duration of the subsequent economic boom (or bust) depends on the degree to which that increase or decrease in inflation is not anticipated or responded to on the supply side of the labor market. Expressed a little differently, the duration of the boom is predicated on the persistence of imperfect information regarding inflation or imperfect response to good, current information on the supply side of the labor market.

Consider, for example, a shock to the economy which results in a specific decrease in the rate of inflation. Figure 4.6 depicts three alternative time paths for the level of output in the economy. As a matter of convenience, assume that in all three cases the rate of change of nominal wages is flexible. In addition, assume that in all three cases labor demanders form their expectations of inflation rationally and are not surprised by the decrease in the rate of inflation.

Path R in Figure 4.6 is based on the assumption that the labor suppliers (as well as labor demanders) form their expectations of inflation rationally and are not surprised by the decrease. Therefore, both labor demand and labor supply curves in $\dot{w},L$ space shift downward at time 0 in proportion to the decrease in inflation. There is no change in employment. There is no change in aggregate output from level Q_0 in Figure 4.6. There is no recession over the time interval after time 0. This dynamic (movement over time) result is analogous to moving directly from point B to point A along the long-run Phillips curve in Figure 4.5. It represents the Neoclassical Case.

Path $A1$ is based on the assumption either that labor suppliers form their expectations of inflation adaptively (and continuously) with a backward-looking lag of one period or that labor suppliers form their expectations rationally but that the fall in inflation was a policy surprise (it was not anticipated when contracts were negotiated) and that there exist stipulations wherein the rate of nominal wage increase is tied to the rate of inflation over the previous period. At time 0 the labor demand curve immediately shifts to the new rate of inflation that is assumed to be fully anticipated and responded to by labor demanders. In contrast, at time 0 the rate of nominal wage increase is tied to the rate of inflation that occurred during the previous period before time 0. The supply curve does

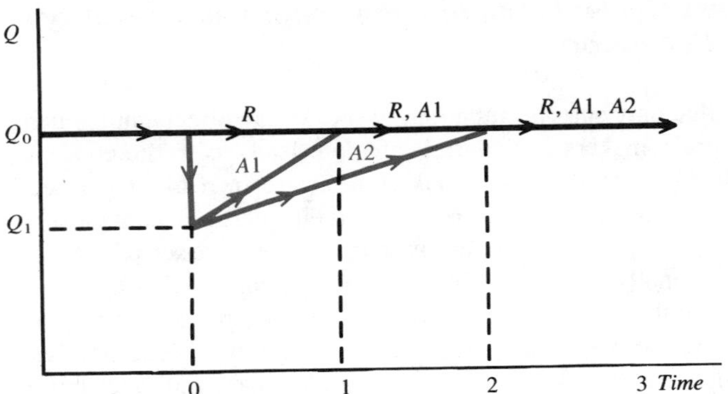

Figure 4.6 Three Recessions of Different Duration Based on Different Formulations of Inflationary Expectations by Labor Suppliers

not shift; therefore, the level of employment declines. At time 0 in Figure 4.6, the level of output declines to Q_1. A recession begins.

During the time interval from time 0 to time 1, the rate of nominal wage increase adjusts gradually to the new lower rate of inflation and the labor supply curve shifts continuously downward in the $\dot{w},L$ space. The level of employment rises. Over the time interval 0,1 in Figure 4.6, the level of output rises back toward Q_0. The economy is pulling out of the recession. By time 1, the rate of nominal wage increase is based entirely on the new rate of inflation that occurred during time interval 0,1. The labor supply curve has shifted downward in proportion to the new rate of inflation. The recession is over. This dynamic result is analogous to movement at time 0 from *B* to *E* and during time interval 0,1 from *E* to *A* along the short-run Phillips curve in Figure 4.5. It reflects the Keynesian case. There is a recession of short duration.

In contrast, path *A*2 is based on the assumption that the rate of nominal wage increase adjusts to inflation with a two-period lag. Under these conditions, the recession begins at time 0 but lasts twice as long because it takes two periods for the wages of workers to adjust. The economy does not pull out of the recession until time 2 when the rate of wage increase is based on the new lower rate of inflation that has persisted over time interval 0,2. This dynamic result is analogous to movement from *B* to *E* at time 0 and from *E* to *A* during time interval 0,2 in Figure 4.5.[9] It too reflects the Keynesian case.

Theories and Forecasting of the Business Cycle

The previous discussion of inflationary shock business cycles is based entirely on the model of the labor market and the assumptions from which it was derived. As explained

[9]Generally, a change in employment and output will occur whenever expectations or responses of labor suppliers lag behind those of labor demanders. As long as this condition of asymmetrical responses holds, whenever inflation accelerates or decelerates, the supply curve will never shift in the same proportion as the demand curve, and the level of unemployment will vary inversely with the rate of inflation. If labor suppliers and labor demanders respond with the same lag (symmetrically) then the labor supply and labor demand curves shift in the same proportion and there is no effect on unemployment.

in footnote 1, the lagged adjustment of nominal wages and the temporary increase in productive effort in the labor market may represent similar responses in other markets for productive inputs and markets in which firms make the decision to produce. As in the labor market, in other markets the increase in productive effort may reflect imperfect price level information or imperfect response to price level information because of fixed price contracts.

Theories are highly simplified views of reality. Nevertheless, even though our approach is simple, it can clarify many things about the real world. For example, the financial pages of mass circulation newspapers and magazines commonly label economic recession, low employment, as a *cause* of a reduction in inflation, and economic boom as a *cause* of inflation. The theory developed here reverses this causality; a deceleration in inflation may *cause* a recession; an acceleration in inflation may *cause* an economic boom; the more severe the acceleration or deceleration, the greater the boom or bust.

Notice that the word *cause* is prefaced with the word *may*. Where expectations are formed rationally, increases or decreases in inflation cause booms or busts only to the extent that they are not fully anticipated or responded to. Movements in the inflation rate that are fully anticipated and responded to on both sides of the labor market can have no effect on employment or output. Thus, modern theory debunks the claim that inflation (or an increase in inflation) is a necessary concomitant of prosperity. In fact, the rational expectations hypothesis suggests that many variations in the rate of inflation may be fully anticipated, and only surprise, unsystematic and basically unforecastable changes in inflation can affect employment and output.

In contrast to the inflationary shock theory of the business cycle presented in this chapter is the theory of the *real business cycle*. Real business cycle advocates minimize the empirical importance of inflationary shocks since market participants are assumed to be rational and would not be surprised by most changes in inflation. These theorists contend that more important shocks arise from changes in productivity (supply shocks). As explained in footnote 4, increases in productivity increase the demand for labor, raise the real wage, and boost employment; reductions in productivity do the opposite. The theory of the real business cycle, unlike the surprise inflationary shock theory developed in this chapter, therefore predicts a positive correlation between real wages and employment and output over time. The real business cycle is discussed at greater length in Chapter Eleven when the concept of supply shocks is developed.

A great many people make a living at the business of forecasting the length and severity of economic upturns and downturns. Some of these economic seers may be applied scientists using elaborate and expensive econometric models containing hundreds of equations. Others simply may be inductivists observing the movement in economic time-series data that are historically highly correlated with subsequent swings in output and employment (for example the so-called *leading economic indicators*). Other forecasters may use the tried and true method of 20/20 hindsight and only "forecast" upturns and downturns after they already occur. Whatever method is used by particular forecasters, many business people and government officials rely on a *consensus forecast,* based on an average of all other forecasts. They realize, from experience, that George Bernard Shaw was correct when he said that if one laid all forecasters end-to-end, they still would never reach a conclusion.

The inflationary shock theory of the business cycle that has been developed here supports the hard headed business person who is wary of all forecasts and who believes Mark Twain's dictum, "The art of prophesy is very difficult, especially with respect to the future." The duration of boom and recession depends on expectational elements—namely, the degree to which changes in inflation are not fully anticipated and responded to. These are not independent of the policy environment. Social scientists, in general, and economists, in particular, know very little about how people really learn. The expectational schemes discussed earlier are merely simplistic hypotheses. Only a small group of theoretical economists have incorporated these hypotheses into their models of the labor market; and this incorporation has occurred only within the last decade and a half. Moreover, the theoretical work cited in footnote 2 of this chapter indicates considerable disagreement over the justification for nominal wage contracts that feature lagged responses to unanticipated inflation. Many of the well-known economic forecasters are not theoretical economists and are virtually completely unencumbered by this area of knowledge. In addition, the theory of the real business cycle, covered briefly above but developed more fully in Chapter Eleven, suggests that productivity shocks are the cause of swings in economic activity. These are notoriously difficult to predict. Thus, modern economic theory warns us to be skeptical the next time an economic forecaster claims to foresee "the beginning of the ending of the upturn of the downturn."

Twenty-Three Years of Applied Theory: The United States Economy, 1964–1987

The usefulness of any theory may be judged by its accuracy in describing historical events. The theory of the relationship between inflation and unemployment can be applied retrospectively, to the past twenty-three years of United States economic history. Figure 4.7 is a highly stylized portrait of inflation and unemployment over the past two decades. In 1964 the annual inflation rate was about 1 percent, and the unemployment rate was at or near full employment. Between 1964 and 1967 the rate of inflation accelerated to about 6 percent per annum. Coming on the heels of about ten years of comparative price level stability, this steady spiraling of prices apparently was not fully anticipated by labor suppliers and the employment rate fell.[10] These were the years of economic boom and low unemployment. As a result, President Lyndon Baines Johnson, was a pretty popular fellow—until the Vietnam conflict.

In 1968, Richard Milhous Nixon was elected, partly on the promise to reduce the rate of inflation. This he did. By early 1971, the rate of inflation was well below its 1967 high. However, the rate of unemployment rose; the economy skidded into a short recession. In 1971, the Nixon administration not only stopped the deceleration of inflation but actually began to preside over a new acceleration of inflation, much of which was temporarily disguised because of the imposition of price controls from late 1971 until 1973. The disguising of inflation apparently duped labor suppliers and generated an economic boom, which, of course, did not hurt Nixon's chances for reelection in 1972. As price

[10]An economic pollster during this period asked a worker why people were ignorant of and apathetic toward inflation. The worker replied that he did not know and he did not care.

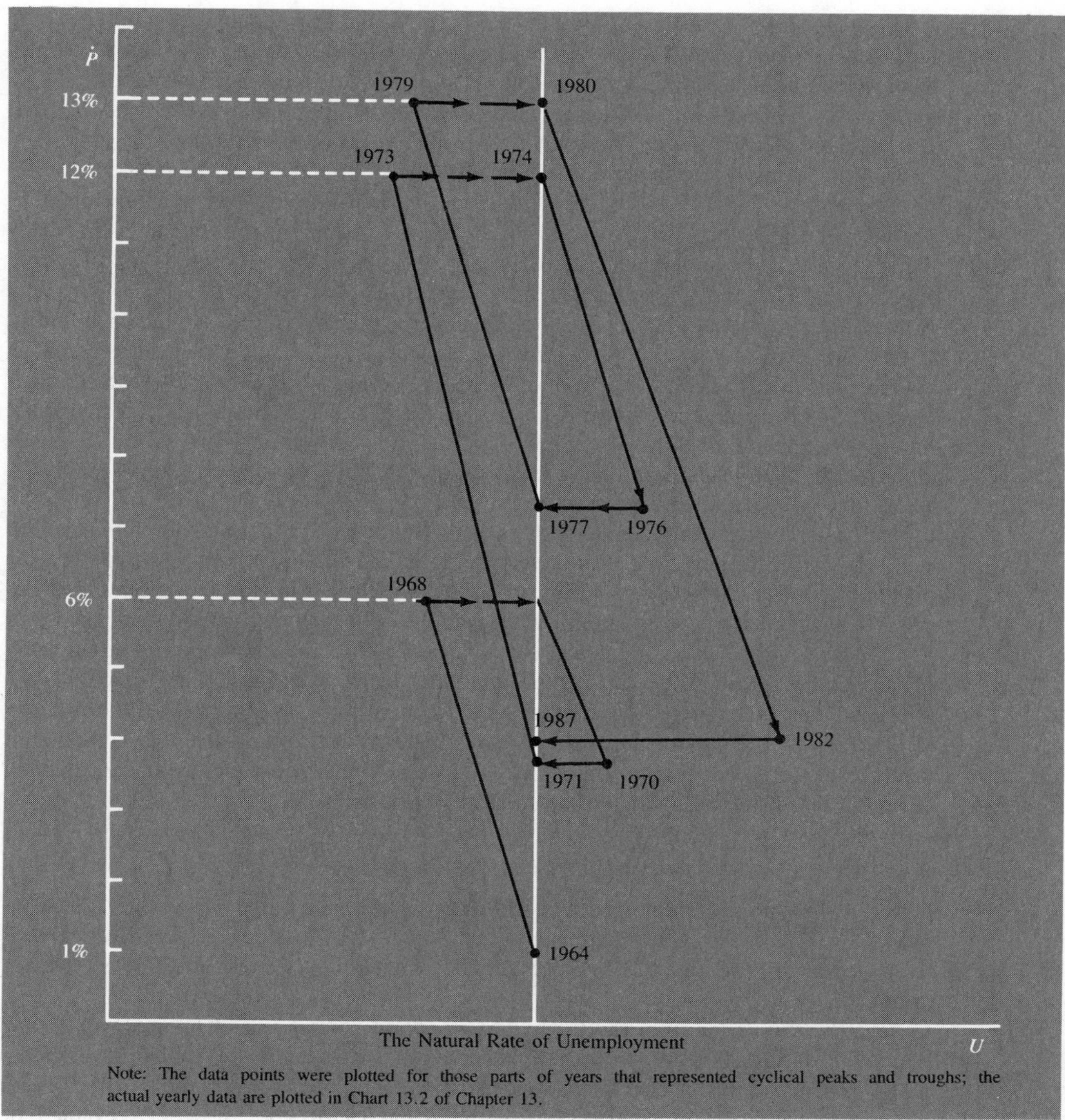

Figure 4.7 Twenty Years of Economic Boom and Bust

controls were gradually lifted, the rate of inflation soared to double-digit levels in late 1973. In that year, the Organization of Petroleum Exporting Countries (OPEC) first raised the price of oil. With this unexpected skyrocketing of inflation, the rate of unemployment fell even further. The economic boom that was launched in 1971 continued well into 1973.

However, by 1974 the public was fed up with inflation. The Nixon-Ford administration launched a militantly anti-inflationary campaign in 1974. The rate of inflation plummeted from double-digit levels in early 1974 down to nearly 6 percent per year in 1976. This severe, and apparently unanticipated, curtailment of inflation plunged the economy into the recession of 1975–1976; unemployment rose to a relatively high rate.

In 1977, Jimmy Carter's administration started the nation back up the economic roller coaster, and by late 1979, the rate of inflation reached its post-war high of around 13 percent per annum. As this astronomical elevation of inflation was apparently not completely expected, unemployment fell drastically; a new economic boom was in full swing.

Then, in 1980, under President Carter, and from 1981 until 1983 under President Ronald Reagan, the nation experienced the most rapid deceleration of inflation in recent United States history. In two years, the rate of inflation fell by over two-thirds. This, of course, launched the most severe and longest recession since the Great Depression.[11] During 1983 the deceleration of inflation stopped and, true to form, a period of economic recovery began and unemployment fell. By 1987, unemployment was restored to its full employment equilibrium level, at an annual rate of inflation of between 3 and 4 percent—a rate that had been virtually unchanged since 1983.

The positive historical correlation between inflation and output and employment provides empirical support for the nominal inflationary shock theory of the business cycle presented in this chapter. According to this theory, the swings of acceleration and deceleration of inflation are apparently responsible for the sorry economic track record of three recessions and three booms in twenty years. Clearly, a stable rate of inflation would resolve this problem. Why can our economy not be so stabilized? The answer to this question requires further knowledge of macroeconomic theory—particularly the theory of the *cause* of inflation. The partial equilibrium models, previously discussed, are insufficient to answer the question. Only a *general equilibrium* approach, described in Chapters Ten through Fifteen, will shed light on this problem.

Trends in the Natural Rate of Unemployment

In Figure 4.7 the full employment equilibrium rate of unemployment was not shown to change over the twenty-three-year span from 1964 to 1987. Indeed, the very term *natural* seems to suggest that this full employment rate of unemployment is somehow cosmically ordained.

Actually, this is far from the truth. The so-called natural rate of unemployment has trended upward and the long-run Phillips curve has drifted rightward for well over thirty years. Recent estimates place the natural rate of unemployment at 4 percent in 1955, and at close to 6 percent in 1979.[12] Very early in the 1950s, the President's Council of

[11]During the Great Depression, the pattern of decelerating inflation and falling real income was quite similar. From 1929 to 1933, the rate of inflation decelerated rather steadily. There was a small positive rate of inflation in 1929. That fell off to a 2 percent rate of *de*flation in 1930. There was a 10 percent rate of deflation in 1931 and a 12 percent rate of deflation in 1932. Over this span of ever-decelerating inflation, real GNP plummeted by over 20 percent. As the rate of inflation stopped decelerating in 1933, real GNP began to recover.

[12]Peter K. Clark, "Potential GNP in the United States, 1948–1980," in *U.S. Productive Capacity: Estimating the Utilization Gap*. St. Louis: Washington University, 1977.

Economic Advisors believed that when less than 4 percent of the labor force was unemployed, the economy was at full employment. Today, the full employment level of unemployment is generally considered to be between 6 and 7 percent of the labor force. Some analysts would even place it above 7 percent.

Why is it now *natural* for an additional 3 percent of the labor force, about three and one-half million more workers, to be defined as unemployed during periods of full employment? To understand this one must have a clear conception of *frictional unemployment*. Frictional unemployment refers to workers who are in the process of changing jobs. If, for example, two workers in twenty quit their jobs every year and take, on the average, six months to find new jobs, the average rate of unemployment will be 5 percent of the labor force. When inflation is unanticipatedly accelerating during the business cycle, the job search interval of the average worker will be shortened and this frictional unemployment rate will fall. When inflation is unanticipatedly decelerating, the job search interval will lengthen and this frictional unemployment rate will rise.

So much for short-term cyclical variations in unemployment. What about the long-term trend, mentioned earlier? The rate of unemployment depends on the length of time that the average worker stays unemployed, looking for work. This, in turn, depends on two costs. One is the opportunity cost of being employed, unemployment compensation and/or welfare benefits. Welfare benefits include food stamps, aid to dependent children, social security benefits, and the like. (For example, among Western European nations, the level of unemployment is highly correlated with the extent of welfare programs.) The rate of unemployment also depends on what economists call labor force participation rates—this measures the tendency or proclivity of the average worker to quit working.

For the last ten of the past thirty years the second cost, the opportunity cost of being unemployed—the average after-tax real wage—has not risen greatly. In fact, it had even fallen in the late 1970s as inflation raised the average worker's nominal income and drove him or her into higher income tax brackets—a process known as *bracket creep*. In contrast, over the past thirty years, the opportunity cost of being employed has risen as untaxed unemployment compensation and welfare payments (often in nonpecuniary form, such as food stamps) have soared. The result of the relatively flat or falling opportunity costs of being unemployed and the rising opportunity cost of being employed has been a slow, upward secular trend in the amount of time the average worker takes between jobs.[13] This suggests a slow, upward trend in the natural rate of unemployment.

Figure 4.8 shows the effect of an increase in the tax rate on the full employment equilibrium level of employment. As the tax rate rises (say, because of bracket creep) from t_0 to t_1, it lowers the after-tax real wage and, because the substitution effect is assumed to dominate the income effect, causes a reduction in the quantity of labor hours supplied. As a result of the leftward shift in the supply curve, the level of employment falls from L_0 to L_1. With an unchanged labor force, the decrease in the full employment equilibrium level of employment results in an increase in the natural rate of unemployment and a rightward shift in the long-run Phillips curve (not shown).

In the 1980s, *supply-side economic policy* has been widely discussed as a means of

[13]In addition, ever-increasing minimum wage laws make it more difficult for low-productivity workers to find employment. This, too, lengthens the job-search interval.

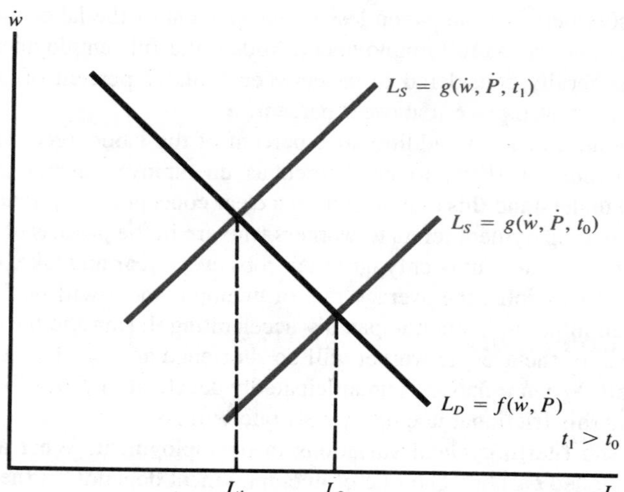

Figure 4.8 Effect of a Change in the Income Tax Rate on Employment

reversing the steady increase in the natural rate of unemployment. One basis for supply-side thinking is the idea that higher, after-tax rates of remuneration will increase productive effort and thereby bolster real income. When applied to the labor market, this reasoning suggests that a reduction in the tax rate on real wages will increase the full employment equilibrium level of employment. Since a rise in employment means more labor input into production processes, aggregate output and real income will rise. In Figure 4.8, a cut in the tax rate from t_1 to t_0 can be seen as shifting the supply curve to the right and causing employment to rise from L_1 to L_0. (There are other aspects of supply-side economic policy; these are discussed more fully in Chapter Fourteen.)

There may be other reasons for the trend in unemployment from the 1950s to the 1980s. One reason is that the changing composition of the labor force has resulted in a lower labor force participation rate. More individuals may be more inclined to drop out of the labor force partly because of a decline in the work ethic. More females in the labor force lower the participation rate because of their time off for pregnancy and early infant care. More teenagers in the labor force also lower the labor force participation rate because they simply quit work more frequently. Finally, an ever-increasing number of those who say they are out of work and drop out of the labor force may be quite profitably but illegally employed in the underground economy (see Chapter Two). On balance, because of a changed composition of the labor force, the average United States worker quits more often (participates less) and, because of the opportunity costs, stays unemployed longer than his or her counterpart in the 1950s.[14]

[14]The relatively high and rising level of the natural rate reflects imperfections in the labor market. For this reason much, if not all, of the unemployment which exists at the natural rate is often referred to as *structural unemployment*. Structurally unemployed individuals are viewed as unemployed because of inefficiencies in the job search process and the insufficient incentives to accept job offers (discussed above).

This does not mean that the United States will continue to be cursed (or blessed, depending on your viewpoint) with a rising trend in the natural rate of unemployment. Recent cuts in welfare should lower the opportunity cost of being employed. Recent cuts in the federal income tax on wages and salaries should raise the opportunity cost of being unemployed. These changes may bring a reversal of the upward trend in the natural rate of unemployment. Ever-changing attitudes toward child rearing could increase female labor force participation rates. And, judging from today's college students, the work ethic is replacing the loaf ethic. These changes may reverse the downward trend in labor force participation.

Concluding Comments

This chapter shows that under conditions of nominal wage contracting and imperfect information on the supply side of the labor market, an increase in the price level, an exogenous variable, results in a jump in employment and aggregate output. Keep in mind that the positive link between price level changes and resulting swings in output is not only the result of labor supplier behavior. Imperfect information and contracting may yield the sort of supplier behavior featured in this chapter in other factor and output markets.

In the labor market, the positive correlation between price changes and employment changes occurs because as the price level rises the marginal revenue product of labor rises. This is reflected in an increased demand for labor. Because workers are assumed to have rigid nominal wages and/or imperfect information regarding the price level (or imperfect contractual response to good current information), the supply of labor does not respond to an increase in the price level. Therefore, the equilibrium level of employment rises in response to an increase in the price level.

The dynamic analog of this model is reflected in movements along a short-run Phillips curve. An acceleration of the rate of inflation that is unanticipated on the supply side of the labor market results in a fall in unemployment (a rise in employment). In the long run, in both static and dynamic analyses, as workers learn about the new price level (static) or rate of inflation (dynamic), the level of employment returns to its long-run equilibrium level.

The degree to which an acceleration or deceleration of inflation is unanticipated depends on how expectations are formed. Where expectations of inflation are formulated adaptively to lagged actual rates of inflation, changes in inflation will always be unanticipated. Where expectations are formed rationally, changes in inflation will be unanticipated only when they come in the form of a random unsystematic "surprise." The rational formulation of expectations suggests that policymakers can affect employment and production only if they "surprise" labor market participants.

Inefficiencies in the job search process are often attributed to the high cost of obtaining and geographically transferring job skills by workers, especially the young and technologically displaced. Thus, structural unemployment is conceived of as unemployment in excess of the "normal" frictional unemployment that would exist in a "perfect" labor market.

An increase or decrease in the price level or rate of inflation has an effect on employment and output, the severity and duration of which is difficult to predict. This is so because, according to the theory presented in this chapter, the effect on employment is based on the degree to which such price movements, inflationary shocks, are unanticipated. This should make one wary of the ability of economic forecasters to predict recessions and boom periods—*the business cycle*. Healthy skepticism toward the art of business-cycle forecasting is entirely warranted by modern economic theory.

The history of the United States economy in the past two decades has been marked by swings in unemployment that are highly correlated with accelerations and decelerations in the rate of inflation. Over the same span, however, there has also been a secularly rising trend in the long-run equilibrium *(natural)* rate of unemployment. This trend has been the product of a number of palpable incentives for workers to remain unemployed for longer periods while changing jobs. These incentives include rising rates of income taxation and unemployment compensation.

While this chapter viewed the labor market in isolated, partial equilibrium, the ultimate purpose of this text is to examine the working of the economy as a whole. The next three chapters examine the working of another key market—the *credit market,* again in partial equilibrium. After these chapters, the partial equilibrium working of the *money market* will be explored. Finally, all three markets—labor, credit, and money—will be combined in a general equilibrium model of the economy as a whole.

EXERCISES

1. How can there be *money illusion* on the supply side of the labor market when money is not involved as a variable?

2. If all welfare payments are eliminated, what will happen to the long-run Phillips curve?

3. According to the theory described in this chapter, outline the only sure way to predict periods of recession and boom in the economy.

4. Evaluate the following statement: "If workers and employers are perfectly aware of the cause of inflation, there can never be cyclical swings in employment."

5. Explain why a short-run decrease in unemployment, depicted as a movement up along a short-run Phillips curve, actually reflects a misallocation of resources.

6. What is the meaning of unemployment when the labor market is in equilibrium in the short run as well as in the long run?

7. Explain whether you agree or disagree with the following statement: "Increased indexation of nominal wages to the Consumer Price Index would reduce swings in employment and production as well as the trend in the natural rate of unemployment."

8. What is the difference between the perfect information assumption and the rational expectations assumption in the labor market model?
9. Using a model of the labor market, list several factors which would determine the severity or magnitude of a recession, then list several factors which would determine the duration of a recession.
10. Do you agree or disagree with the following: "Rigid nominal wages and backward-looking adjustment of nominal wages to inflation violate the tenets of reasonable utility-maximizing behavior for labor suppliers."
11. Critique the following statement from a rational expectations perspective. "One cannot reject on theoretical grounds the idea of the political business cycle, which is the notion that an incumbent governmental administration can manipulate the rate of inflation to systematically generate a period of economic boom prior to Presidential elections.

BIBLIOGRAPHY

Barro, Robert J. "Long-Term Contracting, Sticky Prices and Monetary Policy." *Journal of Monetary Economics* 3 (July 1977), pp. 305–316.

Friedman, Milton. "The Role of Monetary Policy." *American Economic Review* (March 1968), pp. 1–17.

Gilbert, Charles. "The Rational Expectations Hypothesis: Survey and Recent Research." In *Modern Concepts in Macroeconomics*, ed. Thomas M. Havrilesky. Arlington Heights, Ill.: Harlan Davidson, Inc., 1985.

Hall, Robert E., and David Lilien. "Efficient Wage Bargains and Uncertain Supply and Demand." *American Economic Review* 69 (December 1979), pp. 868–879.

Harris, Milton, and Bengt Holmstrom. "Microeconomic Developments and Macroeconomics." *American Economic Review* 73 (May 1983), pp. 223–227.

Humphrey, Thomas. "Some Recent Developments in Phillips Curve Analysis." *Economic Review*, Federal Reserve Bank of Richmond (January/February 1978), pp. 15–23.

Lucas, Robert E., Jr. "Econometric Testing of the Natural Rate Hypothesis." In *The Econometrics of Price Determination*, ed. O. Eckstein. Washington, D.C.: Washington Board of Governors of the Federal Reserve System, 1972.

———. "Some International Evidence on Output-Inflation Tradeoffs." *American Economic Review* (June 1973), pp. 326–334.

Lucas, Robert E., and Thomas J. Sargent. "After Keynesian Macroeconomics. In *Modern Concepts in Macroeconomics*, ed. Thomas M. Havrilesky. Arlington Heights, Ill.: Harlan Davidson, Inc., 1985.

McCallum, Bennett T. *Macroeconomics After a Decade of Rational Expectations: Some Critical Issues*. Working Paper 1050. Cambridge, Mass., National Bureau of Economic Research, (December 1982).

Muth, John. "Rational Expectations and the Theory of Price Movements." *Econometrica* (July 1961), pp. 315–333.

Phelps, Edmund S. *Microeconomic Foundations of Employment and Inflation Theory*. New York: Norton, 1972.

Phillips, A. W. "The Relation between Unemployment and the Rate of Change of Money Wage Rates in the United Kingdom, 1861–1957." *Economica* (November 1958), pp. 282–299.

Sargent, Thomas J. "A Classical Macroeconomic Model for the United States." *Journal of Political Economy,* Vol. 84 (April 1976), pp. 207–238.

______. "Beyond Supply and Demand Curves in Macroeconomics." *American Economic Review* 72 (May 1982), pp. 382–389.

______, and Neil Wallace. "Rational Expectations, the Optimal Monetary Instrument and the Optimal Money Supply Rule." *Journal of Political Economy* (April 1975), pp. 241–254.

Taylor, John B. "Aggregate Dynamics and Staggered Contracts." *Journal of Political Economy* 88 (February 1980), pp. 1–23.

______. "The Role of Expectations in the Choice of Monetary Policy." In *Modern Concepts in Macroeconomics,* ed. Thomas M. Havrilesky. Arlington Heights, Ill.: Harlan Davidson, Inc., 1985.

The Credit Market: Saving and Investment

Chapter 5

Introduction

This text began with a description of several types of markets in our economy. These markets are: factor markets, goods and services markets, and credit markets. The next two chapters focus on the credit markets. (Another name for credit markets is loanable funds markets.) Chapter Two indicated that lenders and borrowers meet in credit markets. This chapter begins by describing how and why lenders and borrowers come together in the credit markets. It then develops the theories of the supply of and demand for credit (loanable funds).

LENDING AND BORROWING

A household or firm frequently spends more than it takes in during a given period. How do aspiring individual capitalists get funds to spend in excess of their income? Do they work hard and save their pennies? Thriftiness is one of the basic capitalistic moralisms, and very well may have been how the free enterprise capitalist got started many decades ago. Individuals may save part of their income for years and then use their accumulated wealth to spend more than they earn in a future year. However, individuals have an easier

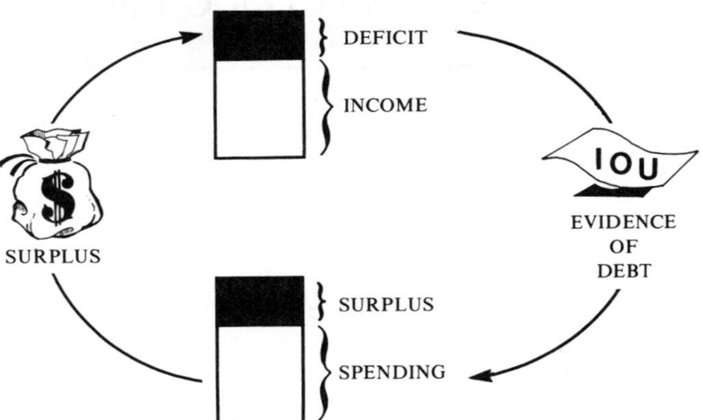

Figure 5.1 Deficit and Surplus Units

way to spend more in a year than they have earned. They can go into debt and borrow the funds. As Josh Billings said, "live within your means, even if you have to borrow money to do it."

The process of spending in excess of earnings works in the following way: First, take any economic decision unit (household, business firm, or governmental) that wants to spend more than it takes in as income in a given period. In Figure 5.1 this economic unit is called a *deficit* unit.

Next, consider an economic decision unit that receives more income than it spends. In Figure 5.1, this economic unit is called a *surplus* unit. Since a deficit is defined as the excess of spending over income, it is reasonable that deficit units should borrow from surplus units.

What induces individuals to sacrifice their earnings? They could easily spend all these earnings. "Generosity" is not the answer. The surplus unit, true to human economic behavior, will sacrifice current enjoyment of goods and services only for the promise of receiving sufficiently greater goods and services in the future through the repayment of principal plus interest. In order to borrow, the deficit unit must convince the surplus unit that its use of the borrowed funds will provide sufficient future income to repay the amount of the debt plus the interest. The deficit unit borrows because it feels it can put present funds to good use to earn more funds in the future.

The lender (surplus unit) must have faith in the future ability of the borrower (deficit unit) to repay the obligation out of future earnings. This faith makes the paper obligation, the newly issued *debt claim* (the IOU in Figure 5.1) valuable. This is why a wag once said, the surest way to establish your credit is to work yourself into a position of not needing any. If the holders of the outstanding debt claims of a particular deficit unit ever lose faith in its ability to meet its obligations, these debts become less valuable.

In short, the newly issued evidence of debt is a claim against the deficit unit. The payment of interest by the deficit unit induces the surplus unit to sacrifice current purchases of goods and services or productive resources. Conversely, borrowed funds allow the deficit unit to make current purchases of goods and services or productive resources.

Thus, the new debt claim signifies a transfer of real resources from surplus to deficit units. Debt enables surplus units to space their consumption over time, in an efficient, interest-earning way. In turn, debt enables deficit units to engage in spending projects that promise future earnings.

Even though credit is vital, finding credit is often a troublesome process. Paying back credit is even more troublesome. This is one reason why there are middlemen in the credit market.

An Overview of the Credit Market

A credit (loanable funds) market is a place where borrowers demand credit, lenders supply credit, and a price (the rate of interest) brings supply and demand into equilibrium. Again, as in the markets for goods and services and productive resources, exchange in the credit market is governed by the general principles of supply and demand. In reality, the credit market consists of a market for long-term credit, called the *capital market,* and a market for short-term credit, called the *money market*. Both terms, *capital* and *money,* are misleading because money and capital goods are *stocks* while credit is a *flow*. (The distinction between stocks and flows was made in Chapters One and Two.) Surplus units (lenders) may be business firms, governments, or households. Deficit units (borrowers), likewise, may be business firms, governments, or households. Generally, however, when viewed from an aggregate sectoral perspective, the household sector is the source of credit while business and government sectors are usually users of credit.

Credit markets are complex. Buyers and sellers must obtain information and organize their transactions. These activities are costly. Investment bankers often act as middlemen to bring buyers and sellers together in an efficient way. However, when lenders have very small amounts of surplus funds and borrowers need big loans, direct transactions are costly to organize. Therefore, special kinds of middlemen pool the small surpluses and deal with the borrowers face-to-face. Economists call these types of middlemen *financial intermediaries*.

In Figure 5.2, the financial intermediary, reverently illustrated as a monumental structure, lends funds when it directly acquires the primary debt claims of deficit units, holds these claims as interest-earning assets and, then, borrows funds from surplus units by directly issuing its own specialized debt claims. Primary debt claims are called promissory notes, mortgages, commercial loans, and consumer loans, among other things, depending on what the borrowing is for, its terms, and its collateral. What the specialized debt claims are called depends on the type of financial intermediary involved in getting the funds from surplus units. Therefore, specialized debt claims may be checking accounts, negotiable order of withdrawal (NOW) accounts, savings shares, money market deposit accounts, pension plans, life insurance policies, and so on. They are always a type of debt claim against (and occasionally an evidence of equity or ownership in) the financial intermediary held by the surplus unit.[1] Some prominent types of financial

[1]Some financial intermediaries are only borrowing intermediaries. They deal directly with surplus units but have no direct dealings with deficit units. They purchase debt claims in the open market, rather than directly from deficit units. An example of a borrowing intermediary is a mutual fund.

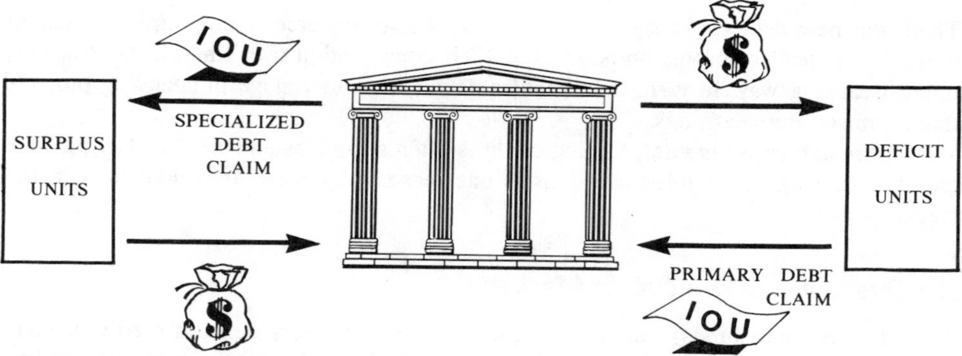

Figure 5.2 The Financial Intermediary in the Credit Market

intermediaries are commercial banks, savings banks, savings and loan associations, credit unions, life insurance companies, and pension funds, among others.[2] Chapter Eight discusses a subset of these financial intermediaries, depository institutions. Depository institutions are financial intermediaries whose specialized debt claims serve as money or as close substitutes for money.

As seen in Figure 5.3, the credit market is viewed by economists as the place where the flow of saving that is supplied out of income by the household sector is demanded by the business sector. Business firms typically use these funds to acquire newly produced capital goods. In this way, the flow of saving increases the stock of capital goods in the economy. Spending on newly produced capital goods is called investment expenditures.

Students are often perplexed by how the act of saving out of income, a flow, adds to the stock of physical capital goods. Reducing the complex market economy to its barest elements by envisioning a one-person economy is often helpful. Consider Robinson Crusoe on a proverbial desert island living entirely by the fish he catches with his bare hands. If Robinson catches five fish daily and can subsist on four, he may save one fish per day, which he stores conveniently in the back of his cave. His saving is real resources that he does not consume. If it takes Robinson an entire day to produce a fishing net, he obviously cannot go fishing on that day, so he may go to the back of his cave and feast on the accumulated saving of four days (ugh!). By this process the saving of real resources out of flow of income, one fish per day, flows into investment expenditures for a newly produced capital good (a fishing net). Robinson saves (abstains from consumption) out of income because he expects a return in the future. The newly produced capital good should enable him to catch more fish in the future.

The parallel to a modern economy should be clear. Just like Robinson Crusoe, individuals in a modern economy save (do not use all their real income on consumption expenditures) because of the existence of interest (an expected future return). Robinson Crusoe knew the amount he had to save to produce a fishing net. In modern market economies, how do households know the right aggregate amount to save to satisfy the aggregate

[2]Some financial intermediaries are only lending intermediaries. They have no direct dealing with surplus units. They sell debt claims in the open market, rather than directly to surplus units. An example of a lending intermediary is a consumer loan company.

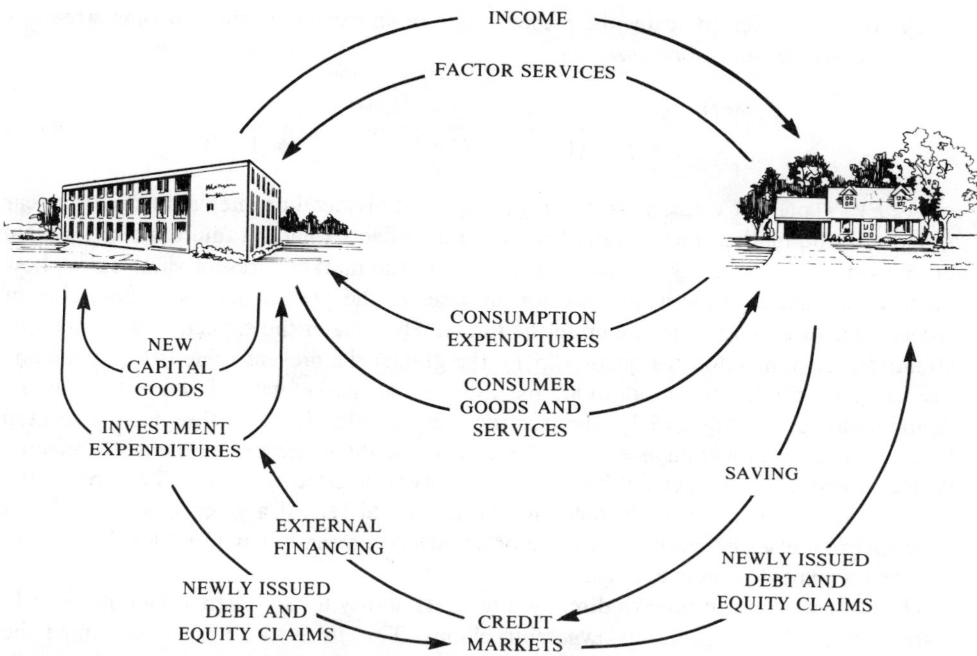

Figure 5.3 The Circular Flow of Income Expenditures and Credit

capital expansion plans of business firms? The answer is that some of the productive resources of the economy are channeled into producing capital goods instead of consumer goods because there should exist in the credit market an equilibrium interest rate, a rate that brings into equality the inflow of saving from households and the outflow of borrowing by business firms. As the borrowing will be used on investment expenditures, the economy's productive resources that are not devoted to the production of consumption goods and services (because of households' saving) will be devoted to the production of capital goods (because of business firms' investment expenditures).

Saving, Investment, Capital Goods, and Wealth

Now, look at the saving-investment process of a market economy. As seen in Figure 5.3, in exchange for its saving, the household sector receives from the business sector either newly issued claims of ownership (equity) or newly issued debt claims in the firms that acquire these newly produced capital goods. Capital goods often serve as collateral for debt claims. These newly issued debt or equity claims are pieces of paper that become part of the stock of wealth of individual households. They add to the assets of individual households. Like many types of wealth, they have value because they are expected to produce income in the future. This is a reasonable expectation because the capital goods that were acquired from the proceeds of issuing these claims are expected to increase the future flow of output of the firms that issued them.

The relation which indicates the present value of an expected future income stream is called the *present value formula:*

$$PV = \frac{y_1}{(1+i)} + \frac{y_2}{(1+i)^2} + \frac{y_3}{(1+i)^3} + \ldots + \frac{y_n}{(1+i)^n} \tag{5.1}$$

where PV = present value, y_j = earnings (expected dividend or interest income) in year j, and i = the market interest rate. Present value reflects what the future income stream of an asset, $y_1, y_2, \ldots y_n$, is worth at present in the market. Present value shows how much a rational investor would pay for an asset in the present for the expectation of receiving a specific income stream in the future. The greater the expected future income stream in the numerator of Equation (5.1), the greater the present value (PV), given any market rate of interest. In addition, the greater the market rate of interest (i) in the denominator of Equation (5.1), the less the present value (PV) of the given, expected future income stream of an asset. This is true because the interest rate reflects the income that an investor could receive if his or her funds were invested elsewhere. The greater the interest rate, the greater the income an investor would earn if a given amount of funds were invested elsewhere and the less he or she would presently pay (PV) for the right to receive the expected income stream, $y_1, y_2, \ldots y_n$.

The ability of a firm to earn directly affects its ability to pay interest income on debt claims or dividend income on ownership claims. This in turn, helps to determine the market value of the outstanding stock of debt or equity claims that it has issued. Outstanding stocks of debt and ownership claims, therefore, have market values that fluctuate because there will be changes in the public's perception of the expected future earnings of the firms that issue these claims. Expected future income is reflected in the numerators of the present value formula. If expected dividend payments increase, the present value of outstanding equity claims will increase. Improvement in the future expected earnings of a business firm will drive up the present value (market prices) of its existing stock of equity claims. Sometimes such increases in the value of equity claims are spectacular. As John Kenneth Galbraith once said, those who want to get rich are advised to have bought IBM stock in 1935.

The market values of the outstanding stocks of debt and ownership claims will also fluctuate because of changes in the market interest rate (i), which is used in the denominator to calculate the present value of a future expected earnings stream. For example, if the market rate of interest rises, present value falls. Therefore, because expected future earnings and interest rates fluctuate, the values of existing debt and equity claims will also fluctuate in the markets in which they are exchanged. Changing market values of the existing stock of debt and equity claims often have a substantial impact on the wealth of the household sector.

Markets for trading equity claims are commonly called *stock markets*. Markets for trading debt claims commonly are called *money markets* and *bond markets*. Changing values are also extremely important because they help to assure an efficient pricing of the stock of capital goods of individual business firms. Therein, they assure an efficient flow of credit, that is, the firms whose outstanding debt and equity claims command the greatest present value because of higher expected future earnings at a given market rate of interest will be able to sell newly issued claims and obtain credit more cheaply.

It is important to understand the relationship between the *flow* of credit and the *stock* of wealth. Viewed from an aggregate sectoral perspective, credit is supplied out of the flow of income by the household sector and demanded by the business sector to finance investment expenditures on newly produced capital goods. In exchange for their flow of saving, households receive newly issued debt or equity claims. New capital goods add to the stock of wealth of the economy, and this is reflected in the increased (value of the) total outstanding equity claims held by households. Thus, even though the physical capital stock rests in the business sector, ownership of it (as evidenced by outstanding equity claims) resides with the household sector.

Actual Credit Flows

Having established the relationship between credit (loanable funds) and wealth, let us now focus on the actual magnitudes of flows in the credit market. According to Figure 5.3, the flow of credit is supplied by the household sector and demanded by the business sector. Households expect to receive interest or dividend income on the newly issued claims they receive from business firms for their saving. Thus, the payment of greater interest or dividend income after federal and state income taxes appears to be an incentive to households to save. On the other hand, interest is a cost to the borrower. Payment of greater interest or dividends would, therefore, appear to be a deterrent to prospective business firm borrowers. Thus, there should exist an interest rate that balances the inflow of saving and the outflow of borrowing in the credit market. An equilibrium interest rate will provide suppliers of credit with sufficient incentive to provide a certain flow of saving and, at the same time, allow demanders of credit sufficient incentive to absorb that flow of saving. This is basically why the interest rate is determined by the supply of and demand for credit in the credit market. (This subject will be explored more rigorously later in this chapter.)

Actually, credit flows are a little more complex than Figure 5.3 would suggest. Economists view the economy as consisting of four sectors, not just two. In addition to the household sector and the business sector, there are the government sector and the foreign sector. While some individual households may borrow, the household sector, viewed as a whole, always supplies credit. The business sector supplies credit in the form of business saving (retained earnings) and capital consumption allowances. (Chapter Two explained why capital consumption allowances [the sum of depreciation expenses of business firms] supply a flow of funds to firms.) However, the business sector also demands credit to finance investment expenditures; these credit demands exceed the level of its retained earnings and capital consumption allowances. Therefore, on balance, the business sector is a net demander of credit. In the government sector, the federal government typically demands credit in order to finance its deficit, while combined state and local governments typically have a surplus and, therefore, supply credit. The foreign sector is neither a consistent demander nor supplier of credit. The foreign sector is de-emphasized in this chapter. Its important interaction with other sectors is taken up in Chapter Fifteen.

Table 5.1 Credit Flows: Saving, Dissaving, and Investment Expenditures 1974–1985 (in billions of dollars)

		1974	1975	1976
Gross Saving		206.3	195.1	236.9
Gross Private Saving		209.5	259.4	272.5
Personal Saving	Household Saving	71.7	80.2	65.9
Undistributed Corporate Profit	Business Saving	.2	16.7	27.6
Capital Consumption Allowances (Depreciation)		137.7	162.5	179.0
Government Surplus or Deficit (−)	Governmental (Dis) Saving	−3.2	−64.3	−35.6
Federal[a]		−10.7	−70.2	−54.0
State and Local		7.6	5.9	18.4
Investment		210.1	201.0	242.5
Gross Private Domestic Investment		214.6	189.1	243.3
Net Foreign Investment		−4.5	11.8	−.9
Statistical Discrepancy		5.8	5.9	5.5

[a]Includes net capital grants received by the United States.
Source: Survey of Current Business (U.S. Department of Commerce)

Table 5.1 presents actual flows of credit for the United States economy for each year from 1974 to 1985. Notice that the household sector consistently supplies credit in the form of a sizable and steady flow of personal saving in each year. The business sector generates saving too. However, the largest part of that flow of business saving is capital consumption allowances (depreciation). As discussed in Chapter Two, capital consumption allowances are the sum total of the flow of depreciation that is necessary to replace the existing capital stock as it wears out. (If capital consumption allowances are subtracted from gross private domestic investment, the result is net domestic investment—additions to the stock of capital goods.) The other part of business saving, the undistributed corporate profit of the business sector, provides a relatively small amount of saving. Moreover, Table 5.1 indicates that undistributed corporate profit varies greatly from year to year. The government sector, as a whole, fairly consistently has a deficit in each year. This occurs because even though state and local government always produce a yearly surplus, it is usually overwhelmed by the persistent annual deficit of the federal government. Thus, Table 5.1 shows how, on balance, household personal saving and undistributed corporate profit provide for the financing of the *net* investment spending needs of the business sector and the deficit spending needs of the government sector.

Consider 1985 as an example of the magnitude of credit flows. Table 5.2 summarizes the sources and uses of credit in 1985. In 1985 household (personal) saving provided a flow of $129.7 billion into the credit market. After subtracting capital consumption allowances, *net* business saving (undistributed corporate profit) was $129.8 billion. Thus, in 1985, the *sources* of credit, combined personal saving and undistributed corporate profit, were $259.5 billion.

1977	1978	1979	1980	1981	1982	1983	1984	1985
(Figures may not balance because of rounding.)								
273.1	324.6	422.8	406.3	477.5	413.9	437.2	551.8	558.7
293.9	324.9	407.3	438.3	504.7	529.9	571.7	674.8	697.7
67.3	72.0	96.7	106.2	130.2	141.1	118.1	156.1	129.7
29.5	36.0	54.5	38.9	44.4	32.0	76.5	115.4	129.8
197.0	216.9	256.1	293.2	330.1	356.8	377.1	403.2	438.3
−19.8	−.3	+14.3	−32.0	−27.2	−116.1	−134.5	−122.9	−139.0
−49.0	−27.7	−16.1	−60.2	−59.0	−147.9	−178.6	−175.8	−197.3
29.2	27.4	30.4	28.2	31.7	31.9	44.1	52.9	58.3
273.3	327.9	421.2	410.1	475.6	414.0	437.7	544.4	559.4
294.2	351.5	423.0	402.4	471.5	421.9	471.6	637.8	670.4
−20.9	−23.5	−1.8	7.8	4.1	−7.9	−33.9	−93.4	−111.0
−.2	3.3	−1.5	3.9	−1.9	−.2	0.5	−7.4	0.6

Table 5.2 Sources and Uses of Credit in 1985 (in billions of dollars)

Sources of Credit		
Household (Personal) Saving		$129.7
Gross Business Saving	$568.1	
Less Capital Consumption Allowances	−438.3	
Undistributed Corporate Profit (Net Business Saving)		129.8
Total Sources		$259.5
Uses of Credit		
Government Deficit		
Federal Deficit	$197.3	
Less State and Local Government Surplus	−58.3	
Government Deficit		$139.0
Gross Private Domestic Investment	670.4	
Less Capital Consumption Allowances	−438.3	
Net Private Domestic Investment		232.1
Foreign Investment		−111.0
Total Uses		$260.1
Statistical Discrepancy		0.6
		$259.5

Now, consider the *uses* of credit. The government sector as a whole had a deficit of \$139.0 billion in 1985. This consisted of a federal deficit of \$197.3 billion less a combined state and local governmental surplus of \$58.3 billion. The total gross domestic investment expenditures of the business sector were \$670.4 billion, but \$438.3 billion of this amount was for the replacement of the existing capital stock provided for by capital consumption allowances. This left \$232.1 billion of *net* domestic investment expenditures as a use of credit. An important *source* of credit in 1985 was the \$111.0 billion of foreign investment into the United States. Table 5.2 demonstrates the importance of household saving in providing for the net investment financing needs of business. It also shows how the government deficit absorbed a good part of the flow of credit in 1985.

Income and Expenditures by Sector

The preceding discussion described the role of business, household, government, and foreign sectors in credit (loanable funds) markets.[3] Now, the sources of each sector's saving and borrowing will be examined.[4] Each sector has earnings which are part of aggregate income. Transfer payments are either added to or subtracted from a sector's earnings. Sectoral earnings plus or minus these transfer payments equal the sector's final receipts. Final sectoral receipts minus sectoral expenditures equal sectoral saving or borrowing. Therefore, for each sector of the economy:

$$\text{Earnings} \pm \text{Transfer Payments} - \text{Expenditures} \equiv \text{Saving or Borrowing}$$

Table 5.3 shows that for each sector there is a budget identity that states that a sector's earnings less its transfer payments equals its final receipts. Table 5.3 also shows that final receipts equal expenditures plus or minus saving.

For the household sector, earnings (Y_h) in column 3 of Table 5.3 consist of wages and salaries (w), rental income of persons (r), net interest (i), and proprietors' income (u). The various transfer payments in row 2 sum to a negative amount ($-T_h$). The sum of earnings and transfer payments in row 3 is called *personal disposable income* (Y_d). Individual households make the decision to consume or save out of personal disposable income. If the sum of household consumption expenditures (C_h) in row 4 is less than all household final receipts (personal disposable income), as it usually is, then there will be a flow of personal saving (S_h) from the household sector in row 5. This flow of saving is a source of credit (a supply of funds) in the credit market. Since interest is paid on newly issued debt claims (and dividends are paid on the newly issued equity claims) that are exchanged for saving, the interest rate is viewed as an inducement to save.

For the business sector, in column 4 of Table 5.3, earnings (Y_b) consists of net corporate profits (π) and depreciation (d). The transfers in row 2 are negative ($-T_b$), and the sum

[3]For most of this text until Chapter Fifteen, the foreign sector is ignored. That is, a *closed economy* is assumed. In Chapter Fifteen exports, imports, exchange rates, and foreign investment are introduced in a general equilibrium model of an *open economy*.

[4]The emphasis here is on credit flows as sectoral residuals after sectoral expenditures and transfer payments have been netted out of sectoral earnings. For further detail on expenditures *and* transfer payments by sector see the discussion of earnings, receipts, and expenditures in Chapter Two.

Table 5.3 Income and Expenditures by Sector

Row	Item	Household	Business	Government	Total
1	earnings	wages and salaries (w) rental income of persons (r) net interst (i) proprietors' income (u) $(w+i+r+u) = Y_h$	net corporate profits (π) and depreciation (d) $(\pi+d) = Y_b$	indirect business taxes minus subsidies (T_i) $T_i = Y_g$	GNP Y
	minus				
2	transfer payments	+ government transfers + dividends − personal income taxes − social security contributions $-T_h$	− dividends − corporate income taxes $-T_b$	− government transfers + personal and corporate income taxes + social security contributions $+(T_h + T_b) = T_g$	0
	equals				
3	final receipts	personal disposable income Y_d	gross business saving S_b	net government receipts T_n	GNP Y
	equals				
4	current expenditures	consumption expenditures C_h	0	government purchases G	$C + G$
	plus or minus				
5	saving	personal saving S_h	gross business saving S_b	government saving (+ surplus or − deficit) S_g $-S_g$	S
6	capital expenditures	0	gross investment expenditures I_g	0	I_g
7	budget identities	$w+i+r+u \equiv C_h+S_h+T_h$	$\pi + d \equiv T_b + S_b$	$T_i \equiv -T_g + G - S_g$	$Y \equiv C_h + S_h + S_b + T_n$
8	financing constraints	$S_n + S_h = \Delta K + \Delta V_g + \Delta M_g$	$\Delta K = I_n = S_n +$ external financing	$S_g = T_n - G = \Delta M_g + \Delta V_g$	
9	private balance sheet identity	$W_n \equiv K + V_g + M_g$			

of these two terms in row 3 is called *gross business saving* (S_b). Individual business firms make the decision to engage in investment expenditures. If the gross investment expenditures (I_g) in row 6 are greater than gross business saving, as they usually are, there will be a net flow of borrowing by the business sector in row 8. This flow of borrowing is called *external financing* and is a use of credit (a demand for funds) in the credit market. Since business firms must pay interest on the debt claims (and dividends on the equity claims) that they issue to attract funds, the interest rate is viewed as a deterrent to borrowing.

In column 5 of Table 5.3, for the government sector, earnings (Y_g) consist of indirect business taxes minus subsidies (T_i). Transfers in row 2 are positive ($+T_g$) and the sum of these two items in row 3 is called *net government receipts* (T_n). If the sum of purchases by governmental entities (G) in row 4 is greater than net government receipts, then there will be a flow of dissaving ($-S_g$) by the government sector in row 5. This flow of borrowing, the *government deficit,* is a use of credit (demand for funds) in the credit market. Another way of defining the deficit of government is to add *government purchases* and the various transfer payments paid *by* government (this sum is called *government expenditures*) and then subtract this total from the transfer payments (taxation) paid *to* government.

Interest (and dividend) payments serve as a deterrent to business borrowing and as an inducement to household saving. The unique interest rate that balances the flow of saving into the credit market with the flow of borrowing out of the credit market is referred to as the equilibrium interest rate; it is the equilibrium price of credit.

Row 7 of Table 5.3 gives budget identities of the three sectors. In column 6 the aggregate budget identity for the economy as a whole indicates that aggregate income is equal to consumption (C_h) plus the saving of households (S_h) and the business sector (S_b) added to net government receipts (T_n). Thus, the flow of aggregate income in the economy (Y) is either used on consumption expenditures (C_h), saved ($S_b + S_h$), or transferred away to government (T_n). Dropping the subscripts and consolidating household and business saving allows the aggregate budget identity to be expressed as: $Y \equiv C + S + T$.

Row 8 uses the private balance sheet identity to show the link between the flow of saving and borrowing and the stock of nonhuman wealth in the economy. The saving of the household sector (S_h) enters the credit market where part of it is tapped by the business sector as a source of external financing of net investment expenditures (I_n). This part helps to increase the economy's physical capital stock (ΔK). In exchange for this flow of saving, households receive either newly issued debt or newly issued equity claims (basically private bonds or shares of stock) from business firms. This reflects part of the increase in the economy's stock of physical capital goods (ΔK).[5] The remainder of net investment expenditures is financed by net business saving (S_n), retained earnings, which

[5]Chapter Two demonstrated the idea that the outstanding stock of privately issued debt claims are not counted as aggregate private wealth because, while private debt claims are the assets of their individual owners, they are the liabilities of the households that own the firms that issue them. Therefore, they cancel out in aggregation. Nevertheless, debt-financed capital expenditures still add to aggregate wealth because they enhance future profits and add to the market value of the outstanding stock of equity claims which are part of aggregate private wealth.

is defined as gross business saving (S_b) minus depreciation, capital consumption allowances (d).

To keep things simple, net business saving should be viewed as flowing directly into net investment expenditures by the firm doing the saving. As this also increases the capital stock of the economy, it is reflected in the wealth of the household sector (as the *value* of *existing* ownership claims increase).

Government taps the rest of personal saving as the means of financing its deficit ($T_n - G$). Households, thereby, also receive newly issued debt claims from governmental entities ($\Delta V_g + \Delta M_g$). In this manner, the saving of the household sector helps to increase its stock of nonhuman wealth where aggregate private nonhuman wealth (W_n) is defined, consistent with the private balance sheet identity, as the value of outstanding equity claims issued by business firms plus the value of outstanding debt claims issued by government ($K + V_g + M_g$). As discussed in Chapter Two and in footnote 5, this concept should be called aggregate private net worth.

The real world is more complex than this discussion might suggest. For example, many interest rates are offered in myriad specialized credit markets. Nevertheless, the preceding discussion describes credit markets in a manner that is compatible with the way economists picture the economy as a whole. This view enables economists to integrate theories of the determination of the interest rate into theories of the determination of employment, output, and the price level.

The Theory of Saving

In the preceding discussion the payment of interest (or dividends) after deducting federal and state taxes on interest (or dividend) income was said to offer a positive incentive to save. This proposition deserves closer inspection. The household sector's budget identity, introduced in row 7 of Table 5.3, provides insight:

$$Y_h \equiv C_h + S_h + T_h \tag{5.2}$$

Equation 5.2 indicates the identity that the income of the household sector (Y_h) is either transferred away (T_h), used for consumption expenditures (C_h), or saved (S_h). Household income less net household transfer payments is called *personal disposable income*. Equation (5.2) indicates that, by definition, personal disposable income is either used for consumption expenditures or saved. Through this identity, the decision of the household to consume out of disposable income is related to its decision to save. A theory of what determines the level of saving is, therefore, identically related to a theory of what determines the level of consumption expenditures. Equation (5.2) suggests that as long as

---

Whether the outstanding debt claims of government should be counted as part of private wealth is a controversial subject. From the accounting perspective of the private balance sheet identity, they should; from the economics perspective of the definition of wealth and income, they should not. The economics perspective on this issue was discussed in Chapter Two.

disposable income is unchanged, any variable that affects consumption expenditures in one direction must, by definition, have an effect on saving that is equal in magnitude but opposite in algebraic sign. For example, if a change in an unspecified variable (x) causes aggregate consumption to decline by \$10 billion, as long as disposable income is unchanged, saving must rise by \$10 billion.

Equation (5.2) also indicates that a change in disposable income must, by definition, be absorbed by a rise in consumption, a rise in saving, or both. For example, if disposable income increases by \$50 billion, the sum of consumption expenditures and saving must rise by \$50 billion.

Having explained the relationship between consumption and saving, a theory of consumption and saving will be developed. The theory of consumption and saving is derived from four fundamental assumptions. These assumptions are:

1. Households maximize their utility,
2. A change in the interest rate has no effect on aggregate real disposable income,
3. Lenders and borrowers, as groups, have the same marginal propensities to consume, and
4. Households have perfect information on current interest rates and their current real disposable income and forecast their real disposable income and future interest rates over their planning horizon.

If and when these assumptions are modified, the theory of consumption and saving will be modified. The theory of consumption and saving is closely related to the general theory of demand. In the general theory of demand, the household is assumed to maximize its utility or satisfaction by allocating its fixed budget across competing uses. The key variables in this decision are the size of the budget, and the prices of the various uses of that budget.

The decision of the household to demand leisure hours (supply labor hours) was presented in a theory-of-demand framework in Chapter Three. The household was assumed to maximize its utility by allocating its budget of hours across two competing uses, labor and leisure. The key variables in this decision were the size of the budget (twenty-four hours per day) and the price or opportunity cost of leisure (the real wage).

The theory of consumption and saving is approached in a very similar and, as we shall see below, interrelated manner. To maximize its utility the household allocates its budget (disposable income) to either present consumption expenditures or present saving. The key variables in this decision are the size of the budget (disposable income), and the *price* (opportunity cost) of present consumption expenditures, the market rate of interest.

The market rate of interest is the *opportunity cost* of present consumption expenditures because it is what the household sacrifices in the future by consuming in the present. If a dollar's worth of present consumption expenditures is forgone, and the household saves the dollar of income instead, it will earn interest. For each dollar of goods that is consumed in the present, more than a dollar's worth of future goods are being sacrificed.

At work here are both an intemporal *substitution effect* and an *income effect*. Assume that an increase in the interest rate is permanent. As the interest rate rises, the price of present consumption relative to future consumption rises. As the interest rate goes up, it costs a household more to consume in the present year. As the interest rate increases, a rational household will tend to substitute the cheaper good, consumption in a future year, for the more expensive one, consumption in the present year. The substitution effect applies unambiguously to all households—lenders (present savers who will save more at higher rates) as well as borrowers (present dissavers who will dissave less at higher rates).[6]

An income effect is also at work. As the interest rate rises, for lenders (savers) the level of their real income (defined to include interest income from dollars saved in the present year) rises. Therefore, if consumption goods in each year are not inferior goods, lenders will increase consumption in present and future years. For borrowers (dissavers) as the interest rate rises, the level of their real income (defined to exclude interest payments on borrowed dollars in the present year) declines. Therefore, if consumption goods are not inferior, borrowers will reduce consumption in all years.

For the economy as a whole, an increase in the interest rate will generate a substitution effect that will cause both present savers (lenders) and present dissavers (borrowers) to consume less. For the economy as a whole, an increase in the interest rate will have an income effect that will cause present savers to consume more and present dissavers to consume less.

If, for the economy as a whole, we assume that a change in the market rate of interest cannot create any new resources, then it cannot advance the level of real income. There will then be no more resources available after the interest rate change than there were before the change. Also assume that the rise in the interest rate having a positive income effect on the consumption of present savers (lenders) is exactly offset by its having a negative income effect on the consumption of present dissavers (borrowers). This means that lenders and borrowers, viewed as groups, are assumed to have the same *marginal propensity to consume* out of current disposable income. The marginal propensity to consume out of current disposable income is the effect of a change in current disposable income on current consumption: $\Delta(C/P)_0/\Delta(Y/P)_{d_0}$.

Under these conditions the income effect of a change in the interest rate on the consumption of savers cancels the income effect of a change in the interest rate on the consumption of dissavers. For the economy as a whole, there can only be an intertemporal substitution effect. Since the substitution effect is unambiguous for lenders and borrowers, aggregate current real consumption varies inversely with the market rate of interest:

$$C/P = h(i) \tag{5.3}$$

Using the sectoral budget identity (expressed now in real terms and without subscripts),

$$Y/P \equiv C/P + S/P + T/P \tag{5.4}$$

[6]It should be recalled from Chapter Three (footnote 7) that a rise in the interest rate motivates workers to substitute future leisure for current leisure. In other words, as the interest rate rises, current leisure declines and current labor increases because the interest rate is the opportunity cost of current leisure. Therefore a rise in the interest rate has a positive substitution effect on the current supply of labor that is consistent with its negative substitution effect on current consumption.

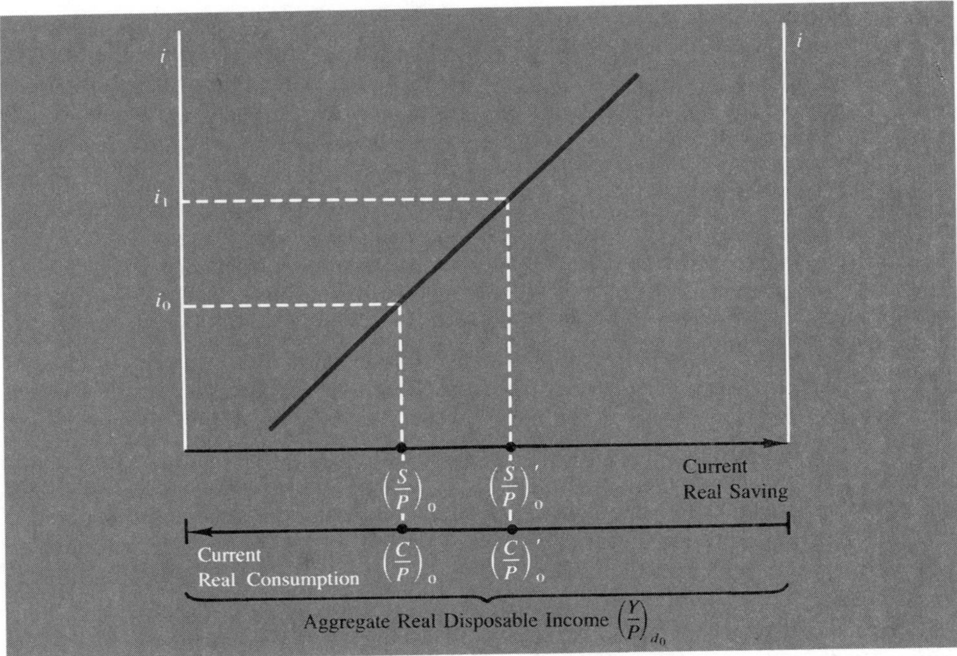

Figure 5.4 The Effect of a Change in the Interest Rate on Aggregate Current Saving and Aggregate Current Consumption

where current real income is unchanged, assuming real transfer payments are not affected by the interest rate, the effect of an interest rate change on aggregate real consumption must be exactly offset by an equal and opposite effect on aggregate real saving. Therefore, for the economy as a whole, aggregate real saving varies positively with the market rate of interest.[7]

$$S/P = \underset{+}{j(i)} \tag{5.5}$$

Figure 5.4 portrays the relationship between aggregate current real disposable income $[(Y/P)_0 - (T/P)_0 \equiv (Y/P)_{d_0}]$, aggregate current real saving $(S/P)_0$, aggregate current real consumption $(C/P)_0$ and the rate of interest (i). The lower horizontal line segment measures the magnitude of aggregate real disposable income. As the interest rate rises from i_0 to i_1 current real saving rises from $(S/P)_0$ to $(S/P)'_0$. Since real disposable income that is not allocated to real saving must be allocated to real consumption, the latter falls from $(C/P)_0$ to $(C/P)'_0$.

[7]This represents further use of the conservation principle developed in Chapter Two, the budget identity. In short, the partial effects of a change in the interest rate or any variable on consumption, saving, and transfers must sum to zero as long as income is unchanged.

Returning once more to the individual household, if a household's real disposable income should increase in year two, the present (year one) value of its real disposable income stream will increase. Likewise, if year one disposable income should increase, the future (year two) value of its current real disposable income will increase. If consumption in any period is not an inferior good, an increase in one year's real disposable income should increase real consumption expenditures in both years.

Assuming that the household has perfect knowledge of the interest rate and current real disposable income and forecasts future real disposable income, the relation between the present value of a real disposable income stream and current real consumption expenditures can be generalized by looking at real disposable income beyond two periods:

$$(C/P)_0 = k(PV)_0 = k \sum_{t=0}^{n} \left[\frac{(Y/P)_{d_t}}{(1 + i)^t} \right], \; 0 < k \leq 1 \tag{5.6}$$

where n is the number of years of the future planning horizon of the household. Equation (5.6) says that a household's real consumption during time 0 varies positively with the present, time 0, value of all future real disposable income. The term k is the marginal propensity to consume out of current disposable income. It reflects the change in current consumption $\Delta(C/P)_0$ with respect to the change in current disposable income $\Delta(Y/P)_{d_0}$. The condition that $k \leq 1$ follows from the constraint that the present value of future consumption is equal to the present value of future disposable income. Therefore, a household can currently consume no more than the present value of its future income. Negative consumption in any period is ruled out as being unreasonable.[8]

The right-hand side of Equation (5.6) is k times the present discounted value of the household's real disposable income stream. The income stream includes current real disposable income as well as future real disposable income. For the time being, real wealth is defined as the present discounted value of future real disposable income *excluding current real disposable income*. Therefore, the present value of a real disposable income stream is, under this definition of real wealth, the sum of current real disposable income and real wealth:

$$(Y/P)_{d_0} + \sum_{t=1}^{n} \frac{(Y/P)_{d_t}}{(1 + i)^t} = \sum_{t=0}^{n} \frac{(Y/P)_{d_t}}{(1 + i)^t} \tag{5.7}$$

[8]If current disposable income changes by $\Delta(Y/P)_{d_0}$, current consumption changes by $\Delta(C/P)_0 = k\,\Delta(Y/P)_{d_0}/(1 + i)^0$. Since $(1 + i)^0$ equals unity, the marginal propensity to consume out of current income is: $\Delta(C/P)_0/\Delta(Y/P)_{d_0} = k$. The marginal propensity to consume out of a future year's income is $k/(1 + i)^t$ where $t > 0$.

The term k will vary across households. As the planning period (n) grows smaller, k grows larger but will always be less than or equal to one. For example, a household consisting of two centenarians may want to consume most of its current disposable income. Its k will be closer to unity because its life expectancy will be shorter. In the aggregate consumption and saving functions k would be a weighted average of individual k's.

Equation (5.6) can be written out to show the effect of current real disposable income and the present value of all future real disposable income, that is, real wealth, on the household's current real consumption:

$$(C/P)_0 = k\left[(Y/P)_{do} + \frac{(Y/P)_{d_1}}{(1+i)} + \frac{(Y/P)_{d_2}}{(1+i)^2} + \ldots + \frac{(Y/P_{d_n}}{(1+i)^n}\right] \tag{5.8}$$

The parameter k, being positive but less than unity, indicates that the household's current real consumption varies directly with the level of its current real disposable income as well as with the level of its real wealth.

The effect of current real disposable income and real wealth on the household's current real saving can now be derived by using the budget identity:

$$(Y/P)_0 \equiv (C/P)_0 + (S/P)_0 + (T/P)_0 \tag{5.9}$$

Rearranging in terms of real disposable income,

$$(Y/P)_{d_0} \equiv (Y/P)_0 - (T/P)_0 \equiv (C/P)_0 + (S/P)_0$$

Substituting Equation (5.8) into (5.9) and rearranging yields

$$(S/P)_0 = (Y/P)_{d_0} - k(Y/P)_{d_0} - k\left[\frac{(Y/P)_{d_1}}{(1+i)} + \frac{(Y/P)_{d_2}}{(1+i)^2} + \ldots + \frac{(Y/P)_{d_n}}{(1+i)^n}\right]$$

$$= (1-k)(Y/P)_{d_0} - k\sum_{1}^{n}\frac{(Y/P)_{d_t}}{(1+i)^t} \tag{5.10}$$

The term $(1 - k)$ is the *marginal propensity to save* out of current disposable income. Thus, current real saving varies positively with current real disposable income but inversely with the level of real wealth, as defined above. This indicates that as long as a current real disposable income is unchanged, when real wealth, defined above to exclude current real disposable income, increases, current real saving will decline. This occurs because if wealth, so defined, rises, current consumption rises. By the budget identity, Equation (5.4), if current consumption rises and current disposable income is unchanged, current saving must decline.

Equation (5.10) shows how current real saving varies with real wealth and real disposable income. Equation (5.8) shows how current real consumption varies with real wealth and real income. A change in real disposable income that lasts only one period will have a smaller effect on current consumption than a change in real disposable income that lasts for the entire n year planning period. A change in the disposable income term in just one numerator of Equation (5.8) will affect current consumption only in the amount $k/(1 + i)^t$ times the change in disposable income. In contrast, an equal-sized change in the disposable income terms in every numerator of Equation (5.8) will affect consumption by:

$$k \sum_{t=0}^{n} \frac{1}{(1 + i)^t}$$

times the change in disposable income. Comparing the two results, where all terms are nonnegative and n is greater than one:

$$k \frac{1}{(1 + i)^t} < k \sum_{t=0}^{n} \frac{1}{(1 + i)^t}$$

Therefore, a change in real disposable income that is permanent, one that affects every year of the n year planning period, has a greater effect on the current consumption and a smaller effect on the current saving of a household than a transitory change in real disposable income.[9]

Disproving the old adage that economic theory is perfectly accurate but absolutely useless, it can be seen that the preceding analysis can have a considerable effect on government's decision to allow the burden of taxation to fall on consumption or on saving. For example, if the level of real taxation $(T/P)_0$ is reduced for just the current year, there will be an increase in real disposable income in just the current year. Equation (5.8) indicates that k of the increase will be consumed. Equation (5.10) indicates that $(1 - k)$ of the increase will be saved. If, however, the reduction in taxation is expected to be permanent, a much greater increase in current consumption and a much smaller increase in current saving will occur.[10] Expressed another way, the marginal propensity to consume out of *transitory income* is less than the marginal propensity to consume out of *permanent income,* and the marginal propensity to save out of *transitory income* is greater than the marginal propensity to save out of *permanent income*.

For the economy as a whole the real saving function is derived by aggregating across individual households. (As explained in earlier chapters, aggregation procedures have a number of technical requirements, the examination of which is beyond the scope of this text.) Figure 5.5 illustrates the relationship between aggregate real saving (as a dependent variable) and the market rate of interest and aggregate real disposable income (as explanatory variables). As the level of aggregate real disposable income increases, the level of aggregate real saving increases at each possible interest rate. (As explained above, the magnitude of the increase varies inversely with the extent to which the rise in disposable income is expected to be permanent.) For every level of aggregate real disposable income

[9]If we were referring to aggregate consumption and aggregate income, it would be reasonable to constrain the term on the right-hand side of this inequality to be less than or equal to unity.

[10]This abstracts from the effect of a cut in the tax *rate* on interest and dividend income. A cut in the rate at which interest and dividend income is taxed will increase the after-tax rate of return to saving. This will increase current saving and reduce current consumption at any given level of disposable income. The relationship between aggregate saving and the after-tax rate of return is estimated to be positive in a paper by Michael Boskin, cited in the bibliography of this chapter. Considerations such as this influence the debates regarding taxation increases to reduce the government deficit, discussed in Chapter Six, and tax reform, discussed in Chapter Fourteen.

Difficulty arises in measuring saving because purchases of consumer durables, such as collectors' items, are really disguised saving. This and other problems in empirical estimation of the determinants of saving behavior are discussed in the recent survey paper by Bowles cited in the bibliography to this chapter.

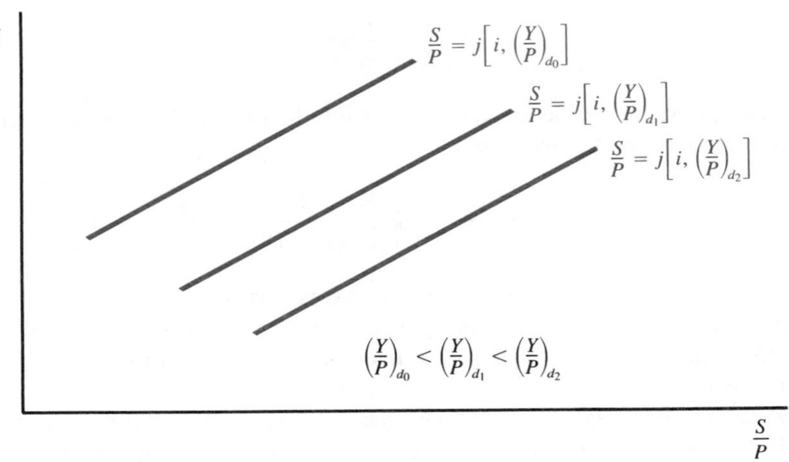

Figure 5.5 Aggregate Real Saving Varies Positively with the Market Rate of Interest and the Level of Aggregate Disposable Income

there is a unique aggregate real saving curve. Therefore, the level of aggregate real saving varies directly with the interest rate as long as aggregate real disposable income is held constant. (In addition, if the interest rate and current real disposable income are held constant, the level of aggregate real saving will vary inversely with the level of aggregate real wealth.) This derivation of the saving curve indicates why it usually takes at least three economists to draw a supply curve: one economist can draw the curve only if the other economists can hold everything else constant.

The Theory of Investment Expenditures

In Chapter Two, gross investment expenditures were defined as the total expenditures of the business sector on newly produced capital goods. Gross investment expenditures less capital consumption allowances is called net investment expenditures.

Therefore, a positive flow of net investment expenditures over a given interval of time generates an increase in the stock of capital goods in the economy. Capital goods are an input into the firm's production process. Thus, to develop the theory of aggregate investment expenditures, one must start with the theory of the firm.

The firm's production function shows the relationship between output and input. In Chapter Three we used the idea of the firm's production function to develop the theory of the demand for labor. Now we will use it to develop the theory of the demand for capital goods. Expenditures on newly produced capital goods are investment expenditures. A theory of the demand for units of a stock of capital goods will, therefore, help to explain the flow of investment expenditures on newly produced capital goods.

The theory of investment expenditures will be derived from five basic assumptions:

1. Diminishing marginal productivity of capital,

2. Purely competitively structured output markets,
3. Purely competitively structured capital goods markets,
4. Business firms maximize the present value of future expected profits minus the cost of capital goods, and
5. Business firms have perfect knowledge of current prices and nominal interest rates and forecast future expected prices and future interest rates.

If these assumptions are modified the theory of investment expenditures will be modified.

In Table 5.4, columns 1 and 2 portray a firm's production function. Notice that as units of capital (K) increase in column 1, units of output (Q) increase in column 2 at a decreasing rate. As inputs of capital are increased by unitary increments in column 1, output rises in column 2, but in ever-decreasing amounts. This illustrates the property of *diminishing marginal productivity* of capital. Diminishing productivity explains why the marginal physical product of capital, in column 3, is positive but declining. In other words, the increment to a firm's output (ΔQ) relative to the increment to units of capital input (ΔK) is positive but decreases as capital input increases. In column 3, the *marginal physical product of capital* is the increment to output with respect to the increment to capital input. The marginal physical product of capital may be expressed as the quotient $\Delta Q / \Delta K$.

Figure 5.6A depicts a smooth production function (given in Table 5.4 in stepwise form). Figure 5.6B depicts the related marginal physical product of capital. In Figures 5.6A and 5.6B all other productive inputs, such as labor, are conceptually held constant. The firm's production function in Figure 5.6A is concave to (bowed out from) the origin, and the marginal physical product of capital in Figure 5.6B in positive but decreasing, exhibiting the property of diminishing marginal productivity.

Table 5.4 The Firm's Demand for Capital

1 Units of Capital K	2 Output Q	3 Marginal Physical Product of Capital $\Delta Q/\Delta K$	4 Price of Output P	5 Marginal Revenue Product of Capital $(\Delta Q/\Delta K)\cdot P$	6 Market Rate of Interest i	7 Present Value PV	8 Price of a Unit of Capital P_k
0	10	—	$100	$ 0			
1	20	10	100	1,000	10%	$10,000	$7,000
2	29	9	100	900	10	9,000	7,000
3	37	8	100	800	10	8,000	7,000
4	44	7	100	700	10	7,000	7,000
5	50	6	100	600	10	6,000	7,000
6	55	5	100	500	10	5,000	7,000
7	59	4	100	400	10	4,000	7,000
8	62	3	100	300	10	3,000	7,000
9	64	2	100	200	10	2,000	7,000

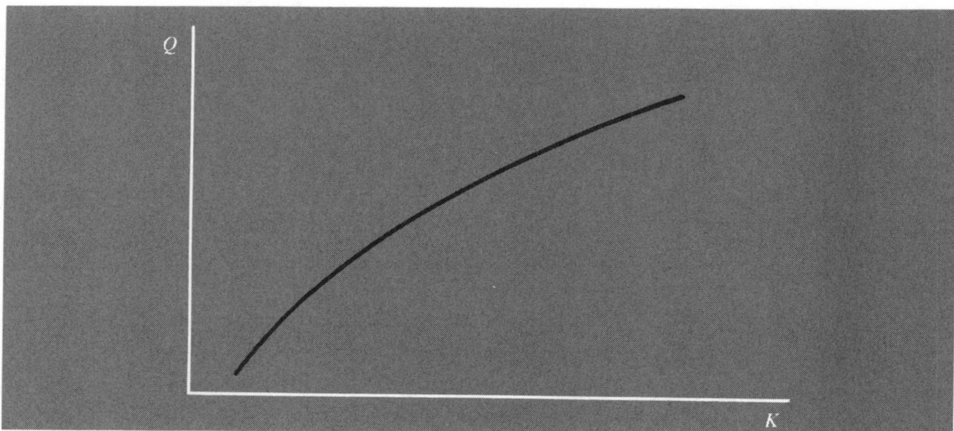

Figure 5.6A The Firm's Production Function

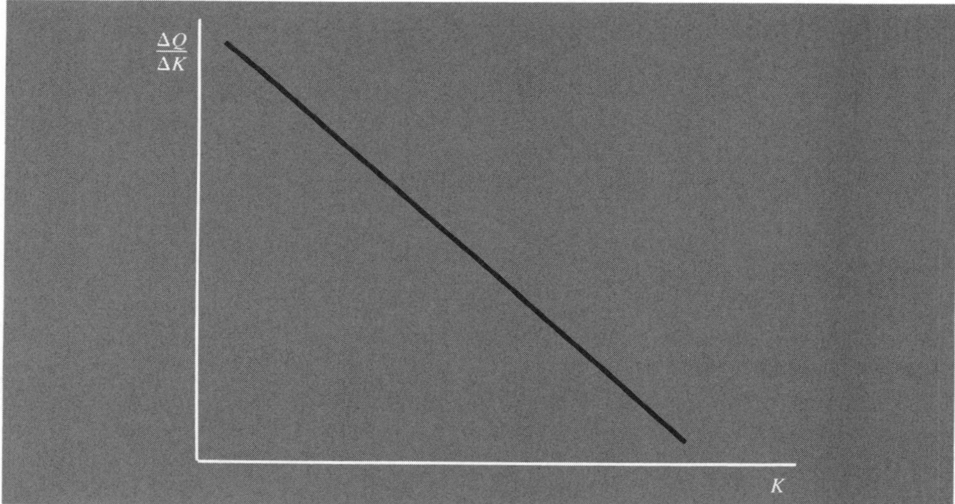

Figure 5.6B The Firm's Marginal Physical Product of Capital

Next, assume that the firm can sell its output at market-determined prices. In short, the market for the firm's output is purely competitively structured such that the firm may sell all the output that it wants to sell at price (P). The market-determined price (P) is shown in column 4 of Table 5.4.

When the price at which output sells is multiplied by the marginal physical product of capital, the *marginal revenue product of capital* is obtained. The marginal revenue product of capital is the increment to the firm's revenue with respect to the increment of capital input. The marginal revenue product of capital is given in column 5 of Table 5.4. Notice that the marginal revenue product of capital, $(\Delta Q/\Delta K)\cdot P$, declines as capital input increases because the marginal physical product of capital $(\Delta Q/\Delta K)$ declines as capital input increases (column 3).

The marginal revenue product of capital represents the stream of dollars that a unit of capital contributes at the margin to a firm's revenue each year. The firm is assumed to forecast future prices. This stream of dollars of revenue is assumed in the present example to continue unchanged until the respective unit of capital completely and suddenly deteriorates. In other words, each unit of capital in column 1 is expected to contribute the dollars of revenue given in column 5 each year for the entirety of its useful life. The dollar amounts in column 5 represent a stream of future dollars. Since there are no future costs associated with these future revenues, they represent future profits. Assuming no tax on business profit, these future revenues represent future after-tax profits.[11]

It is assumed that the firm maximizes net present value (the present value of future expected after-tax profits minus the cost of capital goods). To maximize the present value of future expected after-tax profits minus the cost of capital goods, the firm must acquire units of capital. This is done until the increment to cost from buying a unit of capital is matched by the increment to the present value of the stream of dollars of the future expected after-tax profits. Therefore, the *present value formula* discussed earlier in this chapter can be used again:

$$PV = \frac{y_1}{(1 + i)} + \frac{y_2}{(1 + i)^2} + \frac{y_3}{(1 + i)^3} + \ldots + \frac{y_n}{(1 + i)^n} \qquad (5.11)$$

where y_j is the year j increment to after-tax profit associated with the present increment to the firm's capital stock (in other words, y_j is the marginal revenue product of capital from Table 5.4) and i is the market rate of interest. Returning to Table 5.4, a market rate of interest of 10 percent is given in column 6. As the y and i are assumed to be known by the business firm, it is feasible to calculate the present value of each unit of capital in Table 5.4 (column 7).

Assuming that each unit of capital has an infinite life simplifies the calculations. In this special case, the present value formula reduces to:

$$PV = \frac{y}{i} \qquad (5.12)$$

[11]In the next chapter, we examine the role of actual and expected inflation in the investment expenditures decision. In Chapter Fourteen, we consider the effect of the tax rate on business investment. Also in the next chapter, we distinguish between real and nominal interest rates. If *real* expected profit appears in the numerator of the present value formula, the appropriate interest rate to use in the formula is the expected real interest rate. If *nominal* expected profit appears in the numerator, the nominal interest rate should be used.

In empirical studies of the determinants of aggregate investment expenditures, variables such as expected profit (reflected in the level of aggregate output), the size of the existing capital stock, actual and expected inflation, and the tax rate on profit are explicitly introduced. See the recent survey paper by Naylor cited in the bibliography to this chapter.

Table 5.4, column 7 gives the present value for each unit of capital. For the first unit of capital, the present value of $1,000 per year forever at a market rate of interest of 10 percent is $10,000. In other words, at the current market rate of interest of 10 percent, the expectation of receiving $1,000 of profit per year forever is worth $10,000 today to a rational investor. Viewing it another way, if one could acquire an asset with an infinite life promising to pay $1,000 per year forever at a current market rate of interest of 10 percent, one would rationally pay $10,000 for that asset—no more, no less.

The second unit of capital has a present value of $9,000 to the firm because it is expected to generate $900 of profit per year forever. At the current market rate of interest of 10 percent, this has a present value of $9,000. The third unit of capital has a present value of $8,000 because at the current market rate of interest of 10 percent, $800 of additional profit per year is worth just $8,000.

Next, assume that the market in which the firm may buy capital goods is purely competitively structured. This means that the firm may have all of the capital goods it needs at the market-determined price. In the example, the market-determined price is $7,000 and is listed in Table 5.4 (column 8).

How many units of capital would the firm desire? To answer this, compare column 7 (incremental future after-tax profits expressed as a present value), to column 8 (the incremental cost of a capital good). Assuming that a firm wants to maximize the present value of its future after-tax profits less the cost of capital goods, units of capital should be employed to the point where the increment to present value (the present value of the expected stream of future profits) is matched by the incremental cost of hiring capital: this occurs where $PV = P_k$.

In Table 5.4 the net present value maximizing condition is satisfied where four units of capital are obtained. At this point, the firm will have employed the number of units of capital that maximizes the present value of future profits less the cost of buying capital goods, the net present value.

Suppose that the market-determined price at which output sells rises to $175 per unit and is expected to stay there. If this were to occur, the marginal revenue product of capital in column 5 of Table 5.4 would increase by 75 percent. Marginal revenue product is marginal physical product times price, which has increased by 75 percent. For the first unit of capital, marginal revenue product in column 5 would be $1,750 (= 10 × $175), for the second unit it would be $1,575 (= 9 × $175), for the third $1,400, for the fourth $1,225, and so on. At a 10 percent market rate of interest, the present value of the first unit of capital is $17,500 because the rational investor would pay this amount for the right to receive $1,750 per year forever. The present value of the second unit of capital is $15,750; the present value of the third is $12,250, and so on.

Therefore, if the price of output rises to $175 per unit and is expected to remain there, the firm would desire seven units of capital because the present value of the seventh unit is $7,000 [the marginal revenue product of $700 (the price of $175 times the marginal physical product of 4) divided by the market rate of interest of 10 percent].

Now, suppose that the price at which the firm sells its output is $100 as in Table 5.4, but the price of a unit of capital (P_k) rises to $9,000 in column 8. How many units of capital would the firm desire? The answer is two because at two units, the present value of $9,000 in column 7 is equal to the price of capital of $9,000.

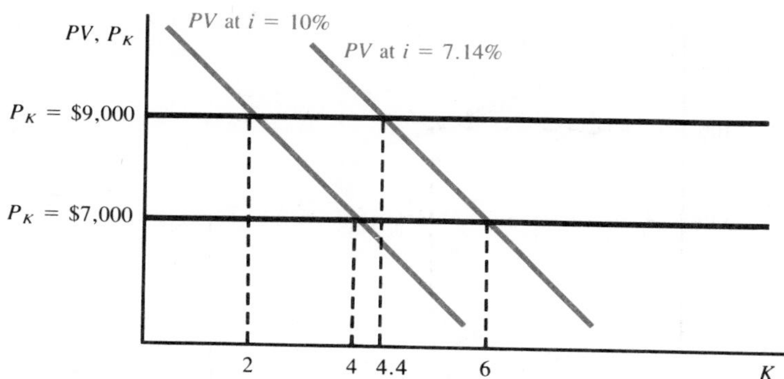

Figure 5.7 The Firm's Demand for Capital Goods

Assume a market rate of interest of 7.14 percent. Each marginal revenue product in column 5 of Table 5.4 now has a greater present value. At a current market rate of interest of 7.14 percent, the present value of the first unit of capital is approximately $14,000 (= $1,000 ÷ .0714). A rational investor would pay $14,000 for the expected profit of $1,000 per year forever. The second unit of capital has a present value of approximately $12,600; the present value of the third is about $11,200. These examples show that the present value of the stream of future after-tax profit that is associated with each unit of capital varies inversely with the market rate of interest. This follows from the fact that the lower the market rate, the greater the amount that would have to be invested to generate any given profit stream. The net present value-maximizing firm would employ six units of capital if the current market rate of interest were 7.14 percent and the price per unit of capital were $7,000. At an interest rate of 7.14 percent the present value of the sixth unit of capital is approximately $7,000.

Figure 5.7 plots the relationships depicted in Table 5.4. On the vertical axis is present value (*PV*), on the horizontal axis are units of capital (*K*). At a market rate of interest of 10 percent the firm will desire four units of capital if the price of capital is $7,000 per unit, as in Table 5.4. If the price is $9,000 per unit, as discussed previously, the firm would like to employ two units of capital at a market rate of interest of 10 percent.

Assume that a change in the interest rate is permanent. As the market rate of interest declines to 7.14 percent, the present value curve in Figure 5.7 shifts rightward. At a price of $7,000 per unit, the firm would desire six units of capital. Figure 5.7 suggests that the lower the current market rate of interest, the greater the present value of each prospective unit of capital. The lower the current market rate of interest the further the present value curve shifts to the right in Figure 5.7.

To translate the preceding discussion of the *desired stock* of capital goods into a theory of (the flow of) investment expenditures, assume that the firm actually will acquire all of the profit-maximizing number of capital goods in the present operating period.[12] This

[12]This is an unrealistic assumption as there are discrete costs of the firm adjusting its capital stock. In fact, as the references on the theory of investment cited in the bibliography of this chapter show, the existence of the investment function derived here depends on adjustment costs. These costs include the costs of installing capital goods and the cost of disrupting production. If adjustment costs rise rapidly as investment increases, the gap between the actual and desired capital stock will close more slowly.

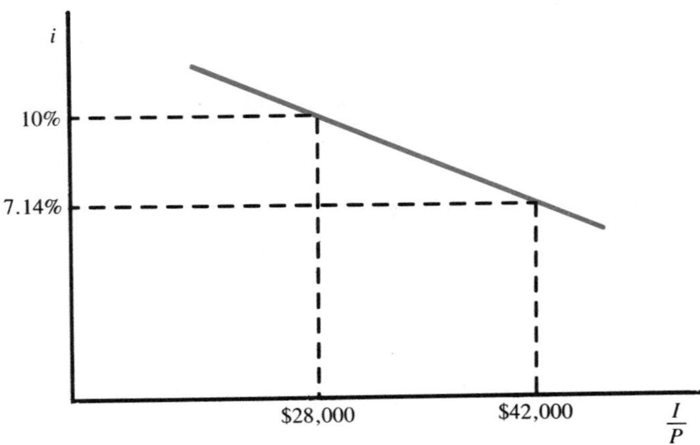

Figure 5.8 The Firm's Investment Expenditures

assumption implies that the firm currently has no capital goods on hand. The actual stock of capital goods is zero. The firm's net investment expenditures are defined as the firm's *desired stock* of capital goods minus its *actual stock* of capital goods. As seen in Figure 5.8 as the interest rate declines from 10 to 7.14 percent the investment expenditures of the firm rise from $28,000 (four units of capital × $7,000 per unit) to $42,000 (six units of capital × $7,000 per unit).

For the economy as a whole the aggregate real net investment expenditures schedule is derived by adding up the net investment expenditures of each firm in the economy at each and every market rate of interest.[13] Thus aggregate real net investment expenditures in the economy vary inversely with the market rate of interest. Whether firms finance internally through retained earnings (net business saving) or externally in the credit market, the lower the market rate of interest, the greater the present value of prospective capital goods, and the greater the demand for capital goods; hence the greater is the level of aggregate real net investment expenditures.

Equation 5.13 expresses the notion depicted in Figure 5.8:

$$I/P = m(\underset{-}{i}) \tag{5.13}$$

[13]As pointed out in Chapter Three, footnote 8, certain conditions must be satisfied before one can aggregate across the factor demand functions of individual firms in order to derive an aggregate factor demand relation. Aggregation procedures have a number of technical requirements, the examination of which is beyond the intended scope of this text.

In addition, in this chapter and throughout the remainder of this book until Chapter Fourteen, we assume that while the flow of net investment expenditures adds to the capital stock, the latter is so large that short-run additions to it are negligible in their effects on the full employment equilibrium level of output and real wages.

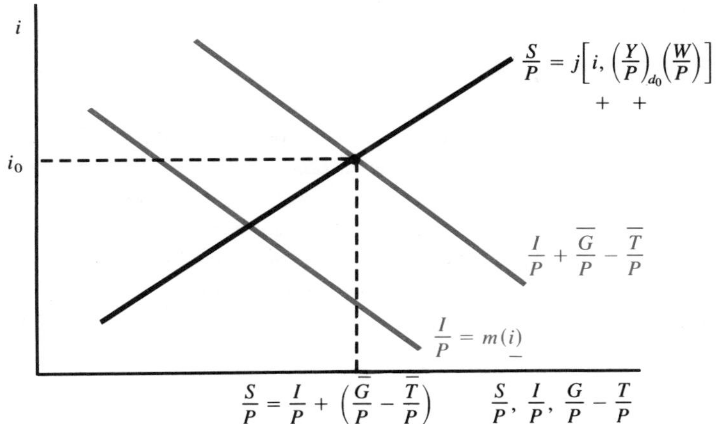

Figure 5.9 The Credit Market

The level of aggregate real net investment (*I*/*P*) varies inversely with the market rate of interest (i).[14]

As discussed earlier, the supply of aggregate real saving varies positively with the market rate of interest, directly with the level of current aggregate real disposable income, and inversely with the level of aggregate real wealth. Aggregate real wealth is defined as the present value of future aggregate real disposable income. Therefore, the flow of resources (saving) from the household sector into the credit market varies directly with the current market rate of interest. The demand for these resources (to finance investment expenditures) by the business sector varies inversely with the current market rate. If the demand for credit by the government sector (to finance the government deficit) is added to the private demand for credit by the business sector, the total market demand for credit is obtained. Given supply and demand schedules for credit, where the level of aggregate real disposable income and aggregate real wealth are assumed constant, the equilibrium interest rate and equilibrium quantity of credit are determined in the credit market. In Figure 5.9, the supply of credit is the aggregate real saving function. The greater the market rate of interest, the greater the flow of real saving, *S*/*P*, out of real disposable income, $(Y/P)_{d_0}$. If real disposable income increases, or if real wealth decreases, real saving increases and the curve shifts to the right. The private demand for credit by firms (*I*/*P*) varies inversely with the market rate of interest. This is the demand for credit to finance aggregate real investment expenditures on newly produced capital goods. To that

[14]As seen from the preceding analysis and the initial assumptions, investment spending is sensitive to expected future after-tax profits. Optimism and pessimism about future profits may shift dramatically depending on the stage of the business cycle. Thus, the aggregate investment expenditures relation may shift procyclically, varying directly with the expected level of future profits. The cyclical volatility of private investment expenditures is discussed in Chapters Six and Seven.

It is also apparent that investment spending responds inversely to the tax rate on profits. The effect of taxes on investment expenditures is discussed in Chapter Fourteen. Considerations such as this influence the debate regarding tax increases to reduce the government deficit, discussed in Chapter Six.

private demand is added the demand of the public sector ($G/P - T/P$), the real government deficit.

Assume that the deficit of the government sector does not vary with the market rate of interest; it is treated as given. The bars above G and T signify that they are exogenously determined. The total demand-for-credit curve is positioned horizontally to the right of the private demand for credit curve by the distance ($\overline{G}/P - \overline{T}/P$). The total demand for credit represents the sum of private demand (I/P) and public demand ($\overline{G}/P - \overline{T}/P$).

The total demand for credit together with the supply of credit determine the equilibrium market rate of interest (i_0). At this rate the market clears (is in equilibrium), and the supply of saving (S/P) is equal to the private demand of firms (I/P) plus the demand of government ($\overline{G}/P - \overline{T}/P$).[15] Equation (5.14) represents the credit market equilibrium condition:

$$\frac{S}{P} = \frac{I}{P} + \left(\frac{G}{P} - \frac{T}{P}\right) \tag{5.14}$$

Concluding Comment

This chapter first discusses the way economists conceptualize the credit (loanable funds) market. The credit market is viewed as a place where surplus units, units in the economy whose income exceeds their expenditures, can lend to deficit units, units whose expenditures exceed their income, at market-determined interest rates. In the aggregate economy, the household sector provides the flow of saving into the credit market, and the business and government sectors receive this flow. Business firms use this flow to engage in investment expenditures to add to their stock of physical capital goods. In this way, the flow of saving from households increases the stock of the economy's wealth. In exchange for its saving, the household sector receives claims on the new, physical capital goods.

Given this picture of the way economists conceive of the credit market, the chapter develops the theory of saving as part of the general theory of demand of a household. This chapter shows that aggregate real saving varies directly with the market rate of interest, directly with the level of disposable income, and inversely with the level of wealth.

Finally, the theory of investment expenditures is developed as part of the general theory of the demand for factors of production of a business firm; capital goods are seen as a factor of production. It is also shown that aggregate real investment expenditures vary inversely with the market rate of interest and directly with expected, future, after-tax profits.

In the next chapter, a theory of the supply of and demand for credit will integrate these theories and analyze the working of the credit market.

[15]Here and throughout this book, it should be remembered that when a nominal magnitude such as S or I is divided by the price level variable P, it means that the relevant decision variable is the quotient, S/P or I/P. Therefore, in a behavioral equation such as (5.13), if the price level in the denominator rises by any percentage the level of nominal magnitude in the numerator will rise by the same percentage such that the quotient, a real magnitude, is unchanged as long as the right-hand side variables are unchanged.

EXERCISES

1. The positively sloped supply curve of credit depends on the assumption that a substitution effect outweighs an income effect.
   a. true
   b. false
2. Clear up the semantic confusion in the following statement: "I have made many investments in the stock market with money from my savings."
3. Explain why households in the aggregate will engage in just the correct amount of real saving so that it is absorbed by the external financing demands of business firms, plus the deficit financing demands of government.
4. How does the flow of real saving add to the stock of aggregate wealth held by households? What if this saving is undistributed corporate profit? What if this saving is used to purchase newly issued debt claims of business firms? What if this saving is used to finance the deficit of government?
5. Using the present value formula, carefully explain why the level of real investment spending varies inversely with the market rate of interest and shifts with changes in the level of expected, future, after-tax profits.
6. Explain and clarify the condition that must hold for the following statement to be true: "If real consumption expenditures are known to vary inversely with the market rate of interest, real saving *must* vary positively with the market rate of interest."
7. How can the business sector be both a source and a use of credit?
8. Explain why capital consumption allowances are a source of funds to finance gross domestic investment expenditures.
9. Explain why you agree or disagree with the following statement: "Gross business saving constitutes the lion's share of total saving in the current economy. Therefore, continued growth in our capital stock need not rely on the personal saving of the household sector."
10. Assume that a household has an infinite planning period, that its disposable income is constant throughout this period and that it is constrained to set the present value of all current and future consumption equal to the present value of all current and future disposable income. Compare the value of the marginal propensity to consume out of a transitory increase in current disposable income to the marginal propensity to consume out of a permanent increase in disposable income.
11. Explain in words why an increase in the level of taxation will have a greater negative impact on current consumption and a smaller negative impact on current saving if the increase is expected to be permanent. How would you modify your answer if the increase in the level of taxation occurs because of a rise in the *rate* at which interest income is taxed?
12. What is the value to society of continually functioning stock and bond markets?

BIBLIOGRAPHY

Ando, Albert, and Franco Modigliani. "The Life Cycle Hypothesis of Saving: Aggregate Implications and Tests." *American Economic Review* 53 (March 1963), pp. 55–84.

Boehm-Bawerk, Eugen von. *Positive Theory of Capital*. New York: Stechent, 1923.

Boskin, Michael J. "Taxation Saving and the Rate of Interest." *Journal of Political Economy* 86 (April 1978), pp. 3–27.

Bowles, David C. "Consumption and Saving through the 1970's and 1980's: A Survey of Empirical Research." In *Modern Concepts in Macroeconomics*, ed. Thomas M. Havrilesky. Arlington Heights, Ill: Harlan Davidson, Inc., 1985.

Brechling, Frank. *Investment and Employment Decisions*. Manchester, England: Manchester University Press, 1975.

Eisner, Robert. "Fiscal and Monetary Policy Reconsidered." *American Economic Review* 59 (December 1969), pp. 897–905.

Fisher, Irving. *Theory of Interest*. New York: Macmillan, 1930.

Friedman, Milton. *A Theory of the Consumption Function*. Princeton: Princeton University Press, 1957.

Gurley, John G. "The Saving-Investment Process and the Market for Loanable Funds." *Proceedings of the 1959 Conference on Savings and Residential Financing*. Chicago: The United States Savings and Loan League, 1960.

Hirschliefer, Jack. *Investment, Interest and Capital*. Englewood Cliffs, N.J.: Prentice-Hall, 1970.

Jorgenson, Dale W., and C. D. Siebert. "A Comparison of Alternative Theories of Investment." *American Economic Review* 58 (September 1968), pp. 681–712.

Keynes, John Maynard. *The General Theory of Employment, Interest and Money*. New York: Harcourt, Brace and Co., 1935.

Lerner, Abba P. *The Economics of Control*. New York: Macmillan, 1944.

Meyer, John, and Edward Kuh. *The Investment Decision*. Cambridge: Harvard University Press, 1957.

Mishkin, Frederic S. "What Depressed the Consumer? The Household Balance Sheet and the 1973–75 Recession." *Brookings Papers on Economic Activity* 3 (1978).

Naylor, John A. "A Survey of Post-1970 Empirical Studies of Investment Expenditures." In *Modern Concepts in Macroeconomics*, ed. Thomas M. Havrilesky. Arlington Heights, Ill.: Harlan Davidson, Inc., 1985.

Ramsey, Frank P. "A Mathematical Theory of Saving." *Economic Journal* (December 1928), pp. 543–549.

Ritter, Lawrence. "The Structure of Flow-of-Funds Accounts." *Journal of Finance* 18 (May 1963), pp. 219–230.

The Credit Market: Crowding Out, Real and Nominal Interest Rates, and the Volatility of Investment Expenditures

Chapter 6

Introduction

Chapter Five examined the basic features of the credit (loanable funds) market. In this chapter the partial equilibrium model of the credit market will be applied to some key problems in our economy.

One of these problems is the effect of an increase in the government's demand for credit on the availability of funds for private expenditures. It is widely believed that when government borrows more in credit markets, less credit is available for the private sector. This chapter examines the *"crowding out" of private expenditures by government expenditures*.

Another problem in our economy is that the expectation of inflation drives up the interest rate. The chapter shows how this process occurs in the credit market, focusing on how the behavior of savers and investors translates the expectation of more inflation into a higher interest rate. Finally, this chapter examines the problem of the volatility of interest rates and the private investment expenditures of business firms.

Before applying our model of the credit market to these key problems, the basic features of credit market behavior will be reviewed. The supply of credit is aggregate real saving which represents the part of the flow of aggregate real income that is neither used for real consumption expenditures nor transferred away to the government sector. The total demand for credit consists of the demand of the business sector plus the demand of the government sector. While some demand for credit comes from individual households, the household sector is, in the aggregate, always a net supplier of credit. Moreover, while business firms usually generate some saving in the form of retained earnings, the business sector is, in the aggregate, always a net demander of credit. The business sector requires credit in order to obtain funds to finance the acquisition of newly produced capital goods—that is, the business sector demands credit in order to finance real investment expenditures.

Finally while state and local government usually generate saving in the form of budgetary surpluses, the government sector, defined to include federal government, is usually a net demander of credit. The government sector needs credit in order to obtain funds to finance the excess of its expenditures over its receipts, the government sector's deficit.

In the previous chapter the supply of aggregate real saving was seen to depend on three variables, the level of aggregate real disposable income, the market rate of interest, and the level of aggregate real wealth. The current level of real income has a positive effect on current real saving because current real saving emanates from real disposable income; it is that part of disposable income that is not used for expenditures. The larger the current level of real disposable income, the larger the current level of real saving. Changes in the level of wealth, defined as the present value of future expected disposable income excluding current disposable income, have a negative effect on current real saving. This is because an increase in wealth causes current consumption expenditures to rise. With current real disposable income unchanged, any rise in current consumption requires a fall in current saving.

The market rate of interest has a positive effect on the level of real saving because the interest rate is the opportunity cost of present consumption expenditures. The greater the market rate of interest, the greater the cost (in terms of interest income that is forgone) of present real consumption expenditures. As discussed in the previous chapter, for the aggregate economy the substitution effect of a rise in the market rate of interest will always outweigh the income effect. Therefore, an increase in the market rate will always cause the substitution of future consumption expenditures for present consumption expenditures. According to the household sector's budget identity, a decrease in present real consumption with real disposable income fixed implies an increase in present real saving. Therefore, a rise in the market rate of interest generates a rise in aggregate real saving.

Based on this reasoning, the aggregate real saving function in general notational form is written:

$$\frac{S}{P} = j\left[\underset{+}{i}, \underset{+}{\left(\frac{Y}{P}\right)_d}, \underset{-}{\left(\frac{W}{P}\right)}\right] \tag{6.1}$$

However, for an economy that sustains full employment, a constant level of real taxation, and no shocks to its productive capacity, the level of current real disposable income, $(Y/P)_d$, and real wealth, (W/P), do not change, and the aggregate real saving function may be simply expressed as:

$$\frac{S}{P} = \underset{+}{j}(i) \tag{6.1'}$$

As discussed in the previous chapter, the level of aggregate real investment expenditures varies inversely with the market rate of interest. As the market rate of interest rises, according to the present value formula, the present value of all prospective physical capital investment projects declines. New physical capital goods will be desired only if their present value exceeds their cost. Therefore, as the present value of all physical capital goods falls, fewer newly produced capital goods will be desired by business firms. Aggregate net real investment expenditures, defined as the increase in the stock of physical capital goods in the economy, therefore, varies inversely with the market rate of interest.

The aggregate net real investment expenditures relation is:

$$\frac{I}{P} = \underset{-}{m}(i) \tag{6.2}$$

Because government interest payments vary directly with the interest rate, the deficit of the government sector could be influenced negatively by the market rate of interest. However, this effect is usually considered insignificant. The level of real income could affect the government deficit to the extent that real income tax receipts vary directly with the level of real income. In this case, real income tax receipts rise and the deficit of the government sector shrinks as the level of real income rises. The government deficit relation in notational form in this instance is:

$$\left(\frac{G}{P} - \frac{T}{P}\right) = h\underset{-}{\left(\frac{Y}{P}\right)} \tag{6.3}$$

However if we assume that the economy sustains a full-employment level of real income and abstract from the effect of bracket creep on tax receipts, real income tax receipts will not change, and the government deficit may be viewed as given:

$$\left(\frac{G}{P} - \frac{T}{P}\right) = \left(\frac{\overline{G}}{P} - \frac{\overline{T}}{P}\right) \tag{6.3'}$$

The bars above the variables indicate that the magnitudes of real government expenditures (G/P) and real government taxation (T/P) are assumed to be exogenously determined.

To round out the credit market model, a credit market equilibrium condition is needed which says that equilibrium will occur when the supply of credit is equal to the demand for credit:

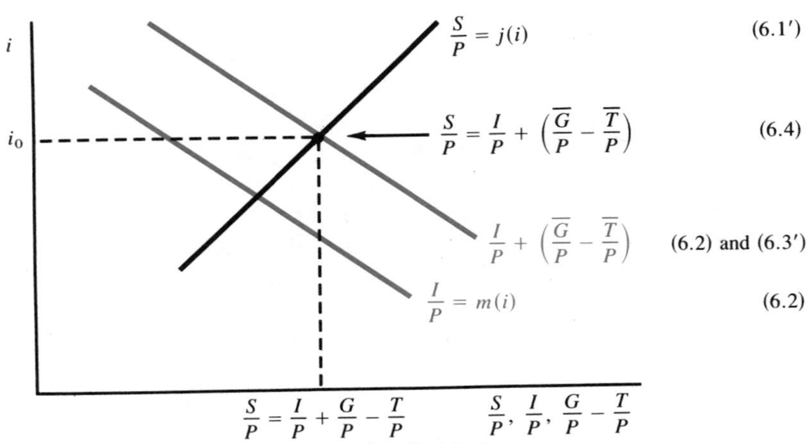

Figure 6.1 Equilibrium in the Credit Market

$$\frac{S}{P} = \frac{I}{P} + \left(\frac{G}{P} - \frac{T}{P}\right) \tag{6.4}$$

where S/P is the quantity supplied and $I/P + (G/P - T/P)$ is the quantity demanded.

Figure (6.1) graphically plots Equations (6.1′), (6.2), (6.3′) and (6.4). At the market rate of interest (i_0) equilibrium is brought to the credit market; at this interest rate supply and demand are in balance. The quantity of real saving that flows into the credit market is just equal to the quantity that is demanded by business firms to finance real investment expenditures plus quantity that is demanded by government to finance its deficit.

Measuring the Government Deficit

Traditionally, members of Congress have found it difficult to promote and vote for increases in taxes. However, it is considerably less difficult for them to vote for increases in government expenditures or to vote for tax cuts. As a result in recent decades our nation has had a chronic government deficit. Science fiction writer Robert Heinlein once described Congress as "a creature that has nine stomachs and no head." Members of Congress seem to behave as though they can deliver the largesse of government spending programs to their constituents without it costing anyone anything since taxes have not increased. In other words, since deficit-financed government purchases of goods and services and government transfer payments to households make some people better off (those who benefit from the government programs) and no one immediately has to pay higher taxes, an increase in the government deficit may appear to be a "free lunch."[1]

This perception is irrational. As pointed out in Chapter Five, any sector that spends more than it takes in is constrained to finance (to borrow) the difference. The government

[1]See, for example, James M. Buchanan and Richard E. Wagner, *Democracy in Deficit* (New York: Academic Press, 1977).

sector, as all sectors, has a *financing constraint*. The financing constraint specifies that when spending exceeds receipts, there is a deficit, and borrowing must equal that deficit. When the government sector increases its real expenditures without increasing its real tax receipts, it must make up the difference by borrowing more in the credit market. An increase in the government deficit is coextensive with an increase in the demand for credit by government.

Table 6.1 reports the actual growth in the size of federal government expenditures and deficits from 1968 to 1985 and the projected growth in these magnitudes to 1990. Since 1968, nominal federal government expenditures have increased almost sixfold. The federal deficit has gone from a small surplus in 1969 to deficits of over $60 billion in 1980 and 1981 and around $200 billion in the mid-1980's. In nine of the eleven years from 1975 to 1985, the deficit has exceeded $40 billion.[2]

Another way to measure the burden of government expenditures and government deficits is to view them as a percentage of gross national product (GNP). Table 6.1 shows that federal government expenditures rose from around 20 percent of GNP in the early 1970s to 24 percent of GNP in 1985. The federal deficit, which was never greater than 2 percent of GNP in the 1960s, has been less than 2 percent of GNP in only two of the eleven years from 1975 to 1985. Table 6.1 also reveals that the deficit varies considerably from year to year. This occurs in part because, as discussed above, the income tax receipts of the federal government rise in years of boom (such as 1973, 1979, and 1986) and fall during years of recession (such as 1970, 1975, and 1980–1982).

Yet another measure of the burden of government deficits is the ratio of outstanding federal debt to GNP. Table 6.1 shows that the outstanding debt rose from $369.8 billion in 1968 to $1,827.5 billion in 1985 and from 35.7 percent of GNP in 1975 to 46.4 percent of GNP in 1985. As we shall see in later discussions, the ratio of debt to GNP is an interesting gauge of our ability to tolerate deficits.

At this writing, prospects for improvement in the near future are uncertain. The tax cuts of the early 1980s (discussed below), together with the relentless growth in defense spending, medicare and Social Security and the interest cost on the exploding federal debt have caused the expenditures-revenue gap to persist. The expenditures projected for 1986 to 1990 are sizable. Expenditures of government are projected to grow steadily, continuing to absorb over one-fifth of GNP. The deficits themselves, however, are projected under two very different scenarios. In column 4 of Table 6.1, the deficit remains rather sizable, still soaking up well over 2 percent of GNP. However, in column 5, under the deficit-cutting provisions of the Gramm-Rudman-Hollings Act (GRH), the deficit shrinks steadily, with a balanced budget arising in 1991 and beyond. This legislation requires specific reductions in the deficit in five successive years from 1987 to 1991. What makes these prospects uncertain is that most of the GRH Act has been declared unconstitutional because it deprives Congress of regular budgetary discretion. Let us assume, however, that Congress will attempt to achieve the GRH goals.

[2]Deficits are not a partisan problem. The evidence in Table 6.1 shows that deficits grow under Republican and Democratic administrations alike. Back in 1980 when Jimmy Carter was piling up $62 billion of red ink, the Republicans warned the nation that if we voted for Carter we would have the biggest deficits in history. Well, many people did vote for Carter and, by golly, the Republicans were right!

Table 6.1 Federal Government Expenditures and Deficits

	Billions of Dollars								Percent of GNP							
Year	Expenditures		Deficits		Debt		Interest		Expenditures		Deficits		Debt		Interest	
1968	178.1		−25.2		369.8		11.1		20.9		−3.0		43.4		1.3	
1969	183.6		3.2		367.1		12.7		19.8		0.3		39.5		1.4	
1790	195.6		−2.8		382.6		14.4		19.8		−0.3		43.6		1.5	
1971	210.2		−23.0		409.5		14.8		19.8		−2.2		38.7		1.4	
1972	230.7		−23.4		437.3		15.5		20.0		−2.0		38.0		1.4	
1973	245.7		−14.9		468.4		17.3		19.1		−1.2		36.4		1.4	
1974	269.4		−6.1		486.2		21.4		19.0		−0.4		34.3		1.6	
1975	332.3		−53.2		544.1		23.2		21.8		−3.5		35.7		1.6	
1976	371.8		−73.7		631.9		26.7		21.9		−4.3		37.2		1.6	
1977	409.2		−53.6		709.1		29.9		21.1		−2.8		36.6		1.6	
1978	458.7		−59.2		780.4		35.4		21.1		−2.7		35.9		1.7	
1979	503.5		−40.2		833.8		42.6		20.5		−1.6		34.0		1.8	
1980	590.9		−73.8		914.3		52.5		22.2		−2.8		34.3		2.0	
1981	678.2		−78.9		1,003.9		98.7		22.7		−2.6		33.6		2.4	
1982	745.7		−127.9		1,147.0		85.0		23.7		−4.1		36.5		2.8	
1983	808.3		−207.8		1,381.9		89.8		24.3		−6.3		41.6		2.8	
1984	851.8		−185.3		1,576.7		111.1		23.1		−5.0		42.7		3.1	
1985	946.3	w/G-R-H	−212.3	w/G-R-H	1,827.5	w/G-R-H	129.4	w/G-R-H	24.0	w/G-R-H	−5.4	w/G-R-H	46.4	w/G-R-H	3.4	w/G-R-H
1986	982.0	979.9	−205.6	−202.8		2,112.0		142.7	23.4	23.4	−4.9	−4.8		50.4		3.4
1987	1,025.9	994.0	−181.8	−143.6		2,320.6		148.0	22.6	21.9	−4.0	−3.2		51.1		3.4
1988	1,077.3	1,026.8	−150.0	−93.6		2,509.0		145.1	22.0	20.9	−3.1	−1.9		51.2		3.2
1989	1,128.1	1,063.6	−138.9	−67.5		2,684.3		136.0	21.4	20.2	−2.6	−1.3		50.9		2.8
1990	1,179.3	1,093.8	−126.3	−35.8		2,841.4		125.6	20.5	19.5	−2.2	−0.6		50.5		2.4

Source: Actual figures for 1968 to 1985, U.S. Department of Commerce. Projected figures for 1986 to 1990 (in dollars of 1986 purchasing power), U.S. Office of Management and the Budget. w/G-R-H means with Gramm-Rudman-Hollings.

Table 6.2 Actual and Cyclically Adjusted Federal Budget Deficits (in billions of dollars)

Year	Cyclically Adjusted Deficit	Actual Deficit
1978	− 46.5	− 29.2
1981	− 55.6	− 60.0
1983	− 77.0	−195.4
1984	−171.3	−185.3
1986	−227.0	−205.6

Source: Actual deficits: U.S. Department of Commerce; cyclically adjusted deficits: Congressional Budget Office.

The first way to achieve these goals is to reduce government expenditures. Column 3 of Table 6.1 indicates that even under GRH sweeping cuts in spending are not considered feasible; government expenditures continue to eat up about 20 percent of GNP. Since government spending is projected to rise, the only way the deficit can be reduced to the GRH target levels is by raising taxation.[3]

The data reported in Table 6.1 do not present the impact of federal deficits relative to other flows in credit markets. In Chapter Five, Table 5.1 revealed that in each year between 1974 and 1985, the federal deficit has absorbed between 15 and 85 percent of total personal saving plus net business saving (retained earnings). It absorbed over half of the sum of personal saving and net business saving in seven of these twelve years. In 1985, the deficit soaked up over 75 percent of personal saving plus net business saving.

Many fiscal analysts prefer to work with the *cyclically adjusted deficit* or *surplus,* sometimes called the structural deficit or surplus. The cyclically adjusted deficit or surplus is calculated by projecting what government tax receipts would have been had the economy been at full employment level of GNP in a given year. (Full employment is defined in two ways: the lowest unemployment rate in the previous business cycle or 6 percent of the labor force.) Thus, the cyclically adjusted deficit is a standardized measure, one which corrects the deficit for changes in income. Because tax receipts rise and expenditures remain unchanged (or even decline) as GNP rises, the magnitude of the actual government deficit varies inversely with GNP, whereas the cyclically adjusted deficit is invariant with respect to changes in GNP.

According to many fiscal analysts, the most desirable high employment budget should generate no deficit or even a small surplus. Fiscal analysts argue that ideally the cyclically adjusted deficit should disappear or even turn into a surplus in boom years. Under this ideal, government does not chronically drain resources from the credit market.

Unfortunately, using the cyclically adjusted deficit concept, federal government in

[3]The official figures presented in Table 6.1 seriously understate the actual deficit for two reasons. First, the government uses an accounting procedure that keeps numerous expenditures "off budget." Off budget borrowing has grown from $1 billion per year in fiscal 1974 to $3 billion per year in fiscal 1985. A second major involvement consists of government-sponsored agencies which guarantee or insure loan principal repayments, for instance, to support private housing or to aid an ailing private corporation. This represents a subsidy by government to select private borrowers. The stock of government debt would be about $350 billion greater if it included the obligations of these institutions.

recent years (and in the foreseeable future) would still drain resources from the credit market in a period of economic prosperity. Table 6.2 reports the actual federal deficit and the cyclically adjusted deficit for 1978, 1981, 1983, 1984 and 1986. These data show that even if these were years of prosperity, the federal government would have absorbed, and will continue to absorb, a significant amount of resources in the credit market.

Four Models of the Crowding Out of Private Expenditures by Government Expenditures

Model I: The Deficit in a Partial Equilibrium Model of a Closed Economy Where Real Disposable Income Is Unchanging. An increase in the demand for credit by government means that resources have to be reallocated. As long as real income is unchanged at the full employment level (discussed in Chapter Three), the pool of real income available to be used for real consumption expenditures, real investment expenditures, or real government expenditures will be unchanged. Therefore, as long as real income is unchanged, and as long as we assume a closed economy with no flow of funds from abroad, if one class of expenditures, say government expenditures, rises, one or both of the other types of expenditures, consumption and investment expenditures, must decline. If the necessary decrease in consumption or investment expenditures does not occur through greater taxation, for instance because of the reluctance of elected officials to raise taxes, then it must be brought about in the credit market, where government must finance its deficit.

This model of the credit market can now be applied to analyze the effect of an increased deficit of the government sector. Assume that the deficit increases because of an increase in government expenditures that is not matched by an increase in government tax receipts. To the initial level of government expenditures minus government tax receipts, $\overline{G}/P - \overline{T}/P$, is added the increase in government spending, $\Delta G/P$.

In this analysis, and in those of the models that follow, there are three conditions. The first is that the increase in government expenditures be permanent. Temporary swings in government spending would not be a significant drain on private resources because they would be quickly reversed in the future. This would mitigate their impact in the other three models.

The second condition is that the gain in utility plus the gain in productivity and output from the *public* services that arise from increased government expenditures do not offset the loss in utility plus the loss in productivity and output from the reduction in private expenditures. If this assumption were not made—if private citizens were, in the aggregate, always as well off after the increase in government expenditures—the effects discussed in this model would not hold.

The third condition is that we abstract from the effects of the increase in government expenditures (in boosting the interest rate, increasing the value of the dollar in terms of foreign currency, or reducing wealth) on the labor market. Specifically, as discussed in Chapter Three, increases in the interest rate or permanent reductions in real income could cause increases in the quantity of labor hours supplied.

Figure 6.2 illustrates the effect of an increased government deficit. The demand for credit shifts to the right by the amount of the increase in government spending ($\Delta G/P$).

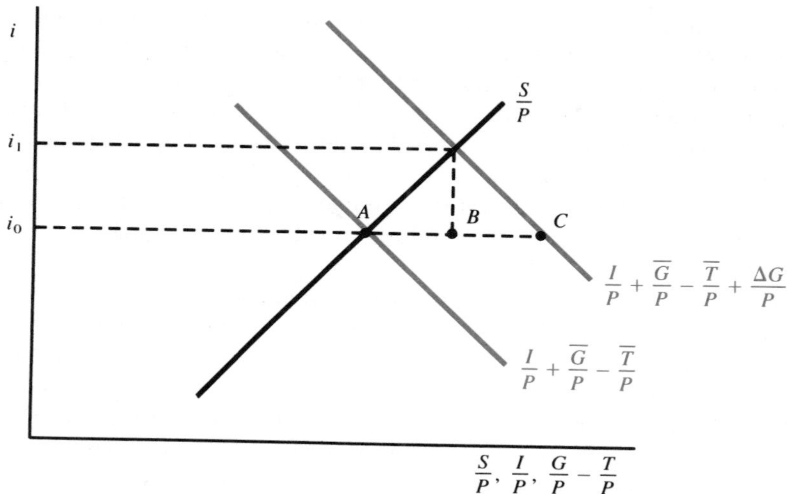

Figure 6.2 Effect of an Increase in the Government Deficit in a Closed Economy Where Real Disposable Income Is Unchanging

The increase in the deficit of government ($\Delta G/P$) is the directed distance AC in Figure 6.2. At the initial equilibrium rate of interest i_0 with the increase in demand, there will be an excess demand for credit. Quantity demanded in Figure 6.2 exceeds quantity supplied by AC. This excess demand should drive up the price of credit, the market rate of interest. As the market rate of interest rises, two things happen which will ultimately restore equilibrium to the credit market: Because of the higher price of credit, quantity demanded will decrease, and quantity supplied will increase. The increase in quantity supplied and the decrease in quantity demanded will, at the new equilibrium interest rate, just offset the initial increase in demand.

Figure 6.2 shows the process whereby supply and demand are balanced. The increased demand for credit spurs the interest rate upward from i_0 to i_1. At the new equilibrium interest rate i_1 there is an increase in the quantity of credit supplied (AB) and a decrease in the quantity of credit demanded (CB). The initial increase in demand (AC) is offset because $AC = AB + CB$.

The increase in the real deficit spending of government $AC(= \Delta G/P)$ causes the interest rate to be bid upward because government is borrowing more heavily to garner the funds to finance its swollen deficit. Part of the jump in government borrowing is offset by a decrease in real private investment expenditures (BC) brought about by the increase in the interest rate from i_0 to i_1. The other part of the boost in borrowing is offset by a decrease in real private consumption expenditures (AB), which is also brought about by the hike in the interest rate. The household sector's budget identity shows that with real income and taxation unchanged, any increase in real saving must result in an equal-sized reduction in consumption expenditures. Therefore, the increase in real saving (AB) is identical to a reduction in real private consumption expenditures.

Thus, in a full employment economy where real income is unchanging, an increase in real government expenditures must be offset by an equal-sized decrease in real private expenditures. In Figure 6.2, the increase in the real deficit expenditures of government (AC) caused an equal-sized reduction in the sum of real private investment expenditures and real private consumption expenditures. In a fully employed economy there will be a *complete crowding out* of private expenditures by government expenditures. Because the deficit is a flow, it will be repeated at this level year after year. All things being equal, the interest rate will remain at i_1, and complete crowding out will persist year after year.[4]

Model II: The Effect of an Increase in the Deficit in a Closed Economy Where Real Income May Change. The preceding analysis is concerned only with the size of the current deficit relative to current saving. It could be argued that a *temporary* rise in the deficit and resulting temporary crowding out is no cause for alarm. According to this view, citizens and policymakers need only be concerned about deficits that are sustained over a long period of time. The preceding analysis also assumed that when the deficit increased current disposable income was unchanging. If current disposable income increased at the same time that the deficit rose, then the saving function and the demand curve for credit would shift rightward at the same time. The interest rate would not increase as much because part of the increased demand for credit would be satisfied by new saving out of the increase in disposable income.

Government bonds are a stock, the deficit is a flow. Government bonds come into existence because of deficits. An increase in the stock of outstanding government bonds in the current period must equal the size of the deficit in that period. In Chapter Five we learned that current aggregate income is the source of all current saving. As income grows, saving increases. Saving can take place in many different forms. One way is for private citizens to buy government bonds. If government bonds are not considered inferior goods, as income increases the demand for government bonds will rise.

Given these principles, it follows that if income and saving are expected to grow as fast as the stock of government bonds, the new debt can be absorbed into private wealth holdings without its having to generate a significantly higher interest rate. In terms of Model I, a rightward shift in the demand for credit on the part of government would be matched by a rightward shift in the supply of credit.

On the other hand, if the stock of government debt is expected to grow faster than aggregate income, those bonds will not be readily absorbed by private asset holders, unless they offer a significantly higher interest rate.

Let the annual stock of outstanding government bonds at time t be noted as B_t; at time $t - 1$, it is B_{t-1}. In nominal terms, government deficit has two components: the "primary deficit," $(G' - T)_t = X_t$, and the interest cost of government, $i \cdot B_{t-1}$. Therefore the stock of government debt at any time grows in the following manner:

[4]One school of thought contends that complete crowding out will occur without a rise in the interest rate. Consumption and investment expenditures will fall in anticipation of higher future taxes to pay the interest on the increased government debt. From this perspective, bond-financed deficits are merely the equivalent of deferred taxation. This is called the *Ricardian equivalence principle* after its original advocate, the early nineteenth century English economist, David Ricardo. It is discussed below.

$$B_t = X_t + (1 + i)B_{t-1} \tag{6.5}$$

Next we reexpress every term in Equation (6.5) as a ratio to nominal income (Y_t):

$$B_t/Y_t = X_t/Y_t + (1 + i)B_{t-1}/Y_t \tag{6.6}$$

If nominal income is growing at the rate g,

$$Y_t = (1 + g)Y_{t-1} \tag{6.7}$$

Substituting this into the last term of Equation (6.6) and expressing the ratios as lowercase letters yields

$$b_t = x_t + \frac{(1 + i)}{(1 + g)\, b_{t-1}} \tag{6.8}$$

If the ratio of government debt to aggregate nominal income is expected to increase in the future, it will cause the current interest rate to rise. The ratio, b_t, would be expected to grow for two reasons: Either the primary deficit is expected to grow relative to aggregate nominal income or the interest rate (i) exceeds the expected growth rate of aggregate nominal income (g). Thus, if we treat the ratio of the primary deficit to nominal income (x_t) as a constant, the interest rate will rise whenever $i > g$.

This result presents an interesting threshold effect. Whenever the interest rate is less than or equal to the growth rate of nominal income, there is still crowding out because the government is absorbing private resources, but the interest rate does not rise and crowding out does not become proportionately greater. However, if the interest rate exceeds the expected growth rate of nominal income, the interest rate and the ratio of the stock of government debt to aggregate nominal income must rise without limit. According to this model, just as soon as the economy trips over the $i = g$ threshold we get runaway debt, an ever-rising interest rate, and crowding out explodes. To avoid this gloomy scenario, policymakers must either control the primary deficit or adopt policies that will make nominal income grow at a rate that exceeds the interest rate.

One problem with this simple-minded partial equilibrium model is that nothing in economics or in nature ever grows without limit. There are indeed constraints to growth in the ratio of government debt to GNP. For instance, we can ultimately allocate no more than our total income to purchasing the newly issued debt of government. But even before this point is reached government bonds become superfluous. The ever rising interest rate will be seen in Chapters Nine and Eleven to cause an ever rising price level. Thus, an unchecked government deficit not only leads to higher and higher interest rates, it will also generate accelerating inflation.

Model III: The Effect of an Increase in Deficit in a Partial Equilibrium Model of an Open Economy. In the previous models we assumed that the economy was closed and that there was no flow of funds from abroad; the additional credit demands of government were met entirely in the domestic credit market. Now let us go to the other extreme and assume that the economy is open and that the additional credit demands of government are met entirely by borrowing abroad. This means that now in addition to real disposable income, the interest rate is also held conceptually constant and prevented from doing the work of clearing the market. We continue to assume a fully employed economy.

In order to finance the increase in the deficit, government is now assumed to have to borrow from foreigners. The borrowing is assumed to take place at an interest rate that is fixed by the world supply of and demand for credit. Other financial flows between the United States and abroad are assumed to be zero. From these assumptions it follows that in order for foreigners to obtain a flow of dollars to lend to our government they must either earn it by selling more of their newly produced goods and services to us or allocate less of the flow of dollars that they have already earned to buying our newly produced goods and services. The market-clearing variable that induces these adjustments is the price of the dollar in terms of a unit of foreign exchange, say, the British pound.

The private demand for dollars by foreigners is assumed to depend only on the flow of real exports (X/P). The higher the pound price of the dollar (£/$), the more expensive for foreigners are goods produced domestically for export and the smaller is the flow demand for dollars:

$$\frac{X}{P} = \underset{-}{X(£/\$)} \tag{6.9}$$

The private supply of dollars by foreigners in this foreign exchange market depends on the flow of real imports (I_m/P). The higher the pound price of the dollar (£/$), the lower the dollar price of the pound ($/£), the greater the domestic demand for goods and services produced abroad, and the greater the flow supply of dollars:

$$\frac{I_m}{P} = \underset{+}{I_m(£/\$)} \tag{6.10}$$

Initially we assume no international financial flows—that is, zero international borrowing or lending—such that imports and exports must be in balance in order for the market to clear:

$$\frac{I_m}{P} = \frac{X}{P} \tag{6.11}$$

Figure 6.3 depicts the foreign exchange market. At the initial value of the dollar, $(£/\$)_0$, the market clears. Imports equal exports. There is no trade deficit or trade surplus.

Next, assume that the government deficit increases by $\Delta G/P$ and it must borrow $\Delta G/P$. Assume that government can attract these funds by offering slightly higher interest

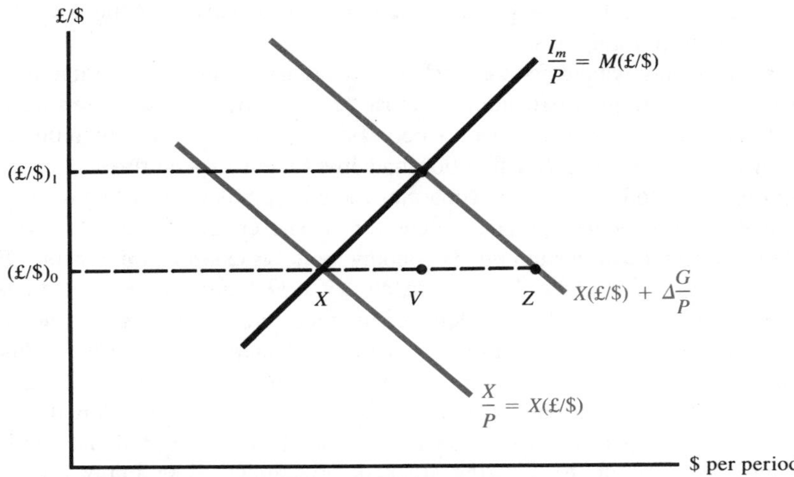

Figure 6.3 Effect of an Increase in the Deficit in an Open Economy

rates on the bonds that it must newly issue in the amount $\Delta G/P$. In order to purchase these bonds, foreigners must first convert $\Delta G/P$ of their currency into dollars. The increased demand for dollars in the foreign exchange market is depicted in Figure 6.3 as a rightward shift in the demand curve from $X(£/\$)$ to $X(£/\$) + \Delta G/P$.

At the initial equilibrium value of the dollar $(£/\$)_0$, with the increase in demand there will be an excess demand of *XZ*. The excess demand should drive up the pound price of the dollar as foreigners exchange their pounds in order to obtain the necessary dollars to purchase the newly issued government debt. As the international value of the dollar rises, two things will happen: The quantity of dollars supplied will increase, and the quantity of dollars demanded will decrease.

Figure 6.3 shows how supply and demand are balanced. The pound price of the dollar is bid upward from $(£/\$)_0$ to $(£/\$)_1$. At the new equilibrium price, $(£/\$)_1$, there is an increase in quantity supplied (*XV*) and a decrease in quantity demanded (*ZV*). The initial increase in demand for dollars (*XZ*) is offset because $XZ = XV + ZV$.

The increase in the quantity of dollars supplied (*XV*) occurs because as the value of the dollar rises against the pound, imports become cheaper and fewer dollars are required to obtain any goods or services produced abroad. Individuals reallocate their fixed disposable income away from purchasing domestically produced goods and services in order to acquire cheaper imports. Thus, domestic expenditures are *crowded out* by import substitution.

The decrease in the quantity of dollars demanded (*ZV*) occurs because as the dollar rises in value against the pound, our goods and services produced for export become more expensive for foreigners. Private expenditures on our exports are crowded out. Because imports now exceed exports, there is a trade deficit. The trade deficit is a symptom of crowding out. In the present model it is coextensive with the flow of government borrowing from foreigners.

Thus, in a full employment economy where government finances its deficit abroad, the increase in real government expenditures must be offset by an equal-sized decrease in real private expenditures consisting of a decrease in private export expenditures and a decrease in private domestic consumption and investment expenditures. In this simple partial equilibrium model of an open economy, there is complete crowding out of import-sensitive and export-oriented private expenditures. The effect of the deficit in a more sophisticated, general equilibrium open economy model is examined in Chapter Fifteen.

Model IV: The Effect of an Increase in Deficit under the Conditions of Ricardian Equivalence. All of the preceding models can be interpreted as having one shortcoming: They are inconsistent with the assumption, made in Chapter Five, that individuals have perfect information and forecast future real disposable income over their respective planning periods. If this assumption is true, then regardless of whether the deficit is financed internally as in Models I and II or externally as in Model III, individuals will realize that the interest costs on the growing stock of government debt imply higher future taxation and lower future real disposable income. If the individual planning period extends to the times in which taxation will be increased, the preceding models are incorrectly specified.

The decision to finance the deficit by borrowing in the current period is, in reality, the *equivalent* of a governmental decision to raise taxation in the future. Even if bonds issued by government are never retired, they generate higher future interest costs for the government. Future taxation must increase to meet these costs. If private individuals plan as far into the future as government, these future increases in taxation must by seen as reducing future real disposable income. As defined in Chapter Five, wealth is the present discounted value of expected future real disposable income. Therefore, these future taxation increases cause a decline in wealth.

This view is consistent with the idea, developed in Chapter Two, that government bonds are not part of aggregate wealth. It is associated with the thought of the early nineteenth-century British economist, David Ricardo.

Ricardian equivalence is based on two general conditions. The first is that individuals have planning periods that go as far into the future as that of government. For instance, if taxation is to be levied on a future generation, present-day households must view this as reducing their wealth. The second condition is that government expenditures must not generate a greater return to society than the private expenditures that they crowd out. That is, government expenditures must not increase aggregate wealth, even though they completely crowd out private expenditures. If these two conditions do not hold, wealth does not decrease as much as the present value of the increase in future taxation.

If these conditions hold, we can depict the effect of an increase in government expenditures that is the equivalent of a rise in future taxation and a decrease in the wealth of prospective taxpayers. Figure 6.4 illustrates this Ricardian equivalence model. The initial point of equilibrium is A. The increase in the real deficit causes the demand for credit to increase by AB. This distance measures the market value of expected future interest income (and principal repayments, if any) on the bonds that were newly issued by

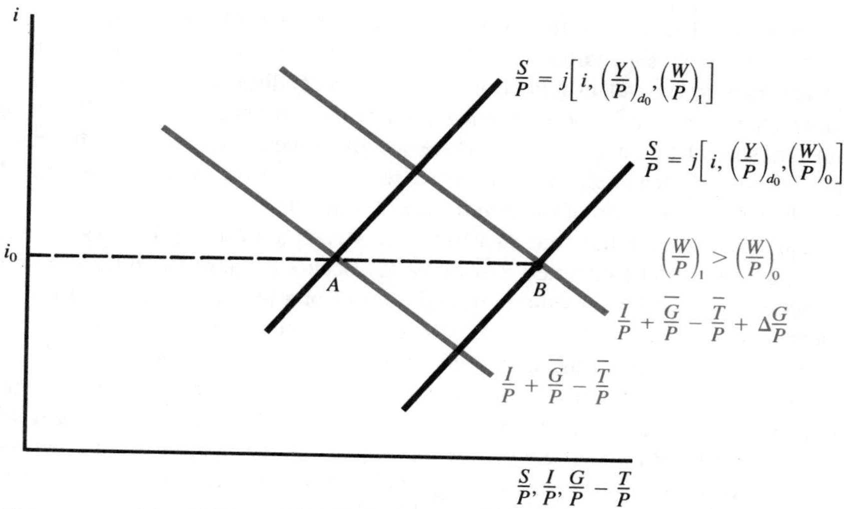

Figure 6.4 Effect of an Increase in the Deficit under Conditions of Ricardian Equivalence

government to finance the deficit. It also measures the present value of the future taxation needed to meet the future interest payments (and principal repayments) of government. Thus, *AB* is also a measure of the decrease in wealth.

In order to set aside resources to enable themselves or their heirs to meet increased future taxation obligations, individuals must currently save *AB* out of current real disposable income. Thus, the demand for and supply of credit both shift rightward by *AB*. The interest rate is unchanged at i_0. Even though the interest rate is unchanged, crowding out is still complete. This follows from the sectoral budget identity, which says that as long as current real disposable income is unchanged, an increase in current real saving requires an offsetting decrease in current real consumption.

Viewed another way, $\Delta G/P$ is the increase in government expenditures. Government exchanges newly issued bonds with a present value of $\Delta G/P$ in order to obtain the resources to make expenditures of $\Delta G/P$. The wealth of individuals who make this trade is unchanged; they have given up resources for bonds. Now taxpayers as a group are less wealthy by the same amount, $\Delta G/P$, because this is the present value of their increased future tax liability to make the interest payments and principal repayments on the newly issued bonds. Current consumption falls and current saving rises by the same absolute amount as the decrease in wealth. Therefore, current saving increases in the same amount by which government expenditures increase.[5]

[5]For further detail on Ricardian equivalence see the articles by Joseph Bryant and Milton Friedman cited in the bibliography to this chapter. Crowding out in an open economy is discussed in the article by the Congressional Budget Office in the bibliography to this chapter. Growth in the ratio of government debt to GNP and its implications are discussed in three separate articles by Preston Miller, Preston Miller and Thomas Sargent, and Michael Darby in the bibliography to this chapter.

Remember that if taxpayers are not fully concerned about future generations or if the increased government expenditures make individuals feel better off (happier and more productive) than an equivalent reduction in private expenditures makes them feel worse off, current saving will not rise (and current consumption expenditures will not fall) in the same (absolute) amount as the increase in government expenditures. In this case, complete crowding out is helped out by the rise in the interest rate, as in Models I and II, or by the rise in the value of the dollar, as in Model III.

It should be kept in mind that in Models I, III, and IV there is always complete crowding out. In Model I complete crowding out occurs because the interest rate rises, and in Model III complete crowding out is the result of a hike in the value of the dollar. The Ricardian equivalence case, Model IV, generates complete crowding out because future taxation is seen as rising and wealth declines. Therefore the sectoral impact of complete crowding out depends on the model one has in mind. In Model I crowding out will occur in interest-sensitive sectors of the economy. In Model III the impact will be on export-oriented and import-sensitive sectors. In Model IV the burden of crowding out is carried by prospective taxpayers. Clearly one's attitude toward the adverse aspects of government deficits depends on how the burden of crowding out is borne.

Of course, in Model II, crowding out will occur, but it need not generate higher interest rates if there is sufficient growth in income to yield the saving that will satisfy the increased borrowing needs of government. In that model if the flow of new saving is sufficiently large relative to the deficit, crowding out will actually decrease over time. This possibility is carried to an extreme in Chapter Seven. There we shall examine a model in which the increase in income is so great that crowding out never even occurs. In that model an increase in the deficit does more than merely absorb some of the saving that arises from ongoing increases in income. In the model of Chapter Seven an increase in the deficit actually *causes* so great a rise in aggregate income that not only is enough saving generated to finance the increase in the deficit but some is left over to allow a rise in private expenditures. This reflects the famous Keynesian multiplier effect.

The Consequences of Crowding Out

An upsurge in the real government deficit necessitates greater government borrowing. Models I and II in the preceding section indicate that increased borrowing drives up the interest rate. At a higher rate of interest, the present values of the prospective private capital spending projects of business firms fall. Part of the potential flow of new investment spending will be delayed or canceled. The level of private capital formation will decline. Fewer new homes, factories, and machines will be built. Fewer new production processes (embodying the latest technology) will be put on line. Increased real government spending will have crowded out real private investment. According to this reasoning, the steady uptrend in the federal deficit as a percentage of GNP since 1968 in Table 6.1 helps to explain the downtrend in private nonresidential fixed investment as a percentage of GNP in Chart 6.2 over the same period. The ratio of investment expenditures to GNP has averaged about 30 percent less in the last decade than it was in the 1950s and 1960s.

The impact of interest rate changes is not uniform across different firms, industries, and sectors of the economy. Interest rate changes will have a more momentous shock on some parts of the economy than on others. In industries where production processes involve capital goods of a relatively lengthy useful life, the impact of variations in interest rate will be greater. The further out into the future that the stream of expected after-tax profit extends, the greater the thrust of an interest rate change on the present values of prospective capital spending projects. According to the present value formula

$$PV = \sum_{j=1}^{n} \frac{y_j}{(1 + i)^j}$$

the greater is j (the number of years into the future the expected after-tax profit stream extends) the higher the power to which $(1 + i)^j$ is carried. An industry that is severely affected by movements in interest rates is housing. Housing capital goods have a relatively long useful life (a relatively large j), thus interest rate increases significantly depress the present values of prospective housing investment projects. Therefore, investment expenditures in housing and in industries which produce housing supplies, such as lumber, are greatly curtailed by increases in interest rates.

Within any industry an advance in interest rates will effect a reallocation of a given capital spending budget toward short-lived, less durable capital spending projects. Reallocation occurs because the longer-lived (more durable) the capital spending project (the greater the j) the greater is the impact of an increase in interest rates on present value. Therefore, projects of a shorter useful life will be less affected than longer-lived projects. On balance, new capital goods will be less durable because of high interest rates. During periods of high interest rates no one should ask, “Why don’t they make ’em (capital goods) like they used to?”

The elevated interest rate associated with crowding out will stimulate real saving and reduce real consumption. At higher interest rates households will find it increasingly expensive to borrow to buy new automobiles, appliances, and vacations on credit. So, households as a whole will borrow less and save more. Again, increased real government spending will have crowded out real private consumption.

Model II in the previous section focused on deficits that persist over a long period of time and generate a steady rise in the ratio of government debt to GNP. Table 6.1 shows that in the United States the ratio of government debt to GNP has risen from .357 in 1975 to .467 in 1985. This increase suggests that either the primary deficit or the interest payments of government, or both, is rising relative to GNP. Table 6.1 reveals that the latter is occurring. The deficit rose from less than 3 percent of GNP in the late 1970s to 5.4 percent in 1985. Interest payments rose from less than 2 percent of GNP in the 1970s to 3.4 percent in 1985. Model II suggests that should this condition be allowed to continue, crowding out will become more and more severe and interest rates will go from out of mind to out of sight.

Model III indicated that crowding out is responsible for the U.S. trade deficit that went from less than \$100 billion in the 1970s to \$149 billion in 1985. According to this model, the impact of the deficit is particularly severe in sectors that depend heavily on exports, such as agriculture. The plight of the American farmer in the 1980s is partly ascribable to the government budget deficit. Also, according to this model the deficit will hit hard those industries that are sensitive to competition from imports. The demise of the U.S. textile and shoe industries, as well as the concern over foreign auto imports, may also be associated, in part, with the government deficit. According to this model, economic adversity in the farm areas of Nebraska and South Dakota, the lumber areas of the Northwest, and the automobile capitol of Detroit are partly the fault of runaway deficits. Hondas crowd Chevrolets out of our parking lots because government spending crowds out private spending in our economy.

Model IV takes a more sanguine view of the crowding out issue. Regardless of how government expenditures are financed, the U.S. taxpayer bears all of the burden. Crowding out does not impact on one sector more than another. It hurts everybody, because government spending requires another turn of the income tax screw, now and in the future.

The persistence of sizable real deficits over many years, implemented for often noble and high-minded purposes such as greater national military might, government aid to deserving groups, and so on, under any of the preceding models implies the crowding out of real private investment expenditures in at least some sectors of the economy. The persistence of deficits means that some parts of the nation's capital stock will not be replaced as rapidly; it will grow more obsolete. As the nation's capital stock fails to embody the latest technology, the productivity (output per person hour) of its workers will deteriorate. Real wages will slide. Efficiency in production will falter, especially when compared to productivity of nations where crowding out is not as pronounced. Real costs per unit of output will mount. As a result, goods and services produced abroad will gain a competitive advantage over domestically produced goods and services in world markets.

In an open economy, it may appear to the uninitiated that crowding out is not occurring because foreigners are supplying the funds needed by government. However, Model III in the preceding section shows that foreigners can buy our government's newly issued debt only if they have dollars. They can obtain these dollars only by selling us more of their output or reducing their purchases of our exports. When government finances its deficit internationally, the greater demand for dollars by foreigners raises the price of the dollar in terms of foreign currency. The stronger dollar causes us to increase our imports and reduce our exports. Therefore, an internationally financed increase in government expenditures causes complete crowding out in export-oriented sectors, such as lumber and agriculture, and in import-sensitive sectors, such as automobiles.

Many economists do not blame the deficit for high interest rates and the strong dollar. The Ricardian equivalence model suggests that an increase in the deficit is matched by a rise in domestic saving such that neither the interest rate nor the value of the dollar in international markets rises. However, even if this model is correct, the deficit is still responsible for complete crowding out. A rise in current saving with real disposable income unchanged requires an offsetting decrease in private consumption.

Crowding Out, the Balanced Budget, and "Supply-Side" Economic Policy

Because persistent crowding out of private expenditures by government deficit expenditures seems to generate economic difficulty, many people support the notion of an annually balanced government budget even if it means another turn of the income tax screw. Some even favor a balanced budget amendment to the Constitution. Others contend that government needs a ceiling on its expenditures, expressed as a percentage of GNP, that is fixed by law. Opponents of balancing the budget by raising income taxes contend that deficits are preferable to higher taxes as a means of financing government expenditures because income taxation falls on efficient and inefficient users of resources alike, while the high interest rate and high value of the dollar induced by the deficit only divert resources away from the least efficient users.[6]

Because of the doomsday view of deficits associated with Model II, the Ricardian equivalence view that a rise in the deficit has much the same effect as an increase in current taxation, and the belief that any increase in income tax rates destroys productive incentives, the emphasis in Congress in the mid-1980s was (1) on attempting to reduce government expenditures and (2) on raising taxes if expenditures could not be cut. The Gramm-Rudman-Hollings (GRH) Act attempted to impose this discipline on Congress. It required reductions in the deficit in specific dollar amounts in five successive fiscal years from 1987 to 1991. If across-the-board spending cuts cannot be effected and the GRH goals are followed, taxation must be raised. If they are achieved, the impact of these Congressional targets on the deficit will be significant. Since much of GRH has been declared unconstitutional, whether these initiatives will be effected or abandoned, particularly during periods of economic stress, is one of the great economic questions of our time.

Many argue that the budget can be balanced by building up our capacity to produce, thereby setting the stage for higher aggregate real income, a greater flow of real federal income tax receipts, a smaller deficit, and eventually, a balanced budget. Moreover, according to Model II, even if the budget is not balanced, as long as income growth is high and the primary deficit is under control, increases in the deficit will not cause crowding out. The key to this last scenario is to first build our productive capacity. Proposals here include reduction of costly government regulation of business; more rapid exploitation of natural resources on federal lands; government-sponsored incentives to encourage saving; and even government subsidies to high tech activities.

Perhaps the best known recent program that was intended to bolster our productive capacity as a nation was the Reagan administration's tax cut package of the early 1980s. These tax cuts were offered as a means of increasing the after-tax real rate of return to saving. They were also intended to increase the flow of future after-tax profit which would boost the present value of prospective private capital formation. As a result it was hoped that real saving and real investment spending would rise. Tax cuts on wage and salary

[6]Many favor a *consumption tax* or *value-added tax* as a means of reducing the deficit without choking off productive effort. See Chapter Fourteen for a discussion of tax reform.

income were intended to raise after-tax real wages so as to increase the supply of labor, as shown in Chapter Three. The resulting expected upsurge in the level of labor and capital inputs into production processes ideally was supposed to promote an increase in aggregate real income.

The partial equilibrium model of the credit market provides some insight into what has been labeled *supply-side economic policy*. If interest income is taxed by government, a cut in the tax rate will increase the after-tax interest return to savers and cause saving to increase at any given interest rate. The saving function in Figure 6.1 will shift to the right. If corporate profit is taxed by government, a cut in the tax rate will increase the expected after-tax profits on new capital spending projects. This will bolster the present values of these projects at any given interest rate. The investment function in Figure 6.1 will shift to the right. As long as the credit demand of government is unchanged or does not balloon because of the tax cuts, the equilibrium levels of saving and investment will rise and new capital formation will be forged. As new capital goods are put into production processes, aggregate output will rise.

The problem with supply-side economic policy tax cuts was that they helped to increase the deficit. Even with the economic boom of the mid-1980s, tax receipts never grew sufficiently to reduce the deficit. Whether the deficit caused crowding out because of a higher interest rate, a higher value of the dollar, or higher expected taxes, by 1987 Congress simply felt that the economy was not going to grow its way out of the deficit problem. Unfortunately, because of strong commitments to defense expenditures and Social Security payments, and because it could not default on its interest payments, there was little room to cut government spending; in the late 1980s, taxation increases loomed large. Because taxation increases require higher income tax rates, it was felt that they compromised the objectives of supply-side economic policy. Thus, coming hard on the heels of likely tax increases in the late 1980s is the issue of *tax reform*.

Tax reform would attempt to eliminate the disincentives for productive effort associated with higher tax rates, discussed above, while still preserving a sufficiently high level of tax receipts to reduce the deficit. To understand supply-side economic policy and to explore the subject of tax reform fruitfully, a general equilibrium model is required. These analyses will be provided in Chapter Fourteen.

Real and Nominal Rates of Interest and Inflationary Expectations

Changes in the rate of inflation affect interest rates. For example, if a lender is to receive a \$100 interest income on a \$1,000 loan for a period of one year, the nominal rate of interest is 10 percent. Nevertheless, if by the date of maturity of the loan, the price level has risen by 7 percent, the actual or *ex post real rate of interest* on the loan (r) will have been approximately 3 percent.[7] The purchasing power value of the principal of \$1,000 will have shrunk by 7 percent or \$70 in that year. Thus, even though interest income is \$100, the lender will have gained *real* purchasing power of only \$30 for a real return of only 3 percent on the principal of \$1,000. This relationship between actual inflation,

[7]The term *ex post* refers to an *actual* magnitude, but *ex ante* refers to an *expected* or *planned* magnitude.

the nominal interest rate, and the actual, or *ex post,* real interest rate may be approximated as

$$i = r + \frac{\Delta P/\Delta t}{P} \tag{6.12}$$

where $(\Delta P/\Delta t)/P$ is the discrete equivalent of $(dP/dt)/P$, or $\dot{P}$ for short, the derivative of the general price level with respect to time, expressed as a percentage.

If debtors and creditors have correct expectations regarding the increase in the future rate of inflation, the current nominal rate of interest will rise in the same amount as the anticipated rate of inflation. This is called the *price inflation expectations effect*. The relationship between expected inflation, the nominal interest rate, and the expected or *ex ante* real interest rate may be expressed as

$$i = r + \dot{P}_e \tag{6.13}$$

where $\dot{P}_e$ is the rate of price inflation that is expected to occur over the period of the loan.[8] From Equation (6.13) it should be clear that the higher the expected rate of inflation, at an unchanged nominal rate of interest, the lower the expected or *ex ante* real rate of interest. Unfortunately, the *ex ante* real rate of interest cannot be directly observed. Instead, taking the current nominal rate of interest, which can be observed in the credit market, and estimating the consensus for the expected rate of price inflation, the *ex ante* real rate of interest can be inferred:

$$r = i - \dot{P}_e \tag{6.14}$$

For example, if the observed, nominal market rate of interest on a one-year loan is 10 percent and the estimated expected rate of inflation for that year is 9 percent, the *ex ante* real rate of interest is approximately 1 percent.[9] This means that if one lends $1,000 for one year, one will receive $100 of interest income at the end of that year. The principal is expected to fall in value by $90 ($1,000 × 9 percent), and the expected or *ex ante* real dollar return on the loan of $1,000 will be only $10. The expected or *ex ante* real rate of interest for the year will be only 1 percent, $10/$1000 = 1 percent.

Unlike the expected, or *ex ante* real rate of interest, the actual *ex post* rate of interest is inferred from actual data on, instead of estimates of, the rate of inflation. Chart 6.1

[8]This is an approximation. More accurately, a $1 security has an expected real rate of interest of r where

$$(1 + i) = (1 + r)(1 + \dot{P}_e)$$

Thus,

$$i = r + \dot{P}_e + r\dot{P}_e$$

In Equation (6.13) the cross-product, $r \cdot \dot{P}_e$, is assumed to be insignificant because it is so small.

[9]More precisely, using the formula in footnote 8, $(1 + i)/(1 + \dot{P}_e) = (1 + r)$, $(1 + .10)/(1 + .09) = 1.00918$. The expected real rate of interest is .918 percent.

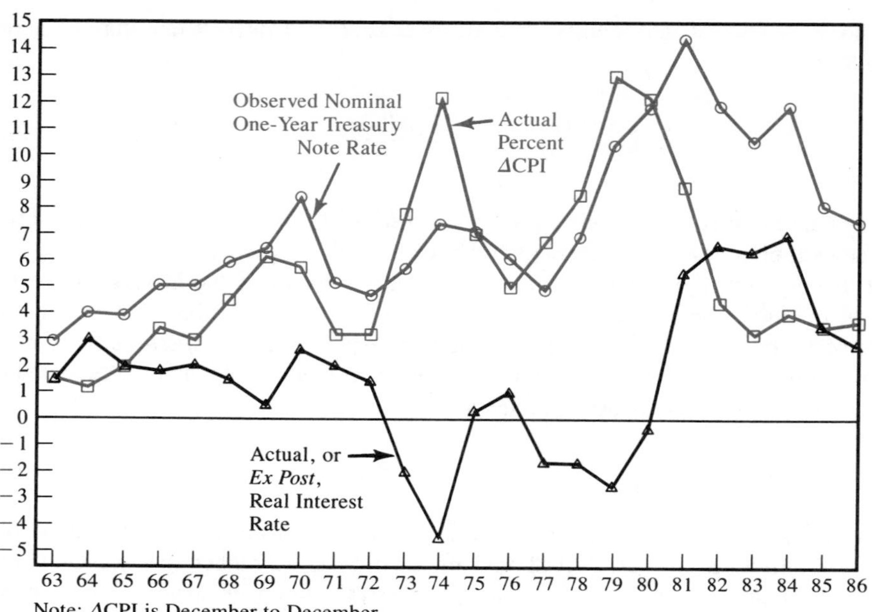

Chart 6.1 Nominal Interest Rate, Actual Inflation, and the *Ex Post* Real Interest Rate

illustrates how a change in the actual one-year rate of inflation that is greater than a change in the nominal one-year interest rate will affect the actual, *ex post* real rate of interest. For example, from 1967 to 1969 the annual rate of inflation leaped from 3 percent to 6 percent while the nominal interest rate on a one-year security only rose from 5 percent to 6 percent. As a result, the actual, *ex post* real rate of interest plunged 2 percentage points to nearly zero. As another example, when the annual rate of inflation dipped from 13 percent in 1979 to 6 percent in 1982, because the nominal interest rate rose from just over 10 percent in 1979 to just over 11 percent in 1982, the *ex post* real rate of interest advanced from minus 3 percent in 1979 to over 6 percent in 1982.[10] From 1983 to 1986, the nominal interest rate moved in the 6 to 9 percent range while inflation stayed between 3 and 4 percent per annum. Thus, the *ex post* real interest rate varied between 3 and 5 percent.

Now consider the effect of anticipated inflation in our model of the credit market. For simplicity, the credit demand of government is omitted. A distinction is now made between real and nominal rates of interest. Aggregate real saving and aggregate real investment depend on the expected real, and not the nominal, rate of interest. This analysis will assume that households and business firms have perfect information regard-

[10] The *ex post* real rate of interest in Chart 6.1 may not be the rate that borrowers and lenders actually expected to prevail. The expected *ex ante* real rate of interest depends on the expected rate of inflation, not the actual rate of inflation. For example, even though the *ex post* real interest rate was negative in 1973, 1974, 1977, 1978, 1979, and 1980, the *ex ante* real interest rate may have been positive. Market participants simply may have underestimated the rate of inflation in these years.

ing the expected rate of inflation. They make their respective decisions to save and invest in real terms. They react to the expected real, not the nominal, rate of interest. The real quantity of aggregate saving depends on the expected real rate of interest. For example, assume the household sector saved \$150 billion in 1988 and the rate of inflation was 10 percent. If the expected real rate of interest were unchanged from 1988, nominal saving in 1989 would be \$165 billion (or \$150 billion in dollars of 1988 purchasing power). If the rate of inflation were 20 percent and the expected real rate of interest were unchanged, nominal saving in 1989 would be \$180 billion (or \$150 billion in dollars of 1988 purchasing power). In both cases, as long as the expected real rate of interest does not change, the flow of real saving holds steady in both years at \$150 billion in 1988 dollars.

Our model of the credit market with government excluded is:

$$\frac{S}{P} = j(\underset{+}{r}) \tag{6.15}$$

$$\frac{I}{P} = m(\underset{-}{r}) \tag{6.16}$$

$$\frac{S}{P} = \frac{I}{P} \tag{6.17}$$

$$r = i - \dot{P}_e \tag{6.18}$$

$$\dot{P}_e = \bar{\dot{P}} \tag{6.19}$$

where Equation (6.18) defines the *ex ante* real rate of interest and Equation (6.19) specifies that the expected rate of inflation $\dot{P}_e$ is equal to the actual rate of inflation $\dot{P}$, which is assumed to be exogenously determined, that is, given outside the model.

In Figure 6.5, saving and investment are plotted on the horizontal axis and the nominal rate of interest on the vertical axis. This format generates unique curves for each and every expected rate of inflation because, given any nominal rate of interest, every time the expected rate of inflation changes, the expected, or *ex ante*, real rate of interest changes in the opposite direction.

In Figure 6.5 the credit market is initially in equilibrium at point X, with the expected rate of inflation $\dot{P}_{e0}$ and the nominal rate of interest i_0. This means that the *ex ante* real rate of interest is r_0. Now assume that the expected rate of inflation rises from $\dot{P}_{e0}$ per year to $\dot{P}_{e_1}$ per year. This implies that at the old nominal rate of interest i_0 the *ex ante* real rate of interest falls from r_0 $(= i_0 - \dot{P}_{e0})$ to r_1 $(= i_0 - \dot{P}_{e_1})$. At a new lower expected real rate of interest two things happen. First, an increase in real investment expenditures occurs because the lower expected real rate of interest increases the present value of, and hence the demand for newly produced capital goods. Second, there is a decrease in real saving because at the lower expected real rate of interest, the opportunity cost of current

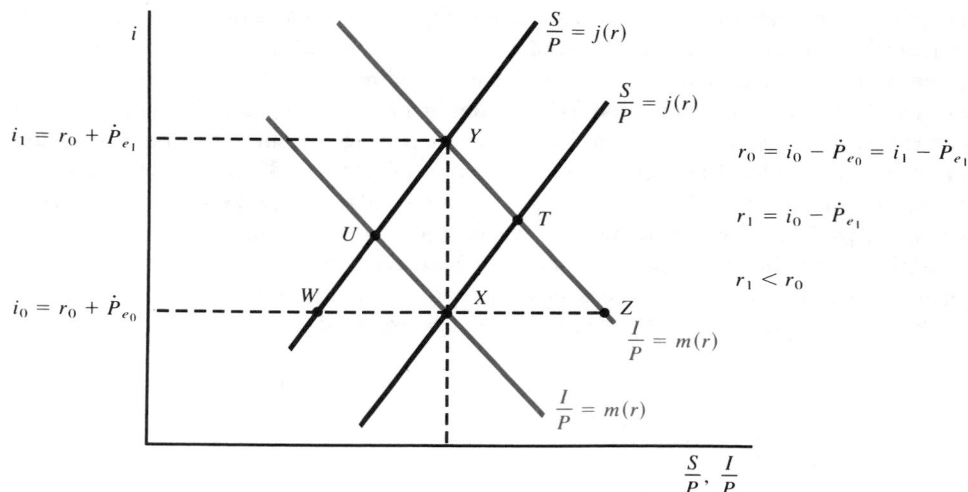

Figure 6.5 The Effect of an Increase in the Expected Rate of Inflation on the Credit Market

real consumption is less. Real consumption expenditures will increase and, according to the household budget identity, real saving will fall.

In Figure 6.5 with the increase in the expected rate of inflation from $\dot{P}_{e_0}$ to $\dot{P}_{e_1}$, the demand for credit shifts rightward by *XZ*; and the supply of credit shifts leftward by *XW*. This occurs because with an unchanged nominal rate (i_0), the expected real rate of interest falls from r_0 to r_1.

Another way to view this is that if real investment expenditures are to remain unchanged, the nominal rate of interest must rise to reflect fully the expected rate of inflation. If the nominal rate adjusts in this manner, the expected, or *ex ante* real rate of interest and the incentive for firms to acquire new capital goods are unchanged. Similarly, if real saving is to be unchanged, the nominal interest rate must rise to reflect fully the expected inflation rate. If the nominal rate adjusts in this manner, the expected real rate of interest and the incentive for households to save are unchanged.

In Figure 6.5 if both the investment and saving functions shift upward by the same amount, then they will intersect vertically above *X* at *Y*. The new equilibrium nominal rate of interest will be i_1, which fully reflects the new expected rate of inflation, $\dot{P}_{e_1}$. Since the nominal rate will have risen by the same amount as the increase in the expected rate of inflation, the expected real rate of interest will remain at its initial equilibrium level (r_0). As the expected real rate of interest is at its initial equilibrium level, the level of real saving and real investment will be at their initial equilibrium levels.

The analysis suggests that as long as household and business participants in the credit market correctly anticipate inflation, and as long as other factors do not cause the real supply and real demand for credit to shift (the *ceteris paribus* condition), the expected, or *ex ante,* real rate of interest will not vary. This will occur because the nominal rate of interest will quickly reflect changes in the correctly anticipated rate of inflation and because all other factors which influence the real rate of interest are constant. If the *ceteris paribus* condition holds and if inflation is correctly anticipated, then the actual, or *ex post,* real rate of interest will equal the expected, or *ex ante,* real rate of interest. The *ex post* and *ex ante* real rates of interest will then be stable over time. For example, if initially the observed nominal interest rate is 8 percent and the expected and actual rate of inflation is 5 percent, then the expected and actual real rates of interest are 3 percent. If the actual rate of inflation ascends to 10 percent and is correctly anticipated, the nominal interest rate immediately rises to 13 percent. The actual and expected real rates of interest are unchanged at 3 percent.

Two Explanations of Cyclical Movements in the Real Rate of Interest Arising from Inflationary Shocks

The preceding discussion describes rapid adjustment of the nominal interest rates to correctly anticipated accelerations and decelerations of inflation and the resultant stability of the *ex post* and *ex ante* real rates of interest, real saving, and real investment over time. This rapid adjustment was based on the assumption of perfect information (perfect accuracy in predicting inflation) and the *ceteris paribus* condition.

Unfortunately, empirical evidence seems to contradict this story. Chart 6.1 demonstrates that the actual, or *ex post*, real rate of interest exhibits a pronounced cyclical pattern. When inflation accelerates, as during the intervals 1967 to 1968, 1972 to 1974, and 1977 to 1979, the *ex post* real rate of interest dips. When inflation plummets, as during the intervals from 1970 to 1971, 1975 to 1976, 1980 to 1982, and 1983 to 1986, the *ex post* real rate of interest soars.

Moreover, real investment expenditures also vary with the business cycle. Chart 6.2 reveals that during cyclical upswings, as during the period from 1972 to 1974, and from 1977 to 1979, private nonresidential fixed investment as a percentage of GNP rises. Chart 6.2 further indicates that during cyclical downturns, as in 1975 to 1976 and 1980 to 1982, this ratio declines. These movements suggest that either the perfect information assumption or the *ceteris paribus* condition, or both, is invalid. Consequently, there are at least two alternative explanations of the cyclical movements in real interest rate and real investment spending. These are either that expectations regarding inflation are formed adaptively or that other variables which affect real saving and real investment are not constant.

Consider a world in which other factors which affect real saving and real investment expenditures, such as aggregate real income, attitudes toward risk, and tax rates, are unchanging but households form their expectations of inflation adaptively. Assume further that business people have perfect information about the inflation rate. In this case, when the actual inflation rate accelerates to $\dot{P}_0$, credit demanders quickly build it into their inflationary expectations, but credit suppliers do not because they are predicting future inflation by looking backward at the past. In Figure 6.5, the demand for credit shifts rightward, but the supply curve does not shift. This means that the credit market equilibrium position temporarily moves to T. As long as equilibrium remains at T, there will be a lower *ex post* real rate of interest. The nominal rate will not have risen suffi-

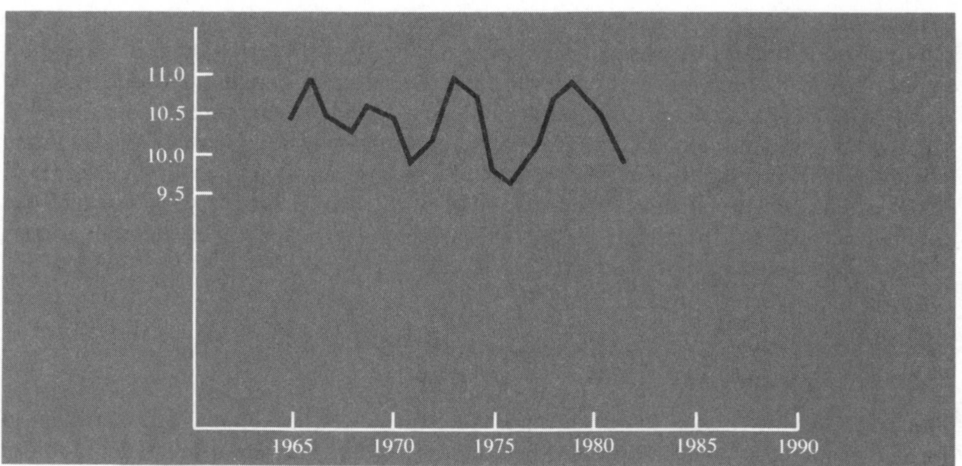

Chart 6.2 Private Nonresidential Fixed Investment as a Percentage of GNP, 1965–1983

ciently (to i_1) to reflect the new, actual rate of inflation. The level of real saving and real investment will rise. There will be a higher rate of capital formation in the economy.

Thus, this analysis of cyclical movements in the *ex post* real interest rate and real investment expenditures is similar to one of the two explanations of the cyclical movements in employment and real wages discussed in Chapter Four. In the labor market, assume that labor demanders have perfect information about the inflation rate and labor suppliers either have imperfect information or are constrained by nominal wage contracts to have imperfect responses to new information. Under this scenario, when inflation accelerates, the demand for labor shifts rightward, the supply of labor does not shift, and employment increases, thus creating a cyclical boom. Unfortunately, the boom lasts only until labor suppliers realize that their real wage has fallen and are able to negotiate a higher rate of nominal wage increase that reflects the new expected rate of inflation.

Similarly, in the credit market, because of an unanticipated acceleration of inflation, credit suppliers may not quickly revise their expectations regarding the rate of inflation. Responding to the increased nominal interest rate because they believe mistakenly that it represents a rise in the real rate, they increase the quantity of real saving, and capital formation rises during this boom period in the economy. Short-run equilibrium is at T in Figure 6.5. This boom lasts until savers realize that the real rate of interest has actually fallen, and they require a higher nominal rate of interest to reflect the new, anticipated rate of inflation. Market equilibrium will then occur at point Y in Figure 6.5.

Thus, remarkable symmetry would exist between the acceleration of inflation and temporary advances in employment and capital formation and temporary declines in the real interest rate and the real wage. This cyclical pattern may be predicated on misperception of the future inflation rate by households acting as labor suppliers and credit suppliers. It can be sustained only as long as that misperception persists. Conversely, a deceleration of the actual rate of inflation, for example from $\dot{P}_1$ to $\dot{P}_0$, would lead to a temporary fall in capital formation (point U in Figure 6.3). Temporary spells of less than full employment and low rates of capital formation (point U in Figure 6.3). Temporary spells of less than full employment and low rates of capital formation and temporary increases in the real interest rate and the real wage would be associated with periods of decelerating inflation in the economy.

The preceding explanation of cyclical movement in the real rate of interest and investment spending and in the real wage and employment is tidy but rather untenable. It is based on the assumption of informational asymmetry on the supply sides of both labor and credit markets. But why should households (suppliers of credit and labor) systematically have worse information than business firms (demanders of credit and labor)? There is little reason to believe that households will systematically err more than business firms.

Even more devastating to this explanation is the fact that it requires credit market suppliers to make systematic errors over time. Every time inflation rises, savers are burned by falling real interest rates. Thus, the adaptive formulation of inflationary expectations would be irrational. It is far more plausible to propose that all credit market participants form their expectations rationally such that they will not make systematic errors over time. We shall see in the next section that if expectations were formed in this way, without relaxation of the *ceteris paribus* condition in the credit market, the *ex ante* real interest rate would not change. The *ex post* real interest rate would vary whenever inflationary expectations were in error. However, these errors would be systematic over time, and the *ex post* real rate would not display the pattern revealed by the data in Chart 6.1. An alternative explanation of the facts involves relaxing the *ceteris paribus* condition in the credit market.

As stated in Chapter Four, to explain the cyclical correlation of employment and inflation arising from inflationary shocks, it is sufficient to assume that rational workers and employers develop labor contracts with nominal wages that adjust to unanticipated inflation with a lag. (There are, of course, markets other than the labor market in which fixed contracts are commonplace.) Thus, a subsequent unanticipated acceleration of inflation may impart a temporary increase in aggregate employment and aggregate real income because the demand curve for labor shifts rightward while the supply curve does not shift. In Chapter Five it was shown that an increase in real disposable income stimulated an increase in real saving. Thus, in the credit market with demand unchanged, a rightward shift in supply would cause the expected and actual real rates of interest to fall and the equilibrium level of real investment expenditures to rise. Even though inflation is assumed to be correctly anticipated by credit market participants, the nominal interest rate does not rise in the same amount as the inflation rate because of the cyclical decline in the underlying real interest rate.

This is shown in Figure 6.6. As in Figure 6.5, equilibrium begins at point X with the expected rate of inflation $\dot{P}_{e0}$ fully reflected in the nominal interest rate i_0. As in Figure 6.5, the increase in the expected rate of inflation to $\dot{P}_{e_1}$ is fully reflected in the new nominal interest rate i_1 at point Y. However, Y is not the new equilibrium. As described above, because of nominal wage contracting in the labor market as inflation rises, employment and aggregate real income rise. With taxation unchanged, real disposable income rises to $(Y/P)_{d_1}$; the saving relation shifts rightward. The new equilibrium is at point

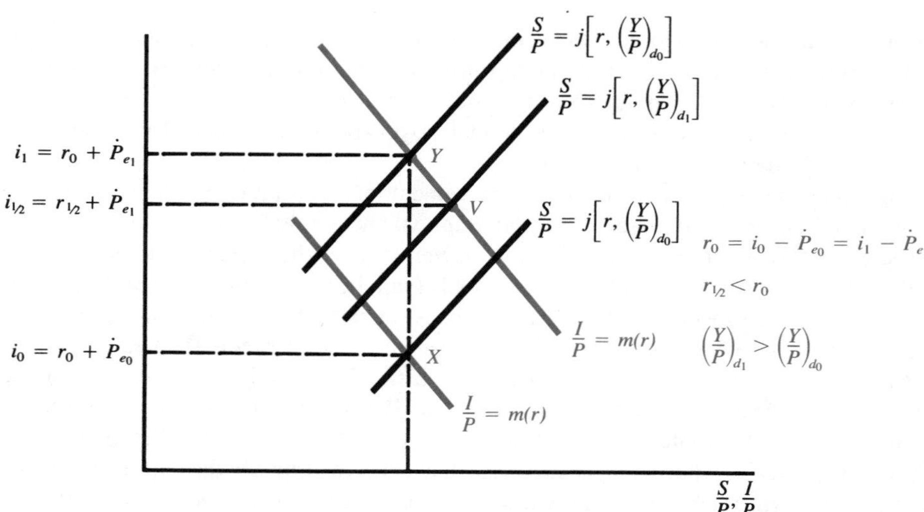

Figure 6.6 The Effect of an Increase in the Expected Rate of Inflation on the Credit Market: Cyclical Boom

V. Here the nominal interest rate, while fully reflecting the increase in expected inflation, has risen to only $i_{1/2}$. This occurs because the underlying *ex ante* real interest rate has been pushed downward to $r_{1/2}$ by the flood of new real saving out of the higher level of real disposable income.

There are other plausible explanations for this pattern, all of which relax the *ceteris paribus* condition in the credit market. One explanation involves the effect of a cyclical boom on savers' attitudes toward risk. If savers are less risk-averse during booms, at each possible *ex ante* real interest rate they will lend more and the saving function in Figure 6.6 will shift rightward. Another explanation involves the effect of the cyclical boom on the actual real deficit. If real taxation varies directly with aggregate real income, because the main source of tax revenue is the income tax, then the real deficit will vary inversely with real income. This is shown early in this Chapter by Equation (6.3). In this situation, the cyclical boom would cause the demand for credit in Figure 6.6 to shift leftward. In either of the preceding cases, the fall in the *ex ante* real interest rate and the rise in the equilibrium level of real investment expenditures shown in Figure 6.6 are exacerbated.

Therefore, there would be a pattern of increases in employment and investment spending and decreases in the actual real interest rate and the level of the real wage during unanticipated accelerations of inflation, inflationary shocks. During periods of decelerating inflation, there would be a pattern of decreases in employment and investment spending and increases in the actual real interest rate and the level of the real wage. To explain the cyclical movement of the *ex post* real interest rate in Chart 6.1 and real investment expenditures in Chart 6.2, it is not necessary to invoke the rather implausible assumption of adaptive expectations on the supply side of the market.

Adaptive Expectations, Rational Expectations, Cyclical Movements in the Real Rate of Interest, and Inflationary Shocks

As stated in Chapter Four, there are two alternative theories of the way expectations are formed. Under an *adaptive expectations* mechanism, the expected rate of inflation is a weighted average of past rates of inflation. Given a change in the inflation rate, as time passes the rate of inflation that is expected by market participants gets closer and closer to the actual inflation rate but is systematically in error over time. According to the New Classical, *rational expectations* critique, it is implausible that market participants would generate expectations of inflation that are systematically wrong. If learning schemes are systematically wrong, rational individuals will scuttle them. It is claimed that an adaptive expectations mechanism is incompatible with rational behavior. According to the rational expectations hypothesis of the "New Classical" brand of Neoclassical economics,[11] individuals will exploit all information about the inflation process. All systematic elements for predicting the rate of inflation will be discovered. The consensual inflationary expectations of market participants will be the most accurate forecast consistent with that knowledge. This implies that, except for strictly random shocks, the market consensus expectation of inflation will not be systematically different from the actual rate of inflation. These results explain the sense in which the rational expectations hypothesis predicts that markets will be efficient. The *efficient markets hypothesis,* discussed in Chapter Thirteen, purports that the consensual expectations of market participants will not be systematically in error.

The rational-versus-adaptive expectations perspective is similar, but not identical, to the perfect-versus-imperfect information scheme. Both adaptive expectations and imperfect information schemes can generate cyclical variation in the *ex post* real rate of interest,[12] while rational expectations and perfect information schemes cannot, unless there are cyclical movements in real income and real saving as explained in the previous section or in attitudes toward risk as explained in footnote 14.

However, there is a significant difference between the two views. The rational expectations hypothesis does not make the strong assumption that information is perfect or that everyone is rational. It only assumes that expectations of inflation are not systematically different from actual inflation. The rational expectations hypothesis does, however, make the fairly strong assumption that the benefits to learning exceed the costs, and that key parts of the economic structure are stable enough to learn systematically at low cost.

Figure 6.7 provides some stylized examples of the time paths of *ex post* real and nominal interest rates under regimes of adaptive formulation of expectations and rational formulation of expectations. Time path R describes what would occur if expectations were formed rationally and there were no unanticipated (inflation-generating) policy changes.

[11]The terms Neoclassical, Monetarist, New Classical, Keynesian, and Neo-Keynesian are defined in Chapter One. These labels are not used in this text because hard and fast boundaries exist between schools of thought, but only because they provide an orderly way to categorize models.

[12]Under adaptive expectations there need not be asymmetry in learning to generate movement in the *ex post* real rate of interest or real wages. Asymmetrical learning is, however, required for cyclical movement in real investment spending and employment.

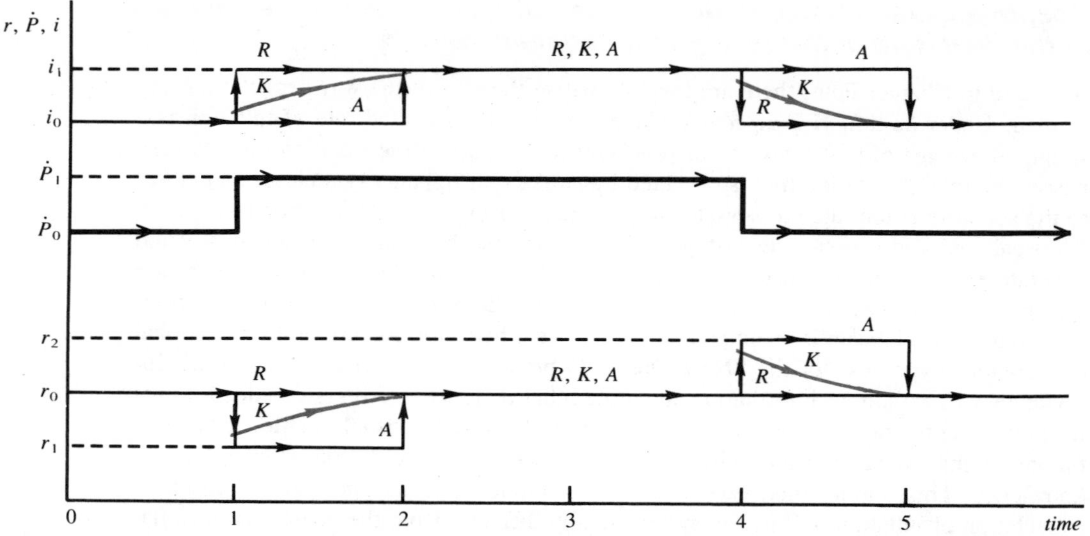

Figure 6.7 Increases and Decreases in Inflation, Inflationary Shocks, and Possible Effects on Nominal and Real Rates of Interest

At time 0 the real rate of interest is r_0, the actual and expected rate of inflation is $\dot{P}_0$, and the nominal rate of interest is $i_0 = r_0 + \dot{P}_{e_0}$. At time 1 the actual rate of inflation rises to $\dot{P}_1$. If the shock that caused this increase were correctly anticipated by market participants, they would fully anticipate the inflationary consequences. The expected rate of inflation would increase immediately. As a result, the nominal rate of interest would rise apace with the actual and correctly anticipated rate of inflation along time path *R*. The new equilibrium nominal interest rate at time 1 would be $i_1 = r_0 + \dot{P}_{e_1}$. The actual and expected rates of interest would be unchanged at r_0 along path *R*. When the actual rate of inflation falls at time 4, the expected rate of inflation correctly adjusts immediately. The nominal interest rate falls along path *R* to i_0, and the actual and expected real rates of interest are unchanged. The static analog of this dynamic pattern is seen in Figure 6.5. There the *ex ante* real interest rate is unchanged at r_0 and the nominal rate rises to i_1 at point *Y*, fully reflecting the rise in expected inflation to $\dot{P}_{e_1}$.

Now assume that inflationary expectations are formed adaptively. Once again, the credit market is in long-run equilibrium at time 0. When the rate of inflation accelerates at time 1, credit market participants are completely uninformed. Assuming that inflationary expectations are formed adaptively after a one-period lag, the nominal rate of interest does not change. It follows path *A* in Figure 6.7 until time 2. Therefore, the *ex ante* real rate of interest does not change but the *ex post* real rate of interest declines at time 1 to $r_1 = i_0 - \dot{P}_1$. The *ex post* real rate of interest stays at this level during interval 1,2 until inflationary expectations are revised at time 2. Credit market participants learn (adaptively) about the new rate of inflation, and it is fully reflected in their inflationary expectations at time 2. The nominal rate of interest then rises to $i_1 = r_0 + \dot{P}_{e_1}$. The *ex post* real rate of interest returns to r_0 along path *A* at time 2. When the rate of inflation falls at time 4, credit market participants are unaware because of the assumed one-period lag in the formation of inflationary expectations. Therefore, the nominal rate of interest does not change along time path *A* until time 5. As a result the *ex post* real interest rate rises along path *A* at time 4. When the credit market fully adapts to the new rate of inflation and it is built into expectations at time 5, the nominal interest rate falls to $i_1 = r_0 + \dot{P}_{e0}$. The *ex post* real rate of interest returns to r_0 at time 5 along path *A*. The static analog of part of this pattern may be seen in Figure 6.5. If the rate of inflation expected by suppliers and demanders of credit stays at $\dot{P}_{e0}$, the nominal interest rate does not change from i_0 at point *X*. But because *actual* inflation rises to $\dot{P}_1$, the actual, or *ex post,* real interest rate falls to $r_1 = i_0 - \dot{P}_1$. When expectations catch up, the equilibrium point moves to *Y;* the nominal interest rate rises to i_1, and the *ex post* real interest rate rises to r_0.

If expectations are formed rationally, and there are no unanticipated inflationary surprises in the credit market, the *ex post* (and *ex ante*) real interest rate could still vary cyclically if nominal wage contracting in labor markets created cyclical variations in real income and, hence, in real saving (and also the real government deficit). Assume a higher level of real income occurs at time 1 and then tapers off, returning to a full employment level by time 2. This will occur if labor demanders and labor suppliers form their inflationary expectations rationally and if these contracts allow only a gradual adjustment of the nominal wage over interval 1,2 should there be an inflationary surprise at time 1.

The initial acceleration of inflation at time 1 would have caused the *R* trajectories to be followed. However, the cyclical increase in real income stimulates real saving (and reduces the real government deficit), and this propels the actual and expected real interest rates downward along path *K*. As nominal wages are gradually adjusted, the boom tapers off during interval 1,2, and the real interest rate returns to r_0 along path *K*. Because the real rate initially declines, even though actual inflation is correctly and immediately reflected in a higher nominal rate, the nominal interest rate initially does not rise in an amount equal to the correctly anticipated rate of inflation. As the real rate rises, the nominal rate of interest only gradually rises along path *K* during time interval 1,2. The static analog of this pattern may be seen in Figure 6.6. The nominal interest rate fully reflects expected inflation, but the *ex ante* real interest rate initially declines to $r_{1/2}$ at point *V* because of the cyclical rise in real saving.

A fall in inflation at time 4 has the effect of decreasing real income and real saving (and increasing the real government deficit). This causes the actual and expected real rates initially to rise abruptly along path *K*. As the decrease in real income tapers off, the real rate of interest returns to r_0 during interval 4,5. Even though actual inflation is immediately and correctly reflected in a lower nominal rate of interest, because of the initial rise in the real rate, the nominal rate initially does not decline in an amount equal to the currently anticipated rate of inflation. As the real rate falls, the nominal interest rate only gradually declines along path *K*.[13]

[13]This analysis abstracts from the effect of income taxes on the relationship between expected inflation and the real interest rate. Because expected inflation forces savers into higher income tax brackets, they demand a higher nominal return. This implies that a higher rate of expected inflation amplifies the changes

A good deal of empirical research has been performed on interest rate behavior. Some of it is cited in the bibliography.[14]

Suppliers and demanders of newly issued short-term debt need only predict inflation over a short future interval. In recent decades, inflation rates have behaved erratically over short periods of time. Therefore, nominal short-term interest rates vary considerably with changes in the rate of inflation. However, despite these changes in short-term nominal interest rates, as seen in Chart 6.1, the actual short-term real interest rate has been very volatile.[15]

Suppliers and demanders of long-term debt need to predict inflation over a long future period. When averaged over long periods of time, the rate of inflation is more stable. Nominal long-term interest rates need vary little with short-lived fluctuations in the rate of inflation. Nevertheless, the actual, or *ex post,* long-term real rate of interest is also fairly volatile over time.

Are market participants generating inflationary expectations rationally or adaptively? For suppliers and demanders of short-term debt who must predict the rate of inflation in the near future, systematic error would result if inflationary expectations were formed adaptively. For suppliers and demanders of newly issued long-term debt, an adaptive, backward-looking formulation of inflationary expectations might be plausible. Short-term shocks to inflation tend to cancel out over long periods of time. Therefore, in the absence of a way of predicting future inflation over long periods of time, participants in the long-term credit market may be behaving reasonably in expecting the inflationary future to resemble the inflationary past.

Because the hypotheses presented here all seem plausible and because conclusive evidence regarding the actual causes of real interest rate volatility has not been produced, it is not yet possible to say that any of the theories here have been falsified. Fluctuation in the real rate of interest, portrayed in Chart 6.1, may reflect the result of several forces: cyclical swings in real income, surprise inflationary shocks, cyclically varying attitudes toward risk, and, since the mid-1970s as revealed by Tables 6.1 and 6.2, an upward trend in the actual and cyclically adjusted government deficit as a percentage of GNP.

---

in nominal rates associated with inflation. This effect works in a direction opposite from the effects described here, wherein nominal rates did not change as much as the inflation rate. However, as pointed out in the works of Milton Friedman and Anna J. Schwartz, and William Kelly and James Miles, cited in the bibliography, such a tax effect has yet to be verified.

[14]Results similar to those shown by the K paths in Figure 6.7 can also be generated if it is assumed that credit market participants are not risk-neutral. The analysis presented here assumes that lenders' and borrowers' attitudes toward risk do not vary over the business cycle. If they did, then during a recession, lenders would be more risk-averse and would insist on higher expected real rates of interest. The opposite would occur during a boom. As a result, the real rate of interest would move cyclically in a fashion similar to the K paths in Figure 6.7. For additional reading on this hypothesis, see the paper by Hansen, Scott, and Singleton in the bibliography to this chapter.

[15]Chart 6.1 shows that the rate of inflation has grown increasingly volatile in the past two decades. The price inflation expectations effect explains why nominal interest rates have also become more volatile. With more volatile nominal interest rates, nominal asset prices are also more volatile. This increases risk to asset holders. An alternative explanation for the rise and persistence of high real interest rates in the 1980s is that credit market participants recognize that increased risk, are risk-averse, and insist on being compensated for it by demanding and receiving higher *ex ante* real interest rates.

So far, the rate of inflation has been determined exogenously, outside the credit and labor markets. The sources of inflation have not yet been explored. Until this is done (and it will be done in the general equilibrium models of later chapters), policy prescriptions for reducing the acceleration and deceleration of the inflation rate will be unintelligible. Nevertheless, it should be clear that policies for stabilizing the inflation rate can have a salutory effect in stabilizing the real rate of interest, the allocation of resources, employment, capital formation, and the overall health of our economy.

The Volatility of Private Investment Spending

Earlier in the chapter we developed two alternative explanations of cyclical variations in the level of investment expenditures. Now we explore a third explanation.

Chart 6.2 shows the volatility of nonresidential private investment as a percentage of GNP. In recession years (such as 1970, 1975, and 1982) this type of spending fell below 10 percent of GNP. In boom years it exceeded 11 percent of GNP.[16]

In Equation (6.20) the terms in the numerators represent the expected future after-tax profit from the capital spending project in question:

$$PV = \frac{y_1}{(1 + i)} + \frac{y_2}{(1 + i)^2} + \frac{y_3}{(1 + i)^3} + \cdots + \frac{y_n}{(1 + i)^n} \tag{6.20}$$

During boom times business people are notoriously ebullient; the future looks bright, and future expected after-tax profits from new projects, the $y_1, y_2, \ldots, y_n$, are viewed in optimistic terms. As a result, the present values (*PV*) of investment spending projects are relatively high. Consequently, there typically will be an investment spending boom during such periods. In Figure 6.8 the demand for credit shifts rightward to $m_1(r) + (\overline{G}/P - \overline{T}/P)$ and the equilibrium level of investment spending is at $(I/P)_1$. During periods of economic boom such investment-spending optimism would drive up the real (and nominal) rate of interest, *ceteris paribus*.

When the economy enters a recession, just the opposite occurs. Business people are depressed; the future looks bleak, and future expected after-tax profits, the $y_1, y_2, \ldots, y_n$, stream in the present value formula Equation (6.20), are viewed in a pessimistic light. As a result, the present values of investment spending projects are relatively low, and investment spending nosedives during such periods. In Figure 6.8 the demand for credit shifts leftward to $m_0(r) + (\overline{G}/P - \overline{T}/P)$, and the equilibrium level of investment spending is $(I/P)_0$.

In the present partial equilibrium, closed economy model the manic-depressive behavior of hardheaded business people would result in the periodic reallocation of resources from investment to consumption spending and vice versa. When real investment spending falls to $(I/P)_0$, real saving declines to $(S/P)_0$ and, if real income does not fall, real consumption must rise. Similarly, when real investment spending rises to $(I/P)_1$, real saving rises to $(S/P)_1$ and, if real income does not rise, real consumption must fall.

[16]As a further example, Table 5.2 of Chapter Five shows that gross private investment declined precipitously in the recession years of 1975, 1980, and 1982.

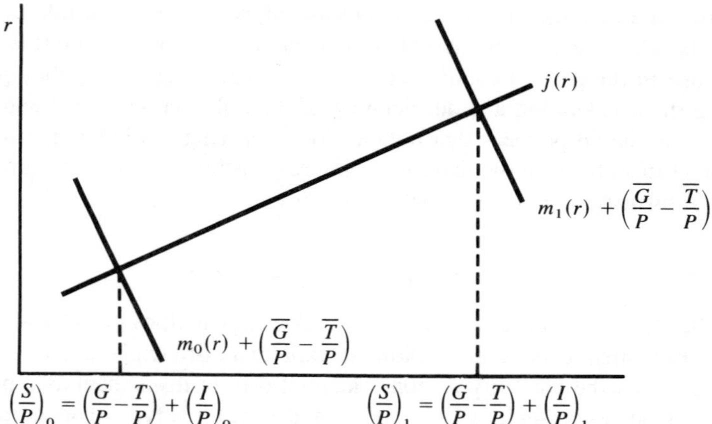

Figure 6.8 The Volatility of Investment Expenditures

Therefore, despite the swings in investment, if real income is stable, total private spending is also stable.

Using other models, however, one cannot be so sanguine. In fact, the volatile temperament of business people historically has troubled many economists who viewed it as a *cause* of sizable fluctuations in aggregate real income and employment. Modern economists call these disturbances private demand shocks. John Maynard Keynes ascribed such swings to the "animal spirits" of business people. Keynes and his followers argued that the cyclical ups and downs in investment spending had a strong impact on total real income. They suggested that swings in investment spending should be counteracted by appropriately timed government spending and taxation policies. Thus, if private investment spending declined because of business pessimism, government would intervene with greater spending. Government spending would keep total (private plus government) spending and, according to Keynes' model, real income and employment on an even keel. To better understand Keynes' views, in the next chapter the saving-investment process is modeled along Keynesian lines.

Concluding Comment

This chapter covers the credit (loanable funds) market and how the market rate of interest is determined in that market. The effect of an increased demand for credit by government is discussed. When an increased government deficit causes government to increase its borrowing in the credit market, fewer resources are available for private spending. This phenomenon is referred to as the crowding out of private expenditures by government expenditures.

Next, the effect of expected inflation on nominal and real interest rates as determined in the credit market is discussed. As the expected inflation rate rises, *ceteris paribus*, the demand for credit rises, and the supply of credit falls. This occurs because when the nominal interest rate remains temporarily unchanged, the expected real interest rate (equal to the nominal interest rate less the anticipated inflation rate) declines. The resulting increase in the demand for credit and reduction in the supply of credit insures that in equilibrium the nominal interest rate will adjust to reflect the expected inflation rate. Because of imperfect anticipation of inflation by credit market participants, or because of swings in real income in response to changes in inflation that are unanticipated in labor market contracts, the observed real interest rate typically falls when inflation increases and rises when inflation decreases.

This chapter closes with a discussion of the volatility of private investment expenditures over time. During periods of recession business people are pessimistic and do not foresee great future profit to investment spending projects. In the eyes of many economists, such pessimism tends to make recessions even more severe. In the next chapter, a model of the saving-investment process is examined. This Keynesian model of aggregate demand is predicated on the view that swings in private spending affect aggregate output and real income.

EXERCISES

1. Explain the following statement: "The supply of and demand for credit depend on the expected *real* interest rate but determine the *nominal* interest rate."
2. Give two alternative explanations for the following statement: "When inflation accelerates, the actual real interest rate is relatively low and investment spending is high. When inflation decelerates, the actual real interest rate is relatively high and investment spending is low."
3. Explain why, after a government deficit increases to a new level and stays there, the real interest rate will not decline in subsequent periods.
4. Outline the conditions under which a continued sizable government deficit would be preferred to a tax increase.
5. Modern psychologists argue that the outlook of business people is subject to waves of bright optimism and bleak pessimism. Use the present value formula to predict the implications of these waves.
6. Explain why you agree or disagree with the following statement: "If increases in government expenditures were financed by raising taxes, there would be no crowding out."
7. "In recent years the United States economy has grown increasingly weak. Productivity has fallen. United States products cannot compete on world markets." Relate this argument to the magnitude of the credit flows in Table 5.1 in Chapter Five.
8. Contrast the cyclically adjusted deficit to the actual deficit. Which is greater in absolute terms during a period of recession? How do they compare in a period of economic boom?

9. Why are long-term nominal interest rates less volatile than short-term nominal interest rates? Does your answer depend on whether inflationary expectations are formed rationally or adaptively?

10. What is the difference between a perfect information model of the credit market and a rational expectations model?

11. Keynes viewed fluctuations in real investment expenditures as a *cause* of movements in real income. Make the case for a reverse causality—fluctuations in real income are a cause of fluctuations in the equilibrium level of real investment expenditures. Which of these interpretations is supported by the behavior of the *ex post* real interest rate in Table 6.1?

BIBLIOGRAPHY

Bryant, John. "How Fiscal Policy Matters." In *Modern Concepts in Macroeconomics,* ed. Thomas M. Havrilesky. Arlington Heights, Ill.: Harlan Davidson, Inc., 1985.

Carlson, John A. "Expected Inflation and Interest Rates." *Economic Inquiry* (October 1979), pp. 597–608.

Carlson, Keith M., and Roger W. Spencer. "Crowding Out and Its Critics." *Review.* Federal Reserve Bank of St. Louis (December 1975), pp. 2–17.

Congressional Budget Office. "The Outlook for Fiscal Policy." In *Modern Concepts in Macroeconomics,* ed. Thomas M. Havrilesky. Arlington Heights. Ill.: Harlan Davidson, Inc., 1985.

Darby, Michael R. "Some Pleasant Monetarist Arithmetic." In *Modern Concepts in Macroeconomics,* ed. Thomas M. Havrilesky. Arlington Heights, Ill.: Harlan Davidson, Inc., 1985.

Fama, Eugene. "Short-Term Interest Rates as Predictors of Inflation." *American Economic Review* (June 1975), pp. 269–282.

Fisher, Irving. *The Theory of Interest*. New York: Macmillan, 1930.

Friedman, Milton. "The Taxes Called Deficits." In *Modern Concepts in Macroeconomics,* ed. Thomas M. Havrilesky. Arlington Heights, Ill.: Harlan Davidson, Inc., 1985.

Friedman, Milton, and Anna J. Schwartz. *Monetary Trends in the United States and the United Kingdom: Their Relation to Income, Prices, and Interest Rates, 1867–1975*. Chicago: University of Chicago Press, 1982.

Gibson, William. "Price-Expectations Effects on Interest Rates." *Journal of Finance* (March 1970), pp. 19–34.

Hansen, Lars, Richard F. Scott, and Kenneth Singleton. "Characterizing Asset Prices." Carnegie-Mellon Working Paper (1983).

Keleher, Robert E. "Supply Side Tax Policy." In *Modern Concepts in Macroeconomics,* ed. Thomas M. Havrilesky. Arlington Heights, Ill.: Harlan Davidson, Inc., 1985.

Kelly, William A., Jr., and James A. Miles. "Darby and Fisher: Resolution of a Paradox." *Financial Review* 18 (August 1983), pp. 341–348.

Keynes, John Maynard. *The General Theory of Employment, Interest and Money*. London: Harcourt Brace, 1936.

Litterman, Robert B., and Laurence Weiss. "Money, Real Interest Rates and Output: A Reinterpretation of Postwar U.S. Data." National Bureau of Economic Research, Working Paper 1077 (February 1983).

Meyer, Lawrence H. "Financing Constraints and the Short-Run Response to Fiscal Policy." *Review,* Federal Reserve Bank of St. Louis (June/July 1980), pp. 24–25.

Miller, Preston J. "Higher Deficit Policies Lead to Higher Inflation." In *Modern Concepts in Macroeconomics,* ed. Thomas M. Havrilesky. Arlington Heights, Ill.: Harlan Davidson, Inc., 1985.

Miller, Preston J., and Thomas J. Sargent. "A Reply to Darby." In *Modern Concepts in Macroeconomics,* ed. Thomas M. Havrilesky. Arlington Heights, Ill.: Harlan Davidson, Inc., 1985.

Minsky, Hyman. *John Maynard Keynes.* New York: Columbia University Press, 1970.

Mishkin, Frederic S. *A Rational Expectations Approach to Macroeconometrics: Testing Policy Ineffectiveness and Efficient Market Models.* Chicago: University of Chicago Press, 1983.

Shiller, Robert. "Rational Expectations and the Dynamic Structure of Macroeconomic Models: A Critical Review." *Journal of Monetary Economics,* 4 (January 1978), pp. 1–44.

Taylor, Herbert. "Interest Rates: How Much Does Expected Inflation Matter?" In *Modern Concepts in Macroeconomics,* ed. Thomas M. Havrilesky. Arlington Heights, Ill.: Harlan Davidson, Inc., 1985.

Wicksell, Knut. *Interest and Prices.* Translated by R. F. Kahn. London: MacMillan, 1936.

Yohe, William P., and Denis S. Karnosky. "Interest Rates and Price Level Changes." *Review,* Federal Reserve Bank of St. Louis (December 1968), pp. 19–36.

The Credit Market and Aggregate Demand: A Keynesian Perspective

Chapter 7

Introduction

The previous chapter discussed how the level of aggregate real saving, aggregate real investment expenditures, and the real government deficit determined the market rate of interest. These factors did not influence the level of aggregate real income which was usually constrained by the working of the labor market to be at the full employment level. In that chapter the market rate of interest adjusted to bring the credit (loanable funds) market into equilibrium. In the present chapter the assumption that aggregate real income is given is relaxed; instead, it is assumed that real income may change and that the market rate of interest is fixed. This means that the level of real income will adjust to bring the credit market into equilibrium. The level of real income will be determined by real saving, real investment expenditures, and the real government deficit. This chapter shows why the Keynesian and Neoclassical partial equilibrium models of the credit market have starkly contrasting implications for the proper role of government spending and taxation policies, including the balancing of the federal budget.

TWO CONTRASTING VIEWS OF THE CREDIT MARKET

Consider the Neoclassical model of the credit market from previous chapters, modified so that real income, rather than real disposable income, influences real saving:

$$\frac{S}{P} = j\left(i, \frac{Y}{P}\right) \tag{7.1}$$

$$\frac{I}{P} = m(i) \tag{7.2}$$

$$\frac{G}{P} - \frac{T}{P} = \left(\frac{\overline{G}}{P} - \frac{\overline{T}}{P}\right) \tag{7.3}$$

$$\frac{S}{P} = \frac{I}{P} + \frac{G}{P} - \frac{T}{P} \tag{7.4}$$

Where the level of aggregate real income is fixed at the full employment level, there are four equations and four unknowns: saving (S/P), investment (I/P), the government deficit ($G/P - T/P$), and the market rate of interest (i). The solution of this Neoclassical model determines the equilibrium rate of interest. (Since the expected rate of inflation is not a variable, changes in the nominal and real interest rates are synonymous.)

Assuming instead that the market rate of interest is given and that real income (Y/P) can change, the four unknowns become S/P, I/P, ($G/P - T/P$), and Y/P. The solution of this Keynesian model determines the equilibrium level of aggregate real income.

Figure 7.1 depicts a solution of the Keynesian model for the equilibrium level of aggregate real income where the interest rate is held constant at i_1, but aggregate real income is variable.

In Figure 7.1 the market is initially in equilibrium at point *A*. An increase in the level of government expenditures, $\Delta(G/P)$, causes the demand for credit to shift rightward. At the interest rate i_1 and level of real income $(Y/P)_1$, there is an excess demand for credit equal to the directed distance *AB*. If real income were fixed and the interest rate were a variable, the market would return to equilibrium at point *C*. The excess demand for credit would be removed by a reduction in private investment expenditures (directed distance *BC'*) and an increase in real saving, which reflects an equal-sized reduction in private consumption expenditures (directed distance *AC'*). In this Neoclassical model there would be a complete crowding out of private expenditures by public expenditures. The additional resources that are needed to finance the increased government spending come entirely from a reduction in private spending.

In contrast, assume that the market rate of interest is fixed, for instance by the monetary authority, and that real income can change. If real saving is an increasing function of real income, the saving function shifts rightward as real income increases. The initial, excess demand for credit is removed, not by a reduction of private expenditures (complete crowding out), but rather by an increase in real saving from the increase in real income. No crowding out occurs in this Keynesian model. The additional resources that are

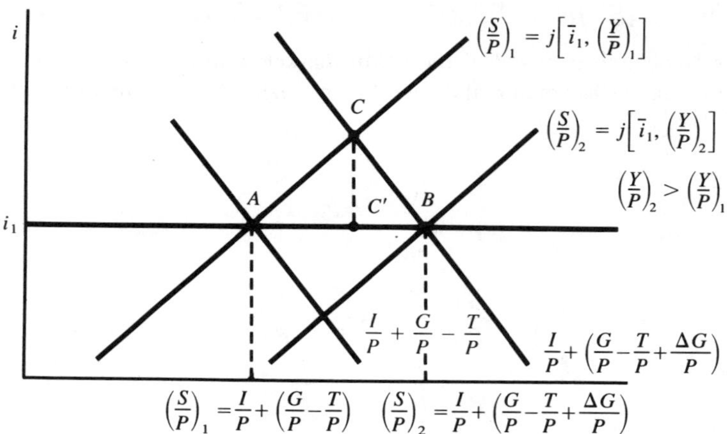

Figure 7.1 With the Market Rate of Interest Constant and Real Income a Variable, an Increase in the Demand for Credit Increases Real Income

needed to finance the increased deficit spending of government come entirely from the rise in real saving out of greater real income.[1]

What utterly contrasting views! In the Neoclassical model an increase in the government expenditures provokes an equal-sized reduction in private expenditures—a rise in collectively enjoyed expenditures results in a fall in *private* living standards within the economy. The swelling of government expenditures—more aircraft carriers, better highways, more public education, and so on—necessitates an offsetting plunge in private expenditures—fewer new homes, automobiles, waterbeds, and personal computers for households, and fewer new factories, trucks, and lathes for business firms. Complete crowding out is an important feature of the Neoclassical model.

In the Keynesian model, because the interest rate is assumed constant and real income is the equilibrating variable, an increase in government expenditures will not produce a reduction in private expenditures. In fact, private (consumption) expenditures actually expand! There is no diminution in private living standards. The increase in government expenditures does not result in fewer private expenditures. Instead, the increase in government expenditures incites greater private expenditures. More government spending stimulates real income. Higher real income generates more real saving and more real consumption out of that income. The boost in saving is used to finance the increased deficit spending of government. Thus, because the interest rate does not rise but real

[1]The linkage mechanism that describes how more real income might be generated by additional government spending is explained in Chapter Twelve. Remember that when G is defined as government expenditures, it includes transfer payments made by government and T is defined as taxation receipts. When G is defined as government purchases, it excludes transfer payments made by government and T is defined as taxation minus these transfer payments.

income does, the increased deficit financing needs of government are satisfied by an expanded flow of saving. Investment does not decrease and consumption actually rises.

The Neoclassical model portrays a pessimistic world of scarcity. Neoclassical muses remind us that there is no such thing as a free lunch. In contrast, the Keynesian world is far more optimistic. The ghost of Keynes assures us that we can spend ourselves rich.

Which view is more realistic? In a sense, both perspectives are unrealistic because both are partial equilibrium models. Both detach the credit market from the rest of the economy, hold one of the five variables constant, and solve for the remaining four. The Neoclassicists hold real income constant; the Keynesians hold the interest rate constant. To judge these contrasting partial equilibrium models for the realism of their pessimistic or optimistic implications, it is necessary to analyze the effects of an increase in the government deficit in a general equilibrium context. This task is reserved for later chapters.

Before analyzing general equilibrium models, it is useful to continue to experiment with the Keynesian partial equilibrium model. This view captured the fancy of teachers, students, and policymakers for nearly forty years, beginning near the end of the Great Depression of 1929–1939. It dominated macroeconomics textbooks for almost as long. Many teachers, students, voters, and policymakers still consider the Keynesian scheme the starting-off point for macroeconomic analysis. Why? Perhaps it is popular because it is so optimistic and gives humanity hope (a false hope, say the gloomy Neoclassicists) that prosperity, good times, and abundance can be engineered by well timed government intervention. Perhaps the Keynesian partial equilibrium model gained widespread endorsement because it helped to rationalize a government that already was destined to grow bigger and bigger. Or perhaps it was embraced because it promised a government spending cure for the periodic economic slumps that seem to plague our economy.

As pointed out at the end of Chapter Six, Keynesians tend to view shifts in private investment spending as a source of instability in real income. With a fixed interest rate and other conditions discussed in Chapter Twelve, such shifts would cause sizable fluctuations in aggregate real income. An active fiscal policy of compensatory movements in government spending (and taxation) could insulate real income from these private demand shocks. Therefore, an examination of the Keynesian model is an interesting exercise in social engineering, as well as a provocative intellectual investigation.

AN IN-DEPTH LOOK AT THE KEYNESIAN PARTIAL EQUILIBRIUM MODEL OF THE CREDIT MARKET

With the interest rate held fixed, the level of real investment expenditures can be treated as given or autonomous. Furthermore, since the interest rate cannot change, real saving can be expressed exclusively as a function of aggregate real income. Aggregate real saving depends positively on aggregate real income, and an increase in aggregate real income will result in an induced increase in aggregate real saving which is smaller than the increase in aggregate real income. Thus, the marginal propensity to save (out of current income), which in a linear relation is the slope of the saving function, is greater than zero but less than unity:[2]

$$0 < \frac{\Delta(S/P)}{\Delta(Y/P)} < 1$$

The theory of saving promulgated by John Maynard Keynes in his *General Theory of Employment, Interest and Money* may be expressed as

$$\frac{S}{P} = \frac{-a}{P} + s\left(\frac{Y}{P}\right) \tag{7.1'}$$

where $-a/P$ is autonomous *dissaving* and s is the marginal propensity to save. The marginal propensity to save measures the increment to current saving with respect to the increment to current income. Another way of looking at the marginal propensity to save is to view it as the effect of an increase in current income on current saving.

The purpose of this chapter is not to present a realistic model of the economy. The assumption that the interest rate, a market-determined price, can be held fixed in a free market economy is patently unrealistic. More relevant, general equilibrium models in which key variables such as the interest rate and real income are simultaneously determined are presented in Chapters Eleven and Twelve.

When real taxation is included in the model, a more sophisticated and realistic version of the real saving relation is specified, as follows:

$$\frac{S}{P} = \frac{-a}{P} + s\left(\frac{Y}{P}\right)_d \tag{7.5}$$

where

$$\left(\frac{Y}{P}\right)_d \equiv \frac{Y}{P} - \frac{T}{P} \tag{7.6}$$

is the definition of real disposable income. Here real saving varies positively with real disposable income $(Y/P)_d$, defined as aggregate real income (Y/P) less the level of real taxation paid to government minus transfer payments received from government (T/P).

A traditional problem in macroeconomic theory is the determination of the equilibrium level of aggregate real income. In the Neoclassical partial equilibrium model of the labor market presented in Chapter Three, the level of aggregate real income is determined by the working of the labor market. In the Keynesian partial equilibrium model discussed

[2]The marginal propensity to save out of current income was also discussed in the theory of consumption and saving presented in Chapter Five. Other variables which might influence current saving and consumption such as expected future income, wealth, and the interest rate are suppressed in the theory presented in this chapter.

here the level of aggregate income is determined by the level of aggregate real expenditures. The condition for equilibrium in the credit market is the equality of real saving (S/P) and real investment expenditures (I/P) plus the real government deficit ($G/P - T/P$)

$$\frac{S}{P} = \frac{I}{P} + \frac{G}{P} - \frac{T}{P} \tag{7.4}$$

In the aggregate budget identity of Chapter Two, aggregate real saving is identically equal to aggregate real income minus aggregate real consumption and aggregate real taxation:

$$\frac{S}{P} \equiv \frac{Y}{P} - \frac{C}{P} - \frac{T}{P}$$

By substituting the aggregate budget identity into the left-hand side of (7.4) and rearranging terms, the equilibrium condition can also be expressed as:

$$\frac{Y}{P} = \frac{C}{P} + \frac{I}{P} + \frac{G}{P} \tag{7.4$'$}$$

which says that aggregate real income equals total aggregate real expenditures, sometimes called *aggregate demand*.

Assuming that investment expenditures, taxation, and government expenditures are *autonomous* (i.e., independent of any other variable in the model) one may write:

$$\frac{I}{P} = \left(\frac{I}{P}\right)_a \tag{7.7}$$

$$\frac{T}{P} = \left(\frac{T}{P}\right)_a \tag{7.8}$$

$$\frac{G}{P} = \left(\frac{G}{P}\right)_a \tag{7.9}$$

The lowercase *a* signifies that the variable is autonomous.

Having written relations for all the components of aggregate expenditures, a simple model of aggregate real income determination can be developed.

Substituting autonomous taxation Equation (7.8) into the definition of real disposable income Equation (7.6) and putting the result into the saving function Equation (7.5) yields:

$$\frac{S}{P} = \frac{-a}{P} + s\left(\frac{Y}{P}\right) - s\left(\frac{T}{P}\right)_a \tag{7.10}$$

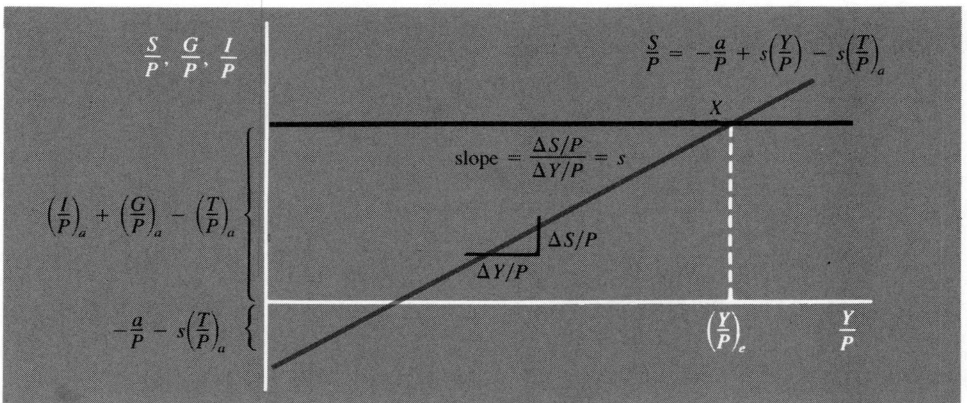

Figure 7.2 Solution for the Equilibrium Level of Real Income

Substituting this result together with autonomous government expenditures Equation (7.9) and autonomous investment expenditures Equation (7.7) into the equilibrium condition Equation (7.4) gives:

$$\frac{-a}{P} + s\left(\frac{Y}{P}\right) - s\left(\frac{T}{P}\right)_a = \left(\frac{I}{P}\right)_a + \left(\frac{G}{P}\right)_a - \left(\frac{T}{P}\right)_a \tag{7.11}$$

Rearranging terms provides the solution for the equilibrium level of real income:

$$\left(\frac{Y}{P}\right)_e = \frac{\frac{a}{P} + \left(\frac{I}{P}\right)_a + \left(\frac{G}{P}\right)_a + s\left(\frac{T}{P}\right)_a - \left(\frac{T}{P}\right)_a}{s} \tag{7.12}$$

The model is depicted graphically in Figure 7.2. Here the saving function Equation (7.10) is graphed to show an intercept consisting of autonomous dissaving ($-a/P$) minus autonomous taxation times the marginal propensity to save $-s(T/P)_a$, and a slope equal to the marginal propensity to save (s). The level of real autonomous investment expenditures $(I/P)_a$ Equation (7.7) plus real autonomous government expenditures $(G/P)_a$ Equation (7.9) less real autonomous taxation $(T/P)_a$ Equation (7.8) are shown as the horizontal line. The equilibrium condition Equation (7.4) is satisfied where real saving equals real investment plus the real government deficit at X in Figure 7.2. This yields the equilibrium level of real income, $(Y/P)_e$.

An Alternative Keynesian Partial Equilibrium Model: The Income and Expenditures Approach

The preceding Keynesian partial equilibrium model of the credit market, like the Neoclassical partial equilibrium model, focused on real saving, real investment, and the real deficit of government—the demand for and supply of credit. The essential difference between the two models is that the equilibrating variable in the Neoclassical model is the interest rate and real income is assumed constant, while the equilibrating variable in the Keynesian model is real income and the market rate of interest is assumed constant.

The Keynesian model is frequently expressed in terms of aggregate real expenditures and aggregate real income, instead of saving, investment, and the government deficit. This alternative aggregate income-aggregate expenditures specification is identically related to the saving-investment-deficit specification. These are two ways of looking at the same partial equilibrium model. The income-expenditures specification, however, emphasizes the power of total spending, including government spending, in determining aggregate real income.

This version of the Keynesian model will be expressed in terms of the alternative equilibrium condition Equation (7.4′) together with autonomous expenditures Equations (7.7), (7.8), and (7.9) and an expression for real consumption expenditures instead of real saving. The consumption function is identically related to the saving function. This is shown simply by taking the saving relation

$$\frac{S}{P} = \frac{-a}{P} + s\left(\frac{Y}{P}\right) - s\left(\frac{T}{P}\right)_a \tag{7.10}$$

and substituting the aggregate budget identity

$$\frac{S}{P} \equiv \frac{Y}{P} - \frac{C}{P} - \frac{T}{P}$$

into its left-hand side

$$\frac{Y}{P} - \frac{C}{P} - \frac{T}{P} = \frac{-a}{P} + s\left(\frac{Y}{P}\right) - s\left(\frac{T}{P}\right)_a$$

and rearranging

$$\frac{C}{P} = \frac{a}{P} + (1 - s)\left(\frac{Y}{P}\right) - (1 - s)\left(\frac{T}{P}\right)_a \tag{7.13}$$

where C/P is total real consumption expenditures, a/P is real autonomous consumption expenditures, and $(1 - s)$ is the *marginal propensity to consume*. Since s is the marginal propensity to save, one minus the marginal propensity to save equals the marginal propensity to consume and the letter b $(= 1 - s)$ will be used to denote the marginal propensity to consume. The marginal propensity to consume is the increment to current consumption expenditures with respect to the increment to current income or the effect of an increase in current income on current consumption expenditures.[3] The consumption function is now expressed:

$$\frac{C}{P} = \frac{a}{P} + b\left(\frac{Y}{P}\right) - b\left(\frac{T}{P}\right)_a \tag{7.13'}$$

The consumption function Equation (7.13′) is simply another way of expressing the theory stated in Equation (7.10), the saving function. The two equations are related through the aggregate budget identity.

In Figure 7.3 the consumption function Equation (7.13′) is graphed to show an intercept consisting of real autonomous consumption, a/P, less real autonomous taxation times the marginal propensity to consume, $-b(T/P)_a$. Each subsequent parallel line in Figure 7.3 adds the level of real autonomous expenditures by an additional sector to total consumption at every level of aggregate real income. First, the autonomous expenditures of the business sector are added, Equation (7.7); then, the autonomous expenditures of the government sector, Equation (7.9), are added. The top line in Figure 7.3 represents the sum of autonomous aggregate demand, $a/P - b(T/P)_a + (I/P)_a + (G/P)_a$, and induced aggregate demand $b(Y/P)$. The latter product represents the level of aggregate expenditures that is induced by the level of aggregate real income. The equilibrium condition, $C/P + I/P + G/P = Y/P$, Equation (7.4′), is graphed as a 45° line from the origin. At any point along this 45° line, directed distances measured horizontally are equal to directed distances measured vertically. Therefore, at every point along this line, aggregate real income and aggregate real expenditures are equal. The intersection of the aggregate demand function and the 45° line yields the same equilibrium level of aggregate real income as the intersection of the saving function with the sum of real autonomous investment and real autonomous government expenditures minus real autonomous taxation, shown in Figure 7.2.

The equilibrium condition in the income-expenditures model is that aggregate real expenditures equal aggregate real income:

$$\frac{C}{P} + \frac{I}{P} + \frac{G}{P} = \frac{Y}{P} \tag{7.4'}$$

Aggregate real expenditures on the left-hand side of (7.4′) are the sum of consumption expenditures Equation (7.13), investment expenditures Equation (7.7), and government expenditures Equation (7.9). This is the top parallel line in Figure 7.3:

$$\frac{C}{P} + \frac{I}{P} + \frac{G}{P} = \left(\frac{a}{P}\right) - b\left(\frac{T}{P}\right)_a + \left(\frac{I}{P}\right)_a + \left(\frac{G}{P}\right)_a + b\left(\frac{Y}{P}\right)$$

[3]The marginal propensity to consume is derived from a more general, theoretical perspective in Chapter Five.

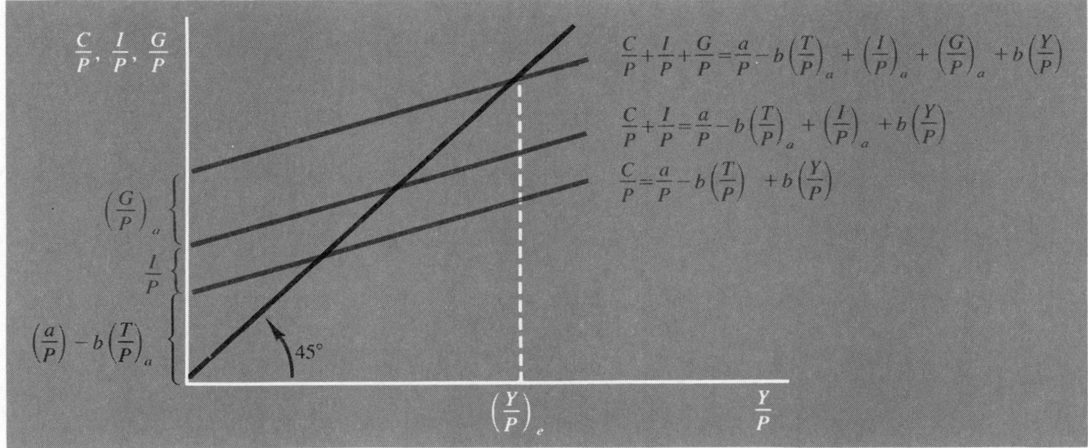

Figure 7.3 Solution for the Equilibrium Level of Aggregate Income

If this expression is substituted into the left-hand side of the equilibrium condition (7.4′) and s is substituted for $(1 - b)$, the equilibrium level of real income may be found:

$$\left(\frac{Y}{P}\right)_e = \frac{\frac{a}{P} + \left(\frac{I}{P}\right)_a + \left(\frac{G}{P}\right)_a + s\left(\frac{T}{P}\right)_a - \left(\frac{T}{P}\right)_a}{s} \tag{7.12}$$

This is the same solution as the one derived in the previous section using the supply of and demand for credit approach.

The Autonomous Expenditures Multiplier

One of the most politically relevant implications of all monetary and macroeconomic theory is the Keynesian autonomous expenditures multiplier. As indicated earlier in this chapter, in the Keynesian partial equilibrium, income-expenditures model an increase in government deficit expenditures does not crowd out private expenditures as it does in the Neoclassical model. Instead, an increase in government deficit expenditures stimulates real income, and the rise in real income assures that new saving will flow into the market to match the financing needs of government. Using the Keynesian model, it will be shown that in order to generate the amount of new saving necessary to bring about equilibrium, real income must increase in a *multiple* of the rise in autonomous government expenditures.

The Keynesian autonomous expenditures multiplier is: $1/(1 - b)$. Any change in the equilibrium level of aggregate income is the product of a change in any element of

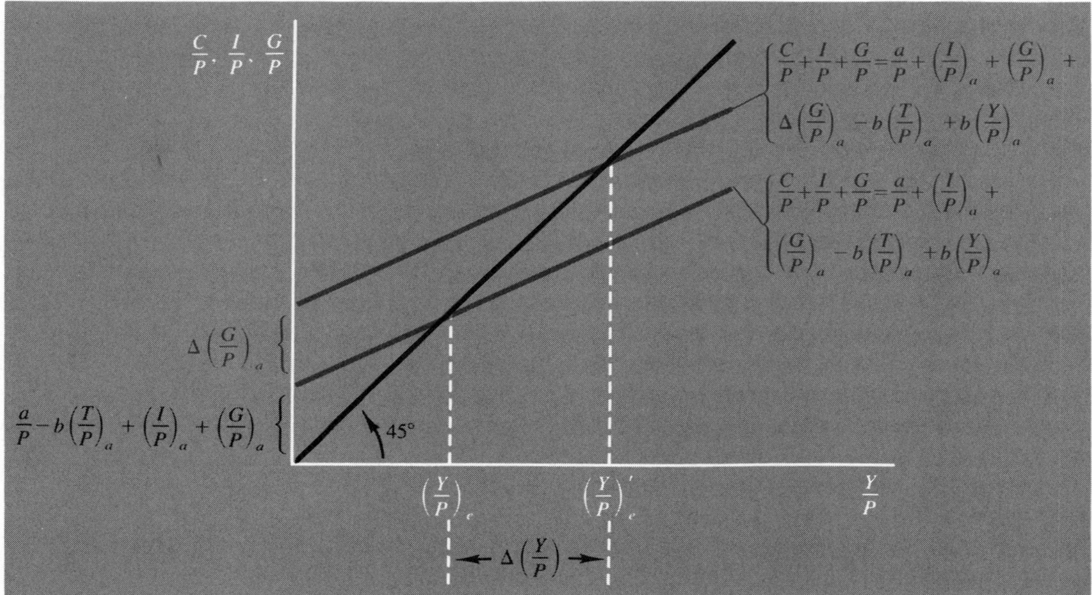

Figure 7.4 The Autonomous Expenditures Multiplier in a Simple Model of Income Determination

autonomous aggregate demand and this multiplier. This can be seen algebraically. Allow the deficit expenditures of government to rise and examine the effect on the equilibrium level of real income. The initial equilibrium level of real income in Figure 7.4 is

$$\left(\frac{Y}{P}\right)_e = \frac{\frac{a}{P} + \left(\frac{I}{P}\right)_a + \left(\frac{G}{P}\right)_a - b\left(\frac{T}{P}\right)_a}{1 - b} \tag{7.14}$$

After allowing any one of the components of autonomous aggregate demand to change, in this case, $\Delta(GP)_a$, a new equilibrium level of income in Figure 7.4 is obtained:

$$\left(\frac{Y}{P}\right)'_e = \frac{\frac{a}{P} + \left(\frac{I}{P}\right)_a + \left(\frac{G}{P}\right)_a - b\left(\frac{T}{P}\right)_a + \Delta\left(\frac{G}{P}\right)_a}{1 - b} \tag{7.15}$$

The change in income is the difference between Equation (7.15) and Equation (7.14):

$$\Delta\left(\frac{Y}{P}\right) = \left(\frac{Y}{P}\right)_e' - \left(\frac{Y}{P}\right)_e = \frac{\frac{a}{P} + \left(\frac{I}{P}\right)_a + \left(\frac{G}{P}\right)_a - b\left(\frac{T}{P}\right)_a + \Delta\left(\frac{G}{P}\right)_a}{1 - b}$$

$$- \frac{\frac{a}{P} + \left(\frac{I}{P}\right)_a + \left(\frac{G}{P}\right)_a - b\left(\frac{T}{P}\right)_a}{1 - \mathrm{b}}$$

$$= \left(\frac{1}{1 - b}\right) \cdot \Delta\left(\frac{G}{P}\right)_a \tag{7.16}$$

Real income is increased $\Delta(Y/P)$ in a multiple of the increase in government expenditures, $\Delta(G/P)_a$. Therefore the *autonomous expenditures multiplier* in this model is

$$\frac{\Delta(Y/P)}{\Delta(G/P)_a} = \left(\frac{1}{1 - b}\right) \tag{7.17}$$

The same multiplier would hold for changes either in autonomous consumption (a) or in autonomous investment expenditures $(I/P)_a$.

The autonomous expenditures multiplier may be viewed in a number of alternative ways. One way is to use the alternative way of expressing income-expenditures equilibrium:

$$\frac{S}{P} = \frac{I}{P} + \frac{G}{P} - \frac{T}{P} \tag{7.18}$$

Assuming that taxation, T/P, is constant, any change in government expenditures, G/P, with investment expenditures, I/P, unchanged must be matched by an equal change in saving, S/P. Similarly, any change in investment expenditures, I/P, with government expenditures, G/P, unchanged must also be matched by an equal change in saving, S/P. Otherwise, the equilibrium condition would not be satisfied. According to the saving relation Equation (7.5), saving will change if and only if income, Y/P, changes in the same direction.

Therefore, assuming a change in autonomous investment expenditures, $\Delta(I/P)_a$, with taxation, T/P, and government expenditures, G/P, unchanged, to sustain equilibrium in income and expenditures,

$$\Delta\left(\frac{S}{P}\right) = \Delta\left(\frac{I}{P}\right)_a \tag{7.19}$$

By Equation (7.5)

$$\Delta\left(\frac{S}{P}\right) = s\,\Delta\left(\frac{Y}{P}\right) \tag{7.20}$$

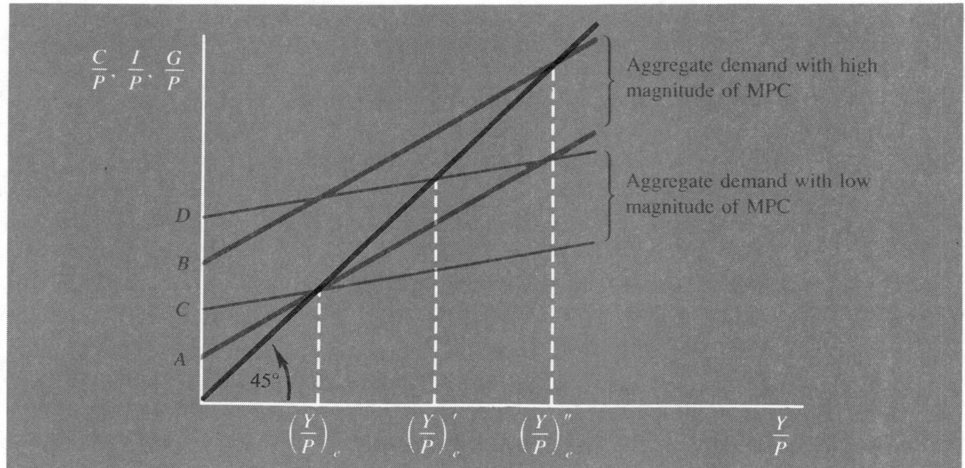

Figure 7.5 Demonstration of the Relationship Between the Size of the Multiplier and the Magnitude of the Marginal Propensity to Consume (MPC)

substituting Equation (7.20) into Equation (7.19) and rearranging yields:

$$\frac{\Delta(Y/P)}{\Delta(I/P)_a} = \frac{1}{s} = \frac{1}{1 - b} \tag{7.21}$$

which is the autonomous expenditures multiplier. The greater the value of the marginal propensity to consume, b, the smaller the value of the marginal propensity to save, s, and the larger the change in income, $\Delta(Y/P)$, that is necessary to generate the necessary change in saving, $\Delta(S/P)$, to match the initial change in autonomous investment expenditures, $\Delta(I/P)_a$.

The autonomous expenditures multiplier process can be portrayed graphically. In Figure 7.4 the change in aggregate income, $\Delta(Y/P)$, is a "multiple" of the change in autonomous aggregate demand, $\Delta(G/P)_a$.

It can also be shown that, given any change in autonomous expenditures, the greater the slope of the aggregate demand relation (the greater the marginal propensity to consume), the greater the change in income from one equilibrium position to the other. This is shown in Figure 7.5. Here two alternative aggregate demand functions are drawn to produce the same equilibrium level of income at $(Y/P)_e$. Then both aggregate demand relations shift upward by the same amount ($AB = CD$) as a result of the increase in autonomous aggregate demand. For the aggregate demand function with the smaller slope or lower marginal propensity to consume (*MPC*), the new equilibrium level of income is $(Y/P)_e{}'$. For the aggregate demand function with the larger slope or the greater marginal propensity to consume, the new equilibrium level of income is $(Y/P)_e{}''$. Figure 7.5 demonstrates graphically that the magnitude of the autonomous expenditures multiplier varies directly with the magnitude of the marginal propensity to consume. It shows that the core of the multiplier principle is the degree to which an initial increase in the level of expenditures generates an even greater expansion in income.

The multiplier process can also be explained intuitively. In equilibrium, aggregate income equals aggregate expenditures. Any shock to equilibrium such as an increase in autonomous expenditures creates disequilibrium. Equilibrium can only be restored if aggregate income rises once again to equal aggregate demand. If the *MPC* is quite small (positive but near zero in magnitude), a relatively small rise in aggregate income can restore equilibrium. In fact, where b is very small, equilibrium can be restored if income rises only by an amount equal to the increase in autonomous aggregate demand (in Equation 7.17 as $b \rightarrow 0$, $[1/(1 - b)] \rightarrow 1$). If, on the other hand, the *MPC* is quite large, only a relatively large increase in aggregate income can restore equilibrium. This happens because as aggregate income rises with a relatively large *MPC*, more aggregate (consumption) expenditures are induced by the rise in income. Where b is large but still less than unity, the size of the autonomous expenditures multiplier approaches infinity (in Equation 7.17 as $b \rightarrow 1$, $[1/(1 - b)] \rightarrow \infty$).

Policy Implications of the Autonomous Expenditures Multiplier

While the multiplier concept may appear to be an arid mathematical and/or graphical exercise, its social implications should not be overlooked. The multiplier indicates that changes in government spending are a lever with which the level of real income can be manipulated. It suggests rather awesome powers for an activist government. In the bleak days of the Great Depression of the 1930s when Keynes first conveyed the autonomous expenditures multiplier to a despairing world, it was social dynamite. While Neoclassical economists, many government officials, and citizens were perplexed about the miserable state of the economy, Keynes and his growing band of followers offered a positive program to get the economy moving again. They argued that autonomous private investment spending had plummeted, that interest rates were fixed or "sticky," and that, as a result, aggregate real income fell. Compensatory increases in government spending (working through the multiplier effect) could revive the wretched economy. The appeal of this argument was magnetic. Economics teachers understood the preceding model fairly easily. As a result, the multiplier concept made its way into the classroom, and several generations of students of economic principles were schooled in it. It was little wonder that the Neoclassical alternative of crowding out seemed so alien when it first began to capture public attention in the 1970s and 1980s.

In the early 1980s, with the economy mired in the deepest recession since the 1930s, Keynesian policy prescriptions reemerged. Many citizens, interest groups, and politicians pressed Congress for government expenditures programs and further tax cuts to stimulate a rip-snorting advance in aggregate output. In bold contrast, adherents to the Neoclassical view insisted that the mounting government deficit would only further impoverish the private sector by increasing interest rates.

Which model is true, the Neoclassical crowding out model or the Keynesian multiplier model? Does an increase in the government deficit reduce private living standards or does it stimulate real income? And, if real income is stimulated, whence come the additional services of the factors of production, such as labor inputs? Are increases in the government deficit a one-way ticket to the poorhouse or are they a means of insuring overall prosperity? Only a general equilibrium view of the world, presented in Chapters Ten through Fifteen, can provide tentative answers to these questions.

Other Multipliers in the Keynesian Partial Equilibrium Income-Expenditures Model: The Autonomous Taxation Multiplier and Its Policy Implications

The Keynesian partial equilibrium model can also be manipulated to yield multipliers premised on changes in the other components of autonomous aggregate demand. For example, changing autonomous taxation $(T/P)_a$ instead of autonomous government expenditures in Equation (7.15) and working through an algebraic process similar to Equations (7.16) and (7.17) yields an autonomous taxation multiplier:

$$\frac{\Delta(Y/P)}{\Delta(T/P)_a} = \frac{-b}{1-b} \tag{7.22}$$

The autonomous taxation multiplier is negative and smaller in absolute magnitude than the autonomous expenditures multiplier. This occurs because any change in autonomous taxation affects autonomous aggregate demand through its effect on autonomous consumption. For example, a lump sum increase in the level of taxation of $\Delta(T/P)_a$ does not reduce autonomous aggregate demand by $\Delta(T/P)_a$, but rather it reduces autonomous aggregate demand by the negative of the marginal propensity to consume $-b$ times the taxation increase or $-b \cdot \Delta(T/P)_a$ through the final term of the consumption function:

$$\frac{C}{P} = \frac{a}{P} + b\left(\frac{Y}{P}\right) - b\left(\frac{T}{P}\right)_a \tag{7.13$'$}$$

Thus, the effect on aggregate income is the decrease in aggregate demand that is induced by the increase in taxation times the autonomous expenditures multiplier, or

$$\Delta\left(\frac{Y}{P}\right) = (-b)\Delta\left(\frac{T}{P}\right)_a \cdot \frac{1}{1-b}$$

which, after rearranging, yields the autonomous taxation multiplier.[4]

$$\frac{\Delta(Y/P)}{\Delta(T/P)_a} = \frac{-b}{1-b} \tag{7.22}$$

[4]The response of consumption expenditures to a reduction in taxation is, in the real world, probably a lot more complicated than portrayed here. The strength of the response depends on whether the effect of the reduction in taxation on real disposable income is viewed by households as being transitory or permanent. There is considerable theoretical evidence that the marginal propensity to consume out of a transitory change in disposable income is less than the marginal propensity to consume out of a permanent change in disposable income. See the discussion of the theory of saving and consumption in Chapter Five.

The *autonomous taxation multiplier* indicates that the level of real income will increase in a multiple of a change in taxation, the tax receipts of government. It shows that taxation policy is also an effective way for government to affect total real income. The only difference between the two multipliers is that in this partial equilibrium model the autonomous taxation multiplier is slightly less than the autonomous expenditures multiplier. In the world of political reality the autonomous taxation multiplier has proven far more relevant than the autonomous expenditures multiplier. Government expenditures are fairly difficult to manipulate as an instrument of countercyclical fiscal policy. In contrast, changing taxation has proven to be a far more feasible means of affecting real income. The autonomous taxation multiplier concept reached its zenith in public acceptance in the early 1960s when Congress passed a tax cut which was proposed by the Kennedy administration. The reduction in taxation was rationalized as an effort to boost aggregate real income and to "get the economy moving again." Thus this battle cry of the early Keynesians of the 1930s and 1940s finally was manifested in law by the activist central government of the 1960s. During the recession of the early 1980s many politicians proposed cuts in taxation as a means of kindling an explosion in the level of real income and ending the recession. The legacy of Keynes' economics has survived!

In contrast, according to the Neoclassical model of the credit market, a reduction in the level of taxation increases the deficit and aggravates crowding out.[5]

Other Multipliers: The Balanced Budget Multiplier

A particularly celebrated concept in Keynesian economics is the *balanced budget multiplier*. The balanced budget multiplier specifies the change in income that will result from any change in autonomous government expenditures that is matched by an equal change in autonomous taxation so that there is no change in the deficit or surplus of the government budget. Thus, the condition for an incrementally balanced budget is:

$$\Delta\left(\frac{G}{P}\right)_a = \Delta\left(\frac{T}{P}\right)_a \qquad (7.23)$$

The initial equilibrium was described by

$$\left(\frac{Y}{P}\right)_e = \frac{\dfrac{a}{P} + \left(\dfrac{I}{P}\right)_a + \left(\dfrac{G}{P}\right)_a - b\left(\dfrac{T}{P}\right)_a}{1 - b} \qquad (7.14)$$

Increases in autonomous government expenditures and autonomous taxation would cause income to rise to

[5]According to yet another Neoclassical perspective, *supply-side economic policy* delineated in Chapter Fourteen, a cut in the *tax rate* may stimulate output, not by increasing spending but by providing incentives for greater productive effort and greater labor and capital inputs in production processes.

$$\left(\frac{Y}{P}\right)_e'' = \frac{\frac{a}{P} + \left(\frac{I}{P}\right)_a + \left(\frac{G}{P}\right)_a - b\left(\frac{T}{P}\right)_a + \Delta\left(\frac{G}{P}\right)_a - b\Delta\left(\frac{T}{P}\right)_a}{1 - b} \tag{7.24}$$

The change in income is the difference between Equations (7.24) and (7.14):

$$\begin{aligned}\Delta\left(\frac{Y}{P}\right) &= \left(\frac{Y}{P}\right)_e'' - \left(\frac{Y}{P}\right)_e \\ &= \frac{\frac{a}{P} + \left(\frac{I}{P}\right)_a + \left(\frac{G}{P}\right)_a - b\left(\frac{T}{P}\right)_a + \Delta\left(\frac{G}{P}\right)_a - b\Delta\left(\frac{T}{P}\right)_a}{1 - b} \\ &\quad - \frac{\frac{a}{P} + \left(\frac{I}{P}\right)_a + \left(\frac{G}{P}\right)_a - b\left(\frac{T}{P}\right)_a}{1 - b}\end{aligned} \tag{7.25}$$

Assume an incrementally balanced budget and substitute Equation (7.23) into Equation (7.25). Simplifying yields:

$$\Delta\left(\frac{Y}{P}\right) = \left(\frac{1 - b}{1 - b}\right)\Delta\left(\frac{G}{P}\right)_a$$

Therefore, the balanced budget multiplier in the present model is unity:

$$\frac{\Delta(Y/P)}{\Delta(G/P)_a} = \left(\frac{1 - b}{1 - b}\right) = 1 \tag{7.26}$$

This can be seen in Figure 7.6. Here, the increase in income, resulting solely from the increase in autonomous government expenditures which is not subject to the incrementally balanced budget condition Equation (7.23), would have been identical to the increase shown in Figure 7.5,

$$\left(\frac{Y}{P}\right)_e' - \left(\frac{Y}{P}\right)_e = \Delta\left(\frac{G}{P}\right)_a\left(\frac{1}{1 - b}\right)$$

However, because the budget must be incrementally balanced, the aggregate demand function has a *net* upward shift of only $\Delta(G/P)_a - b\Delta(T/P)_a$. This is the net result of shifting it upwards by $\Delta(G/P)_a$ (the effect of the increase in autonomous government expenditures) *and* shifting it downwards by $-b\Delta(T/P)_a$ (the effect of the increase in lump sum taxation on autonomous consumption). Since $\Delta(G/P)_a = \Delta(T/P)_a$, by the assumption of an incrementally balanced budget (Equation 7.23), this *net* increase in autonomous

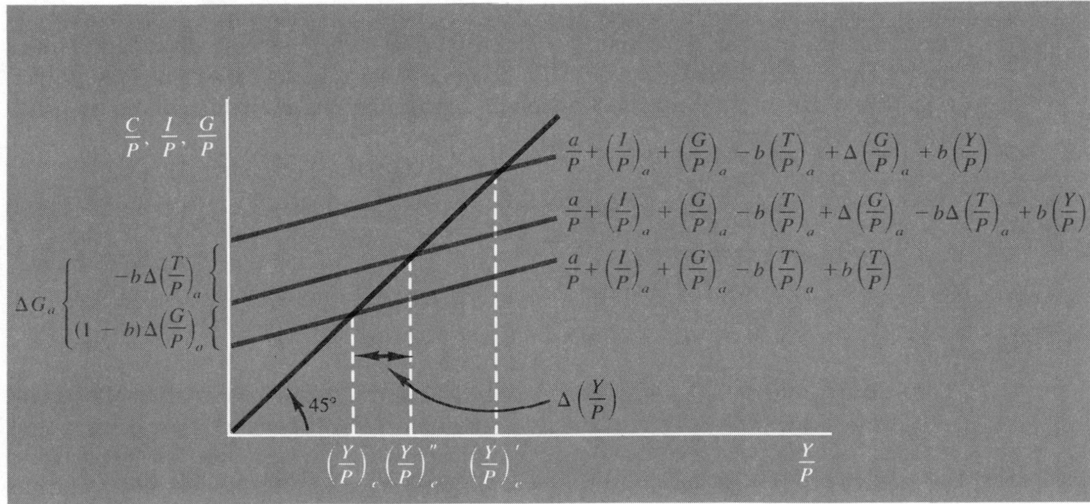

Figure 7.6 Balanced Budget Multiplier

aggregate demand is $\Delta(G/P)_a(1 - b)$, as shown in Figure 7.6. As expressed earlier, the increase in income is equal to the autonomous expenditures multiplier times this net change in autonomous expenditures, or

$$\left(\frac{Y}{P}\right)''_e - \left(\frac{Y}{P}\right)_e = \Delta\left(\frac{Y}{P}\right) = \Delta\left(\frac{G}{P}\right)_a\left(1 - b\right)\left(\frac{1}{1 - b}\right)$$

Collecting terms gives the balanced budget multiplier:

$$\frac{\Delta(Y/P)}{\Delta(G/P)_a} = \left(\frac{1-b}{1-b}\right) = 1 \qquad (7.26)$$

In the income-expenditures model the balanced budget multiplier is clearly less than the autonomous expenditures and autonomous taxation multipliers. During the halcyon days of activist fiscal policy, the balanced budget multiplier was often used to point out the weaknesses inherent in balancing the federal budget. It was argued that the balanced budget approach severely hampered the fiscal power of government to manipulate aggregate real income through its aggregate spending and aggregate taxation policies. Such a program is a far cry from the 1980s when, as discussed in Chapter Six, the crowding out model of the credit market is being used to enlist support for an annually balanced federal budget.

The Automatic Stabilizer

The preceding treatments have all modeled taxation as being autonomous, or independent, of the level of income. As indicated in Chapter Six, this specification violates the facts; it is more realistic to portray aggregate taxation as dependent on the level of aggregate real income. To examine how the level of aggregate income affects government tax receipts and transfer payments, the taxation relation used throughout this chapter, Equation (7.8), will be modified to reflect a marginal tax rate and transfer payments made by government:

$$\frac{T}{P} = \left(\frac{T}{P}\right)_a + t\left(\frac{Y}{P}\right) \tag{7.27}$$

where

$$(T/P)_a < 0 \text{ and } 1 > t > 0$$

This relation indicates that total tax receipts consist of autonomous taxation $(T/P)_a$ plus induced tax receipts $[t(Y/P)]$. Autonomous taxation $(T/P)_a$ is negative since it represents transfer payments that are paid out by government, negative taxation. These payments are assumed to be independent of the level of aggregate real income. Induced tax receipts $[t(Y/P)]$ consist of two terms: the marginal income tax rate (t) times the level of aggregate real income (Y/P).

Induced tax receipts $[t(Y/P)]$ are a constant percentage (t) of real income (Y/P), and autonomous taxation is a negative constant. Therefore, as real income (Y/P) rises, total tax receipts (T/P) climb as a percentage of income. Thus, Equation (7.27) implies a *progressive taxation system*.

If government purchases (G/P) are assumed to be exogenously determined, a rise in aggregate real income will cause the real government deficit $(G/P - T/P)$ to decline. (Notice that $[G/P]$ refers to real government purchases, since real transfer payments by government are now included in $[T/P]$. See footnote 1.) Conversely, a decline in aggregate real income will impel a rise in the real government deficit. Thus, an expansion of real economic activity automatically produces a fiscal policy, as measured by government taxation, that is restrictive, while a dip in the economic activity automatically reduces government taxation and makes fiscal policy more stimulative. This reflects the working of the vaunted *automatic stabilizer* aspect of fiscal policy.

Substituting Equation (7.27) for (7.8) in the preceding model modifies the solution for the equilibrium level of income Equation (7.14):

$$\left(\frac{Y}{P}\right)_e = \frac{\dfrac{a}{P} + \left(\dfrac{I}{P}\right)_a + \left(\dfrac{G}{P}\right)_a - b\left(\dfrac{T}{P}\right)_a}{1 - b + bt} \tag{7.14$'$}$$

This, in turn, alters the multipliers in the following way: The autonomous expenditures multiplier, Equation (7.17), becomes smaller:

$$\frac{1}{1 - b + bt} < \frac{1}{1 - b}$$

The (negative) autonomous taxation multiplier, Equation (7.22), becomes larger (less negative):

$$\frac{-b}{1 - b + bt} > \frac{-b}{1 - b}$$

The balanced budget multiplier, Equation (7.26), becomes smaller (and less than unity):

$$\frac{1 - b}{1 - b + bt} < \frac{1 - b}{1 - b}$$

Thus, the added realism of a marginal income tax rate (t) lowers the absolute magnitude of all the multipliers. This occurs because, with a marginal tax rate, each one dollar increase in real income will increase real disposable income by only ($1 - t$) dollars. Since the increase in real disposable income is less than the increase in real income, the induced effect on consumption expenditures, the basis of all multipliers, will be smaller.

In the Keynesian partial equilibrium model, the automatic response of tax receipts to the pace of economic activity, as reflected in the new smaller multipliers, stabilizes responses in real income to any autonomous (spending) shock. Taxation falls and disposable income and consumption expenditures are automatically stimulated in periods of recession. Taxation rises and disposable income and consumption expenditures are automatically suppressed in periods of boom. This provides an automatic dampener to increases in aggregate demand during periods of economic excitement and to decreases in aggregate demand during periods of economic sluggishness. The boost to consumption spending during recession and the drag on consumption spending during boom restrain economic excesses in either direction. For many decades after Keynes, the concept of an automatic stabilizer for the economy was widely applauded as an important corrective feedback mechanism for the economy.

Contrast this vision with the Neoclassical perspective of the credit market discussed in Chapter Six. Neoclassical economists are wont to point out that larger deficits during recession aggravate the crowding out problem. As seen in Table 6.2 of Chapter Six, during the recession of the early 1980s, the reduction in tax receipts made the federal government deficit approximately \$130 billion greater than it would have been had there been no automatic stabilizer.[6] Keynesians agree that in more realistic models, such as the one presented in Chapter Twelve, the multipliers are smaller because crowding out reduces the stimulatory effect of fiscal policy. However, Neoclassicists contest the alleged stimulatory power of government deficits. They are skeptical of increased deficits or any other policy to increase aggregate real income by systematically stimulating aggregate expenditures. To understand this skepticism, it is necessary to examine fiscal policy from a general equilibrium context, paying careful attention to the role of the formulation of expectations in various markets. This important task will be performed in Chapters Eleven through Fifteen.

[6] In Table 6.1 the actual federal budget deficit for 1985 was \$212 billion. The high employment deficit was \$129 billion. If tax receipts were not tied to real income, the deficit would not have risen as real income fell.

Concluding Comment

This chapter presents the Keynesian alternative to the Neoclassical model of the credit market in partial equilibrium. In the Neoclassical model the interest rate is the variable which brings saving, investment, and the government deficit into equilibrium while the level of aggregate real income is assumed to be constant. By contrast, in the Keynesian model, the level of real income is the variable which brings saving, investment, and the government deficit into balance while the interest rate is assumed to be constant. The models have blatantly different implications for an increase in the government deficit. The Neoclassical model, as seen in Chapter Six, implies a complete crowding out of private expenditures by the deficit of government. The Keynesian model indicates no crowding out; the increased financing needs of government are satisfied by an expanded flow of saving into the credit market based on a higher level of aggregate real income.

Thus, the Keynesian model indicates that a boost in government deficit spending will catalyze a rise in real income. To better explore the nature of the interrelationship between increases in real (autonomous) expenditures and increases in real income, the Keynesian model of credit flows is converted into a model of income and expenditures flows. The two models are synonymous ways of viewing the same economic phenomena. Using the income-expenditures approach, the autonomous expenditures, autonomous taxation, and balanced budget multipliers were derived, their powerful implications for public policy were outlined, and the concept of the automatic stabilizer was discussed.

The stark contrast between Neoclassical and Keynesian models of the same market cannot be overemphasized. Consider the predicted effects of an increase in the government deficit. The Neoclassical model's implications of complete crowding out stand in bold juxtaposition to the Keynesian model's prediction of a briskly stimulated pace of economic activity with no crowding out. Which model is true? In reality, both schemes are unrealistic because they both are models of partial equilibrium, isolated perspectives that hold everything else constant. To better understand the economy and to judge the conditions under which either of the theories is true, one must employ a general-equilibrium perspective of simultaneous interaction between all markets—the labor market, the credit market, and the money market. Then, one can make a better informed judgment about crucial public policy choices to be made by voters.

After examining a model of the money market—the supply of and demand for money—in the next two chapters, general equilibrium analysis, both Neoclassical and Keynesian, will be presented in Chapters Ten through Fifteen.

EXERCISES

1. Prove mathematically that a model of credit (loanable funds) flows is also a model of aggregate expenditures and aggregate output.
2. Explain the autonomous expenditures multiplier principle in words. Why is Keynes' *MPC* so important?

3. Consider the following model of the income-expenditures sector:

   $C = 100 + .8Y_d$

   $I = 200$

   $G = 360$

   $T = 200$

   $C + I + G = Y$

   $Y_d = Y - T$

   a. What is autonomous consumption?
   b. What is the marginal propensity to consume?
   c. What is the marginal propensity to save?
   d. What is the government deficit?
   e. What is the value of the autonomous expenditures multiplier?

4. Explain why you agree or disagree with the following statement: "There is no Neoclassical model of aggregate demand. Aggregate demand is a Keynesian concept."

5. Explain how the Keynesian partial equilibrium model of aggregate expenditures and aggregate real income can be used to justify government activism.

6. Prove that the tax receipts relation, Equation (7.27), implies a system of progressive taxation, defined as a system in which the percentage change in tax receipts always exceeds the percentage change in income.

7. Why is it that the Keynesian partial equilibrium model of income and expenditures flows seems to offer such hope for engineering a healthier economy through government fiscal activism while the Neoclassical partial equilibrium model seems so pessimistic in this regard?

8. Explain why the cyclical variation of government income tax receipts is a good thing in the Keynesian income-expenditures model and a bad thing in the Neoclassical credit market model.

BIBLIOGRAPHY

Brown, E. Cary. "Fiscal Policy in the Thirties: A Reappraisal." *American Economic Review* (December 1956), pp. 857–879.

Dolde, Walter. "Temporary Taxes as Macroeconomic Stabilizers." *American Economic Review* (May 1979), pp. 81–85.

Hansen, Albert H. *A Guide to Keynes*. New York: McGraw-Hill, 1953.

Keynes, John Maynard. *The General Theory of Employment, Interest and Money*. New York: Harcourt, Brace and Co., 1936.

Samuelson, Paul A. "The Simple Mathematics of Income Determination." In *Income, Employment and Public Policy*. New York: W. W. Norton and Co., 1948.

The Money Supply

Chapter 8

Introduction

Previous chapters focused on the labor and credit markets. The next two chapters examine the money market. This chapter begins with a discussion of the role, definition, and determination of the money supply. The next chapter introduces money demand and its interaction with money supply in the money market.

Money commonly is thought of as mere pieces of paper or metal, with a dreary sameness of color and design on each piece. The many slang terms for money such as bread, cabbage, dough, wampum, tin, ducats, skins, lettuce, moola, and zookers are familiar. Some of these terms presumably come from the fact that the items they describe have at one time or another served as money (skins, wampum). Other terms may reflect physical characteristics such as color (cabbage, lettuce) or substance (tin). Still others are of unknown origin (zookers), but teams of highly trained research economists are investigating this problem.

The variety of forms money has taken are fascinating. In recent times, anthropologists discovered huge stones used as money on the island of Yap in the Pacific and dogs' teeth used as money in the Solomon islands. During World War II in many countries and in prisoner of war camps, cigarettes were used as money because conventional forms were valueless and could command no goods or services.

THE FUNCTIONS OF MONEY

Money as a Medium of Exchange

Money may be defined by the functions that it performs. To paraphrase Benjamin Franklin, money is as money does. A medium of exchange is anything that is generally acceptable in exchange for goods or services or in payment of debt. As a medium of exchange, money is accepted not for its own sake but because it can be used to acquire goods and services. Because money is generally acceptable, it is preferable to pure barter, which is the exchange of goods for other goods without the use of money.

As an example of barter, assume that Mr. Adolph wants beer and possesses only frozen Wiener schnitzel, whereas Mr. Bertrand possesses beer and wants Wiener schnitzel. Trading arrangements through the physical exchange of these goods may be feasible under these conditions. If, on the other hand, Mr. Adolph wants beer but possesses wine, and Mr. Bertrand wants Wiener schnitzel but possesses beer, they cannot barter unless they can find a third party who wants wine and possesses Wiener schnitzel. The need for a third party makes exchange less likely, so Mr. Adolph may have to drink wine, and Mr. Bertrand can have a small beer blast until they find a Wiener schnitzel salesperson who wants to party.

A medium of exchange greatly simplifies the trading process. Mr. Adolph can exchange his wine for money (the medium of exchange) when he finds a wine lover. The money he receives is then the temporary abode of the value of the wine he had. He can exchange this money for Mr. Bertrand's beer. Mr. Bertrand would then have money that he, in turn, could exchange for Wiener schnitzel when he found a seller.

Thus, money as a medium of exchange facilitates trade. Money is similar to a "lubricant" on which the engine of exchange runs. Engines without oil break down. It is difficult to imagine a modern economy functioning without money to ease exchange. Because money facilitates exchange, buyers and sellers spend less time and energy in the exchange process, but what is more important, they do not have to be self-sufficient. In fact, they can specialize in the productive tasks they do best.

In the previous example, Messrs. Adolph and Bertrand will be encouraged because of money to specialize in the production of goods or services for which they are best endowed. They know that they can always exchange their labor or output for money and, in turn, use the money to purchase the goods and services they need. When each person does what he or she can do best, more goods are produced and everyone is better off!

Money as a Unit of Account

Money also serves as a unit of account. This means that the value of each good or service is measured in the monetary unit. The money value (price) of a good or service tells the number of money units for which a good or service can be exchanged. For example, the price of a kilogram of tea may be 700 units of money or, in the United States economy, $700. This is denominating, or measuring the value of, tea and other goods in terms of money. Using money in this way provides a unit with which to compare the prices of goods and services and thereby greatly facilitates purchasing decisions.

Under a regime of barter, the price of one commodity would be quoted in terms of many other commodities. A price of home video systems would be quoted in terms of electric toothpicks, a price of Barbie dolls in terms of twenty-four hour visits to Happy Acres Rest Home, a price of 1947 Studebakers in terms of Gumbies, and so on. Market decisions would be difficult, and the world would be an accountant's nightmare. With prices quoted in money, each good or service has one key price, its price in money. This imparts a great benefit to rational economic calculations and is good news to accountants.

Money as a Store of Value

Money also serves a role as a store of value. This role of money becomes apparent when some holders of money hold it without planning to make an imminent purchase. There must be some advantage to holding money and not spending it in the near future. Why is it reasonable for individuals to hold some of their wealth as money when they could hold all of it in the form of consumer durables that provide obvious services, such as a Porsche or a Ronald McDonald cup, or in forms that earn income, such as stocks and bonds?

In answer, consider the kinds of advantages that money does offer. First, it is easily transferred and readily converted into other forms of wealth. Other forms of wealth cannot be so easily transferred. For example, sometimes people cannot sell their used Pintos as quickly as they would like. Second, money does not wear out physically. (Worn currency in circulation can be costlessly replaced.) Other forms of wealth may suffer wear and tear, and therefore incur storage and maintenance costs. Third, money bears no cost of acquisition. In contrast, consider the purchase of stocks or bonds. To acquire or dispose of wealth in this form, a fee must be paid to the stockbroker. Fourth, holding money allows immediate readiness for emergencies or illness without having either to sell assets at a possible loss or to bear the costs (fees or inconvenience) of cashing them in. For example, one may find it fairly difficult, in case of a financial emergency, to find a ready buyer for 1917 Imperial Czarist Bonds.

The Value of Money

Probably every observer of economic life has wondered why money has value. Intuition says that people need it (do they ever!), and that it is scarce; therefore, it has a positive value. In this case, common sense is not misleading. Money is useful because it performs many functions. It is demanded because it performs services for individuals, and they feel better off because of these services. The foremost of these services comes from money's role as a medium of exchange. For a useful thing to retain value, however, it must be scarce. Money (it is no surprise) is relatively scarce. As the ancient Tibetan proverb states, "money does not grow on trees; that's why we are all out on a limb."

Defining the Composition of the Money Stock

What makes up our money supply, and whence does it come? Most of the money supply consists of checkable deposits. These deposits are money because they perform the functions of money, discussed previously. Checkable deposits are issued by depository institutions. They include checking accounts, negotiable orders of withdrawal (NOW) accounts, Super-NOW accounts, automatic transfer service (ATS) accounts, share draft accounts—anything that is transferable by check, draft, wire, or preauthorized payment arrangement.

Checkable deposits are not to be confused with savings accounts, time deposits, money market deposit accounts, or money market mutual funds. Savings accounts, time deposits, money market mutual funds, and money market deposit accounts are close substitutes for money, sometimes called *near monies*. Savings accounts and time deposits are never legally payable on demand. They are not transferred by check but must be withdrawn in the form of cash. In practice, nonetheless, savings accounts and time deposits are usually paid off at once. Money market mutual funds and money market deposit accounts may be transferred by check, but there are usually restrictions on the check writing privilege, such as a limit in terms of a minimum dollar amount per check or number of checks per month. In contrast, checkable deposits are perfectly transferable by check.

A *checkable deposit* is an obligation (liability) of a depository institution which is payable by the institution on demand. This definition identifies a checkable deposit as a debt or liability because a checkable deposit is a debt, obligation, or liability to its issuer, a depository institution, since the institution must pay it on presentation of an order: a check or a negotiable order of withdrawal. Figure 8.1 shows what happens when checks are written. Here Blaze Glory sells his horse to Deadeye. Deadeye pays with a check. The check is the debt obligation of Deadeye's depository institution.

Checkable deposits are considered a form of money because they are generally accepted in exchange for goods and services. Checkable deposits are usually accepted in

Figure 8.1 Transfer of a Checkable Deposit

making purchases; they serve as a medium of exchange. Generally, other assets do not find the universal acceptability of checkable deposits. For example, suppose Blaze Glory is fitted for a new suit at Kwik Kash Kelly's, the local haberdashery. Further assume that the day Blaze goes to pick up the suit he misplaces his checkbook. How will he pay? Kwik Kash wants cash. If Blaze just happened to have brought along his savings account passbook, his fifty shares of stock of X-Rated Video Games, Inc., his lifetime collection of used BBs, or his Han Solo doll, probably none of these would be acceptable to Kwik Kash Kelly (even though Blaze cherishes them). If Blaze had remembered his checkbook, however, he probably would have gotten his suit because checkable deposits are usually more acceptable to business people than other possessions.

This does not mean that only checkable deposits can be used for exchange. For instance, it is conceivable that Blaze's credit card would have been acceptable to Kwik Kash. Yet credit cards are not money because they are not a medium of exchange as are checkable deposits and currency. Credit cards require special arrangements between their issuers and the sellers of goods and services. Furthermore, credit cards are really used to create obligations (of the purchaser to the seller) rather than to settle them, because ultimately the seller is paid off in money.

In addition to checkable deposits, traveler's checks and the currency (bills and coin) that the public holds serve as money. Traveler's checks and currency perform the functions of money. They are generally acceptable for the purchase of goods and services.[1] (Don't leave home without them.) Currency (bills and coin) that is not in circulation is not part of the money supply. For instance, if $50 in coin is in a bank vault, it is not in circulation and cannot be counted as part of the money supply. To count it as such would result in double counting.[2] If $50 in coin is in the hands of a household, it *is* counted in the money supply.

The total money supply of the United States therefore consists of the amount of checkable deposits in the hands of the nonbank public,[3] plus traveler's checks and currency (paper money) and coin in circulation. The money supply, narrowly defined, consists of traveler's checks, currency in circulation, and the deposits upon which checks can be drawn for the payment of debts to third parties. This measure of the money supply is labeled $M1$ by the Federal Reserve. In April 1986, the average total money supply, $M1$, in the United States was approximately $640 billion. About 72 percent of this amount, $465 billion, consisted of checkable deposit liabilities of the nation's depository institutions.[4]

[1]Coin and paper money are called token and fiat money, respectively, since the material from which they are made is not worth their face value. They are, however, *legal tender,* that is, legally acceptable media of exchange.

[2]Vault cash *backs up* as reserves the deposit liabilities of a bank which are counted as money. To count the vault-cash assets as part of our money supply would be a form of double counting. The vast bulk of currency is a liability of the Federal Reserve System. (Coin, totaling a small percentage of our currency in circulation, is a liability of the United States Treasury.)

[3]*Nonbank public* means households and businesses, excluding commercial banks and all government units.

[4]$M1$ does not include deposits held by the United States government, foreign official institutions, and domestic depository institutions.

There are broader measures of money which include deposits that cannot always be used in making payments but can easily be converted into checkable deposits or currency. These near-monies are added to $M1$ to constitute the broadly defined money supply $M2$. The broad money supply $M2$ is approximately four times larger than $M1$. In April 1986, $M2$ totaled $2,580 billion, of which $640 billion was $M1$ and $1,867 billion was savings deposits, small denomination time deposits, money market deposit accounts, and money market mutual funds (other than those of institutional investors), and $73 billion consisted of overnight repurchase agreements and certain Eurodollar deposits. Overnight repurchase agreements are overnight loans to banks. The relevant Eurodollar deposits are those held by United States nonbank residents at Caribbean branches of United States banks. Money market deposit accounts and money market mutual funds, which together exceeded $685 billion in April 1986, generally have limited check writing privileges, but studies show that they are often used for transactions purposes.

Many economists feel that the assets included in $M2$ but not in $M1$ are almost as liquid as those deposits which are payable on demand, checkable deposits, and prefer $M2$ to $M1$. Other economists believe that these assets do not serve as a medium of exchange and prefer $M1$ as the best measure of money because it represents the ultimate in liquidity. Others choose between $M1$ and $M2$ on the basis of statistical criteria such as their correlation with movements in nominal income. Whatever measure is preferred—$M1$, $M2$, an average of the components of $M1$ or $M2$ with each component weighted for its liquidity, or an even broader measure—money is the most liquid of all assets.[5]

OPERATING A DEPOSITORY INSTITUTION

The Balance Sheet

As seen in Chapter Five, depository institutions are a type of financial intermediary. They obtain interest-earning assets, which are primarily debt claims against others, by issuing specialized debt claims against themselves. What distinguishes depository institutions from other financial intermediaries is that depository institutions issue specialized debt claims that are perfectly transferable by check, that is, checkable deposits.

Consider a simple world in which an individual depository institution holds only two forms of assets: cash assets, and interest-earning assets, loans and securities (sometimes

[5]An even broader measure of the composition of the money stock is $M3$. $M3$ consists of everything in $M2$ plus large denomination time deposits of all depository institutions, plus large denomination term repurchase agreements of commercial banks and savings and loan associations, plus money market mutual funds of institutional investors.

Much of the debate over $M1$, $M2$, and $M3$ occurs because innovations by depository institutions can change the relationship between $M1$, $M2$, and $M3$. For instance, a shift in public preferences toward components of $M2$ and $M3$ that are not in $M1$ will cause $M2$ and $M3$ to rise at the expense of $M1$. This will be reflected as a change in the money supply expansion coefficients, discussed later in this chapter. It will also be reflected as a change in the income velocity of $M1$, $M2$, and $M3$. This will be discussed in Chapter Nine.

Table 8.1 The Balance Sheet of a Depository Institution

Cash assets:	Deposits:
Vault cash	Checkable deposits
Deposits at Federal Reserve	Time deposits
Deposits at other institutions	Savings accounts
Checks in collection	Money market deposit accounts
Securities (financial investments):	Other liabilities:
U.S. government securities	Loans from Federal Reserve or other central credit facility
State & municipal bonds	Loans from other institutions
	Nondeposit liabilities
Loans:	Net worth:
Business loans	Outstanding stock (equities)
Personal loans	Retained earnings
Mortgage loans	

called financial, meaning *paper*, investments), and issues various kinds of liabilities. Table 8.1 presents a highly simplified balance sheet of such a depository institution.

Cash assets are important. They enable a depository institution to satisfy the claims that it issues against itself. These claims are issued in order to acquire the interest-earning claims issued by others.[6] Another name for *cash assets* is *primary reserves*. The law requires that each depository institution hold a dollar amount of primary reserves equal to the sum of a legally specified percentage times the dollar amount of each category of deposits. Assets that are eligible to satisfy these legal reserve requirements are called *legal reserves*.[7] (Yet, even if there were no legal reserve requirement, cash assets [primary reserves] would still be held.) The Federal Reserve System's Board of Governors sets these legal reserve requirements within upper and lower boundaries that are established by legislation, the Depository Institutions Deregulation and Monetary Control Act of 1980.

Loans and securities[8] are the *earning assets* of the depository institution. Loans are arranged in face-to-face negotiations. Securities are evidences of interest-bearing debt that the borrowers originally sell on and are traded on the open market. Loans and securities, viewed together, represent that portion of a depository institution's total assets that is held primarily for the (interest) income it earns rather than for its ability to meet deposit claims. Table 8.1 contains several examples of the different types of loans and securities held by depository institutions.

[6]Any action that enables the depository institution to gain cash assets strengthens its ability to acquire earning assets—it strengthens its lending power. As pointed out later, an institution's lending power is advanced by the institution's successfully competing for deposits of cash by borrowing funds, issuing more stock, or increasing retained earnings.

[7]As discussed later, deposits at other institutions and checks in collection are quite liquid or cash-ready (i.e., serve as primary reserves), yet cannot be counted as "legal reserves" for the purpose of satisfying the legal reserve requirement.

[8]Financial investment (purchasing of existing paper assets) is not to be confused with real investment expenditures on newly produced physical capital goods, discussed in Chapter Five.

Liquidity, Lending Power, and Liability Management

Cash assets are the most liquid assets of depository institutions. Cash assets include: (1) vault cash, (2) deposits at a Federal Reserve Bank or other central facility, (3) deposits at other depository institutions, and (4) checks and drafts in the process of collection. Depository institutions maintain a fraction of their total assets as cash items and keep the rest as earning assets. This is called *fractional reserve banking*. Why do depository institutions not keep all their assets as loans and financial (paper) investments and earn even more interest? The reason is that cash assets provide liquidity. Overlooking legal requirements for the moment, among the cash assets, vault cash is held simply because the institution will need cash when a check drawn on a deposit is presented by its owner for currency and coin; the other cash assets, deposits at a Federal Reserve Bank or at other institutions, are held to settle check clearings.

If a depositor writes a check which is then deposited (by the person receiving the check) in a second depository institution, the first institution will need some ready means of paying the second institution. If the institutions have accounts with one another, in a third institution, or in a Federal Reserve Bank or other central facility, they can readily settle the transaction by a simple bookkeeping entry. Thus, since checkable deposits are due on demand, each depository institution must be prepared to honor requests by depositors to withdraw currency or to shift their deposits to other institutions via the check clearing process. The issuance of checks (debt claims which are payable on demand) creates a need for liquid assets by depository institutions.

.The next, most obvious problem is how depository institutions know how much to keep "in reserve." A major premise of fractional reserve banking is that all depositors will not withdraw (in the form of currency drains or deposits in other institutions) all their deposits at one time. As an example, Princess Diana has sizable amounts of deposits in several banks. The typical financial institution welcomes the Princess's money because Charles will seldom need a big portion of her money at one time. The management of the Princess's depository institution then may confidentially keep only a small fraction of these checkable deposit-liabilities backed by cash assets or primary reserves. The rest of the institution's assets can be held in forms that will earn interest income for the institution.

In reality, a depository institution will also try to hold many earning assets in a liquid (readily cashable) form such as short-term U.S. government securities. The bank uses short-term securities as a sort of backstop to protect itself in case of sudden deposit withdrawals or to meet future customer loan demands. Safe earning assets, which have a short maturity and can be actively traded in the securities markets, are called *secondary reserves* to distinguish them from primary reserves. In addition, the regular inflow of cash from loan repayment and maturing securities is an important source of liquidity. Unfortunately, the more liquid forms of loans and securities usually have lower yields than the less liquid forms. For instance, the interest income from some long-term state and municipal bonds is tax free, yet these securities are generally much less liquid than short-term United States government securities. Depository institutions often walk the razor's edge between necessary liquidity and desired profitability when they choose the forms of assets they will hold. This is sometimes disconcerting to the governmental agencies that regulate them, as well as to their stockholders and uninsured creditors.

The need for liquidity is related to the more general desire of the depository institution for a source of *lending power*. Lending power is important to depository institutions that usually feel obligated to stand ready to extend short-term loans to their top customers. One source of lending power is the deposit of cash in return for checkable deposits. Cash assets give an institution a source of lending power. Other sources of lending power, however, usually require a less liquid configuration of assets than checkable deposit liabilities. One source is for institutions to issue claims against themselves which are not legally payable on demand. Table 8.1 contains some examples of noncheckable deposits. For decades, regular savings and time deposits were a small but stable source of funds. Then, in the 1960s, the United States entered an era of intense competition among depository institutions. Commercial banks began competing for more funds by issuing large denomination, negotiable and high interest paying certificates of deposit (large time deposits). Other depository institutions, such as savings and loan associations, were doing the same thing to compete for the deposit dollar. When the interest rates on these instruments reached the legal ceilings set forth by the Federal Reserve in its Regulation Q, there were massive customer withdrawals, called *disintermediation,* because holders could get a higher return from marketable short-term government securities. The lending power of many depository institutions dried up. As a consequence, in the late 1960s Regulation Q ceilings were removed from large certificates of deposit to prevent disintermediation. By 1986, all interest rate ceilings and minimum balance requirements on deposits were completely removed.

The certificate of deposit experiment was just the opening salvo in the competitive war among depository institutions. In the late 1970s, depository institutions became aggressive marketers of small-denomination, nonnegotiable certificates of deposit (small time deposits). In the 1980s, depository institutions offered an ever increasing array of other depository services, including a wide variety of new accounts, such as money market deposit accounts and Super-NOW accounts. As mentioned above, legal ceilings on interest paid on many types of deposits were removed. In an attempt to get stable long-term funds as a source of lending power, more depository institutions began to issue uninsured, long-term nondeposit liabilities against themselves in the bond market, like any borrower. Another source of long-term funds, and an important mollifier for government regulatory agencies which are apprehensive about the solvency of depository institutions, is the issuance of more stock or the retention of bank earnings.[9]

In the process of seeking new sources of lending power, contemporary depository institutions have developed a wide variety of means of satisfying their liquidity needs. In the very short run, institutions can borrow funds from other institutions (Federal funds borrowing) or borrow from the Federal Reserve System or other central credit facilities.

[9]This sketch explains why many depository institutions favor further deregulation of the types of services that they can legally provide and of the geographic areas within which they can provide these services. Such deregulation would allow depository institutions (or their holding companies) to offer new services and enter new geographic markets (by crossing state lines). This would place them more directly in competition with brokerage firms, mutual funds, and other nondepository financial intermediaries that are less regulated. It would provide them with new sources of lending power.

In the short run, depository institutions can issue large denomination time deposits. In the intermediate run, they can compete aggressively for checkable deposits or issue small denomination time deposits. In the long run, they can garner liquidity by issuing long-term uninsured nondeposit debt or equity claims. The practice of selling additional liability claims—borrowing, issuing new deposit claims, and issuing nondeposit liabilities—whenever liquidity needs arise is called *liability management*.

Contemporary depository institutions may encounter profitability problems when interest rates rise if their liabilities are more sensitive to interest rate changes than their assets. This will increase their interest expenses more than it increases their interest income. If assets are more interest-sensitive than liabilities, profitability problems may be encountered when interest rates decline. Modern managers of depository institutions must be conversant with techniques to reduce this risk of a decline in profitability. Steep declines in profitability associated with interest rate changes alarm stockholders and creditors. Because losses threaten an institution's solvency, they also worry regulators such as the Federal Reserve and the Federal Deposit Insurance Corporation.

The Role of the Federal Reserve and the Federal Deposit Insurance Corporation (FDIC)

Realizing that most depository institutions could not possibly pay off all depositors simultaneously, will you and your friends hurry to your bank to withdraw your money and perhaps start an old-fashioned run on the bank? Probably not. You know that checkable deposits are an easy way of carrying out daily transactions or keeping some of your wealth in a liquid form. In addition, since 1933 bank deposits have been insured by the Federal Deposit Insurance Corporation (FDIC) and the deposits of only about a daring, devil-may-care 200 of our 14,000 commercial banks are not insured up to $100,000 per account by the FDIC. (Savings and loan associations and credit unions have similar federal insurance corporations.)

Do not infer from this that depository institutions are never caught short of cash assets or never acquire bad loans and securities. Both occur. The institution caught short of cash assets (primary reserves) will need some time to borrow some from other depository institutions, to borrow from the Federal Reserve or some other central credit facility, to issue large time deposits, to sell some securities, or to contract its loans. The contracting of loans prompted Mark Twain to define a banker as "a fellow who lends you an umbrella when the sun is shining but wants it back again when it begins to rain." If an institution cannot meet its liabilities, it is insolvent. Insolvent or potentially insolvent banks are taken over by the FDIC until they can be merged with stronger banks. If a merger cannot be arranged, the assets of the bank are liquidated and the insured depositors paid off with the proceeds plus FDIC funds. In the 1980s, the number of insolvent depository institutions increased greatly, putting a good deal of pressure on the funds of the deposit insuring agencies.

So far discussion has focused on primary reserves as the most cash-ready assets held by depository institutions. Hereafter, only those forms of primary reserves that satisfy legal reserve requirements by federal law will be considered. By ignoring assets that are primary but not always legal reserves, the word *reserves* can be used unambiguously.[10] The two forms in which legal reserves may be held to satisfy the Federal Reserve System's legal reserve requirements are vault cash and deposits with a Federal Reserve Bank or other central credit facility.

The Federal Reserve Board in Washington, D.C. (called "the Board" by insiders), and the twelve regional Federal Reserve Banks have four major functions: (1) to supervise and control commercial banks, (2) to help the United States Treasury receive and disburse money, (3) to regulate the money supply, and (4) to keep deposits of member depository institutions, much as member institutions keep the deposits of households and firms. The Federal Reserve Bank is a "banker's bank." Deposits of member institutions are a liability of the Federal Reserve and an asset to the member institution.

How does a member institution initially gain a deposit at a Federal Reserve Bank? If a depository institution joins the Federal Reserve System (called "the Fed" by insiders), it may open a deposit at a Federal Reserve Bank simply by sending it some of its vault cash.[11] The institution will have reduced one legal reserve asset, vault cash, and increased another legal reserve asset, its deposit at the Federal Reserve. When a depositor writes a check which is then deposited at another institution, the first institution loses and the second institution gains two things: deposits and reserves.

Under certain conditions the Federal Reserve System acts as a clearinghouse for checks.[12] This transfer occurs in the manner shown in Table 8.2.

Notice that Depository Institution A lost deposits at the Federal Reserve, its reserves, and lost checkable deposits because a check was written on it. Depository Institution B gained deposits at the Federal Reserve, its reserves, and gained checkable deposits because it received a new deposit. The total liabilities of the Federal Reserve do not change. The deposits of Institution A at the Fed fall, and those of Institution B at the Fed rise.

Figure 8.2 shows what happens when Deadeye pays for Blaze Glory's horse with a check. Blaze deposits the check in his own bank account in another city (Blaze Glory's Bank). Assume both banks are members of the Federal Reserve System.

Prudent depository institutions, such as Deadeye's Bank, would always hold primary reserves as some fraction of their deposit liabilities. Depository institutions hold primary reserves to meet probable deposit losses. Aside from the dictates of prudent management, the Depository Institutions Deregulation and Monetary Control Act of 1980 specifies that all depository institutions are required to keep a certain percentage of their checkable deposits as legal reserves. *Required reserves* are the amount of total legal reserves that a

[10]Neither deposits in other institutions nor checks in the process of collection count as legal reserves. Several classes of assets satisfy the definition of primary reserves (cash-ready assets) but do not serve as legal reserves for the purpose of meeting legal reserve requirements.

[11]When it comes to "the Fed," not many people qualify as insiders. In a name-recognition survey conducted in 1983 by the Federal Reserve Bank of Boston, more than half the respondents believed that "Federal Reserve" was a fine Kentucky bourbon, while over 25 percent thought it was a North Dakota Indian reservation. Only 11 percent knew it was our nation's central bank.

[12]Generally, if the institutions are in the same city, they use a local clearinghouse for checks drawn on one another. If they are in the same Federal Reserve District, they use a Federal Reserve Bank. If they are in different districts or if one institution is not a member of the Federal Reserve System, the mechanics are more complicated.

Table 8.2 The Check Clearing Process

Federal Reserve Bank Assets	Federal Reserve Bank Liabilities
	− deposits of member institution A + deposits of member institution B

Depository Institution A Assets	Depository Institution A Liabilities	Depository Institution B Assets	Depository Institution B Liabilities
− deposits at Federal Reserve Bank (reserves)	− checkable deposits	+ deposits at Federal Reserve Bank (reserves)	+ checkable deposits

depository institution is required to hold equal as a legally specified fraction of the institution's deposit liabilities. The *legal reserve requirement ratio* for checkable deposits is set by the Federal Reserve System at 13 percent.

Ignoring the forms of primary reserves that cannot be used to satisfy legal reserve requirements, the phrases *total reserves* and *total legal reserves* may be used interchangeably. A depository institution is required by law to keep reserves as a certain percentage of its deposit liabilities; these are a depository institution's *required reserves*. Now, if a

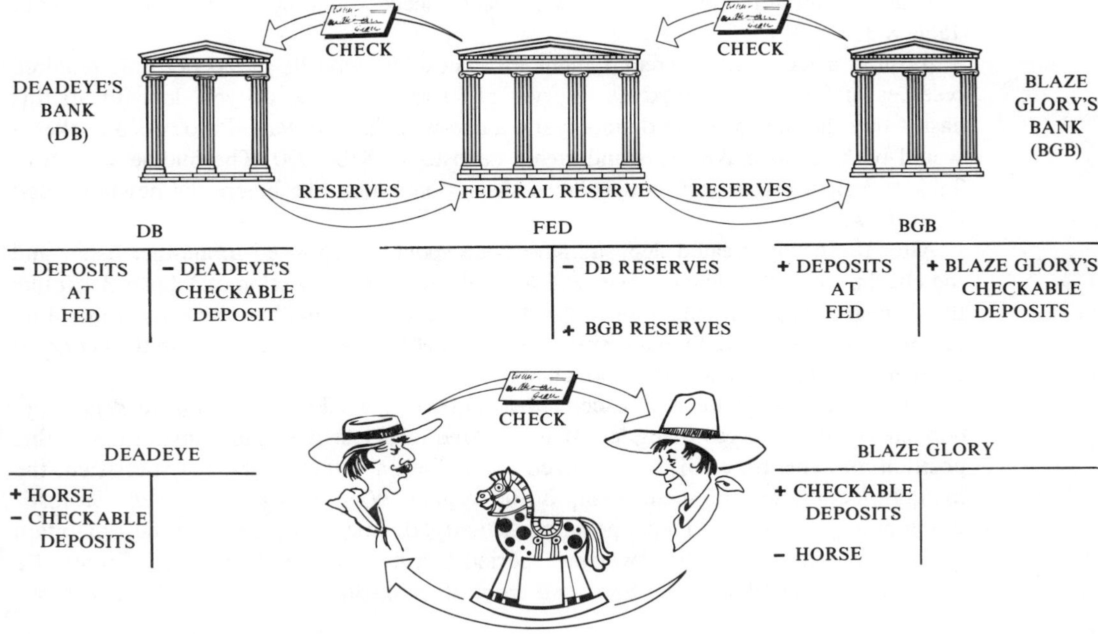

Figure 8.2 Path of a Check

depository institution's total reserves are greater than its required reserves, the (positive) difference is called *excess reserves*.

HOW BANKS CREATE MONEY

Deposits come into existence by the deposit of currency in a depository institution. Conversely, if the currency and coin were withdrawn, deposits would cease to exist. Another way in which deposits can be created is by the depository institution's acquisition of *earning assets*. Similarly, if an institution's holdings of earning assets are reduced, deposits can be destroyed. In other words, deposits can also be created by a depository institution's acquisition of earning assets (by making loans or purchasing securities) or destroyed by the contraction of loans and the sale of securities.

Assume that you are elected "most likely to foreclose" by your class and decide to begin a Bank of Your Own by getting a charter to do business, selling stock, buying a building with the proceeds, and then accepting cash for which you issue checkable deposit liabilities. Checkable deposits are created by the deposit of cash, but new money is not created by the deposit of cash. Checkable deposits increase, but currency in circulation falls. The money supply, defined as checkable deposits plus currency in circulation, is unchanged.

Assume that the stock sale raised $100,000 and the building cost $100,000. Assume that the initial (primary) deposits of cash were $200,000 and that you deposited this cash in your account at the Fed. Your bank's balance sheet would look like the top section of Table 8.3.

Assume a legal reserve requirement for checkable deposits of 20 percent, required reserves of $40,000, and excess reserves of $160,000. What do you do with all this cash—buy the Star of India diamond and a one-way ticket to Pago-Pago? As a banker it would be safer to make loans and create deposits of $160,000. The middle section of Table 8.3 shows what your new balance sheet would look like before the newly created deposits were spent.

After the newly created deposits have been spent, redeposited in another bank, and the checks clear, the balance sheet will look like the bottom section of Table 8.3. Unlike the deposit of cash, which swapped one form of money for another, the acquisition of an earning asset has created money, since total checkable deposits increase[13] in the economy and currency in circulation does not change.

If your bank made loans in excess of $160,000, it would incur a *reserve deficiency,* defined as total reserves being less than required reserves. A member institution in this position for some time will be penalized by the Fed, and if the deficiency persisted, the institution could lose its membership in the System. What does a *reserve deficient* institution do in order to avoid legal penalty? Actually, the member institution must maintain an average deficiency over a two-week period before a penalty is incurred. To avoid a penalty, (1) reserves must be borrowed from other institutions or the Federal Reserve,

[13]Although the checkable deposits that were created may suddenly seem to disappear, this is not true. They stay in existence. They simply appear elsewhere in the depository institution system. Either they become checkable deposits in another depository institution, or they are held as currency in circulation.

Table 8.3 A Bank of Your Own

Assets		Liabilities and Net Worth	
	Opening Balance Sheet		
Reserves	$200,000	Deposits	$200,000
Building	$100,000	Net worth	$100,000
	Before Newly Created Deposits Are Spent		
Reserves	$200,000	Checkable deposits (primary)	$200,000
Loan	160,000		
Building	100,000	Checkable deposits (created by loan)	160,000
		Net worth	100,000
	After Deposits Are Redeposited and Check Clears		
Reserves	$ 40,000	Checkable deposits	$200,000
Loan	160,000		
Building	100,000	Net worth	100,000

Note: Checkable deposits created by the purchase of loans and securities are called *derivative deposits*. These result in money supply expansion. Checkable deposits created by a simple deposit of currency are called *primary deposits*. They do not result in a change in the money supply, since one form, currency, is swapped by the depositor for another form, checkable deposits. Primary deposits increase total reserves. For the institution that creates them, derivative deposits increase earning assets but not total reserves. Therefore, given a legal reserve requirement and a fixed level of primary deposits, there is a maximum total volume of deposits which a depository institution may create by acquiring earning assets. This section explains how deposits may be created (by the purchase of earning assets) in the amount of an institution's excess reserves.

(2) new primary deposits must be attracted, (3) short-term securities must be sold for cash (reserves), or (4) loans, hence checkable deposits, must be contracted.

A single depository institution such as your bank could acquire earning assets and thereby create new deposits in a maximum amount equal to its excess reserves. Seeing how this process works in the depository system as a whole enables one to predict the amount of earning assets the entire system will be able to acquire, and consequently, the amount of new deposits the depository system will be able to create. Knowledge of this process is important because checkable deposits constitute about 70 percent of the narrow money supply. In turn, the supply of money is the most liquid of assets and has a great effect on the economy. The Federal Reserve is enjoined by law to control this process.

The Deposit Creation Process for a Single Bank

For the sake of clarity, assume that the only depository institutions are commercial banks. Commercial Bank A creates money by acquiring an earning asset. Assume that the bank's opening balance sheet is as shown in the top of Table 8.4. Assuming that the loan is repaid in cash by the borrower, the bank's balance sheet looks like the bottom of Table 8.4. Now the bank will probably want to acquire more earning assets.

Table 8.4 Deposit Creation Process for Bank A

Opening Balance Sheet			
Assets		Liabilities	
Vault cash	$ 50	Checkable deposits	$100
Loan	$ 50		
Balance Sheet After Loan Is Repaid			
Vault cash	$100	Checkable deposits	$100
Loan	$ 0		

It seems at first blush that if no borrowers appear, the bank must be content to hold excess reserves it does not want. Indeed, some have argued that the monetary authority, the Federal Reserve, can pump reserves into the banking system, by methods discussed later in this chapter, but it cannot force banks to use them. This argument suggests that the Federal Reserve cannot control the money supply as it is supposed to do. Even cash-obsessed bankers, however, do not allow themselves to sit around and count cash, not with all the interest they might extract in other ways. Remember that the bank can always acquire a second type of earning asset—marketable securities. In reality, whether the bank chooses to hold excess reserves or to acquire one of the many types of loans or securities depends on several variables, including, of course, the rates of return on the various earning assets.

As described earlier, the single bank can create a maximum of new checkable deposits in an amount equal to its excess reserves. Now, the assumptions from which this result was derived are explained. Assume that Bank A now joins the Federal Reserve System. It now becomes "Bank A, Member of the Federal Reserve System." As a consequence, the banker is invited to join the ritziest country club in town while his son, Blaze, is admitted to Harvard, where he plays tackle and gets all A's. Assume further that: (a) the Federal Reserve System requires that an amount equal to 20 percent of all checkable deposits be held in the asset form of vault cash or deposits in a Federal Reserve Bank. (All key assumptions in this discussion are indexed with lowercase letters, and when these assumptions are revised primes are added.)

According to convention, these two assets—vault cash and/or deposits at the Federal Reserve—the most liquid of all a bank's financial assets, are called reserves. When Bank A tenderly wraps up all $100 of its vault cash and delivers it to the Federal Reserve, its balance sheet becomes:

BANK A			
Assets		Liabilities	
Vault cash	$ 0	Checkable deposits	$100
Deposits at Federal Reserve Bank	$100		
Loans	$ 0		
Securities	$ 0		

Since Bank A has \$100 of checkable deposit liabilities, and its total reserves (*RT*) are \$100, it has legally required reserves (*RR*) of \$20 and reserves in excess of the legally required amount (*RE*) of \$80.

How much in earning assets may the profit-maximizing Bank A acquire? How much in new checkable deposits may it create? Assuming (b) that each newly created checkable deposit is redeposited in another bank, (c) that no deposits will be withdrawn as currency or coin (that is, no *currency drain* will occur), and, (d) that the bank wishes to retain zero excess reserves, the answer is \$80. After the loans are made and the newly created deposits are spent the balance sheet will be:

BANK A

Assets		Liabilities	
Reserves	\$20	Checkable deposits	\$100
Loans	\$80		

Now return to the original balance sheet. Then relax assumption (b) and assume (b′)—all newly created deposits are redeposited in Bank A—along with the other original assumptions:

(a) 20 percent legal reserve requirement,
(c) no currency drain will occur, and
(d) the bank retains zero excess reserves.

Under these assumptions, the bank will lose no reserves as the new checkable deposits change hands. Thus, Bank A at all times will retain \$100 in reserves and, with a legal reserve requirement ratio of 20 percent, may create \$400 in new checkable deposits, bringing the total amount of checkable deposits of Bank A to \$500. After the loans are made, its balance sheet is as shown below:

BANK A

Assets		Liabilities	
Reserves	\$100	Checkable deposits	\$500
Loans	\$400		

In the next example, relax assumption (c). Instead, assume (c′)—it is forecast that \$10 of the original (primary) checkable deposit of \$100 will be exchanged for currency by the depositor—along with the original assumptions:

(a) 20 percent legal reserve requirement,
(b) each newly created checkable deposit is redeposited in another bank, and
(d) the bank retains zero excess reserves.

In this situation, only \$72 of checkable deposits will be created initially by Bank A. Because of assumption (c′), \$90 in checkable deposits will remain in Bank A, \$18 of which will be required reserves (20 percent of \$90). The other \$72 are excess reserves, which enable the bank to create new checkable deposits in this amount.

Under assumptions (a), (b′), (c′), and (d′), \$72 in new checkable deposits will be created but ultimately, as they are redeposited at Bank A [assumption (b′)] reserves will remain at \$90, and the bank will create checkable deposits of \$450 (20 percent of \$450 = \$90).

Banks, like individuals, have some uses for idle cash balances. Now relax assumption (d), and assume (d′)—that \$20 of excess reserves will be desired at all times. Then, retaining all other original assumptions (a), (b), and (c), only \$60 in checkable deposits will be created. Even though the bank has some excess reserves, it does not wish to lose them. The bank will make no new loans once its excess reserves have fallen to their desired level.

Checkable Deposit Expansion in the Banking System as a Whole

To look at the big picture, the banking system as a whole, retain all original assumptions for all banks in the banking system:

(a) 20 percent legal reserve requirement,
(b) each newly created checkable deposit is redeposited in another bank,
(c) no currency drain will occur, and
(d) banks retain zero excess reserves.

Consider the chain reaction of deposit expansion that Bank A sets off in the banking system. First, as already shown in the previous section, Bank A creates new checkable deposits (DD′) in the amount of its excess reserves of \$80.

Step one: DD′ = \$80

By assumption (b), when the people who borrow the money spend it, each new dollar of checkable deposits goes to other banks. Suppose the new deposits created by Bank A all go to Bank B. Bank B receives new checkable deposits and new reserves of (DD′) \$80. The legal reserve requirement (r) of 20 percent requires that it retain $DD' \cdot r = \$16$ of reserves. The bank may create new checkable deposits by making loans in an amount equal to its initial gain in reserves (DD'), less its required reserves ($DD' \cdot r$), or the amount of its excess reserves of \$64.

Step two: $DD' - DD' \cdot r = DD'(1 - r) = \$80(1 - .20) = \$64$

Bank C receives new checkable deposits and new reserves of $DD'(1 - r) = \$64$. The legal reserve requirement dictates that it retain $r[DD'(1 - r)] = \$12.80$ of reserves. The bank may create new checkable deposits by making loans in the amount of its excess reserves, \$51.20.

Step three: $DD' - DD'r - r(DD' - DD'r) = DD'r^2 - 2DD'r + DD'$
$= DD'(r^2 - 2r + 1) = DD'(1 - r)^2 = \$80(1 - .20)^2 = \$51.20$

What is the total amount of new money (checkable deposits created by loans) that could be created by the banking system when just one bank gets some excess reserves? In the first five steps, the total amount of new money created is as follows (given the initial $80 excess reserves in Bank A):

Step one, Bank A	$80.00
Step two, Bank B	64.00
Step three, Bank C	51.20
Step four, Bank D	40.96
Step five, Bank E	32.77

The $51.20 in checkable deposits created by Bank C is redeposited in Bank D, which in turn creates checkable deposits in the amount $40.96, which is equal to $DD'(1 - r)^3$. This is deposited in Bank E. Bank E then creates checkable deposits in the amount $32.77 which is equal to $DD'(1 - r)^4$. This process continues because every time a checkable deposit is created, new banks gain reserves, and summing across all n banks, the total amount of new checkable deposits created is:

$$DD' + DD'(1 - r) + DD'(1 - r)^2 + DD'(1 - r)^3 + \ldots + DD'(1 - r)^n$$

Remember $DD' = \$80$. As n becomes large, the sum of this geometric progression approaches:[14]

$$DD'(1/r) = \$400$$

The term $(1/r)$ is the checkable deposit expansion coefficient.

Now repeat the last example, only this time use the balance sheets of the banks involved (to make it easier to follow). First, assume Bank A gets a new primary deposit of $100 (labeled DD_0). With a reserve requirement of 20 percent, it now has $80 in excess reserves. The changes in its balance sheet are:

BANK A

Assets		Liabilities	
Reserves	$100	Checkable deposits (DD_0)	$100

Because Bank A will lose to other banks all the new deposits that it creates, it can create only $80 in new checkable deposits (labeled DD_1):

[14]The sum of the geometric progression is equal to:

$$\frac{(DD') - (DD')(1 - r)^{n+1}}{1 - (1 - r)}$$

and as n, the number of stages, becomes large and since $r < 1$, which it always will be, the expression simplifies to:

$$\lim_{n \to \infty} \frac{(DD') - (DD')(1 - r)^{n+1}}{1 - (1 - r)} = \frac{1}{r} \cdot DD'$$

BANK A

Assets		Liabilities	
Reserves	\$100	DD_0	\$100
Loans	\$ 80	DD_1	\$ 80

After these deposits are spent and redeposited in Bank B, the changes in Bank A's balance sheet are:

BANK A

Assets		Liabilities	
Reserves	\$ 20	DD_0	\$100
Loans	\$ 80		

Bank A cannot create any more new checkable deposits because it is "loaned up." Bank B now has excess reserves with which it can make new loans and create new checkable deposits in the amount of \$64 (labeled DD_2). The changes in Bank B's balance sheet are:

BANK B

Assets		Liabilities	
Reserves	\$80	DD_1	\$80
Loans	\$64	DD_2	\$64

After these deposits are spent and redeposited in Bank C, Bank B has the following changes in its balance sheet:

BANK B

Assets		Liabilities	
Reserves	\$16	DD_1	\$80
Loans	\$64		

Bank B cannot create additional new checkable deposits.

Now, by assumption, all DD_2 were spent and redeposited in Bank C. Therefore, Bank C can create new checkable deposits (DD_3) of \$51.20 because it has this in excess reserves.

Now add up all of the deposits created by Banks A, B, and C. The process is well on the way to the \$400 total of new checkable deposits which will be created after the process is complete.[15] With an initial increment to reserves of \$80, checkable deposits expand by \$400. The checkable deposit expansion coefficient is equal to 5 or 1/.20.

[15]Emphasis here has been on the creation of deposits and money through the acquisition of debt claims by commercial banks. Remember that this process is reversible. If a single bank decides to sell some securities or to let loans come due without making new ones, checkable deposits and the money supply will decrease by the checkable deposit (contraction) coefficient. In addition, just as a deposit of currency injects new (excess) reserves into the banking system and allows multiple expansion, a withdrawal reduces reserves (perhaps causing a reserve deficiency) and allows multiple contraction of checkable deposits.

MONEY SUPPLY MODELS

Model One

This section presents a series of models, each resulting in a single equation that relates the quantity of checkable deposits (*DD*) or quantity of money supplied (M_s) to the behavior assumed for banks and other individuals in the assumptions (a), (b), (c), and (d). The process of expansion, already discussed, will be at work in these models. Now the process of money supply determination is viewed as the solution of a set of equations.

The *monetary base* (*B*) for money supply expansion[16] consists of the total reserves of the banking system (*RT*) plus currency in circulation (*C*). In the following example these components are assumed to be \$100 and zero, respectively.

$$B = RT + C = \$100 + \$0 = \$100 \tag{8.1}$$

Currency is part of the base for money supply expansion, since a (primary) deposit of currency anywhere in the banking system increases total reserves.

Now, as defined previously, total reserves (*RT*) equal required reserves (*RR*) plus excess reserves (*RE*):

$$RT = RR + RE \tag{8.2}$$

By assumption (d), excess reserves are zero:

$$RE = 0 \tag{8.3}$$

By assumption (a), the legal reserve requirement (*r*) is 20 percent against total checkable deposits (*DD*):

$$RR = rDD \tag{8.4}$$

By substituting the right-hand sides of Equations (8.3) and (8.4) into Equation (8.2), and substituting that result into (8.1), Equation (8.5) is derived:

$$DD = \frac{1}{r} \cdot B \tag{8.5}$$

In numerical terms it is: $DD = 1/.20 \times \$100 = \$500$. Again, the checkable deposit expansion coefficient is $1/.20 = 5$.

[16]Sometimes the monetary base is called *high-powered money*.

In the next two models, currency drains and near-monies are introduced as factors that dampen the expansion of checkable deposits by absorbing reserves that would otherwise be available to support checkable deposit expansion.

Model Two

Now, suppose that currency and traveler's checks (C) circulate. As mentioned previously, because a deposit of currency adds to reserves (vault cash), it, too, is part of the base for money supply expansion; therefore,

$$B = RT + C \tag{8.6}$$

Retain all the expressions from Model One:

$$RT = RR + RE \tag{8.7}$$

$$RE = 0 \tag{8.8}$$

$$RR = rDD \tag{8.9}$$

Now revise assumption (c). Assume instead that currency and traveler's checks are held by households and businesses as a fixed percentage ($s = .10$) of checkable deposits:[17]

$$C = sDD \tag{8.10}$$

By substituting the right-hand sides of Equations (8.8) and (8.9) into Equation (8.7) and that result and the right-hand side of Equation (8.10) into Equation (8.6) and rearranging, the result in notational terms is:

$$DD = \frac{1}{r + s} \cdot B \tag{8.11}$$

or in numerical terms: $DD = 1/.30 \times \$100 = \$333.333$. In this case, the checkable deposit expansion coefficient is $1/.30 = 3.333$. When the total money supply is narrowly defined as ($M1$) checkable deposits (DD) plus traveler's checks and currency in circulation (C),

$$M1 = DD + C \tag{8.12}$$

By substituting the right-hand sides of Equations (8.10) and (8.11) into Equation (8.12), the result is:

[17]Checkable deposits may be viewed here as a proxy for total monetary, total liquid, or total financial wealth. It may be realistic to assume that individuals, in aggregate, hold currency as a simple proportion of total monetary wealth. Of course, other arguments and functional forms are also plausible.

$$M1 = \frac{1}{r + s} \cdot B + s \cdot DD \tag{8.13}$$

Now substitute the right-hand side of Equation (8.11) into the last term (*DD*) in Equation (8.13) and get:

$$M1 = \frac{1}{r + s} \cdot B + s\left(\frac{1}{r + s}\right) \cdot B = \frac{1 + s}{r + s} \cdot B, \tag{8.14}$$

or in numerical terms: $M1 = 1.10/.30 \times \$100 = \$366.67$. The narrow money supply expansion coefficient is $1.10/.30 = 3.667$. Since there are no noncheckable deposits or other near-monies assumed to be in existence, the broad money supply expansion coefficient is the same as the narrow money supply expansion coefficient.

Model Three

Retain Equations (8.6) through (8.10) in Model Two, but introduce near-monies, noncheckable deposits (*TD*), which are held as a fixed proportion ($n = 3.00$) of checkable deposits. Noncheckable deposits are defined here to include small denomination time deposits, savings accounts, money market mutual funds, money market deposit accounts, and overnight repurchase agreements—in short, all the components of *M*2 that are not in *M*1. The label *TD* is used because it suggests time deposits:

$$TD = nDD \tag{8.15}$$

As noncheckable deposits have a legal reserve requirement (b), assumed to be .05, Equation (8.9) of Model 2 must be rewritten as

$$RR = rDD + bTD \tag{8.9'}$$

Again, by substituting the right-hand sides of Equations (8.8) and (8.9) into Equation (8.7) and the result into (8.6), we get:

$$B = rDD + bTD + C \tag{8.16}$$

Now substitute Equations (8.10) and (8.15) into Equation (8.16), and rearrange terms to get in notational terms:

$$DD = \frac{1}{r + s + bn} \cdot B \tag{8.17}$$

or in numerical terms: $DD = 1/.450 \times \$100 = \$222.22$. The checkable deposit expansion coefficient is $1/.450 = 2.2222$.

Notice that compared to Model Two, fewer checkable deposits are created because more reserves are now necessary to support the expansion of noncheckable deposits. Since Equation (8.15) says that individuals want to hold near-money (noncheckable deposits) as a fixed proportion of their checkable deposits, these deposits expand along with checkable deposits. In fact, an expression could be developed for the multiple expansion of each of the various kinds of noncheckable deposits, such as money market deposit accounts, small denomination time deposits, and other claims, depending on the form of near-monies the public wants to hold. Just like checkable deposits, this expansion is ultimately supported by the level of the monetary base, which in turn is controlled by the monetary authority.

Again, when the money supply is narrowly defined, as in Equation (8.12) in Model 2, the result in notational terms is

$$M1 = \frac{1 + s}{r + s + bn} \cdot B \tag{8.18}$$

or in numerical terms: $M1 = 2.4444 \times \$100 = \$244.44$. The narrow money supply expansion coefficient is $1.10/.450 = 2.4444$.

When the money supply is broadly defined as $M1$ plus all noncheckable deposits,

$$M2 = M1 + TD \tag{8.19}$$

by substituting Equation (8.17) into Equation (8.15) and substituting the result and Equation (8.18) into Equation (8.19) and collecting terms, we get

$$M2 = \frac{1 + s + n}{r + s + bn} \cdot B \tag{8.20}$$

or in numerical terms: $M2 = 9.1111 \times \$100 = \$911.11$. The broad money supply expansion coefficient is $4.10/.450 = 9.1111$. It is far larger than the narrow money supply expansion coefficient because it includes more types of deposits which have a lower legal reserve requirement. As seen in the next section, in April 1986 the actual narrow money supply expansion coefficient had a value between 2.6 and 2.7. The actual broad money supply expansion coefficient was approximately four times larger. Thus, the magnitudes generated for the expansion coefficients by Model Three of 2.44 and 9.11 only roughly approximate their actual, observed values in April 1986 of approximately 2.65 and 10.7.

These models show that the money stock, defined narrowly as $M1$ or broadly as $M2$, is always a product of the monetary base and the relevant money supply expansion coefficient. The expansion coefficients are functions of bank, household, and business asset-holding behavior; they are not just given. In reality, nonbank demands for currency and noncheckable deposits may not be simply proportional to total checkable deposits. They may well depend on variables such as wealth, income, and various interest rates.[18]

[18]Other variables could be included; for example, empirical studies have shown that the currency to checkable deposit ratio, s, is an increasing function of the level of income and a decreasing function of the

Nevertheless, no matter how complicated the asset holding behavior of the nonbank public, as long as the money supply expansion coefficients are known, the effect of a change in the monetary base (B) on alternative measures of the money supply can be calculated.

Control of the Money Stock

However it is measured, the money supply depends on the relevant money supply expansion coefficient (sometimes called the money multiplier) and the size of the monetary base. The money multiplier depends on the legal reserve requirements set by the Federal Reserve System and the asset preferences of depository institutions and the nonbank public. The monetary base depends on the policy actions of the monetary authority, the Federal Reserve System. Thus, with knowledge of the relevant money multiplier, the Federal Reserve can control alternative measures of the nominal stock of money by controlling the monetary base.

Charts 8.1, 8.2, and 8.3 illustrate recent values of the adjusted monetary base, the money multiplier for $M1$, and the narrow money supply, $M1$. The Charts show that while this money supply expansion coefficient (money multiplier) is not constant, it is stable over extended periods of time. For example, Chart 8.3 shows that from January 1984 until February 1986 the narrow money supply expansion coefficient ranged between 2.58 and 2.67.[19] Because the Federal Reserve knows the value of the multiplier and can control the monetary base, it can fairly easily control the money supply, if it so desires.[20]

Between 1984 and 1986, legal ceilings on interest rates paid on all deposits and all minimum balance requirements were removed. This caused the desired ratio of noncheck-

---

interest rate. Studies also show that the noncheckable deposit to checkable deposit ratio, n, varies positively with the market rate of interest. Because these ratios move in opposite directions when the interest rate changes, responses of the $M1$ and $M2$ expansion coefficients, and hence of the response of $M1$ and $M2$ to changes in the interest rate, are ambiguous.

However, because the noncheckable to checkable deposit ratio is quantitatively more important than the currency to demand deposit ratio, its positive responses to changes in the interest rate would tend to dominate. Therefore, the $M2$ expansion coefficient increases and the $M1$ expansion coefficient decreases when the interest rate rises. These effects of interest changes on the various multipliers are difficult to isolate empirically and are probably of a very small order of magnitude. See footnote 21.

[19]The $M2$ multiplier is not shown in these charts; however, it is approximately four times larger than the $M1$ multiplier. Until 1983, the $M2$ multiplier had trended upward because of the growing popularity of near-monies (noncheckable deposits) relative to checkable deposits. This is reflected in the n term in Equation (8.20).

[20]There has been a downward secular trend in the expansion coefficient for the narrow money supply. The trend is not apparent in Chart 8.2, which covers only a few years. In 1959 this coefficient had a value of approximately 3.2. In 1969 its value was around 3.0. By 1974 the $M1$ multiplier had fallen to about 2.8. Since 1979 it has hovered around 2.6. This trend reflects the secular increase in the desired ratio of noncheckable deposits to checkable deposits, the n term in Equation (8.18). The trend was dampened by the secular increase in the desired ratio of currency to checkable deposits, the term (s) in Equation (8.18). The latter may be taking place because of the increased significance of the underground economy discussed in Chapter Two. Currency transactions are difficult for law enforcement authorities to trace. As the underground economy grows relative to the legitimate economy, the demand for currency grows relative to checkable deposits.

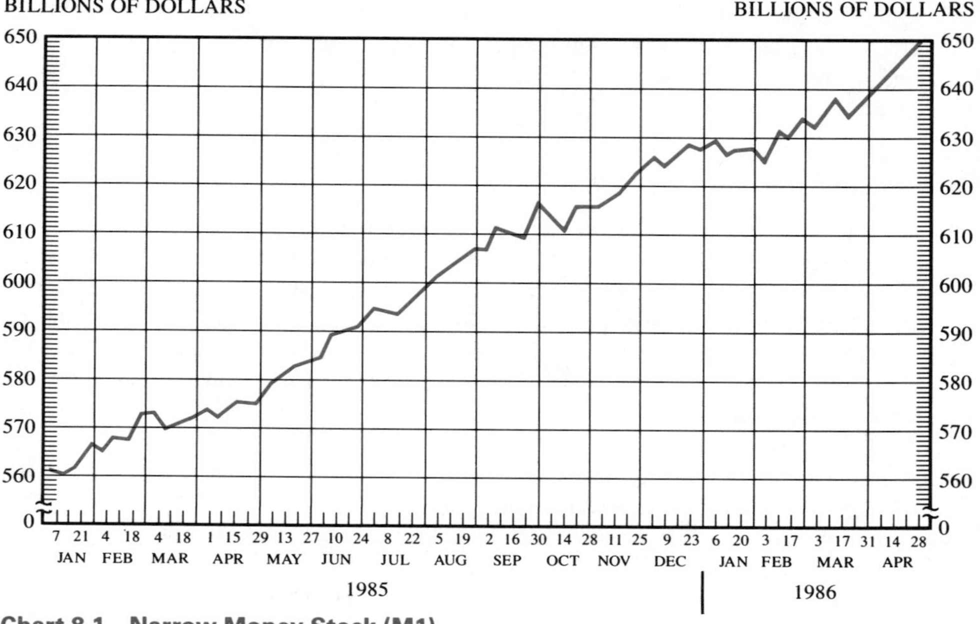

Chart 8.1 Narrow Money Stock (M1)

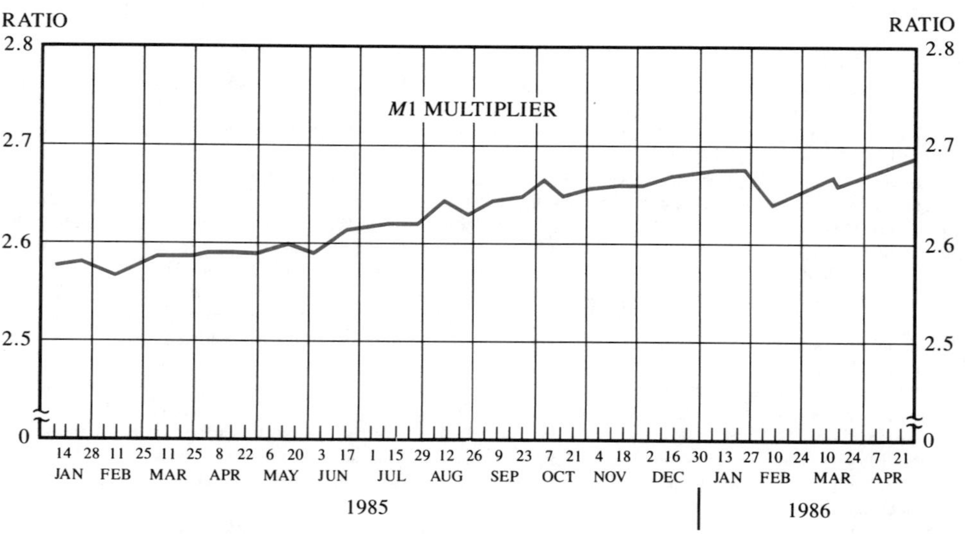

Chart 8.2 Narrow Money Multiplier

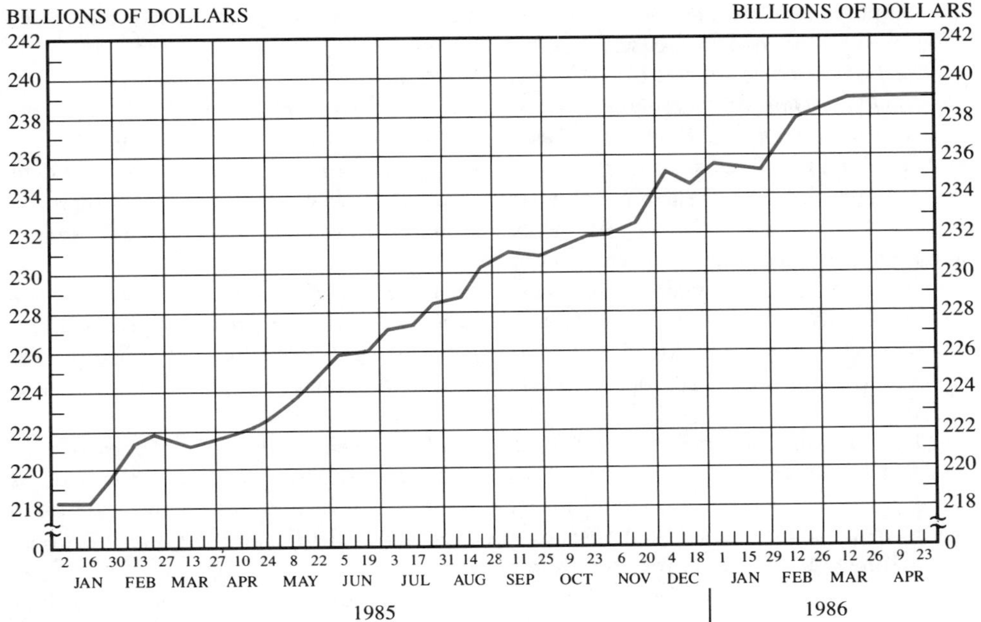

Chart 8.3 Adjusted Monetary Base

able to checkable deposits to fall. As a result, the *M*1 multiplier rose from under 2.6 to a bit under 2.7.[21]

The monetary base depends almost entirely on the assets and liabilities of the Federal Reserve. While the United States Treasury can affect the base by issuing coin or buying and selling its gold or foreign currencies, its actions are taken into account when the Fed decides whether and how to influence its own balance sheet. The Federal Reserve can control the monetary base because it can control the level of its assets.

Table 8.5 shows the factors influencing the size of the monetary base. These factors are called *sources* of the monetary base. The most important source of the monetary base is the Federal Reserve's holding of United States government securities. The Federal Reserve has absolute control over these holdings through its open market operations. In an open market purchase, the Federal Reserve buys a United States government security in the securities markets and pays for it with a check which is deposited at a depository institution by the seller of the security. Such purchases cause United States securities held by the Federal Reserve to rise (a source of the monetary base) and the deposits of that institution at the Federal Reserve (its total reserves) to rise (a use of the monetary base). In an open market sale, this transaction is reversed. The reserves of depository institutions and the Federal Reserve's holdings of securities decline. Thus, an open

[21]The increase in the *M*1 multiplier from 1984 to 1986 may also have been caused by the decline in interest rates over this time span. See footnote 18.

market purchase causes an increase in the monetary base and an open market sale causes a decrease in the monetary base.

The Federal Open Market Committee (FOMC) consists of the seven members of the *Board of Governors of the Federal Reserve System,* plus the presidents of four of the twelve Federal Reserve District Banks. The Board of Governors is comprised of seven presidential appointees with terms of fourteen years. One governor is designated by the President as chairman for a four-year renewable term. Federal Reserve Bank presidents serve on the FOMC on a rotating basis, with the exception of the president of the Federal Reserve Bank of New York, who is a permanent member.[22]

The FOMC meets formally eight times a year to decide on the course of the monetary policy, usually expressed in terms of desired target ranges for the money supply. To affect the money supply, the FOMC directs the manager of the Federal Reserves open market account to engage in the appropriate level of open market sales or purchases until its next meeting.

There are other major sources of the monetary base. Member institutions borrow from the Federal Reserve; their loans ($1.9 billion in Table 8.5) are an asset of the Federal Reserves on the left-hand side and reserves for member institutions on the right-hand side. The discount rate set by the Board of Governors of the Federal Reserve influences the willingness of member institutions to borrow.

Float arises when the Federal Reserve credits reserves to a bank which deposits a check for collection before the account of the paying bank is reduced. The same reserves will be counted by both banks until the paying bank receives the canceled check. Float fluctuates a great deal on a day-to-day basis. In November 1985, the Fed granted $15.4 billion of advance credit to banks in this form. When the volume of checks increases or bad weather delays collections, the amount of float can balloon. Together, holdings of securities, loans, and float equal outstanding Federal Reserve Credit.

The United States Treasury issues gold certificates, coins, and some forms of currency ($32.8 billion in Table 8.5) primarily to the Federal Reserve, but in some cases directly to the public. These issues alter the level of the monetary base. Most of this $32.8 billion reflects the gold the Treasury holds. Long ago, changes in the United States gold stock were a significant cause of fluctuation in the monetary base. Until the 1960s, the expansion of the monetary base was legally limited by the amount of gold held by the United States Treasury. Other minor assets of the Federal Reserve are also a source of the monetary base.

The Treasury holds deposits at the Federal Reserve. These are Federal Reserve liabilities and should be shown, by accounting convention, on the right side of the Fed's balance sheet. But since they reduce rather than expand the money supply supporting capability of the Fed, Treasury deposits at the Fed of $2.9 billion are a negative entry on the left side of Table 8.5. If the Treasury writes a check on its account at the Fed, the check will most likely be deposited in a member institution, which will thereby gain a deposit at the

[22]Because the Fed does not depend on Congress for its budget, the tenure of governors is so long, and the Fed reports its policy objectives only to Congress, it is often said to be independent of political influence. After analyzing various views of the actual behavior of the monetary policy of the Fed in Chapter Thirteen, we will discover that the Fed is about as independent of the White House as Latvia is of Moscow.

Table 8.5 Factors Influencing the Monetary Base, November 1985 (billions of dollars)

Sources		Uses		
Federal Reserve Credit		Reserves of member institutions		$ 27.0
U.S. government securities	$171.2	Deposits at Fed	$24.6	
Loans (discounts)	1.9	Vault cash	2.4	
Float plus other Fed assets	15.4			
Subtotal: Federal Reserve Credit	188.5	Currency held by public		191.4
Treasury deposits at Fed	−2.9			
Gold stock, treasury currency, other	32.8			
Monetary base	$218.4			$218.4

Source: *Federal Reserve Bulletin,* April, 1986

Fed at the same time that the Treasury's deposits decline. Thereby, the monetary base will increase.

A sense of the pivotal role of open market operations in the monetary system can be gained from Table 8.5. Although the Federal Reserve cannot control all accounts in the monetary base equation, it has absolute control over one account, the volume of United States government securities that it chooses to hold in its portfolio. These holdings, totaling $171.2 billion in Table 8.5, give the Federal Reserve an adequate means to offset or supplement changes that occur in any of the other items in the statement. Therefore, control over its own holdings of government securities provides the monetary authority with the necessary power to determine the size of the monetary base.

Currency in the hands of the public ($191.4 billion in Table 8.5) is by far the largest *use* of the base. The remainder of the base serves as the reserves of member banks ($27.0 billion). Most of this latter category consists of deposits at the Fed, although vault cash is also counted as part of their reserves. The uses of the monetary base were specified in the models of money stock determination discussed earlier in this chapter.

TOOLS AND TARGETS OF MONETARY POLICY

The Constitution grants Congress the right "to coin any money [and] regulate the value thereof." For many reasons, this power has been delegated to the Federal Reserve. To control the amount of money, the Federal Reserve must manipulate its policy tools as shown in Table 8.6. Two of these tools are open market purchases and sales of securities and the discount rate.

The tools of monetary policy include only magnitudes which the Federal Reserve controls. The chief tool is open market operations. The Federal Reserve engages in open market operations almost daily. Open market operations are used to control Federal Reserve Credit and the monetary base. The remaining tools of monetary policy are used only occasionally, and then usually for special purposes. For example, the Federal Reserve's discount rate is the interest it charges member institutions on loans to them.

Table 8.6 Tools and Targets of Monetary Policy

Tools of Monetary Policy	Potential Monetary Policy Target Variables
Open market purchases and sales of securities (affects monetary base)	Narrow money supply (*M*1)
Discount rate (affects monetary base)	Broad money supply (*M*2 or *M*3)
Selective credit controls	Bank lending (sometimes called bank "credit")
	Interest rates
	GNP

Institutions often borrow to obtain reserves if they do not have enough to meet their reserve requirements. The discount rate gains its prominence because the Fed sometimes signals major policy changes by moving the rate. However, while it frequently makes the headlines, the influence of the discount rate on actual operations is slight. The discount rate is usually changed merely to keep it in line with market rates of interest. This discourages massive borrowing by members and precludes the need for the Federal Reserve to ration loans to members. As a result, borrowed reserves rarely rise higher than 2 percent of the monetary base. Remember that the monetary authority does not have to alter the discount rate to control the monetary base because it can do so more readily through open market operations.

Selective credit controls are infrequently utilized tools of monetary policy. These include the right of the Federal Reserve to alter the terms or costs of lending by depository institutions. At times, the Federal Reserve has increased the minimum downpayments on consumer or mortgage credit, as well as their repayment terms. In 1980, the Federal Reserve raised by 15 percent the cost of borrowed money that is used to fund additional extensions of consumer credit. This was done by requiring that in a base period, noninterest-bearing reserves equal to 15 percent of the expansion had to be deposited at the Federal Reserve.

The Federal Reserve uses its tools to achieve, insofar as possible, desired values or a desired range of values for certain target variables. Monetary policy target variables consist of variables thought to be strongly influenced but not exactly controlled by Federal Reserve actions. For example, if the Federal Reserve desires a money supply growth of 5 percent per year but money growth is actually 8 percent per year, its policy actions are more stimulatory than desired. In Table 8.6, only one of the potential target variables is the narrow money supply. Other possible target variables include the broadly defined money supply, interest rates, the volume of bank lending, and even GNP. Later chapters examine the quality of the performance of the Federal Reserve in influencing the money supply and other targets.

There has been a considerable amount of debate in recent years concerning the proper targets for monetary policy. Some of the debate concerns the choice of *M*1, *M*2, or *M*3 as the appropriate target. Part of the discussion focuses on the stability of the money multipliers derived in this chapter. If the narrow money supply, *M*1, expansion coefficient is unstable and unpredictable because of unanticipated shifts in its component coefficients, discussed in footnotes 18, 19, and 20, perhaps the Federal Reserve should select a money supply target whose multiplier is more stable and more predictable over time. Some analysts are convinced that $M2$ or $M3$ would be better targets than $M1$ for this reason. Others believe that all money multipliers are unstable and/or unpredictable and favor targets such as total bank lending, interest rates, or even GNP.

Much of the debate over monetary policy targets centers on the stability of the demand for various measures of money and a related magnitude called velocity. As will be seen at the end of Chapter Nine, there are secular trends and cyclical swings in the demand for and velocity of various, narrow and broad, measures of the money stock. It will be seen that changes in the demand for money can cause changes in interest rates, real income and the price level, independent of movements in supply. Under conditions of ever-shifting demand, changes in the supply of money will have uncertain implications for interest rates, real income, and the price level. If demand is shifting unpredictably, these critics might favor a measure of money whose demand appears to be more stable and/or more predictable. Therefore, critics who believe that the demand for and velocity of a certain measure of the money supply is unstable or unpredictable contend that the Federal Reserve should eschew that magnitude as a target variable. Alternately, they might promote an interest rate target or a GNP target for monetary policy.

The debate as to whether some measures of the money supply, interest rates, or GNP are proper targets for monetary policy cannot be pursued fruitfully at this point. These issues cannot be understood unless one clearly understands how a change in the monetary base affects either interest rates, aggregate real income, the price level, or some combination of the three. Understanding this is a formidable task—one that requires the rest of this text to complete. Therefore, the solution to the quest for an ideal target for monetary policy really requires in-depth understanding of alternative hypotheses of how monetary policy affects the economy.

This is no easy task for Federal Reserve officials. What is presented to policymakers and voters as an ideal way to manage monetary policy depends on the presenter's theory of how the economy really works. All too often guidelines for Federal Reserve behavior are based on improperly thought-out theories. There can be answers to the target controversy only to the extent that there are answers to the greater question of how the economy really works.

Concluding Comment

This chapter covers the definition, composition, and determination of the supply of money. It emphasizes the roles played by financial (depository) institutions and the Federal Reserve System. A theory of the *demand for money* and the important impact of the money supply on the economy will be discussed in the next chapter.

EXERCISES

1. What are the functions of money?
2. What is the composition of the money stock, narrowly defined? broadly defined? What are "weighted money aggregates"?

3. Define "checkable deposit." Explain why you would or would not expect this definition to change over time.
4. Explain, in words, how banks create money.
5. Explain, in words, the logic of the money supply expansion process.
6. What are the tools of monetary policy? Which is most important, and why?
7. Identify the following:
   FOMC
   Board of Governors
   Manager of the Open Market Account
8. Analyze and evaluate the following statement: "The Federal Reserve can control total reserves through open market operations; it cannot control currency in circulation; therefore, the monetary base is inferior to total reserves as a control variable or policy instrument."
9. Assume that Congress passes new legislation that permits banks to issue a checking account that not only pays interest equivalent to market-determined rates but also allows the holder to receive a share of bank profits without having to share bank losses. What would be the effect on the narrow money supply coefficient? the broad money supply coefficient? How would your conclusion be modified if checks could not be written on this new type of deposit?
10. Identify the following terms:
    primary reserves
    secondary reserves
    total reserves
    required reserves
    excess reserves
    fractional reserve banking
    primary deposits
    derivative deposits
    Regulation Q
11. Discuss the following concepts of banking operations:
    lending power
    reserve deficiency
    liability management
    disintermediation

BIBLIOGRAPHY

Balbach, Anatol E., and Albert E. Burger. "Derivation of the Monetary Base." *Review* (November 1976), pp. 2–8.

Board of Governors of the Federal Reserve System. *Purposes and Functions*. 6th ed. Washington, D.C.: Government Printing Office, 1974.

Burger, Albert E. *The Money Supply Process*. Belmont, Cal.: Wadsworth Publishing Company, 1972.

Friedman, Milton, and Anna J. Schwartz. *A Monetary History of the U.S., 1867–1960*. Princeton, N.J.: Princeton University Press, 1963.

Gurley, John G., and Edward S. Shaw. *Money in a Theory of Finance*. Washington, D.C.: Brookings Institution, 1960.

Havrilesky, Thomas M., and Robert L. Schweitzer, eds. *Contemporary Developments in Financial Institutions and Markets*. 2d ed. Arlington Heights, Ill.: Harlan Davidson, Inc., 1987.

———, and John T. Boorman. *Money Supply, Money Demand and Macroeconomic Models*. 2d ed. Arlington Heights, Ill.: Harlan Davidson, Inc., 1982.

———, Robert L. Schweitzer, and John T. Boorman, eds. *Dynamics of Banking*. Arlington Heights, Ill.: Harlan Davidson, Inc., 1985.

Rasche, Robert. "A Review of Empirical Studies of the Money Supply Mechanism." *Review*, Federal Reserve Bank of St. Louis (July 1972), pp. 11–19.

The Demand for Money and the Money Market

Chapter 9

Introduction

Money is the vehicle that transforms the supply of factor inputs and finished goods and services into a circular flow of income and expenditures. In serving this function, money is a *medium of exchange*. Individuals (consumers and producers) need money balances for their daily expenditures; that is, they need money to finance day-to-day transactions. Economists call the money balances held for this purpose *transactions balances*. The demand for money to spend, the transactions demand for money, depends on income or wealth, the interest opportunity cost of holding money, the transactions costs of holding nonmoney, and payment and disbursement habits. Money is also held because it is a *store of value*. Economists call money balances held for this purpose *speculative balances*. The speculative demand for money depends on income or wealth and the risks and return (interest) associated with holding nonmoney assets compared to the risks and return from holding money assets.

In a broader sense, the demand for money can be viewed as part of the general theory of demand. In this case, a conceptual separation of transactions and speculative balances is unnecessary. Viewed in this manner, the utility of individuals depends on their holdings of money and nonmoney assets. Utility may be affected by tastes as reflected in payment habits and disbursement habits. Individuals will allocate their total wealth between money and nonmoney in order to maximize that utility subject to a scale variable (wealth or income) and an array of prices. These prices include the risk and interest opportunity cost of holding money and the risk and transactions costs of holding nonmoney. From the general theory of demand perspective, the demand for money depends on income or wealth, interest rates, transactions costs, measures of risk, and payment and disbursement habits.

Knowing the factors that influence the quantity of money individuals want to hold is an important bit of knowledge. When the Federal Reserve increases the nominal quantity of money, its effect on the economy depends on what people do with it. Will people use some of an increase in the money stock to acquire consumer durable goods (wall-to-wall aquariums for their bathrooms)? Will they use some of it to acquire financial assets other than money (Manchu Dynasty Railway Sinking Fund Bonds), or will they hoard some of it (the misers!)? If the Federal Reserve knew, managing the money supply would be an easier task.

TRANSACTIONS BALANCES AND SPECULATIVE BALANCES

Why Everyone Demands Money for Transactions Purposes

All households and business firms have expenditures. All households buy goods, and all business firms buy productive resources. These purchases are made only with certain generally acceptable material: *money*. Money is the material used in exchange for goods and services and thus serves as a medium of exchange. Because all households and businesses have expenditures, they all must hold a stock of transactions balances.

As an example, suppose you receive income once a month and spend a fraction of that income every day of the month. At first glance, it may seem that you have no desire to hold a stock of transactions balances. (After all, nothing gets out of hand as quickly as money.) Yet you must hold transactions balances, however temporarily, in the interval between your receipt of income and your spending of that income. Transactions balances efficiently bridge the gap between income and expenditures. Holding other asset forms in lieu of transactions balances during this interval can be rather costly, because these other asset forms will have to be converted to transactions balances when you want to engage in expenditures.

It may appear irrational to hold money for transactions purposes for any length of time, since other assets usually earn higher interest rates and can be purchased when income is received and sold when cash disbursements must be made. The reason individuals still choose to hold some money and forgo the additional interest income under these circumstances is that there is a cost of converting cash receipts into earning assets and then converting these earnings assets back to spendable cash. These transactions costs include the brokerage fees for buying and selling assets as well as the sheer inconvenience, time opportunity costs, of buying and selling assets every time one receives or needs some cash. As discussed later, technological improvements may reduce the demand for transactions balances. In fact, technological improvements may be able to reduce the costs of

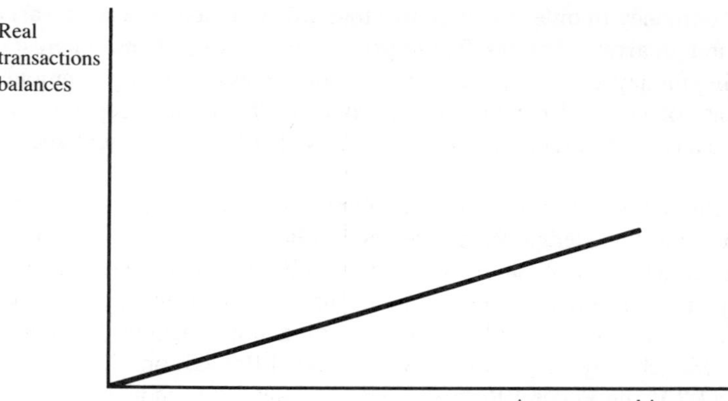

Figure 9.1 The Level of Real Income and the Demand for Real Transactions Money Balances

converting into and out of transactions balances to zero—for example, by an electronic banking program that freely sweeps all checking account balances at the end of every business day into asset accounts that earn higher interest rates. When this occurs, the demand for transactions balances will be close to zero.

The Level of Income and the Demand for Transactions Balances

Money that is narrowly defined to include only checkable deposits, currency in circulation, and traveler's checks is demanded for carrying out transactions because it functions as a medium of exchange. It allows individuals to make expenditures between paydays.

Those who have a higher level of expenditures will need larger transactions balances. The greater the level of a household's real income, the greater its real expenditures; hence the greater the amount of real money balances it will demand for transactions purposes. Therefore, the quantity of real money balances demanded for transactions purposes varies directly with the level of real income.

Now, consider the aggregate demand for transactions balances for the entire economy.[1] The quantity of real transactions balances demanded in the economy as a whole varies directly with the level of aggregate real income. For simplicity, assume that the transactions demand for money varies in direct proportion to the level of real income. As shown in Figure 9.1, if aggregate real income rises by a certain percentage, the aggregate real quantity of transactions balances demanded will rise by an equal percentage. When it comes to real-world behavior, this is not an unreasonable proposition.[2]

[1]The leap from individual behavior to aggregate behavior is often a conceptually mighty one. Nevertheless, as in other chapters, for our purposes, it will not be necessary to discuss the aggregation problem.

[2]Empirical studies of the demand for money, cited in the bibliography which follows this chapter, support this specification.

Payment and Disbursement Habits, the Use of Credit, and the Demand for Transactions Balances

The frequency of payments and disbursements also has an effect on an individual's demand for money. Assume Prince Charles receives an allowance from Princess Diana of $24,000 at the beginning of each month while on a tour of the United States. If he spends $800 daily, his average holding of transactions balances will be the amount he holds halfway through the month, or $12,000. Now suppose Princess Diana changes Charles' payment to $12,000 on the first and fifteenth of the month. Charles' average transaction balance now becomes the amount held at noon on the seventh day of the month, the amount he holds halfway through this 15-day period, or $6,000. More frequent payment dates reduce the need to hold transactions balances.

As another example, assume that instead of spending $800 per day, he spends $8,000 every ten days. Now, his average transactions balance is the amount he holds halfway through the month, or $16,000. Less frequent disbursements increase transactions balances. As a final example, assume that Princess Diana allows Charles to use her credit card. He then charges all purchases during the month and holds $24,000 in transactions balances only on the last day of the month, when he pays his credit card bill. In this case, his average holdings of transactions balances are a weighted average, or $800.

$$\$800 = \frac{29 \text{ days} \times \$0 \text{ balance} + 1 \text{ day} \times \$24{,}000 \text{ balance}}{30 \text{ days}}$$

Clearly, the use of credit reduces the demand for transactions money balances.

While payment and disbursement habits have been stable for decades, the increased use of credit has caused a decrease over time in the demand for transactions balances. The growing use of credit cards means that individuals need less currency on hand and lower checkable deposit balances throughout the month; they need sizable deposits only when it is necessary to pay off their credit card indebtedness. Thus, there has been a slow downward trend in the demand for transactions balances. Steady reductions in the transactions costs of converting between transactions balances and nonmoney assets, discussed earlier, are also a cause of this trend. The effects of that trend are examined later in this chapter.

The Opportunity Cost of Holding Transactions Balances

Economists believe it "costs something" to hold transactions balances. Since money (defined as checkable deposits, plus currency in circulation and traveler's checks) will often earn lower interest than nonmoney assets, this *opportunity cost* is the difference between the interest rate earned on nonmoney assets and the interest rate earned on money balances. The *interest rate,* in this case, means the nominal rate of interest earned on nonmoney assets as opposed to the real rate of interest, discussed in Chapter Six. (Of course, where an expected rate of inflation is assumed constant, changes in the nominal and real rates of interest are the same.) Individuals will economize on their holdings of transactions money balances as the nominal interest rate on United States government bonds and other nonmoney assets rises relative to the nominal interest rate they receive on their holdings of money.[3] Individuals will take advantage of the higher income that results from holding these nonmoney assets and hold fewer transactions balances. (This higher income from interest on nonmoney assets may be assumed to be independent of possible capital gains from increases in the market prices of such assets.)

Nonmoney assets which are easily converted into cash but cannot always serve as a medium of exchange are called *near-monies*.[4] When the interest rate on near-monies is high relative to the interest rate paid on money balances, the rational household or firm is tempted to keep a smaller amount of cash for transactions purposes. Individuals scurry for their checking accounts, negotiable order of withdrawal (NOW) accounts, piggy banks, and cookie jars, where they keep their transactions balances, and reduce these balances and increase the balances in their near-money accounts. They draw down their near-money balances later, when cash is needed for expenditures. When the interest rate on near-monies is high relative to that paid on transactions balances, holding money is more costly (in the sense that the opportunity to earn more interest is lost). Therefore, the average size of real transactions balances demanded over a period of time falls as the rate of interest paid on nonmoney assets rises, relative to the rate paid on transactions balances.

Assume that Joe Sixpack takes a second job so he can take his family on a Bolivian cruise next year. He earns $1,200 monthly and is paid on the first of each month. Assume he deposits his monthly paycheck in his NOW account: His $1,200 becomes a checkable deposit, or a transactions balance. Assume further that Joe spends $1,200 of his income uniformly at $40 per day for thirty days. Joe's average transactions balance during the month is the amount he holds halfway through the month, or $600.

Suppose Joe's depository institution raises the interest rate on its money market deposit account (a near-money) from 5 percent to 15 percent per annum payable on the twentieth of each month but does not raise the interest rate it pays on its NOW accounts. Joe is thereby encouraged to put $400 into his money market deposit account on the first of the month and withdraw it after it earns interest for twenty days and then use it as transactions balances for the final ten days of the month. This is an irksome process, but the additional interest he earns, $3.33 ($400 at 15 percent for twenty days), is considerably more attractive than the previous possible return of $1.11 ($400 at 5 percent for twenty days)—after all, it will buy a sixpack. Assume that the $2.22 increase in interest earnings is high enough to compensate Joe for the transactions costs of shifting his funds twice a month. His average transactions balance for the month, the balance in his NOW account,

[3]Some types of transactions balances—for example, checkable deposits such as NOW accounts—pay an interest rate that varies in nearly the same proportion as the market rate of interest. Other types of transactions balances, such as currency in circulation, earn no interest. Still other types of transactions balances pay an interest rate that does not vary in the same proportion as the market rate. Therefore, the demand for transactions balances as a whole will vary inversely with the nominal market rate of interest earned on nonmoney assets.

[4]Even near-monies, such as balances in savings accounts or money market deposit accounts, which may be transferred by check, often have limitations in terms of the number of checks one can write per month. Thus, near-monies are not perfectly liquid.

will then fall to $400 for the first twenty days and be $200 for the last ten days. In this instance, the rise in the interest rate has caused Joe Sixpack to reduce his average transactions balance.

As another example, Daddy Narcobucks is currently economizing his holding of transactions money balances because of a high rate of return on short-term United States government securities (United States Treasury bills). Assume that this interest rate drops, *ceteris paribus,* while the rate paid on his transactions balances is unchanged. If Daddy's average transactions money balances increase, it is correct to infer that the lower rate is not sufficient to compensate for the transactions costs (selling costs such as brokers' fees and inconvenience) of converting his transactions balances to short-term securities and back. As the rate of interest falls from very high levels, the quantity of transactions balances demanded rises.

These examples show that the aggregate demand for real transactions balances varies inversely with the market rate of interest as long as the interest rate paid on money balances is unchanged. This occurs because the interest rate paid on nonmoney assets minus the interest rate paid on transactions balances is the opportunity cost of holding real transactions balances. The transactions demand for money, therefore, varies inversely with the difference between the rate of interest paid on nonmoney assets and the interest rate earned on money balances. The transactions demand also varies directly with the level of real income, as discussed earlier.

The preceding discussion shows that economists break down the nonhuman wealth of an individual into three categories: transactions balances, near-monies, and nonmoney assets. Where physical goods are ignored, the latter category may be referred to generically as "bonds." If we define "money" to include only transactions balances, we will have developed in the preceding discussion a theory of the demand for transactions balances: The demand for real transactions balances varies directly with the level of aggregate real income and inversely with the interest opportunity cost of holding these balances.

Why Individuals Have a Demand for Assets in the Form of Real Speculative Balances

In analysis of the speculative demand for money, the broad definition of the money stock, $M2$, is usually used.[5] This definition includes everything that is in the narrow, $M1$, definition: checkable deposits, currency in circulation, and traveler's checks, plus near-monies, which include savings accounts, small denomination time deposits, money market mutual funds, money market deposit accounts, overnight repurchase agreements, and

[5]The aggregation of transactions balances ($M1$) and near-monies into the same conceptual category—speculative balances—has not gone unchallenged. Consumer surveys indicate little mixing of near-monies and transactions balances. Their size, turnover, and seasonal and debit characteristics are quite different. Confusion in monetary theory and policy seems to arise because the $M2$ measure contains assets of diverse characteristics. The $M1$ component of $M2$ consists of transactions accounts, whereas the near-monies component of $M2$ consists of savings accounts. The latter are close substitutes for nonmoney financial assets, "bonds," and thus tend to be more interest-sensitive than $M1$. From this perspective, the concept of speculative balances ideally should be redefined to include only near-monies and not transactions balances.

certain Eurodollar deposits. The various near-monies, which were discussed in Chapter Eight, are not as liquid as narrowly defined money because there are usually limitations on drawing checks on these accounts, and therefore, they cannot always be used for small, frequent, day-to-day transactions. However, when it comes to the large, intermittent, periodic transfers that would be made for most speculative transactions, these near-monies are almost perfectly liquid. Moreover, when fully insured by the Federal Deposit Insurance Corporation (FDIC) or some other public or private insurer, near-monies are virtually risk free.

A decline in the market price of an asset leaves the holder with a *capital loss*. Furthermore, if the prices of nonmoney assets fell, individuals would be able to buy them at lower prices, provided they had idle money balances. In short, individuals may wish to hold money, defined as *M*2, as an asset to avoid capital losses on other assets and to take advantage of declining prices on nonmoney earning assets should they occur. To avoid (probable) losses from holding nonmoney assets, it might be wise to hold some wealth in the form of money balances. As old-time humorist Kin Hubbard said, sometimes "the safest way to double your money is to fold it once and put it in your pocket."

The function of money as a store of value was described in Chapter Eight. Money is an asset that can be held for a period and then exchanged for goods and services. Individuals who maintain some of their wealth in the form of idle speculative balances do not earn an inordinate amount of interest income. Nevertheless, they may take full and immediate advantage of stocks, bonds, and other financial assets when their prices fall. Thus, by holding speculative balances, they not only avoid the risk of a decline in the value of nonmoney assets but can also take instant advantage of bargain prices on these assets should they occur.

Before the great stock market crash of 1929–1930, Blaze Glory, Sr., sold all his stocks and bonds for cash and increased his speculative money balances. In April of 1933, when stock prices hit one of the lowest levels of the century (so far!), he made bargain-basement purchases. Mr. Glory later made it big again as the author of a famous book about getting rich in the stock market, *Buy Low, Sell High*.

Basically, Glory held speculative money balances to avoid capital losses and be able to buy nonmoney assets when they were cheap. He satisfied Bernard Baruch's definition of a speculator as "a man who observes the future and acts before it occurs."

THE INTEREST RATE AND THE DEMAND FOR SPECULATIVE BALANCES

Bond Prices and Bond Yields

The quantity of speculative balances held is not constant. It varies because individuals will be tempted occasionally to accept more risk by holding more of their wealth in the form of nonmoney assets and less in the form of money. One important type of nonmoney asset is a *bond*. Bonds promise to pay a fixed nominal dollar income per year. Like any commodity, bonds are traded in the bond market. A change in a bond's price, with the dollar income unchanged, will make the *current yield* (the interest income as a percentage of the price over the life of the bond) change too.

Assume you bought a bond for \$1,000 that promised to pay \$40 per year forever in interest income. Its current yield at the time of purchase was \$40/\$1,000 = 4 percent per year. If an increase in the demand for that type of bond occurred, and its current price rose to \$1,100, its current yield would fall. If someone wanted the bond at the current price, that individual would still get \$40 in income per year, but would pay \$1,100 for it. The current yield would be lower. A bond's price and its current yield are inversely related. If the bond's market price rises, its current yield falls, and vice versa.

The current yield of an obligation may be calculated simply by dividing the dollar amount of the interest paid per year by the current market price of the instrument. The current yield is not a completely satisfactory measure, for it fails to consider the capital gain or loss to be incurred if that obligation is held to maturity. For example, the current yield on an obligation selling for \$950 and paying \$50 per year is \$50/\$950 = .0526, or 5.26 percent. But if the face value of this bond is \$1,000, upon redemption at maturity it will return an additional \$50 above the purchase price to its owner. Thus, if the bond is held to maturity, the owner will realize a capital gain. This gain must be included when calculating the total *yield to maturity* on a security.[6]

From now on in this book, the yield on debt instruments such as bonds will mean the *yield to maturity* instead of the *current yield*.

Yield to maturity may be calculated by a formula for computing the present value of a future stream of returns. To calculate the present value of a single \$50 payment to be made one year from today, *discount* that \$50 according to this formula:

$$\text{present value} = PV = \frac{50}{1 + i}$$

where i is the interest (or discount) rate. For example, the present value of \$50 discounted at 2 percent for one year is

$$PV = \frac{\$50}{1 + .02} = \frac{\$50}{1.02} = \$49.02$$

In other words, \$49.02 invested for one year at 2 percent yields \$50. In general, a single payment of Y dollars to be received two years in the future is currently valued at

$$PV = \frac{Y}{(1 + i)^2}$$

At 2 percent, then, the present value of this single \$50 payment to be made two years from today is

[6]The yield or interest rate discussed here is a nominal, as opposed to a real, interest rate because the price of the debt instrument is expressed in nominal terms as is its interest income stream.

$$PV = \frac{\$50}{(1 + i)^2} = \frac{\$50}{(1 + .02)^2} = \frac{\$50}{(1.0404)} = \$48.06$$

If this formula is generalized, the present value of any payment Y_n to be made n years from now is

$$PV = \frac{Y_n}{(1 + i)^n} \tag{9.1}$$

Therefore, if a debt instrument carries an obligation to pay $50 per year for the next five years and a final repayment of principal of $1,000 at the end of the five-year period, the present value of that stream of returns discounted at a rate of 100i percent per year is

$$PV = \frac{Y_1}{(1 + i)} + \frac{Y_2}{(1 + i)^2} + \frac{Y_3}{(1 + i)^3} + \frac{Y_4}{(1 + i)^4} + \frac{Y_5}{(1 + i)^5} + \frac{\text{principal}}{(1 + i)^5} \tag{9.2}$$

where $Y_1 = Y_2 = Y_3 = Y_4 = Y_5 = \$50$.

For example, if the return demanded by the lender is 6 percent per year, he would be willing to pay $957.87 for a bond with these characteristics:

$$PV = \frac{\$50}{(1.06)} + \frac{\$50}{(1.06)^2} + \frac{\$50}{(1.06)^3} + \frac{\$50}{(1.06)^4} + \frac{\$50}{(1.06)^5} + \frac{\$1,000}{(1.06)^5}$$
$$= \$47.17 + \$44.50 + \$41.98 + \$39.60 + \$37.36 + \$747.26 = \$957.87$$

Alternatively, knowing the current market price of the instrument, the formula to calculate its yield to maturity can be used. For example, if the obligation is currently selling for $950, the yield to maturity is given by the formula:

$$\$950 = \frac{\$50}{(1 + i)} + \frac{\$50}{(1 + i)^2} + \frac{\$50}{(1 + i)^3} + \frac{\$50}{(1 + i)^4} + \frac{\$50}{(1 + i)^5} + \frac{\$1,000}{(1 + i)^5}$$
$$i = .0619 \qquad 100i = 6.19\%$$

This formula shows that the higher the interest rate at which future expected returns are discounted (in the denominators), the lower the present value of that income (the market value of the obligation). Conversely, the lower the rate of discount, the higher the present value. Through variations in the market price of outstanding securities (with fixed payments and a fixed face value), the yield to maturity on those instruments is adjusted to current market conditions.

The formula suggests that when the market rate or yield in the denominator is equal to a 5 percent *coupon rate* (the $50 annual interest payment divided by the $1,000 principal), the bond sells in the market *at par*. This means that its market price is equal to its principal value. When the market rate is greater than the coupon rate, the bond sells *below par*, or at a *discount*. Conversely, when the market rate is less than the coupon rate, the bond sells *above par*, or at a *premium*.

This discussion shows how bond prices adjust (in the market where bonds are traded) to bring a bond's yield to maturity into line with the market rate of interest. Therefore, the market rate of interest is coextensive with yield to maturity. Bond prices vary inversely with the market rate of interest. Thus, there is always a *market risk* associated with holding a bond. This is the risk that its price will fall when the market rate of interest rises.

Finally, the formula indicates that the market prices of longer-term debt instruments will fluctuate more widely for a given change in the market rate than the prices of shorter-term debt instruments. This difference in the fluctuations of bond prices occurs because instruments with a longer term to maturity contain larger powers of $(1 + i)$ in the formula. This means that longer-term bonds are more subject to capital gains and losses than shorter-term bonds. There is greater market risk associated with holding longer-term bonds.

The remainder of this chapter deals exclusively with *consol bonds* because the relationship between the market price of a consol bond and the market rate of interest can be greatly simplified. A consol bond pays interest income indefinitely but does not repay principal. Therefore, the general present value formula, Equation (9.2), is written without the final term for the repayment of principal:

$$(PV) = \frac{Y_1}{(1+i)^1} + \frac{Y_2}{(1+i)^2} + \frac{Y_3}{(1+i)^3} + \ldots + \frac{Y_n}{(1+i)^n} \tag{9.3}$$

Now, multiply both sides of this equation by $1/(1 + i)$:

$$\frac{1}{1+i}(PV) = \frac{Y_1}{(1+i)^2} + \frac{Y_3}{(1+i)^3} + \ldots + \frac{Y_n}{(1+i)^{n+1}} \tag{9.4}$$

Assume that $Y_1 = Y_2 = Y_3 = \ldots = Y_n$ and subtract Equation (9.4) from Equation (9.3):

$$PV\left[1 - \frac{1}{1+i}\right] = \frac{Y}{1+i} - \frac{Y}{(1+i)^{n+1}}$$

Multiply both sides by $(1 + i)$ and rearrange terms:

$$PV = \frac{Y}{i}\left[1 - \frac{1}{(1+i)^n}\right] \tag{9.5}$$

Equation (9.5) is a general expression for the present value of a continuous stream of future interest payments. If an expression for repayment of principal is added, the present value formula can be reformulated by Equation (9.2).

The expression for the present value of a consol is derived by letting the maturity of the bond become infinite. This causes the expression $(1 + i)^n$ to become infinitely large and the term $1/(1 + i)^n$ to approach zero. This adjustment gives:

$$PV = \frac{Y}{i} \tag{9.6}$$

which says that the present value of a consol is inversely proportional to the rate of interest.

The Market Rate of Interest and the Demand for Speculative Balances

An analysis of the demand for speculative balances can now be made. In Chapter Two, an individual household's total nonhuman wealth was defined as consisting of the value of debt claims, the value of equity claims, and the value of consumer durable goods. Debt claims consisted of money and nonmoney debt claims. In this section, as a matter of simplification, assume that individual wealth consists of money, broadly defined, and nonmoney debt, bonds. In short, assume that individual wealth can be held in two forms: bonds and money, broadly defined as $M2$. The advantages of money include its acceptance as a medium of exchange and the fact that the market value of money is usually less subject to volatile swings than the market value of debt instruments. There is little market risk. Moreover, practically everything included in the broad definition of the money stock is insured, so it is virtually free of *default risk*. Traditionally, economists have said that the confluence of these two properties makes money a unique, most "liquid" financial asset.

Assume a world in which there are two financial assets: money, broadly defined, and the short-term bonds of the Pollutaire Corporation. Assume a Pollutaire Corporation bond has a risk of market price decline because the Pollutaire Corporation may be forced out of business and default on its debts. An individual may not be willing to hold that bond and accept the *default risk* if it offers only a 1 percent yield to maturity. Rather, she would hold speculative money balances. They are essentially free of default risk. However, if the yield to maturity on a Pollutaire bond rose to 5 percent per year, the bond's price would fall. At this point, she might choose to purchase some of the corporate bonds. The rise in the yield reduces her demand for speculative money balances and induces acceptance of the default risk associated with holding the bonds.

Now consider a world in which the only types of financial assets are money and long-term bonds which pay a 15 percent yield to maturity. As discussed in the previous section, long-term bonds are subject to the *market risk* of changes in their prices associated with changes in market rates of interest. Many individuals would be induced to accept the market risk of holding the bonds at that relatively high interest rate. A yield of 15 percent may seem to be an attractive bribe for accepting the market risk of holding the bonds. At high yields, individuals hold fewer real speculative money balances relative to their total wealth.

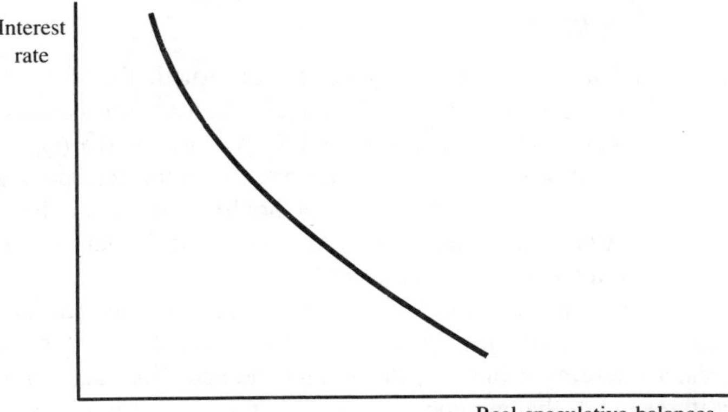

Figure 9.2 The Interest Rate and the Demand for Real Speculative Money Balances

Individuals have a demand for real speculative, sometimes called idle, money balances. The quantity demanded of anything depends on several variables, the most important usually being its own price. As previously discussed, the quantity of real speculative balances demanded is determined by the market rate of interest because the market rate of interest induces individuals to accept or reject the market and default risks of holding nonmoney assets. If nonmoney assets are defined to include equities as well as bonds, market and default risk are still present.[7] For equities, default risk is the risk that the firm will fail.

The quantity demanded of real speculative balances varies inversely with the market rate of interest. This means that the demand curve for money is sloped downward, as in Figure 9.2. A higher interest rate is an inducement to individuals to hold less real speculative balances and assume the risks of holding more nonmoney assets. As the interest rate rises, people are tempted to hold more nonmoney assets and less money because the higher interest rate is a stronger inducement to accept the risks of holding nonmoney assets. The interest rate is the opportunity cost of holding speculative balances. When this cost rises, individuals may increase their utility by substituting nonmoney assets for money.[8]

[7]Introducing physical goods would add realism to the model. Physical goods are subject to the (market) risk of changes in their market value. The benefits in the form of satisfaction and services from holding physical goods are not taxable, while the dividend income from equities and the interest income from bonds are. This explains why individuals in higher tax brackets frequently prefer to invest their wealth in consumer durables such as Roll Royces and Maseratis rather than income-earning assets. Thus, as individuals go into higher income tax brackets, they *seem* to develop a taste for more expensive automobiles. Even when their *real* income is unchanged, the higher their tax bracket, the "cheaper" are their Rolls Royces.

[8]Whenever risk is an inferior good, this analysis assumes that the substitution effect dominates the income effect. Where risk is an inferior good, as the interest rate rises and interest income rises, the income effect causes less risk (fewer nonmoney assets) to be demanded. Whenever risk is not an inferior good, both income and substitution effects work in the same direction, and this assumption is unnecessary.

The Demand for Money

Insofar as the demand for real money balances is concerned, the interest rate has two effects. First, it will inversely influence the demand for transactions balances because the market interest rate less the rate paid on transactions balances is the opportunity cost of holding money. Second, it will inversely influence the demand for speculative balances because the market interest rate is the bribe for holding wealth in the form of risky nonmoney assets. In either case, the demand for real money balances varies inversely with the market rate of interest, *ceteris paribus*.[9]

The level of real income (or wealth) has a direct effect on the total demand for real money balances. First, it will directly influence the demand for transactions balances because the greater the level of income, the greater the need for transactions balances to finance expenditures out of that income. Second, income or wealth will directly influence the demand for speculative balances because the greater the scale of one's income or wealth, the greater one's holdings of all assets, including speculative balances.

When a two-dimensional demand curve is drawn, only two variables can be represented on the axes—quantity demanded and another variable, usually price. Given the hypothesis that money demand is affected by two variables—the interest rate and income—the quantity of money demanded is measured on one axis and either the market rate of interest or the level of income on the other. Assume the remaining variable is held constant. (Remember it takes at least two economists to draw a demand curve—one to draw the curve and the other(s) to hold everything else constant.) According to convention, income is assumed to be constant, while the interest rate is placed on the vertical axis, and the demand function is negatively sloped as in Figure 9.2.

How a Change in the Level of Aggregate Income Affects the Aggregate Demand for Money

The aggregate demand curve for real money balances will shift in the same direction as the change in the level of aggregate real income. When the demand curve for any commodity is drawn as a function of its price and changes occur in some other variable which has an influence on this demand, the demand schedule will shift. When the level of income rises, the demand for most commodities shifts to the right.

This is also true of the demand for money. The aggregate money demand schedule, like any demand schedule, is drawn on the assumption of all things being equal to their previous values. One of these "things" is the level of income. If the level of aggregate real income rises, the aggregate demand for real money balances will shift to the right. As explained earlier, the demand for real transactions balances varies directly with the

[9]This overlooks another type of demand—the precautionary demand for money. *Precautionary balances* are held in reserve for some contingency, such as a personal emergency. Like transactions balances, they may be assumed to vary inversely with the interest rates and directly with the level of income for much the same reasons. Therefore, in the rest of this book simply assume that what is called transactions balances includes some precautionary balances.

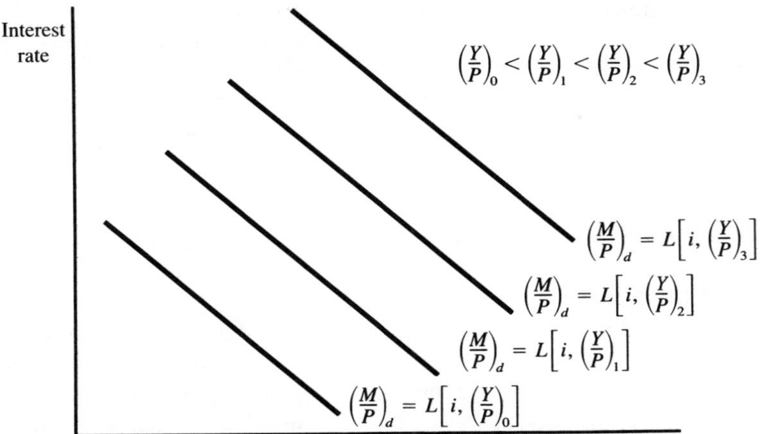

Figure 9.3 A Change in the Level of Aggregate Real Income Causes the Demand for Real Money Balances to Shift

level of real income. As real income rises, individuals require greater money balances to finance their higher level of real expenditures. The demand for speculative balances also varies directly with the level of income because income (or wealth) is a scale variable in the demand relation. The greater the level of aggregate income (or aggregate wealth), the greater the quantity of (noninferior) assets held, including money.

Therefore, there is a separate total demand curve for aggregate real money balances for each and every possible level of aggregate real income shown in Figure 9.3. Here $(Y/P)_0$, $(Y/P)_1$, $(Y/P)_2$, $(Y/P)_3$ are separate levels of aggregate income, and the subscripts order the levels by their relative size $(Y/P)_0 < (Y/P)_1 < (Y/P)_2 < (Y/P)_3$.

The aggregate demand for real money balances, as seen in Figure 9.3, varies inversely with the market rate of interest. It slopes downward for two reasons. First, the market rate less the rate paid on money balances is the opportunity cost of holding real transactions money balances. The greater the interest rate, *ceteris paribus,* the more interest income is sacrificed by holding real transactions money balances and the less the quantity of real transactions money balances demanded. Second, the interest rate is a bribe for assuming the risk of holding wealth in a nonmoney form. The greater the interest rate, the greater the proportion of one's speculative wealth held in risky nonmoney forms and the less the proportion of one's wealth held in the form of real speculative balances.

The aggregate demand for real money balances may be written in the form of an equation:

$$\left(\frac{M}{P}\right)_d = L\left(\underset{-}{i}, \underset{+}{\left(\frac{Y}{P}\right)}\right) \tag{9.7}$$

Equation (9.7) indicates that the aggregate quantity of real money balances demanded $(M/P)_d$ is a function (L) of the market rate of interest and the level of aggregate real income. The algebraic signs under the interest rate and aggregate real income variables indicate how the demand for real money balances is hypothesized to vary with these variables.[10]

THE SUPPLY CURVE OF MONEY

The narrowly defined money stock ($M1$) consists of currency (and coin) in circulation, checkable deposits, and traveler's checks. As was discussed in Chapter Eight, the broadly defined money stock ($M2$) consists of everything in $M1$ plus near-monies identified previously. As also mentioned in the previous chapter, depository institutions create checkable deposits, and the depository system can issue checkable deposits in a multiple of the monetary base. In turn, the monetary base can be controlled by the Federal Reserve System through open market operations.[11] Since neither the narrowly defined nor the broadly defined money supply is a function of the interest rate variable, either measure can be drawn as a perpendicular from the point on the horizontal axis which represents the nominal stock of money in existence,[12] as shown in Figure 9.4.

THE MONEY MARKET

Both the demand and the supply of a commodity are usually functions of the price of that commodity. There usually is a unique price that will set quantity supplied equal to quantity demanded. At any price other than this equilibrium price, either of the following will occur: Quantity supplied will be greater than quantity demanded (a condition of *excess supply*), which will drive the price down, or quantity supplied will be less than quantity demanded (a condition of *excess demand*), which will drive the price up. In either case, the price will change until equilibrium is restored.

[10]Empirical studies support the notion that the demand for real money balances varies inversely with the market rate of interest and directly with the level of real income (or wealth). The bibliography to this chapter cites surveys of several of these studies.

[11]It would be somewhat more precise to develop a model of the money market in terms of the supply of and demand for the monetary base. Since the demand for money implies a demand by banks for reserves and a demand by individuals for currency, the demand for the monetary base would have the same properties as the demand for money from which it would be directly derived. The supply of the monetary base is determined by the Federal Reserve. The implications of such a presentation of the money market would not be substantially different from those derived from the present model which features a supply of and demand for money.

[12]In Chapter Eight, footnote 19, it was shown that the nominal stock of money could vary with the market rate of interest because the money supply expansion coefficient could vary with the interest rate. This realistic feature would make the supply curve in Figure 9.4 less than perfectly (vertical) interest inelastic. However, this would not alter the essentials of the subsequent analysis.

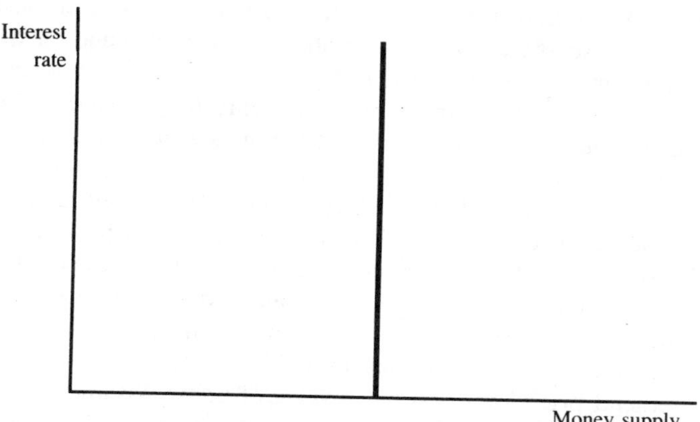

Figure 9.4 The Nominal Stock of Money

Consider the money market in Figure 9.5. In equilibrium, the quantity of real money balances demanded equals the real value of the quantity of nominal money balances supplied, $(M/P)_d = M/P$. Assuming that real income $(Y/P)_0$ and the general price level (P_0) are constant, one can solve this system for the equilibrium interest rate. This rate sets real money balances demanded, $(M/P)_d$, equal to the real value of the nominal quantity of money supplied, M/P_0. If the interest rate is so low that the quantity of real money balances demanded is greater than the real value of the quantity of nominal money balances supplied, an excess demand for money exists. Where individual wealth consists of money plus nonmoney assets, this means individuals will give up their nonmoney assets to obtain money. Consequently, the prices of nonmoney assets will fall. Thus, we are imposing an *aggregate consistency or adding-up condition* on our model. That condi-

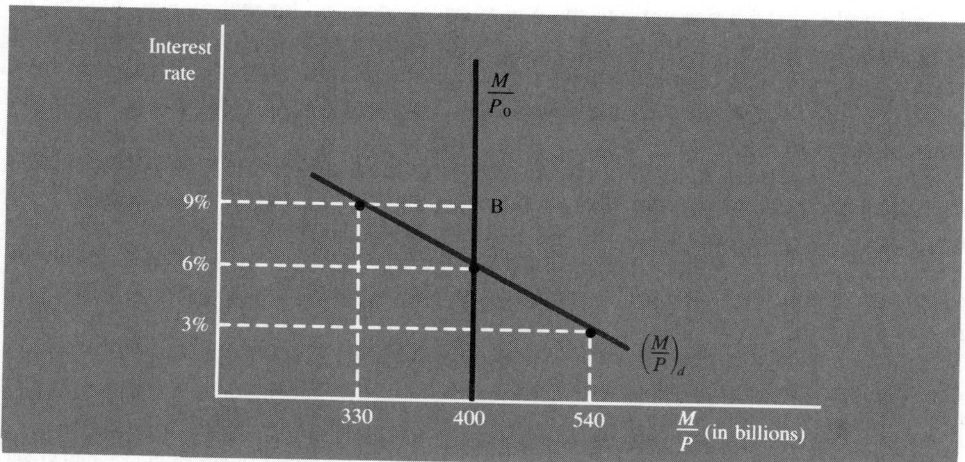

Figure 9.5 The Money Market

tion, known as the Walras Law of Markets, is that if wealth is defined to consist of money, bonds, and goods, an excess supply of one implies an excess demand for the sum of the other two.[13] In this section, we shall assume that an excess supply of money has no effect on the demand for goods. Therefore, it can affect only the demand for bonds. In the present instance, therefore, the excess demand for money implies an excess supply of bonds. Remember: A fall in the price of a bond implies a rise in its yield. As the yield or interest rate rises, the quantity of real money balances demanded decreases. Because individuals are induced to hold more bonds and fewer real money balances as the interest rate rises, we move up along the demand curve. The upward pressure on the interest rate will continue until the quantity of real money balances demanded equals the real value of the nominal quantity of money supplied (until there is no excess demand for money). Then the money market will be in equilibrium, $(M/P)_d = M/P_0$.

Assume the general price level (P_0) has a value of unity. Assume that the monetary authority supplies $400 million of nominal money balances. At the 9 percent interest rate, the quantity of real money balances demanded is $330 billion, the real value of the quantity supplied is $400 billion, and the excess supply of money is $70 billion. Hence, the money market is not in equilibrium.

This excess supply of real money balances means that there is money in circulation that people do not want to hold at the 9 percent rate. Instead, the 9 percent rate induces them to use the excess money to acquire additional bonds. We continue to assume that goods are unaffected. As individuals try to obtain bonds, however, they will bid bond prices up, and as bond prices rise, bond yields will fall.

As the rate of interest falls, individuals will be less willing to accept the risks of holding bonds, and they will be more willing to hold money. In Figure 9.5, the interest rate will fall until the rate of interest equals 6 percent. At the 6 percent rate, the quantity of real money balances demanded will equal the real value of the nominal quantity of money supplied; there will be no excess supply. The money market will be in equilibrium.

Conversely, at the 3 percent rate there is an excess demand for real money balances of $140 billion, and by the same process (working in the opposite direction), the market rate of interest will be bid up. Individuals demand more money than exists. Hence, they sell bonds until the rate rises to 6 percent, and the market is in equilibrium where the curves intersect.

Assume, for example, that the economy is in equilibrium with a total real money supply of $500 billion and an interest rate of 8 percent. If the money supply were to increase by $50 billion to $550 billion, assuming that real income and the general price level were constant, at the 8 percent interest rate, there would be an excess supply of money of $50 billion. This would force interest rates down (as people used the unwanted money balances to buy bonds) until the quantity of money demanded increased from $500 billion to $550 billion to equal the quantity of money supplied. This equality could occur only at a lower interest rate, say, 5 percent.

[13]This consistency or adding-up condition is employed frequently in later chapters involving general-equilibrium analysis. In these later chapters, instead of channeling the excess supply of money into either bonds or goods markets simply by assumption, we set out the conditions under which one or the other or both would occur.

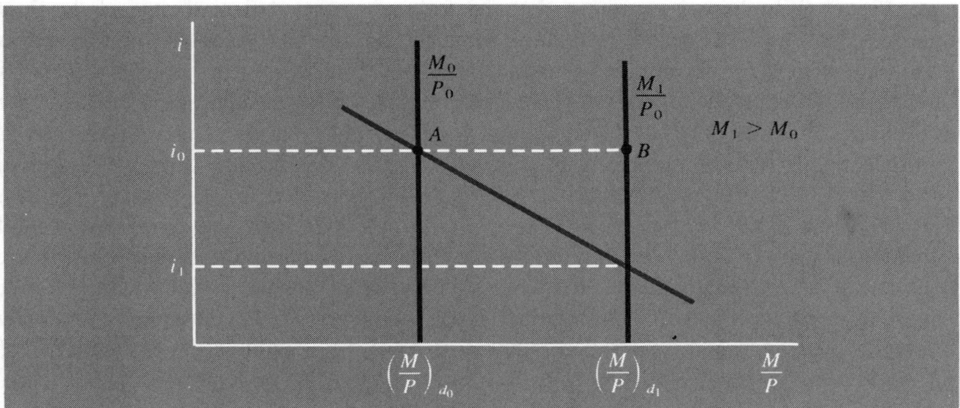

Figure 9.6 The Effect of an Increase in the Supply of Money on the Interest Rate (with the Price Level and Level of Real Income Held Constant)

These relations can be shown graphically. First, consider in Figure 9.6 the effect of an increase in the quantity of money supplied (M_s) from M_0 to M_1 with the price level fixed at P_0 and real income also fixed.[14] In equilibrium the real value of the nominal supply of money (M_0/P_0) equals the total demand for real money balances $(M/P)_{d_0}$ at the equilibrium interest rate i_0. If the supply schedule shifts to the right (to M_1), thus showing an increase in the quantity of money supplied, at the old equilibrium rate there would be an excess supply of money. This is shown on the graph as *AB*. For purposes of this example, continue to assume that goods are unaffected. If individuals had an excess supply of money of *AB*, by definition, they would also have an excess demand for bonds of *AB*. This would drive bond prices up and bond yields (the interest rate) down. As the interest rate falls to i_1, the quantity of real money balances demanded increases to $(M/P)_{d_1}$. At this point demand $(M/P)_{d_1}$ equals supply (M_1/P_0) at a new equilibrium interest rate (i_1).

What Does a Change in the Money Supply Influence— The Interest Rate, Real Income, or the Price Level?

The preceding discussion suggests that an increase in the nominal stock of money will lower the interest rate. This is true if the excess supply of money is used to purchase only bonds. Now let us assume instead that the excess supply of money is used to purchase goods and that the demand for bonds is unaffected (see footnote 13). If the price of goods is conceptually held constant, a rise in the demand for goods requires an increase in the quantity of goods produced. An increase in the level of aggregate output implies a rise in the level of aggregate real income. In the present case, the real income would increase to the level required to restore equilibrium to the money market.

[14] Although the effects are presented here in a simple sequence, they would really occur simultaneously.

In Figure 9.7, there is a unique demand for real money balances at each level of aggregate real income. As the price level remains constant at P_0 and the interest rate is assumed fixed at i_1, because the demand for bonds, and hence the price of bonds, is unchanged, there is one level of aggregate real income $(Y/P)_0$, which gives a demand for real money balances $(M/P)_{d_0} = L[i, (Y/P)_0]$ that is equal to the real value of the stock of nominal money balances supplied, M_0/P_0. This occurs at point A of Figure 9.7. When the nominal stock of money increases from M_0 to M_1, there is an excess supply of money, AB. With the price level conceptually held constant at P_0 and the interest rate held constant at i_0 by previous assumption, this excess supply can be absorbed only if the quantity of real money balances demanded increases to $(M/P)_{d_1} = L[i, (Y/P)_1]$. There it will equal the real value of the nominal supply of money M_1/P_0. This will occur only if the level of aggregate real income increases to $(Y/P)_1$. Equilibrium occurs at B of Figure 9.7.

A third alternative effect of an increase in the nominal stock of money is that it will precipitate an increase in the general price level. Assume, as before, that the excess supply of money is used only to purchase goods and that the demand for bonds is unaffected. As before, this implies that the interest rate is constant at i_0. Now, instead of holding price level constant, assume that the level of aggregate real income is constant at $(Y/P)_0$. In Figure 9.8 this fixes the quantity of real money balances demanded at $(M/P)_{d_0} = L[i_0, (Y/P)_0]$. Since both terms on the right-hand side of the demand-for-money relation are given, at i_0 and $(Y/P)_0$, quantity demanded $(M/P)_{d_0}$ is determined. With the nominal stock of money at M_0 there is only one price level, P_0, which brings about equilibrium. This occurs at point A in Figure 9.8. There the real value of the

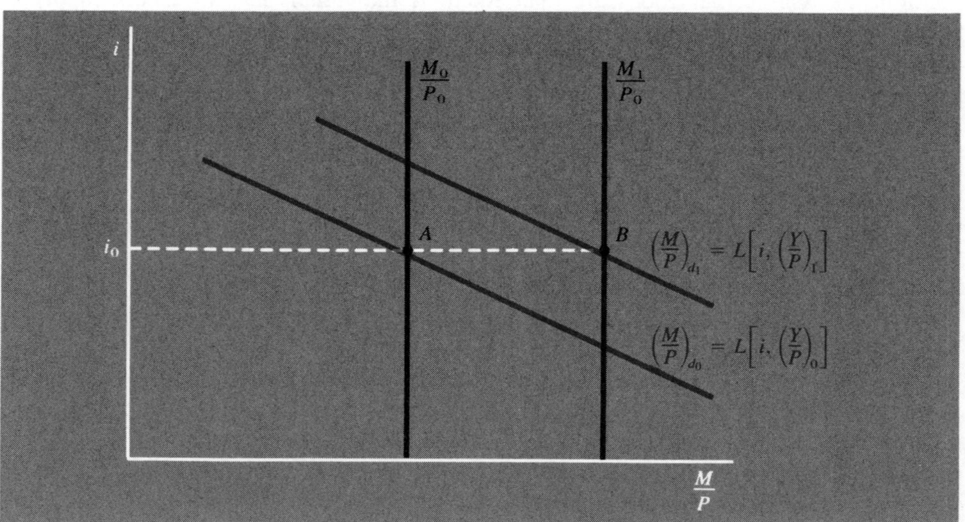

Figure 9.7 The Effect of an Increase in the Supply of Money on Real Income (with the Price Level and the Interest Rate Held Constant)

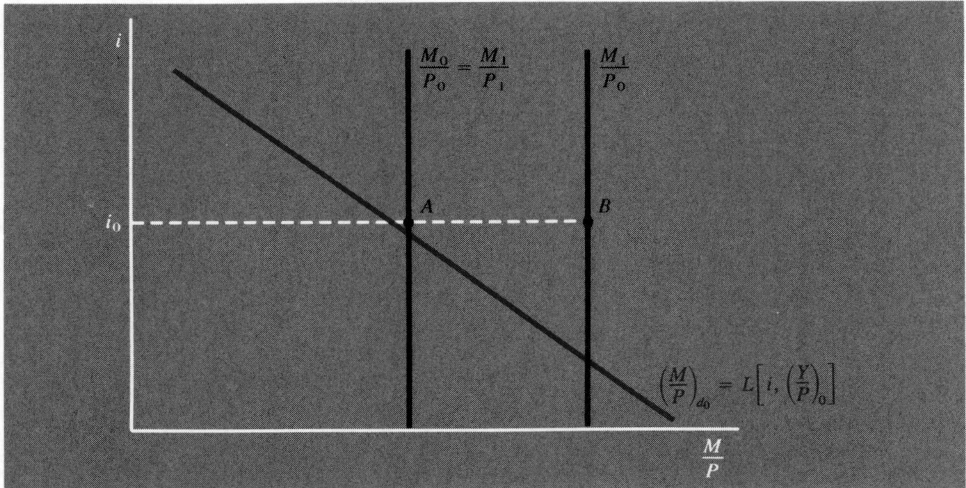

Figure 9.8 The Effect of an Increase in the Supply of Money on the Price Level (with Real Income and the Interest Rate Held Constant)

nominal stock of money M_0/P_0 will equal the quantity of real money balances demanded, $(M/P)_{d_0}$. When the nominal stock of money increases to M_1, since the quantity of real money balances demanded cannot change from $(M/P)_{d_0} = L[i_0, (Y/P)_0]$ because both the interest rate and the level of real income are conceptually held constant, the only adjustment that can reduce the excess supply of money, AB, is an increase in the price level from P_0 to P_1. With the price level at P_1, the real value of the nominal stock of money, M_1/P_1, is again equal to the quantity of real money balances demanded, $(M/P)_{d_0}$. This occurs at point A in Figure 9.8. The general price level has increased in direct proportion to the increase in the quantity of money. This result is called *the quantity theory of money*.[15]

Which of these three scenarios is the most accurate? Will a change in the supply of money affect the interest rate as in Figure 9.6, the level of aggregate real income as in Figure 9.7, or the general price level as in Figure 9.8? Reading the financial press, one often gets the impression that a change in the money supply will always have an effect on the interest rate. However, in reality, a change in the money stock, which may produce a change in the interest rate, will usually have effects on the price level and also, under certain conditions, on the level of aggregate real income. These effects occur because a change in the money supply will affect markets other than the bond market. Alternatively, a change in the money stock may affect the price level or aggregate real income directly, with no effect on the interest rate. These effects occur when a change in the money supply does not affect the bond market at all. Thus, the effect of changes in the money supply

[15]The quantity theory of money is better understood from the perspective of a general equilibrium model. A Neoclassical general equilibrium model that shows the implications of the quantity theory of money is presented in the next chapter.

on the economy as a whole is more complex when the equilibrium of many markets is considered. Analysis of one market viewed in isolation is called partial equilibrium analysis. Analysis of many markets and their interaction is called general equilibrium analysis. In a partial equilibrium model, where aggregate real income and the general price level are conceptually held constant, a change in the money supply will affect the interest rate. In a general equilibrium model, the level of real income and price level are usually endogenous variables, and a change in the money supply may affect the interest rate, the price level, and the level of aggregate real income. In the next chapter, the partial equilibrium analyses of the markets of the preceding chapters are combined in a general equilibrium analysis of all markets. This general equilibrium model will provide a more realistic view of how changes in the money stock affect the economy as a whole.

Recent Developments in the Demand for Money

Two recent developments that have affected the demand for money balances are: (1) the removal of legal ceilings on the payment of interest on checkable (and noncheckable) deposits that varies with the market rate of interest and (2) the increased use of credit cards and technological innovations that reduce the transactions costs of switching from one asset to another.

The payment of interest on checkable deposits that varies with the market rate of interest means that individuals are less likely to switch into and out of money balances when the interest rate paid on nonmoney assets changes. This implies that the demand for real money balances is less interest-sensitive. Any change in the interest rate then generates a smaller change in the quantity of real money balances demanded.[16]

Figure 9.9 shows a partial equilibrium model of the money market where the level of aggregate real income and the price level are held constant. Consider two alternative demand curves for real money balances. The first, $L_1[i, (Y/P)_0]$, reflects a situation where a rate of interest can legally be paid on checkable deposit balances that varies directly with the market rate. The second, $L_0[i, (Y/P)_0]$, reflects a situation where interest payments on checkable deposits cannot vary with the market rate. When interest rates are paid on many forms of money and these rates vary directly with the market rate, individual holdings of real money balances will be less sensitive to movements in the market rate of interest.

Now assume that the nominal stock of money increases from M_0 to M_1 in Figure 9.9. With the less interest-sensitive demand curve $L_1[i, (Y/P)_0]$, there is a greater decrease in the equilibrium interest rate than with the more interest-sensitive curve $L_0[i, (Y/P)_0]$. With the less interest-sensitive curve, a greater decline in the market rate of interest is

[16]Reductions in the interest sensitivity of the demand for money also may be a product of the increased risk of capital loss from holding nonmoney assets. The greater the risk perceived by asset holders, the greater the interest—bribe—they will require to switch from money to nonmoney and the less interest-sensitive will be the demand for money.

Risk of capital loss, as explained earlier, is associated with perceptions of possible fluctuations in the market prices of financial assets. In recent years, factors such as great swings in the government's deficit, sizable variations in inflation, and considerable amplitude in the movement of real income over time have caused sizable variations in interest rates and, hence, in financial asset prices.

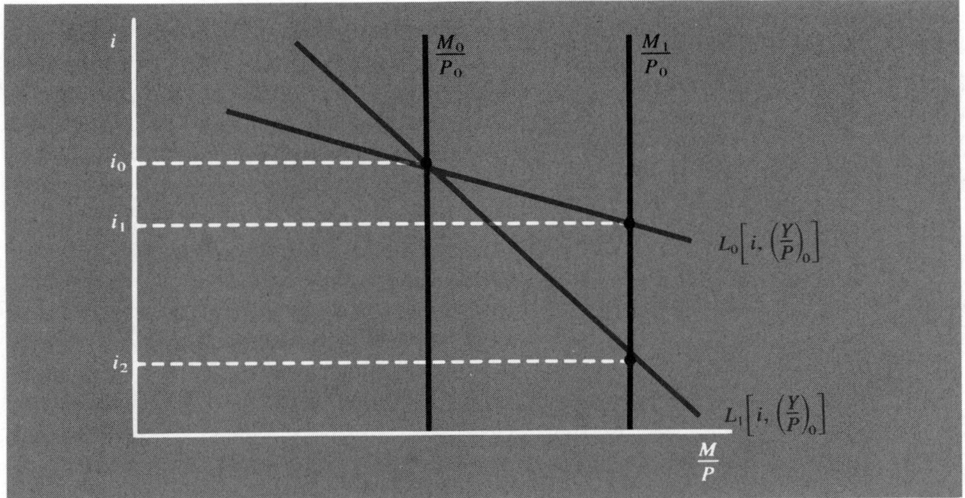

Figure 9.9 The Effect of the Payment of Interest on Checkable Deposits: Makes the Interest Rate More Volatile

required to generate the increase in the quantity of real money balances demanded, which, in turn, is necessary to match the increase in supply and thereby restore equilibrium.

This experiment indicates that the legislation that permitted the interest rates that are paid on checkable deposits to vary with market rates (the Depository Institutions Deregulation and Monetary Control Act of 1980) ushered in an era of greater interest rate volatility. Therefore, one should not be surprised if interest rates continue to fluctuate more in the 1980s and 1990s than they did in the 1960s and 1970s, before this legislation was passed.

In addition to changing the slope of the demand curve, as shown in Figure 9.9, the payment of interest on checkable deposits may have caused it to shift rightward. This increase in the demand for money would take place because interest-bearing transactions balances became more attractive ways of holding wealth. The increase in the demand caused by deregulation is discussed again later in this chapter.

Another recent development has been the increased use of credit cards that has occurred since the early 1960s. Like technological improvements that reduce the transactions costs of switching between money and nonmoney assets discussed earlier, the increased use of credit cards has caused a reduction in the demand for real money balances that are used for transactions purposes. The credit card is a substitute for transactions balances. It is not an asset to its holder. It is merely an efficient means of carrying out transactions by borrowing instead of using money balances. Therefore, it reduces the demand for money to be used to finance transactions.

Now assume a partial equilibrium model of the money market where the level of aggregate real income and the interest rate are held constant. In Figure 9.10 the ever

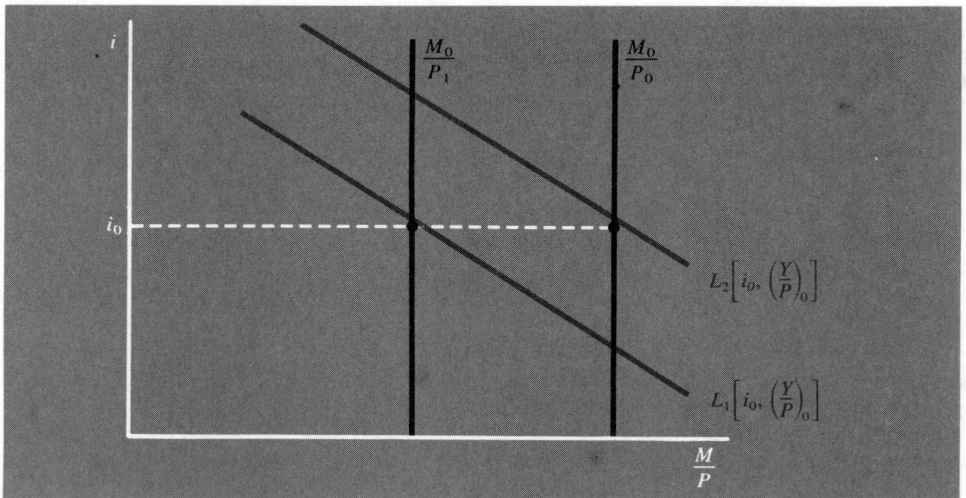

Figure 9.10 The (Secular) Decrease in the Demand for Money because the Increased Use of Credit Cards Raises the Price Level

increasing use of credit cards and technological innovations that reduce the transactions costs of converting from transactions balances to other assets, and vice versa, cause the demand for real money balances to shift steadily leftward from $L_2[i_0, (Y/P)_0]$ to $L_1[(i_0, (Y/P)_0]$. At unchanged interest and real income levels, this creates a condition of an excess supply of money. With the nominal stock of money unchanged at M_0, equilibrium can be restored only if the price level rises from P_0 to P_1. Thus, the secular decrease in the demand for money results in an excess supply of money, which in turn generates an increase in the price level. This suggests that one cause of greater *price inflation* (a continual rise in the price level over time) might be the steady decrease in the demand for money, which is associated with technological improvements that lead to increased credit card usage. In the present model, a steady decrease in the demand for money, *ceteris paribus*, can be just as inflationary as a steady increase in the supply of money.

Velocity and Its Predictability

A secular trend decrease in the demand for real money balances may also be viewed as a secular trend increase in the *income velocity of money*. Conversely, a secular trend increase in the demand for money implies a secular trend decrease in velocity. The income velocity of money is defined as the quantity of money balances demanded, divided into the level of aggregate income. It is the rate of turnover of money balances demanded per period. Velocity denotes how much "work" the average dollar does over a period of time. If the quantity of money balances demanded declines with aggregate income unchanged, velocity increases. Thus, an increase in velocity is analogous to a reduction in the demand for money balances.

As previously mentioned, a sustained decrease in the demand for money (a sustained increase in velocity) is just as inflationary as an increase in the growth rate of the money supply. As the old adage goes, "A nimble sixpence does the work of a slow shilling."

This discussion suggests that it is very important for the Federal Reserve to predict velocity. The data presented in Chart 9.1A show that the income velocity of narrowly defined money, $V1 = Y/M1$, had been trending upward at approximately 3 percent per year from 1965 to 1980. In contrast, Chart 9.1B reveals no discernible trend over the same time span in the income velocity of broadly defined money, $V2 = Y/M2$. The trend in $V1$ is widely believed to have taken place because of the increased use of substitutes such as credit cards for transaction balances and because of reductions in the cost of converting into and out of transactions balances. It should be noted, however, that after 1981, income velocity, $V1$, seems to have stopped its upward trend. It fell until 1983, rose somewhat in 1984, and declined again in 1985 and 1986. Overall since 1981 there has been an average decrease in $V1$ of about 2 percent per year.

Trends in velocity have weighty impact on the money supply growth policies of the Federal Reserve. On one hand, a predicted uptrend in $V1$ would require that moderate targets be set for the growth rate of $M1$ to suppress the potentially inflationary effects of the positive trend in velocity. On the other hand, if $V1$ is projected to remain constant or decline in the late 1980s and beyond, higher targets for the growth rate of $M1$ would not be inflationary.

What changes in the demand for transactions balances could occur in future years? These changes will surely include technological improvements such as more sophisticated automatic teller machines, debit cards, and other transactions cost-reducing services of the heralded "checkless society," which will cause the demand for money to fall and $V1$ to rise. However, they may include the introduction of new interest-bearing forms of $M1$ which could cause the demand for money to rise and $V1$ to fall. When these changes occur, what will be the net effect? Will the desired stock of $M1$ shrink and its velocity rise over time as in the period before 1981, or will the desired stock of $M1$ rise and its velocity shrink as in the 1981–1986 period? How will these developments affect the future time path of $V1$? Will the path of $V1$ be moving strongly downward as in the timespan from 1981 to 1986, or will the path be upward as it was from 1965 to 1979, when there was an average growth rate of velocity of about 3 percent per year? This is a very important problem for the Fed.

Just as there may be predictable secular trend movements in the income velocity of narrowly defined money, there may also be predictable cyclical movements. There are a number of factors which cause a cyclical movement in velocity. The most important of these are cyclical movements in the nominal interest rate and the expected rate of inflation. As seen in Chapter Six, during the recessionary phase of the business cycle, nominal interest rates typically decline. During the boom phase of the cycle, nominal interest rates typically rise. The demand for money varies inversely with the nominal interest rate. The income velocity of money is defined as income divided by the quantity

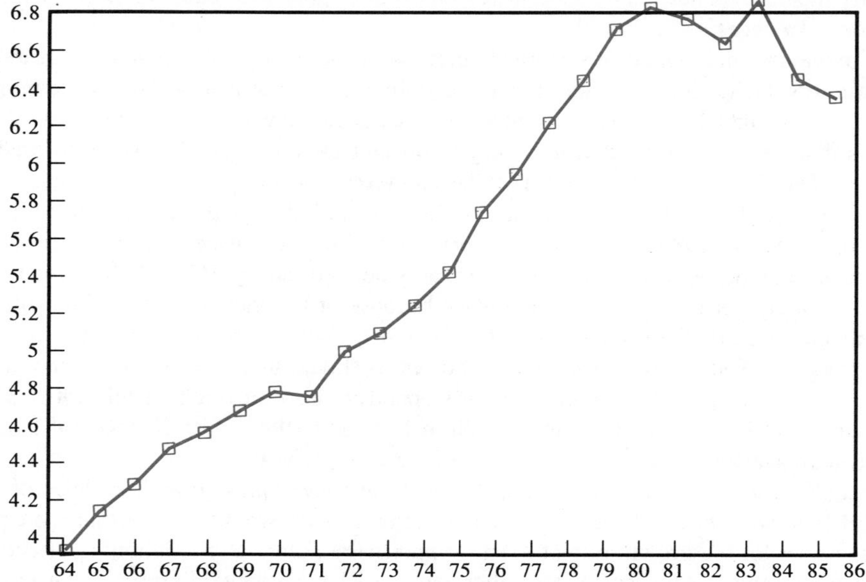

Chart 9.1A The Income Velocity of *M*1

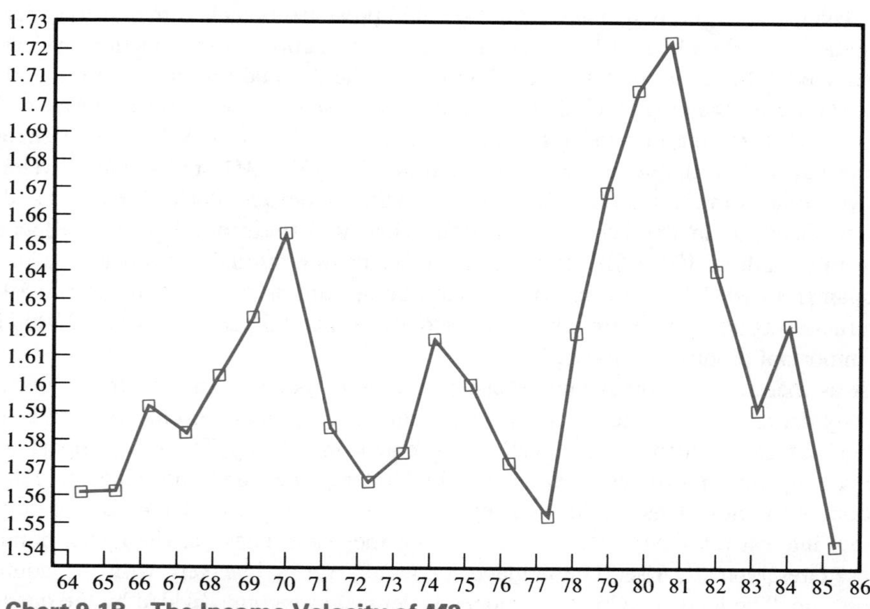

Chart 9.1B The Income Velocity of *M*2

of money, where quantity of money supplied equals quantity demanded. Therefore, the income velocity of money will vary directly with the nominal interest rate and the expected rate of inflation over the course of the business cycle.[17]

The cyclical movement of velocity suggests that any given growth rate of the money supply is less inflationary, *ceteris paribus,* when nominal interest rates are declining, when velocity is low. Conversely, any given growth rate of the money supply is more inflationary, *ceteris paribus,* when nominal interest rates are rising, when velocity is relatively high. This implies that a given growth rate of the money supply will appear to be less inflationary when interest rates are declining and velocity is falling. Under these circumstances, the Fed could be lulled into complacency during an era of falling interest rates, when a high money growth rate does not appear to fuel greater inflation. This occurred in the 1982–1986 period when the Federal Reserve permitted rapid money growth in the face of falling velocity. Such a lax attitude is unwise, because that same money supply growth rate will prove far more inflationary when interest rates are rising. There is considerable evidence that money supply growth has chronically been excessive during cyclical booms when velocity is rising. All this leads to the conclusion that if the Federal Reserve is not ever-alert to trends and cycles in velocity, its objective of controlling inflation will be much more difficult to attain. The Fed's trying to control inflation by controlling money supply growth while ignoring velocity is analogous to a person trying to control her weight through controlling caloric intake while ignoring the rate at which she burns calories through daily activities.

Chart 9.1 reveals cyclical patterns in both the income velocity of narrowly defined money, $V1$, and the income velocity of broadly defined money, $V2$. Because of a trend in $V1$ before 1980 and no apparent trend in $V2$, the cyclical pattern of $V2$ is easier to recognize in the chart. During the cyclical booms of 1966–1969, 1972–1973, and 1977–1980, the income velocity of $M2$ rose; during the recessions of 1970–1971, 1974–1976, and 1981–1982, $V2$ fell. This largely reflects the cyclical pattern of nominal interest rates and expected inflation (see Chart 6.1 in Chapter Six). However, other influences may have been at work on $V2$ and $V1$ in recent years. For example, the pronounced decline of $V2$ and $V1$ between 1981 and 1986 may also have been a reflection of the increased substitution of transactions balances and near-monies for nonmoney assets that occurred when money market mutual funds and money market deposit accounts, both included in $M2$ and NOW and Super-NOW accounts, both included in $M1$ and $M2$, grew in popularity.

In the eyes of some economists, the plunge in velocity, the increase in the demand for money relative to income, in 1981–1986 may be traced to deregulation that allowed

[17]If the demand for money is unit elastic with respect to income, the income velocity of money will not vary with income. The demand for money will increase in the same percentage as income and the quotient, the income velocity of money, will be unchanged. If the demand for money varies inversely with the interest rate, then the income velocity of money will vary directly with the interest rate. Several empirical studies, cited in the bibliography to this chapter, provide evidence that the demand for money varies directly with income and inversely with the interest rate. Some of this evidence supports the assumption of a unitary income elasticity; other evidence does not.

depository institutions to pay interest on the checkable deposit components of transactions balances. According to this view, many of the components of $M1$, such as NOW accounts, now have the characteristics of near-monies. As such, they have become closer substitutes for nonmoney assets. If this is true, the demand for transactions balances may not only have become less interest-sensitive, as discussed earlier, but may have increased as the difference between interest rates paid on transactions balances, on near-monies, and on nonmoney assets narrowed. This would cause velocity to decrease. Difficulties in predicting the demand for money and velocity could arise if the differences between interest rates paid on various components of $M1$ (see footnote 3), on near-monies, and on nonmoney assets vary significantly over time relative to the transactions costs of switching among these assets.

In contrast, other economists are more sanguine. They argue that true transactions balances are identifiable by their size, turnover, and seasonal and debit characteristics and that far greater difficulties occur in prediction when $M1$ is added to near-monies to yield $M2$ (see footnote 5). Some contend that in the emerging world of very low transactions costs, there will be a small but stable demand for transactions balances paying interest rates that fall below those paid in near-monies by a margin that will be stable over time. Still over economists have attempted to unravel the distinction among all of the individual components of $M1$ and near-monies.

In an attempt to identify a measure of liquidity that bears a stable relationship with income over time, economists have been trying to weight the components of $M1$ and $M2$ according to how much is actually issued for spending. Currency and demand deposits get a full weight, while each dollar of NOW or Super-NOW accounts is currently counted as only about 55 cents. Research by Fed analysts shows how much each NOW or Super-NOW account goes for spending. These *weighted money aggregates* are called *Divisia aggregates* and *weighted indexes*.[18]

Ultimately, whether the velocity of $M1$ or the new weighted indexes and Divisia aggregates are more stable, extreme types of cyclical movements in these velocities occur during periods of *hyperinflation*. When hyperinflation sets in, the rate of price level increase goes from out of mind to out of sight. During hyperinflation, the expected rate of inflation and nominal rate of interest are so high that the demand for real money balances falls precipitously and velocity soars. During hyperinflation, an explosion in velocity based on a high expected rate of inflation can propel an astronomical increase in the price level just as readily as a sky-rocketing in the growth rate of the nominal stock of money.[19] Hyperinflation can thus be precipitated by factors that drive up nominal interest rates, such as unbounded growth in the ratio of government debt to GNP (discussed in Chapter Six). This and other causes of inflation are examined in Chapter Thirteen.

[18]For further discussion of the new weighted aggregates, see the article by Barnett and Spindt cited in the bibliography to this chapter. For further discussion of the stability of velocity, see the article by Thornton cited in the bibliography.

[19]Phillip Cagan, "The Monetary Dynamics of Hyperinflation," in Milton Friedman, ed., *Studies in the Quantity Theory of Money* (Chicago: University of Chicago Press, 1956).

Concluding Comment

As this chapter explains, the theory of the demand for money is that the quantity of aggregate real money balances demanded varies directly with the level of aggregate real income (or wealth) and varies inversely with the market rate of interest. The positive relation between quantity of money demanded and real income occurs because income is a scale variable, and an increase in income increases the demand for all wealth forms, including money. In addition, as income increases, the demand for money to be held to finance expenditures out of that income must rise. The negative relation between the quantity of money demanded and the interest rate occurs because the nominal interest rate earned on nonmoney is the opportunity cost of holding money and also because the interest rate is a bribe for assuming the risk of holding one's wealth in nonmoney form.

In a partial equilibrium model of the money market, an increase in the supply of money, *ceteris paribus,* is viewed as creating an excess supply of money in private portfolios. This excess is typically seen as being coextensive with an excess demand for other, nonmoney assets. The excess demand is often said to boost financial asset prices and, according to the present value formula, lower their yield, the market rate of interest. From this perspective, other variables such as aggregate real income and the price level are assumed constant. An alternative view is that the excess demand drives up the price level with the interest rate and real income assumed constant.

The preceding analysis is partial in that it ignores the potential effects of an increase in the supply of money on all of the relevant variables—the interest rate, real income, and the price level. A more realistic view of the effects of an increase in the supply of money would call for a relaxation of the *ceteris paribus* assumption that some of these variables are constant. In the next chapter, the *ceteris paribus* condition is relaxed in a general equilibrium model of the economy as a whole. In a general equilibrium context, the effects of an increase in the supply of money on the interest rate, the level of aggregate real income and the general price level can be fruitfully explored.

EXERCISES

1. "In a world of numerous near-monies, individuals will never hold speculative balances."
   a. true
   b. false
2. Use the present value formula to explain why long-term bond prices are more influenced by interest rate changes than short-term bond prices.
3. Explain the relation between the market rate and the coupon rate when a bond sells above par.
4. Explain how technological improvements which reduce the transactions costs of switching between money and nonmoney assets affect the transactions demand for money and the velocity of $M1$.

5. Give two reasons why the interest rate affects the demand for money.
6. Define the following:
   current yield
   yield-to-maturity
   coupon rate
   default risk
   market risk
7. Explain how technological improvements and depository innovations lead to trends in the demand for money or the income velocity of money which might cause inflation.
8. Why do cyclical variations in velocity require a vigilant Federal Reserve?
9. List the assumptions in a partial equilibrium model under which an increase in the money supply would lower the interest rate.
10. Evaluate: "Because all ceilings on deposit rates of interest will be abolished during the 1980s, the demand for money will be less interest-sensitive because individuals will receive interest on their money balances and will not have to worry about changes in market rates. This means that interest rates will fluctuate a lot less."
11. Suppose the increased attractiveness of near-monies because of depository innovations increased the income velocity of *M*1 and decreased the income velocity of *M*2. What effect should this have on the money supply policy of the Federal Reserve?
12. At present, business firms are prohibited from holding NOW and Super-NOW accounts. What will happen to the demand for narrowly defined money and broadly defined money if these restrictions are removed?

BIBLIOGRAPHY

Barnett, William, and Paul Spindt. "Divisia Monetary Aggregates." In *Modern Concepts in Macroeconomics*, ed. Thomas M. Havrilesky. Arlington Heights, Ill.: Harlan Davidson, Inc., 1985.

Boorman, John T. "A Survey of the Demand for Money: Theoretical Formulations and Pre-1973 Empirical Results." In *Modern Concepts in Macroeconomics*, ed. Thomas M. Havrilesky. Arlington Heights, Ill.: Harlan Davidson, Inc., 1985.

Baumol, William. "The Transactions Demand for Cash: An Inventory Theoretic Approach." *Quarterly Journal of Economics* 66 (November 1952), pp. 545–556.

Friedman, Milton. "The Quantity Theory of Money, A Restatement." In *Studies in the Quantity Theory of Money*, ed. Milton Friedman. Chicago: University of Chicago Press, 1956, pp. 3–21.

———. "The Demand for Money—Some Theoretical and Empirical Results." *Journal of Political Economy* 67 (June 1959), pp. 327–351.

Goldfeld, Stephen. "The Demand for Money Revisited." *Brookings Papers on Economic Activity* (3:1973), pp. 577–638.

Gurley, John G., and Edward S. Shaw. *Money in a Theory of Finance*. Washington, D.C.: The Brookings Institution, 1960.

Havrilesky, Thomas M., "Monetary Modeling in a World of Financial Innovation." In *Electronic Funds Transfers and Payments: The Public Policy Issues,* ed. Elinor Solomon. Boston: Klawer, 1987.

Johnson, Harry G. "Monetary Theory and Policy." *American Economic Review* 52 (June 1962), pp. 335–384.

Jones, David. "The Demand for Money: A Review of the Empirical Literature." Staff Economic Studies of the Federal Reserve System. Paper presented to the Federal Reserve System Committee on Financial Analysis in St. Louis (October 1965).

Judd, John P., and John L. Scadding. "The Search for a Stable Money Demand Function: A Survey of the Post-1973 Literature." In *Modern Concepts in Macroeconomics,* ed. Thomas M. Havrilesky. Arlington Heights, Ill.: Harlan Davidson, Inc., 1985.

Laidler, David. *The Demand for Money: Theories and Evidence*. 2d ed. New York: Dunn-Donnelly Publishing Corp., 1977.

Meltzer, Allan H. "The Demand for Money: The Evidence from the Time Series." *Journal of Political Economy* 71 (June 1963), pp. 219–246.

Thornton, Daniel L. "Why Does Velocity Matter?" In *Modern Concepts in Macroeconomics,* ed. Thomas M. Havrilesky. Arlington Heights, Ill.: Harlan Davidson, Inc., 1985.

Tobin, James. "Liquidity Preference as Behavior Towards Risk." *Review of Economic Studies* 25 (February 1958), pp. 65–86.

———. "Money, Capital, and Other Stores of Value." *American Economic Review, Papers and Proceedings* 51 (May 1961), pp. 26–37.

———. "The Theory of Portfolio Selection." In *The Theory of Interest Rates,* ed. F. H. Hahn and F. P. Brechling. New York: St. Martin's Press, 1965, pp. 3–51.

General Equilibrium Models

Part III

The Neoclassical General Equilibrium Model: Solution Process

Chapter 10

Introduction

The present chapter combines the analysis of the previous chapters into a model of the aggregate economy. In previous chapters, models of the aggregate labor market, the aggregate credit (loanable funds) market, and the aggregate money market were presented as being separate and self-contained entities. Each market was viewed in *partial equilibrium*. The presentation of these markets as unrelated sectors of the economy is unrealistic. They are quite closely interrelated in a number of ways. Interrelation often tends to complicate the analysis a little. The realization of this sort of complication in economic analysis once prompted an economist to remark: "When I was a student, I thought that everything in the world was related to everything else. When I became an economist, I discovered that everything in the economy was related to everything else . . . in at least five different ways."

In this chapter, the interrelatedness of the workings of the three aggregate markets is explored. These markets will be studied in a *general equilibrium,* rather than a *partial equilibrium,* context. However, in order to minimize complication, to keep things as simple as possible, only the basic tools of supply and demand analysis will be used.

This chapter will show how the equilibrium level of aggregate real income, determined in the aggregate labor market, affects the equilibrium rate of interest, determined in the aggregate credit market, and how the level of real income and the interest rate affect the equilibrium price level, determined in the aggregate money market. In other words, we will see how the working of the labor market determines the equilibrium level of employment. Because the level of employment is an input in the aggregate production function, it determines the equilibrium level of aggregate real income. The level of aggregate real income affects aggregate real saving, which in the credit market helps determine the equilibrium rate of interest. With the rate of interest determined by the working of the credit market and the equilibrium level of aggregate real income determined by the working of the labor market, the exact quantity of real money balances demanded in the money market can be found. This holds because the quantity of real money balances demanded depends on the interest rate and the level of aggregate real income. With the quantity of *real* money balances demanded so determined, given any quantity of *nominal* money balances supplied by the money authority, the general price level must adjust until the real value of the stock of nominal money balances supplied by the monetary authority is equal to the quantity of real money balances demanded. Thus, the working of the money market determines the equilibrium general price level.

Therefore, the purpose of this chapter is to show how the interrelated solution of the three sectors of the Neoclassical general equilibrium model supports three hypotheses: (1) The level of employment and production are determined by the working of the labor market; (2) the level of the interest rate is determined by the working of the credit (loanable funds) market; and (3) the general price level is determined by the working of the money market.

THE SOLUTION PROCESS FOR THE NEOCLASSICAL GENERAL EQUILIBRIUM MODEL—THE LABOR MARKET–PRODUCTION SECTOR

The aggregate labor market–production sector of this general equilibrium model of the economy as a whole is the place to begin. In Chapter Three, the labor market and production function were specified as follows:

$$L_D = f(\underset{-}{w}, \underset{+}{P}) \qquad \text{(aggregate demand for labor)} \qquad (10.1)$$

$$L_S = g(\underset{+}{w}, \underset{-}{P}) \qquad \text{(aggregate supply of labor)} \qquad (10.2)$$

$$L_S = L_D \qquad \text{(labor market equilibrium condition)} \qquad (10.3)$$

$$\left(\frac{Y}{P}\right) = \phi(\underset{+}{L}, \underset{+}{\overline{K}}) \text{ with } \overline{K} \text{ given} \qquad \text{(aggregate production function)} \qquad (10.4)$$

The demand for labor, Equation (10.1), varies inversely with the nominal wage (w) and directly with the general price level (P). The supply of labor, Equation (10.2), varies directly with the nominal wage (w) and inversely with the price level (P). The quantity of labor demanded (L_D), in equilibrium, Equation (10.3), equals the quantity of labor supplied (L_S). According to the aggregate production function, Equation (10.4), the equilibrium level of aggregate real income (Y/P) varies directly with the equilibrium level of employment (L), the level of capital input (K) being assumed fixed in the short run.

In the aggregate labor market–production sector there are four equations: (10.1), (10.2), (10.3), and (10.4). With the capital stock assumed given in the short run, there are five unknowns: L_D, L_S, w, P, and Y/P. To solve for the equilibrium values of the five unknowns, one would technically have to add n more equations in $n - 1$ new unknowns. This could be done most simply by specifying that one of the unknowns is given. However, it was seen in Chapter Three that, under the assumption of flexible nominal wages and perfect information, the solution for the equilibrium level of employment and, hence, the equilibrium level of aggregate real income is invariant with respect to the general price level. This is shown graphically in Figure 10.1.

Recall from Chapter Three that the assumption of flexible nominal wages and perfect information means that behavioral agents respond to *real* (purchasing power) values such as the *real* wage, not *nominal* values such as the nominal or money wage. Real magnitudes are nominal dollar magnitudes that are deflated by the general price level.

Figure 10.1 shows that with nominal wage flexibility and perfect information an increase in the price level from P_0 to P_1 or from P_1 to P_2 results in movements in the labor supply and labor demand curves, which, measured vertically, are in the same proportion as the increases in the price level. On the demand side of the labor market, with employment conceptually held constant at any level, the nominal wage offered by employers will increase in the same percentage as the general price level. This follows from the familiar profit-maximizing condition for the firm:

$$\text{nominal wage} = \text{price of output} \times \text{marginal physical product of labor}$$

Since employment (L) is conceptually held constant, output is at a fixed point on the aggregate production function; therefore, the marginal physical productivity of labor is unchanged. Consequently, if the price at which output sells (on the right-hand side of the profit-maximizing condition) rises, the nominal wage that firms are willing to pay (on the left-hand side) must rise in the same proportion.

On the supply side of the labor market, the real wage (w/P) is the opportunity cost of leisure. With labor hours supplied held conceptually constant—that is, conceptually permitting no change in the allocation between labor hours and leisure hours—there can be no change in the real wage. Therefore, when the general price level rises, the nominal wage must rise in the same proportion, such that the real wage and, hence, the allocation of time between labor and leisure is unchanged.

In Figure 10.1, with both labor supply and labor demand curves shifting upward by the same distance, the labor supply and labor demand curves always intersect vertically above the full employment level of employment (L_1). The vertical movement of the supply

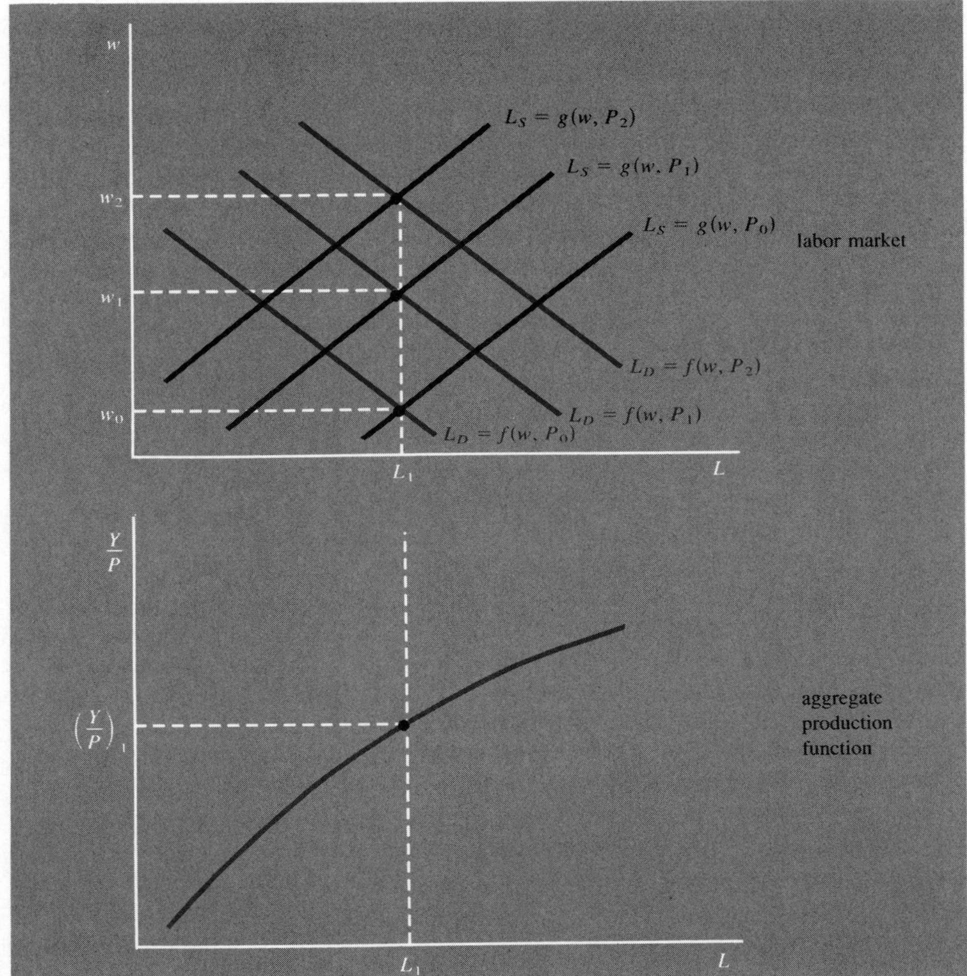

Figure 10.1 The Equilibrium Level of Employment and Aggregate Real Income

and demand curves is proportional to the increase in the general price level, either from P_0 to P_1 or from P_1 to P_2. Thus, when there is nominal wage flexibility and perfect information, the equilibrium level of employment is invariant with respect to the general price level. This is the static analog of the long-run Phillips curve of Chapter Three. Since equilibrium employment is unchanged at L_1, the equilibrium level of aggregate real income, determined by the aggregate production function, is unchanged at $(Y/P)_1$. The marginal physical product of labor and, hence, the real wage are also unchanged ($w_0/P_0 = w_1/P_1 = w_2/P_2$). The nominal wage ($w$) changes in the same proportion as the general price level (P). By the profit-maximizing condition for the firm,

$$\text{nominal wage} = \text{price of output} \times \text{marginal physical product of labor}$$

As the marginal physical product of labor is unchanged, the real wage is also unchanged:

$$\text{real wage} = \frac{\text{nominal wage}}{\text{price of output}} = \text{marginal physical product of labor}$$

THE CREDIT MARKET

Having analyzed the aggregate supply (labor market–production sector) side of this global model, the focus now turns to the aggregate demand side. The aggregate demand side of this model of the economy as a whole has a *flow sector,* the credit (loanable funds) market, and a *stock sector,* the aggregate money market. The flow sector reflects spending and saving behavior in the economy. The stock sector reflects asset holding behavior. The aggregate credit market is specified by the following equations:

$$\frac{S}{P} = j\left[\underset{+}{i}, \underset{+}{\left(\frac{Y}{P}\right)_d}\right] \quad \text{(aggregate saving)} \quad (10.5)$$

$$\frac{I}{P} = m(\underset{-}{i}) \quad \text{(aggregate investment expenditures)} \quad (10.6)$$

$$\left(\frac{G}{P} - \frac{T}{P}\right) = \left(\frac{\overline{G}}{P} - \frac{\overline{T}}{P}\right) \quad \text{(government deficit or surplus)} \quad (10.7)$$

$$\left(\frac{Y}{P}\right)_d = \left(\frac{Y}{P}\right) - \left(\frac{\overline{T}}{P}\right) \quad \text{(definition of disposable income)} \quad (10.8)$$

$$\frac{I}{P} + \left(\frac{G}{P} - \frac{T}{P}\right) = \frac{S}{P} \quad \text{(credit market equilibrium condition)} \quad (10.9)$$

As discussed in Chapter Five, the aggregate supply of real saving, Equation (10.5), responds positively to the nominal rate of interest. In the absence of a change in the expected rate of inflation, a change in the nominal rate of interest is synonymous with a change in the real rate of interest. Aggregate real saving also responds positively to the level of aggregate real disposable income. Equation (10.8) defines real disposable income as real income minus the level of taxation, which is exogenously determined. As also discussed in Chapter Five, the aggregate demand for loanable funds to finance aggregate real investment expenditures by business firms, Equation (10.6), varies inversely with the rate of interest. The aggregate demand for funds to finance the aggregate real deficit of government, Equation (10.7), is exogenously determined. This means that these variables, government expenditures (G) and taxation (T), are determined outside the model and are independent of any of its other variables. The credit market equilibrium condition, Equation (10.9), specifies that the aggregate supply of credit (S/P), in equilibrium, is equal to the total aggregate demand for credit. The total aggregate demand for credit consists of the aggregate private demand for credit by business firms (I/P) plus the aggregate governmental demand for credit ($G/P - T/P$).

Thus, in the aggregate credit market there are five equations—(10.5), (10.6), (10.7), (10.8), and (10.9)—and six unknowns—S/P, I/P, $(G/P - T/P)$, i, $(Y/P)_d$, and Y/P. To solve for the equilibrium values of these six unknowns, one technically would have to add n more equations in $n - 1$ new unknowns. This can be done most simply by specifying one of the unknowns as given. However, it was previously shown that the equilibrium level of aggregate real income is already determined, at a full employment level, by the working of the labor market. Aggregate real income, therefore, is not an unknown but is a *given* in the credit market. Thus, the system is reduced to five equations in five unknowns, S/P, I/P, $(G/P - T/P)$, $(Y/P)_d$ and i. As a consequence, it may be said that the working of the credit market determines the interest rate.

The working of the credit market in determining the interest rate can be seen graphically in Figure 10.2. Because the interest rate is on the vertical axis, the level of aggregate

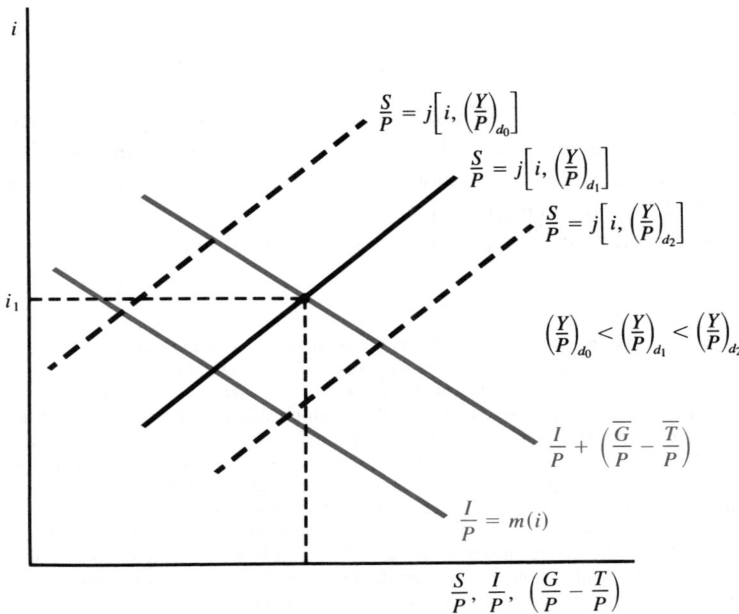

Figure 10.2 Credit Market Equilibrium

real disposable income determines the *position* of the aggregate real saving schedule. There are an infinite number of aggregate real saving curves, one for each level of aggregate real disposable income. However, as the equilibrium value of real income has already been determined in the labor market, and the level of real taxation is exogenously determined, only one of these real saving curves is relevant. The relevant real saving curve is the solid line labeled $S/P = j[i, (Y/P)_{d_1}]$, where $(Y/P)_{d_1} = (Y/P)_1 - \overline{T}/P$ and $(Y/P)_1$ is the full employment level of real income, determined in the labor market–production sector.

With the relevant real saving curve and the total aggregate real demand curve for credit both specified, we may solve for equilibrium values. The equilibrium quantity of credit supplied, the equilibrium quantity of credit demanded, and the equilibrium interest rate are obtained as shown in Figure 10.2. The equilibrium interest rate that is determined by the working of the credit market may be viewed as an equilibrium *real* as well as an equilibrium *nominal* rate of interest. As discussed in Chapter Six, under conditions of perfect information the nominal rate of interest is equal to the expected real rate of interest plus the expected rate of inflation. The equilibrium nominal rate of interest reflects the expected rate of inflation. Thus, while the real supply of and real demand for credit determine the underlying real rate of interest as shown here, expected inflation will affect supply-and-demand behavior such that an (expected) inflation premium is added on to this real rate of interest to yield the equilibrium nominal rate of interest. As long as the expected inflation rate is assumed constant, as it is in the next three chapters, changes in the nominal interest rate are synonymous with changes in the real interest rate.

THE MONEY MARKET

The aggregate credit market is the flow subsector of the aggregate demand portion of the global model. In the credit market the focus is on the flow of spending and saving. The aggregate money market is the stock subsector of the aggregate demand portion of the overall model. In the money market the focus is on the public's demand to hold its stock of assets and the central bank's supply of a stock of nominal money balances.[1]

[1]As explained in Chapter Nine, the market participants' alternative to holding part of this stock of money assets is holding part of the existing stock of nonmoney assets. As discussed in Chapter Five, in the credit market, the flow of new credit demands adds to the stock of assets held by households. Thus, flows and stocks are definitionally related. However, in the analysis which follows, the stock of private wealth is assumed to be so huge compared to this flow that this effect may safely be ignored. The two markets, one dealing in flows, the other in stocks, are related through the interest rate, the price level, and real income. More sophisticated economic theory often links these markets by translating an excess supply of the stock of money into an excess flow demand for credit (an excess supply of newly issued bonds by borrowers) and converting an excess demand for money into an excess flow supply of credit (an excess demand for newly issued bonds). Such an explicit treatment would not add significantly to the simple model presented here. For this and other more advanced treatments, consult the bibliography to Chapter Eleven. All of the works cited in that bibliography deal with the linkage mechanisms of the Neoclassical model.

Specifically,

$$\left(\frac{M}{P}\right)_d = L\left(\underset{-}{i}, \underset{+}{\frac{Y}{P}}\right) \qquad \text{(demand for real money balances)} \qquad (10.10)$$

$$M_s = M_1 \qquad \text{(supply of nominal money balances)} \qquad (10.11)$$

$$\left(\frac{M}{P}\right)_d = \frac{M_1}{P_1} \qquad \text{(money market equilibrium condition)} \qquad (10.12)$$

As discussed in Chapter Nine, the aggregate demand for *real* money balances, Equation (10.10), responds negatively to the nominal rate of interest and positively to the level of real income. As discussed in Chapter Eight, the supply of *nominal* money balances, Equation (10.11), is determined by the monetary authority. The money market equilibrium condition, Equation (10.12), specifies that the quantity of real money balances demanded $(M/P)_d$, in equilibrium, is equal to the real value of the nominal supply of money (M_1/P_1).

In the aggregate money market there are three equations, (10.10), (10.11), and (10.12), in five unknowns, $(M/P)_d$, M_s, i, Y/P, and P. However, the equilibrium level of aggregate real income is already determined at a full employment level by the working of the labor market. Given that level of aggregate real income, the equilibrium interest rate is already determined by the working of the credit market. Therefore, the system is reduced to three equations in three unknowns, $(M/P)_d$, M_s and P.

Figure 10.3 shows equilibrium on the demand side of the money market. Since the interest rate is plotted on the vertical axis, the level of aggregate real income will determine the *position* of the demand curve for real money balances. There are an infinite number of these curves, one for every conceivable level of aggregate real income. However, equilibrium in the labor market implies that only one of these demand curves is relevant—the solid curve labeled $(M/P)_d = L[i, (Y/P)_1]$, where $(Y/P)_1$ is the full employment level of aggregate real income that is determined in the labor market.

Given the position of the demand curve for real money balances, we can identify exactly where we must be on that particular curve, because the equilibrium interest rate has already been determined by the working of the credit market. This is interest rate i_1. Therefore, the exact quantity of real money balances demanded is known because the equilibrium values of both variables on the right-hand side of the demand function are known. In Figure 10.3, the equilibrium quantity of real money balances demanded can only be $(M/P)_{d_1}$.

By Equation (10.12), the money market equilibrium condition, it is known that the quantity of real money balances demanded must, in equilibrium, be equal to the real value of the nominal stock of money supplied. Figure 10.3 shows that with the interest rate at i_1 (as determined by the working of the credit market) and the level of real income at $(Y/P)_1$ (as determined by the working of the labor market), the quantity of real money

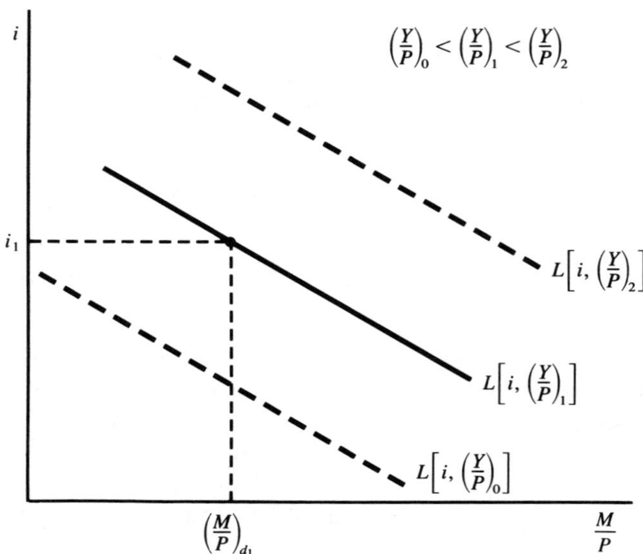

Figure 10.3 The Equilibrium Quantity of Real Money Balances Demanded

balances demanded must be $(M/P)_{d_1}$. The equilibrium condition, Equation (10.12), says that the real value of the stock of nominal money balances supplied must be equal to the quantity of real money balances demanded, $(M/P)_{d_1}$.

As discussed in Chapter Eight, the monetary authority, the Federal Reserve System, controls the stock of nominal money balances supplied. As such, it controls the numerator on the right-hand side of Equation (10.12). However, the *real value* of that stock of nominal money supplied can take on any value depending on the value of the general price level, the denominator on the right-hand side of Equation (10.12). Because the quantity demanded, $(M/P)_{d_1}$, must be equal to the real value of the nominal quantity supplied, the price level will adjust to a value which brings about this equality. In this fashion, the supply of nominal money balances determines the equilibrium price level.

This can also be seen graphically. Figure 10.3 shows that since i_1 and $(Y/P)_1$ are given, the quantity of real money balances demanded is $(M/P)_{d_1}$. No matter what the magnitude of the nominal quantity supplied, the price level will adjust until the real value of that nominal quantity supplied is equal to the quantity of real money balances demanded, $(M/P)_{d_1}$.

Thus, the vertical line or supply curve in Figure 10.4 must pass through point X on the demand curve. No matter what quantity of nominal money balances is supplied, M_1, M_2, M_3, . . . , M_n, the price level will always adjust, P_1, P_2, P_3, . . . , P_n, such that M_j/P_j is equal to $(M/P)_{d_1}$. This indicates that P, the general price level, will always adjust to changes in M, the nominal stock of money, such that M_j/P_j, the real value of the nominal

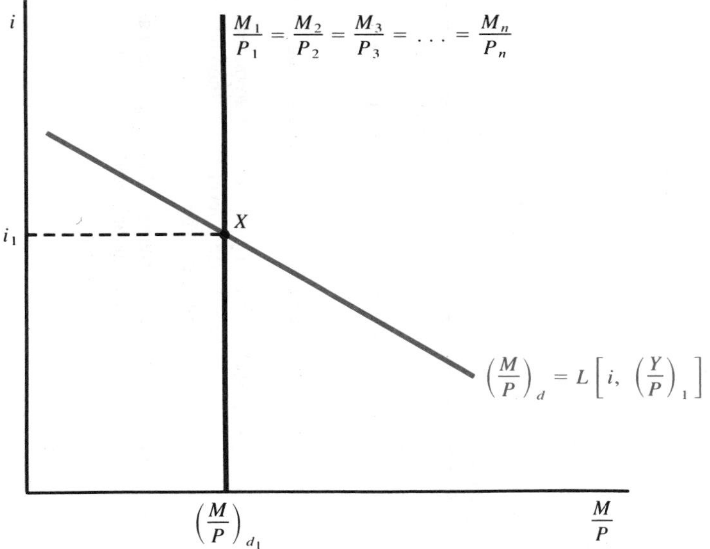

Figure 10.4 The Money Market in Equilibrium

stock of money supplied, is unchanged and equal to $(M/P)_{d_1}$, the quantity of real money balances demanded.[2]

Since the nominal supply of money, M, is in the numerator, and the general price level, P, is in the denominator, and since the quotient must, in equilibrium, remain constant and equal to $(M/P)_{d_1}$, *the general price level will vary in direct proportion to the nominal quantity of money*. This relationship is called *the quantity theory of money*.[3]

THE SOLUTION PROCESS FOR THE NEOCLASSICAL MODEL AS A WHOLE: KEY CHARACTERISTICS

The solution process for the Neoclassical model as a whole may now be demonstrated. In terms of the equations of this model, the solution process is depicted in Table 10.1. Graphically, the solution process is illustrated in Figure 10.5.

The labor market–production sector has three key characteristics. First, in the production function, Equation (10.4), the capital stock is assumed fixed. Therefore, only the

[2]If individuals are holding the desired quantity of real money balances, and if individual real wealth is defined as real money plus real nonmoney wealth, then individuals must be holding the desired quantity of real nonmoney wealth. Thus, when the money market is in equilibrium, other asset markets are also in equilibrium. Expanded definitions of wealth are introduced in the next chapter.

[3]A more general statement would be that the general price level varies in proportion with the excess supply of money. This allows for changes in the price level to occur because of changes in the demand for money with the supply of money unchanged. As discussed in the previous chapter, changes in the demand for money are sometimes expressed as changes in the velocity of money.

Table 10.1 The Solution Process for the Neoclassical General Equilibrium Model

Sector	Equations			Key Characteristics
The labor market–production sector	$L_D = f(\underset{-}{w},\underset{+}{P})$	labor demand	(10.1)	(a) Capital stock assumed fixed at $\overline{K}$.
	$L_S = g(\underset{+}{w},\underset{-}{P})$	labor supply	(10.2)	(b) Solution invariant with respect to P.
	$L_S = L_D$	equilibrium condition	(10.3)	(c) Solution yields full employment equilibrium level of real income $(Y/P)_1$ and real wage.
	$\left(\frac{Y}{P}\right) = \phi(\underset{+}{L}, \underset{+}{\overline{K}})$	production function	(10.4)	(d) Equilibrium level of aggregate real income $(Y/P)_1$, determined in labor market–production sector.
The credit (loanable funds) market	$\frac{S}{P} = j\left[\underset{+}{i}, \underset{+}{\left(\frac{Y}{P}\right)_{d_1}}\right]$	saving	(10.5)	
	$\frac{I}{P} = m(\underset{-}{i})$	investment expenditures	(10.6)	(e) Real income determined in the labor market–production sector $(Y/P)_1$ less exogenously determined taxation $(\overline{T}/P)$ yields real disposable income $(Y/P)_{d_1}$.

	$\left(\frac{G}{P} - \frac{T}{P}\right) = \left(\frac{\overline{G}}{P} - \frac{\overline{T}}{P}\right)$	government deficit or surplus	(10.7)	(f) Solution yields equilibrium interest rate (i_1).
	$\left(\frac{Y}{P}\right)_{d_1} = \left(\frac{Y}{P}\right)_1 - \left(\frac{\overline{T}}{P}\right)$	definition of disposable income	(10.8)	
	$\frac{S}{P} = \frac{I}{P} + \left(\frac{G}{P} - \frac{T}{P}\right)$	equilibrium condition	(10.9)	
The money market	$\left(\frac{M}{P}\right)_{d_1} = L\left[i_1, \left(\frac{Y}{P}\right)_1\right]$	demand for real money balances	(10.10)	(g) Real income $(Y/P)_1$ determined in labor market–production sector.
	$M_S = M_1$	supply of nominal money	(10.11)	(h) Equilibrium interest rate (i_1) determined in credit market. (i) Solution yields equilibrium price level (P_1).
	$\left(\frac{M}{P}\right)_{d_1} = \frac{M_1}{P_1}$	equilibrium condition	(10.12)	(j) Given equilibrium price level, a unique nominal wage (w) is found in the labor market above.

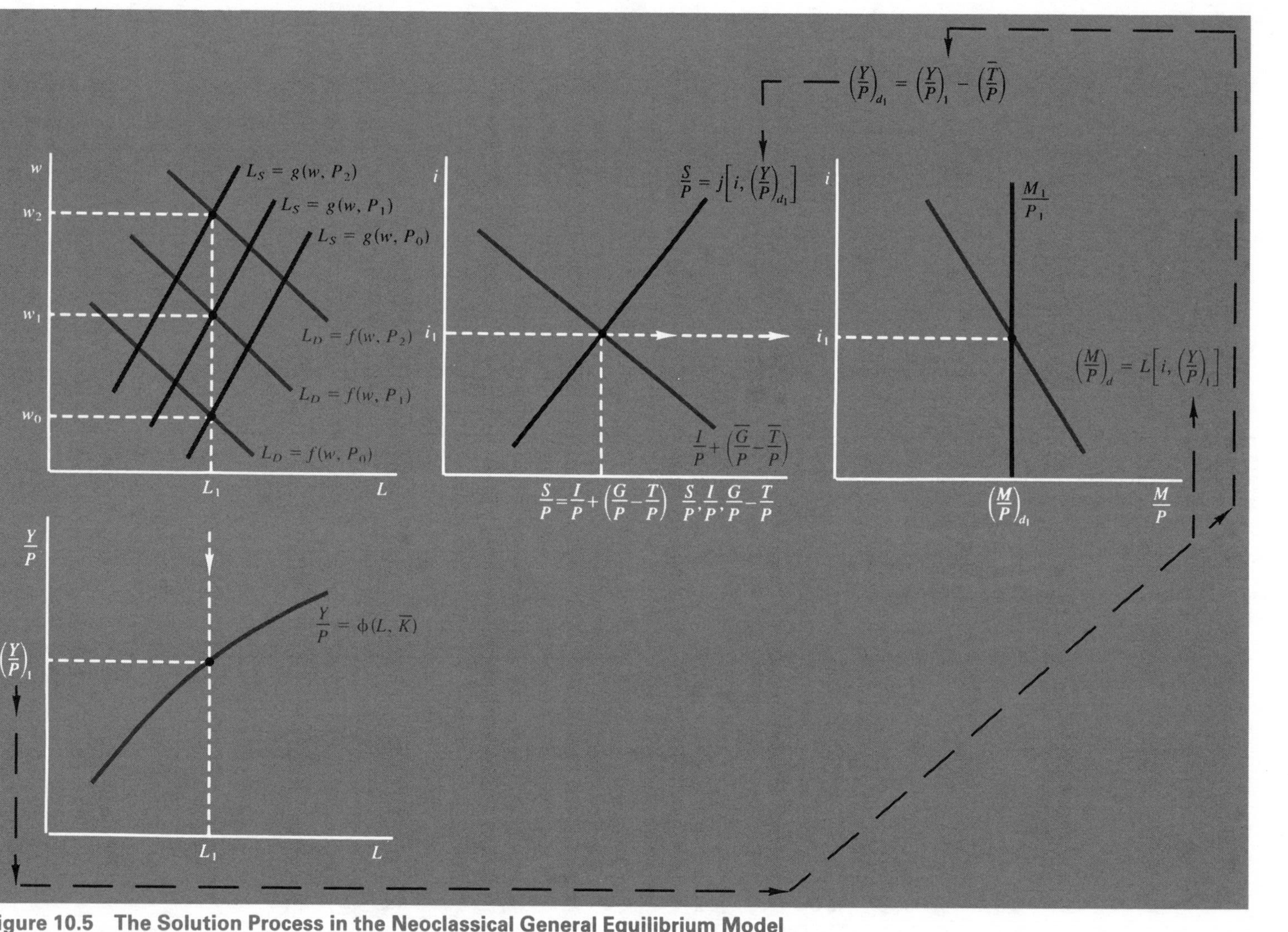

Figure 10.5 The Solution Process in the Neoclassical General Equilibrium Model

employment of labor can affect output. A fixed capital stock is a realistic assumption because even though net investment expenditures are almost always positive in the economy, their yearly magnitudes (about $400 billion in 1987 prices) are so small as to have a negligible effect on the size of the nation's capital stock (over $20 trillion in 1987 prices). The second key characteristic is that even though the general price level affects the demand for and supply of labor, Equations (10.1) and (10.2), the solution for the equilibrium level of employment and aggregate real income is invariant with respect to the general price level. The third characteristic, seen in Figure 10.5, is that the labor market–production sector determines the full employment equilibrium level of employment and aggregate real income. Since the level of employment does not change, the level of output does not change. Therefore, the position on the production function in Figure 10.5 does not change, and the marginal physical product of labor, the real wage, is determined in this sector, as well.

The credit market has two key characteristics. First, while aggregate real disposable income is a variable that influences real saving, Equation (10.6), the full employment equilibrium level of real income has already been determined in the labor market–production sector. Therefore, since the level of real taxation is exogenously determined, the level of real disposable income is also determined, Equation (10.8). The second key characteristic is that the credit market determines only the equilibrium level of the interest rate. This is so because the value of the equilibrium level of aggregate disposable real income is already known.

The money market has four key characteristics. First, while real income is an argument in the demand for money relation, Equation (10.10), the level of real income is determined in the labor market–production sector. Second, while the interest rate is also an argument in the demand for money, Equation (10.10), it is determined in the credit market. The third characteristic is that since the equilibrium level of real income and equilibrium interest rate are both already determined, the money market determines the equilibrium price level. The fourth characteristic is that, with the equilibrium price level (P) so determined, one may then go back to the labor market to solve for the equilibrium *nominal* wage (w) since the equilibrium *real* wage (w/P) has already been determined there.

The Sequential Solution Process for the Neoclassical Model

Perhaps the most striking aspect of the solution process for the Neoclassical model is that it is sequential or recursive. It is solved in a series of four steps. In the first step, the labor market–production sector yields values for the full employment equilibrium levels of employment, real income, and the real wage. In the next step, given the equilibrium level of aggregate real income from step one, the credit market yields a value for the equilibrium interest rate. In the third step, given the equilibrium level of real income from step one, and the equilibrium interest rate from step two, the money market yields the equilibrium price level. In the fourth step, the model is closed by taking the equilibrium price level from step three and returning back to the labor market. Since the equilibrium real wage (w/P) from step one is already known, given the equilibrium price level (P) from step three, one may infer the equilibrium nominal wage (w).[4]

Concluding Comment

This chapter presents our first taste of general equilibrium analysis. Instead of viewing the three markets—labor market, credit market, and money market—separately, they are each seen as part of an interrelated general equilibrium system. The solution process for this general equilibrium system was featured. Making the Neoclassical assumption of flexible nominal wages and perfect information in the labor market allowed determination of the full employment equilibrium level of employment. This, in conjunction with the aggregate production function, yielded the full employment equilibrium level of aggregate real income. With aggregate real income so determined, it was seen how the credit market generated the equilibrium interest rate. Then, with the equilibrium interest rate and the equilibrium level of real income so determined, it was shown how the money market determined the general price level. Thus, in this Neoclassical general equilibrium model of the economy as a whole, the level of employment is determined by the working of the labor market; the interest rate is determined by the working of the credit market; and the general price level is determined by the working of the money market.

In Chapter Twelve, a Keynesian general equilibrium model of the economy as a whole is presented using the same three markets. The same assumptions and the same relations will be made as in the Neoclassical model save for two. The assumptions that there are perfectly flexible nominal wages and perfect information in the labor market will be relaxed.

EXERCISES

1. "The quantity theory of money can be fully understood only in general equilibrium analysis."
   a. true
   b. false
2. Why is it realistic to assume that capital is fixed in most general equilibrium models?
3. Discuss and evaluate the following statement: "While the level of the nominal wage is determined by the working of the labor market in the partial equilibrium model

[4]The sequential nature of this solution process would be altered somewhat if the price level became a separable variable in the credit market. This could occur if the real value of the nominal stock of money, M/P, influenced saving behavior in the credit market. (This would hold if real wealth, of which real money is a component, influenced saving as discussed in Chapter Five.) In this sort of model, the labor market–production sector would still determine the full employment equilibrium levels of employment, aggregate real income, and the real wage in the first step. However, instead of the equilibrium values of interest rate and price level being found sequentially in the two subsequent steps, they would be found simultaneously in a single step. Nevertheless, even with this variation, a change in the money supply would still affect only the price level and would have no effect on the equilibrium real interest rate in the long run.

of that market where the price level is exogenous, in a general equilibrium context, the level of the nominal wage is determined by the money market."

4. In the Neoclassical model, why do real saving and real investment determine only the interest rate when real saving also depends on real income?
5. "Velocity is constant in the Neoclassical model." Would you agree or disagree?
6. What is meant by a recursive solution? Describe in words the solution process of the Neoclassical model.

BIBLIOGRAPHY

Fisher, Irving. *Theory of Interest*. New York: Macmillan, 1930.

———. *The Purchasing Power of Money*. New York: Macmillan, 1911.

Friedman, Milton. "A Theoretical Framework for Monetary Analysis." *Journal of Political Economy* (March/April 1970), pp. 193–238.

Habeler, Gottfried. *Prosperity and Depression*. London: Alland and Unwin, 1958.

Hadjimichalakis, Michael. *Modern Macroeconomics*. Englewood Cliffs, N.J.: Prentice-Hall, 1982.

Keynes, John Maynard. *A Treatise on Money*. London: Macmillan, 1930.

———. *A Tract on Monetary Reform*. London: Harcourt Brace and World, 1923.

Marshall, Alfred. *Money, Credit and Commerce*. London: Macmillan, 1925.

Patinkin, Don. *Money, Interest and Prices*. 2d ed. New York: Harper and Row, 1965.

Pigou, A. C. "The Value of Money." *The Quarterly Journal of Economics* 32 (November 1917), p. 41.

Samuelson, Paul. "What Classical and Neoclassical Monetary Theory Really Was." *Canadian Journal of Economics* 1 (February 1968), pp. 1–15.

Wicksell, Knut. *Interest and Prices*. Trans. R. F. Kahn, 1898. London: Macmillan, 1936.

Experiments with the Neoclassical Model

Chapter 11

Introduction

The solution process for the Neoclassical model was unveiled in the previous chapter. To some economists, developing and working with models is an interesting problem in itself. However, other economists prefer to apply their theories to predicting real-world events.

The model will now be applied to some real-world situations. Specifically, the model will be used to predict the outcome of three separate events:

1. the effect of a change in the supply of money,
2. the effect of a change in the government deficit, and
3. the effect of a supply shock such as a change in the price of an imported raw material.

THE EFFECT OF A CHANGE IN THE MONEY SUPPLY

The Federal Reserve System controls the nominal stock of money in our economy, as discussed in Chapter Eight. Viewing the money market in partial equilibrium, it is easy to get the impression that the Federal Reserve can control the interest rate by changing the supply of money. (As long as the expected rate of inflation is assumed constant, as it is in the static models of the next two chapters, changes in the nominal interest rate are synonymous with changes in the real interest rate.)

Figure 11.1 shows how, in partial equilibrium, a change in the nominal supply of money from M_1 to M_2 with the price level unchanged at P_1 and the level of aggregate real income unchanged at $(Y/P)_1$ will cause the interest rate to fall, *ceteris paribus*. This experiment was discussed at length in Chapter Nine. This isolated, partial equilibrium view of the effect of an increase in the money supply has led many to conclude that the monetary authority can control the interest rate and should be blamed for high interest rates. The trouble with this conclusion is that it is often drawn from a limited view of the economy. The *ceteris paribus* condition (that all things are held equal) of the partial equilibrium model of the money market is simply unrealistic. Instead of this partial equilibrium view, consider the effect of an increase in the supply of money in the context of the Neoclassical general equilibrium model.

When the money supply increases at the initial price, interest rate, and real income levels, there is an excess of the supply of money over the demand for money. The excess supply of money means that wealth holdings of individuals are out of balance, that is, their portfolios are in disequilibrium. With an excess supply of money in private portfolios, individuals have too much money relative to other, nonmoney, ways of holding their stock of wealth. Portfolios, wealth holdings of individuals, are excessively "liquid." Individuals will employ this excess liquidity, this excess supply of money, to buy other types of nonmoney wealth.

What sort of nonmoney wealth will they acquire? Consistent with the concepts developed in Chapters Two, Five, and Nine, individual nonhuman real wealth is defined as consisting of real money balances, the real value of debt claims, the real value of equity claims, and the real value of existing consumer durables. As a matter of simplification, debt and equity claims are considered perfect substitutes and are lumped together and

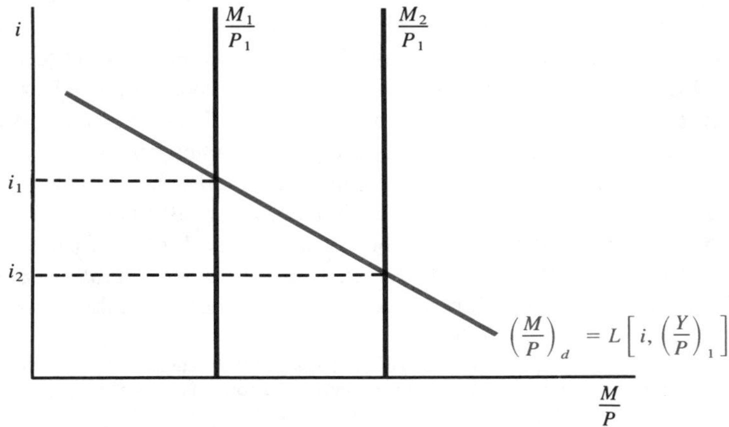

Figure 11.1 The Possible Effect of an Increase in the Nominal Supply of Money on the Interest Rate

called "bonds." As a further simplification, it will be assumed that the demand for existing consumer durables is unchanged.

It is extremely important to make one assumption explicit at this time. It will be assumed initially that individuals either form their expectations of future prices rationally but do not anticipate the increase in the aggregate money supply, or else they form their expectations adaptively. Under the first assumption, individuals experience an increase in the liquidity of their portfolios but do not associate it with a rise in the nation's nominal money stock, and, therefore, do not predict higher price levels. Under the second assumption, whether they are aware of the increased aggregate money supply or not is irrelevant because future prices are assumed to be extrapolated from past prices.[1]

If bonds and money are close substitutes in portfolios, if an individual's real wealth is unchanged, and if there is no change in the demand for existing consumer durables, an excess supply of money implies an excess demand for bonds of the same absolute magnitude. This reflects the aggregate consistency or adding-up condition discussed in Chapter Nine. In the model of the aggregate money market in panel c of Figure 11.2, at the initial interest rate i_1, when the money supply increases from M_1 to M_2, there is an excess supply of money over the demand for money. The line segment AB represents an excess supply of money. By the assumptions outlined above, this excess supply of money is coextensive with an excess demand for bonds. The excess demand for bonds drives up bond prices. Assume that these bonds have a fixed interest income and a variable, market-determined price. The bond's price represents the present (market) value of a fixed expected future stream of bond interest income and principal repayment. Therefore, the *present value formula,* last discussed in Chapter Nine, is relevant here:

$$PV = \sum_{j=1}^{n} \frac{y_j}{(1 + i)^j} + \frac{Z_n}{(1 + i)^n}$$

where Z_n = principal repayment in year n, i = market rate of interest, and y_j = expected future interest income. By the present value formula with interest income and principal repayment fixed, as the bond's market price (PV) rises, the bond's yield-to-maturity (the market rate of interest) i must fall.[2] Therefore, the excess supply of money, excess demand for bonds, propels the price of bonds upward and the market rate of interest downward. Individuals are using their undesired money balances to obtain bonds.

Panel c of Figure 11.2 shows that as the interest rate falls, the quantity of real money balances demanded increases. Individual nonhuman real wealth is defined as consisting of real money balances, the real value of bonds, and the real value of existing consumer durables. Therefore, with the demand for existing consumer durables assumed to be unchanged, as the quantity of real money balances demanded rises, the quantity of bonds

[1]Where expectations of future prices are formed rationally and the increase in the liquidity of portfolios is associated with an increase in the aggregate money supply, the consequences of an increase in the money stock will be quite different. They are discussed in the next section of this chapter. The adaptive expectations hypothesis and rational expectations hypothesis were discussed in detail in Chapters Four and Six and are discussed further in this chapter.

[2]Yield-to-maturity was defined in Chapter Nine. It is synonymous with *the* market rate of interest.

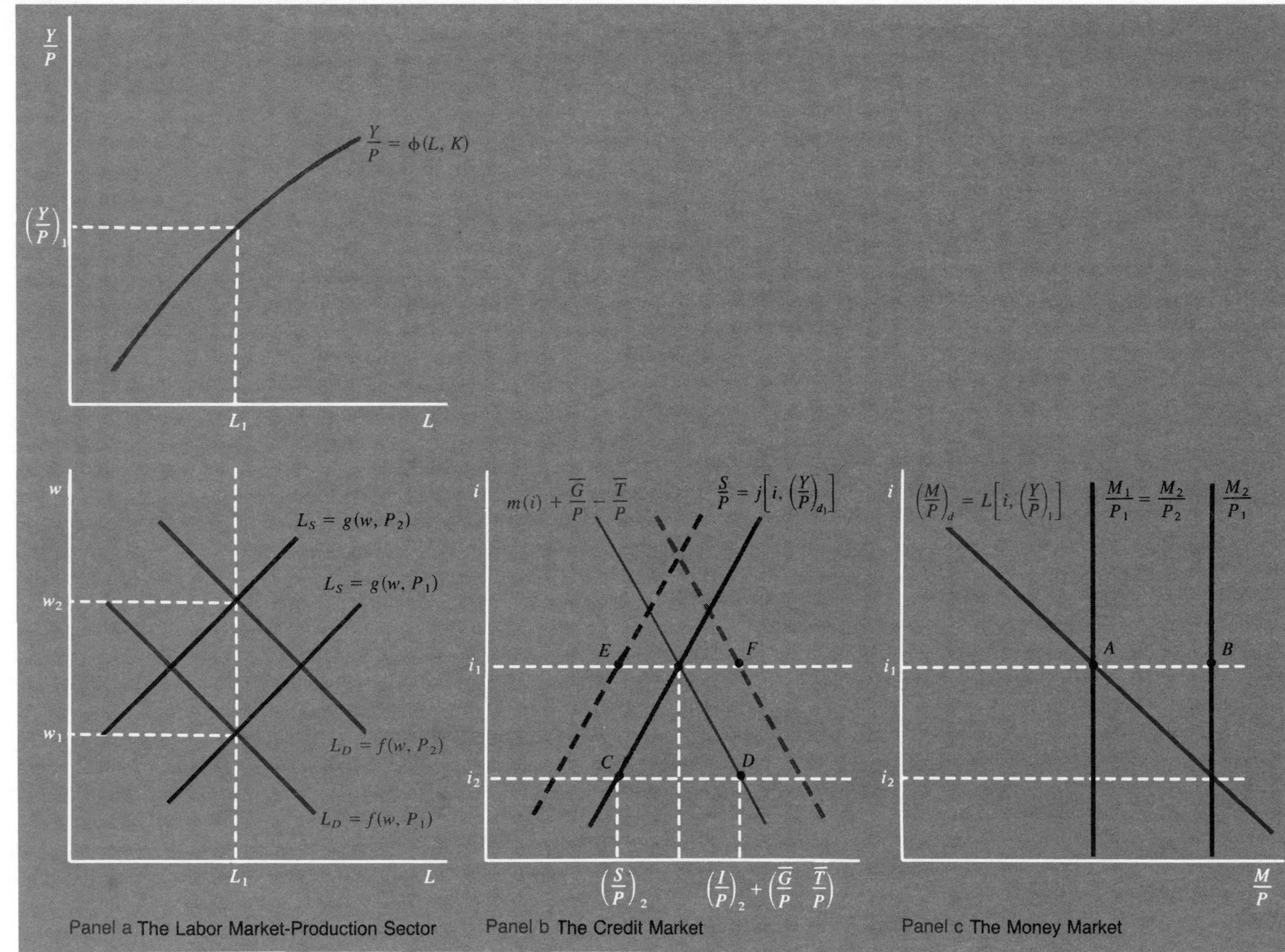

Figure 11.2 The Effect of an Increase in the Supply of Money in the Neoclassical General Equilibrium Model

demanded must fall. The quantity of real money balances demanded will increase until at a new lower interest rate, i_2, the money market is in equilibrium. In equilibrium, the quantity of real money balances demanded is equal to the real value of the new quantity of money supplied, M_2/P_1. Individuals are now willing to hold the newly created money. With the money market in equilibrium at i_2, the bond market must also be in equilibrium.[3]

While the money market, panel c in Figure 11.2, is in equilibrium at the new interest rate i_2, the credit market in panel b of Figure 11.2 is in disequilibrium. While the aggregate wealth-holding positions, stocks, of individuals are in balance, there is imbalance in credit flows. The quantity of real credit supplied, $(S/P)_2$, is less than the quantity of real credit demanded, $(I/P)_2 + (\overline{G}/P - \overline{T}/P)$. There is an excess demand for credit depicted by the directed distance CD. Because part of the economy, the credit market, is not in equilibrium, the economy as a whole is not in general equilibrium. Let us identify the forces that are at work to restore equilibrium in this disequilibrium situation.

Consider the aggregate budget identity first developed in Chapter Two:

$$\frac{Y}{P} \equiv \frac{C}{P} + \frac{S}{P} + \frac{T}{P} \tag{11.1}$$

This expression, a conservation principle in economics, says that aggregate real income must, by definition, either be used on consumption expenditures (C/P), saved (S/P), or transferred away to government in the form of income taxes (T/P). Rearranging the terms of this identity yields:

$$\frac{S}{P} \equiv \frac{Y}{P} - \frac{C}{P} - \frac{T}{P} \tag{11.1$'$}$$

This says that real saving (S/P) is identical to real income (Y/P) less real consumption expenditures (C/P) and less real taxation (T/P).

Now consider the disequilibrium condition, the inequality, that exists in the credit market, panel b, at interest rate i_2:

$$\frac{S}{P} < \frac{I}{P} + \frac{G}{P} - \frac{T}{P} \tag{11.2}$$

Substitute (11.1′) into (11.2):

$$\frac{Y}{P} - \frac{C}{P} - \frac{T}{P} < \frac{I}{P} + \frac{G}{P} - \frac{T}{P}$$

[3]An increase in aggregate real wealth occurs as the interest rate falls to i_2 and bond prices rise. This would increase (shift rightward) the demand for money and the demand for bonds. Because the decline in the interest rate is temporary, this increase in real wealth is also temporary and is ignored in the analysis. Moreover, the inclusion of this effect would introduce unnecessary complications to our model.

Rearrange:

$$\frac{Y}{P} < \frac{C}{P} + \frac{I}{P} + \frac{G}{P} \tag{11.3}$$

This says that, at interest rate i_2, real income, (Y/P), is less than aggregate real expenditures, $C/P + I/P + G/P$. In other words, the disequilibrium at i_2 may be viewed in two identically related ways. One is that the flow of real credit supplied is less than the flow of real credit demanded; there is an excess demand for credit:

$$\frac{S}{P} < \frac{I}{P} + \frac{G}{P} - \frac{T}{P} \tag{11.2}$$

The other is that the flow of aggregate output falls short of the flow of aggregate real expenditures; there is an excess of aggregate real expenditures over aggregate output:

$$\frac{Y}{P} < \frac{C}{P} + \frac{I}{P} + \frac{G}{P} \tag{11.3}$$

An excess demand for credit, Equation (11.2), is therefore tantamount to an excess demand for newly produced goods and services, Equation (11.3). They represent two identically related ways of looking at the same condition.

When the sum total of the nation's output falls short of the nation's real spending on that output, shortages develop. Such shortages have different manifestations. Inventories of goods are depleted. Waiting lines and waiting lists develop for various services. Factory orders increase, and suppliers' backlogs materialize. Given such an excess demand for newly produced goods and services, business firms might like to produce more to satisfy their customers. However, panel a of Figure 11.2 shows that real output is constrained to be at the full employment level. Under conditions of perfectly flexible nominal wages and symmetrical responses to information on both sides of the labor market, no more labor hours can be acquired by firms.[4] The economy is at full employment capacity. No more output can be produced. Therefore, when the demand for newly produced goods and services increases, market-determined prices of these goods and services rise. In this way, the excess demand for credit, in panel b of Figure 11.2, which is equivalent to excess demand for newly produced goods and services, makes the general price level rise.

As the price level rises, in panel a, the nominal wage ascends in the same proportion. If the nominal wage and all individual prices climb in the same proportion, costs of

[4]A stronger assumption would be to assume perfectly flexible nominal wages and rational formation of price level expectations with an anticipated increase in the money supply on both sides of the labor market. However, the same result, no effect on employment and output, can be obtained if the increase in the money supply is unanticipated or if expectations are assumed to be formed adaptively just as long as responses are symmetrical on both sides of the labor market. See Chapter Four for a detailed discussion of the alternative scenarios that would sustain a continued full employment equilibrium.

production rise in the same proportion, and there is no change in employment and output.[5]

As the general price level (P) rises at interest rate i_2 in panel c of Figure 11.2, the real value of the stock of nominal money balances (M/P) declines. Consequently, at i_2, at any price level below P_2, there is an excess of the quantity of real money balances demanded over the real value of the nominal stock of money supplied. As long as it is assumed that the demand for existing consumer durables in individual portfolios is unchanged, there is an excess supply of bonds in private portfolios of an equal absolute magnitude.[6] Once again, this reflects the aggregate consistency or adding-up condition discussed in Chapter Nine. Individuals try to sell bonds to obtain money balances to bring their portfolios back into balance; this drives bond prices down. According to the present value formula, as bond prices (present values) plunge, bond yields and the market rate of interest rise. In panel c of Figure 11.2, as the market rate of interest goes up, the quantity of real money balances demanded falls.

The price level will continue to ascend until at its new equilibrium level P_2 the real value of the nominal stock of money supplied is equal to the quantity of real money balances demanded at the interest rate i_1. Now, at price level P_2 and interest rate i_1, there is equilibrium in the money market as well as equilibrium in the credit market.[7]

[5]There may be an inconsistency between the expectational assumptions posited here for money and credit market participants in order for the increased money supply to cause temporarily lower interest rates and the expectational assumptions posited for labor market participants in order for employment and output to remain unchanged. In the former markets, individuals are assumed either to formulate expectations adaptively or to formulate them rationally and not to anticipate the increase in the aggregate money supply. In the latter market, there are two possibilities. One is to assume that individuals form price expectations rationally and anticipate the increase in the money supply. Unfortunately, it is not reasonable to assert that households and business firms behave one way in the labor market and quite a different way in asset and credit markets. This inconsistency may be resolved if it is instead assumed either that labor market expectations are formed rationally and the increase in the money supply is unanticipated or that labor market expectations are formed adaptively. In these cases, there will be no effect on employment and output as long as expectations and responses to these expectations are symmetrical on both sides of the labor market. See Chapter Four for further discussion.

[6]In this and all future analyses, under the assumption of an unanticipated disturbance whenever prices begin to rise, it would be reasonable to assume that the price level increase is fueled not only by the lower interest rate, i_2, but also by the adaptively formed expectation of higher future prices. Consumption and investment expenditures would rise in anticipation of higher prices of newly produced goods and services. In panel b of Figure 11.2, this modification would shift the supply and demand curves up and hasten the movement of the price level to its new equilibrium. These shifts would be caused by an excess supply of money at any combination of an interest rate below i_1 and a price level below P_2. When the price level reaches its new equilibrium level, P_2, and the real value of the money supply contracts to M_2/P_2, the supply and demand curves in panel b return to their initial positions. There is no change in the equilibrium interest rate or level of output.

[7]Individual portfolios return to their initial positions; real money balances and the real value of existing consumer durables are unchanged at price level P_2 and interest rate i_1. The real value of private bond holdings is unchanged because at the higher price level, private bond issuers must supply and private bond holders must demand a nominal quantity of bonds that has increased in proportion to the rise in the price level. Thereby, balance sheets are unchanged in real terms because the nominal quantity of private bonds and the price level change equiproportionately and the real value of bonds is unchanged. In all the experiments of this and the following chapters, it should be assumed that the nominal quantity of private bonds varies equiproportionately with the price level. As explained in the next section, the real value of government bonds in private hands is irrelevant.

The labor market (panel a of Figure 11.2) stays at full employment equilibrium at the new price level. As the price level moves up, the supply of and demand for labor shift upward in the same proportion. As a result, the levels of employment, output, and the real wage do not change. Only the nominal wage changes; it goes up from w_1 to w_2, in direct proportion to the hike in the general price level from P_1 to P_2.

Therefore, the labor market–production sector is in equilibrium at w_2, P_2, L_1, and $(Y/P)_1$; the credit market is at equilibrium at i_1 and $(Y/P)_1$; and the money market is in equilibrium at i_1, P_2, and $(Y/P)_1$. There is general equilibrium.

Conceptualizing the Linkage Mechanism

Now, let us review the sequence of effects in the Neoclassical general equilibrium model of an increase in the nominal stock of money. To impart more realism, assume that this is brought about by an open market purchase of bonds by the Federal Reserve, which increases the monetary base, as discussed in Chapter Eight.

In an open market purchase the Federal Reserve buys existing bonds from individuals in the market where bonds are traded. The Federal Reserve pays for these bonds with checks. These checks are deposited in depository institutions. The portfolios of these institutions become more liquid. Depository institutions will use this excess liquidity to acquire bonds. Thus, the increase in the supply of money depresses the interest rate from i_1 to i_2 in panel c of Figure 11.2. At the new lower interest rate, the new liquidity is held.[8]

The increase in the money supply initially drives the interest rate down from i_1 to i_2 in panel c of Figure 11.2. This new lower interest rate, i_2, will prompt an excess demand for credit in panel b. Through the aggregate budget identity, this implies an excess demand for newly produced goods and services. The latter will force up the price level from P_1 to P_2. At price level P_2, the real value of the nominal stock of money is restored to its initial level at the original interest rate i_1. At this stage, all markets are in equilibrium; there is general equilibrium.

Thus, under the assumptions discussed earlier, an increase in the nominal quantity of money has the short-run effect of lowering the interest rates from i_1 to i_2. This is the *liquidity effect* of money on interest. However, this liquidity effect is followed by a *nominal income effect* of money on interest which propels the interest rate back up to i_1. The nominal income effect occurs because at i_2 there is an excess demand for newly

[8]In the process of withdrawing bonds from and injecting money into individual portfolios, the Federal Reserve bids up bond prices and causes the interest rate to decline. However, the interest rate decline does not stop here. As discussed in Chapter Eight, open market purchases increase the monetary base, and this results in a multiple expansion of the money supply as depository institutions purchase even more bonds (debt claims) with newly created deposits.

Depository institutions would be willing to buy bonds at higher bond prices and nonbank individuals would be willing to hold the newly created money balances only if they did not, respectively, anticipate lower bond prices and higher prices of newly produced goods and services in the future. If market participants anticipated higher future prices of goods and services, depository institutions would only be willing to buy bonds at the initial bond prices, conforming to the initial interest rate, i_1, and nonbank individuals would immediately use their newly created money to acquire newly produced goods and services. The interest rate would not change, and the general price level would rise immediately. This alternative scheme is discussed in the next section.

produced goods and services, and the price level ascends from P_1 to P_2. The increase in the price level reduces the real value of the money supply, and the interest rate must rise back to i_1.

The movement from i_2 back to i_1 is called the nominal income effect because as the price level rises, by the definition of nominal income, $Y \equiv P \times Q$, the level of nominal income rises in the same proportion. Thus, an increase in the quantity of money will initially drive down the rate of interest (i_1 to i_2), the liquidity effect of money on interest, but soon the interest rate will climb back to its initial equilibrium level (i_2 to i_1), the nominal income effect of money on interest.[9]

An increase in the quantity of money, therefore, has no effect on employment and aggregate output and has only a transitory effect on the (nominal and real) interest rate. An increase in the quantity of money has only one lasting effect in the long run. It causes the general price level to rise.[10] The implication that changes in the quantity of money have no effect on the interest rate or output is often called *the neutrality of money*.

Neutrality requires the assumption that government debt is not wealth. In Chapters Two and Six, it was asserted that while government debt benefits its holders, it increases the future tax liabilities of private citizens to meet interest payments and principal repayments. Whether these bonds are held by private individuals or by the central bank makes no difference; they still represent a liability to taxpayers. An open market operation merely shifts government bonds from private individuals to the central bank, or vice versa. It does not relieve taxpayers of any tax liability. It does not affect aggregate wealth. Therefore, the ratio of government bonds to total wealth in private portfolios is of no concern to private market participants.[11] Only the impact of open market operations on portfolio liquidity is important.

Some economists simplistically argue that an increased stock of money incites the price level to rise because more money in circulation "chases" the same quantity of goods produced. As seen in the next section, this naïve view may be quite accurate. However,

[9]If the increase in the aggregate money supply were anticipated by money market participants, there would be no initial liquidity effect and no subsequent nominal income effect. Just as soon as the money supply rose, aggregate expenditures on newly produced goods and services would rise. The price level would leap immediately. The newly created money would not be held in portfolios as bond yields are bid downward; instead, it would immediately be spent on newly produced goods and services. This scenario is discussed in the next section.

[10]This quantity theory of money result would hold true even if the increase in the money supply could influence real saving (since, as pointed out in footnote 3, the open market purchase could temporarily lower the interest rate and thereby temporarily affect real wealth, and real saving varies inversely with real wealth, as discussed in Chapter Five). In this case, an increase in the supply of money would cause the saving curve in Figure 11.2 to shift leftward. However, the subsequent rise in the price level (one that is proportionate to the increase in the money supply) would restore the saving curve to its initial position at the initial equilibrium interest rate, and the Neoclassical implications would still hold. Individual portfolios would return to their initial position (see footnote 7). The bibliography to this chapter contains further readings on the *neutrality of money*.

[11]The open market purchase lowers the ratio of the aggregate real value of government bonds to aggregate real wealth in the new equilibrium as compared to the original equilibrium. This may appear to violate neutrality since it would seem to require a fall in the interest rate and a rise in the real value of bonds in order to restore the ratio. However, as explained above, as long as government bonds are not wealth, this ratio is irrelevant.

it is not always based on general equilibrium thinking and can lead to conceptual pitfalls and misunderstandings about the way the economy works. Money is a *stock,* and the production of goods is a *flow*. Money is measured at a *point* in time. Output is measured over an *interval* of time.

When an excess supply of money occurs, private financial portfolios are immediately out of balance at that point in time by, say, hundreds of millions of dollars. Unless they anticipated the increase in the aggregate money supply and hence the eventual jump in the prices of goods and services, market participants would not attempt to correct an instantaneous imbalance in their individual wealth-holding positions by making payments and down payments on more newly produced goods and services with these excess money balances.

Unless higher prices for newly produced goods and services were anticipated in the short run, market participants would have no incentive to employ these hundreds of millions of dollars of excess money holdings by placing orders for more newly produced goods and services, such as haircuts, new homes, bubble gum, new automobiles, suits, sixpacks, and dolls. They would, however, quickly and efficiently balance their portfolios, getting rid of the excess money, by purchasing closer substitutes for money, existing bonds (and other forms of existing financial assets) from middlemen (brokers and financial intermediaries, discussed in Chapter Eight). It should be remembered that we are assuming that the demand for existing consumer durables is unchanged.

It is important to view money as a stock, not a flow. Where the change in this stock, and, hence, in the price level is not anticipated, and where the demand for existing consumer durables is assumed unchanged, disequilibrium in the money market is most efficiently corrected by individuals purchasing financial assets. Financial asset (bond) prices, and, hence, interest rates, would reflect this correction in the very short run. The prices of newly produced goods and services adjust in the longer run because the changes in interest rates, wrought by short-run portfolio adjustments to absorb the excess supply of money, in turn effect a change in the demand for newly produced goods and services. Thus, the general price level eventually comes to reflect the excess supply of money. Therefore, where the change in the money stock is unanticipated, the linkage mechanism from changes in the stock of money to changes in the prices of newly produced goods and services is not direct and immediate, but is indirect and takes time. This linkage or transmission mechanism is indicated by the dashed trajectory in Table 11.1. This Table summarizes the adjustment of the economy to a change in the supply of money.[12]

Even under the assumptions outlined above, the liquidity effect of money on interest is transitory, a purely short-run phenomenon. As the price level and therefore nominal income begin to rise, this liquidity effect will disappear because of the nominal income effect of money on interest. Historically, the plea for the Federal Reserve to lower interest rates, based on the partial equilibrium view of the money market portrayed in Figure

[12]In the case of either a perfectly interest-sensitive (horizontal) money demand curve or perfectly interest-insensitive (vertical) credit demand and supply curves, a change in the money supply will have no effect on the price level or, in a Keynesian model, on output. This case is discussed in Chapter Twelve in the section "Money Does Not Matter versus Only Money Matters."

Table 11.1 Linkage Mechanism: Effect of an Increase in the Money Supply in the Neoclassical Model

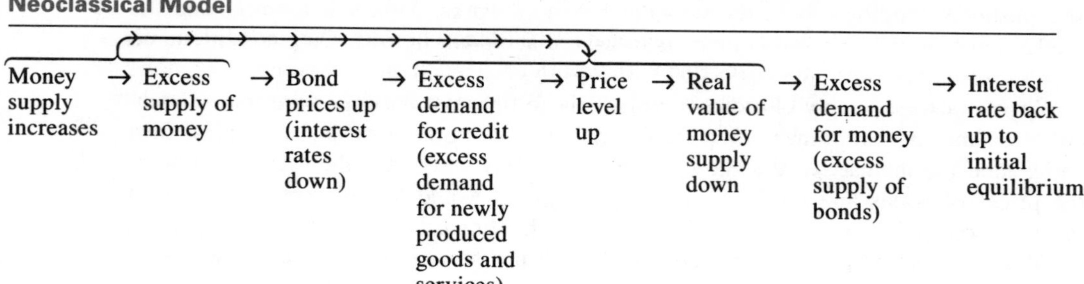

Money supply increases	→ Excess supply of money	→ Bond prices up (interest rates down)	→ Excess demand for credit (excess demand for newly produced goods and services)	→ Price level up	→ Real value of money supply down	→ Excess demand for money (excess supply of bonds)	→ Interest rate back up to initial equilibrium

Note regarding the expectations of credit and money market participants:
→ → →Assuming rationally formed expectations and an unanticipated increase in money supply, or assuming adaptively formed expectations (see footnote 4)
———→Assuming rationally formed expectations and an anticipated increase in the money supply

11.1, is often made with inadequate consideration of the general equilibrium perspective of Figure 11.2 and Table 11.1. A partial equilibrium view often leads to misunderstandings of the way the economy works.

A Rational Expectations, "New Classical" View of an Anticipated Change in the Money Supply

Now, consider the effect of an increase in the money supply where it is assumed that expectations of future prices are formed rationally, and the increase in the aggregate nominal money stock is anticipated by market participants.

According to the rational expectations hypothesis of the New Classical branch of Neoclassical economics, individuals will exploit all information about future prices. All systematic elements for predicting future prices will become known, and the consensual price expectations of market participants will be the most accurate forecast consistent with that knowledge. This implies that, except for unavoidable surprises, the market consensus expectation of the price level will not be systematically different from the actual price level.

If monetary policy is systematic, it is predictable. Therefore, as soon as the money supply rises and the Federal Reserve engages in open market purchases, money and credit market participants correctly associate the increase in the liquidity of their portfolios with an increase in the nation's money supply. Small changes in the market rate of interest may signal market participants that a shock is occurring. They then turn to published money supply data to confirm their anticipation of this shock. They, therefore, correctly and immediately predict the rise in the general price level with no change in the interest rate. Under these conditions market participants would not use these excess money supply balances to acquire bonds at higher bond prices. The interest rate would not be bid downward. There would be no transitory liquidity effect of money on interest (followed by an offsetting nominal income effect). Instead, market participants would use their excess money balances to acquire newly produced goods and services in anticipation of higher future prices. The aggregate consistency or adding-up condition, discussed in Chapter Nine, indicates that with wealth unchanged, an excess supply of money implies an excess demand for bonds and goods. If the excess supply of money does not cause the demand for bonds to increase, it must cause the demand for goods to rise. Even if the newly produced goods and services could not be immediately delivered, individuals would use their excess money balances as down payments for future delivery. In this case, the naive view that an increase in the quantity (stock) of money in circulation directly "chases" an unchanged quantity (flow) of newly produced goods and services is not inaccurate.

In Figure 11.2, the adjustment would take place in the following way: The initial excess supply of money, *AB* in panel c, would be used to finance private expenditures in a like amount, *EF* in panel b. The saving function would shift leftward (because consumption expenditures increase), and the investment expenditures plus government deficit function would shift rightward (because investment expenditures increase) to the positions indicated by the broken lines in panel b of Figure 11.2. At the unchanged interest rate i_1, there would be an excess of expenditures over output, measured by the directed distance *EF*. This condition would cause the general price level to rise to P_2. The real value of the nominal stock of money would contract to M_2/P_2, an amount equal to the quantity of real money balances demanded at interest rate i_1 and real income level $(Y/P)_1$. Because the excess supply of money would disappear, there would be no excess money balances to fuel the higher level of real expenditures. The supply and demand curves would return to their initial positions indicated by the solid lines in panel b, intersecting again at i_1.

As a result, the price level would immediately rise with the increase in the money stock. In Table 11.1, all of the immediate steps depicted by the dashed trajectory illustrating the linkage between an increase in the money supply adjustments in the interest rate and the increase in the price level would not occur. Instead, the long-run effect of an increase in the price level would obtain directly and immediately. The linkage or transmission mechanism is indicated only by the solid trajectory in Table 11.1.

In a rational expectations world, market participants have an incentive to anticipate systematic changes in the money supply. They would obviously want to avoid acquiring bonds at the temporarily higher bond prices associated with interest rates below i_1 in Figure 11.2. If bond prices rose, they would not be expected to persist because when the interest rate rose back to its initial level, i_1, bond prices would fall and individuals would incur capital losses. Market participants would have an incentive to monitor the money supply–creating behavior of the Federal Reserve in order to avoid such losses.

In the labor market, it is also assumed that nominal wages are flexible and that expectations are formed rationally. An anticipated increase in the money supply would stimulate immediate upward adjustment in the nominal wage. There would be no change in employment and output.

In a world where expectations are rationally formulated in all markets, an anticipated increase in the money supply has an immediate effect on the price level with no transitory effects on the interest rate or on employment and output.[13] Long-run equilibrium conditions occur at once.

The Effect of a Change in the Government Deficit[14]

An increase in the government deficit, when viewed simply in terms of the credit market in partial equilibrium analysis for a closed economy, drives up the rate of interest, as seen in Chapter Six. In this section, we reconsider this experiment in terms of the Neoclassical general equilibrium model rather than just the partial equilibrium view of the credit market in isolation.

The following discussion ignores the Ricardian equivalence principle, which suggests that a larger deficit will result in complete crowding out without a change in the interest rate. According to this approach, as the government deficit increases, the government issues bonds for the resources, which it then spends as ΔG. The newly issued bonds represent wealth (from future interest income) to the individuals who gave up resources for them. Because these individuals simply exchanged resources for bonds, their wealth is unchanged. However, for taxpayers in general, wealth has fallen because of the increase in future taxation that is required in order to enable government to make the future interest payments on the newly issued bonds. This loss in aggregate wealth causes individuals to increase their current saving in order to meet the increased future taxation obligations. As a result, the supply of credit increases (shifts rightward) in the same magnitude as the demand for credit and the interest rate does not change. According to the Ricardian equivalence approach, since the interest rate does not change, there will be no excess supply of money and no rise in the price level.

In the following discussion, we assume that the increase in future taxation is not expected and that the expected gain in private welfare from the increase in government expenditures exceeds the expected loss from any related decrease in private expenditures such that there is no decrease in aggregate wealth. Since the resources of the economy are unchanged, real income is at a full employment level; crowding out must occur via a rise in the interest rate.

In panel b of Figure 11.3, there is equilibrium at i_1 where $S/P = I/P + G/P - T/P$. Using the aggregate budget identity, this translates to $Y/P = C/P + I/P + G/P$. Thus, there is neither an excess demand for nor an excess supply of credit or aggregate output. Other markets, depicted in panels a and c, are also in equilibrium; there is general equilibrium.

In the analysis that follows, it is assumed either that market participants formulate their expectations of future prices and interest rates rationally but do not anticipate the

[13]For a discussion of the rational expectations hypothesis as it applies to the labor market and the credit market individually, see Chapters Four and Six, respectively. The bibliography to Chapter Six cites a number of studies which utilize a rational expectations perspective to repudiate any causal link between the money supply and the *ex ante* real rate of interest, the liquidity effect.

[14]If the newly issued government bonds were part of aggregate wealth, saving would fall and the demand for money would rise, thereby increasing the initial impact of the deficit on the interest rate. For further discussion, see footnote 7 in Chapter Twelve. The pros and cons of including government bonds in the definition of aggregate private wealth were discussed in Chapters Two and Five.

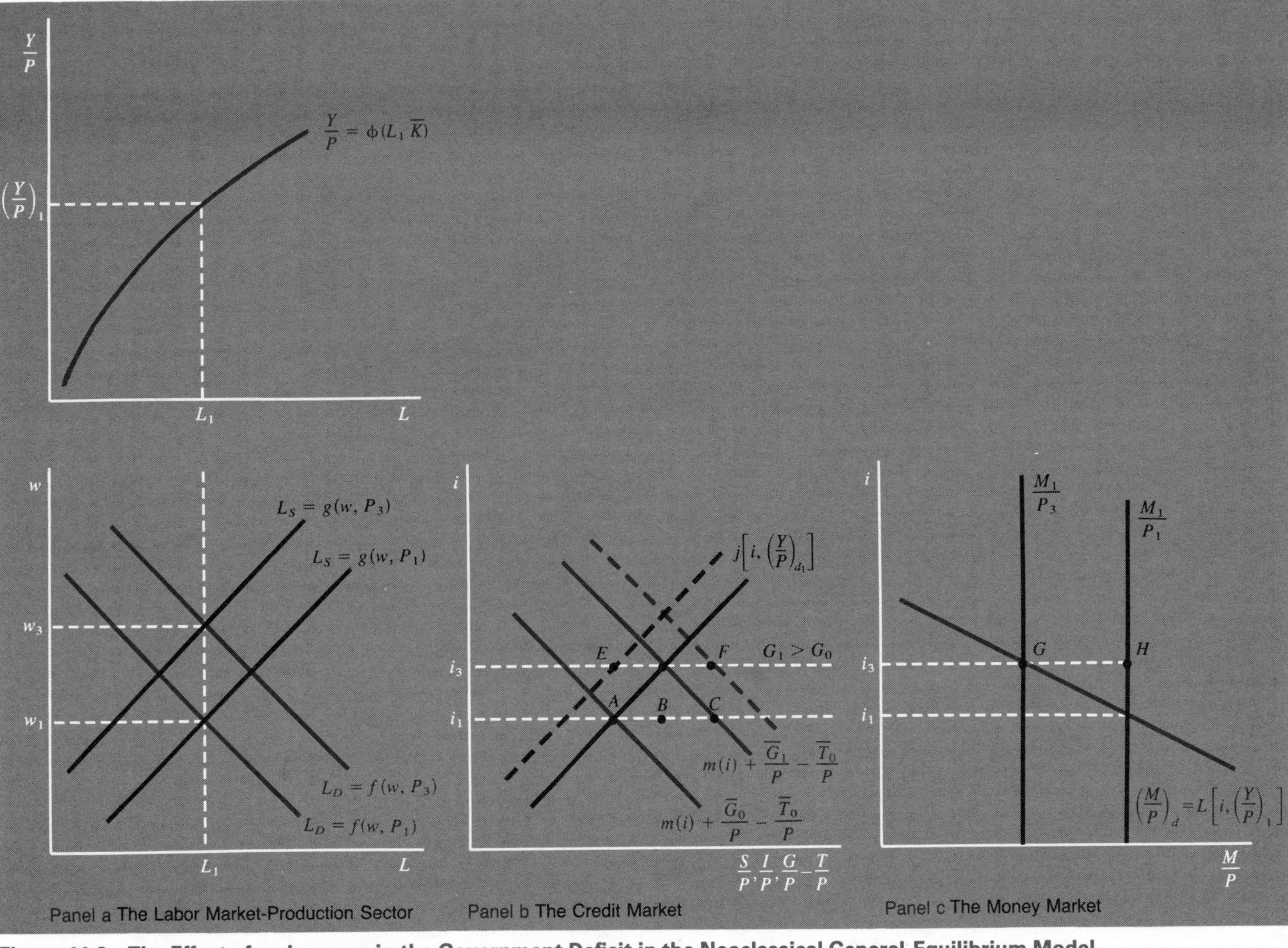

Figure 11.3 The Effect of an Increase in the Government Deficit in the Neoclassical General Equilibrium Model

increase in the deficit or that they formulate their expectations adaptively. In the next section, it will be assumed that expectations are formed rationally and that the increase in the deficit is anticipated.

An increase in government expenditures from G_0 to G_1 causes the deficit to rise from $(\overline{G}_0 - \overline{T}_0)$ to $(\overline{G}_1 - \overline{T}_0)$. The excess demand for credit, the directed distance AC at the initial interest rate, i_1, has the tendency to increase the nominal and the real interest rates. In a partial equilibrium model, equilibrium is restored at i_3, because the quantity of real saving increases by AB and the quantity of real investment expenditures decreases by CB. But with all other variables unchanged, other markets are *not* in equilibrium at an interest rate above i_1. Specifically, as the interest rate rises in panel c of Figure 11.3, the quantity of real money balances demanded declines. This creates an excess supply of money. With the nominal quantity of money at M_1 and the price level at P_1, for any interest rate greater than i_1 there is an excess of quantity supplied over quantity demanded. At any interest rate above i_1, as long as there are no other adjustments, the overall model is not in equilibrium because the money market is not in equilibrium.

We have assumed that the increase in the deficit and, hence, the eventual rise in the interest rate to i_3 and the price level to P_3 are unanticipated. Market participants only know that at any interest rate above i_1 they have undesired liquidity in their portfolios and want to correct the imbalance efficiently. By the aggregate consistency or adding-up condition, an excess supply of money implies an excess demand for the sum of bonds and goods. However, individuals have no incentive to place orders for newly produced goods and services, using the excess money balances in payment or down payment. In addition, as a means of simplifying the analysis, it is assumed that the demand for existing consumer durables is unchanged. As a result of these assumptions, the excess supply of money induces an excess demand for bonds of equal absolute magnitude. Therefore, the excess supply of money will impede the rise in the interest rate to i_3. Excess liquidity will be used to purchase bonds; this will temporarily bolster bond prices and, temporarily, keep the interest rate below its equilibrium level i_3. As long as the interest rate is less than i_3 (panel b of Figure 11.3), there is an excess demand for credit in the credit market:

$$\frac{S}{P} < \frac{I}{P} + \frac{G}{P} - \frac{T}{P} \tag{11.2}$$

Substituting the aggregate budget identity,

$$\frac{S}{P} \equiv \frac{Y}{P} - \frac{C}{P} - \frac{T}{P} \tag{11.1}$$

into the left-hand side of Equation (11.2) reveals that the excess demand for credit in (11.2) implies an excess of aggregate real spending over aggregate output:

$$\frac{Y}{P} < \frac{C}{P} + \frac{I}{P} + \frac{G}{P} \tag{11.3}$$

As seen earlier, this generates upward pressure on the general price level, as the excess demand for newly produced goods and services persists over time.

As the price level goes up in panel c of Figure 11.3, the real value of the nominal stock of money goes down. As the real value of the nominal stock of money falls, the impediment (of excess liquidity) to the rise in the interest rate will dissipate. When the price level finally climbs to P_3, the real value of the stock of money (M_1/P_3) will be equal to the quantity of real money balances demanded at the interest rate i_3. At i_3 and P_3 the credit market and the money market are both in equilibrium.

In panel a of Figure 11.3, under the assumption of perfect nominal wage flexibility and symmetrical responses on both sides of the labor market, the supply of and demand for labor shift upward in proportion to the increase in the price level from P_1 to P_3.[15] As a result, the nominal wage jumps from w_1 to w_3 with no change in employment, output or the real wage. The labor market is in equilibrium.

Thus, viewing the effect of an increase in the government deficit in the partial equilibrium context of the credit market alone is misleading. In a general equilibrium perspective, the increase in the demand for credit does, of course, cause the interest rate to rise; however, the rising interest rate will impart an excess supply of money. As the increase in the deficit and the eventual rise in the price level are assumed to be unanticipated, market participants will use excess money balances to acquire bonds. This, in turn, will impede the progress of the interest rate to its new equilibrium level at i_3. The effect of the excess supply of money in suppressing the immediate increase of the interest rate to i_3 will cause an excess demand for credit to persist over time. The aggregate budget identity indicates that an excess demand for credit is tantamount to an excess of aggregate spending over aggregate production. The persistence of excess demand for newly produced goods and services over time will lead to a rising price level. The rising price level will eliminate the excess supply of money, and full equilibrium will be restored to both markets at interest rate i_3 and price level P_3.

Therefore, the Neoclassical general equilibrium model shows that an increase in the government deficit not only causes the (nominal and real) rate of interest to rise and complete crowding out, as suggested by the partial equilibrium model of Chapter Six, but also causes the price level to rise because the rising interest rate creates an excess supply of money.[16] In the absence of nominal wage inflexibility and asymmetrical responses in the labor market, there is no effect on employment and aggregate output.

In Table 11.2, the dashed trajectory summarizes the transmission mechanism in the economy from an increase in the government deficit and a rise in the interest rate to an increase in the price level under the assumptions previously outlined.[17]

[15]See footnotes 4 and 5 in this chapter.

[16]In the special case of a perfectly interest-insensitive (vertical) demand curve for money, no excess supply of money will arise with the higher interest rate and fiscal policy will have no effect on prices (or, in a Keynesian model, on output). This case is discussed in the section in Chapter Twelve entitled, "Money Does Not Matter versus Only Money Matters."

[17]As shown in one of the partial equilibrium models in Chapter Six, an increase in the deficit can also be viewed as affecting the value of the dollar in international markets. This case is treated in greater detail in the open economy general equilibrium model of Chapter Fifteen.

Table 11.2 Linkage Mechanism: Effect of an Increase in the Government Deficit in the Neoclassical Model

Deficit increases	Interest rate rises in credit market	→ Rising interest rate creates excess supply of money in money market	→ Rise in interest rate in credit market impeded by excess supply of money	→ Excess demand for credit implies excess of aggregate expenditures over aggregate output	→ Price level rises	→ Increase in price level reduces real value of nominal stock of money	→ Excess supply of money is eliminated and equilibrium is restored at new, higher price level and interest rate

Note regarding the expectations of money and credit market participants:
→ → →Assuming rationally formed expectations and an unanticipated increase in the government deficit, or assuming adaptively formed expectations (see footnote 4)
———→Assuming rationally formed expectations and an anticipated increase in the government deficit

The Rational Expectations, New Classical View of the Effect of an Anticipated Increase in the Government Deficit

Now consider the effect of an increase in the deficit where it is assumed that expectations of future prices and interest rates are formed rationally and the increase in the deficit is anticipated by market participants. Small changes in the interest rate may signal market participants that a shock is occurring. They then turn to published estimates of the government deficit to confirm their anticipation of this shock. In anticipation of the permanently higher interest rate and resulting excess supply of money, individuals will acquire newly produced goods and services just as soon as the deficit increases. They will not use these excess money balances to acquire bonds, thereby temporarily impeding the rise in the interest rate to i_3. They will want to avoid the capital losses associated with acquiring bonds at interest rates below i_3 because they would expect the rate to rise to i_3 and bond prices to fall. As a result of the excess demand for goods and services at interest rate i_3 and price level P_1, the price level is immediately bid upward to P_3.

Even if newly produced goods and services could not be immediately acquired, the excess money balances would be used in downpayment for future delivery. As a result, all of the intermediate steps in the linkage mechanism depicted by the dashed trajectory in Table 11.2 will not occur. Instead, the solid trajectory would be followed, leading directly and immediately from an increase in the deficit and a higher interest rate to a higher price level.

In a rational expectations world, market participants have an incentive to anticipate systematic changes in the deficit. They would want to avoid capital losses associated with purchasing bonds at interest rates below i_3. Market participants would have an incentive to monitor the budgetary plans of Congress and the President.

In Figure 11.3, the adjustment would take place in the following way. At the new interest rate i_3 there is an excess supply of money, *GH* in panel c. These balances would be used to finance private expenditures in a like amount, *EF* in panel b. The saving function would shift leftward and the investment plus government deficit function would shift rightward to the positions indicated by the broken lines in panel b of Figure 11.3. At the unchanged interest rate i_3, there would be an excess of expenditures over output measured by the directed distance *EF*. This condition would cause the general price level to rise to P_3. The real value of the nominal stock of money would shrink to M_1/P_3, an amount equal to the quantity of real money balances demanded. Because the excess supply of money would disappear, there would be no excess money balances to fuel the higher expenditures. The supply and demand curves in panel b would return to their initial positions, denoted by solid lines in panel b, intersecting at i_3.

In the labor market, it is assumed that nominal wages are flexible and that expectations are formed rationally. Therefore, an anticipated increase in the deficit would stimulate immediate upward adjustment in the nominal wage. There would be no change in employment and output. In conclusion, in a world where expectations are rationally formulated in all markets, an anticipated increase in the government deficit has an immediate effect on the price level and the interest rate with no transitory effects on the interest rate or on employment and output.

Deficits and Inflation

Because an increase in the government deficit leads to an increase in the price level, one should not infer that the quantity theory of money is invalidated. On the contrary, the increase in the general price level is directly associated with the excess supply of money brought about by a rising interest rate, which reduces the quantity of real money balances demanded, while the total money supply is unchanged. An increase in the price level can be brought about by an increase in the supply of money with demand unchanged or by a reduction in the quantity of money demanded with supply unchanged. In either case, the resulting excess supply of money creates an excess demand for newly produced goods and services and drives up the price level in proportion to the excess supply. The quantity theory of money, discussed in Chapter Ten, holds. There can be no increase in the general price level that is not associated with an equiproportional excess supply of money.

Over the years, the public has come to associate a high rate of inflation with a large but not increasing deficit. This seems to contradict the preceding theory, which indicates that only a continual *increase* in the deficit can steadily increase the interest rate and continually create an excess supply of money to fuel inflation. There are at least four possible theoretical connections between a large, unchanging deficit and inflation. The first is that a large, unchanging deficit can generate continual increases in the supply of money, as the monetary authority tries to ameliorate the effect of the large deficit on the interest rate by increasing the supply of money. This process, the *monetization of the deficit*, is explored in detail in Chapter Thirteen.

In Chapter Six, it was shown that an unchanging deficit could nevertheless cause a steady rise in the ratio of the stock of government debt to GNP. The demand for most forms of wealth varies proportionately with wealth and income. If the stock of debt is growing faster than GNP, supply is growing faster than demand. The continual excess supply of government debt will depress bond prices and push the interest rate to high levels. As the interest rate steadily rises, the demand for money continually declines, creating an ongoing excess supply of money. Thus, there is a second link between a large but unchanging deficit and inflation.

A third possible connection between a large but steady government deficit and the rate of inflation is through the indirect effect of the deficit causing a continual decrease (leftward shift) in the demand for money. (Notice that a decrease in demand is not the same as a decrease in quantity demanded. The latter is movement along a demand curve, the former is a leftward shift in the curve.) An unchanging, large deficit implies a continually high interest rate. The interest rate is the opportunity cost of holding money. A persistently high opportunity cost will, over time, induce technological improvements that will reduce the demand for money. A good example of such improvements was discussed in Chapter Nine: the increased use of credit, particularly credit cards. This causes the demand for real money balances to shift leftward. A continual leftward shift in money demand will generate a chronic excess supply of money and inflation.[18]

A fourth possible link between a large, unchanging deficit and inflation is through crowding out. Continual crowding out could reduce private capital formation. This, in turn, could lower real income and real saving over time. The persistent fall in real saving causes a continual rise in the interest rate. With a steady rise in the interest rate and a steady fall in real income, the quantity of real money balances demanded falls continually. The resulting continual excess supply of money fuels a steady rise in the price level.

Cost Push, Supply Shock, and the Scapegoat Theory of Inflation

During the decade of the 1970s, the prices of many raw materials rose by leaps and bounds, propelling costs of production and the prices of consumer goods upward and thereby generating a high rate of inflation. In certain years, as inflation rose, the level of employment and aggregate real income fell. The apparent confluence of a stagnating level of output and employment with a higher rate of inflation came to be branded with the label *stagflation*. It seemed to many observers that rising individual raw material prices were impeding our ability to produce. Analysts reasoned that more expensive imported raw materials raised production costs in many industries, causing less output to be produced at higher prices. Thus, the notion of a *supply shock* to the economy was born.

[18]A reduction in the quantity of real money balances demanded with real income unchanged is often referred to as an increase in the *income velocity of money*—the rate at which money balances turn over against income. Thus, an increase in velocity can fuel inflation, *ceteris paribus*. See Chapter Nine for further discussion of trends in velocity.

In the 1950s and 1960s similar reasoning was applied to union wage increases that exceeded productivity gains because of an increase in the monopoly power of the labor union. In that era, it was argued that such wage increases forced up production costs in these industries, causing less output to be produced at higher prices. This was the origin of the concept of a *cost push*.

If we generalize, it can be seen that an exogenous increase in the price of any variable labor or raw material input used in production processes could increase production costs for any level of industry output. This would tend to result in higher prices and less output. Thus, the concepts of supply shock and cost push are closely related.

Many analysts relate the simultaneous price level hikes and output declines of the 1970s (stagflation) to supply shocks. In 1974–1975, the price of petroleum on the world market increased 400 percent because of the increase in the monopoly power of the OPEC oil cartel. Inflation soared, and output and employment plummeted. Conversely, when oil prices fell between 1983 and 1986, the reverse occurred. Inflation plunged and output and employment skyrocketed.

There is, however, an alternative view of the supply shock and cost push concepts. This view contends that supply shocks and cost pushes are not always significant and do not always have much impact on output and prices in equilibrium. The reasons for this contention are discussed in the next two sections. These critics argue that the concepts of cost push and supply shock are often used to cover up the true source of much inflation—the monetary and fiscal policies of government. The supply shock and cost push phenomena in this perspective serve as excuses for mismanaged monetary and fiscal policy.

In regular public announcements, the Bureau of Labor Statistics associates a rise in the cost of living with increases in the components of the price index, such as an increase in the price of certain foods, a price increase in a certain industry, or an increase in the price of an imported raw material, such as oil. Whenever the cost of living rises in a magnitude that arouses the ire of voters, or there is other bad economic news, highly placed government officials tend to use these announcements to focus on a scapegoat. Critics call this hallowed Washington tradition the *scapegoat theory of inflation*. Convenient scapegoats in the past have been business people who raise prices, union leaders who demand higher nominal wages, the leaders of cartels who try to control the prices of raw materials such as oil, and even dear old Mother Nature, who sporadically causes bad weather that leads to higher food prices because of crop failures, livestock losses, and fish kills.

Despite historical correlation between increases in the price level and increases in relative prices, we should not conclude that relative price increases lead to a rise in the equilibrium price level. In our general equilibrium model, given the full employment equilibrium level of real income and the interest rate, there is a unique equilibrium price level. This price level cannot change unless an excess supply of money arises. We have already examined two kinds of shocks that lead to an excess supply of money. Therefore, cost push or supply shock can cause a higher price level only if it gives rise to a similar condition. Let us consider the concepts of cost push and supply shock using our general equilibrium model.

Aggregate Supply Shock in the Neoclassical Model without a Capacity-Reducing Effect[19]

Assume an unanticipated hike in the price of an imported raw material or in the price of a domestic product wrought by a union wage increase which raises production costs. (In this section, the focus is on supply shock; a cost push analysis would be quite similar.) Let the more expensive imported raw material be anchovies but assume that this has no effect on the economy's productive capacity. The price of imported anchovies and anchovy-based products, such as fertilizer, will go up in the price index. This index, the general price level, will rise in the same proportion as the price of imported anchovies because the prices of domestically produced goods increase in the same proportion as the increase in the price of foreign-produced anchovies.[20]

In Figure 11.4, panel c, the upsurge in the price level from P_1 to P_2 reduces the real value of the nominal stock of money balances from M_1/P_1 to M_1/P_2. This immediately initiates an excess demand for money, depicted in panel c as the directed distance AB. According to the aggregate consistency or adding-up condition, an excess demand for money is tantamount to an excess supply of bonds; bond prices dip as individuals attempt to rebalance their portfolios by selling bonds to obtain money. As already discussed, lower bond prices are related, through the present value formula, to higher rates of interest. As the market rate of interest rises in panel c to i_2, the quantity of real money balances demanded declines until at interest rate i_2 the money market will be in equilibrium.

Unfortunately, at interest rate i_2, the credit market (panel b of Figure 11.4) is not in equilibrium. The directed distance CD represents an excess supply of credit:

$$\frac{S}{P} > \frac{I}{P} + \frac{G}{P} - \frac{T}{P} \tag{11.2}$$

Using the aggregate budget identity,

$$\frac{S}{P} \equiv \frac{Y}{P} - \frac{C}{P} - \frac{T}{P} \tag{11.1}$$

[19]The effects on the model of a private *demand shock* arising from an increase in autonomous private investment expenditures or private consumption expenditures are similar to the effects of an increase in the government deficit. As discussed in Chapters Seven and Twelve, disturbances in private spending are considered significant in Keynesian analysis.

In this analysis it will be assumed that supply shocks are random events and, as such, are probably unanticipated by market participants. This assumption may violate the facts. A small increase in the producers' price index or interest rate may signal market participants that a shock has occurred. They might then search data resources for changes in components of price and production indexes to confirm their anticipation of the shock.

[20]As shown in Chapter Fifteen, if the price of foreign-produced goods, P^*, rises with the exchange rate, e, initially held constant; the terms of trade, $e \cdot P^*/P_d$, rise. This creates an excess of exports over imports. This is tantamount to an excess of expenditures over output and drives up the price of domestically produced goods, P_d, in proportion to the rise in the price of imports, so as to restore equilibrium at the initial terms of trade. The overall price level P is a geometrically weighted average of the price of domestically produced goods and foreign-produced goods, $P = P_d^a \cdot (e\,P^*)^{1-a}$, where $1 - a$ reflects the percentage of imports in the GNP.

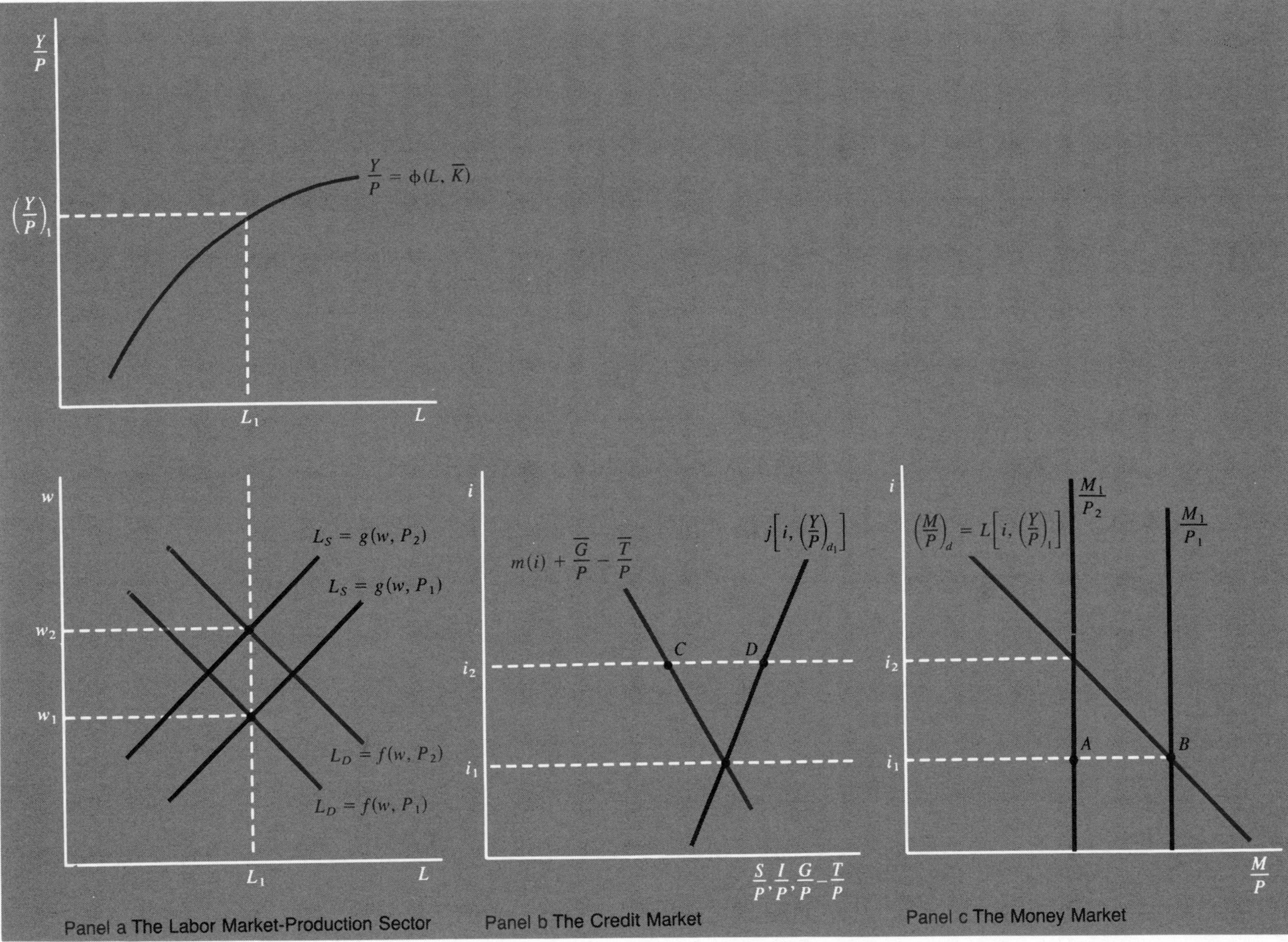

Figure 11.4 The Effect of an Increase in the Price of an Imported Raw Material in the Neoclassical General Equilibrium Model

Table 11.3 Linkage Mechanism: The Effect of an Aggregate Supply Shock in the Neoclassical Model with No Capacity-Constraining Effects

Price of raw material goes up (price level rises)	→ Real value of nominal stock of money falls	→ Excess demand for money in money market (excess supply of bonds)
→ Interest rate rises (bond prices down)	→ Excess supply of credit implies excess supply of newly produced goods and services	→ Price level falls
→ Real value of nominal stock of money rises	→ Interest rate and price level return to original equilibrium levels	

we see that this implies an excess of aggregate output over aggregate real expenditures:

$$\frac{Y}{P} > \frac{C}{P} + \frac{I}{P} + \frac{G}{P}$$

This will lead to a slide in the prices of newly produced goods and services even though the price of the imported raw material remains at its higher level.[21]

The decrease in these prices will lower the price index. As it subsides back to P_1, the real value of the nominal stock of money increases, and the resulting excess supply of money drives interest rates back down to i_1. At interest i_1 and price level P_1, general equilibrium (equilibrium in all markets) is restored. There is one—and only one—general price level consistent with general equilibrium given the equilibrium full employment level of income *(Y/P_1)* in panel a and the equilibrium interest rate *(i_1)* in panel b.

In the labor market (panel a of Figure 11.4), under the assumption of perfect nominal wage flexibility and symmetrical responses, the initial increase in the general price level from P_1 to P_2 causes the demand for and supply of labor to shift upward in the same proportion. As a result, the nominal wage rises from w_1 to w_2, but the levels of employment, output, and the real wage remain unchanged. When the price level declines from P_2 to P_1, this movement is exactly reversed: The nominal wage goes back to w_1 and, once again, there is no effect on employment, output, or the real wage.[22]

Table 11.3 summarizes the transmission mechanism in the economy associated with an aggregate supply shock in the form of an unanticipated increase in the price of an

[21]As shown in Chapter Fifteen, a decrease in (the real value of) the nominal stock of money and subsequent excess of output over aggregate expenditures will lower the exchange rate and prices of domestically produced goods, P_d, in the same proportion so that the equilibrium terms of trade, $e \cdot P^*/P_d$, are unchanged. Therefore, the overall price index, $P = P_d^a \cdot (e\,P^*)^{1-a}$, falls in the same proportion as the decrease in domestic price level.

[22]The demand for labor in this experiment is properly a function of the price of domestically produced goods, and the supply of labor is a function of the overall price level (the cost of living). As discussed in footnotes 20 and 21, the price of domestically produced goods increases and decreases in the same proportion as the increase in the overall price level.

imported raw material. (The linkage mechanism for a cost push would be virtually identical.)

Aggregate Supply Shock in the Neoclassical Model with a Capacity-Reducing Effect

The preceding analysis must be qualified to the extent that the aggregate supply shock or cost push reduces the productive capacity of the economy. If there is no close substitute for the higher-priced raw material such as imported oil, and if technological innovations that will reduce the need for this raw material are not immediately forthcoming, then the supply shock will cause the long-run equilibrium level of output to decline.[23] This will transpire not only because less of the raw material is available but also because resources will be diverted to search for alternate sources and to economize on the scarce input.[24] Thus, we assume that this shock is not temporary and that the productive capacity of the economy is reduced.

Begin from the short-run positions depicted by points E, C, D, and F in Figure 11.5. Because of the supply shock, the price level has already risen to P_2 and the nominal wage level has risen to w_2. The labor market is at point E in panel a. In the money market, since the price level has already risen to P_2, the real value of the stock of nominal money balances has contracted to M_1/P_2. The money market is at point F in panel c. At the interest rate i_2 the credit market is not in equilibrium. The excess supply of credit CD (panel b) is tantamount to an excess of aggregate output over aggregate demand. As a result, the price level declines.

In the previous section, which did not consider capacity-reducing effects, the price level descended all the way to its original level, P_1, because the prices of other newly produced goods and services fell even though the price of the imported raw material remained at its higher level. However, in the present case, the decline in the availability of the higher-priced raw material reduces production and aggregate output. This is reflected in a downward shift of the production function from $\phi(L, \overline{K})$ to $\phi'(L, \overline{K})$ in panel a of Figure 11.5. The equilibrium level of aggregate output tumbles to $(Y/P)_0$. With less of the raw material available and more labor diverted to searching for alternative sources and to economizing on existing supplies of the raw material, existing inputs of labor are less productive, and the marginal physical product of labor, the real wage, declines.[25] This may be seen as a leftward shift in the demand for labor. As a result, there is a decrease in employment in panel a of Figure 11.5. Labor market equilibrium occurs

[23]In the case of a cost push, productive capacity would also decline if the workers displaced by wage increases in excess of productivity gains in the unionized sector were not as productive at their new jobs in other sectors.

[24]In the long run, technological innovation eventually will generate means of substituting for the expensive raw material and the capacity-restraining effects will dissipate. Thus, after a long period of time, the analysis of the preceding section does not violate the facts.

[25]As discussed in Chapter Three, a rise in the interest rate and decline in aggregate real income could cause an increase in the quantity of labor supplied. This effect would reduce the decline in real income, the rise in the interest rate, and the rise in the price level. In Figure 11.5 and the discussion that follows, we abstract from this effect, however, it is part of the theory of the real business cycle discussed in the next section.

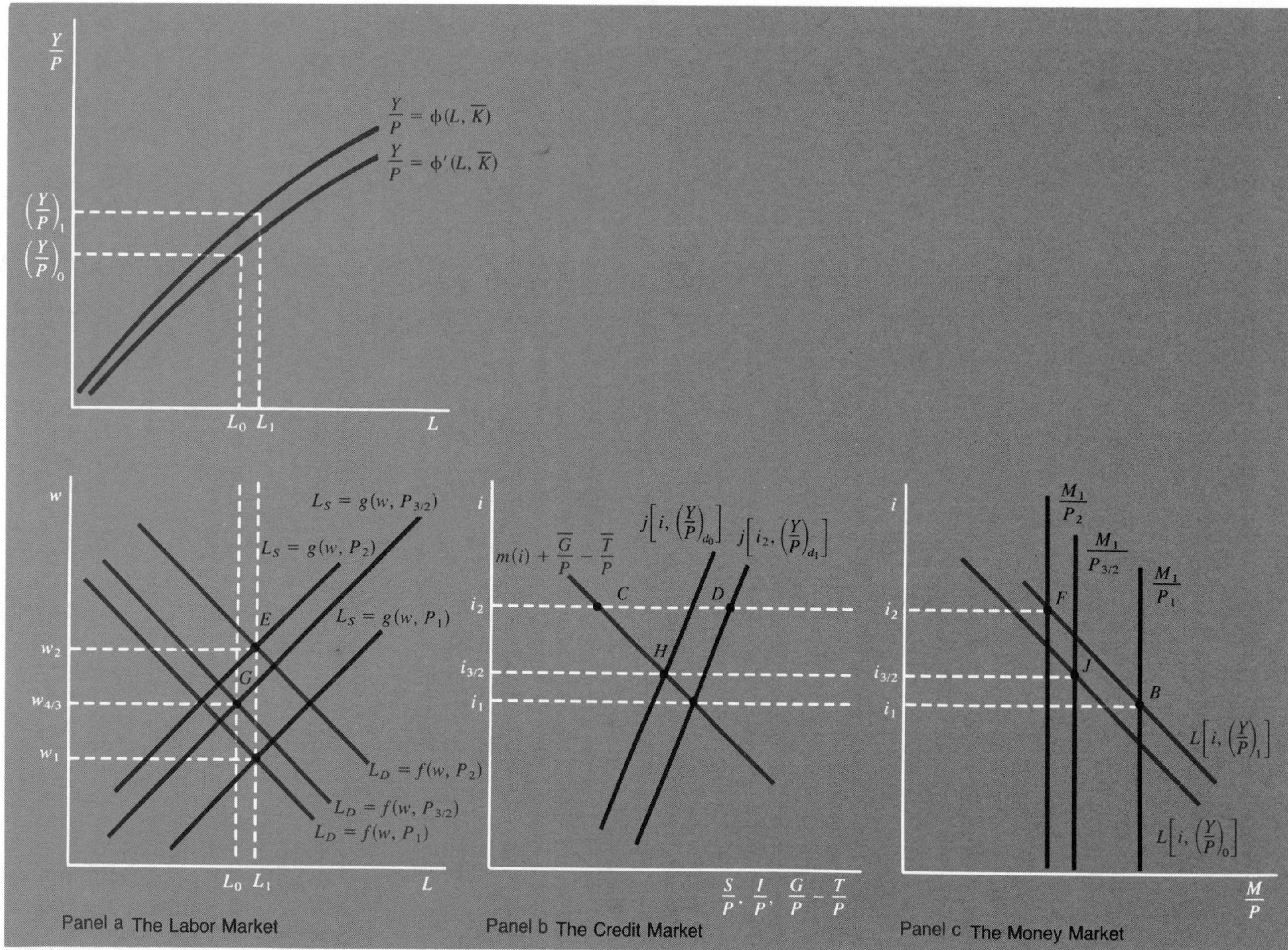

Figure 11.5 The Effect of an Increase in the Price of an Imported Raw Material in the Neoclassical General Equilibrium Model with a Capacity-Reducing Effect

at point G at a lower nominal wage ($w_{4/3}$) and price level ($P_{3/2}$). Because the nominal wage has declined ($w_2 - w_{4/3}$) more than the price level ($P_2 - P_{3/2}$), the real wage has fallen from w_2/P_2 to $w_{4/3}/P_{3/2}$. With a lower equilibrium level of real income, there is a leftward shift in the saving relation in the credit market (panel b). Hence, the equilibrium rate of interest rises to $i_{3/2}$ at point H.

Because of the overall decrease in productivity, the marginal productivity of capital can also be expected to decline. This would reduce investment expenditures at each possible interest rate and result in a leftward shift in the demand for credit in panel b. In addition, the permanent decline in aggregate real income would result in a reduction in wealth that would cause an increase in current saving. Thus, these two effects would reduce, or possibly even eliminate, the rise in the interest rate and reduce the subsequent increase in the price level discussed below. However, for simplicity's sake, we shall not consider them in Figure 11.5 or the analysis that follows.

With the lower equilibrium level of real income and the higher equilibrium interest rate, the demand for real money balances declines. As a result, the long-run equilibrium price level does not return all the way back to P_1 but goes only to $P_{3/2}$. Equilibrium occurs at point J rather than at point B.

Thus, the reduction in the productive capacity of the economy drops real income from $(Y/P)_1$ to $(Y/P)_0$; this causes the interest rate to climb from i_1 to $i_{3/2}$ and results in a hike in the price level from P_1 to $P_{3/2}$. As mentioned earlier, the concurrent fall in real income and rise in the price level are sometimes called stagflation.

In this case, an increase in the price of an imported raw material may be said to *cause* an increase in the price level. (A similar conclusion would be reached for a capacity-reducing cost push.) It should not be inferred, however, that this invalidates the quantity theory of money. By comparing initial equilibrium conditions to new equilibrium conditions, it can be seen that the price level varies in proportion with the excess supply of money. The capacity-reducing effect on real income depresses real saving. This spurs the interest rate up to $i_{3/2}$. The decline in real income causes the demand for money to shift leftward, and the higher interest rate reduces the quantity of real money balances demanded. At the initial equilibrium price level, an excess supply of money forms. This excess supply of money results in the equilibrium price level rising from P_1 to $P_{3/2}$. The increase in the price level is still proportional to the excess supply of money.

We may conclude from these experiments that supply shock (or cost push) forces could cause the general price level to rise in equilibrium if such forces constrain the productive capacity of our economy. To the extent that there are no close substitutes for the higher-priced input and to the extent that the input is important to overall production, as in the case of imported oil, there will be capacity-inhibiting effects. Output will fall, and the interest rate and the general price level will rise. However, even in this case, it cannot be said that the increase in the price level is not a monetary phenomenon because the reduction in real income and the rise in interest rates reduce the demand for money and thereby generate an excess supply of money that is the proximate cause of the higher equilibrium price level. To the extent that a higher-priced input is not significant to our economy's overall production or has a close substitute, as in the case of imported anchovies, capacity-constraining effects are quite limited and there will be very small effects on real income, the interest rate, and the price level. Supply shock (or cost push) forces under these circumstances are not so significant.

Can we attribute the periodically high inflation rates, interest rates, and unemployment of the 1973–1982 period to aggregate supply shocks? On the one hand, the oil price shocks of 1974 and 1979 would appear to be legitimate causes of a higher price level, interest rates, and unemployment. Crude oil was of enormous significance as a productive input, and in the near term, substitution of other energy sources for oil was severely limited. Of course, just as there are capacity-reducing shocks, there are capacity-enhancing ones. In the period from 1983 to 1986, oil prices declined significantly. As a result, output increased, interest rates declined, and the rate of inflation fell. These effects were consistent with the notion of a capacity-enhancing supply shock. The economic boom of the mid-1980s was, in large part, a product of the steady decline in the price of imported oil. In addition, without this favorable aggregate supply shock, the hemorrhaging federal deficit probably would have provoked much more severe inflation and even higher interest rates.

When government officials blamed the huge increases in the price level in 1977 and 1978 on such minor disruptions as the failure of the Peruvian anchovy crop or a four-week-long truck drivers' strike, we were probably witnessing the scapegoat theory of inflation. Work disruptions are usually preceded and followed by overtime employment, workers who become unemployed in one industry often find jobs and drive down wages and prices in another, and there are close substitutes for anchovies in fertilizer as well as in pizza production.

Keep in mind that the scapegoat theory of inflation also works in the opposite direction. In the 1983–1986 period, government officials were not at all reluctant to take credit for the economic boom and the low rate of inflation. Yet, without the capacity-enhancing aggregate supply shock precipitated by the tremendous slide in the price of foreign-produced oil, there probably would have been no boom and inflation would have been much worse. In addition, without the favorable capacity-enhancing supply shock, the government deficit would have pushed the interest rate even higher. An expanded version of the scapegoat theory might be: "When bad things happen to the economy, find a scapegoat; when good things happen, even when associated with forces beyond our control, take credit."

The Theory of the Real Business Cycle

The general agreement that the oil supply shocks of the 1970s and 1980s led to the swings in employment, real income, real wages, interest rates, and the price level, described above, gave impetus to a revival of interest in the role played by supply shock events in causing business cycles. (Recently, the menu of capacity-changing shocks has been expanded to include technological innovations and shifts in consumer demand from one sector of the economy to another, but the focus has mainly been on supply shocks.)

An important argument in favor of the real or supply shock explanation of cyclical movements in employment and output is that alternative demand shock explanations, discussed earlier in this chapter, require the assumption that such shocks and the resulting price level changes come as a surprise to market participants. Many researchers believe that in a world where market participants formulate their expectations rationally such strictly unanticipated monetary and fiscal shocks would be rather rare. Advocates of the real business cycle are more comfortable in not relying so heavily on the assumption of unanticipated shocks, related wage and price inflexibility, and a delay in the return to long-run full employment equilibrium. Under the supply shock explanation employment and output fall, not because of lagged responses of (labor) market participants and a delayed return to (long-run) full employment equilibrium, but because changes in the productive capacity of the economy alter the long-run full employment equilibrium position of the economy. For example, in the case of a capacity-enhancing supply shock, the full employment equilibrium level of employment rises because the demand for labor increases. This increase in demand is associated with an increase in productivity. As a result, the equilibrium level of the real wage rises. In addition, the full employment equilibrium level of real income goes up and the equilibrium interest rate declines. In the case of a capacity-reducing shock the reverse of these movements occurs.

Another important feature in favor of real business cycle theory is its prediction of a positive correlation between employment and real wages. This correlation squares fairly well with the actual cyclical patterns of real wage and employment movements in the real world.

In addition, as indicated in the previous section, there are good reasons to believe that, given a capacity-changing supply shock, the full employment equilibrium positions in the economy will change over time in ways that correspond to actual cyclical movements. For example, given a capacity-reducing supply shock, the full employment equilibrium levels of employment and output fall, real wages fall, interest rates rise, and the price level rises. Over time, however, the behavior of the market participants will cause a movement back toward the initial, preshock, full employment equilibrium values of these variables. For example, the reduction in wealth arising from lower real income will cause saving to rise, which will reduce the interest rate, increase investment spending, and eventually raise the level of real income and lower the price level. In addition, the decline in wealth will cause the supply of labor to increase, further causing real income to rise, interest rates to decline, and the price level to fall.

At the present stage in its development the real business cycle theory may be viewed as an interesting response to two recent developments. One is the shortcomings of surprise, or demand shock, explanations of cyclical movements fostered by the rational expectations critique. The other development is the impact of capacity-changing supply shocks on the economy in recent years. A more complete understanding of business cycles surely requires an integration of both theories, the inflationary surprise, demand shock theory and the real, supply shock theory.

Wage and Price Controls (Incomes Policies)

As discussed earlier, the notion that the price level can be forced up by increases in the monopoly power of cartels, unions, or big business has often been called the cost push theory of inflation. If, because of significant capacity-reducing effects, monetary and fiscal policymakers cannot control the resulting inflation or can do so only at the cost of a possible recession (discussed in the next chapter), proponents of the cost push theory often favor *wage and price controls* (sometimes called *incomes policies*) as a direct way of halting it. They sometimes assert that if one cartel or big business raises its prices, other businesses (and unions) will be tempted to exploit their unused monopoly power and raise their prices (and wages) in order to keep up. They suggest that one way to stop the cost push process is for a monitoring government agency to institute rules about higher prices and higher wages and to punish the violators in order to constrain them from exploiting their unused monopoly power.

Advocates of controls contend that, in concert with monetary and fiscal policies, they can restrain inflation better with a smaller cost in terms of recession than monetary or fiscal measures working alone. Proponents of controls say that they signal a "get tough" policy stance with regard to inflation. They sometimes even argue that inflation can be propelled by expectations of inflation alone and that price and wage controls can effectively dampen inflationary expectations.[26]

Price controls have been around for a long time. The Emperor Diocletian instituted a price control program in 301 A.D. Anyone caught disobeying the Emperor's 890 different price categories was executed by drowning. Price controls worked for Diocletian as a form of population control as well as inflation control.

The Continental Congress instituted price controls during the American Revolution. Again inflation was reduced. However, at Valley Forge, George Washington found that he had enormous problems buying provisions for his troops at controlled prices. It is not widely known that in 1775 General Washington discovered one of the flaws of price controls: If they are effective, they create shortages at the artificially low controlled prices.

During World War II under President Franklin Roosevelt, the United States again reverted to controlling prices. Again, however, there were significant shortages at the official, controlled prices. In the early 1970s, the Nixon administration tried price controls. Again shortages developed in the economy at the official prices.[27]

The historical record speaks for itself. Price controls do not really work because when the market-clearing price of a good or service exceeds the official controlled price, a shortage appears, and illegal trading at unofficial prices (a black market) or lower product quality develops. Price controls only make it seem as though inflation has been licked. Actually, inflation is only repressed. As soon as controls are lifted, prices shoot up to reflect the shortages and distortions that take place at the artificially controlled, official prices. In the meantime, the costs of administering controls and a loss of economic freedom are imposed on individual citizens.

[26]See the section of Chapter Thirteen titled "Can Inflation Be Sustained by Expectations Alone?"

[27]In the 1960s, the Kennedy and Johnson administrations tried *wage-price guidelines*. Guidelines are controls with no explicit enforcement procedures except for the threat of loss of government contracts or antitrust measures against violators. To the extent that they are unenforceable, wage-price guidelines neither suppress inflation nor create shortages.

Concluding Comment

This chapter discusses three experiments with the Neoclassical general equilibrium model: an increase in the supply of money, an increase in the government deficit, and an increase in the price of an imported raw material.

In the money supply experiment, the initial excess supply of money causes an excess demand for credit which, by use of the aggregate budget identity, is tantamount to an excess of aggregate expenditures over aggregate output. This condition results in a rise in the general price level. As the price level rises, the real value of the nominal stock of money contracts. As long as there are flexible nominal wages and symmetrical responses in the labor market, the increase in the money supply has no effect on employment and output. The increase in the money supply has the solitary effect of driving up the price level.

In the second experiment, an increase in the government deficit makes the interest rate rise. The increase in the interest rate causes a reduction in the quantity of real money balances demanded. This results in an excess supply of money which, in turn, generates an increase in the general price level. Thus, the increase in the government deficit brings about an increase in the interest rate as well as an increase in the general price level. Once again, in the absence of impediments to symmetrical adjustment on both sides of the labor market, there is no effect on employment and aggregate output.

In the third experiment, a supply shock in the form of an increase in the price of an imported raw material initially drives up the price level. Initially, it is assumed that this has no effect on productive capacity. At the new, higher price level, the real value of the nominal stock of money shrinks. The excess demand for money spurs the interest rate upward. The higher interest rate creates an excess supply of credit which is tantamount to an excess of aggregate output over aggregate expenditures. This produces a decline in the general price level to its initial equilibrium level wherein the real value of the nominal stock of money returns to its initial equilibrium level, as does the market rate of interest. Thus, while an increase in the price of an imported raw material initially causes the general price level and the interest rate to rise, in the long run the price level returns to its initial equilibrium level with no effect on the interest rate, employment, or aggregate output.

If there are no close substitutes for the imported raw material and it plays a significant role in production processes, the supply shock will cause the equilibrium level of real income to decline. This, in turn, lowers real saving and generates a rise in the equilibrium interest rate. With lower real income and a higher interest rate, the demand for real money balances declines. The resulting excess supply of money generates an increase in the equilibrium price level.

This chapter demonstrates that a large but unchanging government deficit cannot cause the price level to rise (except where it forges a continual contraction in saving, a continual reduction in the demand for money, or a continual rise in the debt-to-income ratio). It also reveals that a supply shock such as an increase in the price of an imported raw material (or a cost push) cannot cause the price level to rise (except when it hampers productive capacity and results in a reduction in the demand for money). Why, then, does the public associate these things with increases in the price level which, if sustained over time, are called *inflation?* The Neoclassical general equilibrium model predicts that only an excess supply of money can cause the price level to rise. The resolution of this question requires closer inspection of the link between the government deficit and supply shocks on the one hand and the manner in which the Federal Reserve manages the money supply on the other. This is one of the subjects of Chapter Thirteen.

EXERCISES

1. Evaluate the following statement: "It is an excess supply of money or excess expenditures that drives up the price level, not an excess demand for credit."
2. Explain why you agree or disagree with the following statement: "The nominal income effect is a misnomer because it is the change in the price level, not nominal income, which causes the interest rate to change."
3. Explain why only an ever-increasing deficit and not a large but unchanging deficit can cause an ever-increasing price level.
4. "In the Neoclassical model, an increase in the deficit can cause an increase in the price level; therefore, the quantity theory of money is invalid." True or false?
5. "In the Neoclassical model, a shift in the demand for money can create a change in the price level; therefore, the quantity theory of money is invalid." True or false?
6. Why might an increase in the price of a raw material hamper the productive capacity of an economy? Why might a cost push reduce productive capacity? What would be the effects on prices, employment, and interest rates? Would these effects be permanent? Could monetary policy be used to ameliorate any of these effects?
7. Under what conditions does the injection of liquidity into portfolios immediately drive up prices of newly produced goods and services? Under what conditions does it drive up financial asset prices? Which set of conditions seems in closer accord with a full employment model of the labor market?
8. Discuss at least two pitfalls that arise from the partial equilibrium view of the money market.
9. "The price level always varies in proportion to the excess supply of money." Evaluate this statement from the perspective of the Neoclassical model.
10. In what sense can wage and price controls "work"? In what sense do they not "work"?
11. On the evening news, a government spokesman blames the increase in the latest consumer price index on the higher price of food associated with the impact of a bout of cold weather on the Florida citrus crop. Will the crop failure cause a higher equilibrium price level?

12. Develop a rational expectations model of supply-shock inflation.
13. Why would money and credit market participants have an incentive to anticipate changes in monetary and fiscal policy? What about labor market participants?
14. Analyze wage and price controls policy from a rational expectations perspective.

BIBLIOGRAPHY

Allais, Maurice. "A Restatement of the Quantity Theory of Money." *American Economic Review* 56 (December 1966), pp. 1123–1157.

Bailey, Martin. *National Income and the Price Level*. New York: McGraw-Hill, 1971.

Friedman, Milton. "Factors Affecting the Level of Interest Rates." *Proceedings of the 1968 Conference on Savings and Residential Financing*. Chicago: United States Savings and Loan League, 1969, pp. 11–27.

———. "The Quantity Theory of Money—A Restatement." In *Studies in the Quantity Theory of Money*, ed. Milton Friedman. Chicago: University of Chicago Press, 1956, pp. 1–21.

Gilbert, Charles. "The Rational Expectations Hypothesis: Survey and Recent Research." In *Modern Concepts in Macroeconomics*, ed. Thomas M. Havrilesky. Arlington Heights, Ill.: Harlan Davidson, Inc., 1985.

Hadjimichalakis, Michael G. *Modern Macroeconomics*. Englewood Cliffs, N.J.: Prentice-Hall, 1982.

Kydland, Finn E., and Edward C. Prescott. "Time to Build on Aggregate Fluctuations." *Econometrica*, 50 (December 1982), pp. 1345–1371.

Lucas, Robert E., and Thomas J. Sargent. "After Keynesian Macroeconomics." In *Modern Concepts in Macroeconomics*, ed. Thomas M. Havrilesky. Arlington Heights, Ill.: Harlan Davidson, Inc., 1985.

Meltzer, Allan H. "The Case for a Monetary Rule." In *Modern Concepts in Macroeconomics*, ed. Thomas M. Havrilesky. Arlington Heights, Ill.: Harlan Davidson, Inc., 1985.

Mishkin, Frederic. *A Rational Expectations Approach to Macroeconomics: Testing Policy Ineffectiveness and Efficient Markets Models*. Chicago: University of Chicago Press, 1983.

Motley, Brian. *Money, Income and Wealth*. 2d ed. New York: D. C. Heath, 1976.

Niehans, Jurg. *The Theory of Money*. Baltimore: The Johns Hopkins University Press, 1978.

Park, Yung Chul. "Some Current Issues in the Transmission Process of Monetary Policy." *Staff Papers*. Washington, D.C.: International Monetary Fund, March 1972, pp. 1–43.

Patinkin, Don. *Money, Interest and Prices*. 2d ed. New York: Harper and Row, 1965.

Shiller, Robert J. "Rational Expectations and the Dynamic Structure of Macroeconomic Models." *Journal of Monetary Economics*, 4 (December 1978), pp. 1–44.

Taylor, John B. "The Role of Expectations in the Choice of Monetary Policy." In *Modern Concepts in Macroeconomics*, ed. Thomas M. Havrilesky. Arlington Heights, Ill.: Harlan Davidson, Inc., 1985.

The Keynesian General Equilibrium Model: Solution Process and Two Experiments

Chapter 12

Introduction

A Neoclassical general equilibrium model of the economy as a whole was presented in Chapter Ten. In that model, the level of aggregate real income was determined by the working of the labor market. The interest rate was determined by the supply of and demand for credit (which are identically related to the level of aggregate real expenditures and output). The general price level was determined by the working of the money market.

Now a Keynesian general equilibrium model of the economy as a whole will be examined. A Keynesian model is characterized by conditions of nominal wage inflexibility and asymmetrical response to information regarding the general price level in the labor market. Specifically, when the price level changes, the demand for labor will change but the supply of labor will not change sufficiently to keep the level of employment unchanged. Therefore, the level of employment will be affected by variations in the price level. As a consequence, swings in the level of aggregate real expenditures (brought about by disturbances such as movements in the money supply or by movements in the government deficit) which affect the price level will also have an impact on aggregate real income.

To the extent that changes in the money supply have an effect on real income and do not cause a proportional change in the price level, monetary impulses will have an effect on the equilibrium interest rate. Therefore, the equilibrium interest rate is not viewed as being determined exclusively by the level of aggregate real expenditures independently of the money market as it was in the Neoclassical model.

THE KEYNESIAN GENERAL EQUILIBRIUM MODEL: SOLUTION PROCESS

The Keynesian model in Table 12.1 is identical to the Neoclassical model of the previous chapter except for the specification that there is nominal wage inflexibility and imperfect information or imperfect response to information on the supply side of the labor market.[1] This is indicated by the infinity sign under the nominal wage variable and the zero sign under the price level variable in the labor supply equation, (12.2). The zero sign means that laborers do not respond to changes in the price level; the infinity sign means that the nominal wage is perfectly rigid. This alteration of the model has a significant effect on the solution process.

The most striking characteristic of this model is that it requires a simultaneous solution involving all three markets. For example, unlike the Neoclassical model, the labor market–production sector does not automatically yield full employment solution values for the levels of employment, aggregate real income, and the real wage. Let us examine the labor market–production sector in order to see why this is so. Figure 12.1 depicts the labor market–production sector with a Keynesian specification of the labor supply curve, which conforms to Equation (12.2). As the exogenously determined price level increases from P_1 to P_2, the demand for labor increases but the supply of labor does not because workers are assumed either to be uninformed about or unable to respond to the increased cost of living. Moreover, it is assumed that the nominal wage is fixed at w_0. Therefore, the increase in demand has no effect on the nominal wage but has a tremendous impact on employment. The equilibrium level of employment rises from L_1 to L_2, and aggregate real income goes from $(Y/P)_1$ to $(Y/P)_2$. The price level increases from P_1 to P_2. Because this jump in the price level is either not fully apprehended or not responded to by labor suppliers, the rightward shift in the demand for labor results in an increase in employment from L_1 to L_2 and an increase in output from $(Y/P)_1$ to $(Y/P)_2$. The level of employment and real income are not invariant with respect to the general price level as they were in the Neoclassical model. We cannot solve for the equilibrium level of aggregate real income independently of the other markets.

[1]The imperfect response specification reflects implicit or explicit nominal wage contracting with lagged adjustment of the nominal wage to changes in the price level that were unanticipated when the contract was negotiated. The lagged response to such price level information makes it appear that workers systematically have worse information than employers. Actually, they may have information that is as good as anyone else's but may simply be subject to implicit or explicit contracts which inhibit quick responses to that information. If labor demanders have and respond to information, the lagged responses of labor suppliers would generate a systematic positive linkage between changes in the price level and changes in employment. See Chapter Four for further discussion of the rationale for contracts under which workers forfeit immediate adjustment to information that was unanticipated when the contract was made.

Table 12.1 The Keynesian Model

Sector	Equations			Key characteristics
Labor Market–Production	$L_D = f(w,P)$ $- \quad +$	labor demand	(12.1)	cannot solve for (Y/P) or any variable independently of credit and money markets
	$L_S = g(w,P)$ $\infty \quad 0$	labor supply	(12.2)	
	$L_S = L_D$	equilibrium condition	(12.3)	
	$\left(\frac{Y}{P}\right) = \phi(L, \overline{K})$ where K is fixed	production function	(12.4)	
Credit (Loanable Funds) Market	$\frac{S}{P} = j\left[i, \left(\frac{Y}{P}\right)_d\right]$ $+ \quad +$	saving	(12.5)	cannot solve for i or any variable independently of labor and money markets
	$\frac{I}{P} = m(i)$ $-$	investment expenditures	(12.6)	
	$\left(\frac{G}{P} - \frac{T}{P}\right) = \left(\frac{\overline{G}}{P} - \frac{\overline{T}}{P}\right)$	government deficit or surplus	(12.7)	
	$\left(\frac{Y}{P}\right)_d = \left(\frac{Y}{P} - \frac{\overline{T}}{P}\right)$	definition of disposable income	(12.8)	
	$\frac{S}{P} = \frac{I}{P} + \left(\frac{G}{P} - \frac{T}{P}\right)$	equilibrium condition	(12.9)	
Money Market	$\left(\frac{M}{P}\right)_d = L\left[i, \left(\frac{Y}{P}\right)\right]$ $- \quad +$	demand for real money balances	(12.10)	cannot solve for P or any variable independently of labor and credit markets
	$M_S = M_1$	supply of nominal money	(12.11)	
	$\left(\frac{M}{P}\right)_d = \frac{M_1}{P}$	equilibrium condition	(12.12)	

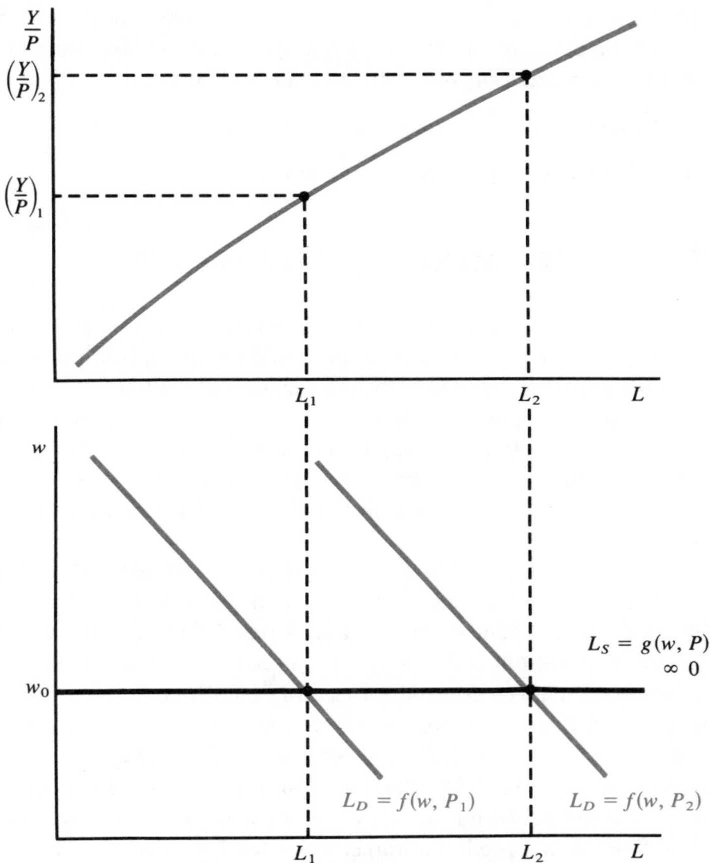

Figure 12.1 Keynesian Partial Equilibrium Model of Labor Market-Production Sector

Turn next to the flow subsector of the aggregate demand side of the model in Table 12.1. In the credit (loanable funds) market, without knowledge of the level of real income, we cannot isolate a unique real saving curve. Therefore we cannot solve for the equilibrium interest rate independently of the other markets. In the stock subsector of the aggregate demand side of the global model, the money market, we cannot solve for the price level independently of the other markets.

Thus, the solution process for the Keynesian model cannot be neatly presented as a stepwise, sequential procedure as in the Neoclassical model. Fortunately, this does not mean that the Keynesian model is more difficult to understand than the Neoclassical model. Simple supply and demand reasoning is used to understand both models. The fact that the solution process is simultaneous does not require complicated graphs or mathematics. It is not necessary to "muddy the water so that it may appear deep." To understand the simultaneous solution process for the Keynesian model, we shall proceed directly to two of the experiments that were performed on the Neoclassical model using only the basic time-honored tools of supply and demand curves:

1. the effect of a change in the money supply, and
2. the effect of a change in the government deficit.

THE EFFECT OF A CHANGE IN THE MONEY SUPPLY

Figure 12.2 presents the Keynesian general equilibrium model. Initially, the money market is in equilibrium at point A. The credit market is in equilibrium at point A'. The labor market is in equilibrium at point A''. These are points of long-run, full employment equilibrium. Assume an increase in the nominal stock of money from M_1 to M_3. This is depicted as a rightward shift in the supply curve from M_1/P_1 to M_3/P_1 in the money market (panel c). At the initial equilibrium interest rate, there is an excess supply of money (AB). Portfolios, the ways in which individuals hold their nonhuman wealth, are not in balance.

As in previous chapters, individual nonhuman wealth is defined to consist of real money balances, the real value of debt claims, the real value of equity claims, and existing consumer durables. As in Chapter Eleven, it is assumed that debt and equity claims are perfect substitutes and are lumped together as "bonds." As a means of simplifying the analysis, it is assumed that the demand for existing consumer durables does not change. Finally, it is assumed that market participants either form their expectations of future prices rationally but do not anticipate the increase in the money supply or form their expectations adaptively. Under the first assumption, individuals experience an increase in the liquidity of their portfolios but do not associate it with a rise in the nation's money stock and, therefore, do not predict a higher price level. Under the second assumption, whether or not they are aware of the increased money supply is irrelevant because expected future prices are extrapolated from past prices.

Under these assumptions bond prices are bid upward as individuals use their excess money balances to acquire bonds. As in Chapters Nine and Eleven, the aggregate consistency or adding-up condition continues to hold. The advance in the price of bonds is related (by the present value formula) to a decline in the market rate of interest. As the interest rate falls, the quantity of real money balances demanded comes into balance with the real value of the nominal stock of money (M_3/P_1). At C (panel c), the money market is in (temporary) equilibrium. (As the expected rate of inflation is assumed constant throughout this chapter, changes in the nominal interest rate are synonymous with changes in the real interest rate.)

While the money market is in equilibrium at i_2, the credit market in panel b is not. At i_2 there is an excess demand for credit, illustrated by the distance $C_0'\ C_1'$. Substitution of the aggregate budget identity ($S/P \equiv Y/P - C/P - T/P$) into the left-hand side of the excess demand for credit ($S/P < I/P + G/P - T/P$) implies that the line segment $C_0'\ C_1'$ also depicts an excess of real aggregate demand over real aggregate income

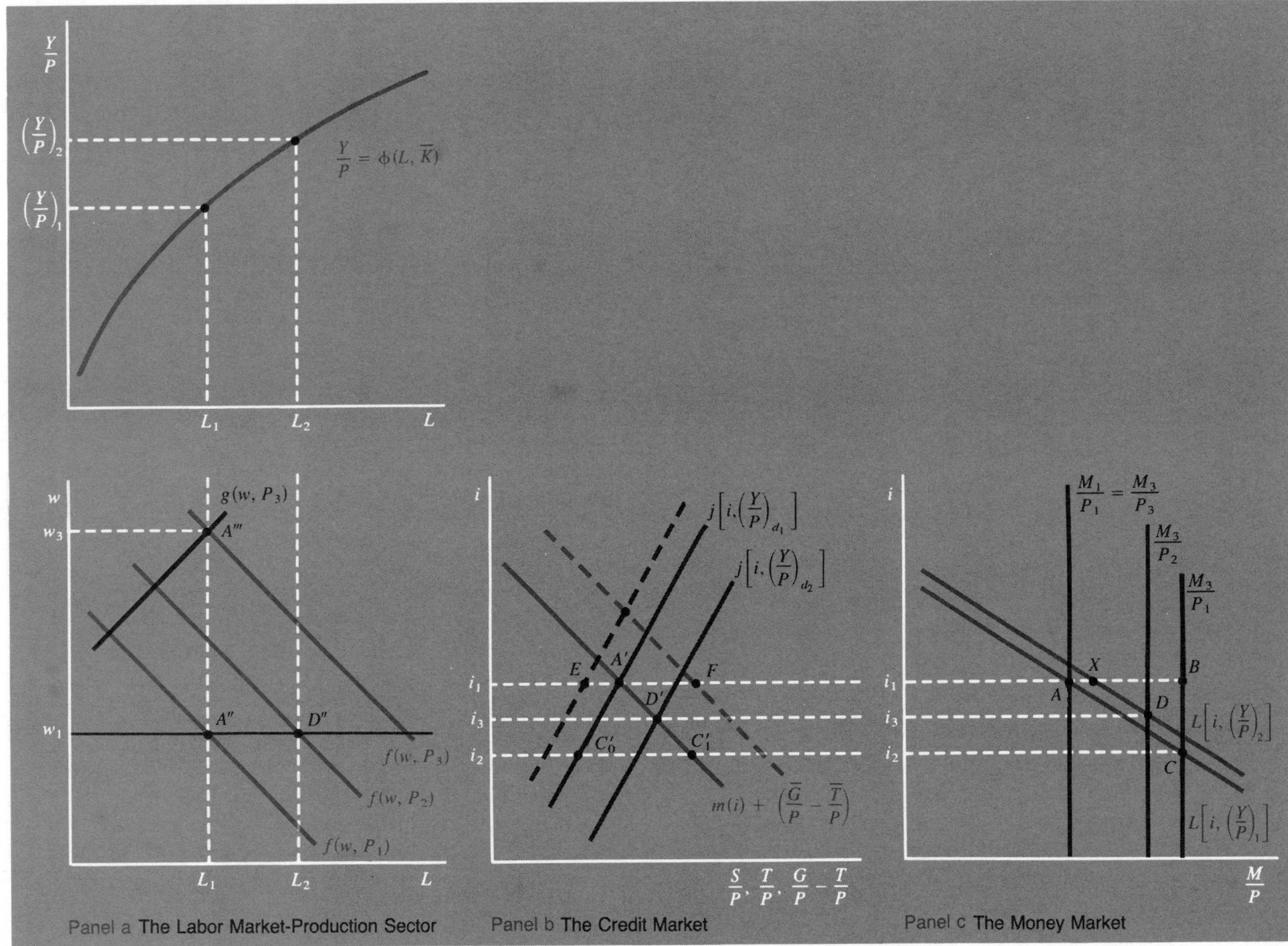

Figure 12.2 **An Increase in the Money Supply in the Keynesian General Equilibrium Model**

($Y/P < C/P + I/P + G/P$). Because this excess demand will persist over time, prices of newly produced goods and services will begin to go up. When real aggregate expenditures exceed real aggregate output, the prices of newly produced goods and services are bid upward and the general price level (P) climbs.

If we alter the expectational assumption made earlier and assume that expectations in the credit and money markets are formed rationally and the increase in the money stock is anticipated, credit and money market participants will use the excess supply of money, AB in panel c, to finance private expenditures in a like amount, EF in panel b. The aggregate consistency or adding-up condition holds. Now the excess supply of money implies an excess demand for goods. Small changes in the market rate of interest may signal market participants that a shock is occurring. They then turn to published money supply data to confirm their anticipation of this shock. The saving function would shift leftward (because consumption expenditures increase), and the investment plus government deficit function would shift rightward (because investment expenditures increase) to the positions indicated by the broken lines in panel b of Figure 12.2. At the unchanged rate, i_1, there would be an excess of expenditures over output, measured by the directed distance EF. This condition would cause the price level to rise.

Up to this point, under either set of expectational assumptions regarding the behavior of credit and money market participants, the preceding alternative descriptions of the effect of an increase in the supply of money are the same in the Keynesian model as in the Neoclassical model. Under either set of assumptions, the increase in the money supply incites a rise in the price level. Beyond this point, however, the two models differ. Under the Neoclassical model, the price level is bid up to P_3 and the real value of the money stock plummets to M_3/P_3 (panel c of Figure 12.2). General equilibrium in both the money and credit markets is restored at the initial interest rate i_1 with no effect on the labor market–production sector. There is no effect on employment because of the assumption of perfect nominal wage flexibility and symmetrical responses on both sides of the labor market, and the nominal wage rises to w_3.[2]

Under the Keynesian model, however, as the price level is bid upward by excess aggregate demand, it has an impact on employment in the labor market. In panel a of Figure 12.2, the higher price level P_2 thrusts the demand for labor rightward to $f(w, P_2)$. Firms realize that at a higher price level, the marginal revenue product of labor is higher. However, the supply of labor does not shift upward because workers are assumed to be unaware of or unable to respond to the higher price level [the sign under the P variable in Equation (12.2) is zero]. The nominal wage is assumed rigid at w_1, as depicted by the horizontal labor supply curve (panel a) and the infinity sign under the w term of Equation (12.2). Therefore, as the price level rises, there is an enormous increase in employment (from L_1 to L_2) and in real output [from $(Y/P)_1$ to $(Y/P)_2$, panel a]. Equilibrium occurs at point D'' (panel a). The increase in aggregate real expenditures provoked by an increase in the money supply is not totally absorbed by rising prices as it was in the Neoclassical model. Part of the increase in expenditures is absorbed by higher output.

[2]In expectational terms, a stronger assumption would be nominal wage flexibility and the rational formulation of price expectations with anticipation of the money supply increase by labor market participants. See the section "Rational Expectations versus Adaptive Expectations" in Chapter Four for an explanation of why these assumptions are similar but not identical.

As explained at the outset of Chapter Four, the positive link between output and the price level may arise from su y decisions in many markets other than the labor market. We focus on the labor market as a reflection of behavior in many markets for productive inputs and outputs. In these markets, a rise in the general price level may cause more productive inputs to be supplied and more output to be produced under two alternative approaches: imperfect information or nominal contracting. Under the imperfect information approach, associated with the article by Lucas and Sargent cited in the bibliography to this chapter, a rise in the general price level is incorrectly perceived as an increase in the input suppliers' or output producers' own price relative to the general price level. Under the nominal contracting approach, associated with the work by Taylor cited in the bibliography, a rise in the general price level indicates an increase in demand to which input suppliers or output producers are contractually obligated to respond without raising their own prices. Keeping this in mind, we may now return to the general equilibrium model.

Because real income increases with taxation unchanged, real disposable income rises. Because disposable income rises, real saving also increases. In panel b, the real saving function shifts to the right with $j[i, (Y/P)_{d_2}]$. As explained in Chapter Six, the rise in real saving could also occur because lender attitudes toward risk are more optimistic during periods of cyclical expansion of aggregate real income. Thus, the leap in real saving makes it unnecessary for the interest rate to stay at its initial equilibrium level, i_1. Equilibrium is restored to the credit market at interest rate i_3 at point D' (panel b).

The expansion in the equilibrium level of real disposable income from $(Y/P)_{d_1}$ to $(Y/P)_{d_2}$ stimulates the supply of credit, real saving, in the credit market, thereby precluding a return of the interest rate to i_1 (panel b). It also causes the demand for real money balances to increase to $L[i, (Y/P)_2]$ in panel c. The higher equilibrium level of real income, together with the fact that the new equilibrium interest rate, i_3, is lower than it would have been if real saving had not increased, means that the quantity of real money balances demanded is greater than it would have been had the level of real income not risen and the interest rate gone all the way back up to i_1. As a result, the price level does not have to soar all the way to P_3 to restore the real value of the quantity of nominal money balances to its original level ($M_3/P_3 = M_1/P_1$). Equilibrium occurs at point D in panel c of Figure 12.2 with a price level of P_2 and real money balances of M_3/P_2. In the Keynesian model, the price level does not rise in proportion to the increase in the nominal quantity of money. The quantity theory of money does not hold. This is because the higher level of real income, $(Y/P)_2$, and lower interest rate, i_3, cause the quantity of real money balances demanded to rise. This rise absorbs part of the increase in the money supply. Only the remainder of the increase fuels the rise in the price level. Nevertheless, the price level does rise. The increase in the demand for money can never be so great as to prevent a rise in the price level because without it there would be no stimulus to increased employment in the labor market and no increase in real income. Equilibrium is restored to the money market with a price level of P_2 and with real money balances of M_3/P_2 at point D of panel c. Points D, D', and D'' are referred to as positions of short-run, super-full employment equilibrium.

Table 12.2 displays the linkages from an increase in the supply of money to changes in the interest rate, the price level, employment and output in the Keynesian model.

Table 12.2 Linkage Mechanism: The Effect of an Increase in the Money Supply in the Keynesian Model

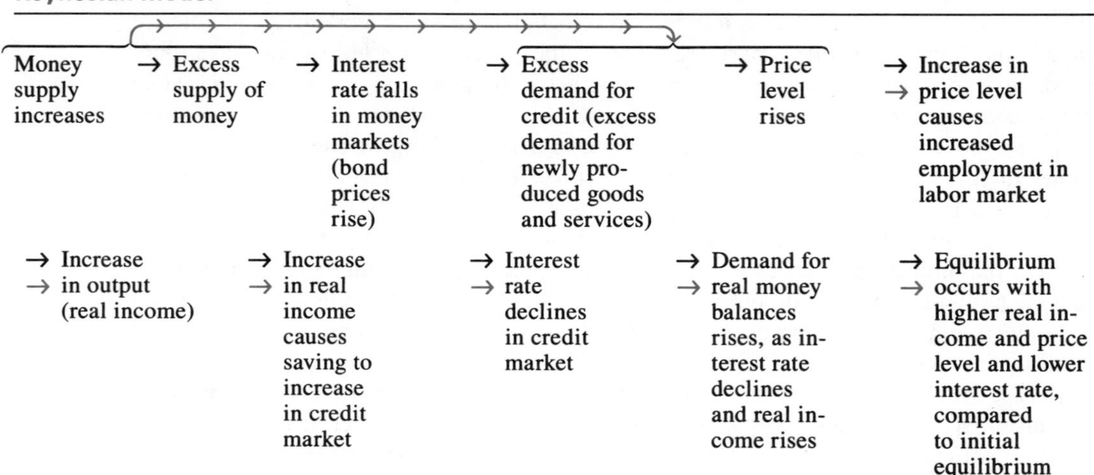

Money supply increases	→ Excess supply of money	→ Interest rate falls in money markets (bond prices rise)	→ Excess demand for credit (excess demand for newly produced goods and services)	→ Price level rises	→ → Increase in price level causes increased employment in labor market
→ → Increase in output (real income)	→ → Increase in real income causes saving to increase in credit market	→ → Interest rate declines in credit market	→ → Demand for real money balances rises, as interest rate declines and real income rises	→ → Equilibrium occurs with higher real income and price level and lower interest rate, compared to initial equilibrium	

Note regarding the expectations of money and credit market participants:
→ → → Assuming rationally formed expectations and an unanticipated increase in the money supply or assuming adaptively formed expectations
→ → → Assuming rationally formed expectations and an anticipated increase in the money supply

An initial expansion of the money supply stimulates aggregate expenditures. The higher level of aggregate expenditures makes prices rise and also makes output increase. This boost in real income stimulates real saving, which prevents the return of the interest rate to its original level. Thus, the increase in the money supply lowers the equilibrium interest rate, causes the price level to rise, and increases the equilibrium level of real income. This result conforms to the Keynesian hypotheses that the level of real income can be influenced by real aggregate expenditures and the interest rate can be influenced by the monetary authority.

It is important to point out that the New Classical rational expectations view of the economy is not incompatible with the Keynesian model. Money market and credit market participants may be assumed to formulate their price expectations rationally and to anticipate the increase in the money supply. Under this condition, the increase in the money stock translates immediately to a rise in the price level. There is no liquidity effect of money on interest. The linkage or transmission mechanism between changes in the money supply and the rest of the economy is modified by the colored trajectory in Table 12.2.[3]

[3]The New Classical interpretation does not rely on adaptive expectations to generate a linkage between the money supply and the interest rate. As long as real income is affected by money supply changes, interest rates will also be affected. Moreover, the effect of money on real income does not depend on expectational or informational asymmetry in the labor market. Labor suppliers agree to contracts wherein they essentially forfeit the opportunity to respond immediately to unanticipated changes in the price level caused by unanticipated changes in money supply. See Chapter Four for a discussion of the rationale behind such contracting.

Employers and workers in the labor market can also be assumed to form their expectations rationally and to anticipate certain systematic money supply increases at the time contracts are made. However, because of nominal wage contracting, featuring lagged adjustment to the effects of increases in the money stock that were unanticipated when contracts were negotiated, resulting price level increases that were therefore unanticipated when labor contracts were negotiated could generate a rise in employment. If labor market participants form their expectations rationally, we shall assume that the present increase in the money supply was unanticipated when labor contracts were made. Thus, when the price level increases, real income goes up and the interest rate falls as depicted by the black trajectories in the second row of Table 12.2.

Money Does Not Matter versus Only Money Matters

A traditional controversy in economics centers on the power of monetary policy in affecting real income in Keynesian models. In the 1940s and 1950s, many policy advisers contended that changes in the supply of money could have no effect on real income; that is, they believed that "money does not matter" for manipulating income and employment. Their argument was derived from two possible theoretical extremes. In case one, sometimes called *the liquidity trap,* the demand curve for money would be horizontal—perfectly interest elastic (panel c of Figure 12.2). In case two, the demand and supply curves for credit would be vertical—perfectly interest inelastic—and identical at the equilibrium level of real income (panel b of Figure 12.2). In neither case would a change in the supply of money affect real income. In case one, an excess supply of money could not occur. In case two, an excess supply of money would presumably have no effect on spending. In either of these extreme situations, only fiscal policy (a change in the government deficit) could affect output by shifting the demand curve for credit directly.

The antithesis of the "money does not matter" view is the perspective that "*only* money matters." According to this notion, the demand curve for money would be vertical and perfectly interest inelastic (panel c of Figure 12.2). In this situation, a change in the demand for credit would impel the interest rate upward but would not generate a change in output because no excess supply of money could occur.

This debate was once prominently featured in economics textbooks but has been rendered obsolete by two developments: (1) empirical studies (cited in the bibliography to Chapter Nine) show that the money demand curve is neither perfectly vertical nor perfectly flat and that the credit demand curve is not perfectly vertical; and (2) the focus of controversy has shifted from whether money matters in affecting output to whether *any* policy, monetary or fiscal, can have *any* significant systematic effect on output and employment. This controversy will be taken up shortly.

A Change in the Money Supply: Short Run versus Long Run

It is often said that Keynesian economics is the economics of the short run and that Neoclassical economics is the economics of the long run. This view is captured in Figure 12.2, which shows the result of the eventual adjustment in nominal wages paid to workers.

As time passes, workers are willing and able to contract for higher nominal wages. This is predicated on a greater demand for their services and a realization that at D'' (panel a of Figure 12.2) their real wage is lower than at A'', $w_1/P_2 < w_1/P_1$. The real wage is lower because the price level has risen to P_2, but the nominal wage w_1 has not changed. The supply of labor shifts upward to $g(w,P_3)$. When the nominal wage rises, costs of production for business firms rise and market-determined prices must increase. As the price level rises, the marginal revenue product of labor rises and the demand for labor moves up to $f(w,P_3)$. The nominal wage rises to w_3, employment falls to L_1, output goes to $(Y/P)_1$, and the real wage returns to its original level, $w_3/P_3 = w_1/P_1$. Equilibrium occurs at A''' in panel a. This is a position of long-run, full employment equilibrium.

In the credit market (panel b of Figure 12.2), the decrease in real disposable income to $(Y/P)_{d_1}$ causes the real saving function to shift leftward to $j[i, (Y/P)_{d_1}]$. The equilibrium interest rate is bid back up to i_1 at point A' (panel b), its long-run equilibrium level.

In the money market (panel c of Figure 12.2), the now higher interest rate (i_1) and the lower level of real income $(Y/P)_1$ provoke a decrease in the quantity of real money balances demanded and create an excess supply of money (AX) at price level P_2. The excess supply of money propels the price level upward to P_3 in the manner discussed in the previous chapter. As the price level increases to P_3, the real value of the nominal stock of money drops to M_3/P_3. Long-run equilibrium is restored at point A. The price level rises to P_3, increasing in proportion to the increase in money supply from M_1 to M_3. In the long run the quantity theory of money holds.

Thus, the upswing in real income and the dip in the interest rate caused by an increase in the money supply should be viewed as short-run phenomena, predicated on a lagged adjustment of nominal wages on the supply side of the labor market. As time passes, labor suppliers learn about the price level and are willing and able to negotiate higher nominal wages.[4] In the long run, the Neoclassical tenets are restored, and the increase in the money supply produces only a proportionate rise in the price level and the nominal wage with no lasting effects on real income, the interest rate, or the real wage.

Therefore, the Keynesian and Neoclassical theories of how the economy works are not irreconcilably and inexorably opposed. They are readily synthesized. Over a limited range of time, the short-run Keynesian theory is true. Over a longer interval, the long-run Neoclassical theory is true.

How short is the short run? How long is the long run? Economists disagree. Many Neoclassical economists believe that the short run is too short for monetary policymakers to try to manipulate real income or interest rates. Many Keynesian economists think that the long run is either of little consequence or else consists of a series of short runs so that monetary policy should be oriented toward influencing interest rates and real income.

Archetypal Keynesians believe that the economy is always in a short-run condition because it is continually being bombarded by significant and sizable disturbances from the private sector. These disturbances include the expansions and contractions of auton-

[4]The lag in the response of labor suppliers can be premised on a learning lag (an adaptive expectations scheme) or a response lag resulting from a rational expectations scheme where changes in the money supply were unanticipated at the time that implicit or explicit labor contracts were made and workers forfeited the opportunity to immediately adjust to the effects of these changes.

omous investment expenditures (private demand shocks) discussed in Chapter Seven, as well as the private sector supply shocks featured in Chapter Eleven and later in this chapter. (The effects of private demand shocks on the model are similar to the effects of changes in the government deficit.) In such an environment, there are repeated unanticipated variations in prices. As a consequence, employment and output are highly variable over time.

In contrast, many Neoclassicists believe that most swings in investment expenditures are not autonomous but reflect responses to cyclical variations in the real rate of interest and expected profits, as discussed in Chapter Six, and that many alleged supply shocks are only marginally significant despite what policymakers are often wont to claim, as discussed in Chapter Eleven. Instead, Neoclassicists view (unanticipated) swings in monetary and fiscal policy as significant disturbances to the economy. Some regard these as *the* most important sources of unanticipated price variations that, as previously discussed, give birth to most of the cyclical variations in employment, output, and the real interest rate. Other Neoclassicists believe that capacity-affecting supply shocks are a major source of cyclical movement. (See the discussion of the Real Business Cycle in Chapter Eleven.)

Keynesians counter the Neoclassical contention with the argument that the informational and expectational assumptions of the Neoclassical economists, especially those of the New Classical school, are unrealistic. They maintain that the assumption that market participants use all available sources of information to form expectations rationally disregards the cost of gathering information. Moreover, they argue that, in a realistic world featuring inflexible nominal wage contracting, the short run is of sufficiently long duration to be the focus of macroeconomic stabilization policy.

Implications for Macroeconomic Stabilization Policy

From the Keynesian perspective, monetary and fiscal policies are capable of combating demand shocks originating from the private sector or from previous macroeconomic policy. Neoclassical economists often say that even if shocks from the private sector are significant, they are too unpredictable to be the legitimate focus of macroeconomic policy. According to the New Classical variation on this Neoclassical theme, if demand shocks from the private sector were anticipated, there would be no need for a monetary or fiscal policy response because market participants would anticipate their effects on the price level and there would be no change in employment or output. If such private demand perturbations cannot be anticipated by market participants, they could not be anticipated by macroeconomic policymakers either. As long as private demand shocks are unanticipated, the policymaker, as well as the private decision maker, lacks the information to respond to them. If private demand shocks are anticipated, there is no need for policy action to counteract them. Because of the foregoing view of stabilization *policy ineffectiveness,* the New Classical school envisions a limited role for macroeconomic policy: a role of eliminating the unanticipated changes in monetary and fiscal policy which propel the economy away from its long-run, full employment equilibrium. Many Keynesians retort that policymakers often have an informational advantage and can effectively counteract demand shocks that emanate from the private sector because market participants, particularly labor market participants, are bound to nominal contractual arrangements that do not always correctly anticipate future policy.

Therefore, when certain segments of the body politic, certain interest groups, and certain political leaders become alarmed about high levels of unemployment and urge the Federal Reserve to engage in easier monetary or fiscal policy to relieve the unemployment problem, they may find support from Keynesian economists. When other interest groups and political leaders become incensed about high levels of interest rates and prompt the Federal Reserve to engage in easier monetary policy to bring interest rates down, they too may elicit aid from Keynesian economists. Typically, these same groups will find Neoclassical economists insensitive to their needs when it comes to using monetary or fiscal policy as a cure for high unemployment and/or high interest rates.

Archetypal Neoclassical economists envision monetary or fiscal policy as being incapable of manipulating unemployment and interest rates on anything except a very short run and/or unsystematic basis. Those interest groups and officials who rank price instability number one on their personal worry meters and want monetary policy to cure it will find wholehearted support from Neoclassical economists. Neoclassical economists often assert that monetary and fiscal policy responses that attempt to counteract private demand and supply shocks make macroeconomic policy less predictable and generate greater price instability. In their eyes, the unanticipated changes in macro policy account for most of the variation of output and employment.

Of course, the world of economics does not consist of two kinds of people; many economists are neither die-hard Keynesians nor rabid Neoclassicists. In the real world, economists fill the spectrum between these two polar positions. These eclectic individuals might, under certain circumstances, view the short run as being just long enough to justify the use of monetary policy to bring relief from low levels of real income and/or high interest rates. For those with Neoclassical leanings, such circumstances might include only the abysmally high unemployment associated with a particularly deep recession or a terrifying level of business bankruptcies associated with astronomically high interest rates, caused, for example, by a severe supply shock. Others still closer to the Neoclassical end of the spectrum might be very reluctant to promulgate an easy money fix for the same levels of unemployment and interest rates. These economists would tend to think that the inflationary aftermath of monetary or fiscal cure might be worse than the high unemployment or high interest rate illness. It is fair to conclude that if there are indeed only two kinds of economists in the world, the two groups do not consist of Keynesians and Neoclassicists but are comprised of economists who believe there are only two kinds of economists in the world and economists who do not.

This diversity of opinion among economists explains not only why economists can be found in all political camps but also why some so facilely switch their policy positions. Politicians can often reward economists who support their own, often improperly thought out, conclusions on monetary and fiscal policy. This situation leaves many people thoroughly confused as to whose economic theory is correct or whether any theory can be worthwhile. The public may get the impression that economic theories are like the New England soil—highly cultivated but naturally barren.

THE EFFECT OF A CHANGE IN THE GOVERNMENT DEFICIT

Figure 12.3 shows the effect of an increase in the government deficit on the Keynesian general equilibrium model. We begin from positions of long-run, full employment equilibrium. The money market is in equilibrium at A, the credit market is in equilibrium at A', and the labor market is in equilibrium at A'' (in panels c, b, and a, respectively). Assume an increase in the real deficit of government $(G/P - T/P)$ is wrought by an increase in government expenditures, ΔG. This shifts the demand for credit upward from $m(i) + (\overline{G}/P - \overline{T}/P)$ to $m(i) + (\overline{G}/P - \overline{T}/P + \Delta\overline{G}/P)$[5] (panel b). At the initial equilibrium interest rate this would create an excess demand for credit, the directed distance $A'X'$ in panel b. As in Chapter Eleven, we assume that the Ricardian equivalence proposition does not hold. In the partial equilibrium model of Chapter Six, excess demand would simply propel the interest rate to i_3, at B' in Figure 12.3. However, in the present general equilibrium model, at interest rate i_3, with the nominal stock of money M_1 and the price level P_1, there is an excess supply of money. This is measured by the directed distance BZ in panel c. It is assumed that individual nonhuman wealth consists of real money balances, the real value of bonds and existing consumer durables, and that the demand for consumer durables is unchanging. Finally, it is assumed either that market participants form their expectations of future prices rationally but do not anticipate the higher deficit or else form their expectations adaptively. Under these assumptions, individuals do not anticipate that the interest rate or the price level will rise. They have no incentive to acquire newly produced goods and services with these excess money balances. They can, however, efficiently balance their portfolios by employing these balances to acquire bonds, which are a closer substitute for money.

Under these conditions, at any rate greater than i_1 there is an excess supply of money which is equivalent to an excess demand for bonds. As individuals try to balance their portfolios by purchasing bonds, bond prices advance and the market rate of interest is prevented from rising to i_3, the rate that would place the credit market in equilibrium. Thus, the excess demand for credit persists over time at all rates of interest below i_3. The persistence of excess demand over time forges upward pressure on the prices of newly produced goods and services. This obtains because the condition of an excess demand for credit $(S/P < I/P + G/P - T/P)$ is related, through use of the aggregate budget identity, to the condition of an excess of real aggregate demand over real aggregate income $(Y/P < C/P + I/P + G/P)$. As this excess demand for newly produced goods and services persists, the prices of newly produced goods and services will be bid upward. The general price level will begin to rise.

If we alter the expectational assumption made earlier and assume that expectations are formed rationally and the increase in the deficit is anticipated, credit and money market

[5]If the increase in the deficit occurred because of a cut in taxation $(-\Delta T)$ and saving were specified to be a function of real *disposable* income $(Y/P - T/P)$, then a tax cut would increase real saving by a fraction, the marginal propensity to save, of the cut in taxation. However, the demand curve would shift further right than the supply curve, and the effects portrayed here would still hold.

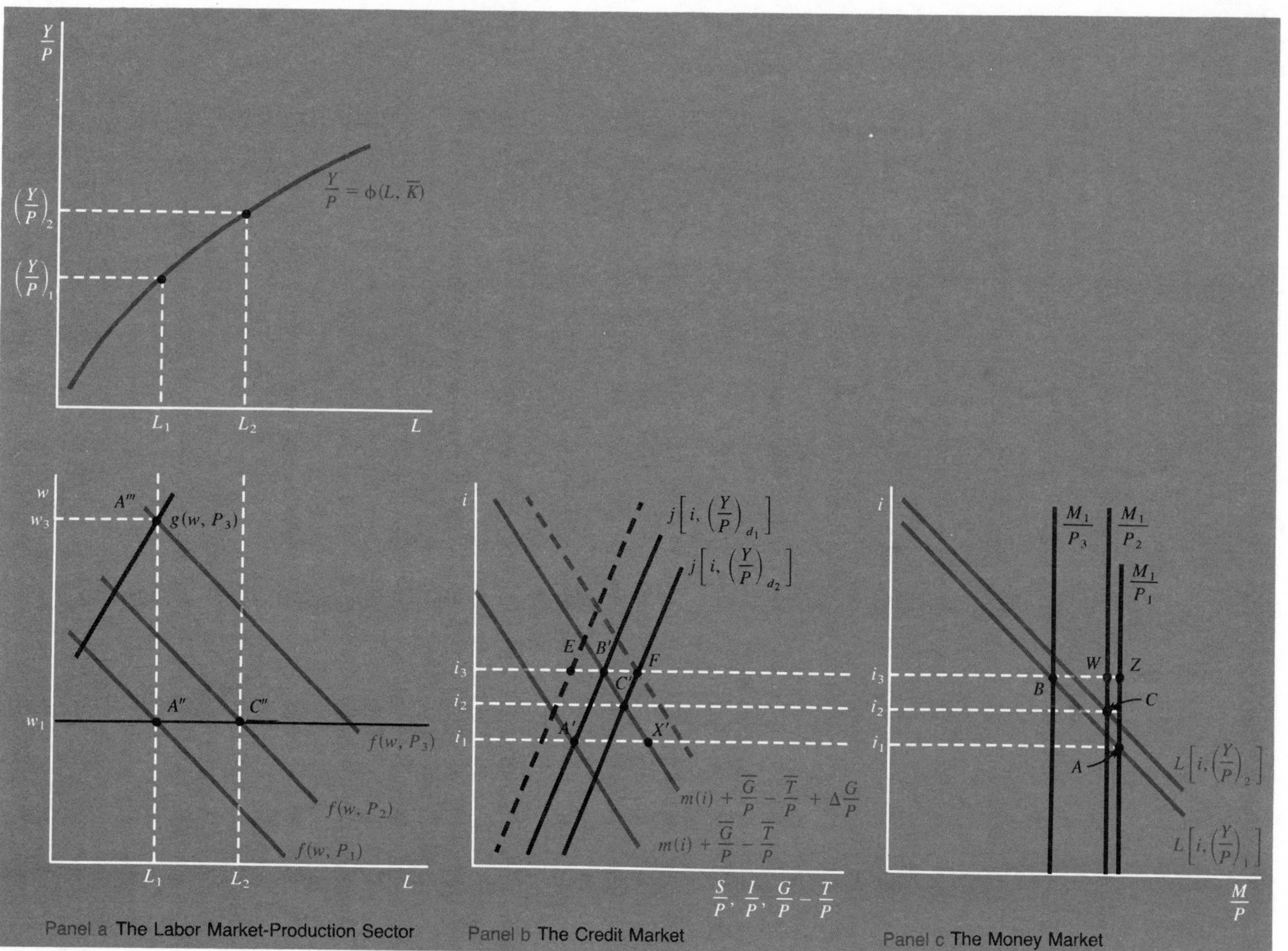

Figure 12.3 An Increase in the Government Deficit in the Keynesian General Equilibrium Model

participants will use the excess supply of money, BZ in panel c, to finance private expenditures in a like amount, EF in panel b. Small changes in the interest rate may signal market participants that a shock is occurring. They then may turn to published estimates of the government deficit to confirm their anticipation of this shock. The saving function would shift leftward (because consumption expenditures have increased), and the investment plus government deficit function would shift rightward (because investment expenditures have increased) to the positions indicated by the broken lines in panel b of Figure 12.3. At the unchanged interest rate i_3, there would be an excess of expenditures over output, measured by the directed distance EF. This condition would cause the price level to rise.

Up to this point, under either set of assumptions regarding the behavior of credit and money market participants, the preceding descriptions of the effect of an increase in the deficit are the same in the Keynesian model as in the Neoclassical model. Under either set of assumptions, the increase in the deficit incites a rise in the price level. Beyond this point, however, the two models differ. In the Neoclassical model, the price level goes to P_3 and the real value of the money stock contracts to M_1/P_3 (panel c of Figure 12.3). Equilibrium is restored to both money and credit markets at interest rate i_3 at points B and B'. There is no effect on employment and aggregate real income in the labor market–production sector as the nominal wage rises to w_3, proportional to the increase in the price level.

Under the Keynesian model, in contrast, as the price level is bid upward, it has an impact on the labor market. In panel a, the higher price level P_2 makes the demand for labor rise to $f(w, P_2)$ as firms realize that the marginal revenue product of labor is greater. However, because workers are assumed to be unaware of or unable to respond to the new price level, the supply of labor does not shift upward. The sign under the P term in Equation (12.2) is zero. The nominal wage is assumed rigid at w_1 [as depicted by the horizontal labor supply curve in panel a and the infinity sign under the w term in Equation (12.2)]. Therefore, there is an enormous jump in employment from L_1 to L_2 and an upswing in real income from $(Y/P)_1$ to $(Y/P)_2$. Equilibrium occurs at point C'' in panel a.

In short, the expansion of real income occurs because the increase in demand for credit associated with the enlarged government deficit provokes an increase in the interest rate. This results in an excess supply of money. The excess supply of money causes the excess of aggregate expenditures over aggregate output to persist. Because of imperfect information or imperfect response to information on the supply side of the labor market, the rise in aggregate expenditures is not totally absorbed by rising prices as it was in the Neoclassical model. Instead, part of the increase in expenditures is absorbed by higher real output.

As discussed in a previous section, imperfect information or imperfect response to information need not be confined to the labor market alone. These conditions may also exist in markets for other productive inputs and in output markets. If information is imperfect, suppliers who notice that the prices of their own products have risen might not associate the increase with a rise in the overall price level and increase the quantity supplied. If contracting exists, increases in demand for their products might require a quantity adjustment rather than a price adjustment. Therefore, the increase in aggregate real income that follows from a rise in the price level does not work exclusively through the labor market.

Because real income increases with taxation unchanged, real disposable income rises. Because real disposable income increases, real saving increases. In panel b of Figure 12.3, the real saving function shifts to the right to $j[i, (Y/P)_{d_2}]$. As explained in Chapter Six, the rise in real saving could also occur because lender attitudes toward risk are more optimistic during periods of cyclical expansion of aggregate real income. The expansion in real saving makes it unnecessary for the interest rate to ascend all the way to i_3. Equilibrium is restored to the credit market at interest rate i_2 at point C' (panel b of Figure 12.3).

The rise in the equilibrium level of real income from $(Y/P)_1$ to $(Y/P)_2$ generates the increase in the supply of credit (real saving) in the credit market. It also prompts the demand for real money balances to increase to $L[i, (Y/P)_2]$ (panel c). The higher equilibrium level of real income and the fact that the new equilibrium interest rate, i_2, is lower than it would have been had real saving not increased, $(i_2 < i_3)$, means that the quantity of real money balances demanded is greater than it would have been had the level of income not risen and the interest rate gone all the way to i_3. As a result, the price level does not have to move all the way up to P_3. The price level does not rise in proportion to the initial excess supply of money BZ as it did in the Neoclassical model. This is because the increased demand for real money balances at interest rate i_2 and real income level $(Y/P)_2$ absorb part of the initial excess supply of money. Only the remainder of that excess supply fuels the rise in the price level. Equilibrium is restored to the money market at a price level of P_2 and with real money balances of M_1/P_2 at point C (panel c). Points C, C' and C'' represent positions of short-run, super-full employment equilibrium.

The increase in the deficit of government causes the interest rate to rise. The higher interest rate actuates an excess supply of money balances. The resulting persistence of aggregate real expenditures over aggregate real output causes prices to rise. Because of imperfect information or imperfect response to information on the supply side of the labor market in this Keynesian model, the increase in prices causes real output to increase. The rise in real income stimulates real saving, which dampens the rise in the interest rate. Thus, an elevation of the real government deficit in this Keynesian model increases the interest rate, causes the price level to rise, and increases the equilibrium level of aggregate real income. This result conforms to the Keynesian hypothesis that the level of real income is determined by the level of real aggregate demand.

Table 12.3 summarizes the linkages in the Keynesian model. In the case where money and credit market participants form their price expectations rationally and anticipate the expanded deficit, it translates immediately to a rise in the price level. The linkage mechanism is modified by the colored trajectory in Table 12.3. Employers and workers can also be assumed to formulate their expectations rationally and to anticipate certain systematic changes in the deficit at the time labor contracts are made. However, because of nominal wage contracting featuring lagged adjustment to the effects of increases in the deficit that were unanticipated when contracts were made, resulting price level increases

Table 12.3 Linkage Mechanism: The Effect of an Increase in the Government Deficit in the Keynesian Model

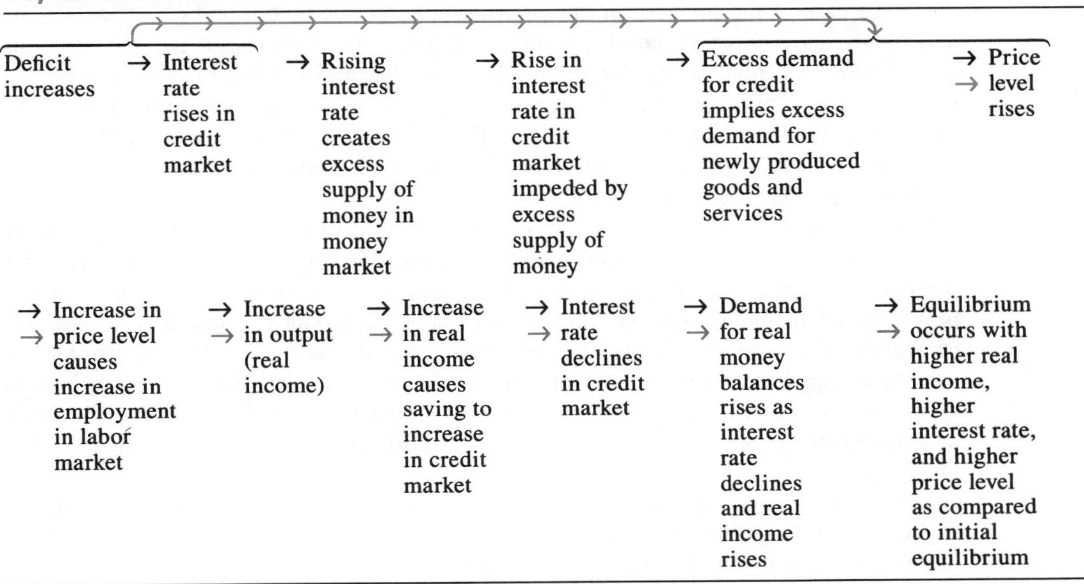

Deficit increases	→ Interest rate rises in credit market	→ Rising interest rate creates excess supply of money in money market	→ Rise in interest rate in credit market impeded by excess supply of money	→ Excess demand for credit implies excess demand for newly produced goods and services	→ → Price level rises
→ → Increase in price level causes increase in employment in labor market	→ → Increase in output (real income)	→ → Increase in real income causes saving to increase in credit market	→ → Interest rate declines in credit market	→ → Demand for real money balances rises as interest rate declines and real income rises	→ → Equilibrium occurs with higher real income, higher interest rate, and higher price level as compared to initial equilibrium

Note regarding the expectations of money and credit market participants:
→ → → Assuming rationally formed expectations and an unanticipated increase in the government deficit or assuming adaptively formed expectations
→ → → Assuming rationally formed expectations and an anticipated increase in the government deficit

could, therefore, generate a rise in employment.[6] If labor market participants form their expectations rationally, we shall assume that the present increase in the deficit was unanticipated when labor contracts were made. As a result, when the price level increases, real income goes up and the interest rate declines as depicted by the black trajectory in the second row of Table 12.3.

A Keynesian autonomous expenditures multiplier is at work here. An increase in government expenditures results in a rise in the (short-run) equilibrium level of aggregate real income. Because the increase in the deficit also causes the interest rate to rise, and the higher interest ràte chokes off some private expenditures, there is partial crowding out of private expenditures. Here the multiplier is not as great as the multiplier for the Keynesian model where the interest rate is assumed constant. In the latter model, discussed in Chapter Seven, there was zero crowding out.[7]

[6]Labor suppliers essentially forfeit the opportunity to respond to unanticipated changes in the government deficit. See Chapter Four for a discussion of the rationale behind such contracting.

[7]Additional crowding out could occur if the deficit were financed by the government selling newly issued bonds, which would cause the demand for money to rise if they were assumed to generate an increase in private wealth and/or a decrease in private liquidity. There would be an even greater rise in the interest rate and a smaller rise in the price level and real income because the demand for money would shift to the right

A Change in the Deficit: Short Run versus Long Run

As in the case of the increase in the money supply, points C, C', and C'' (panels a, b, and c, respectively, of Figure 12.3) represent positions of short-run but not long-run equilibrium. As time passes, labor suppliers are able and willing to ask for a higher nominal wage. This is predicated on two factors: an increased demand for their services and their realization that at C'' in panel a, the real wage w_1/P_2 is lower than at A'', $w_1/P_2 < w_1/P_1$. The real wage is lower because the price level has risen to P_2, but the nominal wage, w_1, has not changed.

The preceding discussion reveals what happens in the short run. In the longer run, as nominal wages respond, the supply curve of labor shifts upward to the line $g(w, P_3)$ through A''' (panel a). When the nominal wage rises, costs of production for business firms go up and market-determined prices of newly produced goods and services increase. As the general price level rises, the marginal revenue product of labor rises and the demand for labor shifts rightward to $f(w, P_3)$. The equilibrium nominal wage climbs to w_3, the real wage goes back up to its initial level, $w_1/P_1 = w_3/P_3$. The level of employment returns back down to L_1. The equilibrium level of real income returns to $(Y/P)_1$.

In the credit market (panel b of Figure 12.3), as real disposable income falls back to $(Y/P)_{d_1}$, real saving shifts back to $j[i, (Y/P)_{d_1}]$ and the interest rate goes to i_3 at point B'. We return to a position of complete crowding out.

In the money market (panel c of Figure 12.3), the now higher interest rate (i_3) and lower level of real income, $(Y/P)_1$, create an excess supply of money (BW) at price level P_2. This excess supply of money impels the price level upward to P_3 in the fashion discussed in the previous chapter. Long-run equilibrium is restored at point B.

Thus, the increase in real income should be viewed as a short-run phenomenon based on the lagged response to information on the supply side of the labor market. In the long run, labor suppliers respond to the higher price level and negotiate a higher nominal wage.[8] In the long run, there can be no increase in real income above the full employment level $(Y/P)_1$, and the expansion in the government deficit brings only a rise in the interest rate and an increase in the price level while, under conditions discussed in the previous chapter, Neoclassical results could occur in the short run in the present context. The distinction between short run and long run is the basic difference between Keynesian and Neoclassical macroeconomic theories.

---

in panel c of Figure 12.3. If there were an increase in the demand for money, and if the newly issued bonds were poor substitutes for money and were viewed as making portfolios very illiquid, then crowding out conceivably could be complete. The fiscal policy multiplier would be zero even in the short run. See the bibliography to Chapter Six for further reading on crowding out in Keynesian general equilibrium models.

The effects on the model of a private demand shock arising from increases in autonomous private investment expenditures or private consumption expenditures are similar to the effects of an increase in the government deficit. As discussed in Chapter Seven, disturbances in private spending are considered significant in Keynesian analysis.

[8]As discussed earlier, the lagged response of workers can result from a learning lag based on adaptive expectations or on a response lag based on rational formulation of expectations where changes in the government deficit were not anticipated at the time implicit or explicit labor contracts were made.

Implications for Fiscal Policy

For fiscal policy, as in the case of monetary policy, the short-run–long-run distinction explains the conflicting policy positions of economists regarding fiscal policy. From a short-run Keynesian perspective, an increase in the government deficit is viewed as stimulating employment and output (a multiplier effect) without bidding interest rates up too much. Therefore, increases in the government deficit would be acceptable during periods of recession. From a longer-run, Neoclassical perspective, enlarged deficits are not seen as having any effect on employment and real income but only as causes of higher prices and higher interest rates. In turn, higher interest rates reflect the crowding out of private expenditures by government expenditures.[9]

Concluding Comment

This chapter presents the effect of two experiments in a Keynesian general equilibrium model of the economy. The Keynesian model is distinguished from the Neoclassical model of the previous chapter by the presence of lagged responses on the supply side of the labor market.

The two experiments that are described involve (1) an increase in the quantity of money and (2) an increase in the government deficit.[10] In the money supply experiment, the initial excess supply of money creates an excess of aggregate expenditures over aggregate output which pushes the price level up. Given this increase in the price level, the presence of asymmetrical responses in the labor market results in an expansion in employment and real income in the short run. The rise in real income causes real saving to rise and the interest rate to decline relative to their initial long-run equilibrium levels. With a higher level of real income and a lower interest rate, the quantity of real money balances demanded rises. This precludes a great rise in the price level in the short run. In the long run, in the labor market, employment and real income return to their long-run equilibrium levels. As real income declines, so does real saving. As real saving falls, the interest rate rises to its long-run equilibrium level. With real income falling and the interest rate rising to their long-run equilibrium levels, the quantity of real money balances demanded falls to its long-run equilibrium level. As a result, the price level rises to its long-run equilibrium level. The jump in the price level is proportional to the increase in the quantity of money.

In the deficit experiment, the enlarged deficit initially causes the interest rate to rise and provokes an excess supply of money. The ensuing rise in the price level, given the presence of asymmetrical responses in the labor market, instigates an increase in the equilibrium levels of employment and real income in the short run. The increase in real

[9]As discussed in Chapter Fourteen, the deficits associated with the Reagan administration's tax cuts were widely seen as leading to crowding out. However, benefits in the form of greater economic growth were expected later in the decade.

[10]A handy comparison of the effects of these two experiments appears in Table 1.3 of Chapter One. This table summarizes in condensed form Tables 11.1, 11.2, 11.3, 12.2, and 12.3.

income makes real saving rise and the interest rate decline relative to their previous levels. With a higher level of real income and lower interest rates, the quantity of real money balances demanded rises, precluding a great rise in the price level in the short run. In the long run, employment and real income return to their long-run equilibrium levels. When real income falls, so does real saving. The decline in real saving forces the interest rate to rise to its long-run equilibrium level. The decline in real income and rise in the interest rate to their long-run equilibrium levels forces the quantity of real money balances demanded to fall to its long-run equilibrium level. As a result, an excess supply of money propels the price level to its long-run equilibrium.

EXERCISES

1. What result or results make a model Keynesian? What key assumptions produce Keynesian results? How does less than full employment equilibrium arise?
2. What is "stagflation"? Give two explanations of stagflation using a Keynesian general equilibrium model. What is the appropriate monetary policy response?
3. Explain why Keynesian models cannot be clearly understood in the partial equilibrium context of Chapter Seven, but instead require a general equilibrium outlook.
4. Why does an increase in the government deficit not result in complete crowding out in a Keynesian model?
5. Evaluate the following statement: "In a Keynesian model, the quantity theory holds because an increase in the money supply drives up the price level."
6. In a Keynesian general equilibrium model, why does the money supply influence the equilibrium interest rate? Does this represent a liquidity effect of money on the interest rate?
7. Evaluate the following statement: "The notion that Keynesian economics is true in the short run and that Neoclassical economics is true in the long run is too simple-minded. The two theories differ in so many complex ways and are so inexorably opposed that simple reconciliation is impossible."
8. Using a Keynesian general equilibrium model, predict the effect of a decrease in the price of an imported raw material.
9. Evaluate the following statement: "Even though the quantity theory of money does not hold in a Keynesian model, an increase in the price level is still motivated by an excess supply of money."
10. If credit and money market participants form expectations rationally and anticipate the deficit, how can an increase in the deficit be linked causally to a change in real income in a Keynesian model? Are labor market participants behaving rationally in this case?

11. Assume that there are significant demand shocks emanating from the private sector of the economy. Under what conditions would an active macroeconomic stabilization policy of counteracting these shocks be justifiable?

12. What determines the magnitude of the autonomous expenditures multiplier in a Keynesian general equilibrium model?

BIBLIOGRAPHY

Gilbert, Charles. "The Rational Expectations Hypothesis: Survey and Recent Research." In *Modern Concepts in Macroeconomics,* ed. Thomas M. Havrilesky. Arlington Heights, Ill.: Harlan Davidson, Inc., 1985.

Hansen, Alvin. *A Guide to Keynes*. New York: McGraw-Hill, 1953.

Hicks, John R. "Mr. Keynes and the 'Classics': A Suggested Interpretation." *Econometrica* 12 (1937), pp. 147–159.

Hines, A. G. *On the Reappraisal of the Economics of Keynes*. London: Martin Robertson, 1971.

Keynes, John Maynard. *The General Theory of Employment, Interest and Money*. New York: Harcourt, Brace and Co., 1936.

Klein, Lawrence. *The Keynesian Revolution*. New York: Macmillan, 1947.

Leijonhufvud, Axel. *On Keynesian Economics or the Economics of Keynes*. New York: Oxford University Press, 1968.

Lucas, Robert E., and Thomas J. Sargent. "After Keynesian Macroeconomics." In *Modern Concepts in Macroeconomics,* ed. Thomas M. Havrilesky. Arlington Heights, Ill.: Harlan Davidson, Inc., 1985.

Mishkin, Frederic. *A Rational Expectations Approach to Macroeconomics: Testing Policy Effectiveness and Efficient Markets Models*. Chicago: University of Chicago Press, 1983.

Modigliani, Franco. "The Monetarist Controversy, or Should We Forsake Stabilization Policies?" *American Economic Review* (March 1972), pp. 1–18.

______. "Liquidity Preference and the Theory of Interest and Money." In American Economic Association, *Readings on Monetary Theory*. New York: McGraw-Hill, 1951, pp. 186–240.

Park, Yung Chul. "Some Current Issues on the Transmission Process of Monetary Policy." *Staff Papers*. Washington, D.C.: International Monetary Fund, March 1972, pp. 1–43.

Shiller, Robert J. "Rational Expectations and the Dynamic Structure of Macroeconomic Models." *Journal of Monetary Economics* 4 (December 1978), pp. 1–44.

Smith, Warren. "A Graphical Exposition of the Complete Keynesian System." *Southern Economic Journal* (October 1956), pp. 115–125.

Taylor, John B. "Aggregate Dynamics and Staggered Contracts." *Journal of Political Economy* 88 (February 1980), pp. 1–23.

______. "The Role of Expectations in the Choice of Monetary Policy." In *Modern Concepts in Macroeconomics,* ed. Thomas M. Havrilesky. Arlington Heights, Ill.: Harlan Davidson, Inc., 1985.

Tobin, James. "Inflation and Unemployment." *American Economic Review* (March 1972), pp. 1–18.

______, and William Buiter. "Long Term Effects of Fiscal and Monetary Policy on Aggregate Demand." In *Monetarism,* ed. Jerome Stein. Amsterdam: North Holland, 1976, pp. 37–59.

The Causes and Consequences of Changes in Money Supply Growth

Chapter 13

Introduction

Chapters Ten, Eleven, and Twelve developed two different general equilibrium models of the economy, Keynesian and Neoclassical. Chapter Eleven analyzed the effect of three types of exogenous shocks on the Neoclassical model: (1) a demand shock in the form of an increase in the supply of money, (2) a demand shock in the form of an increase in the government deficit, and (3) a supply shock in the form of an increase in the price of an imported raw material. Chapter Twelve analyzed the effect of just the first two of the shocks on the Keynesian model. Each exogenous shock was treated as an isolated, one-time-only phenomenon.

In reality, our economy does not always work this way. Shocks are often interrelated. For example, a large, unchanging level of the government deficit (a flow) is often accompanied by continual increases in the money supply (a stock) on the part of the Federal Reserve System. Moreover, other things influence the money supply policy of the Fed.

Because of these interrelationships, the growth rate of the money supply is not steady; it fluctuates, sometimes drastically. What are the effects of pronounced accelerations and decelerations in the growth of the money supply? Will interest rates, asset prices, the prices of newly produced goods and services, output, and employment rise, fall, or be unaffected by such changes? The answer to these questions depends on whether the structure of the economic real world is Neoclassical or Keynesian. This, in turn, depends on the extent to which market participants anticipate and respond to changes in money growth.

The major purpose of this chapter is to apply the general equilibrium reasoning of the previous chapters to the problem of concurrent shocks to the economy. The interrelationships of the government deficit and other factors on the money supply policy of the Federal Reserve System will be examined. Another purpose of this chapter is to apply this general equilibrium reasoning to the consequences of ever-changing growth rates of the money supply. In short, this chapter explores the causes and consequences (for interest rates, asset prices, the price level, output, and employment) of changes in money supply growth.

SOURCES OF MONETARY INSTABILITY

There are essentially two sources of monetary instability: the response of monetary policy to the magnitude of the government deficit, and the response of monetary policy to shocks to the economy that emanate from the private sector.

No link necessarily exists between the level of the real government deficit and the supply of money. As indicated in Chapter Five, the real deficit ($G/P - T/P$) is a flow. As such, it occurs over an interval of time. The United States Treasury finances the federal deficit by periodically selling newly issued bonds in the credit market. The periodic selling of new bonds by the Treasury to finance the deficit does not necessarily tie-in to the money stock determining activity of the Federal Reserve, a separate agency.

One of the partial equilibrium, closed economy models of Chapter Six demonstrates that an increase in the real government deficit boosts the interest rate. The Neoclassical general equilibrium, closed economy model of Chapter Eleven shows that a hike in the real government deficit makes the interest rate ascend to a new level and forces the price level to increase also. In the Keynesian model of Chapter Twelve, an increase in the deficit not only elevates the interest rate and price level, but also generates a (temporary) rise in employment and real income. As in previous chapters, as long as the expected rate of inflation is constant, a change in the real interest rate is synonymous with a change in the nominal interest rate.

The real deficit is a flow. If the real deficit does not change from one year to another, the magnitude of the real demand for credit (loanable funds) will not vary, *ceteris paribus*. According to the first partial equilibrium model in Chapter Six, there can be no change in the equilibrium interest rate. With no variation in the level of the real deficit and the equilibrium interest rate, there can be no excess of aggregate real expenditures over aggregate output. Therefore, an unchanging deficit, no matter how large, apparently can generate no pressure for the general price level to rise.

Despite these unambiguous, theoretical predictions, conventional wisdom has come to associate a large but unchanging deficit with a high rate of price inflation. In Chapter Eleven, four possible reasons were established for this connection. First, it was argued that the high interest rate brought about by a large deficit could induce a steady economizing in the demand for money. A continual leftward shift in the demand for money would generate inflation in the general equilibrium model.

The second reason is that a large deficit leads to continued crowding out. This, in turn, lowers real income and real saving over time. The continual fall in saving causes a continual rise in the interest rate. With a steady rise in the interest rate and a steady fall in real income, the quantity of real money balances demanded falls continually. The resulting continual excess supply of money fuels a steady rise in the price level, *ceteris paribus*.

A third reason is that the large deficit could cause a steady rise in the ratio of the stock of government debt to GNP. As discussed in Chapter Six, the demand to hold most forms of wealth varies proportionately with income. If the stock of debt is growing faster than GNP, supply is growing faster than demand. The continued excess supply of government debt will depress its price and raise the interest rate. A continually declining interest rate will cause a steady reduction in the quantity of real money balances demanded, creating a continual excess supply of money. This will cause a continual rise in the price level. Thus, there is a third plausible link between a large and unchanging deficit and inflation.

A fourth, and most important reason why an unchanging deficit could lead to inflation, is that the size of the federal budget deficit sometimes influences the money supply policy of the Federal Reserve. Because of political antipathy toward high interest rates caused by a large and unchanging real federal deficit, historically, the Federal Reserve has often sought to reduce the interest rate by increasing the money supply. Therein, a link between a large, unchanging deficit and continuing inflation is forged by political pressure on the Federal Reserve's Federal Open Market Committee (FOMC) to *monetize the deficit*.

Now, assume that because the increased government deficit has crowded out real private expenditures, there is considerable public antipathy toward the higher equilibrium rate of interest. Assume further that attempts to bring down the interest rate by reducing the deficit through raising taxes or cutting government expenditures are politically infeasible. As pointed out in Chapters Eleven and Twelve, under certain conditions changes in the money supply can allow the Federal Reserve to manipulate the interest rate in the short run. Pressure will be brought upon the Federal Open Market Committee (FOMC) to "do something" about interest rates. Pressure could come directly from the Oval Office or Congress and indirectly from lobbying groups for certain interest-sensitive sectors of the economy, such as home builders, mortgage lenders, construction firms, building materials industries, actual and potential homeowners, debt-sensitive business firms, and financial intermediaries.

Pressures can arise from within government itself.[1] A chilling fact of economic life is that it ultimately may not be feasible to finance a sizable, perennial government deficit without money supply accommodation. As discussed above, a large unchanging deficit adds to the outstanding government debt year after year. If the government debt grows faster than GNP, interest payments on that debt grow without limit, thereby eventually forcing government into insolvency. Federal Reserve monetization of deficits may be demanded in order to forestall, if only temporarily, the snowballing of interest costs that would lead to insolvency.

[1]Two studies by the author reporting evidence of White House pressure on Federal Reserve policy are cited in the bibliography to this Chapter.

Because of these multiple pressures, political fortunes of members of Congress and the President are extremely sensitive to the level of interest rates. This fact once prompted a wag to suggest that the FOMC be renamed CREEP, the Committee to Re-elect the President.

Another source of pressure on the Federal Reserve System to increase the money supply might be associated with the effects of a supply shock, such as an increase in the price of an imported raw material.[2] The raw material price increase initially boosts the general price level. As the general price level rises, the real value of money balances contracts, and this shortage of liquidity temporarily increases the interest rate. In addition, as discussed in Chapter Eleven, as long as the supply shock significantly curtails our productive capacity, employment and output would permanently contract, and the interest rate would permanently ascend to a higher level. Thus, the increase in the price of an imported raw material could provoke temporarily, as well as permanently, higher levels of the interest rate and unemployment.

To stave off impending economic discomfort, the FOMC might be tempted to respond to a noncapacity reducing supply shock by expanding the money supply. Under certain conditions, a jump in the money supply could prevent the temporary hike in the interest rate. A rise in the money supply could block the initial boost in the interest rate associated with the original decline in real money balances, brought about by the initial increase in the price level. If the money supply swells in response to the threat of a temporarily higher interest rate, the initial elevation in the price level brought about by the increase in the price of the raw material will persist. There will be no necessity for the price level to subsequently decline. The initial increase in the price level will have been "validated" or "ratified" by the monetary authority.

If the supply shock significantly constrains the productive capacity of our economy, a process of money supply expansion cannot alter the eventual contraction in real income and the rise in the interest rate. Nevertheless, it could temporarily postpone these ultimate consequences by stimulating an economic boom in the short run.

In anticipation of these consequences, many people both in and out of the Federal Reserve will argue that the Federal Reserve can and should "do something" about a high rate of interest and a high level of unemployment. What the Federal Reserve apparently can do is bring the interest rate down by increasing the supply of money. Many believe that the Federal Reserve can lower the rate of interest for one or more of the following three immediate reasons: (1) They take a partial equilibrium view of the money market (such that any increase in the money supply is believed to have the "obvious" liquidity effect of forcing down the interest rate); (2) they have a Keynesian general equilibrium view of the economy (such that an increase in the money supply stimulates a boom and lowers the interest rate and unemployment in the short run); or (3) they have a Neoclassical general equilibrium view of the economy, but it is accompanied by an overwhelmingly short-run orientation, for instance, caring about crowding out at current interest rates and heavily discounting the future inflationary consequences of trying to bring

[2]A private demand shock emanating from a substantial change in autonomous consumption or autonomous investment expenditures could also elicit pressure on the Federal Reserve. The effects of a private demand shock on the model are similar to the effects of a change in the government deficit.

interest rates down through monetary stimulation (for example, the possible liquidity effect of money on interest). All three of these immediate reasons are premised on the implicit assumption that either the expectations of money, credit, or labor market participants are formed rationally and the proposed expansion in the money supply will be unanticipated or the expectations of market participants are formed adaptively.

In light of these pressures and beliefs, Federal Reserve officials historically have often responded to a large but stable government deficit, to a supply shock, or to a private demand shock (see footnote 2) by unleashing the money supply. Now the consequences of such a response will be examined in terms of our general equilibrium model.

Figure 13.1 presents a picture of only the credit and money markets. The labor market-production sector is temporarily ignored. Suppose that a supply shock has curtailed productive capacity such that the market rate of interest is i_1, the price level is P_1, and the level of real income is $(Y/P)_1$. The model would tend to remain in equilibrium at points A and A' (panels b and c, respectively).

The increase in the supply of money from M_1 to M_2 (panel b of Figure 13.1) with the price level unchanged in the short run creates, at the initial equilibrium interest rate i_1, an excess supply of money. This excess supply of money is shown as a line segment $A'B'$ (panel c). As discussed earlier, an excess supply of money places individual portfolios in disequilibrium.

As in Chapter Eleven, there are two alternative conceptions of the linkage between an excess supply of money and its effect on the price level. One is based on the assumption that market participants form their expectations adaptively or form their expectations rationally and do not anticipate the excess supply of money. The alternative is that market participants form their expectations rationally and anticipate the excess supply of money. Assuming initially that the expectations of credit and money market participants in Figure 13.1 are formed adaptively or are formed rationally and the money supply increase is unanticipated, the resulting excess demand for bonds jacks up bond prices and, as can be seen from the present value formula, causes the bond yield, the market rate of interest, to decline to i_0. As the market rate falls, the quantity of real money balances demanded rises. At C' (panel c) the quantity of real money balances demanded equals the real value of the nominal stock of money, M_2/P_1. The money market is in equilibrium.

However, at i_0 the credit market is not in equilibrium; there is an excess demand for credit, as measured by the line segment C_0C_1 (panel b). This translates, via the aggregate budget identity, into an excess of aggregate real expenditures over aggregate output. The excess aggregate demand for goods and services propels the general price level upward to P_2. This causes the real value of the nominal supply of money to fall to M_2/P_2 in panel c. The interest rate rises back to i_1 and equilibrium is restored to both markets at points A and A', respectively. (These effects of an increase in the money supply were discussed in detail in Chapter Eleven.)

Thus, the initial liquidity effect of money on interest is the decline in the interest rate from i_1 to i_0, wrought by the excess supply of money (liquidity). This effect is followed by a nominal income effect of money on interest, the rise in the interest rate from i_0 back to i_1. The nominal income effect is generated by the excess of aggregate expenditures over aggregate output at the interest rate i_0. Excess aggregate demand for goods and

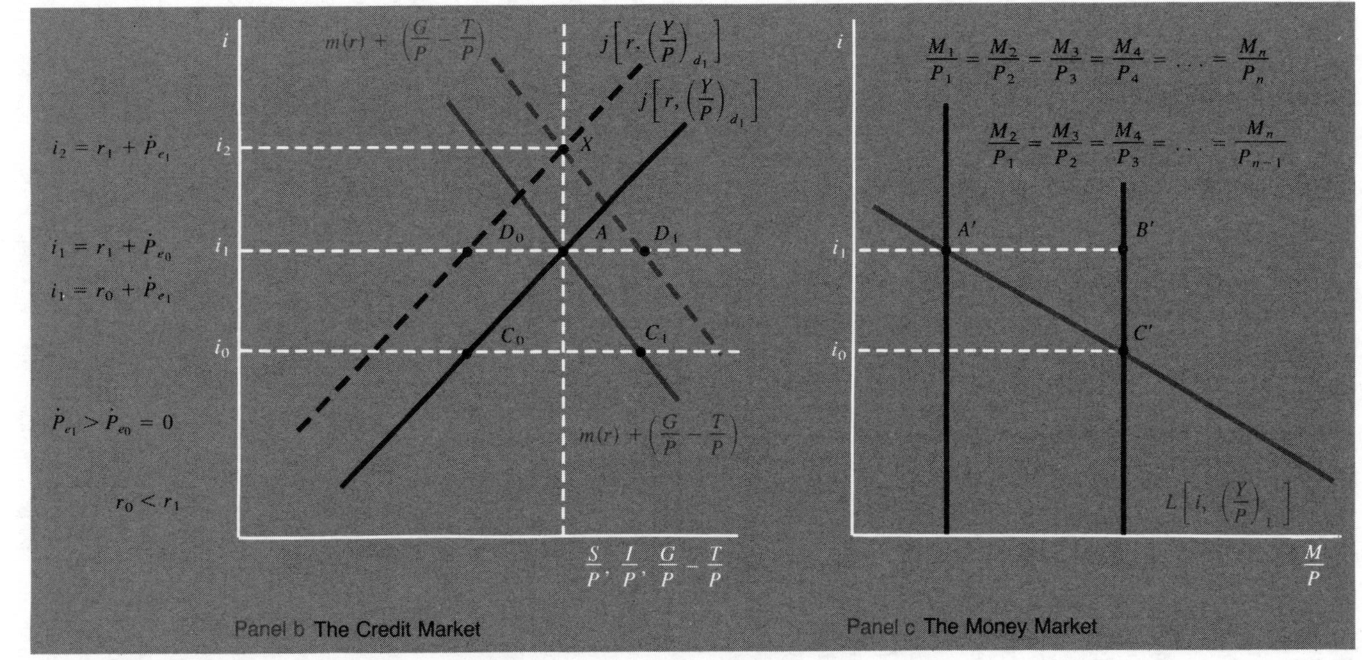

Figure 13.1 The Federal Reserve Attempts to Reduce the Market Rate of Interest

services pushes up the price level to P_2 and, obviously, increases aggregate nominal income, which, by definition, is the product of the price level and (unchanged) real income $[P \cdot (Y/P) \equiv Y]$. Therefore, the conscious attempt by the Federal Reserve to lower the interest rate can only work, if at all, in the short run by way of the liquidity effect. In the longer run, the nominal income effect takes hold and the interest rate returns to its initial level.

As an alternative, where the expectations of money and credit market participants are formed rationally and where the increase in the money supply is anticipated, the initial excess supply of money is not used to acquire bonds. Market participants expect that any fall in the interest rate will be temporary, and bonds acquired at an interest rate below i_1 will fall in price when the interest rate rises. Therefore, the excess supply of money $A'B'$ is used to make downpayments on newly produced goods and services. At interest rate i_1, there is an excess of expenditures over output. This is reflected in the upward shift in both supply and demand functions in panel b to the positions denoted by the broken lines. At interest rate i_1, the excess supply of money $A'B'$ fuels the excess of expenditures over output D_0D_1. There is no temporary liquidity effect of money on interest, and the price level immediately rises to P_2.

Under either set of expectational assumptions, it should be remembered that if there are asymmetrical responses to the higher price level in the labor market, the level of employment and output will temporarily rise. If real disposable income does temporarily rise, real saving will also temporarily increase. If real disposable income rises to a level greater than $(Y/P)_{d_1}$, this will temporarily lower the interest rate as the saving function in panel b will shift to the right of $j[r, (Y/P)_{d_1}]$. (As discussed in Chapter Six, a rise in real income will also increase real tax receipts, reduce the government deficit, and further lower the interest rate.) Thus, the jump in the money supply will provide a temporary respite from the interest rate i_1 as well as a temporary boom in employment and output. (This pattern is not depicted in Figure 13.1 but is discussed at length in Chapter Twelve.)

Regardless of which of the alternative linkage mechanisms holds in reality, there is no reason to suppose any diminution in pressures on the Federal Reserve to bring the interest rate down and/or to stimulate employment and output. Again, the Federal Reserve will increase the nominal quantity of money—this time to M_3 from M_2 (panel c of Figure 13.1). Again, the new quantity of money, M_3 at the initial price level P_2, generates an excess supply of money—liquidity ($A'B'$ in panel c). This excess supply of money under either of the preceding expectational schemes provokes an excess of aggregate real expenditures over aggregate output. The price level rising to P_3 implies that real money balances shrink back to M_3/P_3 (panel c). This restores equilibrium at points A and A'. Again, because of the expectational behavior of money, credit, and market participants, increasing the money supply may have a transitory effect on the interest rate as well as a transitory effect on employment and output.

Is there any reason to believe that pressure on the Federal Reserve will cease? Many market participants savor the possible temporary relief provided from high interest rates and high unemployment but psychologically block out the disappointment of the eventual rise in interest rates and rise in unemployment. Once again, the Federal Reserve will increase the nominal stock of money, and, once again, there may be relief—but, alas, it will be only temporary. What will be the end result of the Federal Reserve's *easy money* policy?

Period after period, the Federal Reserve has increased the money supply, first from M_1 to M_2, then from M_2 to M_3, then from M_3 to M_4, then from M_4 to M_5, and so on. This results in a higher *growth rate* of the money supply of $\dot{M}_1$:

$$\dot{M}_1 = \frac{M_2 - M_1}{M_1} = \frac{M_3 - M_2}{M_2} = \frac{M_4 - M_3}{M_3} = \frac{M_5 - M_4}{M_4} = \ldots = \frac{M_n - M_{n-1}}{M_{n-1}}$$

where $\dot{M} = (\Delta M/\Delta t)/M$ and Δt is an interval of time.

The only lasting effect of the higher growth rate of the money supply is a period-after-period increase in the general price level which results in a positive rate of inflation, $\dot{P}_1$:

$$\dot{P}_1 = \frac{P_2 - P_1}{P_1} = \frac{P_3 - P_2}{P_2} = \frac{P_4 - P_3}{P_3} = \ldots = \frac{P_n - P_{n-1}}{P_{n-1}}$$

where $\dot{P} = (\Delta P/\Delta t)/P$ and Δt is an interval of time. In essence, a new rate of money supply growth $\dot{M}_1$ results in the long run in a new, proportionately higher rate of inflation, $\dot{P}_1$. This result conforms to the *quantity theory of money,* which was discussed in Chapters Nine through Twelve.

As discussed in Chapter Six, the behavior of credit market participants will always assure that, in equilibrium, the nominal rate of interest is equal to the expected, or *ex ante,* real rate of interest plus the expected rate of inflation:

$$i = r + \dot{P}_e$$

Initially, before the onset of new, higher rate of money supply growth, the rate of growth of the money supply was zero and there was a zero expected rate of inflation, $\dot{P}_{e_0} = 0$ such that the nominal and real rates of interest were equal:

$$i_1 = r_1 + \dot{P}_{e0} \qquad (13.1)$$

where $\dot{P}_{e_0} = 0$, i is the nominal rate of interest, and r is the expected, or *ex ante,* real rate of interest.

To keep the analysis simple, assume that the expected rate of inflation is equal to the actual rate of inflation (this assumption will be relaxed later in the chapter):

$$\dot{P}_e = \dot{P} \qquad (13.2)$$

In this situation, as long as the nominal rate of interest is at i_1, the expected real rate will fall to r_0 when the expected rate of inflation rises to $\dot{P}_{e_1}(= \dot{P}_1)$:

$$i_1 = r_0 + \dot{P}_{e_1} \qquad (13.3)$$

where $r_0 < r_1$.

Real saving behavior and real investment behavior depend on the real rate of interest, not the nominal rate of interest, as discussed in Chapter Six. A lower expected real rate of interest, instigated by the expectation of a higher rate of inflation with the nominal rate unchanged, will cause the real saving (supply) function to shift leftward to the position denoted by the broken line in panel b of Figure 13.1. This leftward shift occurs because real saving varies directly with the expected real rate of interest. As long as the nominal rate of interest is unchanged at a higher expected rate of inflation, the expected real rate must decline. A lower expected real rate of interest will also cause the investment (demand) function to shift rightward to the position denoted by the broken line in panel b. This rightward shift occurs because real investment expenditures vary inversely with the expected real rate of interest, and, as long as the nominal rate of interest is unchanged, given the higher expected rate of inflation, the expected, or *ex ante,* real rate must fall.

These movements in real saving and real investment functions can also be viewed as vertical shifts. For the level of real saving and the level of real investment to remain the same, the expected real rate of interest must not vary. For the expected real rate to remain unchanged, the nominal rate of interest must rise sufficiently to reflect fully the expected rate of inflation. For this to occur, the real saving and real investment functions must each shift upward by the expected rate of inflation to the positions denoted by the broken lines in panel b.

As the supply and demand curves shift upward in the same proportion, they will intersect at point X (panel b of Figure 13.1). The resulting equilibrium nominal rate of interest will completely capture the new, expected rate of inflation $\dot{P}_{e_1}$:

$$i_1 = r_0 + \dot{P}_{e_1} \tag{13.3}$$

With the nominal rate of interest now fully reflecting expected inflation, the expected, or *ex ante,* real rate of interest returns to its initial level r_1. At the same real interest rate, r_1, real saving and real investment are unchanged from their initial equilibrium values at A in panel b.

Ironically, the attempts of the Federal Reserve to hold down the real rate of interest and stimulate real income by letting money supply growth soar generate, in the long run, not a lower real rate of interest and more output but an unchanged real rate of interest and an unchanged level of output. Moreover, the nominal rate of interest will not decline; it will, in fact, rise to fully reflect the higher rate of inflation.

These rather bleak long-run predictions of economic theory do not deter practical-minded individuals from pressing for an easy money policy. As indicated at the outset of this section, there are powerful motivations for easy money. Anterior to all of these motivations is the implicit assumption that either the expectations of money, credit, or labor market participants are formed rationally and increases in the money supply are unanticipated or that the expectations of market participants are formed adaptively. When imputed to the expectational behavior of money and credit market participants, this implicit assumption nurtures the hope for a temporary liquidity effect of money on interest. When imputed to the expectational behavior of labor market participants, it nourishes the hope for a transitory expansion of employment and real income and a transitory decline in interest rates, all fueled by money supply expansion.

Are these wishes idle fantasy? Are expectations formed adaptively or are money supply expansions generally unanticipated by market participants such that they actually can catalyze an economic boom and/or depress the real interest rate? In other words, can policymakers fool a lot of the people a lot of the time? In the next section we will look at the facts. We will examine the data regarding money supply growth and subsequent movements in interest rates, inflation, and employment.

THE EMPIRICAL RELATIONSHIPS BETWEEN MONEY GROWTH, INFLATION, UNEMPLOYMENT, AND INTEREST RATES

Chart 13.1 illustrates a close relationship between money growth and inflation. Both money and the price level are plotted as annual, average rates of change. A pronounced increase or decrease in the growth rate of the money supply, one that lasts for many months, is followed after about one and a half to two years by a noticeable change in the

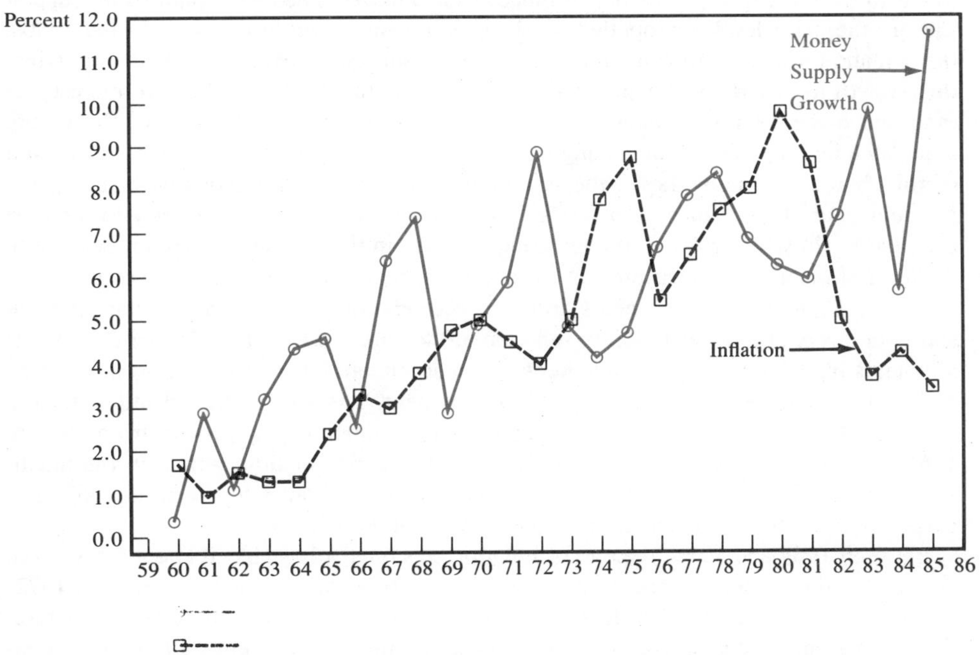

Note: Inflation is shown by the dotted line. Money supply growth is shown by the solid line.

Chart 13.1 Inflation and Money Supply Growth in the Short Run

rate of inflation. Consider the period of prolonged acceleration in money supply growth that began in 1960 at about 1 percent per year and ended in 1965 at almost 5 percent per year. The associated rate of inflation climbed from about 1 percent per year in 1961 to over 3 percent per year in 1966, a lag of over one year. The acceleration in money supply growth from less than 4 percent per year in 1969 to over 9 percent in 1972 resulted in a dizzying acceleration in the rate of inflation from around 4 percent annually in 1972 to about 9 percent annually in 1974.

Most of the rise occurred in 1973 and 1974 because of price controls that were in effect from late 1971 until 1973. The tremendous deceleration in money growth that took place from 1972 to 1974 resulted in a rapid slide in the rate of inflation between 1975 and 1976. In 1976, the annual rate of inflation was under 6 percent. The acceleration of money growth from between 5 percent and 6 percent per annum in 1975 to over 8 percent per annum in 1978 generated the rebound in inflation from just under 6 percent per year in 1977 to almost 9 percent per year in 1980. The deceleration in money growth from over 8 percent annually in 1978 to around 6 percent annually in 1982 resulted in a precipitous nosedive in inflation from over 9 percent per year in 1981 to less than 4 percent per year in 1983.

After 1983, the relationship between money growth and inflation appears to break down. As shown in Chart 13.1, M_1 grew at an annual rate of over 10 percent in the 1982–1986 period, when the average annual rate of inflation was only 3.7 percent. Does this invalidate the quantity theory of money? The answer is no. As explained in Chapter Eleven, the price level is propelled by changes in supply *and* in demand. In the 1980s, the demand for money grew more rapidly than the supply. As explained in Chapter Nine, this growth in demand was explained in large part by the decline in the real interest rate (and hence the nominal interest rate) and also by the rise in real income. Both were stimulated by the capacity-enhancing decline in oil prices from 1982 to 1986. As a result of this favorable supply shock, the rate of inflation fell off dramatically, bringing the nominal interest rate down even further and causing the demand for money to increase even more. (In Chapter Nine, the resulting increase in the demand for money relative to the level of income was measured as a decline in the income velocity of money.)

The apparent short-run benefits from an acceleration of inflation and the apparent short-run costs of a deceleration in inflation are featured in Chart 13.2. The data reveal an interesting correlation over time between an acceleration (or deceleration) of inflation and related decreases (or increases) in unemployment. The acceleration of inflation from 1962 to 1969, a visible product of the explosion in money supply growth from 1960 to 1968 in Chart 13.1, seems to be correlated with a corresponding retreat in the unemployment rate from approximately 5.5 percent in 1962 to about 3.5 percent in 1969. The graph for 1961 to 1969 seems to trace out a short-run Phillips curve.

Between 1969 and 1971, the rate of inflation was relatively stable at about 5.5 percent per year, and the unemployment rate rose to almost 6 percent of the labor force in 1972. This suggests movement back toward a vertical long-run Phillips curve with a natural rate of unemployment of just under 6 percent. From late 1971 until 1973, price controls were in effect and the rate of inflation was artificially suppressed below 6 percent per year.

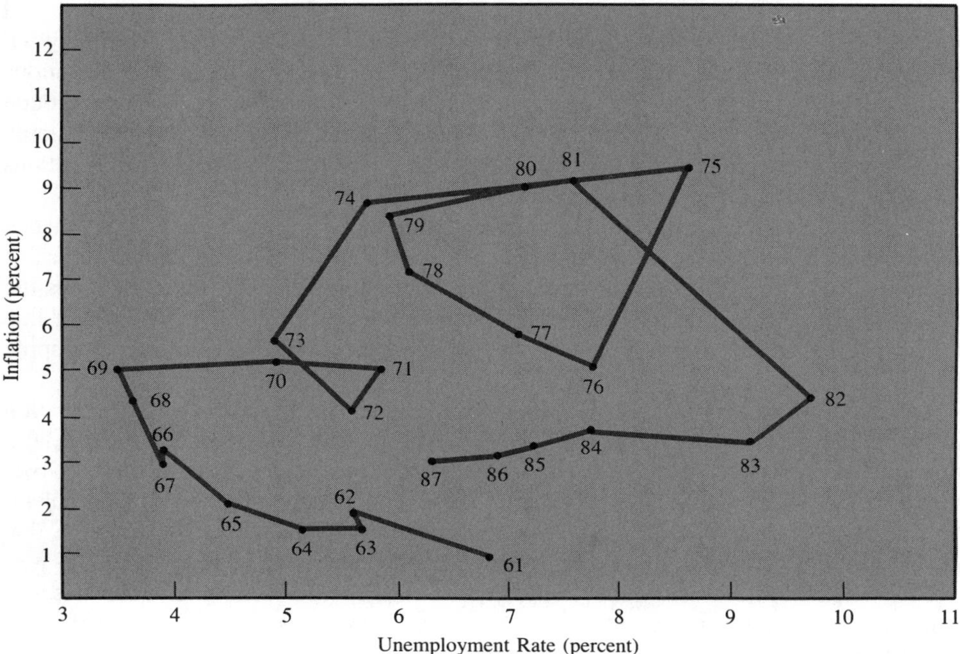

Chart 13.2 Relationship between Acceleration (or Deceleration) of Inflation and Related Decreases (or Increases) in Unemployment, by Year

However, in 1973 and 1974, as the lid on prices was removed and the price of imported oil soared, inflation blasted off to almost double-digit levels. As a result, a distinct short-run Phillips curve is not revealed for 1972 and 1973. In these years, unemployment declined, but inflation could not accelerate because of price controls. The deceleration of inflation from near double-digit levels in 1974 to under 6 percent in 1976, and its subsequent acceleration from around 5.5 percent in 1976 to well over 8 percent in 1979, again seems to outline another short-run Phillips curve. Unemployment swelled from under 6 percent in 1974 to nearly 8 percent in 1976 and retreated from over 7 percent in 1977 to under 6 percent in 1979. Between 1979 and 1980, the rate of inflation was fairly stable and the unemployment rate rose, suggesting movement back toward a long-run Phillips curve, which, as discussed in Chapter Four, had apparently drifted rightward over the span from 1961 to 1981. This suggests a natural rate of unemployment of over 7 percent in the early 1980s. As inflation decelerated from 1981 to 1982, the unemployment rate mounted, outlining yet another short-run Phillips curve. Then in 1983, as inflation held fairly steady at less than 4 percent per year, the unemployment rate subsided.

Between 1983 and 1987, the rate of inflation held steady at under 4 percent per year and the unemployment rate fell back toward a natural rate of around 6 percent. This noninflationary boom in the economy was, in the minds of many analysts, a product of the capacity-enhancing oil supply shock of 1982–1986.

The relationship between accelerations and decelerations in money supply growth and accelerations and decelerations in inflation in Chart 13.1 and the relationship between inflation and the unemployment rate in Chart 13.2 suggest that unanticipated fluctuations in the growth rate of the money supply instigate cyclical movements in employment and output. Thus, observation of a negative correlation between unanticipated money supply growth and movements in the unemployment rate provide an answer to the questions posed at the end of the previous section.

Further evidence of this causal connection is provided by Chart 13.3. The shaded vertical bars denote periods of economic recession as defined by the National Bureau of Economic Research. The upward-trending line in the middle of the chart measures the twenty-quarter (60-month) moving average rate of money supply growth. The jagged line fluctuating about this trend measures the two-quarter average rate of money supply growth.

The chart shows that each of the periods of recession was preceded by a deceleration of the growth rate of the money supply below its trend. (The only pronounced deceleration that did not seem to bring on an officially defined recession occurred in 1966–1967.) Similarly, each period of recovery from the five recessions was preceded by an acceleration of money growth above trend.[3] These correlations further support the notion that unanticipated variations in money supply growth affect output and employment.

Unanticipated increases in money supply growth do indeed seem to have the effect of stimulating employment and output. Cyclical expansions in economic activity seem to generate lower real interest rates, as discussed in Chapter Six. Cyclical recessions have the opposite effect. To these cyclical impacts of unanticipated changes in money growth on real interest rates, we must add the effect of anticipated money supply growth. Because of the effect of anticipated money supply growth on expected inflation, trends in money growth have a direct effect on the price inflation expectations premium that is built into nominal interest rates. Therefore, in order to predict nominal interest rate movements, the forecaster, or market participant, will have to separate cyclical swings from long-range trends in money supply growth.

For excursions into the maze of empirical data, the explorer ought to be well equipped. Unfortunately, it is assumed that the average reader of this text has only a meager kit of statistical and econometric tools at his or her disposal. That is why our analytical methods are limited to the good old-fashioned technique of eyeballing Charts 13.1 through 13.3.

Regardless of the statistical techniques used to uncover and interpret the facts and of the theory used to explain the facts, they seem to indicate strong correlations between changes in money supply growth and movements in interest rates and unemployment in the short run.

With such politically popular near-term effects, there should be little wonder that the recent economic history of the United States has been characterized by prolonged periods of excessive money growth. However, the "high" that the economy receives from ex-

[3]Chapter Four contains the theoretical background for understanding these movements along short-run Phillips curves and drifts in the long-run Phillips curve. Chapter Twelve presents the theory of why unanticipated changes on money supply growth generate variations in real income.

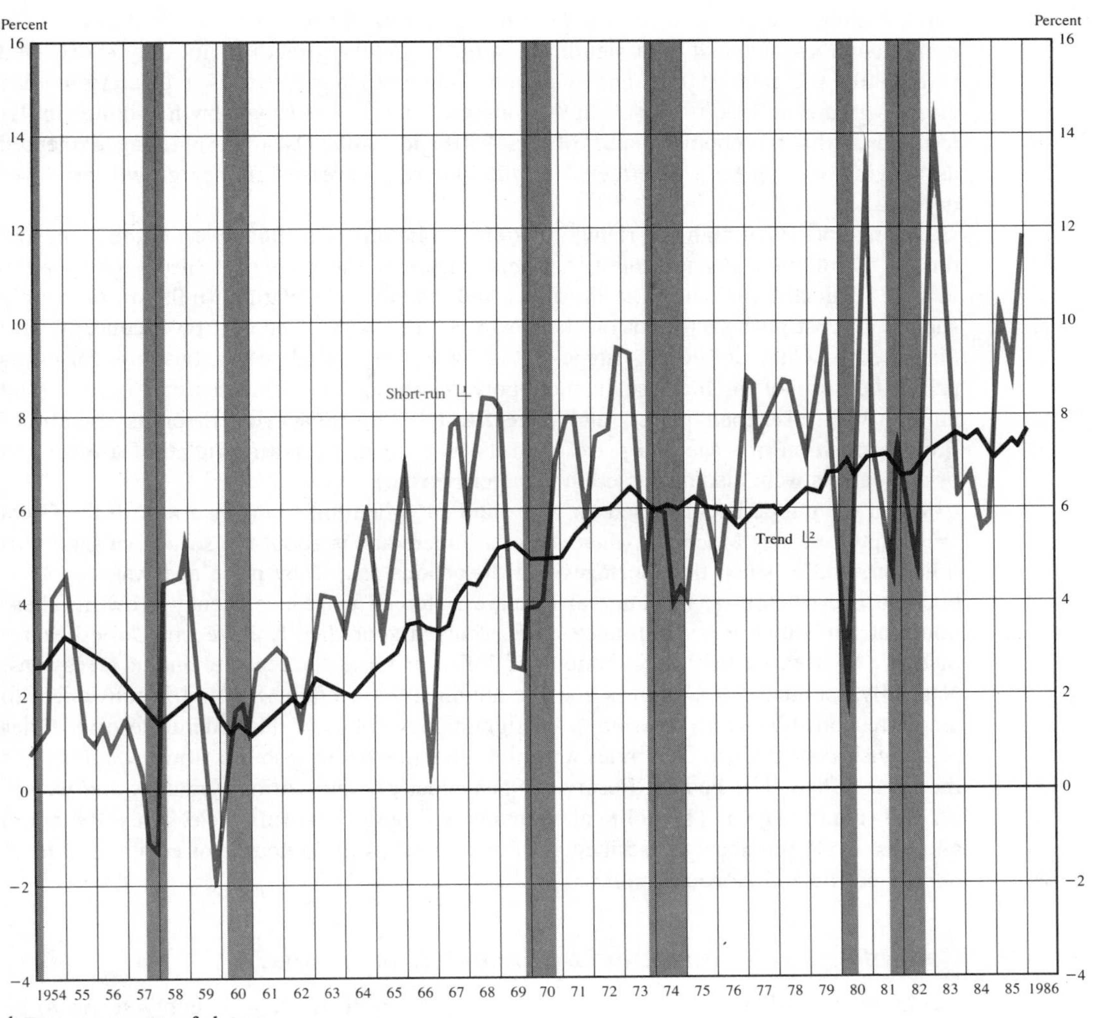

[1] Two-quarter rate of change.

[2] Twenty-quarter rate of change; data prior to 1st quarter 1964 are M_1 on the old basis.

Shaded areas represent periods of business recessions.

Source: Federal Reserve Bank of St. Louis.

Chart 13.3 Rates of Change in Money Stock *(M_1)*

panded money supply growth is only temporary. Like a drug-induced "high," the economic euphoria induced by a significant surge in money growth is not only short-lived (eventually the interest rate and unemployment rise) but also has a deleterious side effect—greater inflation. In fact, in the long run, runaway money growth is quite similar to the drug that the popular pianist of the 1930s and 1940s, Oscar Levant, once lamented as "having *nothing but* side effects." In the long run, excessive money growth produces nothing but inflation.

During periods of high and rising inflation, public officials often revert to the scapegoat theory of inflation. As indicated in Chapter Eleven, the scapegoat theory of inflation involves officials, including the President and his advisers, blaming inflation on supply shock and cost push factors or on their own predecessors.[4] The cost push concept, also discussed in Chapter Eleven, suggests that when one cartel or big business raises its prices because of an increase in monopoly power, other businesses and cartels (and unions) will raise their prices (and wages) to keep up. Scapegoat theorists sometimes favor imposition of wage and price controls as a means of halting inflation. (Wage and price controls were also discussed in Chapter Eleven.)

When the public becomes fed up with the Fed, when folks have had it with the Great Washington Money Machine, when voters are incredulous about the scapegoat theory of inflation, and/or when the shortages and distortions caused by price and wage controls become overwhelming, the Federal Reserve is forced to reduce money growth. These bouts of anti-inflationary militance have occurred sporadically in recent United States history. As seen earlier, decelerations of inflation typically seem to incite recessions. Naturally, members of Congress and the administration often will find it convenient to assign responsibility for recession to the tight money policy of the Federal Reserve. Cries of anguish over high interest rates and high unemployment resound from Congress and the Oval Office. The Federal Reserve comes under pressure for easy money, and we are off and running again. The political economy will have come full cycle. Thus, the boom and bust cycle previously described is often viewed as the outcome of erratic and thoroughly politicized monetary policy.

Can Inflation Be Sustained by Expectations Alone?

As discussed earlier in this chapter, excessive growth in the money supply seems to be brought on by efforts of the monetary authority, either to try to keep interest rates below their equilibrium level or to prevent temporary increases in unemployment. As seen from Chart 13.1, money growth is highly correlated with inflation. Some economists claim that inflation, once it is well rooted in the expectational behavior of business people, workers, lenders, borrowers, and asset holders, is difficult to reduce; they argue that inflationary expectations, built into wage and price contracts, are hard to root out because market participants anticipate continued money supply growth to accommodate these expectations. This explains the widespread publicity given to the concept of an underlying

[4]Only one President of the United States never blamed the ills of the economy on his predecessor—George Washington.

or *core rate of inflation*. This claim will now be examined using our general equilibrium model.

In Figure 13.2, the labor, credit, and money markets are in equilibrium at points A (panel a), A' (panel b), and A'' (panel c), respectively. In the labor market–production sector (panel a), there is full employment equilibrium at employment level L_0 and a $\dot{w}_1$ rate of nominal wage increase. The latter matches the rate of inflation $\dot{P}_1$ so that the real wage is unchanging. In the credit market (panel b), the equilibrium nominal rate of interest i_1 equals the equilibrium real rate of interest plus the expected rate of inflation ($\dot{P}_{e_1}$). In the money market (panel c), with an equilibrium interest rate of i_1 and a level of aggregate real income of $(Y/P)_0$, the recent rate of money supply growth ($\dot{M}_1$) is consistent with the current observed rate of inflation ($\dot{P}_1$). The expected rate of inflation ($\dot{P}_{e_1}$) is equal to the current observed rate ($\dot{P}_1$).

To see whether inflationary expectations alone can sustain the current observed inflation rate ($\dot{P}_1$), assume that because of a wave of anti-inflationary sentiment emanating from the White House, the Federal Reserve reduces money supply growth to zero ($\dot{M}_0 = 0$). The money supply stays at level M_n. Assuming either that inflationary expectations are formed rationally and the deceleration in money growth is unanticipated or that expectations are formed adaptively, the rate of inflation persists because it is deeply ingrained in the behavior of business people, workers, lenders, and borrowers. In the very short run, it seems that the expectation of inflation can cause inflation. However, when the price level increases to P_{n+1} (panel c), and the money supply is unchanged, the real value of the nominal stock of money plummets to M_n/P_{n+1}. This creates an excess demand for money, segment XA'', which elevates the interest rate to i_2. The liquidity effect of money on interest is $i_2 - i_1$. Money market equilibrium in the short run occurs at point B''.

In the credit market (panel b), the ascension of the nominal interest rate to i_2 with the expected rate of inflation at $\dot{P}_{e_1}$ means an increase in the expected real rate of interest to r_1. At this higher rate of interest there is an excess supply of credit, directed distance $C'B'$. Through application of the aggregate budget identity (demonstrated in earlier chapters), an excess supply of credit is the equivalent of an excess of aggregate output over aggregate real expenditures (real aggregate demand). This condition produces pressure for the rate of inflation to decelerate. In this particular example, because money growth is now zero, the price *level* must actually decline from P_{n+1} since P_{n+1} has not been sustained by an increase in the money supply. Thus, the expectation of an underlying or *core rate of inflation* cannot sustain actual inflation beyond the very short run.

As the price level declines from P_{n+1} back to P_n in the money market (panel c), a condition of an excess supply of money is created at interest rate i_2. Excess liquidity of line segment $B''Z''$ causes the interest rate to fall back to i_1. This is the nominal income effect of money on interest. At price level P_n and interest rate i_1, it would seem that equilibrium is restored to the money and credit markets (panels c and b, respectively), at points A'' and A'. However, now that the new money growth rate is $\dot{M}_0 = 0$, the rate of inflation is $\dot{P}_0 = 0$. In the credit market (panel b), the expected rate of inflation is still $\dot{P}_{e_1}$ based on the old rates of inflation and money growth, $\dot{P}_1$ and $\dot{M}_1$ respectively. When

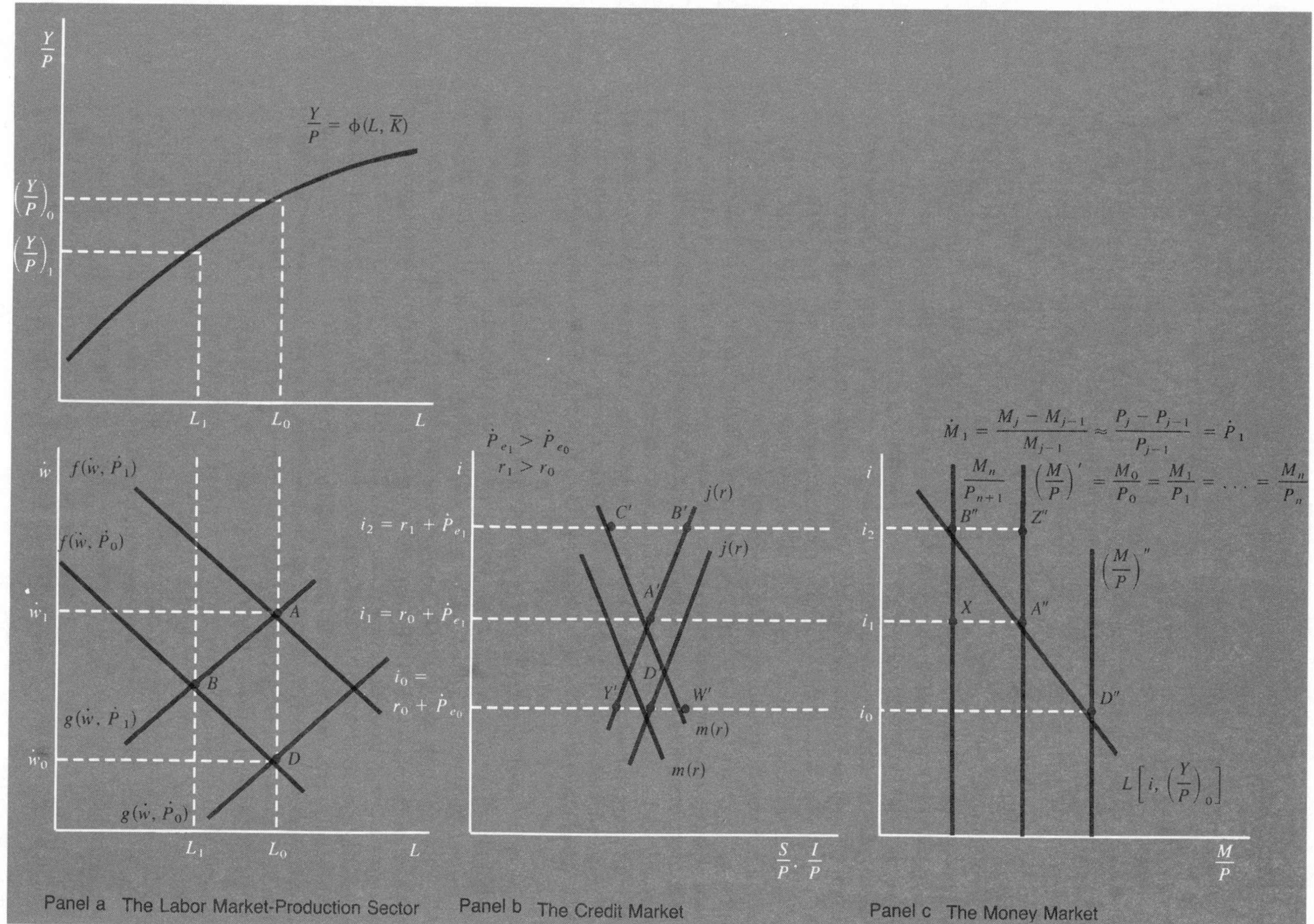

Figure 13.2 Inflationary Expectations and Money Supply Growth in the General Equilibrium Model

credit market participants realize that the actual rate of inflation has decelerated from $\dot{P}_1$ to $\dot{P}_0$, they will become aware that if inflation is sustained at $\dot{P}_0$, as long as the market rate of interest is unchanged at i_1, the real rate of interest will be higher than r_0. When lenders and borrowers come to expect that the new rate of inflation will be sustained at $\dot{P}_0$, it will affect their expectations.

Assuming that the expectation of future inflation adjusts to $\dot{P}_{e0}$ (panel b), with the nominal rate of interest at i_1, the expected real rate of interest rises. The rising real interest rate stimulates real saving, and the real saving function shifts rightward by the directed distance $Y'D'$. The boost in the expected real rate of interest stifles real investment expenditures, and the demand for credit shifts leftward by $W'D'$.

As a result, the equilibrium nominal rate of interest settles at i_0, which is equal to the equilibrium real rate of interest (r_0) plus the expected rate of inflation ($\dot{P}_{e0}$). The credit market is in long-run equilibrium at D'. At the new nominal rate of interest, the money market is in equilibrium at D''. The labor market is in long-run equilibrium at D.

In the labor market, while the rate of price inflation was decelerating from $\dot{P}_1$ to $\dot{P}_0$, there might have been a transitory drop in employment. In the short run, because of asymmetrical responses of participants in the labor market (panel a), equilibrium could have occurred at B and aggregate output could have fallen from $(Y/P)_0$ to $(Y/P)_1$. As discussed in Chapter Four, this would have been consistent with a movement down along a short-run Phillips curve. Therefore, a temporary hike in unemployment (a recession) is often one of the costs of "breaking the back" of inflation and inflationary expectations. In this case, the temporary contraction of real income would cause real saving to decline, and the temporary leftward shift in the saving function would cause the real rate of interest to stay above r_0 and the nominal rate to stay above i_0 as long as the recession persists. (This is not depicted in Figure 13.2, panel b).

Where the expectations of all market participants are formed rationally, the deceleration of money growth is anticipated, and the rate of nominal wage increase is flexible, the rates of price and wage inflation would immediately adjust to $\dot{P}_0$ and $\dot{w}_0$, respectively. The interest rate would immediately fall to i_0 at the new expected rate of inflation, $\dot{P}_{e0}$. There would be no liquidity or nominal income effects of money on the real interest rate. There would be no change in employment and output and no rise in the real interest rate because of a temporary contraction of real income. Under these conditions, the concept of an underlying or core rate of inflation is not supportable, even in the very short run.

Alternative Dynamic Effects of a Change in Money Supply Growth

Figure 13.3 presents a stylized illustration of alternative dynamic effects of a permanent increase in the growth rate of the money supply on the nominal interest rate and inflation. The level of aggregate real income is assumed to be constant. It is assumed that expectations of inflation are formed either adaptively or rationally. Under a rational formulation of inflationary expectations, market participants may be able to anticipate changes in the trend growth rate of the money supply and, assuming they have knowledge of velocity

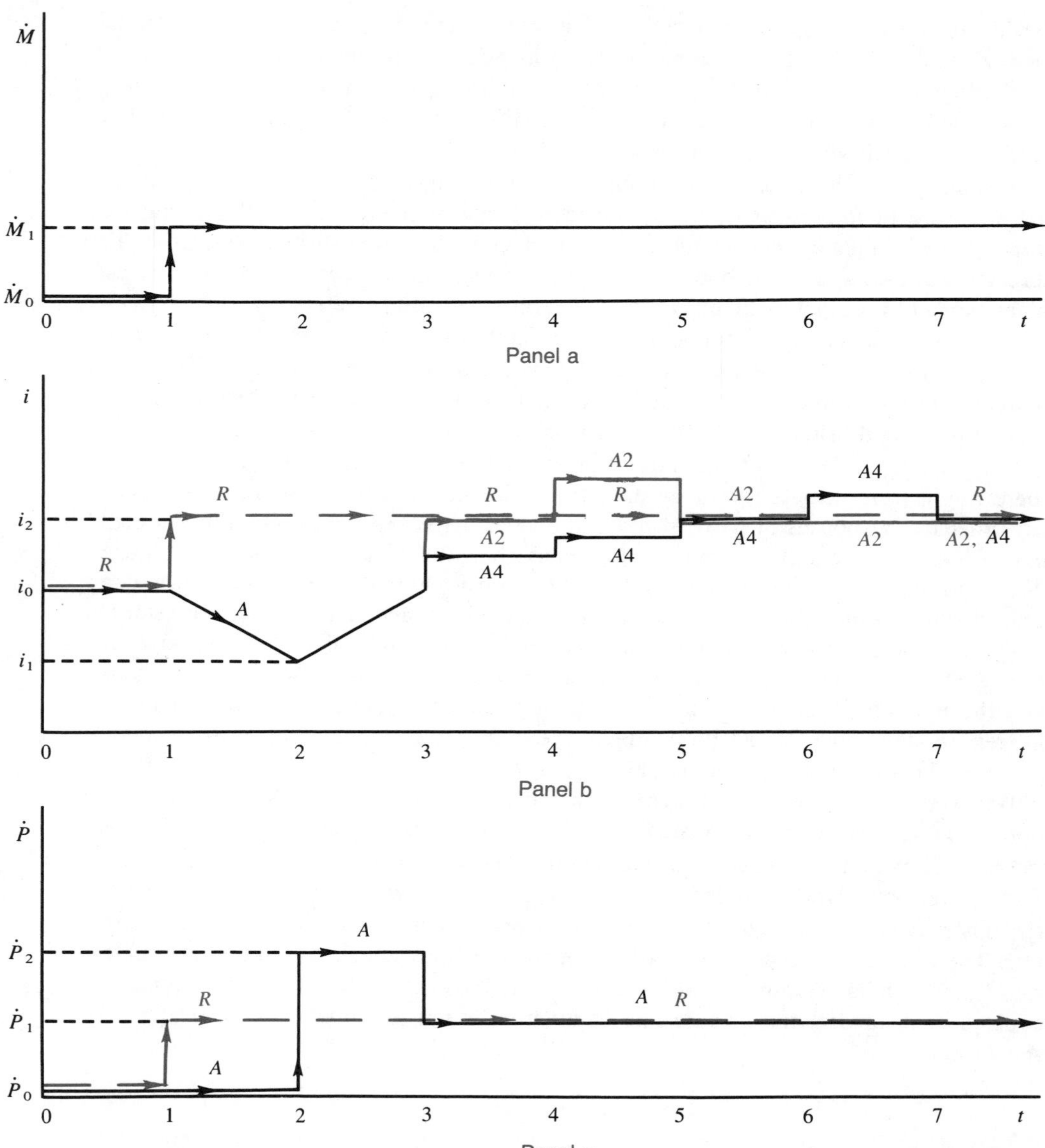

Figure 13.3 Alternative Dynamic Effects of an Increase in the Growth Rate of the Money Supply on Interest Rates with Real Income Assumed Constant

and aggregate output, may be able to generate a new expected rate of inflation just as soon as the new anticipated growth rate occurs. This is shown in Equation (13.5) and is labeled *R* for rational expectations. Under this condition there are unique time paths for the interest rate, inflation, and output:

$$(R) \qquad \dot{P}_{e_t} = f(\dot{M}_t) \qquad (13.5)$$

However, where the change in money supply growth is unanticipated, market participants are assumed to revert to an adaptive formulation of inflationary expectations.

Where expectations are formed adaptively, a number of alternative time paths for inflation, the interest rate, and aggregate output are feasible. Results are sensitive to the length of the lag in the formulation of expectations. We will consider just three possible adaptive expectations-generating relations. Equation (13.6) indicates that inflationary expectations depend on actual inflation in the two preceding periods and is labeled $A2$. Equation (13.7) indicates that inflationary expectations depend on actual inflation in the three preceding periods. It is labeled $A3$. Equation (13.8) says the expectation of inflation depends on actual inflation in the preceding four periods and is labeled $A4$.

$$(A2) \qquad \dot{P}_{e_t} = a\,\dot{P}_{t-1} + a\,\dot{P}_{t-2} \qquad (13.6)$$

$$(A3) \qquad \dot{P}_{e_t} = b\,\dot{P}_{t-1} + b\,\dot{P}_{t-2} + b\,\dot{P}_{t-3} \qquad (13.7)$$

$$(A4) \qquad \dot{P}_{e_t} = c\,\dot{P}_{t-1} + c\,\dot{P}_{t-2} + c\,\dot{P}_{t-3} + c\,\dot{P}_{t-4} \qquad (13.8)$$

To make this exercise easy to follow, assume that the weights within each relation are equal, $a = .5$, $b = .33$, and $c = .25$. A more realistic pattern might involve weights that geometrically decline as one looks back in time. To further simplify the analysis, variables are assumed to change at discrete points in time rather than continuously over intervals of time, and all functions in our general equilibrium model are assumed to be linear.

Initially, the system is in equilibrium during time interval 0, 1 with money growth of $\dot{M}_0 = 0$, inflation of $\dot{P}_0 = 0$, and a nominal and real interest rate of i_0 (where $i_0 = r_0 + \dot{P}_{e0}$ and $\dot{P}_{e0} = 0$).

In panel a, the rate of growth of the money supply accelerates at time 1 to $\dot{M}_1$ and stays there. Under a regime of adaptive expectations, or under a regime of rational expectations where the acceleration in money growth is unanticipated, individual portfolios become more liquid for as long as the rate of inflation stays at zero. As money growth $\dot{M}_1$ exceeds inflation $\dot{P}_0$, real liquidity will grow over the interval between time 1 and time 2. In panel b, the nominal interest rate will follow trajectory A as money market participants substitute financial assets (bonds) for money. Remember that individual market participants do not know that aggregate money growth has increased. They are individually experiencing a growth in their own real liquidity, and they are balancing their portfolios by purchasing financial assets, substituting bonds for money. They are not yet associating their individual experiences with a more rapid growth in the money supply in the economy as a whole. They do not, therefore, expect a higher rate of inflation. The resulting liquidity effect of money on interest $(i_1 - i_0)$ is completed over time interval 1, 2. As the expected rate of inflation has not changed, this represents a decline in the real as well as the nominal interest rate. As a result of the lower interest rate, market participants increase their holdings of real money balances over time interval 1, 2. If real income does not increase over this interval, the income velocity of money will decline.[5]

[5]See the latter part of Chapter Nine for a discussion of cyclical and trend movements in velocity.

As the lower rate of interest creates an excess of aggregate expenditures over aggregate output, the prices of newly produced goods and services begin rising at time 2 along path *A* in panel c. If the excess real liquidity injected into portfolios during time interval 1, 2 is to be absorbed, the rate of inflation must temporarily exceed the rate of money supply growth ($\dot{M}_1$). When viewed alone, the effect of the lower interest rate in creating an excess of aggregate expenditures over aggregate output would only drive the rate of inflation to $\dot{P}_1$. The rate of inflation over interval 2, 3 will be twice the rate of money growth only if individuals increase their expenditures over and above the level warranted by the new lower interest rate i_1. Credit and money market participants will do this if they notice the price increases and, in response, raise their expenditures in order to beat future price increases. They can do so by purchasing newly produced goods and services with the additional real money balances acquired during time interval 1, 2. For these two reasons, the lower interest rate and the anticipation of higher future prices, over interval 2, 3 the rate of price inflation will be $\dot{P}_2$ and not $\dot{P}_1$. Because inflation exceeds money growth during interval 2, 3, by time 3 the real liquidity of portfolios will have shrunk, and the interest rate will have risen along path *A* in panel b. The nominal income effect of money on interest ($i_0 - i_1$) is completed by time 3.

It is important to note that the expectation of future inflation, by Equations (13.6), (13.7), or (13.8), is formulated at distinct points in time. Therefore, at time 2 and during time interval 2, 3 the expectation of future inflation is still zero. It is an average of inflation experienced in previous periods. Market participants will not reformulate their expectation of zero inflation until time 3. The rapid rate of inflation during time interval 2, 3 is not the result of the expectation of a higher *rate* of inflation at time 2. It reflects only the joint effects of greater expenditures in anticipation of a higher price *level* and greater expenditures in response to an interest rate that is lower than i_0.

If credit market participants generate their expectation of inflation with a two-period lag, according to Equation 13.6, the expected rate of inflation at time 3 is $\dot{P}_e = \dot{P}_1 = .5\,\dot{P}_0 + .5\,\dot{P}_2$. In response to this expectation, as shown by the trajectory *A*2 in panel b, the full price inflation expectations effect ($i_2 - i_0$) occurs at time 3. However, there is a temporary one-period overshoot above i_2 at time 4, when expected inflation is $\dot{P}_e = .5\,\dot{P}_2 + .5\,\dot{P}_1$. At time 5, the interest rate returns to *i* and stays there. If credit market participants generate inflationary expectations with a four-period lag, according to Equation (13.8), the full price inflation expectations effect occurs at time 5.

Clearly, in a regime of adaptive expectations, the lag in the adjustment of the interest rate to inflation depends on how backward-looking market participants are. Suppliers and demanders of long-term loans are interested in expected rates of inflation over a long future period. Therefore, with an adaptive formulation of expectations, they may extrapolate expected future inflation on the basis of inflation that occurred over a fairly lengthy past historical period. The trajectory of a long-term interest rate might follow a path more similar to *A*4 than to *A*2 in panel b. In contrast, suppliers and demanders of short-term loans are interested only in expected rates of inflation in the near future. Therefore, with an adaptive formulation of expectations, they may predict future inflation only on the basis of more recent past inflationary experiences. The trajectory of a short-term interest rate might follow a path more like *A*2 than *A*4 in panel b.

If, in contrast to adaptive expectations schemes, it is assumed that money and credit market participants generate expectations rationally and anticipate an acceleration of money growth, a different story emerges. Prior to time 1, market participants will have planned to increase their purchases of newly produced goods and services whenever the anticipated extra money balances become available. Even if these newly produced goods and services cannot all be delivered during interval 1, 2, they can be ordered and paid for as money balances become available during interval 1, 2. Because of the immediate increase in aggregate expenditures financed out of ever growing money balances, the rate of price inflation immediately goes to its equilibrium level as shown by the broken line, trajectory R, in panel c of Figure 13.3. There is no liquidity effect because the new money balances are not used to acquire bonds. It would be irrational for participants to use the new money balances to buy bonds at higher bond prices (lower interest rates) if they expected bond prices to fall (interest rates to rise) in the future. Credit and money market participants generate their expectations of inflation according to Equation (13.5), and the inflationary expectations effect of money on interest $(i_2 - i_0)$ is fully and immediately realized at time 1 as shown by trajectory R in panel b of Figure 13.3. Under these circumstances, it is said that markets are efficient. The *efficient markets hypothesis* is the kissing cousin of the rational expectations hypothesis. If transactions costs are low relative to expected changes in bond prices, markets will be efficient; all available information will be immediately exploited by market participants (see footnote 17).

Figure 13.4 illustrates some alternative effects of a permanent increase in the growth rate of the money supply on inflation and real income. Under a rational formulation of expectations where the money growth rate is anticipated by all (money, credit, and labor) market participants, at time 1 in panel b on trajectory R the rate of inflation rises to reflect anticipated inflation, and the level of output remains at a full employment level as shown by trajectory R in panel c.

Next, consider three possible effects in the labor market of an increase in money supply growth where all labor market participants form their expectations rationally and the increase is not anticipated or where all labor market participants form their expectations adaptively. As discussed earlier, assume that the rate of inflation follows trajectory A in panel b of Figure 13.4.

Labor market participants generate inflationary expectations as a weighted average of prior periods' rates of inflation. If there is complete symmetry between the expectational formulations of labor suppliers and those of labor demanders, both groups will be using the same expectations-generating relations (either Equations 13.6, 13.7, or 13.8). Labor supply and labor demand curves shift upward in the same proportion, and there is no effect on employment. The rate of wage inflation matches the rate of price inflation. Trajectory $A1$ prevails in panel c of Figure 13.4.

In contrast, assume a more backward-looking formulation of inflationary expectations by labor suppliers than by labor demanders. Assume labor demanders utilize the two-period lag expectations relation, Equation (13.6). If labor suppliers generate their expectations of inflation using a three-period lag, Equation (13.7), labor demand shifts rightward at time 3 and time 4 more than labor supply shifts leftward. The result is a temporary rise in employment and a boom period during the interval from time 4 to time

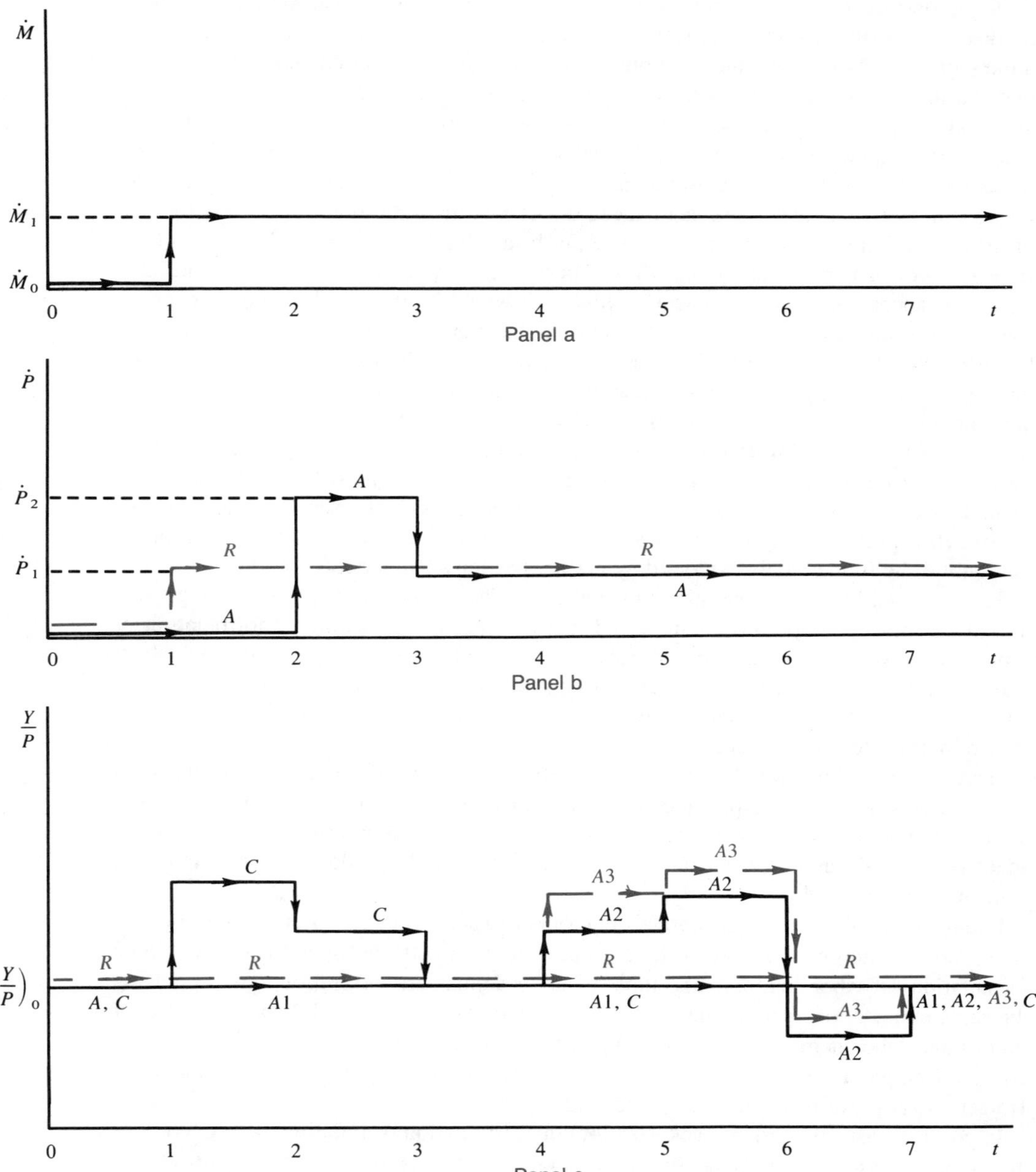

Figure 13.4 Alternative Dynamic Effects of an Increase in the Growth Rate of the Money Supply on Real Income

6. This is followed by a moderate drop in output at time 6 and a return to a full employment level at time 7. The time path of output during this boom is shown by trajectory *A*2.

If labor demanders have a two-period lag in their expectations formation but suppliers have a four-period lag, a somewhat more pronounced boom in the economy occurs as trajectory *A*3 is followed. Thus, similar to the static model of Chapters Four and Twelve, increases in the rate of inflation that were not as well anticipated by labor suppliers as labor demanders generate a greater cyclical variation in employment and aggregate output.

Finally, assume that money and credit market participants form their inflationary expectations rationally and try to anticipate the increase on money supply growth, but labor market participants have implicit or explicit nominal wage contracts, and when these contracts were made the acceleration in money growth was not anticipated. Moreover, assume that workers forfeit the right to an immediate adjustment in the rate of nominal wage increase.[6] Instead, assume that by explicit or by tacit contractual agreement the rate of increase of nominal wages adjusts to actual inflation over two previous intervals, as described by Equation (13.6).

When the rate of inflation accelerates at time 1 along path *R* in panel b, labor demanders immediately increase the demand for labor, but the supply of labor does not shift leftward until time 2. However, because nominal wage adjustments are made with a two-period lag, the labor supply does not fully adjust until time 3. Along trajectory *C* in panel c, the level of real income rises at time 1, tapers off at time 2 but is still above the full employment level, and returns to the full employment level at time 3.

The Dynamic Effects of Changes in Money Supply Growth on Financial Asset Prices

This section will demonstrate how it may be possible to anticipate future movements in stock and bond market prices by observing current money supply growth. Knowledge of modern macroeconomic theory might enable you to make your fortune in securities markets by anticipating the future and acting before it occurs. But before you dash to the phone to call your stock broker, read the rest of this chapter carefully. We said being informed *might* make you rich, not that it *would* make you rich.

Figure 13.5 shows a number of plausible alternative effects of an acceleration in money growth on inflation, the nominal interest rate, the real interest rate, and the price of equity. In panel a, money supply growth accelerates at time 1. Three different alternative paths for the nominal interest rate, the real interest rate, and the price of equity are plotted in panels b, d, and e, respectively.

The *R* paths in these panels reflect the assumption that money, credit, and labor market participants all form their inflationary expectations rationally and anticipate the increase in money supply growth. In panel b, the nominal interest rate moves up at time 1 along

[6]See Chapter Four for a discussion of the rationale behind such contracts.

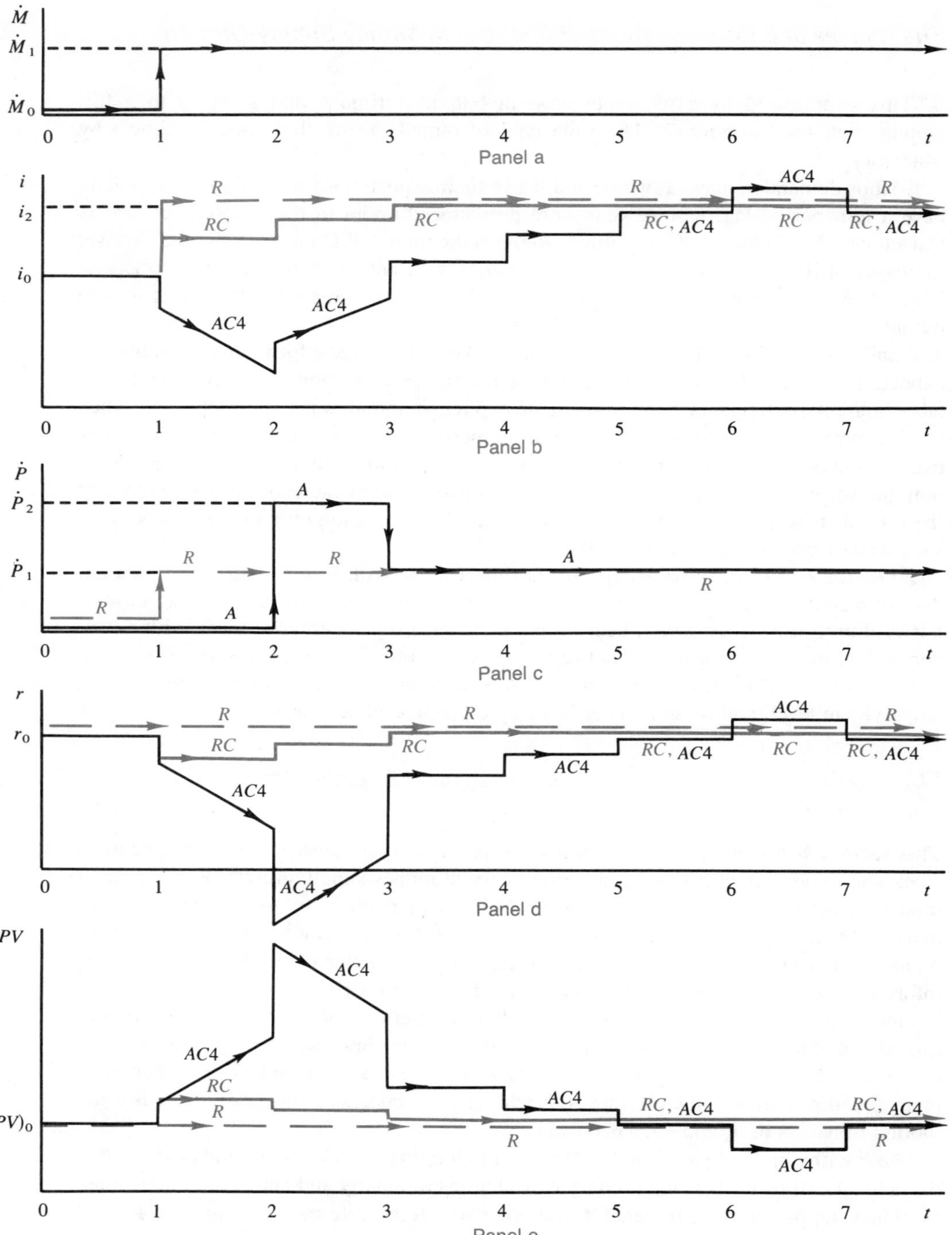

Figure 13.5 Alternative Dynamic Effects of an Acceleration in Money Supply Growth on Nominal and Real Interest Rates and on the Price of Equity with Real Income Not Assumed Constant

path R to reflect fully the new rate of inflation. In panel c, the rate of inflation follows path R.[7] Because there is no effect on real income (see panel c of Figure 13.4), real saving does not increase. Because there is no change in the real saving and because the rate of inflation is fully reflected in the nominal rate, the actual and expected real rate of interest does not change along path R in panel d.

In panel e, the price of equity represents the present value (PV) of future expected nominal profits discounted at the nominal rate of interest. Since the rate of inflation is fully anticipated, it will be fully reflected in increased expected nominal profits. As the nominal rate of interest and expected nominal profits both fully reflect the new rate of inflation, the price of equity (PV) does not change along path R in panel e. There is no way for an individual to systematically beat the market by exploiting information regarding money growth in stock market trading. The market will already have quickly and systematically assimilated and utilized this information. In this sense, under a regime of rationally formed expectations, the stock market and all other markets are *efficient*.

Next, assume that money and credit market participants form their expectations rationally and anticipate the increase in the money supply growth but that labor market participants do not. Assume that because of a lagged adjustment of nominal wages to the new rate of inflation that occurs at time 1, the level of real income follows path C in panel c of Figure 13.4. Real saving increases and the actual and expected real interest rate follows trajectory RC in panel d of Figure 13.5. Therefore, even though inflationary expectations are immediately and correctly built into the nominal rate of interest at time 1, the nominal rate does not immediately rise to i_2. Instead, it follows path RC in panel b.

In the equity market, while expected nominal profits increase to fully reflect the new rate of inflation, the nominal interest rate at which these profits are discounted has not increased in the same proportion. (Put another way, while expected real profits are unchanged, the real rate of interest has fallen.)[8] As a result, the price of equity rises at time 1 along path RC in panel e, tapers off at time 2 and returns to PV_0 at time 3.

Finally, assume that real income follows path C in panel c of Figure 13.4 and participants in money and credit markets form expectations adaptively or form them rationally but do not anticipate the growth. If inflationary expectations are formed with a four-period lag (Equation 13.8), the nominal rate will fall along trajectory $AC4$ in panel b of Figure 13.5 during interval 1, 2, and rise during interval 2, 3, reflecting the liquidity and nominal income effects of the increase in the money supply on interest rates. Then, after time 3, the nominal interest rate will eventually reflect the rate of inflation. These effects were described in conjunction with the discussion of path $A4$ in panel b of Figure 13.3. Unlike that earlier description, in the present case real income is not assumed to be constant but follows path C in panel c of Figure 13.4.

[7]Actually, the inflation rate would initially overshoot $\dot{P}_1$ at time 1 in panel c and then move back toward $\dot{P}_1$. This would occur because the rising nominal interest rate in panel b would reduce the demand for money balances and create an (additional) excess supply of money. This additional excess supply can be erased only by inflation in excess of $\dot{P}_1$. This property applies to both path R and path RC.

[8]As discussed in footnote 13, the real interest rate may fall even further because of cyclical reduction in the risk premium required by lenders.

In panel b of Figure 13.5, the nominal interest rate falls during interval 1, 2 along path *AC*4 for two reasons: (1) the increase in real income which lowers the real interest rate and (2) the aforementioned liquidity effect of the increased growth in the money supply. During interval 2, 3 the nominal interest rate rises because real income is somewhat lower than during interval 1, 2 and because of the nominal income effect. After time 3, real income is at its long-run equilibrium level, and the nominal rate slowly adjusts to the rate of inflation along path *AC*4 (as described earlier).[9]

In panel c, there initially is no increase in inflation because of the increased demand for money as the nominal interest rate falls. At time 2, the inflation rate overshoots $\dot{P}_1$ because the decreasing demand for money helps to fuel inflation. At time 3, the equilibrium rate of inflation is restored. (Actually, $\dot{P}_1$ would be only gradually approached from above because of the gradually decreasing demand for money associated with the gradually rising nominal interest rate in panel b.)

In panel d, trajectory *AC*4 is a plot of the *ex post* real rate of interest. It represents the difference between the nominal interest rate on path *AC*4 in panel b and the actual rate of inflation in path *A* in panel c. During interval 1, 2 the actual real rate of interest falls for the same reasons that the nominal rate fell in panel b. During interval 2, 3 the rate of inflation zips up from zero to $\dot{P}_2$ on path *A* in panel c. As a result, along trajectory *AC*4 the *ex post* real interest rate initially plunges at time 2, becoming negative, and then rises along with the nominal rate in panel b.[10]

In panel e, the price of equity on path *AC*4 mirrors the movements in the real interest rate. Stock prices explode during interval 1, 2 as the nominal rate of interest declines and nominal profits are unchanged. At time 2, expected nominal profits soar with inflation but the nominal interest rate rises only slowly. (Conversely, expected real profits are steady, while the *ex post* real rate of interest plummets.) After time 2, with nominal (and real) profits holding steady and the nominal (and real) interest rate rising, stock prices slowly retreat.[11]

[9]Movements in the nominal rate of interest in recent years are reported in Chapter Six.

[10]Movements in the *ex post* real rate of interest in recent years are reported in Chart 6.1 in Chapter Six. There it can be seen that the *ex post* real interest rate plunged and even became negative during periods of rapidly accelerating inflation.

[11]A more realistic portrayal of the trajectories in Figures 13.3, 13.4 and 13.5 would involve continuous, smooth, rather than discrete, paths. For example, along the *A* paths inflation would begin smoothly accelerating between time 1 and 2, overshoot $\dot{P}_1$ after time 2, and slowly approach it from above well after time 3. The liquidity effect, if any, would therefore end before time 2. Output would therefore respond well after time 1 and follow a smoothed version of the discrete *A* paths in panel c of Figure 13.4.

Precise estimates of the timing of these *A*-type responses are not available; however, empirical studies provide rough impressions. A liquidity effect, if any, seems to last less than two months. Output begins to respond to an acceleration of money growth after three to nine months. Inflation approaches its equilibrium rate about two years after an acceleration, but the entire pattern of output and inflation adjustment takes perhaps four years. The exact nature of the *A*-type time paths would, however, be very sensitive to the changing formation of expectations.

The rough correspondence of *A*-type paths to the data should not suggest that *R*- or *RC*-type time paths are not plausible or consistent with the facts. Recent empirical studies show that the expectational hypotheses lying behind the *R* and *RC* time paths explain the data in Charts 13.1 through 13.3 quite well. One of the great shortcomings of modern macroeconomic theory is that the formation of expectations, and hence the modeling of labor, credit, and money market behavior, is not invariant with respect to the stance of macroeconomic policy. Therefore, the actual configuration of these time paths is difficult to predict.

Path *AC*4 suggests that a pronounced acceleration of money supply growth, such as occurred at time 1 in panel a, may serve as a signal or a predictor of the preceding type of movement in stock (and bond) prices. On trajectory *AC*4 in panel e of Table 13.5, stock prices peak at time 2 and remain high until time 5, long after the initial acceleration in money supply growth at time 1.[12]

If the assumptions lying behind paths *AC*4 regarding the formulation of inflationary expectations hold in the real world, you may, armed with this bit of knowledge, now be well poised to make billions systematically as a stock market speculator just by learning to anticipate changes in money supply growth. (Hint: Buy before time 2 and then sell before time 3.) However, the rest of this chapter is so exciting that you should probably defer enrolling in a course in Fed watching until you finish it.[13]

Predicting the Business Cycle

Where the expectations of labor suppliers are more backward looking than those of labor demanders or when their responses are constrained by nominal wage contracts, there will be a period of super-full employment and an economic boom associated with an acceleration of inflation and a period of less than full employment and recession associated with a deceleration of inflation. As suggested by discussion of panel c in Figure 13.4, the greater the asymmetry in responses between employers and workers, or the longer the period covered by nominal wage contracts, the greater the magnitude of the boom (and conversely, the greater the magnitude of a recession). Where there is no asymmetry, there will be no change in employment following an acceleration or deceleration of inflation. In Figure 13.4, trajectory *R* will prevail.

This result at once suggests the difficulty of predicting the length, severity, and even occurrence of cyclical swings in output and employment (the business cycle). As discussed in Chapter Four, even with a sophisticated economic theory, economists do not know enough about how market participants respond to information. There is considerable debate regarding why it seems to take time and how much time it takes for workers and employers to translate observations or predictions of a greater demand for newly produced goods and services into increased nominal wages.[14] It should also be kept in

[12]If the economic boom between time 1 and time 3 raised real profits, and this, in turn, stimulated an expectation of even greater future expected real profits, the price of equity could rise even more than depicted on *AC*4.

[13]The stories told here regarding the alternative responses of nominal and real interest rates to changes in money supply growth are not exhaustive. Other plausible tales include the assumption that during recessions lenders are very risk-averse, and insist that greater risk premiums be built into *ex ante* real interest rates but that during booms lenders are less risk-averse, and these premiums fall. As a result, in a world where credit and money market participants form their expectations rationally and anticipate the acceleration in money growth, the real interest rate and the price of equity vary cyclically in a manner similar to that shown by trajectories *RC* in panels d and e, respectively.

Other tenable stories would include the effect of inflation on the taxation of nominal interest income. This too would cause real after-tax rates of interest to vary in the cyclical manner described previously. See Chapter Six for further discussion of the effect of inflation on real after-tax rates of interest. See the bibliography to Chapter Six for studies of these phenomena.

[14]See the bibliography to Chapter Four for a sampling of this literature. As pointed out in footnote 11, one of the shortcomings of modern macroeconomic theory is that its models are not invariant with respect to the policy environment. Therefore, answers to these questions and usable, accurate, predictions and forecasts are rather scarce.

mind that cyclical swings in output do not arise solely from imperfect information or imperfect response to information in the labor market. As pointed out in the previous chapter, these conditions could also exist in other markets for productive inputs as well as in markets for output. Also as indicated in Chapter Eleven supply shocks may generate a "real" business cycle that has nothing to do with private demand-side shocks.

Sometimes theories are useful not because they help us to predict but because they tell us what we cannot easily predict given the current limitations on human knowledge. Modern macroeconomic theory suggests that a good deal of caution be employed when it comes to predicting periods of recession and prosperity. Just look at the varied assortment of plausible time paths that real income can take in panel c of Figure 13.4! It is no surprise, then, that economic pundits have such a bad track record when it comes to predicting the length and severity of recession and boom periods.[15] It is probably this bad track record that once prompted a businessperson to remark that the best indicator that an economic crisis is over is when economic forecasters begin to recognize that it has already occurred.[16]

Predicting Movements in the Stock Market

Now we focus our attention on everybody's favorite charity: the stock market. Empirical studies reveal a high positive correlation between peaks in the prices of stocks traded on the major exchanges and later cyclical upswings in real income. The beginning of upswings in real income follow the peaks in the stock markets by an average of two to seven months. Many casual observers have been fascinated by these empirical studies. Some have jumped to the conclusion that highly trained financial speculators are able to anticipate movements in output and real income. They claim that the big boys on Wall Street buy securities before real income (and corporate profits) improve and sell securities before real income (and corporate profits) fall.

Our theory tells us that such a conclusion is unwarranted. Correlation is not causality. Changes in stock prices reflect changes in the real interest rate and real profits. Changes in real income reflect the presence of asymmetrical responses in the labor market. In Figures 13.4 and 13.5, the unanticipated acceleration of money supply growth causes *both* the decline in the real interest rate and the rise in real income. Speculators in financial markets do not necessarily drive up stock prices in anticipation of an economic boom; they may simply be responding to lower interest rates. Participants in securities markets are neither omniscient nor omnipotent. In Figure 13.5, they most assuredly do not drive up stock prices at time 1 in anticipation of the boom in real income that occurs between time 1 and time 3 in Figure 13.4.

[15]The National Bureau of Economic Research (a nonprofit organization) defines a recession as three consecutive quarters of falling GNP. There are no theoretical underpinnings for this operational definition. However, this official designation generates systematic definitions of recessions that come in handy.

[16]To make matters worse, economists do not agree as to the cause of the business cycle. Some say that supply shocks (discussed in Chapter Eleven) raise and lower real wages and cause regular variations in the equilibrium level of employment. This theory of the "real" business cycle was discussed in Chapter Eleven.

Modern macroeconomic theory indicates that by predicting pronounced and prolonged changes in money supply growth rates, one *may* be able to predict movements in interest rates and in stock market prices. However, if some other market participants are generally able to predict swings in money supply growth, and if expectations are formed rationally, then interest rates and equity prices will not vary in the manner portrayed by the *AC*4 trajectories in Figure 13.5. Instead, they will move along the *R* paths. In a pure rational expectations world, there is not much potential for an individual to earn billions in the stock market by currently anticipating changes in money supply growth and systematically picking the right time to buy and sell stocks.[17] This may explain why the denizens of Wall Street are interested in whether the tenets of the New Classical school are true. A hypothesis which is related to the rational expectations hypothesis is the *efficient markets hypothesis*. If markets are efficient—that is, if market participants behave rationally and if transactions costs are low—a lot of speculators and their highly paid advisers should go into early retirement or find other work. Specialists will, on average, only earn a return commensurate with the risks they assume. The efficient markets hypothesis suggests that the pickers on Wall Street are no better than the pickers in Nashville.

The Limited Role for Stabilization Policy in a Rational Expectations World

The rational expectations hypothesis, if true, should also increase the job search activities of many government policymakers and their highly paid advisers. In a rational expectations, New Classical world, there is no meaningful role for macroeconomic stabilization policy. This is often referred to as the *policy ineffectiveness proposition* of New Classical economics. In both Keynesian and Neoclassical models, changes in monetary or fiscal policy may affect output because of unanticipated shocks to the economy, including unanticipated changes in macroeconomic policy. The rational expectations, New Classical view is that labor suppliers and labor demanders are rational and do not make systematic errors in forecasting. If policy actions may be anticipated, so too will be related, subsequent changes in inflation. Only unanticipated policy moves can excite output and employment because only unanticipated moves will have an effect on the price level that cannot be predicted.

How should macroeconomic policy respond to demand shocks to the economy that emanate from the private sector, such as shifts in private investment expenditures? As discussed in Chapters Seven and Twelve, many Keynesians contend that such private demand shocks are a source of instability in aggregate real income and employment. According to the rational expectations, New Classical perspective, if such variations are anticipated, there would be no need for monetary or fiscal policy response. Labor sup-

[17]It was indicated earlier that being informed about macroeconomic theory *might* make you rich. If everyone is "smart," in the rational expectations sense, there are no systematically exploitable gains in stock market speculation. As indicated earlier, markets will be efficient in the sense that no unexploited information will be "lying around." This is why a hard-core rational expectations enthusiast once refused to pick up a $100 bill that he *thought* he saw lying in the street. He said to himself, "If it were *really* there, someone else would have already picked it up."

pliers and demanders would anticipate the effects on inflation, and there would be no change in output and employment.

What if demand shocks from the private sector are unanticipated by behavioral agents including labor demanders and labor suppliers? In this case, related price level effects cannot be anticipated, and there might be an impact on output and employment. Is there not a role for monetary and fiscal policy in such a case?

The problem here is that under the assumption of rationally formed expectations, if market participants cannot foresee private demand shocks, neither can policymakers. As long as such shocks are unanticipated, policymakers as well as market participants lack the information. Once the shock is anticipated by policymakers, it is also anticipated by market participants, and there is no need for policy action to counteract it.

The rational expectations, New Classical approach, therefore, somewhat dourly concludes that there is a limited role for monetary and fiscal stabilization policy. Such a role would eliminate unanticipated policy moves that would take the economy away from its long-run full employment equilibrium by causing behavioral agents to make errors in forecasts.[18]

The preceding discussion focused on private demand shocks. Supply shocks generate another dilemma because, as discussed in Chapter Eleven, since they affect production and productivity relations, they have long-lived impacts on real income and interest rates regardless of whether they are anticipated. As discussed earlier in this chapter, capacity-reducing supply shocks may provoke monetary policy surprises to offset their adverse effects on output and interest rates while aggravating their inflationary consequences. In contrast, capacity-enhancing supply shocks, such as the 1982–1986 retreat in imported oil prices, require no policymaker responses, except taking undeserved credit for the consequences.

Concluding Comment

Previous chapters treat the three exogenous shocks to our general equilibrium models (a change in the deficit, a change in the money supply, and a supply shock in the form of a change in the price of an imported raw material) as being strictly independent. The present chapter shows how they are often related. The linkage occurs because a large, unchanging government deficit or an adverse supply shock often generates political pressure for faster money supply growth. A large deficit means a high interest rate. A capacity-reducing increase in the price of an imported raw material implies a permanently higher interest rate and a permanently higher unemployment level. Certain sectors of the economy will become distressed by high interest rates. Other sectors will be upset by high unemployment. Because of this unrest, many believe that relief is spelled M-O-N-E-Y. Unfortunately, the relief, if any, can be only temporary; excessive money growth

[18]The Keynesian reply to the New Classical critique is that market participants, particularly labor market participants, may be bound to nominal contractual arrangements that do not always correctly anticipate future policy. For the Keynesian reply to the rational expectations critique, see the sections entitled "A Change in the Money Supply: Short Run versus Long Run" and "Implications for Macroeconomic Stabilization Policy" in Chapter Twelve.

in the long run generates only inflation and an even higher nominal interest rate. The quest for relief may explain why our recent economic history has been marred by prolonged periods of accelerating money growth and only sporadic episodes of decelerating money growth (see Chart 13.1). It may also explain why even during episodes of money supply growth deceleration, there occur intermittent bursts of money growth acceleration. In Chapter Eight, it was shown that the money supply can be easily managed; in the present chapter, we explore the possibility that it may be systematically mismanaged to generate short-run, transitory, cosmetic reductions in interest rates and unemployment at the cost of excessive inflation.

Accelerations and decelerations of money supply growth may have a number of temporary effects. They may temporarily alter interest rates; they may temporarily change financial asset prices, including the price of stocks (equity shares); they may temporarily affect unemployment. This chapter takes a dynamic look at these effects and their interactions. Accelerations and decelerations of money supply growth lead to a number of plausible alternative responses in interest rates, financial asset prices (including stock market prices), the rate of inflation, employment, and output. The alternative time paths for these variables depend on how market participants generate their expectations about inflation. If expectations are formed rationally and money growth is anticipated, then the economy promptly moves to its long-run equilibrium state with no fluctuations in employment, a swift increase in inflation, an immediate and direct rise in the nominal interest rate to reflect inflationary expectations, and no variation in the price of equities. If expectations are formed adaptively or if they are formed rationally and money growth is not anticipated, then there will be pronounced fluctuations in the rate of inflation, interest rates, equity prices, and unemployment. Macroeconomic theory in its current state of development teaches how little can really be predicted with certainty. It merely informs us to be highly skeptical of individuals (no matter what devices they employ) who claim to be able to divine the economic future with regard to interest rates, stock prices, output, and employment.

EXERCISES

1. Why do people commonly infer that a large but unchanging deficit causes inflation?
2. Why would the monetary authority want to validate an increase in the price of an imported raw material?
3. Name at least three reasons why money growth rates have been excessive for extended periods of time.
4. Why are recessions typically so short lived?
5. Evaluate the following statement: "The modern, highly trained portfolio manager on Wall Street has access to the best minds, the latest computer software, and the most recent information. Therefore, stock market experts can foresee recessions.

That is why the stock market always turns down before the onslaught of a recession and up before an economic boom."

6. The Great Depression was marked by a 20 percent decline in real GNP from 1929 to 1934. What do you believe the growth rate of the money supply was doing over this time span?

7. Assume a demand shock in the form of an unanticipated, exogenously caused drop in autonomous investment expenditures. How would this affect the interest rate, the price level, and output? Which of these three effects would create pressure for the Federal Reserve to respond?

8. What does the rational expectations hypothesis have to say about the following:
   a. people's ability to forecast the business cycle;
   b. the proper role for macroeconomic stabilization policy;
   c. the ability of stock market speculators to systematically outguess the market;
   d. the notion that the expectation of an underlying or core rate of inflation can sustain actual inflation.

9. Examine the time paths of interest rates and the price of equity in Figure 13.5. Which paths do you believe to be most realistic? Why?

10. A stock market prognosticator claims to show a 99.9 percent correlation between the color of the bands on wooly caterpillars and subsequent movements in the Dow Jones Industrial Average. Critique the ability to use this correlation from a rational expectations perspective.

11. Between mid-1982 and mid-1983, the narrowly defined money supply increased by $64 billion and interest rates fell significantly. Is there a causal link between the two? If so, identify it.

BIBLIOGRAPHY

Borins, Sanford. "The Political Economy of the Fed." *Public Policy* (1972), pp. 175–198.

Buchanan, James M., and Richard Wagner. *Democracy in Deficit*. New York: Academic Press, 1977.

Cobham, David. "The Politics of the Economics of Inflation." *Lloyds Bank Review* (April 1978), pp. 19–32.

Friedman, Milton. "Factors Affecting the Level of Interest Rates." *Proceedings of the 1968 Conference on Savings and Residential Financing*. Chicago: United States Savings and Loan League, 1969, pp. 11–27.

Friedman, Milton, and Anna J. Schwartz. *A Monetary History of the United States*. Princeton, N.J.: Princeton University Press, 1963.

Gilbert, Charles. "The Rational Expectations Hypothesis: Survey and Recent Research." In *Modern Concepts in Macroeconomics,* ed. Thomas M. Havrilesky. Arlington Heights, Ill.: Harlan Davidson, Inc., 1985.

Gordon, Robert J. "The Demand and Supply of Inflation." *Journal of Law and Economics* (December 1975), pp. 807–836.

Havrilesky, Thomas. "Monetary Policy Signaling from the Administration to the Federal Reserve." *Journal of Money, Credit and Banking* (February 1988).

Havrilesky, Thomas. "A Partisanship Theory of the Fiscal and Monetary Regime." *Journal of Money, Credit and Banking* (August 1987).

Hibbs, Douglas. "Political Parties and Macroeconomic Policy." *American Political Science Review* (1977), pp. 1467–1487.

Jevons, William Stanley. *Investigations in Currency and Finance*. London: Macmillan and Company, 1909.

Kane, Edward J. "Politics and Fed Policymaking: The More Things Change, the More They Remain the Same." *Journal of Monetary Economics* (April 1980), pp. 199–211.

Lindbeck, Assar. "Stabilization Policy in Open Economies with Endogenous Politicians." *American Economic Review* (May 1976), pp. 10–19.

Laney, Leroy, and Thomas Willet. *The Political Economy of Global Expansion: The Causes of Monetary Expansion in the Major Industrial Countries*. Washington, D.C.: American Enterprise Institute, 1982.

Lombra, Raymond K., and Willard K. Witte, eds. *Political Economy of International and Domestic Monetary Relations*. Ames, Iowa: Iowa State University Press, 1982.

Maisel, Sherman, *Managing the Dollar*. New York: W. W. Norton, 1973.

Miller, Preston J. "Higher Deficit Policies Lead to Higher Inflation." *Quarterly Review*, Federal Reserve Bank of Minneapolis (Winter 1983), pp. 8–19.

Mishkin, Frederic S. *A Rational Expectations Approach to Macroeconometrics: Testing Policy Ineffectiveness and Efficient Markets Models*. Chicago: University of Chicago Press, 1983.

Mullineaux, Donald. "Efficient Markets, Interest Rates and Monetary Policy." In *Modern Concepts in Macroeconomics,* ed. Thomas M. Havrilesky. Arlington Heights, Ill.: Harlan Davidson, Inc., 1985.

Nordhaus, William. "The Political Business Cycle." *Review of Economic Studies* (April 1975), pp. 169–190.

Santoni, G. J., and W. W. Brown. "Monetary Growth and the Timing of Interest Rate Movements." *Review,* Federal Reserve Bank of St. Louis (August/September 1983), pp. 16–25.

Sargent, Thomas J., and Neil Wallace. "Some Unpleasant Monetarist Arithmetic." *Quarterly Review,* Federal Reserve Bank of Minneapolis (Fall 1981), pp. 1–7.

Shiller, Robert J., and Jeremy Siegel. "The Gibson Paradox and Historical Movements in Real Interest Rates." *Journal of Political Economy* 85 (October 1977), pp. 891–907.

Taylor, Herbert. "Interest Rates: How Much Does Expected Inflation Matter?" In *Modern Concepts in Macroeconomics,* ed. Thomas M. Havrilesky. Arlington Heights, Ill.: Harlan Davidson, Inc., 1985.

Tufte, Edward. *Political Control of the Economy*. Princeton, N.J.: Princeton University Press, 1978.

Economic Growth and Supply-Side Economic Policy

Chapter 14

Introduction

Models of the economy discussed so far have implied that aggregate real income was either at an unchanging full employment equilibrium level or could vary only cyclically about that full employment level. Temporary changes in real income were associated with accelerations and decelerations in the rate of inflation. Nevertheless, the equilibrium level of aggregate output was fixed in the long run. However, from the perspective of economic growth, the full employment level of aggregate output can increase slowly over time for three reasons:

1. an increase in the full employment equilibrium level of labor input;
2. an increase in the capital stock of the economy; or
3. technological improvements in production processes.

In the Neoclassical or Keynesian models of previous chapters, the full employment equilibrium level of aggregate output depended on the levels of aggregate labor and aggregate capital inputs into production processes. This relationship was reflected in the aggregate production function. Capital input, the economy's capital stock, was always assumed fixed and labor input, the full employment level of employment, was determined by the working of the labor market. Moreover, production technology was assumed to be unchanging. In the present chapter, the conditions of a fixed aggregate capital stock, an unchanging full employment equilibrium level of employment, and an unchanging technology of production processes will be relaxed. These three things will be allowed to change slowly over time. In so doing, the sources of growth in the full employment level of aggregate output will be examined.

SOME GENERAL PRINCIPLES

The aggregate production function (Figure 14.1) reveals how the level of aggregate output depends on aggregate labor input, capital input, and the technology of production.[1] With the capital stock and the state of technology fixed, an increase in the equilibrium level of employment increases aggregate output, raises the marginal physical product of capital ($\Delta Q/\Delta K$), and lowers the marginal physical product of labor ($\Delta Q/\Delta L$). In panel a of Figure 14.1, an increase in labor input, with the capital stock and technology assumed fixed, is depicted as an upward shift in the aggregate production function because aggregate output (on the vertical axis) increases, while the capital stock (on the horizontal axis) is constant. The slope ($\Delta Q/\Delta K$) at B exceeds the slope ($\Delta Q/\Delta K$) at A, showing that the marginal productivity of capital has risen. In panel b, the same experiment is depicted as a rightward movement along the aggregate production function as labor input increases. The slope ($\Delta Q/\Delta L$) at B' is less than the slope ($\Delta Q/\Delta L$) at A', showing that the marginal physical product of labor has fallen.

Figure 14.2 shows that with the equilibrium level of employment and technology fixed, an increase in the capital stock increases aggregate output, raises the marginal physical product of labor, and lowers the marginal physical product of capital. In panel b, an increase in capital input, with labor input and technology assumed fixed, is depicted as an upward shift in the aggregate production function. Aggregate output (on the vertical axis) increases, while labor input (on the horizontal axis) is constant. Since the slope ($\Delta Q/\Delta L$) at B is steeper than the slope ($\Delta Q/\Delta L$) at A, the marginal productivity of labor has risen. In panel a, the same change is depicted as a rightward movement along the aggregate production function as capital input increases. The slope ($\Delta Q/\Delta K$) at B' is less than the slope ($\Delta Q/\Delta K$) at A', showing that the marginal physical product of capital has fallen.

In reality, neither the economy's capital stock nor full employment level of employment are constant in the long run; rather, both are normally increasing at all times. The capital stock usually increases every year because the flow of aggregate private net investment expenditures is usually positive. Business firms are acquiring newly produced capital goods faster than old ones wear out.

[1]To derive the aggregate production function from the production functions of different firms, it is necessary to assume that the production functions of all firms are concave and homogeneous of degree one. As in previous chapters, we will not discuss the important but somewhat advanced subject of aggregation procedures.

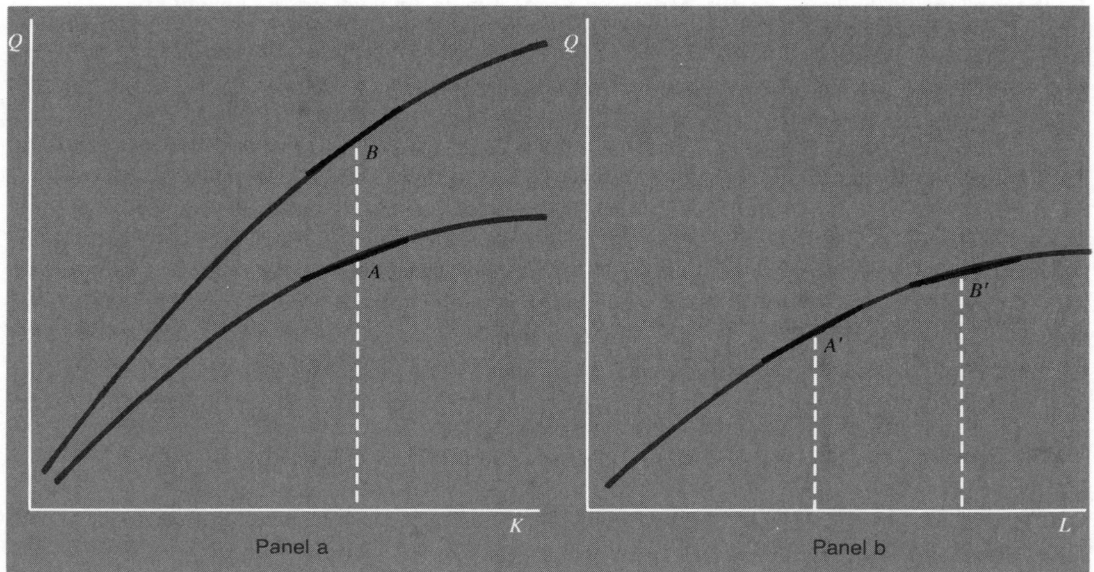

Figure 14.1 The Aggregate Production Function: The Effect of an Increase in the Labor Force

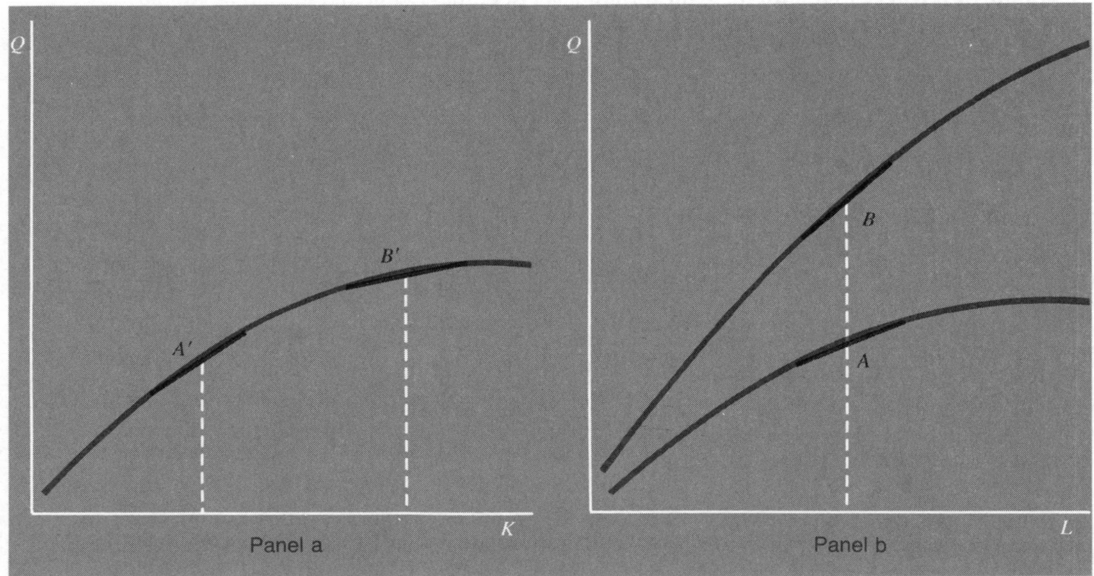

Figure 14.2 The Aggregate Production Function: The Effect of an Increase in the Capital Stock

However, while the capital stock in the economy grows, it does not grow at a fixed rate. The level of net investment expenditures, the rate of growth of the capital stock, is not constant over time. The level of net investment expenditures varies because the present value of capital spending projects is not perceived by business people as being constant over time. In Chapter Five, it was shown that the present value of prospective capital spending projects depends on the expected future after-tax profits (the expected marginal revenue product of capital net of costs) and the interest rate at which these expected returns are discounted. If business people are optimistic about expected future after-tax profits (or if the interest rate falls), present value increases and the rate of growth of the capital stock increases. If business people are pessimistic about expected future after-tax profits (or if the rate of interest rises), present value decreases and the rate of growth of the capital stock decreases. Later in this chapter, the effect of governmental policies designed to increase expected future after-tax profits will be examined. An increase in expected future profits raises the rate of capital formation and stimulates greater growth in the full employment equilibrium level of aggregate output.

In a similar sense, the full employment equilibrium level of employment usually increases every year because the labor force is growing as the population increases. Like the growth of the capital stock, the rate of growth of the equilibrium level of employment has not been constant over time. It may be greater than or less than the rate of growth of the population depending on the incentives that workers have to engage in labor, as opposed to leisure. As discussed in Chapter Three, the decision to allocate time between labor and leisure depends on the opportunity cost of leisure, the after-tax real wage. In Chapter Four, in discussing the *natural rate of unemployment*, factors other than the after-tax real wage were included in the opportunity cost of leisure. It was argued that a more complete version of the opportunity cost of leisure would be the after-tax real wage less unemployment compensation and welfare benefits. This opportunity cost might steadily increase over time as unemployment compensation and welfare benefits are steadily cut. In this case, the allocation of time to labor would steadily increase over time, and labor inputs into production would grow at a faster rate. Later, this chapter will examine the effect of governmental policies designed to increase the allocation of time to labor and, hence, to raise the growth rate of the equilibrium level of employment and promote the growth of aggregate output in the economy.

Output can also increase over time because of technological improvements in production processes. In the real world, technological improvements are as vital to economic growth as capital deepening. It is often realistic to view technological changes as though they increase both the productivity of labor and the productivity of capital. Such technological changes could be viewed as a combination of Figure 14.1, panel a, and Figure 14.2, panel b. Technological changes of this sort are labeled *neutral*.

Technological improvements can be *labor saving*, *capital saving*, or *neutral*. Labor-saving improvements increase the marginal productivity of labor but reduce or have no effect on the marginal productivity of capital. Capital-saving improvements raise the marginal productivity of capital but reduce or have no effect on the marginal productivity of labor. Technological improvements in production processes often occur because of the introduction of new types of capital inputs or new types of (better trained) labor inputs.

New technology is often embodied in new capital inputs and new labor inputs. Neutral technological changes result in increases in the productivity of both labor and capital.

THE THEORY OF STEADY-STATE ECONOMIC GROWTH

With improvements in the technology of production processes assumed neutral, the percentage growth rate of aggregate output may be viewed as a weighted average of the percentage growth rate of the capital input, the percentage growth rate of the labor input, and the percentage growth rate of technological improvements. The following statement expresses this notion: growth rate aggregate of output = $(1 - a) \times$ growth rate of capital input + $(a) \times$ growth rate of labor input + growth rate of technological improvements. The weighting factor a is less than one and greater than zero. The factor a represents labor's share of aggregate income; the factor $1 - a$ represents capital's share. Using the notation $\dot{Q}$, $\dot{K}$, $\dot{L}$, and $\dot{A}$ to represent rates of growth of aggregate output, aggregate capital input, aggregate labor input, and technological improvements, respectively, this relationship may be written as[2]

$$\dot{Q} = a\dot{L} + (1 - a)\,\dot{K} + \dot{A} \tag{14.1}$$

where $0 < a < 1$.

It follows from this definition of the growth rate of aggregate output that if capital inputs are growing more quickly than labor and technological inputs, the ratio of output to labor (Q/L) is rising, and the ratio of output to capital (Q/K) is falling. The ratios Q/L and Q/K represent output per unit of the respective inputs, or the *average* productivity of labor and capital, respectively. When the growth rate of capital exceeds the growth rate of labor and the growth rate of technological improvements, the average physical product of labor, and hence, the marginal physical product of labor, rises, and the average physical product of capital, and hence, the marginal physical product of capital, falls.[3] Therefore, as the marginal physical product of labor for the profit-maximizing firm under conditions of pure competition equals the real wage, the real wage rises. Also, as seen in Chapter Five, for the profit-maximizing firm, as the marginal physical product of capital declines, expected future after-tax profits fall and the present value of capital spending projects declines. Thus, it can be seen that for periods when the rate of growth of the capital stock exceeds the rates of growth of the labor force and technological improvements (periods

[2]This is derived from the more general production function $Q = A\,L^aK^{1-a}$, where A is a technological factor which converts input units into units of output. Since $a + 1 - a = 1$, there are constant returns to scale. Constant returns to scale means that equiproportionate increases in labor and capital inputs with technological change held constant result in an equiproportionate increase in output. Dividing the total differential of $Q = AL^aK^{1-a}$ by Q, we get Equation (14.1), $\dot{Q} = a\dot{L} + (1 - a)\,\dot{K} + \dot{A}$, where the dot over a variable refers to a percentage time rate of change.

[3]We assume marginal product is less than average product. Therefore, when marginal product is falling, average product is falling. When marginal product is greater than average product and is falling, average product is rising.

of *capital deepening*), the real wage rises and the present value of capital spending projects falls.

This condition of capital deepening does not persist indefinitely. From Equation (14.1), it can be seen that a decline in the growth rate of capital will cause the growth rate of output to fall. As capital deepening persists, the present value of prospective capital spending projects steadily declines, fewer and fewer projects have a present value in excess of the cost of the capital good, and the capital stock will grow at an ever slower rate. This trend will continue until the growth rate of capital declines to a point where it is equal to the growth rate of the slowest growing remaining input. From Equation (14.1), it can be seen that where the growth rate of capital equals the growth rate of labor and the growth rate of technological improvements, they generate the equilibrium growth rate of output. At this point, the ratio of output to labor (Q/L) and the ratio of output to capital (Q/K) will stop changing, the real wage will stop rising, and expected future after-tax profits, the expected return to capital, will stop declining. With no further decline in the expected returns to capital, the growth rate of capital will stop falling. At this point, a *steady-state growth rate* of output will be achieved. Therefore, the steady-state equilibrium growth rate of aggregate output will occur only when capital, labor, and technological inputs are growing at the same rate.

In the interval of time during which the growth rate of output is above its steady-state rate, the economy is enjoying a growth bonus. The interval during which the capital stock is deepening and higher growth is being realized will be called a period of *intermediate-run economic growth*. During intermediate-run periods of higher than steady-state rates of growth, the full employment equilibrium level of real income is expanding.

The preceding analysis indicates that in the steady state, the long-run growth rate of an economy does not depend on the percentage of its income that is saved. If the ratio of saving to income, the economy's saving rate, rises, so too must its flow of net investment spending relative to income. Since added net investment expenditures boost the economy's capital stock, a higher saving rate implies a higher rate of capital formation. This implies an improved growth rate of income and sets the stage for greater intermediate-run growth. As shown by Equation 14.1, the growth rate of income is a weighted average of the growth rates of all inputs. As we have seen, in the long-run steady state, the growth rate of the capital stock is constrained not to exceed the growth rate of output. Therefore, an increase in the saving rate of an economy will kindle economic growth in excess of the steady-state growth only in the intermediate run. In the long run, the steady-state growth rate of output is determined by the growth rate of the labor force and the rate of technological change.

Tax Incentives for Economic Growth

The work of Edward Denison indicates that over the period from 1929 to 1969, United States economic growth averaged 3.2 percent per year. Of that growth, Denison attributes 1.4 percent to growth in labor and capital inputs and 1.8 percent to growth in factor productivity. The growth of output fell considerably below this rate in the 1970s to about

2.6 percent per year.[4] If growth had continued at the pre-1969 rate, the level of real GNP would have been over 16 percent greater in 1987. The most prominent feature of this nosedive in growth seems to have been a dismal decline in the rate of growth of the capital stock of the economy and a depressing drop in the growth rate of factor productivity.[5]

Concern over our sagging growth in the 1970s gave birth to a program called *supply-side economic policy*. Supply-side policy focuses on factor supplies (capital and labor) and technological improvements as sources of a higher growth rate of real income. Proponents of supply-side economic policy recognize that long-run growth is constrained by the growth of the labor force and technological improvements. Nevertheless, in the intermediate run, these supply-side advocates propose more rapid growth in technology and in labor and capital inputs through tax incentives. These incentives are to be directed at the rate of saving, the level of investment expenditures, and the supply of labor.[6]

In the 1970s, supply-side proponents argued that inflation had raised nominal incomes so as to push workers, savers, and investors into higher and higher marginal income tax brackets. This *bracket creep* reduces the after-tax return to productive effort. Therefore, it stifles productive activity. Since 1985, taxes have been subject to *tax indexation,* which ends bracket creep by adjusting tax brackets for inflation.

Moreover, even without bracket creep, inflation reduces the real return to saving and investment expenditures because taxes are levied on nominal incomes. For example, assume that the tax rate on nominal income is 50 percent and the rate of inflation is zero. If the nominal rate of interest is 4 percent, the real after-tax rate of return is 2 percent. If inflation jumps to 10 percent, the nominal rate of interest soars to 14 percent, and the real before-tax rate of return is 4 percent. However, the real after-tax rate of return is a negative 3 percent: $4\% - (1 - .50) \times 14\% = -3\%$.

As another example, consider a return in the form of a capital gain on the value of a share of stock (purchased out of saving). If the value of the stock goes up 20 percent in one year, and the income tax is 50 percent, the after-tax gain is 10 percent. If, however, inflation is 10 percent, the increase in the real value of the stock is 10 percent, but the real after-tax gain is zero because the nominal gain of 20 percent is taxed at a 50 percent rate.

For these reasons supply-side advocates contend that an inflationary environment makes it mandatory that tax rates on wages, interest, and profits be cut.

Increases in the after-tax real wage, net of unemployment compensation and welfare benefits, provide an incentive to workers to allocate more time to labor and less to leisure. As seen in Chapter Three, as long as the substitution effect outweighs the income effect, the incentive of an increase in the after-tax real wage increases employment. An increase in labor inputs, *ceteris paribus,* increases the level of aggregate output.

[4]Edward Denison, *Accounting for Slower Economic Growth* (Washington: Brookings Institution, 1979).

[5]Papers by Bosworth and Jorgenson cited in the bibliography to this chapter indicate that about 10 percent of the decline was associated with a decline in capital growth. Most of the decline arose from a plunge in the growth of factor productivity.

[6]In addition to the tax incentives, deregulation, including environmental, financial, and product safety deregulation, is sometimes proffered as a means of increasing the growth in the productivity of labor and capital inputs.

As seen in Chapter Five, increases in expected future after-tax profits provide an incentive for business firms to step up their acquisition of capital goods. An increase in capital inputs, *ceteris paribus,* raises the equilibrium level of aggregate output.

As also seen in Chapter Five, improvements in the after-tax return to saving stimulate saving. In the United States over the past thirty-five years, the ratio of personal saving to personal income has varied between 4 and nearly 8 percent. While international comparisons are difficult to draw inferences from, in other countries the ratio of personal saving to personal income is much higher. In Japan, the ratio of saving to income is 20 percent, in France it is 17 percent, and in West Germany it is 14 percent. These nations provide for lower taxation of interest income. As seen in earlier chapters, an increase in saving raises the equilibrium level of private capital formation.[7]

Intermediate-run economic growth depends on technological changes as well as growth in labor and capital inputs. Supply-side advocates insist that to increase the growth of aggregate output, governmental policies should be designed to boost the after-tax wage, net of unemployment compensation and welfare benefits, to bolster the after-tax return to saving and to enhance expected future after-tax profits. Growth policies which focus on private capital formation and productivity growth are especially important.[8]

In Chapter Six, it was shown that the lack of private capital formation could serve as a serious detriment to adequate growth in output. Moreover, insufficient private capital formation implies an insufficient embodiment of new technology into production processes. This could not only arrest the growth in productivity but also impair the competitiveness of a nation's industries in international markets.

A Tax Cut in the Static General Equilibrium Model

As indicated at the beginning of this chapter, economic growth is a process that occurs over time. Therefore, analysis of the effects of a tax cut on economic growth would normally require dynamic modeling wherein time is an explicit variable. Unfortunately, dynamic modeling usually requires more mathematics than is assumed for the average reader of this text. Therefore, static modeling will be used.

Static models obviously cannot easily be used to trace the path of economic variables over time. Static analysis can examine markets only at certain points in time. Neverthe-

[7]There are a number of problems in using saving and/or investment ratios as indicators of actual domestic capital formation. One problem is that international capital flows, discussed in Chapter Fifteen, allow one country's saving to flow abroad. Another problem is that the underground economy and other factors, discussed in Chapter Two, distort all international comparisons. A third problem is that research and development costs are recorded as current expenditures rather than capital outlays and, therefore, are never reflected in investment expenditures. A fourth problem is that investment in human capital, such as educational expenses, are counted as consumption. As a result, a nation's actual investment expenditures are always understated.

[8]The focus on private capital formation is usually justified by data, such as those cited in papers by Denison, Bosworth, and Jorgenson in footnotes 4 and 5, which show that capital growth accounts for about 10 percent of the growth in output. These same sources also emphasize a tremendous decline in the growth of productivity in the 1970s. The decline in productivity may have been a one-time phenomenon associated with the (oil) supply shocks and new environmental and other regulations of the 1970s. The easing of oil prices and deregulation policies in the 1980s revived the growth in productivity. (See Chapter Eleven for an analysis of the capacity and productivity effects of a significant supply shock.)

less, by focusing on certain markets at carefully selected points in time, static analysis can provide an adequate idea of how a tax cut affects economic growth.

To be able to use a static model to tell the "story" of a tax cut's effect on the economy, important individual stages of the story have to be selected. These stages include: a point in time just before the tax cut, *stage one*; a point in time just after the tax cut but before intermediate-run growth has occurred, *stage two*; and a point in time after the interval of intermediate-run economic growth has taken place, *stage three*. To further simplify matters, our old friend the static general equilibrium (supply and demand) model will be used to tell the story.

To discuss the effects of policy incentives in this model, a new variable, the income tax rate (t), will be introduced. This single variable cannot capture with complete accuracy all of the policy incentives for increasing technological improvements and labor and capital inputs into production processes; however, the income tax rate can serve as a proxy for a wide array of incentives. Incentives to increase labor inputs include reductions in welfare benefits, unemployment compensation payments, and the personal income tax rate on labor income. Incentives to increase capital inputs include reductions in the corporate income tax rate, reductions in the personal income tax rate on interest and dividend income, and greater allowances for depreciation expenses in business income tax returns.

An increase in the income tax rate shall be specified as having negative effects on the quantity of labor supplied (L_S), the level of aggregate real saving (S/P), and the level of aggregate real investment expenditures (I/P) and as having a positive effect on the level of government tax receipts (T/P). Thus, a change in the tax rate will affect the economy in several ways. The purpose of this chapter is not only to view these effects in each separate market but also to trace their impact on the economy as a whole, viewed in a general equilibrium context.

The general equilibrium model containing these effects is specified as follows:

Labor Market–Production Sector

$$L_D = \underset{-\ \ +}{f(w, P)} \qquad \text{labor demand} \qquad (14.2)$$

$$L_S = \underset{+\ \ -\ \ -}{g(w, P, t)} \qquad \text{labor supply} \qquad (14.3)$$

$$L_S = L_D \qquad \text{labor market equilibrium} \qquad (14.4)$$

$$\left(\frac{Y}{P}\right) = \underset{+\ \ +}{\phi(L, K)} \qquad \text{production function} \qquad (14.5)$$

Credit Market

$$\frac{S}{P} = j\left[\underset{+}{i}, \underset{+}{\left(\frac{Y}{P}\right)_d}, \underset{-}{t}\right] \qquad \text{saving} \qquad (14.6)$$

$$\frac{I}{P} = \underset{-\;-}{m(i\,,\,t)}$$ investment expenditures (14.7)

$$\frac{G}{P} - \frac{T}{P} = \frac{\overline{G}}{P} - t\left(\frac{Y}{P}\right)$$ government deficit or surplus (14.8)

$$\frac{S}{P} = \frac{I}{P} + \frac{G}{P} - \frac{T}{P}$$ credit market equilibrium (14.9)

$$\left(\frac{Y}{P}\right)_d = \left(\frac{Y}{P}\right) - \left(\frac{T}{P}\right)$$ definition of disposable income (14.10)

Money Market

$$\left(\frac{M}{P}\right)_d = L\left[\underset{-}{i}, \underset{+}{\left(\frac{Y}{P}\right)}\right]$$ money demand (14.11)

$$M_S = M_1$$ money supply (14.12)

$$\left(\frac{M}{P}\right)_d = \frac{M_s}{P}$$ money market equilibrium (14.13)

Equation (14.3) indicates that whenever the tax rate (on labor income) is cut, the aggregate quantity of labor hours supplied at any given real wage rises. This is consistent with the notion developed in Chapter Three that the relevant opportunity cost of leisure is the after-tax real wage and the assumption that the substitution effect of a change in the after-tax real wage dominates the income effect. Therefore, when the tax rate on labor income is reduced, even though the real wage is unchanged, the after-tax real wage rises, and the supply of labor shifts rightward.

Equation (14.6) indicates that whenever the tax rate on interest (and dividend) income is cut, the level of aggregate real saving at any level of real disposable income and any interest rate increases. This is consistent with the idea that the relevant opportunity cost of consumption is the real, after-tax rate of interest. Therefore, when the tax rate on interest income is reduced, even though the interest rate and real income are unchanged, the after-tax rate of return to saving rises. The supply curve of credit shifts rightward. In addition, as the tax rate is cut, the level of taxation falls, and real disposable income rises. An increase in real disposable income also causes real saving to rise.[9]

Equation (14.7) indicates that whenever the tax rate on business profit is cut, the level of aggregate real investment expenditures rises. This follows from the notion developed in Chapter Five that the present value of prospective capital spending projects depends not only on the interest rate and the expected future profits on those projects but also on the rate at which those profits are taxed. Therefore, when the tax rate is cut, the expected after-tax profits on prospective capital spending projects rise (the numerators in the present value formula rise). At an unchanged interest rate, present value increases and the level of investment spending goes up.[10] The demand curve for credit shifts rightward.

Equation (14.8) indicates that the level of the real tax receipts of government, rather than being assumed exogenous ($\overline{T}/P$) as in previous chapters, is now endogenous to the general equilibrium model. Tax receipts are a product of the tax rate (t) and the level of real income (Y/P). With real government expenditures ($\overline{G}/P$) assumed exogenous, whenever the tax rate (t) is cut, the level of real tax receipts $t(Y/P)$ falls and the government deficit $[G/P - t(Y/P)]$ rises.

It should be emphasized that the present model assumes a constant and proportional rate of taxation. This implies that real tax receipts (T/P) rise in proportion to real income (Y/P). In contrast, progressive taxation means that real tax receipts rise in greater proportion than the rise in real income. Progressive taxation would be somewhat more consistent with the present income tax codes but would unnecessarily complicate the analysis by requiring a more complicated functional form of Equation (14.8). Also, the present model assumes that the tax rate is uniform with regard to labor income, interest income, and business profit. Different tax rates on different sources of income would be more realistic but, once again, would unnecessarily complicate the analysis by requiring several new equations.

The Stages of the Tax Cut in the Static General Equilibrium Model

The effect of a cut in the tax rate in the static general equilibrium model will now be described. As indicated earlier, our method will be to view the economy at three different stages over a long interval of time. At stage one, it is assumed that the economy is at its

[9]In Chapter Five, according to the theory of consumption and saving, if the decrease in the level of aggregate taxation is viewed as being permanent, the effect on aggregate saving will be very small (the marginal propensity to save out of a permanent change in disposable income is very small). In the present analysis, the focus is primarily on the effect of the tax rate, not the level of aggregate taxation, on aggregate saving. Therefore, if there is a permanent cut in the tax rate and the level of aggregate taxation declines, the former may have a sizable positive effect on aggregate saving, while the latter will have a very small positive effect on aggregate saving.

[10]This result follows because payments out of profits are not fully deductible for income tax purposes as in the case of dividend payments on equity claims. This result would also follow when the tax cut is in the form of more rapid permissible depreciation, which reduces the firm's taxable income but does not change its before-tax cash flow (profit plus depreciation). Finally, it would follow when the tax cut is in the form of an investment tax credit. The last represents a reduction of income tax liability as a percentage of current investment expenditures.

As pointed out in footnote 11 of Chapter Five, the existence of an investment expenditures relation depends on the presence of costs of adjusting the desired capital stock to the actual capital stock.

steady-state growth rate. To simplify the analysis, it is assumed that the steady-state growth rate is zero. It is also assumed that there is a zero rate of inflation in this steady state. Real income is at a full employment equilibrium level. There is no growth in the labor force. There is no technological change. There is no growth in the capital stock. The level of saving is just sufficient to satisfy the replacement investment expenditures needs of business firms and the deficit of government. Stage one will present the initial short-term effect in the credit market of an anticipated future cut in the tax rate.

At stage one, a tax cut has been enacted by Congress. The government is assumed to demand more credit in anticipation of the reduction in tax revenue without an offsetting decrease in government expenditures. At this stage, the incentive effects of the tax cut on real saving, real investment, and the labor supply have not yet occurred. The Treasury is assumed to initiate more borrowing in the credit market in anticipation of less tax revenue in the near future. The upshot of the larger government deficit will be, at stage one, a higher interest rate, crowding out of private expenditures, and a rise in the price level. (As in previous chapters, as long as the expected rate of inflation is assumed constant, changes in the real interest rate are synonymous with changes in the nominal interest rate.) There is a lapse of time between stage one and stage two. It is assumed that in stage one, government is borrowing in anticipation of the shortage in tax revenues that will materialize as soon as tax rates are cut. (Alternatively, credit market participants could be assumed to anticipate the future increased borrowing needs of government.) The result will be that even though the actual tax cut has not yet occurred, the rate of interest rises. This approach allows us to isolate the crucial crowding out aspects of the tax cut.

Stage two of the analysis reveals the effects of the cut in the tax rate on labor supply, real saving, and real investment, but assumes these effects have not yet had an impact on real output. The economy is still at its steady-state growth rate of zero. This assumption permits, in a static framework, a separation of the tax cut's effect in stimulating greater labor and capital inputs from its ultimate effect in increasing the level of real output. A lag between the two effects occurs because it takes time for the enlarged flow of investment spending to increase significantly the stock of capital goods in the economy. Four things happen in stage two. First the level of employment climbs. Second, private capital formation advances. Third, the before-tax real wage declines. Fourth, as the rate of interest remains higher than its initial level, the crowding out of private expenditures continues.

Stage three presents the economy after the effect of increased labor and capital inputs have been fully felt on the level of aggregate output. Between stage two and stage three the intermediate-run effect of a higher than steady-state rate of growth of output has occurred. At stage three the full employment equilibrium level of real income is at a higher level. The economy has returned to steady-state growth. However, because the capital stock and the level of employment are greater, the level of aggregate output has expanded.

As real income has risen, real saving has increased, and the real government deficit may have declined from its initial level. (See footnote 18.) As a result of both of these effects, the interest rate has fallen. Crowding out has abated. Because the interest rate has subsided, the ensuing excess demand for real money balances has caused the price level and the rate of inflation to decline. Because of the increased stock of capital goods relative to labor, the marginal product of labor, and hence, the demand for labor has risen. This has fostered an increase in the before-tax real wage.

Tax Cut—Stage One

Figure 14.3 depicts stage one, the most immediate consequences of an (anticipated) tax cut. Initially, equilibrium occurs at points A'', A', and A, in panels a, b, and c, respectively.

In panel b, the anticipated reduction in the tax rate from t_1 to t_0 means that the tax receipts of government are expected to fall from $t_1 \cdot (Y/P)_1$ to $t_0 \cdot (Y/P)_1$. Because the level of real government expenditures is assumed unchanged at $\overline{G}/P$, the real deficit of government is expected to rise from $[\overline{G}/P - t_1 \cdot (Y/P)_1]$ to $[\overline{G}/P - t_0 \cdot (Y/P)_1]$. In anticipation of additional financing needs, the government's demand for credit increases by the directed distance $A'B'$ in panel b.

The resulting rise in the interest rate above i_1 produces an excess supply of money (BD) in panel c. As discussed in earlier chapters, the excess liquidity condition in panel c sustains a continued excess demand for credit ($A'B'$) in panel b. The aggregate budget identity implies that the excess demand for credit is identical to an excess of aggregate real expenditures over aggregate output. This forces up the prices of newly produced goods and services. As the general price level ascends to P_2, in panel c, the excess supply of money disappears and equilibrium is restored to both markets at price level P_2 and at interest rate i_2. Equilibrium occurs at point D' in the credit market and at point D in the money market.[11]

At the new, higher interest rate i_2 a *complete crowding out* of aggregate private expenditures by government expenditures occurs. In panel b, the increase in the real deficit ($A'B'$) results in a decrease in private investment expenditures ($B'C'$) and a decrease in private consumption expenditures ($A'C'$).

This model suggests that in the initial stages of a tax cut, the promised stimulus to the economy will seem remote indeed. As private expenditures fall, the interest rate rises and real income and employment do not improve.

In the labor market, the supply and demand for labor both shift upward by the same magnitude in response to the higher price level (P_2), the nominal wage rises to w_2, and

[11]The preceding description assumes that credit and money market participants either form their expectations rationally but do not anticipate the increased deficit or form their expectations adaptively. If it were assumed that expectations are formed rationally and the increase in the deficit is anticipated, the excess supply of money would be used to place orders for newly produced goods and services, and the price level would rise directly and immediately. There would be no intervening suppression of the rise in interest rates because a temporary liquidity effect would not occur. See Chapter Eleven for further discussion of the alternative linkages between an increase in the government deficit and rises in the price level and the interest rate.

The preceding discussion also ignores the possibility that crowding out could occur without a rise in the interest rate. This would transpire if credit market participants discounted back to the present the increase in future income tax liabilities associated with the swollen indebtedness of government. This effect, the *Ricardian equivalence principle,* was discussed in Chapter Six.

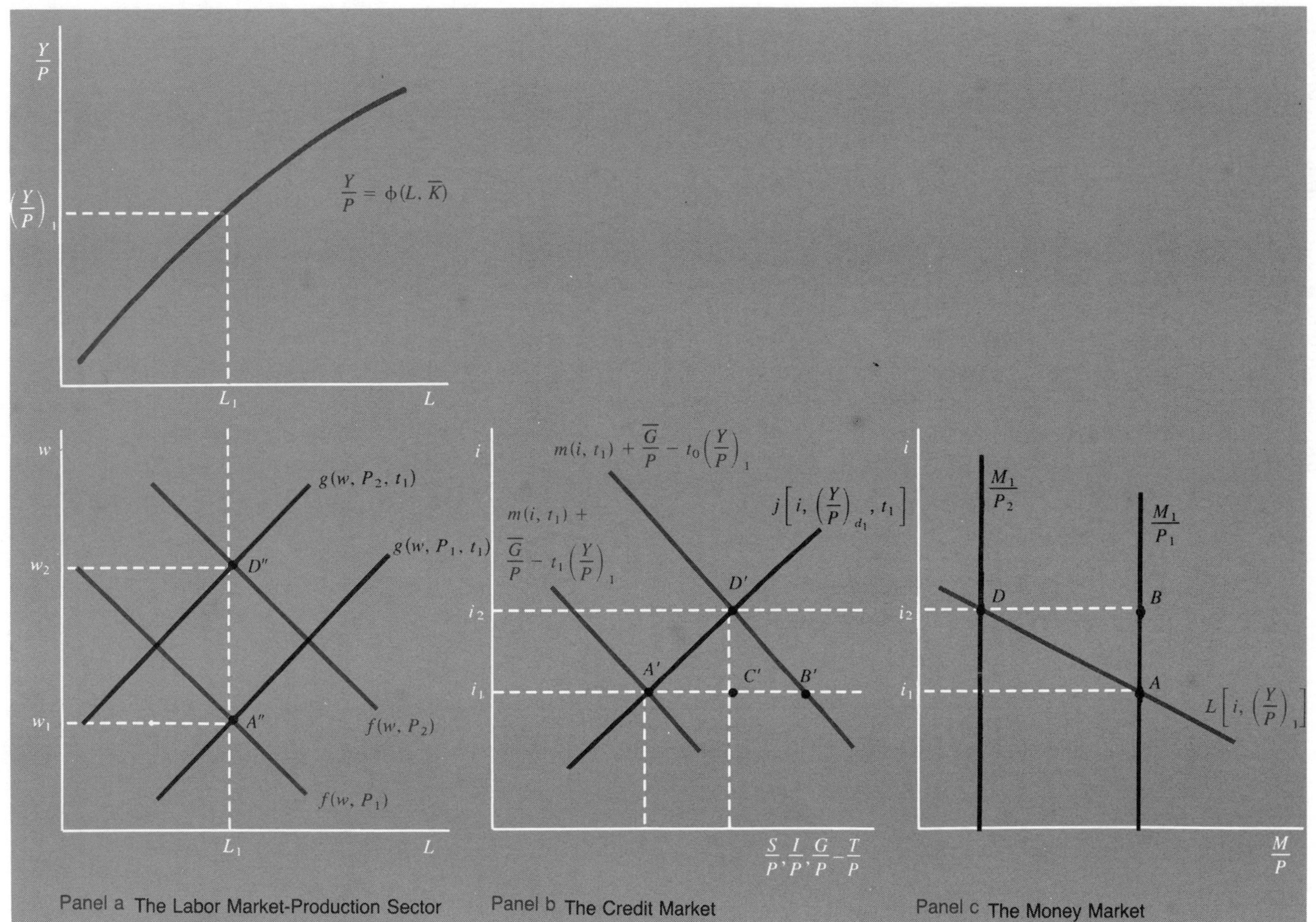

Figure 14.3 Tax Cut—Stage One

the level of employment is unchanged at its full employment equilibrium level, L_1. Equilibrium occurs at point D'', and the level of real income is unchanged at $(Y/P)_1$.

If labor market responses to the increase in the price level are not symmetrical, the tax cut could result, *ceteris paribus,* in a (temporary) rise in employment and real income, as discussed in Chapter Twelve. Of course, the *ceteris paribus* condition may not obtain. For example, if the rate of inflation is falling because of an independent policy of reducing money supply growth, the level of employment and real income might temporarily fall during this stage of a tax cut.

The preceding analysis conforms fairly closely to the initial effects felt throughout the 1980s of the fairly sizable sequence of tax cuts enacted by Congress in 1981, 1983, and 1986. The increase in the deficit of government caused the interest rate to rise and choked off private expenditures. This resulted in a pronounced plunge in private capital formation, especially in certain interest-sensitive sectors of the economy.

In addition, as will be seen in Chapter Fifteen, a rise in domestic interest rates increases the flow of funds from foreign economies into the domestic credit market. This increases the value of the dollar relative to foreign currencies, which in turn increases imports of foreign goods and reduced exports. Thus, even though part of the deficit needs of government was being satisfied by foreign saving, greater imports and reduced exports may have caused a reduction in private expenditures on domestically produced goods. Thus, there may have been crowding out in export-oriented and import-sensitive industries felt throughout the 1980s as a result of the enlargement of the government deficit which was brought about, in part, by the 1981, 1983, and 1986 tax cuts.

Thus, crowding out in interest-sensitive, import-sensitive and export-oriented industries will be a consequence of an increase in the deficit. At stage one, this effect makes the promised stimulus to aggregate real income seem a rather distant prospect.

In the 1981–1987 period, crowding out brought depressed conditions to many industries. Special interest groups petitioned Congress for relief. Concerts and demonstrations were held to raise funds to aid individuals in ailing export-oriented sectors such as agriculture. Some analysts blamed the lack of government protection for the depressed state of many industries. Crowding out, brought about by the tax cut, may have been a major culprit.

In 1986, Congress enacted the Gramm-Rudman-Hollings bill, which targeted specific reductions in the federal deficit for each year from 1986 to 1991. These reductions were to be achieved by slashing government expenditures. If expenditure cuts could not be effected, taxation would have to be increased.[12] In 1987, major portions of the Gramm-Rudman-Hollings Act were declared unconstitutional because they deprived Congress of its right to use discretion in budgetary matters. Nevertheless, the great debate of the late 1980s and early 1990s will center around the ability of Congress to reduce the deficit and its effect on certain sectors of the economy. If pursued, the Gramm-Rudman targets will ease the pressure on interest-sensitive, export-oriented, and import-sensitive sectors.

[12]As discussed below, because reductions in government spending were politically difficult to bring about, in the 1982 and in the 1984 budgets, taxes had to be raised to reduce the deficit and give some sectors of the economy relief from crowding out.

But this will have adverse impacts on sectors that benefit from government expenditures programs. If taxation must be increased, the impact will depend on whether it is carried out by a turn of the income tax screw or by tax reform measures as part of the scenario. Higher income tax rates will have dramatic effects that will be opposite from those discussed in the next two sections. Tax reform promises to be number one on the national economic worry meter in the late 1980s and beyond. It is reviewed later in this chapter.

Tax Cut—Stage Two

Figure 14.4 envisions the state of the economy as the tax cut begins to have an effect on the behavior of households and business firms. In this stage, only the positive incentive effects of the tax cut are portrayed. They increase the level of employment, the level of saving, and the level of investment expenditures relative to income. To simplify the analysis, it is assumed that the level of real income has not yet responded. The growth rate of real income remains at the steady state which, together with inflation, is assumed to be zero. Intermediate-run growth from a higher level of factor inputs is assumed to occur between stage two and stage three. With the price level at P_2 and the nominal wage at w_2, labor market equilibrium is initially at point D'' in panel a. The lower tax rate (t_0) increases the after-tax real wage. As a result, the supply curve of labor shifts rightward from $g(w, P_2, t_1)$ to $g(w, P_2, t_0)$.[13] Assuming that the level of output is not yet affected by an increase in the capital stock, the demand for labor does not shift. Therefore, the before-tax nominal wage declines to $w_{3/2}$. Equilibrium occurs at point E''. Since the equilibrium before-tax nominal wage has fallen but the price level has not, the equilibrium before-tax real wage falls to $w_{3/2}/P_2$. Because workers allocate more time to labor, it is clear that even though the before-tax real wage has fallen, the after-tax real wage has risen.

The reduction in the rate of taxation on interest income from t_1 to t_0 causes the saving function to shift rightward to $j[i, (Y/P)_{d_1}, t_0]$ (panel b) because the after-tax rate of return increases. The supply of credit increases.[14] Because the tax cut from t_1 to t_0 expands expected future after-tax profits from prospective capital spending projects, and thereby increases the present value of these projects, the demand for credit also increases. The

[13]Empirical estimates indicate for married males a labor supply elasticity with respect to the after-tax real wage of .2 to .3. For married females it is upwards of .8. An elasticity of .3 means that for a 10 percent increase in the after-tax real wage, labor supply increases by 3 percent. See the articles by Jerry Hausman and Don Fullerton listed in the bibliography.

[14]Actually, the reduction in the tax rate (t) would also increase disposable real income (Y/P_d) because it reduces the level of taxation $t(Y/P)$. This could also stimulate saving. The magnitude of this effect depends on whether or not the tax cut is believed to be permanent. As shown in Chapter Five, if the increase in disposable income is believed to be permanent, the effect on saving will be quite small. The marginal propensity to save out of a permanent change in income is quite small. On the assumption that the tax cut is permanent, the present example abstracts from the effect of a lower tax rate reducing the level of taxation and increasing disposable income (see footnote 5).

The elasticity of saving with respect to the tax rate has been estimated at between .2 and .4. This means that for a 10 percent decrease in the tax rate, saving will increase by between 2 and 4 percent. See the articles by Michael Evans and Michael Boskin and the article by David Bowles that surveys the literature on the effects of taxes on saving that are cited in the bibliography.

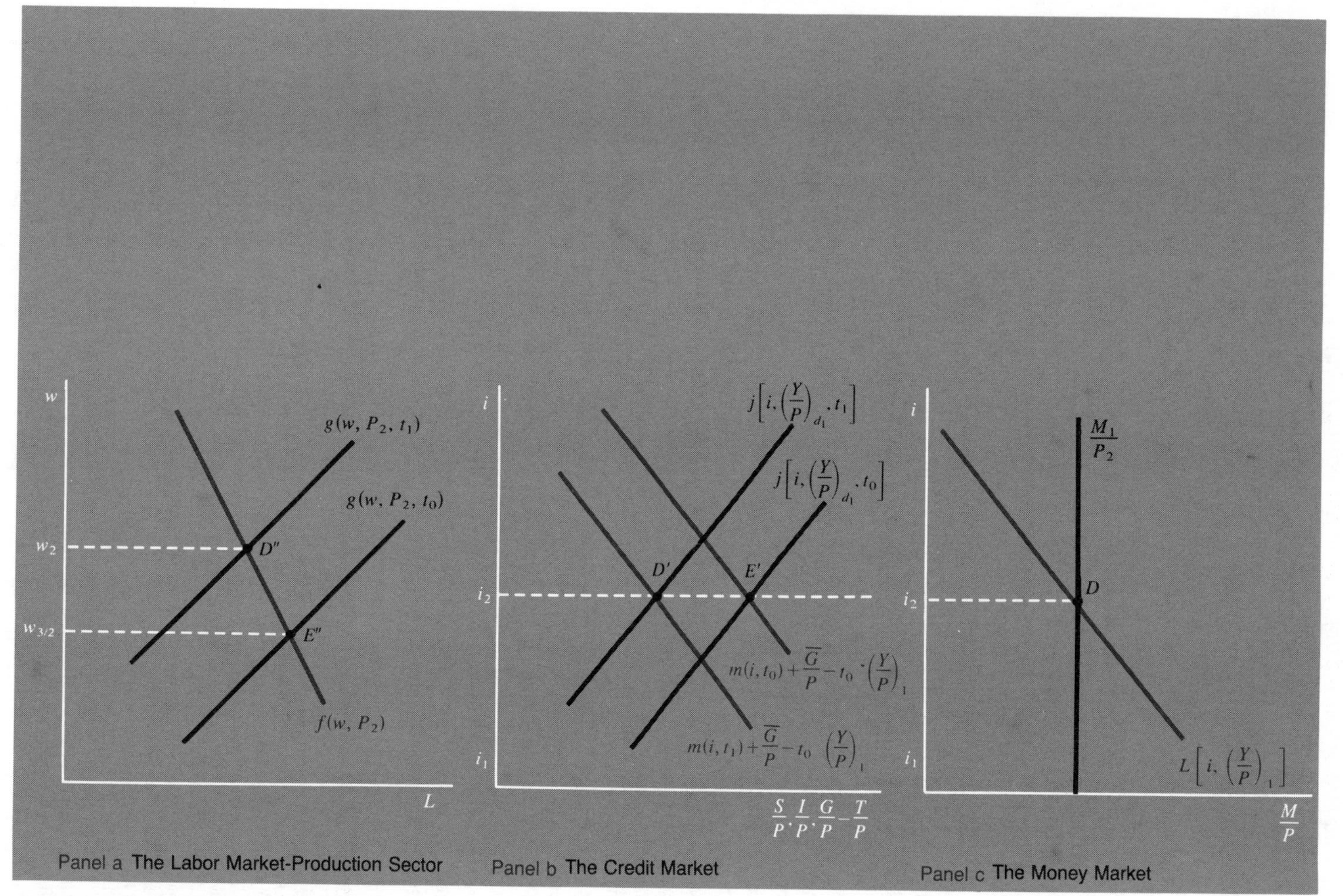

Figure 14.4 Tax Cut—Stage Two

demand for financing investment expenditures jumps to $m(i, t_0)$ from $m(i, t_1)$.[15] Since the level of real income is unchanged at $(Y/P)_1$, the real deficit and related credit demands of government are unchanged at $\overline{G}/P - t_0(Y/P)_1$. Equilibrium in the credit market now occurs at point E'. Both supply and demand curves shift to the right. As a matter of convenience, it is assumed that real saving and real investment both shift by the directed distance $D'E'$ in panel b.[16] As a result, the interest rate remains at i_2. Because real income has not yet increased, the real government deficit is still unchanged at the higher level initially brought about by the tax cut. Therefore, the interest rate is still "high" at i_2, and there is still considerable crowding out in stage two of the tax cut.

In panel c, the equilibrium position of the money market is unchanged at D because the interest rate is still at i_2. The level of real income is still at $(Y/P)_1$.

At this stage of the tax cut, the expected stimulus to the equilibrium level of employment and investment expenditures is depicted, but because capital formation takes time, the effect on the full employment equilibrium level of aggregate real income is not shown. At this stage real income is assumed constant; therefore, the real deficit is unchanged. The full effect of the tax cut in generating a higher level of real income will take time to develop, as the increased flow of real investment expenditures slowly builds up the economy's stock of physical capital goods.[17]

Tax Cut—Stage Three

Figure 14.5 shows the ultimate effect of a cut in the tax rate; namely, an increase in the full employment equilibrium level of aggregate real income. As mentioned earlier, this represents the level of aggregate real income that is reached after the spurt of higher intermediate-run growth. In stage three, the economy has returned to steady-state growth, which, as a matter of convenience, is assumed to be zero.

In panel b, the improvement in the level of real income has two effects. First, real saving increases from $j[i, (Y/P)_{d_1}, t_0]$ to $j[i, (Y/P)_{d_2}, t_0]$, directed distance $E'G'$ in panel b (see footnote 14). Second, the real deficit decreases from $\overline{G}/P - t_0 (Y/P)_1$ to $\overline{G}/P - t_0 (Y/P)_2$, by directed distance $E'H'$.[18] The increase in the supply of and reduction in the

[15]The elasticity of investment expenditures with respect to the tax rate is estimated at $-.3$ for the corporate tax rate and -1.1 for depreciation allowances. This means that a 10 percent cut in corporate income tax rates raises investment expenditures by 3 percent and a 10 percent increase in depreciation allowances raises investment expenditures by 11 percent. See the article by Otto Eckstein and the article by John Naylor that surveys the literature on the effects of taxes on investment expenditures cited in the bibliography.

[16]The equiproportionate shift—both supply and demand—is not a necessary implication of the tax cut. It is assumed here merely as a matter of convenience. One curve could shift more than the other, and the equilibrium rate of interest could be lower or even higher than i_2.

[17]In the United States economy, the private capital stock in dollars of 1987 purchasing power was well over \$25 trillion. In 1987, gross private domestic investment expenditures were only about \$600 billion. Thus, it would take many years of increased investment expenditures to raise the stock of capital goods in the economy by a significant amount.

[18]The new full employment equilibrium deficit $(G/P) - t_0 (Y/P)_2$ may not be smaller than the original, full employment equilibrium deficit $(G/P) - t_1 (Y/P)_1$. For it to be smaller the percentage increase in income will have to be greater than the percentage decrease in the tax rate. This, in turn, requires a higher

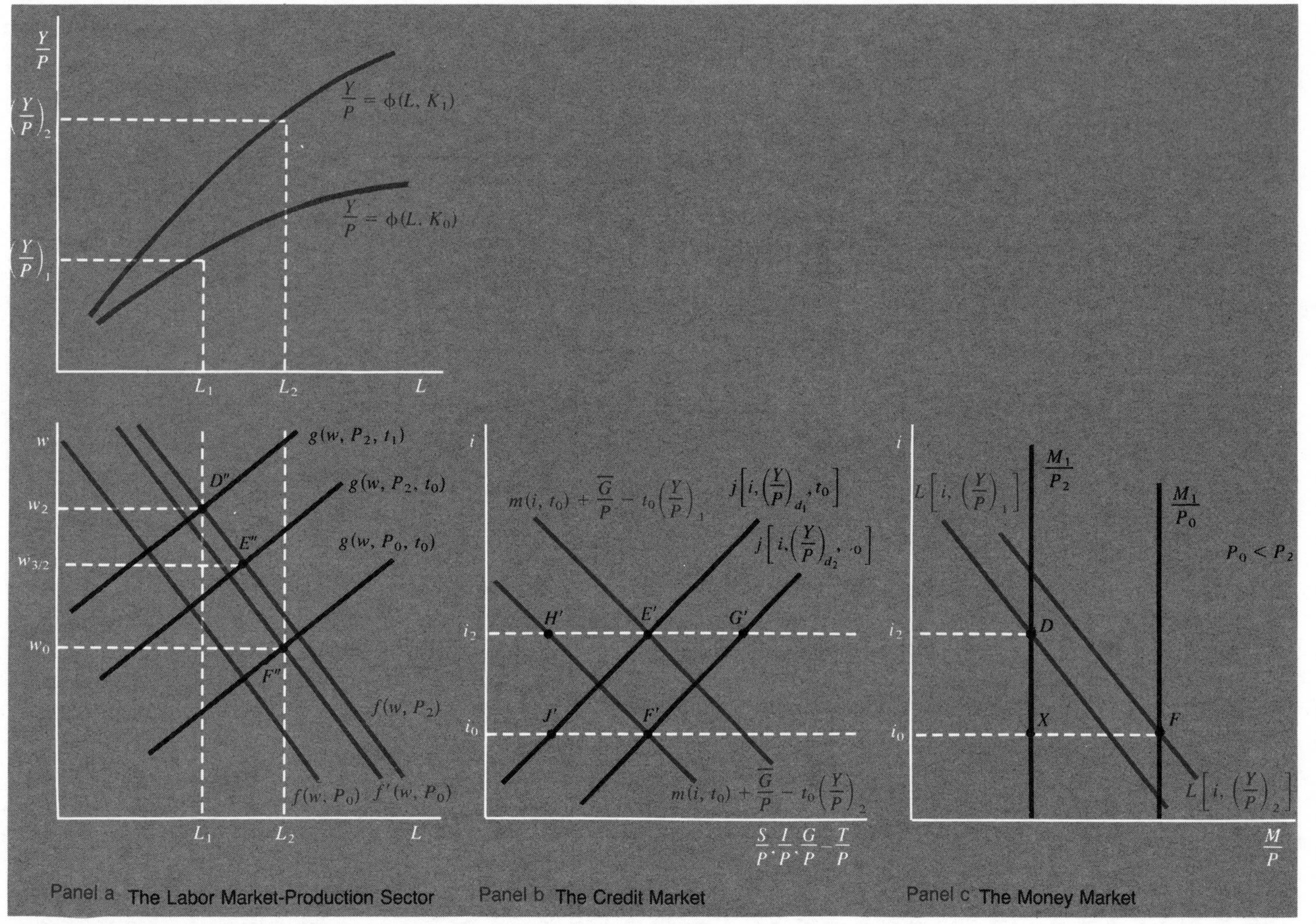

Panel a The Labor Market-Production Sector

Panel b The Credit Market

Panel c The Money Market

Figure 14.5 Tax Cut—Stage Three

demand for credit cause the interest rate to decline to i_0. The interest rate retreats because real saving increases and the real deficit decreases. The initial crowding out of private expenditures by government expenditures that occurred in stage one and persisted in stage two is considerably reduced because the interest rate drops to i_0. (It is eliminated if i_0 in Figure 14.5 is less than i_1 in Figure 14.3.) The equilibrium levels of real investment expenditures and real consumption expenditures increase as the interest rate falls from i_2 to i_0 in panel b. Equilibrium occurs at point F'.[19]

It should be recalled that according to the Ricardian equivalence model of Chapter Six (also discussed in Chapter Eleven), a rise in the deficit would not initially raise the interest rate to i_2 from i_1 in stage one. This would occur because the increase in future taxation would reduce current wealth and increase current saving in an amount equal to the rise in the deficit. In stage three, the interest rate, under Ricardian equivalence, would not decline to i_0. This would occur because the increase in aggregate wealth associated with a permanent boost in the level of real income and the reduction in future taxation would cause real saving to shift rightward to intersect the new demand for credit at the initial (stage one) interest rate, i_1.

The lower interest rate i_0 and the higher level of real income $(Y/P)_2$ increase the quantity of real money balances demanded in the money market (panel c). This creates an excess demand for money XF which drives down the equilibrium price level to P_0. Equilibrium occurs at point F.

In the labor market–production sector (panel a), the higher level of capital input (K_1) relative to labor input (L_2) causes the aggregate production function to shift upward. The higher level of capital input (K_1) relative to labor input (L_2) raises the marginal physical product of labor and makes the demand for labor increase to $f'(w, P_0)$ from $f(w, P_0)$. The supply of labor which had already increased to $g(w, P_2, t_0)$ from $g(w, P_2, t_1)$ now goes up to $g(w, P_0\ t_0)$. Since both demand and supply increase, employment rises to L_2 and the labor market is in equilibrium at point F''. With the greater capital stock (K_1) and greater employment (L_2), aggregate output expands to $(Y/P)_2$. Because capital input has risen relative to labor input, the real wage at the new full employment equilibrium at point F'' is greater than the real wage at the initial equilibrium point D''. When compared to the initial full employment equilibrium prior to stage one, the tax cut finally results in a greater level of real income $(Y/P)_2 > (Y/P)_1$ and a higher real wage $w_0/P_0 > w_2/P_2$.[20]

---

degree of responsiveness of the labor supply, saving, and investment to the cut in the tax rate. Empirical studies suggest an elasticity of tax revenues with respect to the tax rate of about $-.6$ such that a tax cut of 10 percent raises tax revenues by only 6 percent and the new deficit is not smaller than the old one. See the article by Jerry Hausman in the bibliography.

[19]While investment expenditures and saving are greater in the new steady state, the capital stock is now larger. Therefore, a larger flow of saving and investment expenditures is required to replace the larger capital stock as it wears out. In fact, with the assumed zero steady-state growth, all investment expenditures are for replacement.

[20]In this model, we abstract from the possibility that the income effect would dominate the substitution effect because of the permanent boost in aggregate real income and, hence, in labor's real income. This dominance was prominent in the late 19th and early 20th centuries, as discussed in Chapter Three. It would cause the labor supply curve in panel a to shift leftward, raising the equilibrium after-tax real wage but

Implications for Policy: Can We Make It to Stage Three? Tax Reform in the 1980s and Beyond

While there may be some skepticism regarding the actual, empirical effect of incentives for increased employment, real saving, and real investment expenditures (stage two), there is little doubt that, if they actually work, considerable time must elapse before they will have an effect on output. Tax cut packages such as the Reagan administration's Economic Recovery Tax Act of 1981 (ERTA), and additional cuts in 1983 and 1986, are often promoted, for political reasons, as a quick fix for a nation's economic ills. Nothing could be further from the truth. The time that elapses between the tax cut (stage one) and the observable impact on aggregate output (stage three) could be many years.

ERTA featured a 23 percent cut in personal income tax rates in all but the top brackets, *tax indexation* (of tax brackets, personal exemptions, and the zero bracket amount in 1985 and beyond), a speed-up of depreciation allowances, and "safe harbor leasing" provisions that allow firms to sell unused tax credits to businesses that can use them. *Tax indexation* refers to the concept that brackets and exemptions are to be increased by the percentage increase in prices. Its final enactment was delayed until 1987. Because the actual effective magnitude and empirical effects of a tax cut on labor supply, real saving, and real investment expenditures are not well known, tax programs such as ERTA are economic experiments. At the time the Reagan administration pushed through the tax packages of 1981, 1983, and 1986, there was little research to show the actual effects on the supply of labor, the supply of saving, and investment expenditures. People do respond to incentives. The big questions are: How big are the effective incentives and how big are the responses?

Despite these significant cuts, the effective tax rate on personal income may have declined very little because, while income tax rates were reduced in 1981, 1983, and again in 1986, the Tax Equity and Fiscal Responsibility Act, TEFRA, of 1982 curtailed the "safe harbor leasing" and accelerated depreciation arrangements of ERTA. Moreover, Social Security taxes and indirect taxes rose and inflation forced individuals into higher and higher income tax brackets. Therefore, the tax cuts of 1981, 1983, and 1986 may really have represented reductions in the effective increases that would have occurred in their absence. Critics of the current tax policy point out that because of the 1982 offsets under TEFRA, bracket creep, higher Social Security taxes, and higher indirect taxes, the overall tax structure does not provide new incentives. Critics also contend that the responses of labor supply, saving, and investment expenditures to any tax incentives are rather modest.[21]

In addition, unlike experiments in the physical sciences, policy experiments in economics use the real world as a laboratory. Unlike laboratory experiments in the physical sciences, policy experiments in economics do not benefit from laboratory controlled

---

reducing employment from L_2 and real income from $(Y/P)_2$. In addition, an increase in labor's share of income would follow from an increase in the capital/labor ratio if the elasticity of substitution of labor for capital were low. This would strengthen the possibility that the income effect could overpower the substitution effect. For further detail, see the article by Michael Boskin cited in the bibliography to this chapter.

[21]For estimates of the relevant elasticities involved, see footnotes 13, 14, 15, and 18 in this chapter.

conditions. For example, during the first two years of the Reagan tax cut experiment, the *ceteris paribus* condition of textbooks did not hold. The economy was in a recession (because of the administration's avowed pledge to reduce the rate of inflation). Aggregate real income was depressed, as were tax receipts. Because of these conditions, it was difficult to tell if the tax program was having any incentive effects. Finally, the deficit, which was already swollen by the tax cut, ballooned. In addition, as real income declined, so did real saving. The cyclical reduction in saving, increase in the deficit, and other factors discussed in Chapter Thirteen spurred the real rate of interest to even higher levels. Even without a recession, crowding out would have been formidable. With a recession, it was politically intolerable. Moreover, the recession-tempered pessimism of business people may have dampened investment expenditures even further.[22]

Then, from 1982 to 1987, falling oil prices generated a capacity-enhancing supply shock for the economy. As discussed in Chapter Eleven, real income grew. By the mid-1980s, the economy had entered a boom phase. The tax receipts of government rose because of the rise in real income ignited, in part, by the favorable supply shock. Still, the deficit persisted, and interest rates and the value of the dollar continued to be widely regarded as being too high. Clearly, Congress was compelled to control the deficit or face the consequences outlined in Chapters Six and Eleven.

Crowding out, high real interest rates, and the high value of the dollar against foreign currencies forced Congress to try to either reduce government expenditures or raise taxation. The urgency of this need was reflected in the Gramm-Rudman-Hollings bill of 1986, first discussed in Chapter Six. If the targets of GRH are met in the late 1980s, the bill will have a beneficial effect on sectors harmed by crowding out but an adverse effect on sectors damaged by spending cuts or tax rate increases. In order to offset the harm done by expected future tax increases, Congress will probably continue to debate tax reform measures throughout the late 1980s into the 1990s. Let's consider some basic types of tax reform.

Tax Base Broadening. Some experts argue that the erosion of the income tax base through exclusions and deductions has created problems of equity in distributing the tax burden and has prompted higher tax rates than would otherwise be necessary. Comprehensive broadening of the tax base would make compliance and administration easier, improve equity by not taxing different kinds of income differently, and would also allow the same revenue to be raised with significantly lower marginal tax rates, thereby reducing the disincentive of high marginal rates for productive effort.

Unfortunately, rate reductions would not be distributed evenly among taxpayers. Individuals benefiting from tax preferences would owe more taxes when their particular exclusions, deductions, exemptions, or credits were returned to the tax base. Individuals not now benefiting from such preferences would owe less.

Flat Rate Income Tax. Instead of a graduated rate schedule, such as is used in the current income tax, a flat rate income tax applies a single rate to the income base. Flat

[22]As discussed in Chapter Six, some analysts do not worry about the size of the deficit. They claim that in the absence of tax reform (discussed below), current taxation falls upon efficient and inefficient users of resources alike whereas government borrowing impacts upon the least efficient users of resources.

rate tax proposals also usually propose some base broadening in order to simplify compliance and permit a lower tax rate. Like tax base broadening, a flat rate income tax would reduce the high marginal tax rates paid by upper-income classes and increase productive effort. However, also like tax base broadening, the flat tax would probably redistribute the tax burden.

Because the current income tax structure is progressive, some redistribution of the tax burden would result from adoption of a flat rate tax. Experts agree that even with an elimination of all personal exemptions and deductions and taxation of all capital gains, taxpayers in the lower-income groups would receive large tax increases and high-income taxpayers would receive large tax reductions. Because of the increase in tax payments for low-income groups, most flat tax rate proposals include some form of low-income relief. It should be pointed out, however, that some middle- and upper-income groups would be worse off following a change to a flat rate tax because of the loss of deductions and exclusions.

An Indirect Consumption Tax. There are two kinds of indirect consumption taxes—the value-added tax and the retail sales tax. Both are essentially flat rate consumption taxes. A consumption-type value-added tax (VAT) exempts investment goods from taxation and levies a tax on the difference between a firm's sales and the value of its purchased inputs, including capital goods. This is the "value added" to output by the firm. With taxes being passed on at every stage of production, the final consumer bears the burden of the VAT. Although both the VAT and the retail sales tax are collected from sellers, the latter is a single-stage tax collected only at the retail level.

Like the expenditures tax, the VAT and a federal retail sales tax would increase saving and investment when compared with the current income tax. One advantage over the expenditures tax is that a VAT or retail sales tax cannot be evaded by participants in the underground economy. However, both the sales tax and the VAT are regressive; low-income taxpayers, who allocate a higher percentage of their incomes to consumption, would bear a heavier tax burden than would high-income taxpayers. Some of this regressivity could be reduced by exempting from taxation certain classes of consumer spending, such as for food, medical care, clothing, and housing.

An Expenditures Tax. An expenditures tax is another way of taxing consumption instead of income. Under an expenditures tax system, an individual would be taxed on his or her income less his or her saving. An expenditures tax would increase the incentive to save by increasing the after-tax rate of return. As with an income tax, the broader the base of an expenditures tax, the lower the rates needed to provide the same revenue. Moreover, the adoption of an expenditures tax implies progressivity, because if proportional taxation of consumption were wanted, an indirect consumption tax such as a value-added tax or a federal retail sales tax could be used. Because of its fairness and incentive effects, many experts favor an expenditures tax.[23]

[23]One criticism of all the tax reform proposals that encourage saving and discourage consumption is that they downplay the productivity growth associated with human capital investment expenditures that are counted and taxed as consumption. See Chapter Two for a discussion of human capital investment expenditures.

Concluding Comment

Previous chapters treat the full employment equilibrium level of aggregate output as unchanging. In reality, the level of aggregate output increases over time because of increases in the level of labor and capital inputs into production processes, as well as technological improvements in these processes. Increases in labor input, *ceteris paribus,* raise output, increase the marginal productivity of capital, and reduce the marginal productivity of labor. Increases in capital input, *ceteris paribus,* raise aggregate output, increase the marginal productivity of labor, and reduce the marginal productivity of capital. Improvements in technology increase aggregate output and have varying effects on the productivity of labor and capital depending on whether the improvement is neutral, labor saving, or capital saving.

This chapter shows that when the growth rate of the capital stock exceeds the growth rate of output, output will grow at a higher rate. This higher rate is called intermediate-run economic growth. In the long run, the growth rate of capital and output are constrained to be equal to the growth rate of the slowest growing input, labor or technological improvements. This long-run growth rate is called the steady-state growth rate.

Despite the ultimate constraint of steady-state growth, this reasoning suggests that policies designed to stimulate a higher rate of capital formation can increase the level of real income. Supply-side economic analysis focuses on the theoretical and empirical impact of incentives to increase the level of saving, investment, labor supply, and technological change and thereby raise the full employment productive capacity of the economy.

A reduction in income tax rates is viewed as one of the main stimuli to intermediate-run economic growth. An income tax cut is viewed as increasing the supply of labor because it increases the real after-tax wage. It is also seen as stimulating real saving because it increases after-tax interest income. Finally, an income tax cut is conceived as increasing real investment expenditures because it increases the flow of expected future after-tax profits.

The effect of a tax cut is plotted using the static general equilibrium model. Because that model is static, the effects of an income tax cut are separated into three stages. In stage one, the tax cut is mapped out as increasing the government deficit because government must finance the ensuing deficit; however, effects on real saving, investment, and labor supply are suppressed until stage two. As a result, the increased deficit drives up the interest rate and increases the crowding out of private expenditures by government expenditures. At the higher interest rate, the excess supply of money causes the price level to increase.

In stage two, the reduction in the income tax rate is modeled as having a positive impact on real saving, real investment expenditures, and the supply of labor. However, the effect on aggregate output of the resulting increase in labor and capital inputs is suppressed until stage three.

In stage three, real income rises, real saving increases, and the tax receipts of government rise, thereby reducing the increased deficit induced by the tax cut. As a consequence, the interest rate declines and the crowding out that occurred in stage one is reduced.

The Economic Recovery Tax Act of 1981 was the initial one of a series of tax cuts in the 1980s. While there is growing evidence that these tax cuts do increase productive effort, the initial (stage one) impact of the resulting larger government deficit was substantial. Increased government deficits crowd out expenditures in interest-sensitive, import-sensitive, and export-oriented sectors of the economy. These effects and the persistence of deficits, despite the capacity-enhancing oil supply shock of the mid-1980s, required that Congress act. The Gramm-Rudman-Hollings legislation of 1986 targets deficit reductions through 1991. These reductions are to be brought about first by spending cuts; if expenditures cannot be slashed, taxation must be raised. The problems of disincentives for productive effort associated with higher income tax rates, discussed earlier in this chapter, are legendary. In order to minimize these disincentives, tax reform promises to be a thoroughly explored issue in the late 1980s and beyond. It is probably fair to infer from the political responses that the tax cut programs of the 1980s are interesting economic experiments that have encountered and will continue to encounter formidable political obstacles.

EXERCISES

1. Critique the following statement: "An income tax increase will encourage leisure instead of labor."
2. Evaluate the effects of an increase in the growth rate of the capital stock in excess of the growth rate of the labor force.
3. Will the presence of volatile investment expenditures behavior discussed in Chapter Seven make the effects of an income tax cut more predictable or less predictable?
4. Review the various effects of high income tax rates in discouraging saving and investment.
5. Under what conditions could a current tax cut lead to a smaller government deficit in the future?
6. How does the confluence of inflation and the taxation of nominal income inhibit real saving?
7. A spokesman for the United States automobile industry claims that that sector of the economy has been in an "economic recession" for seven years. Clarify this assertion, and relate it to the magnitude of the government deficit.
8. Discuss the obstacles that barred the economy in the early 1980s from the promised payoff from the tax cut program enacted in 1981.
9. What is the difference between tax cuts and tax reform? Enumerate the various proposals for tax reform discussed in this chapter.

10. Evaluate the following: "Depository innovations permitted by the Depository Institutions Deregulation and Monetary Control Act of 1980 encourage saving." (Chapter Nine discusses these innovations.)

BIBLIOGRAPHY

Bechter, Dan M. "Budget Deficits and Supply Side Economics: A Theoretical Discussion." *Economic Review* (June 1982). Federal Reserve Branch of Kansas City, pp. 14–27.

Blinder, Allen S. *Economic Policy and the Great Stagflation*. New York: Academic Press, 1979.

Boskin, Michael J. "Taxation, Saving, and the Rate of Interest." *Journal of Political Economy*, 86 (April 1978), S3–S27. The University of Chicago. Reprinted in Bruce Bartlett and Timothy P. Roth, eds. *The Supply Side Solution*. Chatham, N.J.: Chatham House Publishers, 1983.

———. "Some Issues in Supply-Side Economics." In *Supply Shocks, Incentives and National Wealth*, ed. Karl Brunner and Allan Meltzer. Amsterdam: North-Holland Publishing Co., 1981, pp. 201–220. Reprinted in Bruce Bartlett and Timothy P. Roth, eds. *The Supply Side Solution*. Chatham, N.J.: Chatham House Publishers, 1983.

Bosworth, Barry P. "Capital Formation and Economic Policy." *Brookings Papers on Economic Activity* 2 (1982), pp. 273–317.

Bowles, David C. "Consumption and Saving Through the 1970's and 1980's: A Survey of Empirical Research." In *Modern Concepts in Macroeconomics*, ed. Thomas M. Havrilesky. Arlington Heights, Ill.: Harlan Davidson, Inc., 1985.

Denison, Edward F. *Accounting for Slower Economic Growth*. Washington, D.C.: Brookings Institution, 1979.

Eckstein, Otto. "A Time for Supply Economics." In Congress of the United States, Forecasting the Supply Side of the Economy: Hearing before the Joint Economic Committee, 96th Congress, 2nd session. Washington, D.C.: Government Printing Office, 1980, pp. 24–31. Reprinted in Bruce Bartlett and Timothy P. Roth, eds. *The Supply Side Solution*. Chatham, N.J.: Chatham House Publishers, 1983.

Evans, Michael K. "The Bankruptcy of Keynesian Econometric Models." *Challenge* (January/February 1980), pp. 13–19. Armonk, NY: M. E. Sharpe, Inc. Reprinted in Bruce Bartlett and Timothy P. Roth, eds. *The Supply Side Solution*. Chatham, N.J.: Chatham House Publishers, 1983.

Froyen, Richard T. *Macroeconomics: Theories and Policies*. New York: Macmillan, 1983.

Fullerton, Don. "Can Tax Revenues Go Up When Tax Rates Go Down?" Washington, D.C.: Department of the Treasury, Office of Tax Analysis, Paper 41, September 1980. Reprinted in Bruce Bartlett and Timothy P. Roth, eds. *The Supply Side Solution*. Chatham, N.J.: Chatham House Publishers, 1983.

Hausman, Jerry A. "Labor Supply." In *How Taxes Affect Economic Behavior*, ed. Henry J. Aaron and Joseph A. Pechman, Washington, D.C.: Brookings Institution, 1981, pp. 27–64. Reprinted in Bruce Bartlett and Timothy P. Roth, eds. *The Supply Side Solution*. Chatham, N.J.: Chatham House Publishers, 1983.

Jorgenson, Dale W. "Taxation and Technical Change." *Technology in Society* 3 (1981), pp. 151–171.

Keleher, Robert E. "Supply Side Tax Policy." In *Modern Concepts in Macroeconomics*, ed. Thomas M. Havrilesky. Arlington Heights, Ill.: Harlan Davidson, Inc., 1985.

Kendrick, John W. *The Formation and Stocks of Total Capital*. New York: National Bureau of Economic Research, 1976.

Meyer, Stephen A. "Tax Cuts: Reality or Illusion." *Business Review,* Federal Reserve Bank of Philadelphia (July–August 1983), pp. 3–16.

Naylor, John. "A Survey of Post-1970 Empirical Studies of Investment Expenditures." In *Modern Concepts in Macroeconomics,* ed. Thomas M. Havrilesky. Arlington Heights, Ill.: Harlan Davidson, Inc., 1985.

Phelps, Edmund S. "Second Essay on the Golden Rule of Accumulation." *American Economic Review* (September 1965), pp. 232–248.

Shapiro, T., and W. L. White, eds. *Capital for Productivity and Jobs*. Englewood Cliffs, N.J.: Prentice-Hall, 1977.

Solow, Robert M. "A Contribution to the Theory of Economic Growth." *Quarterly Journal of Economics* (February 1956), pp. 65–94.

Swan, Thomas. "Economic Growth and Capital Accumulation." *Economic Record* (November 1956), pp. 334–361.

Tannenwald, Robert E. "Should We Adopt an Expenditures Tax?" In *Modern Concepts in Macroeconomics,* ed. Thomas M. Havrilesky. Arlington Heights, Ill.: Harlan Davidson, Inc., 1985.

Tobin, James. "A Dynamic Aggregative Model." *Journal of Political Economy* (April 1955), pp. 121–135.

An Open Economy

Chapter 15

Introduction

Previous chapters focused exclusively on a one-country, closed economy. This chapter introduces economic interaction between countries—our domestic economy and that of the rest of the world, which is assumed for purposes of analytical simplification to consist of one other country. This requires an increase in the number of variables in the basic model. The model will have an exchange rate between domestic and foreign currency, a foreign price level, a foreign interest rate, and a level of foreign aggregate real income. There will be a foreign exchange market in which the currencies of each country are traded and in which their relative price, the *exchange rate,* is determined. Each country is assumed to have its own currency. There is a wide variety of currencies from which to choose: United States dollars, Canadian dollars, British pounds, French francs, Polish zlotys, Malaysian ringgits, and Banalian zookers, to name a few. However, to keep matters simple, the two currencies chosen will be dollars ($) for our country and pounds (£) for the other country. The foreign currency will also be called *foreign exchange*. The *exchange rate* (e) is the relative price of foreign currency (the price of foreign exchange). The exchange rate is the number of dollars one needs to exchange for a single pound ($/£).

This chapter begins by examining a partial equilibrium model of the foreign sector of the domestic economy. Several new concepts will be introduced. One of these concepts is the *current account balance,* another is *net capital flows*. The *balance of payments* is simply the sum of the current account balance and net capital flows. The current account balance is defined as exports minus imports plus net factor payments. Exports and imports will be specified to depend on the exchange rate, the price of domestic goods, the price of foreign goods, domestic real income, and foreign real income. Net capital flows are the difference between foreign funds being invested in domestic financial assets and domestic funds being invested in foreign financial assets. Net capital flows will be specified to depend on the domestic interest rate and the foreign interest rate.

Perfect mobility of international capital flows is assumed. This assumption, together with the assumption of fixed foreign and domestic price levels and real income levels, implies that imports and exports will be brought into equilibrium by adjustments in the exchange rate. After viewing the foreign exchange market in a partial equilibrium context, a foreign exchange market is introduced implicitly into the general equilibrium model by incorporating it into the credit market—flow sector—of the general equilibrium model of the economy as a whole.

Initially, a Neoclassical general equilibrium model with a flexible exchange rate (sometimes called a freely floating exchange rate) will be used. The first experiment will be used to increase the domestic money supply using that model. The same experiment will then be carried out with a Keynesian general equilibrium model that also has a perfectly flexible exchange rate. Then, using a Neoclassical general equilibrium model with a flexible exchange rate, the experiment involving an increase in the government deficit will be performed. The final experiment under a flexible exchange rate involves an increase in the government deficit using a Keynesian general equilibrium model. In each experiment, consideration is given to the linkage between either the money supply or the deficit shock and the endogenous variables of the model under alternative assumptions regarding the formation of expectations by market participants.

The subsequent section will examine the case of a fixed exchange rate, a rate that is not permitted to fluctuate with changes in supply and demand. Three experiments will be performed here. The first involves an increase in the government deficit in a Neoclassical general equilibrium model. The second explores the implications of an increase in the government deficit using a Keynesian model. The third examines the effects of an increase in the domestic money supply under Neoclassical conditions.

The chapter closes with a review of the evolution of the present international payments system from a fixed exchange rate to a flexible exchange rate mechanism. The discussion focuses on the forces that have caused the breakdown of the fixed exchange rate system. It attends to some of the difficulties of maintaining freely fluctuating exchange rates and describes the development of the present loose constellation of managed floating exchange rates.

A PARTIAL EQUILIBRIUM MODEL OF THE FOREIGN SECTOR

Foreign purchases of domestically produced goods and services are called *exports*. Domestic purchases of foreign-produced goods and services are called *imports*. Exports are part of the flow of domestic expenditures. Imports are a leakage from domestic income because they represent expenditures on foreign production. Exports and imports each depend on the price of domestic goods relative to the price of foreign goods. This relative price is defined as the ratio of the price of goods produced abroad (P^*) to the price of goods produced domestically (P_d) times the exchange rate (e) *measured in dollars per pound* (\$/£). The product ($e \cdot P^*$) measures the price of foreign goods in terms of dollars, and the term (P_d) measures the price of domestic goods in dollars. If import prices ($e \cdot P^*$) rise relative to the price of domestic goods ((P_d), there is a deterioration in the *terms of trade*. The terms of trade are the relative price of imports. They are the number of units of domestic goods that are given up to obtain one unit of foreign production from abroad. As they are a price that is denominated in goods rather than nominal dollars, the terms of trade are a real variable, not a nominal variable.

If both the foreign price level (P^*) and the price of domestic goods (P_d) are held constant, the terms of trade move with the exchange rate. If the exchange rate increases (if e rises), then import prices increase in terms of domestic currency. Exchange rate appreciation thus raises the relative price of imports, the terms of trade. It also makes domestic goods relatively cheaper. Therefore, exchange rate appreciation (a decline in the value of the dollar), or a rise in e, leads to an increase in exports and a decrease in imports. Furthermore, if the exchange rate and foreign prices are held constant, an increase in the domestic price level increases the relative price of domestic goods. It reduces the relative price of the foreign goods, the terms of trade. This induces a rise in imports and a decline in exports.

Current Account Trade Balance

The *current account trade balance* expresses the difference between real exports and real imports. Real exports (X/P) depend on the terms of trade and the level of real income in the importing country. Real imports (Im/P) depend on the terms of trade, $e\,P^*/P_d$, and the level of domestic real income such that:

$$\frac{X}{P} = X\left[\underset{-}{\frac{e\,P^*}{P_d}}, \underset{+}{\frac{Y^*}{P^*}}\right], \text{ and} \tag{15.1}$$

$$\frac{Im}{P} = M\left[\underset{-}{\frac{e\,P^*}{P_d}}, \underset{+}{\left(\frac{Y}{P}\right)_d}\right] \tag{15.2}$$

In Equation (15.1), the term Y^*/P^* is the level of foreign aggregate real income. In Equation (15.2), the term $(Y/P)_d$ is the level of domestic aggregate real disposable income. The term e is the price of pounds in dollars; P_d is the price of domestic goods, and P^* is the price of foreign goods. The notations X [ ] and M [ ] mean "a function of." When used in this way, the symbol M does not stand for the money supply.

The current account trade balance (A/P) is the difference between real exports and real imports.[1]

$$\frac{A}{P} = X\left(\frac{e\,P^*}{P_d}, \frac{Y^*}{P^*}\right) - M\left[\frac{e\,P^*}{P_d}, \left(\frac{Y}{P}\right)_d\right] \tag{15.3}$$

With the price of foreign goods (P^*) held constant, an increase in the price of domestically produced goods reduces exports and increases imports. Therefore, an increase in P_d reduces the current account trade balance. An increase in the exchange rate, an increase in e, boosts exports and reduces imports because the purchasing power of foreign currency in terms of the dollar has increased. Therefore, it increases the current account trade balance.

Capital Flows

In the study of international finance, movements of foreign funds into the domestic economy are called *capital inflows*. Movements of domestic funds abroad are called *capital outflows*. The label "capital" here may be misleading because heretofore it has referred to the *stock* of capital goods. In the present context, it is associated with a *flow* of funds. In the present context, a better label would be *credit inflows* and *outflows*. In Chapter Five, Table 5.1, it was seen that in recent years foreign "capital" inflows added many billions of dollars to the domestic credit market each year. In 1987, net capital inflows were over $100 billion.

Capital outflows $(N/P)_0$ can arise from more than one source. They can come from residents who purchase foreign financial assets abroad or from loans to foreigners (residents acquiring foreign financial assets). Capital inflows $(N/P)_i$ represent movements of foreign funds into the domestic economy. They arise from residents of foreign countries who invest in domestic financial assets (foreigners acquiring domestic financial assets):

$$\frac{N}{P} = \left(\frac{N}{P}\right)_i - \left(\frac{N}{P}\right)_o \tag{15.4}$$

Net capital flows (N/P) are the difference between inflows and outflows. They depend negatively on the foreign interest rate and positively on the domestic interest rate. A lower domestic interest rate encourages net outflows; a higher one spurs net inflows. Throughout this chapter, the assumption of *perfect international capital mobility* is maintained.[2] Under this assumption, the domestic interest rate will be equal to the foreign interest rate. This condition reflects the notion that, in the absence of political risk, arbitrage

[1]The current account is the sum of the current account trade balance and net factor payments. Net factor payments are the sum of interest and dividend income (interest and dividends earned from foreign assets less interest and dividends paid to foreigners) plus net labor remittances from nationals working abroad. For a description of different ways of reporting the balance of payments, see Leland B. Yeager, *International Monetary Relations: Theory, History and Policy*, 2d ed. (New York: Harper and Row, 1976).

[2]This assumption is mildly at odds with the facts. However, the opposite assumption, one of zero capital mobility, so grossly violates the facts that analysis premised on such an assumption is useless.

between countries will equalize interest rates. It implies that lenders are indifferent between lending domestically or lending abroad and that borrowers are similarly indifferent between borrowing domestically or borrowing abroad.[3] Thus, $i = i^*$.

The Balance of Payments

The balance of payments (B/P) is the sum of the current account balance (A/P) and net capital flows (N/P):[4]

$$\frac{B}{P} = \frac{A}{P} + \frac{N}{P} \tag{15.5}$$

There is balance of payments equilibrium ($B/P = 0$) where net imports ($A/P = X/P - Im/P$) equal net capital inflows (N/P) or when net exports equal net capital outflows. Thus, net capital inflows mean that imports exceed exports, and net capital outflows mean that exports exceed imports. The condition of balance of payments equilibrium is called *external balance*. The label *external* refers to transactions external to the domestic economy—transactions with foreign economies.

The Market for Foreign Exchange[5]

The balance of payments can be interpreted in terms of the supply of and demand for foreign exchange. In Chapter Six, we interpreted it in terms of the supply of and demand for dollars. That treatment placed the price of the dollar in terms of a foreign currency on the vertical axis and the quantity of dollars on the horizontal axis. Here we place the price of the foreign currency in terms of the dollar bn the vertical axis and the quantity of foreign currency on the horizontal axis. One treatment is the equivalent of the other. The supply of foreign exchange (F_s) emanates from exports (X/P) and from capital inflows $(N/P)_i$. Exports and capital inflows require the sale of foreign currency by foreigners for dollars. These dollars enable foreigners to purchase domestic goods and services and domestic financial (paper) assets. The demand for foreign exchange (F_d) emanates from imports (Im/P), and from capital outflows $(N/P)_0$. Imports and capital outflows require the sale of dollars by domestic individuals to buy foreign currency. Foreign currency

[3]Somewhat more realistically, the expected return on domestic lending will equal the expected return on foreign lending, as viewed by a domestic resident. The expected return on foreign lending is the foreign interest rate plus the expected change in the exchange rate. Perfect substitutability of foreign for domestic lending implies that in equilibrium the interest rate differential between two countries just equals the expected change in the exchange rate. This is the theory of *interest rate parity*. An exchange rate differential will widen if lenders expect a foreign currency will appreciate or depreciate in the future. This expectation depends in turn on differences in expected future inflation rates between the two countries. Speculators buy and sell foreign exchange for the purpose of profiting from expected changes in exchange rates. To survive over time, speculators must buy when the exchange rate is below equilibrium and sell when it is above equilibrium. Thus, speculators, in the long run, stabilize exchange rates.

[4]To simplify this analysis we assume that net factor payments are zero. Therefore, the current account trade balance is equal to the current account. See footnote 1 for further discussion.

[5]The foreign exchange market is not in any one location. Rather it is a worldwide market that is electronically connected. It has the largest trading volume of any market and never closes. See Robert Z. Aliber, *The International Money Game*, 3d ed. (New York: Basic Books, 1979).

enables domestic residents to purchase foreign goods and services and foreign financial (paper) assets.

A supply and demand, partial equilibrium model of the foreign exchange market is specified as follows:

$$F_s = \frac{X}{P} + \left(\frac{N}{P}\right)_i \tag{15.6}$$

$$F_d = \frac{Im}{P} + \left(\frac{N}{P}\right)_o \tag{15.7}$$

$$F_s = F_d \tag{15.8}$$

For simplicity, assume a zero net capital flow. In this case, the supply of foreign exchange (F_s) is coextensive with exports (X/P), and the demand for foreign exchange is coextensive with imports (Im/P).

If both the price of domestic goods (P_d) and the price of foreign goods (P^*) are assumed constant, then the supply of and demand for foreign exchange, exports and imports respectively, determine the exchange rate (e).[6] Figure 15.1 depicts equilibrium in the (flow) market for foreign exchange.

If the level of domestic real disposable income rises, there will be an increase in imports. This causes the demand for foreign exchange to increase. There is an excess demand (AB) at the old equilibrium exchange rate. The condition of excess demand drives up the equilibrium exchange rate to e_1 (depreciates the value of the dollar). At the new, higher exchange rate, real imports are more expensive in the domestic market, and real exports are less expensive to foreigners. As the exchange rate rises, there is a decrease in the quantity of real imports measured by directed distance BC and an increase in the quantity of real exports measured by directed distance AC. Equilibrium is restored at the new exchange rate e_1.

THE GENERAL EQUILIBRIUM MODEL

Now that the elements of the foreign sector in a partial equilibrium context have been defined, they are introduced into a Neoclassical general equilibrium model of the economy as a whole. Table 15.1 presents that model.

The labor market–production sector is exactly the same as that of the Neoclassical model for a closed economy with one exception. The demand for labor (Equation 15.9) varies inversely with the nominal wage (w) and directly with the price of domestic goods (P_d) rather than the overall price level (P). This is because the demand for labor varies

[6]This exchange rate is the spot rate, the price of foreign exchange rate for immediate delivery. The forward exchange rate is the price of foreign exchange for delivery at a specific future date. The equilibrium spot rate is thus determined by the forces determining the price levels, and real income levels, in each country.

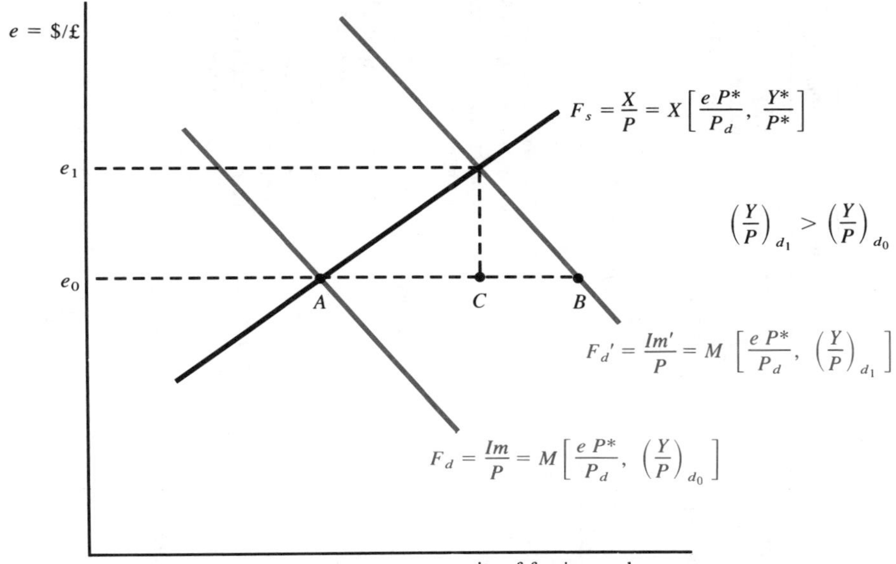

Figure 15.1 The Market for Foreign Exchange

directly with the marginal revenue product of labor, which is in turn affected only by domestic prices. The supply of labor, Equation (15.10), varies directly with the nominal wage (w) and inversely with the overall price level (P).

The overall price level (P), the cost of living, is defined by Equation (15.25) as a geometrically weighted average of the dollar price of domestic goods (P_d) and the dollar price of foreign goods ($e\ P^*$). The weight "a" reflects expenditures on domestically produced goods as a percent of total domestic budgets. The weight "$1 - a$" reflects expenditures on foreign goods as a percentage of total domestic budgets. Where $0 < a < 1$, the two weights sum to unity and the implicit exponent on the overall price level is unity.

The labor market determines the full employment equilibrium level of employment and the equilibrium real wage. Substituting the equilibrium level of employment into the aggregate production function, Equation (15.12), yields the equilibrium level of real income.

The credit (loanable funds) market for an open economy is quite different from the credit market for a closed economy. The terms of trade ($e\ P^*/P_d$) and the level of foreign aggregate real income (Y^*/P^*) are new variables. There is an exports relation, Equation (15.16), and an imports relation, Equation (15.17). The assumption of perfect international capital mobility implies that the domestic interest rate is exogenously determined in the world capital market at level i_0 specified in Equation (15.19). The level of foreign aggregate real income is also exogenously determined as specified by Equation (15.20). Next, turn to the saving relation, Equation (15.13). Since the level of domestic aggregate real income is determined by the working of the labor market, and since both the level

Table 15.1 The Neoclassical Model of an Open Economy

Sector	Equations			Key Characteristics
Labor market–production sector	$L_D = f(\underset{-}{w}, \underset{+}{P_d})$	Labor demand	(15.9)	(a) Gives the full employment equilibrium level of employment and the equilibrium real wage.
	$L_S = g(\underset{+}{w}, \underset{-}{P})$	Labor supply	(15.10)	
	$L_S = L_D$	Labor market equilibrium	(15.11)	
	$\frac{Y}{P} = \phi(\underset{+}{L}, \underset{+}{K})$	Production function	(15.12)	(b) With the capital stock given, yields the full employment equilibrium level of real income.
Credit (loanable funds) market	$\frac{S}{P} = j\left[\underset{+}{i}, \underset{+}{\left(\frac{Y}{P}\right)_d}\right]$	Saving	(15.13)	(c) With a domestic income given by working of labor market, with foreign real income exogenous, and with domestic interest rate determined in world capital market, the credit market yields the equilibrium terms of trade.
	$\frac{I}{P} = m(\underset{-}{i})$	Investment expenditures	(15.14)	
	$\frac{G}{P} - \frac{T}{P} = \frac{\overline{G}}{P} - \frac{\overline{T}}{P}$	Government deficit	(15.15)	
	$\frac{X}{P} = X\left[\underset{+}{e\frac{P^*}{P_d}}, \underset{+}{\left(\frac{Y^*}{P^*}\right)}\right]$	Exports	(15.16)	

	$\frac{Im}{P} = M\left[\underset{-}{e\frac{P^*}{P_d}}, \underset{+}{\left(\frac{Y}{P}\right)_d}\right]$	Imports	(15.17)	
	$\frac{I}{P} + \frac{G}{P} - \frac{T}{P} + \frac{X}{P} = \frac{S}{P} + \frac{Im}{P}$	Credit market equilibrium	(15.18)	
	$i = i_0$	Fixed interest rate	(15.19)	
	$\left(\frac{Y^*}{P^*}\right) = \left(\frac{\overline{Y}^*}{\overline{P}^*}\right)$	Fixed level of foreign income	(15.20)	
	$\left(\frac{Y}{P}\right)_d = \frac{Y}{P} - \frac{\overline{T}}{P}$	Definition of disposable income	(15.21)	
Money market				
	$\left(\frac{M}{P}\right)_d = L\left[\underset{-}{i}, \underset{+}{\frac{Y}{P}}, \underset{+}{\left(e\frac{P^*}{P^d}\right)}\right]$	Demand for money	(15.22)	(d) With domestic income determined in the labor market–production sector, the interest rate determined in the world capital market, the foreign price level exogenously determined, and the terms of trade determined in the domestic credit market, this market yields the price of domestic goods and the overall price level.
	$M_S = M_0$	Money supply	(15.23)	
	$\left(\frac{M}{P}\right)_d = \frac{M_S}{P}$	Money market equilibrium	(15.24)	
	$P = P_d^a \cdot (e\,P^*)^{1-a}$	The price level	(15.25)	
	$P^* = \overline{P}^*$	Fixed price of foreign goods	(15.26)	

of taxation and the interest rates are exogenously determined, the level of aggregate real saving is known. Similarly, with the interest rate exogenously determined, the level of real investment expenditures, Equation (15.14), is also known. Equation (15.15) says that the level of the real government deficit is exogenously determined. Therefore, in the credit market the levels of real saving, real investment expenditures, and the real government deficit are all known.

Next, consider real exports in Equation (15.16). As the level of foreign real income is exogenously determined, real exports can only vary (positively) with the terms of trade ($e\ P^*/P_d$). Similarly, because the level of domestic aggregate real income (and therefore aggregate real disposable income) is determined by the working of the labor market, real imports, Equation (15.17), can only vary (negatively) with the terms of trade. Therefore, credit market equilibrium, Equation (15.18), is brought about exclusively through adjustment in the terms of trade. Thus, equilibrium in this (flow) sector of the economy determines the terms of trade.

The concept of equilibrium in the credit market in the general equilibrium model is broader than the concept of equilibrium in the foreign exchange market in a partial equilibrium context. The latter involves only the exchange rate. The price of domestic goods, the price of foreign goods, and the overall price level are held constant. In a general equilibrium context, the price of domestic goods and the overall price level are variables, and we solve for the equilibrium terms of trade, not just the equilibrium exchange rate.

The term "credit market" is a carryover from all previous chapters. It refers to the flow subsector of the overall general equilibrium model. Sometimes the term "loanable funds" is used instead of credit. In the credit market of an open economy model, domestic credit flows (saving, investment, and government flows) are added to international credit flows (the supply of and demand for foreign exchange). As in earlier chapters, it is sometimes useful to interpret this flow subsector in terms of aggregate expenditures and aggregate output rather than in terms of supply of and demand for credit.

If the aggregate budget identity is used to translate the credit market equilibrium condition into an aggregate-expenditures-equals-aggregate-output equilibrium condition, it follows that equilibrium between aggregate expenditures and aggregate output is brought about by adjustment in the terms of trade.[7]

[7]Take the credit market equilibrium condition,

$$\frac{I}{P} + \frac{G}{P} - \frac{T}{P} + \frac{X}{P} = \frac{S}{P} + \frac{Im}{P}$$

substitute the aggregate budget identity,

$$\frac{S}{P} + \frac{Im}{P} \equiv \frac{Y}{P} - \frac{C}{P} - \frac{T}{P}$$

on the right-hand side, and rearrange:

$$\frac{C}{P} + \frac{I}{P} + \frac{G}{P} + \frac{X}{P} = \frac{Y}{P}$$

Compared to the general equilibrium model of a closed economy in previous chapters, the money market is modified in one respect. The demand for real money balances, Equation (15.22), varies directly with the terms of trade. This obtains because nonmoney assets now include foreign bonds whose prices vary directly with the terms of trade. The outstanding stocks of domestic money and the two types of bonds, foreign and domestic, are given at any point in time in private portfolios. (In this analysis, as in previous chapters, the demand for existing consumer durables is assumed not to change.) The direct relationship between the demand for money and the terms of trade can best be understood by recalling that an increase in the domestic interest rate is synonymous with a decrease in domestic bond prices. A decrease in the domestic bond prices reduces the quantity of real money balances demanded. Similarly, a decrease in foreign bond prices, brought about by a reduction in the terms of trade, also reduces the quantity of real money balances demanded.

The level of domestic real income is determined by the working of the labor market. The domestic interest rate is exogenously determined in the world capital market. The terms of trade are determined in the credit market. Thus, the quantity of real money balances demanded, Equation (15.22), is known. Equation (15.23) specifies the nominal domestic stock of money supplied by the domestic monetary authority. The money market equilibrium condition, Equation (15.24), indicates that the price level (P) will adjust until the real value of the nominal stock of money supplied, M/P, equals the known quantity of real money balances demanded, $(M/P)_d$.

The price level is specified by Equation (15.25) as a geometrically weighted average of the dollar price of domestic goods (P_d) and the dollar price of foreign goods ($e\,P^*$). The price of foreign goods (P^*) is exogenously determined in Equation (15.26). Therefore, the adjustment of the overall price level occurs as a result of the adjustment of the price of domestic goods and the exchange rate.

With the equilibrium terms of trade determined in the credit market at $(e\,P^*/P_d)_0$, the overall price level determined in the money market at $P_0 = P_d^a \cdot (e\,P^*)^{1-a}$, and the price of foreign goods exogenously determined at $\overline{P}^*$, we may solve these two equations for the equilibrium exchange rate, e_0, and the equilibrium price of domestic goods, P_{d_0}. With the price of domestic goods determined in this way and the overall price level determined in the money market, we may then solve for the equilibrium nominal wage in the labor market.

Figure 15.2 illustrates the solution process for this Neoclassical general equilibrium model of an open economy with perfect international capital mobility and a flexible exchange rate. In the labor market–production sector (panel a), the solution for the full employment equilibrium level of employment (L_0) is invariant with respect to the price of domestic goods (P_d) and the overall price level (P) as long as both prices change in the same proportion. The price of domestic goods (P_d) influences labor demand, as it affects the marginal revenue product of labor. The overall price level (P), the cost of living, influences labor supply, as it affects the opportunity cost of labor. The overall price level (P) is a geometrically weighted average of the dollar price of domestic goods (P_d) and the dollar price of foreign goods ($e\,P^*$).

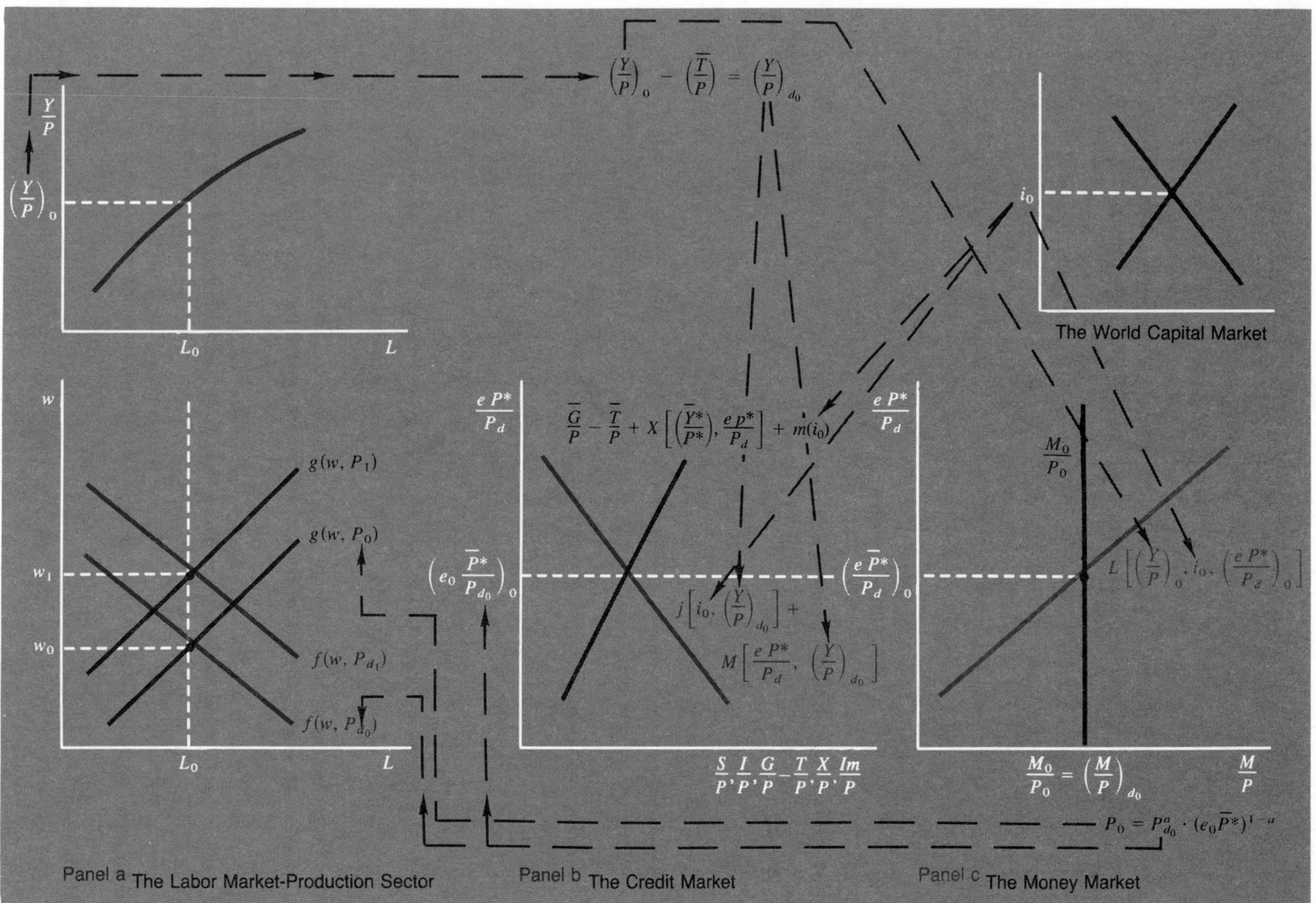

Figure 15.2 The Solution Process in the Neoclassical General Equilibrium Model of an Open Economy with Perfect International Capital Mobility and a Flexible Exchange Rate

For the time being, it is simply assumed that the general price level and the price of domestically produced goods always change in the same proportion. (Later in this chapter, this condition will be demonstrated rather than assumed.) The full employment equilibrium level of employment in the aggregate production function (panel a) yields the full employment equilibrium level of domestic aggregate real income $(Y/P)_0$.

In panel b, the domestic interest rate is exogenously determined at i_0, in the world capital market. This fixes the level of real investment expenditures at $m(i_0)$. The level of domestic aggregate real income $(Y/P)_0$ enters from the labor market–production sector. Since the level of taxation $\overline{T}/P$ is assumed given, the level of real disposable income $(Y/P)_{d_0}$ is determined. This, together with the exogenously determined interest rate (i_0), fixes the level of real saving at $j[i_0, (Y/P)_{d_0}]$. The real government deficit is exogenously determined at $(\overline{G}/P - \overline{T}/P)$. With foreign real income exogenously determined at $(\overline{Y}^*/\overline{P}^*)$, the level of exports can only vary (directly) with the terms of trade. With domestic aggregate real income given by the working of the labor market at $(Y/P)_0$ and the level of taxation exogenously determined, real disposable income $(Y/P)_{d_0}$ is given, and the level of imports can only vary (inversely) with the terms of trade.

As the terms of trade decrease, the level of real imports rises and the level of real exports falls. Therefore, at terms of trade below the equilibrium level, imports exceed exports, the supply of credit exceeds the demand for credit, and aggregate output exceeds aggregate expenditures. At terms of trade above the equilibrium level, exports exceed imports, the demand for credit exceeds the supply, and aggregate expenditures exceed aggregate output. The upward-sloping curve in Figure 15.2 (panel b) is the demand curve for credit. The downward-sloping curve is the supply curve of credit. Therefore, credit market equilibrium yields a solution for the equilibrium terms of trade: $(e\, P^*/P_d)_0$.

In panel c, the domestic interest rate enters the money demand relation as being exogenously determined in the world capital market (i_0). The level of domestic real income enters as being determined by the working of the domestic labor market–production sector at $(Y/P)_0$. Therefore, the position of the demand for money curve is known. Because the terms of trade are determined in the credit market at $(e\, P^*/P_d)_0$, the equilibrium point on that money demand curve is known. All three variables in the demand for money function are determined outside of the money market. With the quantity of real money balances demanded so determined, and given the stock of nominal money balances M_0, the overall price level adjusts to equate the real value of the nominal stock of money supplied, M_0/P_0, to the quantity of real money balances demanded, $(M/P)_{d_0}$.

This adjustment in the overall price level to (P_0) comes entirely through the adjustment of the price of domestic goods and adjustment of the exchange rate because the price of foreign goods is assumed to be exogenously determined at $(\overline{P}^*)$.

With the equilibrium terms of trade determined in the credit market at $(e\, P^*/P_d)_0$, the overall price level determined in the money market at $P_0 = P_d^a \cdot (e\, P^*)^{1-a}$, and the price of foreign goods exogenously determined at $\overline{P}^*$, we may solve for the equilibrium exchange rate, e_0, and the equilibrium price of domestic goods, P_{d_0}.

Since the real wage is equal to the marginal product of labor and that magnitude is known from the equilibrium position on the aggregate production function, the real wage is known. As the equilibrium price level, P_0, and the equilibrium price of domestic goods, P_{d_0}, have been determined, this permits solution for the nominal wage, w_0. This completes the solution process for the Neoclassical model of an open economy with perfect international capital mobility and flexible exchange rates.

FOUR EXPERIMENTS WITH THE GENERAL EQUILIBRIUM MODEL UNDER A FLEXIBLE EXCHANGE RATE

In previous chapters, closed economy models were perturbed by changes in the money supply and changes in the deficit, and the effects were analyzed. In the present chapter, we will shock our open economy models in the same two ways. Two models will be used: a Neoclassical general equilibrium and a Keynesian general equilibrium model. Thus, four experiments will be performed under the condition of a flexible exchange rate.

An Increase in the Nominal Stock of Money: The Neoclassical Model

Figure 15.3 shows the effect of an increase in the quantity of money in the Neoclassical model. All markets are initially in long-run, full employment equilibrium at points A'', A', and A. In panel c, an increase in the quantity of money creates the condition of an excess supply of money, depicted by line segment AB.

Assume that there are four forms in which individuals may hold their wealth: money, domestic bonds, foreign bonds, and consumer durables. As in previous chapters, as a means of analytical simplification, the demand for existing consumer durables is assumed unchanged. Similar to the model of a closed economy, there are two expectational alternatives. One is to assume either that expectations are formed adaptively, or that they are formed rationally and the money supply increase is unanticipated by credit and money market participants. The other is to assume that expectations are formed rationally and that the increase in the money supply is anticipated by credit and money market participants.[8]

We begin with the first expectational alternative. When individual credit and money market participants experience an excess supply of money, they are not aware that the overall aggregate supply of money has risen. Once they notice a rise in the exchange rate, they do not associate it with an increase in the money supply. Therefore, they have no incentive to use their excess money balances to order newly produced goods and services. As bonds are a close substitute for money, market participants have no reason not to balance their portfolios efficiently by substituting foreign bonds for their excess money balances.

[8]A rational expectations analysis of open economy models is a challenging task because there are more variables and plausible shocks than in a closed economy. Some of these disturbances will be less anticipatable and/or less verifiable by market participants. For example, under a flexible exchange rate, the exchange rate adjusts to shocks. The exchange rate is readily observable. Therefore, market participants know that a shock has occurred when the exchange rate varies and may be able to infer the source in order to confirm their expectations. In contrast, under a fixed exchange rate, central bank holdings of foreign currency reserves adjust to disturbances. Data on these holdings are not continuously reported. Therefore, market participants can neither easily discern that a shock has occurred nor confirm an anticipated shock.

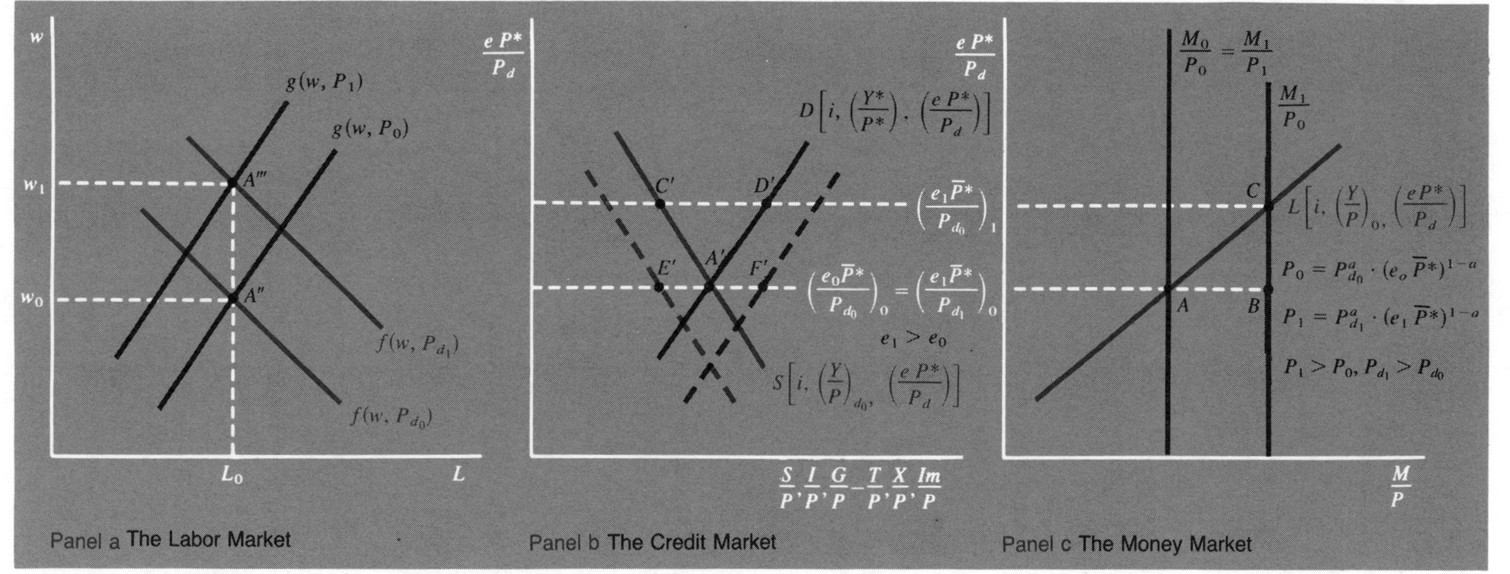

Figure 15.3 The Effect of an Increase in the Money Supply on the Neoclassical General Equilibrium Model of an Open Economy with Perfect International Capital Mobility and a Flexible Exchange Rate

As the level of real income and the domestic interest rate (and hence domestic bond prices) are exogenously determined, the excess supply of money is synonymous with an excess demand for foreign bonds. Individuals use their excess money balances to acquire foreign financial assets. This increases the demand for foreign currency which increases the number of dollars necessary to purchase a unit of foreign currency from e_0 to e_1 and causes the equilibrium terms of trade in the money market to rise from $(e_0 \overline{P}^*/P_{d_0})_0$ to $(e_1 \overline{P}^*/P_{d_0})_1$. The increased demand for foreign exchange has raised the terms of trade by causing the exchange rate to rise from e_0 to e_1. At the new, higher terms of trade, the money market is in equilibrium at point C (in panel c) but the credit market is not. In panel b, at the new, higher terms of trade there is an excess demand for credit as measured by the directed distance $C'D'$. The line segment $C'D'$ indicates that the demand for credit exceeds the supply.[9] There is disequilibrium in the credit market because the new, higher terms of trade stimulate exports (*X*/*P*) and reduce imports (*Im*/*P*):

$$\frac{G}{P} - \frac{T}{P} + \frac{X}{P} + \frac{I}{P} > \frac{S}{P} + \frac{Im}{P} \tag{15.27}$$

The aggregate budget identity can be used to translate this inequality into an expression of imbalance between aggregate output and aggregate real expenditures.

$$\frac{Y}{P} \equiv \frac{C}{P} + \frac{S}{P} + \frac{T}{P} + \frac{Im}{P} \tag{15.28}$$

This says that real income can only be used for real consumption expenditures, saved, taxed away, or used for expenditures on imports. Rearranging yields:

$$\frac{S}{P} \equiv \frac{Y}{P} - \frac{C}{P} - \frac{T}{P} - \frac{Im}{P} \tag{15.29}$$

Substituting into inequality (15.26) and rearranging, the result yields:

$$\frac{Y}{P} < \frac{C}{P} + \frac{I}{P} + \frac{G}{P} + \frac{X}{P} \tag{15.30}$$

This inequality indicates that at terms of trade $(e_1 \overline{P}^*/P_{d_0})_1$, the level of real aggregate expenditures exceeds the level of aggregate output. This disequilibrium condition exists because at exchange rate e_1, dollars are cheaper in terms of foreign currency. Therefore, at exchange rate e_1, *ceteris paribus*, real exports are greater and real imports are less than at exchange rate e_0.

The budget identity indicates that with real income, taxation, and saving unchanged, a decrease in imports (*Im*/*P*) implies an equal-sized rise in consumption expenditures

[9]Recall that the *upward-sloping* curve in panel b is the *demand* curve and the *downward-sloping* curve is the *supply* curve.

(C/P). Therefore, the excess of exports over imports in Equation (15.27) implies an equal-sized excess of aggregate expenditures (consisting of unchanged I/P and G/P and increased C/P and X/P) over aggregate output. This disequilibrium condition means that the price of newly produced domestic goods and services will be bid upward. The domestic price level rises in the same proportion as the exchange rate such that the terms of trade return to their initial equilibrium level, $e_0 \bar{P}^*/P_{d_0} = e_1 \bar{P}^*/P_{d_1}$, at point A'.

In panel c, the price of domestic goods and services rises from P_{d_0} to P_{d_1} in the same proportion as the rise in the exchange rate from e_0 to e_1. Therefore, the overall price level rises in the same proportion from $P_0 = P_{d_0}^a \cdot (e_0 \bar{P}^*)^{1-a}$ to $P_1 = P_{d_1}^a \cdot (e_1 \bar{P}^*)^{1-a}$. The real value of the nominal stock of money declines from M_1/P_0 to M_1/P_1. Equilibrium is restored to the money market at point A at the initial terms of trade $(e_1 \bar{P}^*/P_{d_1})_0 = (e_0 \bar{P}^*/P_{d_0})_0$. The overall price level rises in proportion to the quantity of money.

As the exchange rate rises from e_0 to e_1, the domestic price level rises in the same proportion to P_{d_1} to restore the terms of trade to their initial equilibrium level. Both the exchange rate and the price level ascend in proportion to the increase in the quantity of money. The quantity theory of money holds in this Neoclassical model of an open economy. The dollar shrinks in value in international markets in the same proportion that its domestic purchasing power shrinks.[10]

In the credit market (panel b), the initial equilibrium terms of trade restore equilibrium because:

$$\left(e \frac{\bar{P}^*}{P_d}\right)_0 = e_0 \frac{\bar{P}^*}{P_{d_0}} = e_1 \frac{\bar{P}^*}{P_{d_1}}$$

There is no excess demand for credit or excess of aggregate expenditures over aggregate output.

In the labor market (panel a), it is assumed, as in all Neoclassical closed economy models, that nominal wages are flexible and the responses of workers and employers are symmetrical. The price of domestic goods and the overall price level have increased in the same proportion. Therefore, there are proportional shifts in the labor demand and labor supply relations. This drives the nominal wage up to w_1. The nominal wage rises in proportion to the overall price level; the equilibrium real wage is unchanged: $w_1/P_1 =$

[10]According to the *theory of purchasing power parity*, the exchange rate moves quickly to keep the effective prices equal across countries. (Of course, this has to be modified for transportation costs and tariff barriers.) Domestic prices increase more than world prices increase, resulting in an immediate appreciation of the foreign exchange rate. For a review of the issues, see Lawrence H. Officer, "The Purchasing Power-Parity Theory of Exchange Rates: A Review," *International Monetary Fund Staff Papers* (March 1976), pp. 1–61.

Responses of the exchange rate that exceed domestic price level adjustments are consistent with recent evidence of exchange rate volatility discussed at the end of this chapter. This volatility is explained by a number of alternative hypotheses. One hypothesis involves the effect of current money supply changes on expected future exchange rate appreciation, which in turn leads to current exchange rate appreciation. Another hypothesis explains the overshoot in exchange rate adjustments because domestic prices are slow to adjust. A third hypothesis explains exchange rate volatility as reflecting the absence of perfect substitutability between domestic and foreign financial assets. For a survey and synthesis of these and other views on modern exchange rate volatility, see the paper by Bergstrand in the bibliography to this chapter.

w_0/P_0. Employment and output are unchanged. The point of full employment equilibrium is A'''.

Now consider the same model with the same money supply shock under the alternative assumption of rationally formed expectations and the anticipation of the increased money supply by market participants. Under this alternative, credit and money market participants are aware that increases in their individual liquidity are associated with a greater aggregate stock of money. (Small changes in the exchange rate may signal them that a shock is occurring. They then turn to published money supply data to verify their anticipation of this shock.) As soon as an increase in individual liquidity is experienced, market participants predict higher prices for newly produced goods and services. Therefore, the initial excess supply of money, *AB* in panel c, is not used to acquire foreign bonds. Market participants know that acquiring bonds at terms of trade higher than $(e\ P^*/P_d)_0$ will lead to capital losses when the terms of trade return to their long-run equilibrium and the purchasing power value of foreign bonds declines. They will not use their new money balances to acquire foreign bonds. They will use all of the new money balances to order newly produced goods and services. Thus, at the initial terms of trade, an excess of aggregate expenditures over aggregate output immediately occurs. This is reflected in panel b as an increase (a rightward shift) in the upward-sloping demand relation and a decrease (a leftward shift) in the downward-sloping supply relation to the corresponding dashed lines. The resulting excess demand, $E'F'$, is fueled by the corresponding excess supply of money, *AB*.

As a result of this immediate excess of expenditures over output, the domestic price level and the exchange rate are immediately and directly bid upward. Market participants initially use a portion of their excess money balances to order foreign goods (imports) and this boosts the exchange rate and induces more exports and fewer imports. Market participants use the remaining portion of their excess money balances to order domestically produced goods.[11] The combination of greater exports and greater domestic expenditures drives up the domestic price level. The overall price level increases in proportion to the rise in the exchange rate and the rise in the domestic price level. (The terms of trade remain at their initial equilibrium level.) Therefore, in the labor market, supply and demand curves shift upward in the same proportion, and there is no change in employment.

In this Neoclassical general equilibrium model of an open economy with perfect capital mobility and flexible exchange rates, an increase in the domestic money supply, under either set of expectational assumptions, incites the overall price level, the price of domestic goods, the nominal wage, and the exchange rate to rise in the same proportion as the increase in the money supply. Output, real wages, and the terms of trade are unchanged.

An Increase in the Nominal Stock of Money: The Keynesian Model

The Keynesian general equilibrium model is marked by asymmetrical responses in the labor market. Plausible explanations of this asymmetry are provided in Chapters Four

[11]These portions are $(1 - a)$ and (a), respectively, in Equation (15.25).

and Twelve. The result is that when the price level rises, employment rises. The price of domestic goods and the exchange rate go up because the initial excess supply of money, AB, generates an excess of aggregate spending over aggregate output.

The excess of expenditures over output can come about in two alternative ways. If credit and money market participants form their expectations adaptively or form their expectations rationally and do not anticipate the rise in the money supply, they will acquire foreign bonds. This initially boosts the terms of trade to $e_1 \overline{P}^*/P_{d_0}$ which forges an excess of exports over imports shown by distance $C'D'$ in panel b of Figure 15.4. The related excess of expenditures over output forces the domestic price level up to $P_{d_{1/2}}$. Alternatively, where credit and money market participants form their expectations rationally and anticipate the increase in the money supply, an excess of expenditures over output occurs immediately in the amount $F'G'$ at the initial terms of trade. This immediately and directly drives up the exchange rate to e_1 and the domestic price level to $P_{d_{1/2}}$.

The rise in employment occurs because at the higher price of domestic goods the demand for labor shifts rightward to $f(w_1, P_{d_{1/2}})$ (in panel a of Figure 15.4), but the supply of labor does not shift. Responses in the labor market are asymmetrical. The point of short-run, super-full employment equilibrium is E''. Employment rises to L_1. The real wage declines to $w_{1/4}/P_{1/2}$, where $P_{1/2} = P^a_{d_{1/2}} \cdot (e_1 \overline{P}^*)^{1-a}$.

As employment jumps from L_0 to L_1, domestic aggregate real income increases from $(Y/P)_0$ to $(Y/P)_1$. Because of the greater real disposable income, real saving and real imports rise. This is reflected as a rightward shift of the (downward-sloping) supply curve of credit in panel b from $S[i, (Y/P)_{d_0}, (e\ P^*/P_d)]$ to $S[i, (Y/P)_{d_1}, (e\ P^*/P_d)]$. Higher domestic real saving constitutes a greater supply of funds into the credit market. This bids up the terms of trade. The rightward shift in supply causes the equilibrium terms of trade to go to $e_1 \overline{P}^*/P_{d_{1/2}}$. When compared to the initial equilibrium at A', the higher terms of trade cause exports to rise and imports to fall. The short-run equilibrium point is E' (in panel b).

In the money market (panel c), there is an increase in the quantity of real money balances demanded. The higher level of real income makes the demand for real money balances shift rightward to $L[i, (Y/P)_1, (e\ P^*/P_d)]$. At the new equilibrium terms of trade $(e_1 \overline{P}^*/P_{d_{1/2}})$, the price level needs to rise only to $P_{1/2}$ to bring the real value of the nominal stock of money $(M_1/P_{1/2})$ into balance with the demand for real money balances. Short-run equilibrium occurs at point E in panel c.

Thus, in a Keynesian general equilibrium model, an increase in the domestic money supply causes the terms of trade to rise and the level of domestic aggregate real income to rise in the short run. There will be a rise in the domestic price level but a proportionately greater rise in the exchange rate. The overall price level will not increase in proportion to the increase in the money supply. The quantity theory of money does not hold.[12]

[12]In the Keynesian closed economy model of Chapter Twelve, an increase in the money supply caused the interest rate to decline. In the present model, the interest rate is assumed to be determined in the world capital market. However, a slight modification would allow the interest rate to be affected by an increase in the money supply. This would involve the effect of future expected changes in the exchange rate on the interest rate. See footnote 3.

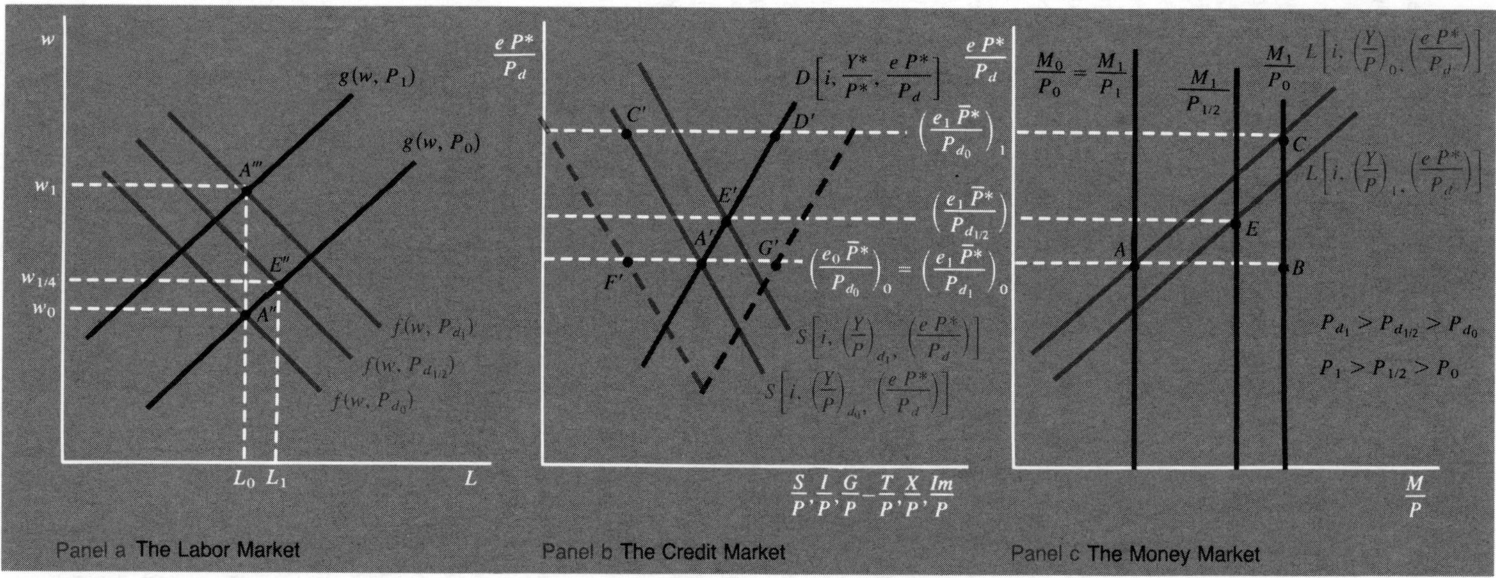

Figure 15.4 The Effect of an Increase in the Money Supply in a Keynesian General Equilibrium Model of an Open Economy with a Flexible Exchange Rate

In the long run, the asymmetrical responses disappear from the labor market. The labor supply curve shifts upward in proportion to the shift in the labor demand curve. In panel a, the level of employment returns to L_0, its initial full employment equilibrium level. Real income declines to its original level. In the credit market (panel b), the supply curve shifts leftward to its original level $S[i, (Y/P)_{d_0}, (e\,P^*/P_d)]$. The terms of trade return to their initial equilibrium level. In panel b, equilibrium occurs at point A'. In the money market (panel c), the decline in real income impels the demand for real money balances to shift leftward to its initial position, $L[i, (Y/P)_0, (e\,P^*/P_d)]$. At the lower terms of trade, the price level must rise all the way to P_1 in proportion to the increase in the money supply. Equilibrium is restored at point A. As the terms of trade are unchanged, the exchange rate and price of domestic goods must also rise in the same proportion. Thus, in the long run, the Neoclassical conditions are restored. Increases in the domestic money supply result only in proportionate price level, nominal wage, and exchange rate increases.

This model shows that exchange rates and price levels cannot be treated as unrelated variables since policies that affect one tend to affect the other. Exchange rates are determined by monetary policy and are not independent policy instruments. Changes in exchange rates reflect variations in domestic (and foreign) money supplies. Exchange rate fluctuations are not a cause of inflation; they are symptoms of inflation. Governments can help to eliminate problems of price level and exchange rate fluctuations by adhering to stable monetary policy.

An Increase in the Government Deficit: The Neoclassical Model[13]

Figure 15.5 shows the effect of an increase in the government deficit, which is assumed to occur because of an increase in government spending without an increase in taxation. Initial full employment equilibrium is at points A'', A', and A in Figure 15.5. In panel b, the (upward-sloping) demand for credit shifts rightward in the amount of the increase from $D[i, (Y^*/P^*), (e\,P^*/P_d)]$ to $D'[i, Y^*/P^*, (e\,P^*/P_d)]$. At the initial terms of trade, there is an excess demand for credit denoted by directed distance $A'B'$. The increased demand for credit by government implies a rush of foreign funds into the domestic credit market. This occurs because the initial increase in the demand for credit by government causes the domestic interest rate to rise by a minuscule amount. Under our assumption of perfect international capital mobility, foreigners enter the domestic credit market to purchase domestic financial assets to take advantage of this infinitesimally higher domestic interest rate.

The inflow of foreign funds to purchase domestic financial assets increases the relative price of dollars in terms of foreign currency. This lowers the relative price of foreign currency, the exchange rate, e, and depresses the equilibrium terms of trade. The unfettered inflow of capital keeps the interest rate from rising in the face of greater government

[13]The following discussion ignores the Ricardian equivalence principle, which states that a larger deficit will result in crowding out without a change in the terms of trade. See Chapter Six for further discussion in the context of a closed economy.

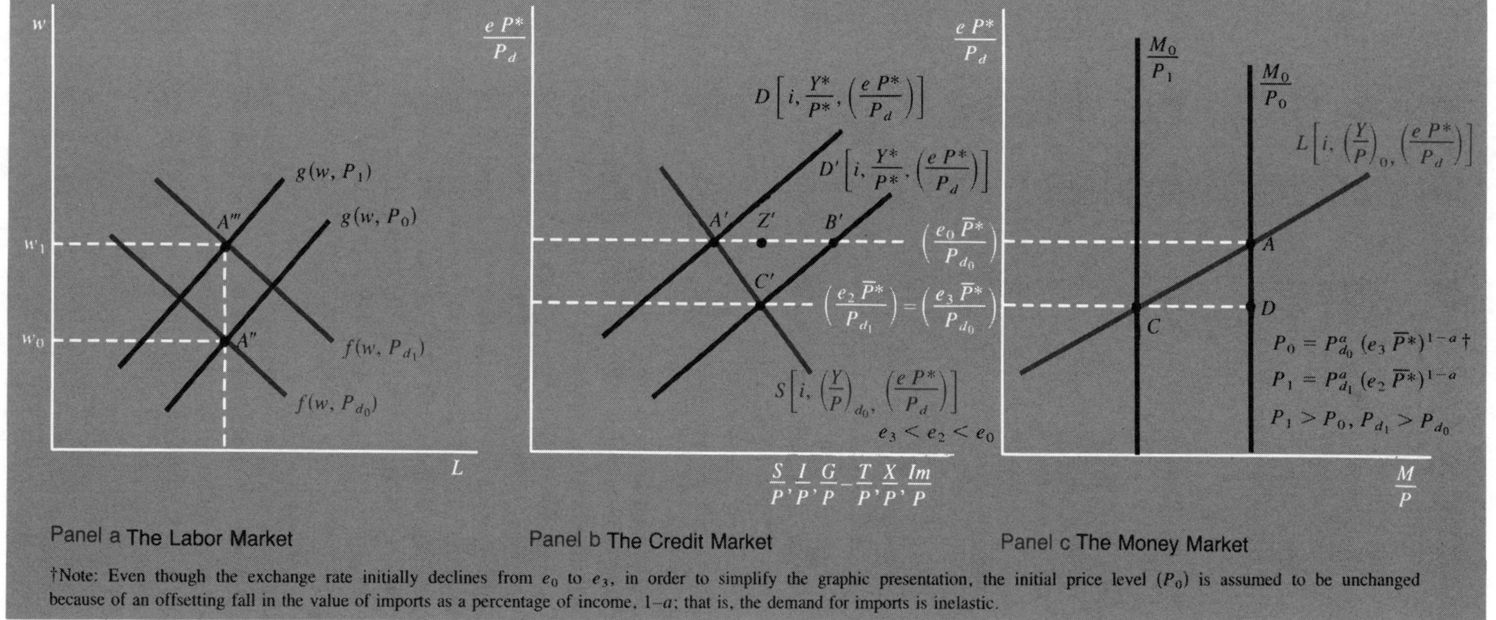

†Note: Even though the exchange rate initially declines from e_0 to e_3, in order to simplify the graphic presentation, the initial price level (P_0) is assumed to be unchanged because of an offsetting fall in the value of imports as a percentage of income, $1-a$; that is, the demand for imports is inelastic.

Figure 15.5 The Effect of an Increase in the Government Deficit on the Neoclassical General Equilibrium Model of an Open Economy with Perfect International Capital Mobility and Flexible Exchange Rates

borrowing (see footnote 15). Therefore, the decrease in the terms of trade is associated with a decrease in the exchange rate. The dollar rises in value against foreign currency as foreigners acquire dollars to purchase domestic financial assets. As this occurs, real imports rise by the directed distance $A'Z'$, and real exports decline by the directed distance $B'Z'$ in panel b of Figure 15.5. The new equilibrium terms of trade are $(e_3 \overline{P}^*/P_{d_0}) < (e_0 \overline{P}^*/P_{d_0})$, where $e_3 < e_0$.

The new, lower terms of trade imply that the increased deficit of government is financed by a reduction in real exports and an increase in real imports. In this open economy model, as long as the deficit, a flow, remains at the new higher level, the funds to satisfy the borrowing needs of government will be obtained from foreigners. As long as this flow of credit persists, the terms of trade will be lower, the flow of real exports will be at a reduced level, and the flow of real imports will be at an increased level. By the aggregate budget identity, it can be seen that with real income, real saving, and real taxation unchanged, an increase in imports requires an offsetting decrease in domestic consumption expenditures. The increase in our imports provides foreigners with part of the flow of funds which they use to purchase the newly issued bonds of our government. The other part of the flow of funds from abroad is provided by a reduction in our exports which is tantamount to a reduction in imports by foreigners. Rather than purchase our newly produced goods and services, foreigners now use that part of their income to buy our government's newly issued bonds. Therefore, there is a complete crowding out of domestic private (export and consumption) expenditures by government expenditures.[14]

The new, lower terms of trade create an excess supply of money (panel c of Figure 15.5). The excess supply is depicted by directed distance CD. This is because the quantity of real money balances demanded at terms of trade $e_3 \overline{P}^*/P_{d_0}$ is less than the real value of the nominal stock of money, M_0/P_0.

To analyze the linkage mechanism beyond this point requires making one of two alternative sets of expectational assumptions. If credit and money market participants form their expectations adaptively or form their expectations rationally but do not anticipate the increase in the deficit, they will not foresee the permanent fall in the terms of trade to a new level. Therefore, they will be willing to use their excess money balances to acquire foreign bonds at terms of trade higher than $e_3 \overline{P}^*/P_{d_0}$. Credit and money market participants would not foresee a fall in the price of foreign bonds because they do not foresee the decline in the terms of trade to the new, permanently lower level. Under these circumstances, the excess supply of money will impede the decline in the terms of trade. This occurs because market participants will use their excess money balances to acquire foreign bonds, which are close substitutes. They have no incentive to use their excess balances to order newly produced goods and services. To obtain foreign bonds, individuals require foreign currency. The increased demand for foreign currency lowers the rela-

[14]Domestic crowding out will not be complete if the resource needs of government are, in part, being satisfied by a flow of funds from abroad over and above that generated by the reduction in exports and increase in imports. This would occur, for example, if we modified our model to allow for significant international interest rate differentials. In this case, there would be crowding out abroad as foreign saving was being diverted to our economy. In terms of the world economy as a whole, crowding out would be complete.

tive price of the dollar in terms of foreign currency. It impedes the decline in the exchange rate to e_3.

At terms of trade greater than $e_3\,\overline{P}^*/P_{d_0}$ (panel b), there is an excess demand for credit associated with an excess of exports over imports. The aggregate budget identity indicates that an excess of exports over imports is synonymous with an excess of aggregate real expenditures over aggregate output. Thus, at terms of trade greater than $e_3\,\overline{P}^*/P_{d_0}$, the price of domestic goods and services and the exchange rate will be bid upward in the same proportion, to P_{d_1} and e_2, such that the equilibrium terms of trade do not change.

Now consider the alternative expectational assumption. In a world where market participants are assumed to form their expectations rationally and anticipate the larger deficit, they would avoid using the excess money balances to acquire foreign bonds. Small changes in the terms of trade may notify market participants that a shock is occurring. They would then turn to estimates of the government deficit to confirm their anticipation of this disturbance. They would foresee that any terms of trade above $e_3\,\overline{P}^*/P_{d_0}$ would be temporary and would want to avoid the subsequent capital losses incurred from acquiring foreign bonds when the terms of trade were above the equilibrium level. Credit and money market participants would directly and immediately place orders for newly produced domestic and foreign goods and services at the new terms of trade. As a result, the price of domestic goods and the exchange rate would be bid upward in the same proportion, to P_{d_1} and e_2, respectively, such that the equilibrium terms of trade would not change. (To keep the picture uncluttered, this case is not depicted in panel b; it simply involves a temporary shift in the supply and demand curves generating a temporary excess of expenditures over output equal to the excess supply of money *CD* at the equilibrium terms of trade.)

As the overall price level rises (panel c), the real value of the nominal stock of money declines. With the new, higher price of domestic goods P_{d_1}, and higher exchange rate e_2, the overall price level rises to $P_1 = P_{d_1}^a \cdot (e_2\,\overline{P}^*)^{1-a}$. The real value of the nominal stock of money declines to M_0/P_1. Equilibrium is restored to the money market at point *C* at terms of trade $e_2\,\overline{P}^*/P_{d_1}$. The equilibrium terms of trade are:

$$e_2\frac{\overline{P}^*}{P_{d_1}} = e_3\frac{\overline{P}^*}{P_{d_0}} < e_0\frac{\overline{P}^*}{P_{d_0}}$$

where $e_3 < e_2 < e_0$. In the credit market (panel b), equilibrium occurs at point C'.

Thus, an increase in the government deficit causes the equilibrium terms of trade to decline. The increased deficit is financed partly by a reduction in exports and partly by an increase in imports which reflects an equal reduction in domestic consumption expenditures. The decline in the terms of trade means that the expenditures in certain export-oriented and import-sensitive sectors of the domestic economy will be *crowded out* by government deficits. In contrast, for a closed economy, the impact of crowding out will be in interest-sensitive sectors of the economy, such as housing and building materials. For the Neoclassical model of an open economy, the crowding out of private expenditures by government expenditures is still complete. It occurs in the same magnitude as in the Neoclassical model of a closed economy. The difference is masked by the flow of resources from abroad which become available in our domestic market as a concomitant of the reduction in our exports and the increase in our imports.

The decline in the terms of trade fosters an excess supply of money which elevates the price of domestic goods, the exchange rate, and the overall price level in the same proportions. The quantity theory of money holds.

In the labor market (panel a), symmetrical responses of employers and workers are assumed. Proportional increases in the price of domestic goods and in the overall price level cause the demand for and supply of labor to shift upward in the same proportion. As a result, the nominal wage increases in proportion to the increase in the price level. There is no change in employment or in the equilibrium real wage. The new long-run, full employment equilibrium is at point A'''.

In the Neoclassical general equilibrium model of a closed economy (Chapter Eleven), a larger deficit propels the interest rate upward. This chokes off private investment expenditures and private consumption expenditures. The impact of crowding out in such a world will be most heavily felt on interest-sensitive sectors, such as housing and building materials. In the Neoclassical model of an open economy, a larger deficit forces the terms of trade down. This stimulates imports and depresses exports. Using the aggregate budget identity, with real income, real saving, and taxation unchanged, a rise in imports implies a fall in consumption expenditures. Thus, the impact of crowding out in an open economy is most heavily felt in export-oriented and import-sensitive sectors. For the United States economy in the 1980s, a good example of an export-oriented sector is the agricultural sector and good examples of import-sensitive sectors are the steel and auto industries. It should also be remembered that the massive net inflow of capital into the United States to finance our federal deficit means that foreigners hold an expanding stock of claims against us. In the future, a growing portion of private expenditures must be crowded out in order to pay the interest on this debt. Finally, increases in the holdings of foreigners could at some point lead to their portfolios being saturated with debt claims against the United States.

Depressed conditions in certain domestic sectors resulting from larger government deficits are often confused with overall economic recession. Spokespersons and lobbyists for these industries may bring pressure on Congress and the administration to generate a recovery from these depressed conditions. They may attempt to have protectionist bills, involving higher tariffs or quotas on imports, or subsidy bills, involving higher price supports on government aid to agriculture. Foreign governments may also be upset because of other effects of the new terms of trade. There may be pressure on the Federal Reserve for monetary ease. Increases in the money supply, as seen in the previous section, could generate temporary increases in the terms of trade and thereby stimulate exports and constrain imports. Nevertheless, in the long run only a higher price level and unchanged terms of trade can result. In the 1980s, considerable pressure was placed on Congress to pass protectionist trade and farm aid legislation. From 1985 and 1987, the Federal Reserve intervened in foreign exchange markets and increased money growth in an attempt to reduce the international value of the dollar (increase the value of foreign currency in terms of the dollar). Thus, political responses to the domestic and possible foreign crowding-out effects of an increase in the government deficit have actually sparked government responses, the wisdom of which are often called into question. The preceding policy actions to reduce the dependence on foreign capital flows only obscure the fundamental cause of the problem: the government budget deficit.

An Increase in the Government Deficit: The Keynesian Model

The Keynesian general equilibrium model in Figure 15.6 features asymmetrical responses in the labor market. This means that when the price level rises, employment rises. The boost in employment occurs because the demand for labor shifts rightward to $f(w, P_{d_{1/2}})$ (panel a), but the supply of labor does not shift. The point of short-run, super-full employment equilibrium is E''. Employment rises to L_1; real wage declines to $w_{1/4}/P_{1/2}$.

As employment increases from L_0 to L_1, domestic aggregate real income rises from $(Y/P)_0$ to $(Y/P)_1$. The rise in real disposable income stimulates real saving and real imports. This is reflected as a rightward shift of the supply curve (panel b) from $S[i, (Y/P)_{d_0}, (e\ P^*/P_d)]$ to $S[i, (Y/P)_{d_1}, (e\ P^*/P_d)]$. This shift in supply, together with the rightward shift in demand from $D[i, Y^*/P^*, (e\ P^*/P_d)]$ to $D'[i, Y^*/P^*, (e\ P^*/P_d)]$ caused by the increased government deficit, results in short-run equilibrium at point E'. The new terms of trade are slightly lower than the initial equilibrium level at A' but are not as low as in the Neoclassical model. The increased government deficit is not financed entirely through a reduction in real exports and an increase in real imports. In this Keynesian model, there is an increase in real domestic saving out of the increase in real disposable income.

In the money market (panel c), the increase in domestic aggregate real income causes the demand for real money balances to shift rightward to $L[i, (Y/P)_1, (e, P^*/P_d)]$. At the new equilibrium terms of trade, the price level need only rise to $P_{1/2}$ to bring the real value of the nominal stock of money, $M_0/P_{1/2}$, into balance with the quantity of real money balances demanded. Short-run equilibrium occurs at point E.

Thus, in a Keynesian general equilibrium model, an increase in the government deficit prompts the terms of trade to decline and the level of domestic aggregate income to rise in the short run. Because of the rise in real income and, hence, in real saving, the terms of trade do not decline as much as in the Neoclassical model. The enlarged deficit is partly financed out of increased saving and not exclusively through a reduction in net exports. There is not the open economy equivalent of complete crowding out that holds in the Neoclassical model.

In the long run, the asymmetrical responses disappear from the labor market. The labor supply curve shifts upward in proportion to the shift in the labor demand curve. The level of employment returns to L_0 (panel a of Figure 15.6). Real income declines to its initial full employment equilibrium level, $(Y/P)_0$. In the credit market (panel b), the supply curve shifts leftward to its initial level, $S[i, (Y/P)_{d_0}, (e\ P^*/P_d)]$. The terms of trade fall further to their new long-run equilibrium level. In panel b, equilibrium occurs at point C'. Once again, the increase in the government deficit is financed entirely out of an increase in imports and a reduction in exports. The larger government deficit has completely crowded out private expenditures in this model of an open economy. In the money

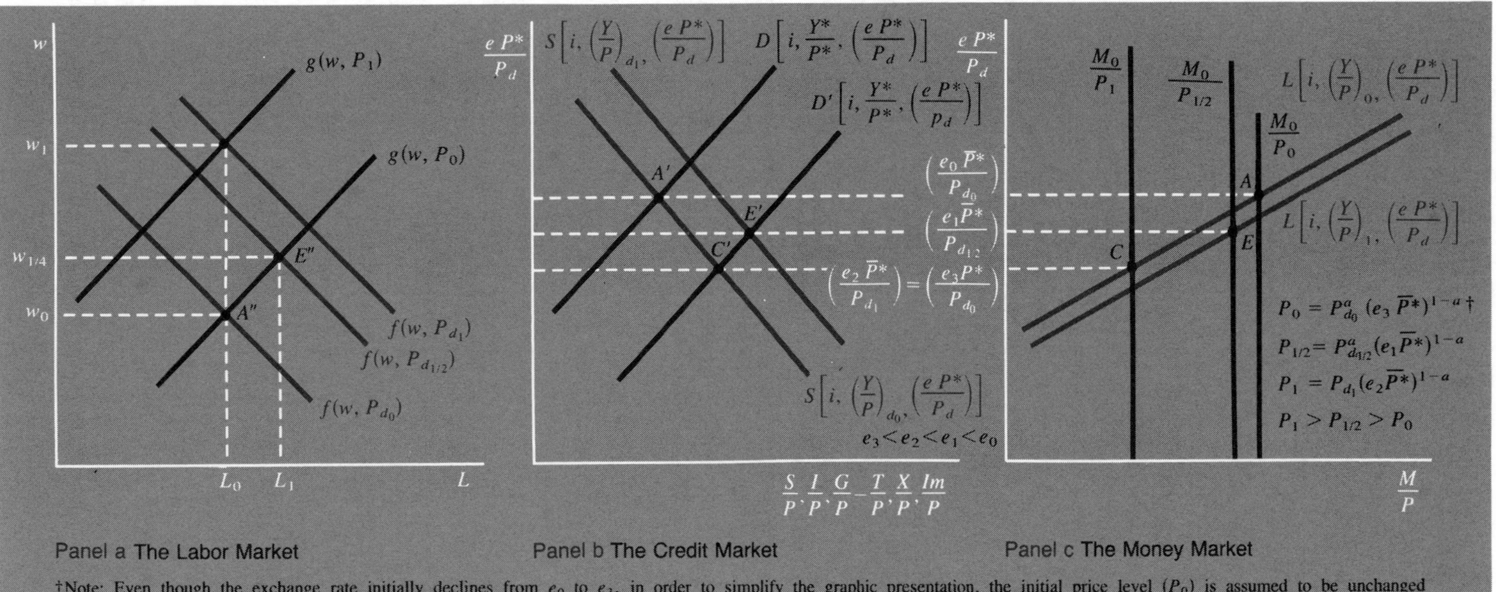

†Note: Even though the exchange rate initially declines from e_0 to e_3, in order to simplify the graphic presentation, the initial price level (P_0) is assumed to be unchanged because of an offsetting fall in the value of imports as a percentage of income, $1-a$; that is, the demand for imports is inelastic.

Figure 15.6 The Effect of an Increase in the Government Deficit on the Keynesian General Equilibrium Model of an Open Economy with a Flexible Exchange Rate

market (panel c), the decline in real income causes the demand for real money balances to shift leftward to its initial position $L[i, (Y/P)_0, (e\,P^*/P_d)]$. At the lower terms of trade, the price level must rise to P_1. Again, in the long run, the Neoclassical conditions are restored.[15]

Aggregate Supply Shocks: The Neoclassical Model

In Chapter Eleven, we examined the impact of noncapacity-reducing and capacity-reducing aggregate supply shocks in the Neoclassical model of a closed economy. Now we engage in the same experiments with a Neoclassical model of an open economy.

A noncapacity-reducing supply shock begins with an increase in the price of foreign-produced goods, P^*. This raises the terms of trade, $e \cdot P^*/P_d$, and creates an excess of exports over imports. The resulting excess of aggregate expenditures over aggregate output drives up the price of domestically produced goods, P_d, in proportion to the rise in the price of imports. This restores equilibrium at the initial terms of trade. The new, higher overall price level decreases the real value of the nominal stock of money, and the subsequent excess of output over aggregate expenditures will lower the exchange rate, e, and lower the price of domestically produced goods, P_d, in the same proportion. Thus, the equilibrium terms of trade, $e \cdot P^*/P_d$, are unchanged. Therefore, the overall price index, $P = P_d^a \cdot (e\,P^*)^{1-a}$, falls in the same proportion as the decrease in the domestic price level, P_d. Both return to their initial equilibrium levels.

Therefore, a noncapacity-reducing supply shock would have no effect on the equilibrium values of the key domestic macroeconomic variables. Even though the price of the foreign-produced good rose and remained higher, as long as it had no impact on our productive capacity, it would have no effect on real income, the terms of trade, or the price level.

A capacity-reducing aggregate supply shock begins in the same way as the preceding shock. Unfortunately, it is not so easily absorbed by the economic mechanism. An increase in the price of a foreign-produced good that is crucial to domestic production processes and for which no close substitute exists precipitates a downward shift in the aggregate production function (and a leftward shift in the demand for labor). The resulting decline in aggregate real income causes domestic saving to decrease (shift leftward). In models where the tax receipts of government depend positively on the level of aggregate real income, the government deficit will also increase. These two effects lower the terms of trade in the same manner as that discussed in the preceding sections concerning the deficit. This lowering leads to a decline in domestic private expenditures, also exactly as discussed in the preceding sections. The new, lower terms of trade create an excess supply of money that creates an equiproportionate increase in the exchange rate, e, and the domestic price level, P_d.

[15]The assumed absence of any effect of a change in the government deficit on domestic interest rates is unrealistic for open economies which, because of their size, have a discernible impact on world interest rates. In such cases, there will be crowding out of private investment expenditures and consumption expenditures because of higher domestic interest rates, as well as crowding out of exports and consumption expenditures because of lower terms of trade. For example, the high interest rates in the United States during the span from 1980 to 1986 are frequently thought to have influenced world interest rates.

A noncapacity-reducing aggregate supply shock would arise, for example, if the price of New Zealand's kiwi fruit rose. The mighty United States' economic engine could neatly absorb such a shock even though it might provoke mass emigration of kiwi fruit fanatics. In contrast, consider the effect of an increase in the price of foreign-produced oil. This would be a capacity-reducing aggregate supply shock. Economic engines, like mechanical engines, literally run on oil. As no close substitutes exist, aggregate output, the terms of trade, and the price level would be severely affected. Of course, as discussed in Chapter Eleven, there are favorable as well as adverse supply shocks. In the 1980s, the price of foreign-produced oil declined rather steadily. This provoked a tremendous increase in our productive capacity, boosted real income, and impeded massive deterioration in the terms of trade and increase in the price level that was being caused by the hemorrhaging federal deficit.

EXPERIMENTS WITH THE GENERAL EQUILIBRIUM MODEL UNDER A FIXED EXCHANGE RATE

Next, the money supply and government deficit experiments will be undertaken with the Neoclassical general equilibrium model under the condition of a fixed exchange rate.

In a fixed exchange rate system, the central banks of various nations must stand ready to buy and sell foreign currencies at a price fixed in terms of dollars. In a fixed rate system, central banks must finance any balance of payments surplus or deficit. Central banks do this by buying or selling all the foreign exchange that is necessary at the fixed price. Therefore, fixed exchange rates are a price support scheme. Central banks are obligated to satisfy the excess demand for a foreign currency out of their inventory of that currency. They must also be ready to absorb an excess supply of a foreign currency into their inventory. For example, if the United States has a balance of payments deficit with Great Britain, at the official, fixed exchange rate there is an excess supply of dollars in Britain and an excess demand for pounds in the United States. The British central bank must be prepared to buy up those dollars and pay for them with pounds at the official, fixed exchange rate. The Federal Reserve, our central bank, must be prepared to sell pounds in exchange for dollars. So long as our central bank has the necessary reserves of pounds, it can intervene in foreign exchange markets.[16]

Central banks hold inventories of foreign currencies as assets. Foreign currencies are part of the source monetary base, discussed in Chapter Eight. Therefore, the monetary base changes when foreign currencies are bought or sold to finance balance of payments deficits or surpluses. This implies that in the case of a balance of payments deficit, our central bank will decrease the domestic monetary base and the domestic money supply. The Federal Reserve will have to provide pounds out of its inventories to satisfy the excess demand for pounds that exists at the fixed exchange rate. In the act of selling

[16]When the selling central bank runs out of reserves, it may decide it can no longer support the official, fixed exchange rate and generally must devalue its currency. See the second article by Batten and Ott in the bibliography to this chapter.

pounds, it buys up dollars. The assets of the Fed decline. The monetary base shrinks, and the domestic money supply falls. In the case of a balance of payments surplus, the Federal Reserve will be increasing our domestic money supply by buying up excess pounds with dollars. The monetary base and the money supply expand. Therefore, under a system of fixed exchange rates, the balance of payments is causally linked directly to the domestic money supply. In terms of the Neoclassical general equilibrium model of an open economy, outlined in Table 15.1, there is now one simple modification:

$$M_s = M_0 + B \qquad (15.23')$$

This equation says that the domestic nominal money stock has two components. One part (M_0) is autonomous, and the other component (B) depends on the payments balance.

The solution process for the general equilibrium model is exactly as outlined earlier. The level of employment and aggregate real income are determined in the labor market–production sector. The terms of trade are determined in the credit market. The domestic price level is determined in the money market. The only difference is that with the exchange rate now fixed at $\bar{e}$ and the foreign price level exogenously determined, any balance of payments disturbance which affects the equilibrium terms of trade must be resolved entirely through adjustments to the domestic price level.[17]

An archetypal fixed exchange rate system was the classical gold standard as it functioned for many decades in much of the world during much of the nineteenth century and early twentieth century. Under the gold standard, the value of each currency was defined in terms of gold. Money was either gold or was fully redeemable in gold. The exchange rates between currencies were defined by their respective gold content.

Whenever a balance of payments deficit was incurred *vis-à-vis* a trading partner's balance of payments surplus, gold was shipped to that country to correct the imbalance. As a result, the money supply and domestic price level of the country that shipped gold fell, and the money supply and price level of the country that received the gold rose. Thereby, an automatic correction of the payment's imbalance was produced. No central bank intervention was required. In this form, the classical gold standard is often enshrined as the apotheosis of the laissez-faire Invisible Hand. In order to make other kinds of fixed exchange rate systems function smoothly, the Visible Hand of central bank intervention must be relied upon. As discussed later in this chapter, this Visible Hand has not always been so steady and reliable.

An Increase in the Government Deficit: The Neoclassical Model[18]

In Figure 15.7, assume that an increase in the government deficit creates an increase in the demand for credit. The demand curve shifts to $D'[(Y^*/P^*), (e\, P^*/P_d)]$.

[17]Under the regime of a perfectly flexible exchange rate system, the balance of payments is always zero.

[18]The expectational alternatives outlined in all previous experiments are not made explicit here. Under a system of a fixed exchange rate, shocks such as increases in the money supply and increases in the government deficit may be less discernible. Anticipations of such disturbances may be less confirmable. This could occur because a fluctuating exchange rate is a source of information for market participants. See footnote 8 for further discussion.

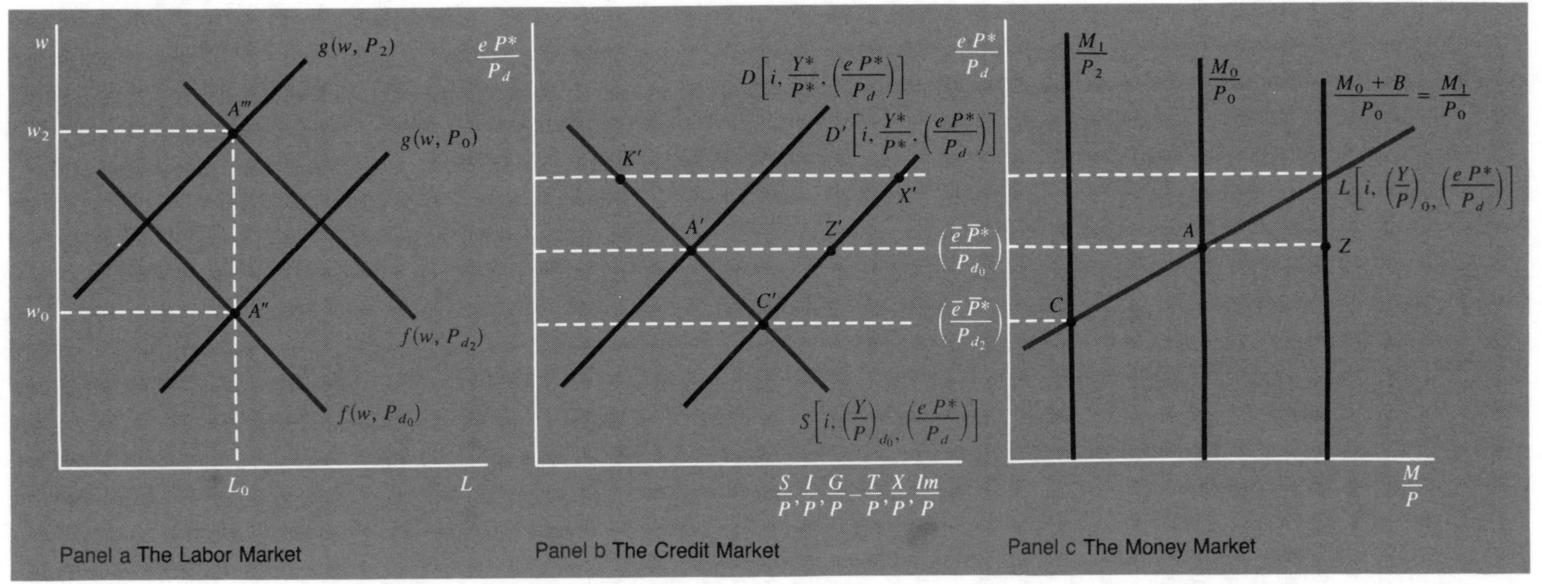

Figure 15.7 The Effect of an Increase in the Government Deficit in the Neoclassical General Equilibrium Model of an Open Economy with a Fixed Exchange Rate

Because of the assumption of perfect international capital mobility, the increased government deficit attracts a flow of foreign funds into the domestic credit market. This results in a balance of payments surplus at the initial terms of trade, $(\bar{e}\,\bar{P}^*/P_{d_0})$. This is shown by the directed distance $A'Z'$ (panel b). By the aggregate budget identity, directed distance $A'Z'$ is synonymous with an excess of aggregate expenditures over aggregate output. Under a flexible exchange rate, this excess demand would lead to the exchange rate decline and the price level increase, as described earlier. However, under a fixed exchange rate, the exchange rate cannot vary. Rather, the domestic money supply increases by the amount of the balance of payments surplus, $M_0 + B = M_1$. The increase in the money supply from M_0 to $M_0 + B$ occurs because in order to maintain the fixed exchange rate, $\bar{e}$, the central bank is obliged to buy up foreign currency with dollars. The monetary base and the money supply increase. The resulting excess supply of money, line segment AZ (panel c), causes an even greater excess of aggregate expenditures over aggregate output, shown by directed distance $K'X'$ (panel b), $K'X' = A'Z' + AZ$.

The result of the excess of aggregate spending over aggregate output is an increase in the price of domestic goods from P_{d_0} to P_{d_2}. The price of domestic goods is driven upward not only by the initial excess demand (the excess of exports over imports $A'Z'$) but also by the increase in excess demand caused by the increased money supply.

When the price of domestic goods rises to P_{d_2}, the terms of trade decline $\bar{e}\,\bar{P}^*/P_{d_2}$, and equilibrium is restored at point C' (panel b). At the price of domestic goods P_{d_2}, the overall price level rises to P_2. At the new terms of trade, the quantity of real money balances demanded has fallen, and equilibrium is restored at point C (panel c). In the labor market, the increase in the price of domestic goods to P_{d_2}, and the rise in the price level to P_2 generate equiproportionate shifts in supply and demand curves with no effect on the full employment equilibrium level of employment or on the real wage.[19] Equilibrium occurs at A''' (panel a).

Thus, an increase in the government deficit with a fixed exchange rate still causes the terms of trade to decline. Despite the injection of money into the domestic economy to peg the exchange rate, the increased deficit still is entirely financed by a reduction in net exports. There is still the open economy equivalent of crowding out.[20]

An Increase in the Government Deficit: The Keynesian Model

In the Keynesian case, the rise in the price level creates an increase in employment because of asymmetrical responses in the labor market. As a result, aggregate real income

[19]By buying up foreign currency with dollars at the fixed exchange rate, the central bank promotes an increase in imports with no reduction in domestic expenditures. This is because the market for foreign exchange no longer rations scarce foreign currency by upward adjustments in its price. The fixed exchange rate system is a price support scheme wherein increased demand for foreign exchange is satisfied by the price controller, the central bank, releasing new supplies. This feeds the demand for imports at an unchanging level of real income. In price level Equation (15.25), this may be interpreted as causing a rise in P_d (without a change in its exponent) and as causing a rise in the exponent on $e\,P^*$ such that the overall price level increases in proportion to the domestic price level. The exponents no longer are assumed to sum to unity.

[20]See footnotes 13, 14, and 15.

increases, real saving rises, and real imports increase. The increase in the supply of credit is reflected as a rightward shift of the supply curve. This reduces the balance of payments surplus and results in a much smaller rise in the money supply. This, together with the fact that the demand for real money balances rises with the increase in real income, implies that the excess supply of money is much smaller than in the Neoclassical case. As a result, the subsequent rise in the price level and reduction in the terms of trade are much smaller. There is not as much crowding out of private expenditures by the larger deficit as in the Neoclassical model. In the long run, Neoclassical conditions are restored.

An Autonomous Increase in the Domestic Money Supply[21]

Assume that the central bank attempts to increase the money supply independently of balance of payments considerations. In Figure 15.8 (panel c), the increase in the domestic money supply from M_0 to M_1 at the fixed exchange rate $\bar{e}$ creates an excess supply of money. The excess supply of money is denoted by directed distance AB (panel c). This generates a higher price of domestic goods P_{d_1}.[22] The terms of trade decline from $\bar{e}\,\bar{P}^*/P_{d_0}$ to $\bar{e}\,\bar{P}^*/P_{d_1}$. The lower terms of trade create an excess supply of credit. This implies an excess of aggregate output over aggregate expenditures which is coextensive with an excess of imports over exports, a balance of payments deficit $(-B)$. The balance of payments deficit is depicted by directed distance $F'H'$ (panel b). As discussed earlier, because of the balance of payments deficit $(-B)$, to maintain the exchange rate at $\bar{e}$ the central bank must now exchange its reserves of foreign currency for dollars. This reduces the money supply from M_1 to $M_1 - B = M_0$. The subsequent reduction in the money supply from M_1 back to M_0 causes the initial price level P_0 to be restored.

This experiment demonstrates that under a fixed exchange rate, the central bank cannot conduct an independent monetary policy. The balance of payments induces changes in the domestic money stock that are necessary to restore the equilibrium terms of trade. The results suggest that under a regime of fixed exchange rates, it is not possible for a country to manipulate its own price level. This implication has dramatic portents in Keynesian models where unanticipated increases in the money supply generate increases in employment and domestic aggregate real income. For example, an expansionary monetary policy might temporarily reduce unemployment, but would lead to balance of payments deficits that require the central bank to contract the money supply. Thus, under fixed exchange rates, monetary policy is about as useful as a breathalyzer test in a brewery.

[21]See footnote 18.

[22]Since foreign prices and the exchange rate are assumed constant, additional foreign goods and services cannot initially be obtained and the entire excess supply of money is directed toward acquisition of domestically produced goods and services. In the price level Equation (15.25), this may be interpreted as causing the value of a to go to unity and the general price level to rise in the same proportion as domestic prices.

The assumption of a fixed foreign price level is unrealistic because the money supply of one country will have some influence on prices in other countries, especially if that country looms large in world economic affairs.

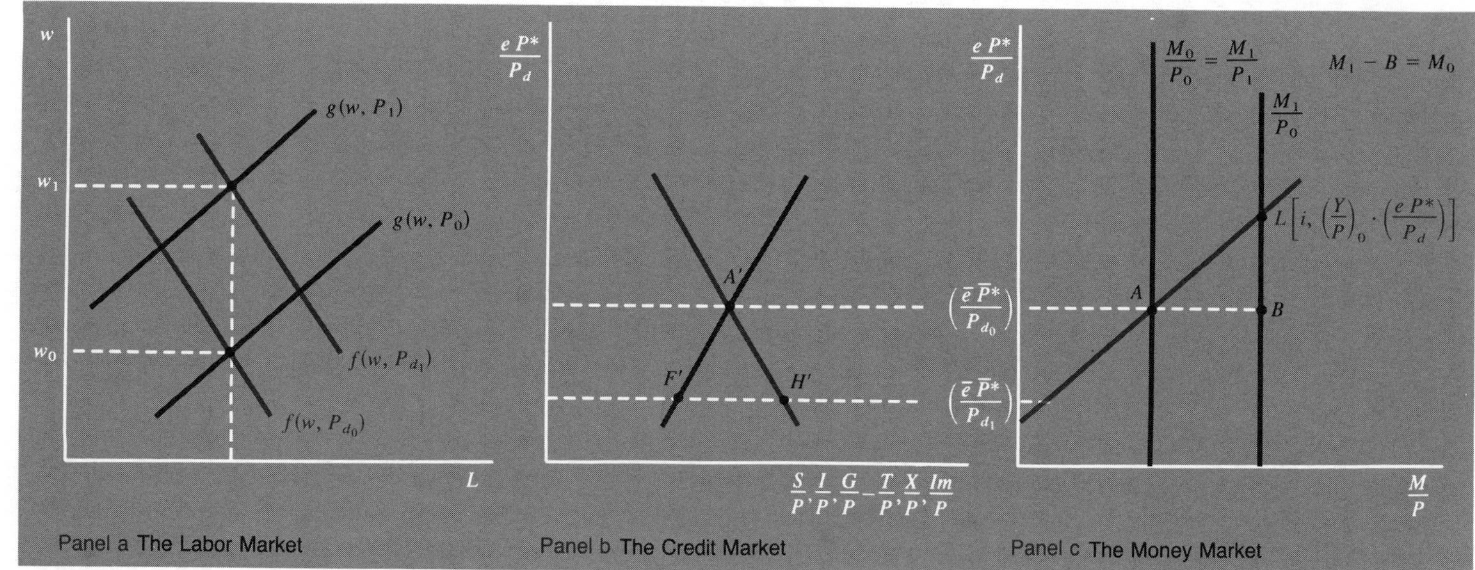

Figure 15.8 The Effect of an Increase in the Money Supply in the Neoclassical Model of an Open Economy with a Fixed Exchange Rate

In contrast, in a regime of flexible exchange rates, a country can determine its own price level. In the Keynesian analysis, this means that the level of employment and aggregate income might, under conditions described earlier, also be manipulated in the short run through monetary and fiscal policy without adverse balance of payments implications and the resulting need for central bank intervention.

Toward the Managed Float and Beyond

The current international monetary system, if it is a "system" at all, features neither completely fixed nor completely flexible exchange rates. The current arrangement is a cross between fixed and flexible exchange rates, which is called a *managed float*. How did we get into this situation?

The 1944 *Bretton Woods Conference* of the Allies instituted a system of fixed exchange rates among most currencies. Under this system, the United States dollar was fixed in terms of gold, and other currencies were pegged to the dollar (within 1 percent of either side of the pegged rate). The United States did not intervene in the market but left the problem to foreign central banks. The *International Monetary Fund (IMF)* was organized to administer the agreement. Under the Bretton Woods Agreement, a country was to be able to revalue its exchange rate if it found there was "fundamental disequilibrium" in its balance of payments. Such adjustments proved politically difficult to implement because no government wanted to signal failure of its domestic policies or the domestic policies of its trading partners.

In the first decade after Bretton Woods, the United States typically had balance of payments surpluses because its major trading partners had been devastated by the war and relied on imported American goods. As industrial Western nations and Japan regained their productive strength and as United States monetary policy was increasingly used to stimulate employment and to keep interest rates low, United States exports declined relative to United States imports, and the United States began to run balance of payments deficits. As long as the United States payments deficits were not sizable, foreign central banks were willing to sell their currencies to obtain dollars to hold since the dollar was an official reserve currency. Dollar reserve holdings rose from $21 billion in 1960 to $38.5 billion in 1968.

However, foreign central banks also converted much of their dollar reserves to gold in the 1960s. The United States gold stock fell by 50 percent from 1950 to 1970. Foreign central banks could no longer absorb dollar reserves, nor could they demand payment in gold since the United States gold stock was seriously depleted. The death blow for the system came on August 15, 1971, when President Nixon eliminated the right of central banks to convert holdings of United States dollars into gold. This led to the Smithsonian Agreement of December 1971, in which exchange rates were realigned through the devaluation of the dollar.

This pact was short-lived. In the face of the huge increases in oil prices that created large balances of payments deficits, in March 1973 the United States adopted a flexible exchange rate policy that has evolved into today's *managed float*.

Our central bank now participates in the foreign exchange market only when it decides a movement in the exchange rate is undesirable. There is no formal commitment to defend a particular exchange rate. In the 1974–1980 period, there were frequent interventions by the Federal Reserve in the foreign exchange market. Then in 1981, the Reagan administration announced that there would be intervention only when necessary to prevent disorder in exchange markets during crises.

During the 1974–1980 interval, our central bank frequently responded to shifts in the demand for and supply of domestic currency by buying or selling enough currency for the exchange rate to adjust slowly to its new equilibrium. However, even with the absence of regular United States intervention, as during the 1981–1983 period, the price of the dollar still did not float freely. This is because foreign central banks still regularly bought and sold dollars to influence their exchange rates against the dollar. Thus, the managed float persisted even though our central bank was doing little of the managing. During the 1985–1986 period, because of the high value of the dollar in terms of foreign exchange, the Reagan administration increased its intervention.[23] When the dollar fell in 1987 intervention continued.

Where do we go from here? Advocates of flexible exchange rates point out how they free domestic monetary and fiscal policy from a balance of payments concern. Proponents of fixed exchange rates contend that they provide a more stable trade environment in which business managers need not worry about exchange rate fluctuation. Some even argue that the balance of payments' influence on domestic monetary and fiscal policy imposes discipline on policies that would otherwise be excessively inflationary. Flexible rate devotees counter by pointing out that under fixed rates risk is not eliminated; it is merely shifted from risk of exchange rate fluctuations to risk of price level and/or real income fluctuations. Moreover, under flexible rates business managers can hedge against exchange rate variations by making transactions in the forward market. For example, an American computer sales company which expects to receive payments in Japanese yen in thirty days can contract to sell yen for dollars in one month. Another, less viable option is for the American firm to hold a diversified currency portfolio. Both tactics eliminate risk of fluctuation in the dollar price of yen. In retort, opponents of flexible rates argue that huge speculative flows of "stateless money" can shift exchange rates as much as 2 percent per day. This volatility imposes sizable transactions costs on firms which must hedge or hold currency portfolios.[24]

Despite sizable exchange rate fluctuations, world trade continues to grow under the present setup. While central bankers tend to favor the fixed rate system, strong sentiment for independent monetary and fiscal policies insures continued support for some type of exchange rate flexibility. Moreover, even the most ardent advocates of fixed rates can foresee no return to that system until worldwide inflation abates further. At this writing, the outcome of the debate is uncertain. One thing is sure: The controversy over fixed

[23]Political decisions that result in trade barriers and capital controls interfere with the economic forces bearing on exchange rates. Dramatic events such as the nationalization of banks in France in 1982 or the breathtaking plunge in the value of the German mark in 1983 make investments appear riskier and lead to capital outflows from these nations. The political stability of the United States makes it a natural recipient of such flows and makes the dollar appreciate at such times. It is especially during such crises that our central bank intervenes.

[24]See footnote 10 for hypotheses regarding the causes of sizable exchange rate fluctuations. For further discussion, see the articles by Batten and Ott in the bibliography to this chapter.

versus flexible exchange rates will persist no matter how the present arrangement is modified.

Concluding Comments

This chapter begins with a partial equilibrium model of the market for foreign exchange. It then incorporates the concepts developed in that model into a general equilibrium model of an open economy. Under assumed conditions of perfect international capital mobility and flexible exchange rates, two experiments are performed: an increase in the domestic money supply and an increase in the government deficit. Implications are developed for both Neoclassical and Keynesian variants of the open economy general equilibrium model. In all experiments, consideration is given to the linkage between money supply and deficit shocks under alternative expectational assumptions.

Under Neoclassical conditions, an increase in the money supply results in equiproportionate increases in the domestic price level and exchange rate with all real variables including the terms of trade unchanged. An increase in the government deficit results in a reduction in the terms of trade and the crowding out of private expenditures by government expenditures. Under Keynesian conditions, the quantity theory results of an increase in the money supply and the crowding out results of an increase in the government deficit are ameliorated in the short run by temporary increases in aggregate real income.

The chapter next examines the effects of these same two experiments under the condition of perfect international capital mobility and fixed exchange rates. An increase in the government deficit creates a balance of payments surplus. The rules of the game, under a fixed exchange rate regime, require central bank intervention to absorb the excess supply of foreign exchange associated with the payments surplus. This increases the domestic money supply and thus increases the price of domestic goods and lowers the terms of trade. The lower terms of trade result in the crowding out of private expenditures by government expenditures.

The chapter closes with a brief review of the evolution of the present international payments system from a fixed exchange rate to a flexible exchange rate mechanism. The discussion focuses on the forces that caused the breakdown of the fixed exchange rate system. It attends to some of the difficulties of maintaining freely fluctuating exchange rates and describes the development of the present precarious arrangement of managed floating exchange rates.

EXERCISES

1. Define the following terms:
   current account balance
   international capital flows
   balance of payments
   foreign exchange rate
   terms of trade

2. Explain whether you agree or disagree with the following statement: "Under a regime of flexible exchange rates, higher exchange rates cause inflation because they make imports more expensive."

3. Explain whether the following statement is true or false: "In an open economy, there is no crowding out of private expenditures by government deficit expenditures because domestic interest rates will not be bid upward. The deficit can be financed by borrowing from foreigners."

4. Explain why there can be no independent monetary policy under a regime of a fixed exchange rate.

5. Relax slightly the assumption of perfect international capital mobility, and discuss the implications of an increase in the government deficit for an open economy with flexible exchange rates.

6. Assume a short-run Keynesian perspective on the part of government policymakers. If government wants to influence output and employment, which system is preferable—fixed exchange rates or flexible exchange rates?

7. Describe the effect on the domestic economy of an increase in the money supply of a trading partner under a regime of flexible exchange rates.

8. Who manages the present exchange rate arrangement of a managed float?

9. It is often said that flexible exchange rates insulate the domestic economy from foreign shocks. Outline the effects on the Keynesian general equilibrium model under flexible exchange rates of a change in foreign real income that is unanticipated by domestic market participants.

10. Assume an unanticipated increase in the prices of foreign-produced goods and services. What effects would this have in a Neoclassical general equilibrium model with flexible exchange rates?

11. Why is the assumption of anticipation of demand shocks (induced by changes in the money supply and government deficit) somewhat less plausible under a fixed exchange rate regime than under a flexible exchange rate regime?

BIBLIOGRAPHY

Aliber, Robert Z. *The International Money Game*. 3d ed. New York: Basic Books, 1979.

Branson, William H. "Exchange Rate Dynamics and Monetary Policy." In Assar Lindbeck, ed., *Inflation and Employment in Open Economies*. Amsterdam: North Holland, 1979.

Batten, Dallas, and Mack Ott. "Five Common Myths about Floating Exchange Rates." In *Modern Concepts in Macroeconomics*, ed. Thomas M. Havrilesky. Arlington Heights, Ill.: Harlan Davidson, Inc., 1985.

———. "What Can Central Banks Do about the Value of the Exchange Rate?" In *Modern Concepts in Macroeconomics,* ed. Thomas M. Havrilesky. Arlington Heights, Ill.: Harlan Davidson, Inc., 1985.

Bergstrand, Jeffrey H. "Selected Views of Exchange Rate Determination after a Decade of 'Floating'." In *Modern Concepts in Macroeconomics,* ed. Thomas M. Havrilesky. Arlington Heights, Ill.: Harlan Davidson, Inc., 1985.

Caves, Richard E., and Ronald W. Jones. *World Trade and Payments: An Introduction*. 3d ed. Boston: Little, Brown and Company, 1981.

Corden, W. Max. *Inflation, Exchange Rates and the World Economy*. Oxford, England: Clarenden Press, 1977.

Dornbusch, Rudiger. "Expectations and Exchange Rate Dynamics." *Journal of Political Economy* 84 (December 1976), pp. 1161–1176.

Frenkel, Jacob, and Harry G. Johnson, eds. *The Monetary Approach to the Balance of Payments*. Toronto: University of Toronto Press, 1976.

Humphrey, Thomas. "Explaining Exchange Rate Behaviors: An Augmented Version of the Monetary Approach." *Economic Review,* Federal Reserve Bank of Richmond (May–June 1981), pp. 3–11.

Mundell, Robert A. *International Economics*. New York: Macmillan, 1968.

Officer, Lawrence H. "The Purchasing Power–Parity Theory of Exchange Rates: A Review." *Staff Papers,* International Monetary Fund (March 1976), pp. 1–61.

Richardson, J. David. *Understanding International Economics: Theory and Practice*. Boston: Little, Brown and Company, 1980.

Yeager, Leland B. *International Monetary Relations: Theory, History and Policy*. 2d ed. New York: Harper and Row, 1976.

Glossary

Above par When the market price of a debt claim is greater than its face value

Adaptive expectations The formulation of expectations of future prices by looking back at past prices

Adding-up condition An excess supply of money must equal the sum of an excess demand for bonds and an excess demand for goods

Aggregate An adjective meaning the sum of

Aggregate budget identity An equation that defines aggregate income as the sum of consumption expenditures, transfer payments, and saving

Aggregate output The purchasing power or real value of a volume of goods and services that are newly produced in an economy during a period of time

Aggregate private balance sheet identity See **Aggregate private net worth**

Aggregate private net worth The sum of the value of equity claims, the value of debt claims of government, the value of consumer durables, and the value of human wealth

Aggregate private nonhuman wealth Aggregate private wealth minus the value of human wealth

Aggregate private wealth The sum of the value of equity claims, the value of consumer durables, and the value of human wealth; aggregate private net worth minus the value of the debt claims of government

Aggregate real income The real value of the earnings generated by the production of goods and services during a period of time

Aggregate wealth identity An equation that defines aggregate private wealth as the sum of the value of equity claims, the value of consumer durables, and the value of human wealth

At par When the market price of a debt claim equals its face value

ATS account Automatic transfer services account: checkable deposits that are transferable by preauthorized arrangement; available since January 1978

Automatic stabilizers The automatic countercyclical variation of government tax receipts and hence the government deficit. In Keynesian models, the countercyclical movement of these variables is thought to stabilize cyclical variations in the level of aggregate output and employment

Autonomous consumption expenditures Consumption expenditures that are independent of all other variables in the model in question

Autonomous expenditures multiplier In Keynesian models, the effect of a change in autonomous expenditures in generating a change in real income in a multiple of that change

Autonomous investment expenditures Investment expenditures that are independent of all other variables in the model in question

Autonomous taxation Taxation that is independent of all other variables of the model in question

Autonomous taxation multiplier The effect of a change in autonomous taxation in generating a change in real income in a multiple of that change

Balanced budget multiplier The effect of a change in autonomous government expenditures which is matched by an equal change in autonomous taxation in generating a change in real income in a multiple of that change

Balance of payments The current account balance plus net capital flows

Barter Economic transactions without the use of money as a medium of exchange

Behaviorial relations Equations that reflect the behavior of individuals or groups of individuals

Below par When the market price of a debt claim is less than its face value

Board of Governors of the Federal Reserve System The ruling body of the Federal Reserve System consisting of eight presidential appointees

Bond A debt claim that may be traded in an organized market

Bond markets Markets for trading newly issued and existing debt claims

Bracket creep The effect of inflation forcing individuals into higher nominal income tax brackets

Business cycle A pattern involving intervals of greater than full employment and less than full employment that recur over time, usually with varying frequency and periodicity

Business cycle: inflationary shock or monetary surprise A pattern involving intervals of greater than full employment and less than full employment that recur over time, usually with varying frequency and periodicity. Caused by surprise changes in money growth, inflation, and/or other nominal demand shocks. Compare to **Real business cycle.** See also **Short-run Phillips curve.**

Business saving, gross Net business saving plus capital consumption allowances

Business saving, net Undistributed corporate profits; retained corporate earnings; corporate profits minus corporate income taxes minus dividends

Capital consumption allowance The sum of aggregate depreciation, which is, in turn, an estimate of the amount of investment expenditures used to replace the aggregate stock of capital goods as it wears out (see **Depreciation**)

Capital deepening An increase in the level of capital inputs relative to other inputs in production processes

Capital expenditures Expenditures on newly produced capital goods

Capital goods The produced means of producing more goods and services

Capital inflows Foreign purchases of domestic securities

Capital loss A reduction in the market value of an asset

Capital markets The part of the credit markets where long-term debt claims and equity claims are exchanged

Capital outflows Domestic purchases of foreign securities

Cash assets The most liquid assets of a depository institution

Ceteris paribus All things being held equal or constant

Checkable deposit A claim on a depository institution that is transferable by check, wire, or preauthorized arrangement, e.g., checking accounts, NOW accounts, Super-NOW accounts, and ATS accounts

Closed economy The domestic economy as a whole viewed as being isolated from other economies

COLA clauses Cost of living adjustments in rates of remuneration, often used in reference to labor contracts

Complete crowding out The dollar-for-dollar displacement of private expenditures by an increase in government expenditures

Consensus forecast An average of a large number of forecasts

Consistency condition See **Adding-up condition**

Consol bonds Debt claims that are never legally redeemable by the holder, thereby paying interest income in perpetuity

Consumer price index A weighted average of the prices of the newly produced consumption goods and services

Consumer surplus The sum of the differences between the sum of the value that each consumer would have paid for a certain quantity of a good or service minus the sum of what he or she actually does pay for that good or service at the market-determined price

Consumption expenditures The (current) expenditures by households on newly produced goods and services

Consumption tax An income tax that legally exempts taxation of the entire portion of income that is saved

Core inflation The underlying rate of inflation that could persist for a period of time because of expected systematic monetary accommodation of supply shocks and demand shocks

Cost of living See **Consumer price index**

Cost push A type of supply shock typically associated with an increase in union monopoly power that results in increases in nominal wages in excess of productivity gains and causes increases in costs of production and the prices of newly produced goods and services (see **Supply shock**)

Coupon rate The face rate of interest on a debt claim; the interest income on a debt claim expressed as a percentage of par or face value

Credit Part of the flow of income that is saved and hence, in equilibrium, loaned to borrowers; loanable funds

Credit, sources of The saving of household, business, and government sectors

Credit, uses of The borrowing of household, business, and government sectors

Credit markets Where the saving of lenders is exchanged at a market-determined price, the interest rate, for newly issued debt and equity claims of borrowers; loanable funds markets

Crowding out The displacement of private expenditures by increases in government expenditures

Currency to checkable deposit ratio The ratio of currency in circulation to checkable deposits; a parameter in the money supply expansion coefficient

Currency drain The reduction in deposits that occurs when currency in circulation increases

Current account balance Exports minus imports plus net factor payments

Current account trade balance Exports minus imports

Current expenditures Expenditures on newly produced noncapital goods and services

Current yield The interest income on a debt claim expressed as a percentage of its current market price

Cyclically adjusted deficit The magnitude of the government deficit when income is at a high employment level

Debt claims Evidences of debt or liability

Default risk The risk that the value of a debt claim will vary in price if the debtor defaults on interest payments or principal repayments

Deficit An excess of expenditures over income

Demand for labor, theory of An abstract representation of the factors that determine the quantity of labor demanded by business firms, frequently including the nominal wage, the price level, and the income tax rate

Depository innovations New types of specialized debt claims offered by depository institutions; usually encouraged by technological changes and deregulation of depository institutions

Depository institutions Financial intermediaries whose specialized debt claims serve as money

Depreciation The portion of the historical cost of a capital good that is allocated by a business firm to current production as an expense in each year of its useful life

Derived deposits Deposits created from a new loan by a depository institution

Diminishing marginal productivity Holding all other inputs constant, as one input increases, output increases at a decreasing rate

Diminishing returns See **Diminishing marginal productivity**

Discount A verb meaning to calculate the present value of a future dollar amount(s)

Discount rate The interest rate set by the Board of Governors at which member institutions may borrow from the Federal Reserve

Disintermediation The massive withdrawal of deposits from depository institutions and acquisition of marketable securities with these funds by depositors

Disposable income See **Personal disposable income**

Dissaving For households, the excess of consumption expenditures over disposable income

Dynamic analysis Examination of a relationship or set of relationships wherein the values of variables change over time

Earnings The income of the factors of production; for households: wages, net interest, the rental income of persons, and proprietor's income; for business firms: net corporate profits plus depreciation; for government: indirect business taxes

Easy money A policy of increasing the money supply or its rate of growth in excess of the latest long-term trend growth rate

Economic forecasting Attempts to predict the future path of employment, output, interest rates, and inflation

Economic model An abstract representation of the market behavior of individuals or aggregations of individuals

Efficient markets hypothesis The postulate that market participants will not be systematically in error in predicting future prices so that systematic opportunities for profit will always have been exploited

Employment level The number of workers that are employed

Employment rate The percentage of the labor force that is employed

Endogenous variable A variable whose solution value is determined within the model in question

Equilibrium conditions Relations that specify that a market or sector of the economy is in balance with no tendency to change

Equity claims Evidences of ownership

ERTA Economic Recovery Tax Act of 1981; a series of tax cuts enacted largely in the interest of stimulating productive effort

Evidence of debt An IOU, a liability, a debt claim

Excess demand When quantity demanded at the market price exceeds quantity supplied

Excess reserves Total reserves less required reserves

Excess supply When quantity supplied at the market price exceeds quantity demanded

Ex ante An adjective meaning planned, anticipated, or expected

***Ex ante* real rate of interest** The expected real rate of interest, approximately equal to the nominal rate of interest minus the expected rate of inflation over the period of the loan

Exchange rate The price of a foreign currency in dollars

Exogenous variable A variable whose value is determined outside the model in question

Ex post An adjective meaning actual or realized

***Ex post* real rate of interest** The actual real rate of interest, approximately equal to the nominal rate of interest minus the actual rate of inflation over the period of the loan

Exports Foreign purchases of newly produced domestic goods and services

External balance The absence of a balance of payments deficit or surplus

External financing Financing expenditures by issuing new debt or equity claims in the credit market

FDIC Federal Deposit Insurance Corporation; the quasi-governmental agency that insures the accounts of depositors in banking institutions

FOMC Federal Open Market Committee; the group that directs the open market operations of the Federal Reserve System, consisting of the Board of Governors plus the presidents of four Federal Reserve Banks

Factor markets Where the services of the factors of production are exchanged at market-determined prices, thereby generating earnings for their owners

Factors of production Inputs into the production process—typically labor, capital, entrepreneurial services, and land; viewed by economists as being owned by households and sold to business firms in factor markets

Federal Reserve System The central bank of the United States directed by a Board of Governors and consisting of twelve Federal Reserve Banks

Final sales The total sales of all business firms less all interfirm noncapital expenditures during a period of time

Financial assets Items of wealth other than physical goods and human wealth; "paper" assets; debt and equity claims

Financial intermediaries Institutions that operate in credit markets, acquiring primary debt claims of borrowers and issuing specialized debt claims against themselves to lenders

Financing constraint An equation which says that excess of expenditures over income must, by definition, be financed by issuing new debt claims or new equity claims

Flat tax All individuals pay the same income tax rate, and all deductions and progressivity are eliminated

Float The increment to Federal Reserve assets and to the aggregate deposits of member institutions that occurs when receiving banks get an increase in their accounts at the Fed for checks deposited with them while paying banks have not yet lost their deposits at the Fed; float increases when checks are slow to clear through the paying bank

Flows Quantities that are measured between two points in time

Foreign exchange The quantity of a flow of foreign currency available in the foreign exchange market

Fractional reserve banking Keeping less than a dollar of cash assets for each dollar of deposits

Frictional unemployment The rate of unemployment associated with the natural rate of employment; the percentage of the labor force that is changing jobs at the natural rate of unemployment

Full employment equilibrium When a market or markets is/are in equilibrium at a level of employment obtained when all factors of production which seek employment at prevailing and correctly anticipated future wage and price levels are able to find it

General equilibrium model An equilibrium model of several markets or sectors of the economy

General notation Mathematical notation indicating a relationship between a left-hand side, dependent variable and right-hand side, explanatory variables but not specifying functional form

General price level A weighted average or index of the nominal prices of goods and services

Gold standard The ultimate type of fixed exchange rate system; the value of all currencies fixed in terms of gold

Government deficit Government expenditures less government taxation or government purchases plus government transfers less government taxation

Government expenditures Government purchases of newly produced goods and services plus government transfers to other sectors

Government saving Government surplus; government expenditures less government taxation

Government transfers Transfer payments from the government sector to all other sectors; does not include taxation received by the government sector

Great Depression, the The period of prolonged less-than-full employment lasting from approximately 1929 until 1939

Gross corporate profits Net corporate profits plus depreciation

Gross investment expenditures Total aggregate expenditures on newly produced capital goods, including investment expenditures for replacement of capital goods as estimated by capital consumption allowances

Gross national product The market value of the flow of newly produced goods and services and the income generated thereby over a given interval of time

Growth rates See **Steady-state growth rate** and **Intermediate-run growth rate**

High employment deficit The magnitude of the government deficit when the level of income is at a high employment level

High-powered money The monetary base

Human capital The present value of the flow of income from future labor services

Human capital consumption allowance An estimate of the part of consumption expenditures necessary to replace the aggregate stock of human capital as it "wears out"

Human wealth See **Human capital**

Hyperinflation The condition of extremely high inflation that results in a minimal demand for real money balances because of extremely high expected inflation and extremely high nominal interest rates

Identities Equations that always hold by definition

Imperfect information Incomplete knowledge of present and future prices

Implicit GNP price deflator An index of the prices of all the newly produced goods and services in GNP

Imports Domestic purchases of newly produced foreign goods and services

Imputations Adjustments to aggregate income made for value added by households and government; additions to value added by the business sector

Income effect Allocation of part of a budget that has been enlarged by a change in the price of a good or service toward or away from that good or service

Incomes policies Systematic, and sometimes flexible, programs of wage and price controls or wage and price guidelines

Indexation Correction of a nominal dollar magnitude for inflation so as to maintain an unchanged real magnitude

Indirect business taxes Sales taxes plus excise taxes less government subsidies

Inflation The rate of change of the general price level over a period of time

Inflationary shock See **Business cycle: inflationary shock or monetary surprise**

Interest rate The price of future consumption in terms of current consumption

Interest rate parity, theory of The proposition that the interest rate differential between two countries equals the expected change in their exchange rate

Intermediate-run growth rate Growth in output which occurs when the growth rate of one factor input into production processes exceeds the growth rate of other factor inputs

Investment expenditures Expenditures on newly produced capital goods and therefore part of the flow of output that is allocated to the production of newly produced capital goods

Investment expenditures, theory of An abstract representation of the variables that explain the level of aggregate investment expenditures; these variables include the rate of interest, expected future after-tax profits, and the price of capital goods

Keynesian economics Macroeconomic analysis that indicates that changes in government expenditures, taxation, and the money supply can and should be applied to systematically affect interest rates, employment, and aggregate output

Labor force The total number of persons currently able and available for employment

Labor force statistics Measurements of employment, unemployment, and participation of individuals in the labor market

Labor market equilibrium condition Quantity of labor supplied equals quantity of labor demanded

Law of diminishing returns As inputs into production increase, output increases at a decreasing rate

Leading economic indicators Measures which are purported statistically to predict or anticipate cyclical changes in output and employment

Legal reserves Vault cash plus deposits at the Federal Reserve or other central credit facilities

Legal reserve requirement ratio See **Reserve requirement ratio**

Legal tender Anything dictated by government to serve as a medium of exchange and circulate at its face value against all other media of exchange

Liquidity The cash-readiness of an asset or of an entire balance sheet

Liquidity effect The possible effect of an increase or decrease in the money supply in depressing or raising the market rate of interst, *ceteris paribus*

Liquidity trap The idea that changes in the money supply have no effect on the interest rate because the demand for money is perfectly interest sensitive

Loan A debt claim that is exchanged in face-to-face negotiation between borrower and lender and is not usually traded in an organized market

Loanable funds See **Credit**

Long run In macroeconomics, a long interval of time

Long-run equilibrium No tendency to change no matter how much time passes

Long-run Phillips curve The trade-off between inflation and unemployment (usually zero or a small order of magnitude); associated with the natural rate of unemployment

M1 The narrowly defined money supply consisting of currency in circulation, checkable deposits, and travelers' checks

M2 The broadly defined money supply consisting of everything in M1 plus savings accounts, small time deposits, money market mutual funds, money market deposit accounts, overnight repurchase agreements, and overnight Eurodollar accounts

Macroeconomics The study of the behavior of aggregate economic entities

Marginal physical product of capital The increment to output with respect to the increment to capital input

Marginal physical product of labor The increment to output with respect to the increment to labor input

Marginal propensity to consume The increment to consumption expenditures with respect to the increment to income

Marginal propensity to save The increment to saving with respect to the increment to income

Marginal revenue product of labor The increment to revenue with respect to the increment to labor input

Marginal tax rate The increment to taxation with respect to the increment to income

Market risk The risk that the market value of a debt or equity claim will vary in price as the earnings of the debtor and market rates of interest change

Market system The subsystem of the social system in which the organizational principle is exchange or *quid pro quo* reciprocity

Medium of exchange A function of money; money viewed as serving the need for a means of conducting payments and disbursements

Microeconomics The study of the behavior of individual economic entities

Monetarist A label commonly applied to that part of the Neoclassical macroeconomic analysis that emphasizes the role of the money supply in macroeconomic stabilization policy and concludes that stable money supply growth is a superior objective for such policy

Monetary base, sources of Basically, the assets of the Federal Reserve System plus United States Treasury currency minus deposits of the Treasury and other minor liabilities of the Federal Reserve

Monetary base, uses of Total reserves plus currency in circulation

Monetary surprise See **Business cycle: inflationary shock or monetary surprise**

Monetization of the deficit Financing the government deficit by increasing the money supply rather than by increasing the stock of government bonds in the hands of the public

Money Anything that serves the functions of money: a medium of exchange, store of value, and unit of account

Money illusion Basing a decision on nominal, rather than real, purchasing power magnitudes

Money market In ordinary business language, the part of the credit markets where short-term debt claims are exchanged. Alternatively, in macroeconomic theory, where suppliers and demanders of money and nonmoney assets meet

Money market deposit account A near money; a deposit that pays interest that fluctuates with market rates, usually has limited check-writing privileges, and requires a minimum balance

Money multiplier The money supply expansion coefficient

Money supply, broadly defined The money supply consisting of currency in circulation, checkable deposits, travelers' checks, saving accounts, money market deposit accounts, small-time deposits, money market mutual funds, overnight repurchase agreements, and overnight Eurodollar accounts; M2

Money supply, narrowly defined The money supply consisting of currency in circulation, checkable deposits, and travelers' checks; M1

Money supply expansion coefficient A combination of behavioral parameters, such as the currency to checkable-deposit ratio and legal reserve requirement ratios which, when multiplied by the monetary base, yield the money supply

Multiplier principle The idea perfected by John Maynard Keynes during the Great Depression that a change in some element of autonomous expenditures would generate a change in real income in a multiple of the change in autonomous expenditures

National income Net national product less indirect business taxes; aggregate income measured at factor cost

Natural rate of unemployment The rate of unemployment that occurs at full employment equilibrium when labor market participants anticipate all price changes and nominal wages are flexible; coextensive with the rate of frictional unemployment

Near money Anything that serves all of the functions of money but cannot serve as the medium of exchange and function as costlessly as the money, narrowly defined. Many types of near money are included in the M2 definition of money stock but not in the M1 definition

Neoclassical economics Macroeconomic analysis that indicates that changes in government expenditures, taxation, and the money supply may affect employment and aggregate output but that such effects either are too short-lived or too unsystematic to serve as a basis for government macroeconomic stabilization policy

Neo-Keynesian See **Keynesian economics**

Net aggregate income See **Net national product**

Net capital flows The difference between foreign purchases of domestic securities and domestic purchases of foreign securities

Net government receipts Indirect business taxes plus or minus government transfers and government income tax receipts

Net investment expenditures Gross investment expenditures less capital consumption allowances; additions to the economy's stock of capital goods

Net national product Gross national product less capital consumption allowances; aggregate income less expenditures for replacement of the capital stock

Neutrality of money The condition that an increase in the nominal stock of money has an effect on nominal values, such as the price level, and not on real values or real quantities; an implication of the quantity theory of money

New Classical economics Macroeconomic analysis that indicates that changes in the government expenditures, taxation, and money supply can affect employment and aggregate output only when unsystematic and hence unanticipated by market participants and concludes that such a basis is not a justifiable premise for macroeconomic stabilization policy; macroeconomic analysis associated with the rational expectations hypothesis

Nominal An adjective meaning "dollar value of"

Nominal income effect The effect which follows sequentially the liquidity effect when the market rate of interest returns to initial equilibrium level as the price level (and hence, nominal income) adjusts, *ceteris paribus*

Nominal rate of interest The observed market rate of interest; subtracting the actual rate of inflation yields the actual or *ex post* real rate of interest; subtracting the expected rate of inflation yields the expected or *ex ante* real rate of interest

Nominal wage inflexibility See **Nominal wage ridigity**

Nominal wage rigidity Inflexibility of the dollar wage because of nominal wage contracts or because of money illusion or other imperfections

NOW accounts Negotiable order of withdrawal accounts; checkable deposits which pay interest (up to some legal ceiling) and have check-writing privileges, available on a nationwide basis since January 1981

Open economy The domestic economy viewed in conjunction with other economies

Open market operations The purchase and sale of government securities by the Federal Reserve so as to affect the monetary base and the money supply and/or interest rates

Opportunity cost The return or reward sacrificed in order to engage in an activity

Opportunity cost of being employed The amount of benefits such as unemployment compensation that one gives up by employment

Opportunity cost of being unemployed The real after-tax wage that one gives up by being unemployed

Partial equilibrium model An equilibrium model of a market or sector of the economy where variables determined in other markets or sectors are assumed constant

Perfect information The condition that all relevant present and future prices are known to market participants

Perfect international capital mobility The unrestricted flow of funds across international boundaries

Permanent income Income that is expected to occur over the entire planning horizon of a decision making entity such as a household

Personal disposable income Household earnings plus or minus various transfer payments such as income taxes, dividends, social security contributions, and unemployment compensation payments

Personal saving Personal disposable income minus consumption expenditures

Policy ineffectiveness proposition The idea that macroeconomic stabilization policy cannot be effective, in terms of changing real income or real interest rates, because shocks to the economy are anticipated by private market participants as readily as by government policymakers

Political business cycle Incumbent politicians purposely encourage monetary surprises so as to stimulate real output and lower unemployment prior to an election

Post-Keynesian The label applied to the macroeconomic analysis that insists that the original theories of John Maynard Keynes have been misinterpreted by Neoclassical, New Classical, and Keynesian (Neo-Keynesian) analysts

Precautionary balances Money balances held as a contingency for future cash needs

Present value formula An equation that generates market value by using the market rate of interest to discount an expected stream of future income

Price index	A weighted average of the prices of individual goods and services
Price-inflation expectations effect	The addition by market participants of the expected rate of inflation (inflation premium) to the real rate of interest; helps determine the nominal rate of interest
Primary deposits	Deposits arising from a deposit of currency in a depository institution
Primary reserves	The cash assets of depository institutions
Private nonhuman wealth	See **Aggregate private nonhuman wealth**
Product markets	Where newly produced goods and services are exchanged at market determined prices thereby generating dollar expenditures
Production function	A technical relation between the level of output of a good or service and the level of productive inputs employed in its production
Progressive taxation	When the percentage change in taxation exceeds the percentage change in income
Purchasing power parity, theory of	The proposition that the exchange rate moves (quickly) to keep the price of one country's goods in terms of another country's goods equal across countries, modified for transportation costs and tariff barriers
Purely competitive markets	Markets where buyers or sellers are so numerous that individual buyers and sellers cannot influence prices
Quantity theory of money	The prediction that the general price level and all other nominal values such as the nominal wage level and the exchange rate will vary in direct proportion to an excess quantity of money
Rational expectations hypothesis	The postulate that the expectations of market participants will not be systematically wrong in predicting future prices
Real	An adjective meaning purchasing power value of
Real business cycle	Swings in output employment and interest rates are caused by capacity changing supply shocks. Consistent with the positive correlation between real wages and employment over time and the notion that the economy is always in long-run full-employment equilibrium
Real wage	The purchasing power value of the nominal wage, the nominal wage adjusted (deflated) for changes in the cost of living
Relative price	The price of a good or service in terms of the price of another good or service
Repurchase agreements	Short-term loans to depository institutions by nonbank individuals
Required reserves	The sum of the dollar amount of each class of deposits that must be held in reserve in order to satisfy legal reserve requirements; required reserves must be held in the form of vault cash or deposits at the Federal Reserve or some other central credit facility
Reserve requirement ratio	The percentage of each class of deposits that must be held as reserves in order to satisfy legal reserve requirements
Retained earnings	See **Undistributed corporate profits**
Ricardian equivalence theorem	The concept that an increase in the government deficit will result in complete crowding out without a rise in the interest rate because private market participants discount future tax increases associated with a larger present deficit

Saving Part of flow of income that is not transferred to government or used for consumption expenditures; a source of loanable funds in the credit market

Scapegoat theory of inflation The notion that government officials will blame inflation on seemingly uncontrollable forces, such as supply shock or cost push factors, when these factors are, in fact, virtually insignificant and the true source of inflation is government macroeconomic policy

Secondary reserves The liquid noncash assets of a depository institution

Sectoral budget identity An equation which says that the earnings of a sector plus or minus the transfer payments of that sector always equal its expenditures plus its saving

Short run In macroeconomics, a short interval of time

Short-run equilibrium No tendency to change over a short period of time

Short-run Phillips curve The trade-off, usually negative, between inflation and unemployment that may exist in the short run

Specialized debt claims Evidences of liability issued by financial intermediaries

Speculative balances Balances held in order to have a liquid means of holding wealth in order to be able efficiently to acquire nonmoney assets as needs arise, often inclusive of near-monies

Stagflation Label given in ordinary language to the simultaneous occurrence of high inflation and high unemployment

Static analysis Examination of a relationship or set of relationships at a point in time; movement over time is not considered

Steady-state growth rate The growth rate of output that occurs when all productive inputs are growing at the same rate

Stocks Quantities that are measured at a point in time

Stock markets Markets for trading newly issued and existing equity claims

Store of value A function of money serving the need for a liquid way of holding wealth

Substitution effect Allocation of a larger share of a fixed real budget to a good or service whose price has fallen

Super-full employment equilibrium Short-run equilibrium featuring a level of employment greater than the full employment equilibrium level

Super-NOW accounts Checkable deposits which pay interest that fluctuates with market rates, have unlimited check-writing privileges but require a minimum balance

Supply of labor, theory of The abstract representation of the things that determine the quantity of labor supplied by households including the nominal wage, the price level and the income tax rate

Supply shock A change in the price of an input into production processes that initially raises costs of production and the prices of newly produced goods and services, often associated with changes in the price of imported raw materials but also arising from other sources. See **Cost push**

Supply-side economic policy The idea that productive effort and the level of aggregate output can be increased by incentives such as cuts in taxes on income and deregulation of market activities

Surplus An excess of expenditures over income

Targets of monetary policy Variables that are usually endogenous to macroeconomic models that the Federal Reserve may try to influence through manipulation of the tools of monetary policy so as to ultimately influence the price level, employment output, and interest rates

Tax indexation The adjustment of income taxes to correct for the effect of bracket creep

Tax reform The philosophy that changes in the basic tax codes will stimulate productive effort. See **Consumption tax, Value added tax,** and **Flat tax**

Technical relations Equations that show an interdependence that is based on a technological process

Technological change, capital saving Technological change that increases the marginal productivity of labor and does not raise the marginal productivity of capital

Technological change, labor saving Technological change that increases the marginal productivity of capital and does not raise the marginal productivity of labor

Technological change, neutral Technological change that increases the marginal productivities of capital and labor

Terms of trade The number of units of domestic goods that are given up to obtain one unit of foreign production from abroad

Time deposit to checkable deposit ratio A parameter in the money supply expansion coefficient

Tools of monetary policy Open market operations and the discount rate

Total reserves Required reserves plus excess reserves; total reserves consist of vault cash plus deposits at the Federal Reserve or some other central credit facility

Transactions balances Money balances held in order to finance transactions; often associated with the narrowly defined money supply (M1) or a weighted money aggregate

Transfer payments One-way or unilateral nonmarket flows between sectors of the economy such as personal income tax payments from the household sector to the government sector; transfer payments do not generate output or earnings

Transitory income Income that is expected to occur only for a short period of the entire planning horizon of a decision-making entity such as a household

Underemployment equilibrium Short-run equilibrium featuring a level of employment less than the full employment level

Underground economy Income and output not reflected in GNP because certain income-generating transactions are not reported to the Internal Revenue Service

Undistributed corporate profits Net corporate profit minus corporate income taxes and dividends; net business saving

Unemployment level The number of workers that are not employed

Unemployment rate The percentage of the labor force that is not employed

Unit of account The use of money as a means of denominating values

Value added Increment to aggregate income added by each business firm in the economy; sales less payments to other firms for noncapital goods and services

Value added tax (VAT) A tax on value added; similar to a sales tax on a national level

Vault cash Currency and coin in the vault of a depository institution

Velocity Aggregate income divided by the money stock; the rate at which money turns over against income

Wage and price controls A policy of placing legal ceilings on wages and prices and punishing violators; usually intended as a means of reducing inflation

Wage indexation Tying the nominal wage to the cost of living, usually through labor contracts

Wage-price guidelines Wage and price controls without well-defined penalties for violation

Weighted money aggregates An index derived by weighting the components of M1 or M2 for their value in carrying out transactions

Yield-to-maturity The percentage return on a debt claim which accounts for interest income as well as future capital gains or loss when the debt claim is redeemed at par

Zookers The currency of Banalia

Author Index

Subject Index